TAKING SIDES

Clashing Views on Controversial Social Issues

6th edition

Clashing Views on Controversial Social Issues

6th edition

Edited by

Kurt Finsterbusch
University of Maryland

and

George McKenna
City College, City University of New York

The Dushkin Publishing Group, Inc.

To John, Alec, Ned, Laura, Maria, and Christopher, who must live these issues now and in the years ahead.

Taking Sides ® is a registered trademark of The Dushkin Publishing Group, Inc.

Library of Congress Catalog Card Number: 89-81547

Manufactured in the United States of America

Sixth Edition, First Printing
ISBN: 0-87967-858-5

PREFACE

The English word *fanatic* is derived from the Latin *fanum*, meaning temple. It refers to the kind of madmen often seen in the precincts of temples in ancient times, the kind presumed to be possessed by deities or demons. The term first came into English usage during the seventeenth century, and it was used to describe religious zealots. Soon after, its meaning was broadened to include a political and social context. We have come to associate the term fanatic with a person who acts as if his or her views were inspired, a person utterly incapable of appreciating opposing points of view. The nineteenth-century English novelist George Eliot put it precisely: "I call a man fanatical when . . . he . . . becomes unjust and unsympathetic to men who are out of his own track." A fanatic may hear, but is unable to listen. Confronted with those who disagree, a fanatic immediately vilifies opponents.

Most of us would avoid the company of fanatics, but who among us is not tempted to caricature opponents instead of listening to them? Who does not put certain topics off limits for discussion? Who does not grasp at euphemisms to avoid facing inconvenient facts? Who has not, in George Eliot's language, sometimes been "unjust and unsympathetic" to those on a different track? Who is not, at least in certain very sensitive areas, a *little* fanatical? The counterweight to fanaticism is open discussion. The difficult issues that trouble us as a society have at least two sides, and we lose as a society if we hear only one side. At the individual level, the answer to fanaticism is listening.

This book contains thirty-eight selections presented in a pro and con format. A total of nineteen different controversial social issues are debated. The sociologists, political scientists, economists, and social critics whose views are debated here make their cases vigorously. In order to effectively read each selection, analyze the points raised, debate the basic assumptions and values of each position, in other words, in order to think critically about what you are reading, you will first have to give each side a sympathetic hearing. John Stuart Mill, the nineteenth-century British philosopher, noted that the majority is not doing the minority a favor by listening to its views; it is doing *itself* a favor. By listening to contrasting points of view, we strengthen our own. In some cases we change our viewpoint completely. But in most cases, we either incorporate some elements of the opposing view—thus making our own richer—or else learn how to answer the objections to our viewpoint. Either way, we gain from the experience.

Organization of the book   Each issue has an issue *introduction*, which sets the stage for the debate as it is argued in the YES and NO selections. Each issue concludes with a *postscript* that makes some final observations and points the way to other questions related to the issue. In reading the issue and forming your own opinions you should not feel confined to adopt one or the other of the positions presented. There are positions in between the given views or totally outside them, and the *suggestions for further reading* that appear in each issue postscript should help you find resources to continue your study of the subject. At the back of the book, beginning on page 364, is a listing of all the *contributors to this volume*, which will give you information on the social scientists whose views are debated here.

A word to the instructor An *Instructor's Manual with Test Questions* (multiple-choice and essay) is available through the publisher. A general guidebook, called *Using Taking Sides in the Classroom*, which discusses methods and techniques for integrating the pro/con approach into any classroom setting, is also available.

Acknowledgments We received many helpful comments and suggestions from our friends and readers across the United States and Canada. Their suggestions have markedly enhanced the quality of this edition of *Taking Sides* and are reflected in the eight totally new issues and the updated selections.

Our thanks go to those who responded with suggestions for the sixth edition: Stephen Beach, Avila College; Lanny R. Bowers, Walters State Community College; Trudie Coker, Florida International University; Keith Crew, University of Northern Iowa; Raymond D'Angelo, St. Joseph's College-Brooklyn; Marvin D. Free, Jr., University of Wisconsin-Marathon Center; Madeleine Giguere, University of Southern Maine-Gorham; Susan Greenwood, University of Maine-Orono; Ronald Haverlandt, College of Great Falls; Colleen Hyden, Washington and Jefferson College; Frank McVeigh, Muhlenberg College; John Molloy, Michigan State University; Cindy Moniz, University of New Hampshire-Plymouth; John Moore, University of South Carolina-Lancaster; Richard L. Ogmundson, University of Victoria; Fred Pincus, University of Maryland-Baltimore; Stephanie Shanks-Meile, Indiana University Northwest; and Bahram Tavakolian, Denison University.

We also wish to acknowledge the encouragement and support given to this project over the years by Rick Connelly, president of the Dushkin Publishing Group. We are grateful as well to Mimi Egan, program manager for the Taking Sides series. Finally, we thank our families for their patience and understanding during the period in which we prepared this book.

Kurt Finsterbusch
College Park, MD

George McKenna
New York City

CONTENTS IN BRIEF

CONTENTS

Professor Lawrence Kohlberg argues that an awareness of ethics and values will develop in young people through a relaxed, nondirective approach to moral education. Educator Edward A. Wynne favors the method of indoctrination for transmitting moral values to the young.

Media analyst and former publisher of the *National Review* William Rusher makes the case that liberal opinions are promoted in the media through a deliberate bias against conservatives. In contrast, professors Edward S. Herman and Noam Chomsky argue that the media function as a "propaganda mill" operating on behalf of the wealthy and powerful.

Novelist and essayist Marilyn French argues that feminism offers a serious and coherent alternative to patriarchal thinking and structures. Writer

Nicholas Davidson disagrees with the feminist perspective, which he feels is a one-dimensional interpretation of human existence. He argues that "the Feminist Era is over."

Basing their remarks on a national survey, Shirley Wilkins and Thomas Miller show that most women want to combine work and family, even though it has its difficulties. Social critic George Gilder argues that women are much less committed to careers than men, and he uses various data to support his conclusions.

Sociologist Steven Goldberg believes there are inherent, unchangeable differences between men and women that make patriarchy inevitable. Professor Cynthia Fuchs Epstein contends that the passage of the time has destroyed any plausibility Goldberg's thesis might once have had.

Social commentator George Gilder praises the American political economy that provides so many incentives for people to get ahead and make money, and he claims that the economic system is dynamic and that all classes benefit from it. Psychologist William Ryan contends that income inequalities in America are excessive and immoral because they vastly exceed differences in merit and result in tremendous hardships for the poor.

Professor Edward Banfield suggests that it is the cultural outlook of the poor that tends to keep them in poverty. Psychologist Ryan responds that this view is a form of "blaming the victim."

Sociologist William Julius Wilson argues that class, rather than race, is now the dominant factor in determining a person's life chances. Educator Charles V. Willie counters that race remains the primary consideration.

Harvard professor Glenn Loury contends that insistence on "ill-suited" civil rights strategies makes it impossible for blacks to achieve full equality in American society. Professor Herman Schwartz argues that we must somehow undo the cruel consequences of racism that still plague our society and those who are subject to it.

Political scientist Charles E. Lindblom contends that corporate leaders hold a privileged position in U.S. society that is inconsistent with democratic theory and vision. Professor David Vogel counters that business influence is limited and that large corporations pose no threat to democratic thought and structures.

Political scientist John J. DiIulio, Jr., argues that poverty and many of America's social ills are traceable to the depraved street criminals who prey on inner-city communities. Criminologist Jeffrey H. Reiman takes the opposite view, and he describes to the harmful effects of white-collar crimes and the menace they pose for all Americans.

Writer and philosophy student Claudia Mills contends that the financial and social costs of fighting drugs using conventional methods is excessive and not productive. She argues for durg legalization. Political scientists James W. Wilson and John J. DiIulio, Jr., argue that legalizing drugs would only worsen an already staggering social problem.

Professor James Q. Wilson argues that imprisoning everyone convicted of a serious crime for several years would greatly reduce these crimes. He contends that incapacitation is the one policy that works. Judge David L. Bazelon discusses the moral and financial costs of the incapacitation approach and argues that society must attack the brutal social and economic conditions that are the root causes of street crime.

Population Institute representatives Hal Burdett, Werner Fornos, Sheila
Kinkade, and David Meyer state in their report to the 101st Congress that
overpopulation is a crisis affecting Africa's future. Philosophy student Ray
Percival maintains that overpopulation problems are lessening rather than
worsening.

Economist Julian L. Simon believes the public has been misled by the media
with frightening tales of environmental problems, which can be alleviated
through human effort and inventiveness. Worldwatch Institute environmentalists Lester R. Brown, Christopher Flavin, and Edward C. Wolf argue that
the earth's fragile ecological support system is being eroded with potentially
disasterous consequences.

Historian Paul Kennedy warns that the United States, like other great
powers, must strike a balance between its international military commitments and its own economic development or it will continue to decline.
Political scientist Samuel P. Huntington is optimistic that the decline is
temporary and reversible, and he argues that the future holds promise for
renewal.

INTRODUCTION

Debating Social Issues

Kurt Finsterbusch

George McKenna

WHAT IS SOCIOLOGY?

"I have become a problem to myself," St. Augustine said. Put into a social and secular framework, St. Augustine's concern marks the starting point of sociology. We have become a problem to ourselves, and it is sociology that seeks to understand the problem and, perhaps, to find some solutions. The subject matter of sociology, then, is ourselves—people interacting with one another in groups.

Auguste Comte (1798–1857), the French mathematician and philosopher who is considered to be the father of sociology, had a vision of a well run society based on social science knowledge. Social scientists (all of whom he called sociologists) would discover the laws of social life and then determine how society should be structured and run. Society would not become perfect because some problems are intractable, but he believed that a society guided by scientists and other experts was the best possible society.

Unfortunately, Comte's vision was extremely naive. For most matters of state there is no one best way of structuring or doing things that sociologists can discover and recommend. Instead, sociologists debate more social issues than they resolve.

The purpose of sociology is to throw light on social issues and their relationship to the complex, confusing, and dynamic social world around us. It seeks to describe how society is organized and how individuals fit into it. But neither the organization of society nor the fit of individuals is perfect. Social disorganization is a fact of life—at least in modern, complex societies such as the one we live in. Here, perfect harmony continues to elude us, and "social problems" are endemic. The very institutions, laws, and policies that produce benefits also produce what sociologists call "unintended effects"— unintended and undesirable. The changes that please one sector of the society may displease another, or the changes that seem so indisputably healthy and good have a dark underside to them. The examples are endless. Modern urban life gives people privacy and freedom from snooping neighbors that the small town never afforded; yet, that very privacy seems to breed an uneasy sense of anonymity and loneliness. Or take another example: Hierarchy is necessary for organizations to function efficiently, but hierarchy leads to the creation of a ruling elite. Flatten out the hierarchy, and you may achieve social equality—but at the price of confusion, incompetence, and low productivity.

This is not to say that all efforts to effect social change are ultimately futile and that the only sound view is the tragic one that concludes "nothing works." We can be realistic without falling into despair. In many respects, the human condition has improved over the centuries and has improved as a result of conscious social policies. But improvements are purchased at a price—not only a monetary price but one involving human discomfort and discontent. The job of policymakers is to balance the anticipated benefits against the probable costs.

It can never hurt policymakers to know more about the society in which they work or the social issues they confront. That, broadly speaking, is the purpose of sociology. It is what this book is about. This volume examines social issues that are central to the study of sociology.

SOCIALIZATION AND VALUES

A common value system is the major mechanism for integrating a society, so it is essential that young people become socialized to internalize the basic elements of the society's value system. How should this be done? What is the best way for children to become moral and responsible adults? The traditional method is indoctrination. Parents and teachers essentially pursue indoctrination methods to instruct children as to the society's value system. Progressive educators, however, think that young people need to work out their moral systems throug dialogue with parents, educators, other authorities, and friends. Lawrence Kohlberg's research on the cognitive and moral development of children greatly strengthened this viewpoint. Some of his work, and that of a traditionalist, Edward A. Wynne, is presented in Issue 1. Issue 2 switches to another socializing system, the media. The debate here is over whether or not the media, on average, are basically conservative, and teach compliance with the existing arrangements of society, or liberal, and act as social critics.

SEX ROLES AND THE FAMILY

An area of tremendous value change in the last several decades is sex roles and the family. Women in large numbers have rejected major aspects of their traditional sex roles and family roles while remaining strongly committed to much of the mother role and to many feminine characteristics. In fact, on these issues women are deeply divided. The ones who seek the most change identify themselves as feminists and they have been in the forefront of the modern women's movement. Now a debate is raging as to whether the feminist cause really helps women. (See Issue 3.) Feminist Marilyn French identifies positive changes that feminists have accomplished and many changes that are still needed. Nicholas Davidson attacks feminism as intellectually unsound and generally harmful. Issue 4 is more concrete. Can women combine careers and families? Shirley Williams and Thomas Miller present evidence that they can, while George Gilder comes to the opposite conclusion.

STRATIFICATION AND INEQUALITY

Issue 5 is both a feminist issue and a stratification issue. How do we explain the supposed finding that patriarchy or male dominance is possibly universal? Stephen Goldberg presents an unrelenting argument that it is genetically based and cannot be readily changed. Cynthia Fuchs Epstein says it is not universal nor genetically based but results from systematic domination and subordination of women, which democratic societies must end.

Issue 6 centers around a perennial sociological debate about whether inequality is beneficial (functional) to society. George Gilder claims that it is and William Ryan argues that inequalities should be greatly reduced. Closely related to this debate is the issue of why the poor are poor. The "culture of poverty" thesis maintains that most long-term poverty in America is the result of a culture that is all too common among the poor. The implication is that those who always seek immediate material gratification will not climb out of poverty, even if they are helped by welfare and social programs. Others see most of the poor as victims of adverse conditions; they ridicule the culture of poverty thesis as a way of "blaming the victim." In Issue 7 we present a clear-cut exchange on this issue, with Edward Banfield saying "yes" to the question of whether "lower-class" culture perpetuates poverty, and William Ryan saying "no."

The next two issues deal with lively debates on the black civil rights movement. Has oppression because of race significantly declined in America, or does it remain as bad as it was in the recent past? Two black sociologists, William J. Wilson and Charles V. Willie, differ in Issue 8. Then there is the controversy over affirmative action or racial quotas. Is equality promoted or undermined by such policies? Professors Glenn Loury and Herman Schwartz take opposing sides on this question in Issue 9.

POLITICAL ECONOMY

Sociologists study not only the poor, the workers, and the victims of discrimination but also those at the top of society—those who occupy what the late sociologist C. Wright Mills used to call "the command posts." The question is whether the "pluralist" model or the "power elite" model is the one that best fits the facts in America. Does a single power elite rule the United States or do many groups contend for power and influence so that the political process is accessible to all? In Issue 10, political scientist Charles E. Lindblom argues that the business elite have a dominating influence in government decisions and that no other group has nearly as much power, while David Vogel sees the business class as one of many groups with power.

But what kind of political economy does the single or plural elites control? The United States is a capitalist welfare state. The economy is based on private enterprise and the relatively free markets of capitalism, with the full support of the state. The state, however, is also committed to the welfare of those who are not provided for by the labor market.

In Issue 11, economist John Kenneth Galbraith and former Treasury Secretary William Simon debate the question of whether American government has become too big. In Issue 12, writer Charles Murray argues that the welfare programs of the "Great Society" are colossal failures and should be abandoned. On the other hand, Professor Christopher Jencks thinks the data indicate that welfare programs have been successful and that to abolish the programs would spell disaster for the poor.

The last political economy issue moves up to the global level. According to world systems theory, which is now the dominant view in sociology, the core capitalist countries in the West develop in part by exploiting Third World countries and thereby retarding their development. This view is developed by Gerald J. Kruijer in Issue 13, while Peter Berger points out that multinational corporations, in most cases, contribute greatly to the Third World countries in which they operate.

CRIME AND SOCIAL CONTROL

Crime is interesting to sociologists because crimes are those activities which society makes illegal and will use force to stop. Why are some acts made illegal and others which are more harmful not made illegal? Surveys indicate that concern about crime is extremely high in America. Is the fear of crime, however, rightly placed? Americans fear mainly street crime, but Jeffrey Reiman argues in Issue 14 that corporate crimes cause far more death, harm, and financial loss to Americans than street crime. In contrast, John DiIulio points out the great harm done by street criminals, even to the point of social disintegration in some poor neighborhoods. Much of the harm that he describes is related to the illegal drug trade, which is having such bad consequences that some people are seriously talking about legalizing drugs in order to kill the illegal drug business. Claudia Mills at the Institute for Philosophy and Public Policy argues this view in Issue 15, while James Q. Wilson and John J. DiIulio argue that legalization would greatly expand the use of dangerous drugs and the personal tragedies and social costs resulting therefrom. Another issue is whether adults should be allowed to make their own decisions on matters like drugs. Finally, we examine whether deterrence or tough sentencing of criminals will stop crime. The debate is whether our society should focus on deterrence by meting out sentencing on a tougher and more uniform basis. Or should our emphasis be on rehabilitating criminals and eliminating the social conditions that breed crime? These alternatives are explored in the debate between Judge David Bazelon and political scientist James Q. Wilson in Issue 16.

THE FUTURE

Many social commentators speculate on "the fate of the earth." The environmentalists have their own vision of apocalypse. They foresee the human race overshooting the carrying capacity of the globe. The resulting collapse could lead to the extinction of much of the human race and the end of free societies. Population growth and increasing per capita levels of consumption, say some experts, are leading us to this catastrophe. We examine two issues that have been much debated since the ecology movement began in the late 1960s. In Issue 17, Ray Percival and Hal Burdett and his colleagues argue over whether the world is really threatened by "overpopulation." Issue 18 features Julian Simon arguing with ecologists Lester Brown, Christopher Flavin, and Edward C. Wolf over whether the world's physical environment is getting better or worse. Finally, we turn to projections of America's future from a different perspective.

The last issue in this book deals with the future role of America in the world. Historian Paul Kennedy argues that America has overextended itself militarily and is in the process of decline similar to the decline of previous empires. He predicts America's fortunes, therefore, on the basis of a theory of the rise and fall of empires. This makes him the present heir of an intellectual tradition going back to the English historian Arnold Toynbee (1889–1975) and the classical tradition in sociology. Kennedy's critic Samuel P. Huntington, however, does not debate theories of empire but rather argues that the trends that Kennedy points to are only temporary and will soon be reversed, so his thesis is beside the point.

OBJECTIVTY AND SUBJECTIVITY

The topics presented in this book range far and wide—from patriarchy to welfare to the U.S. capitalist economy. What they all have in common is that they are at once subjective and objective issues. The point deserves some discussion.

When St. Augustine said "I have become a problem to myself," he was pondering the problem of how he could remember forgetfulness. If to forget means to obliterate from memory, how can forgetfulness be remembered? It was that riddle (which need not concern us here) that set him thinking about the vast difference between physical science and humanistic investigations. "For I am not now investigating the tracts of the heavens, or measuring the distance of the stars, or trying to discover how the earth hangs in space. I am investigating myself, my memory, my mind." The distinction is between the subjective, what is "in our heads," and the objective, that which is "out there." This is a valuable distinction, but it needs to be qualified. There is a third area, the public realm, that is partly subjective and partly objective. It consists of the actions and interactions of human beings and leads to all sorts of objective happenings; yet the subjective obviously plays a role in what happens. People act on what they believe and think and feel, and their minds, in turn, are influenced by the public environment.

At its best, sociology attempts to hold together both the objective and the subjective without allowing either to overwhelm the other.

CONCLUSION

Writing in the 1950s, a period in some ways like our own, the sociologist C. Wright Mills said that Americans know a lot about their "troubles," but they cannot make the connections between seemingly personal concerns and the concerns of others in the world. If they could only learn to make those connections, he said, they could turn their concerns into *issues*. An issue transcends the realm of the personal. According to Mills, "An issue is a public matter: some value cherished by publics is felt to be threatened. Often there is a debate about what the value really is and what it is that really threatens it."

It is not only personal troubles but social issues that we have tried to present in this book. The variety of topics in it can be taken as an invitation to discover what Mills called "the sociological imagination." This imagination, said Mills, "is the capacity to shift from one perspective to another—from the political to the psychological; from examination of a single family to comparative assessment of the national budgets of the world. . . . It is the capacity to range from the most impersonal and remote transformations to the most intimate features of the human self—and to see the relations between the two." This book, with a range of issues well suited to the sociological imagination, is intended to enlarge that capacity.

United Nations/Milton Grant

PART 1

Socialization and Values

Sociologists recognize that a society's view of what is acceptable, or worthy, or moral, is subject to change as that society's culture evolves. The values of a society—and the social skills needed for an individual to function within that society's framework of values—can be inculcated in many ways. To what extent does society rely on the schools to imbue its young people with moral values? How should that be accomplished? What role does the news media play in transmitting values, particularly political values? Are they advocates of one political view or another? These are some of the questions sociologists face in a dynamic, rapidly changing, highly industrialized society.

Teaching Moral Values in the Schools: Is Indoctrination the Wrong Approach?

Are Liberal Values Propagated by the News Media?

1

ISSUE 1

Teaching Moral Values in the Schools: Is Indoctrination the Wrong Approach?

YES: Lawrence Kohlberg, from "The Cognitive-Development Approach to Moral Education," *Phi Delta Kappan* (June 1975)

NO: Edward A. Wynne, from "The Great Tradition in Education: Transmitting Moral Values," *Educational Leadership* (December 1985/January 1986)

ISSUE SUMMARY

YES: Lawrence Kohlberg, a noted educator and author, suggests that an open-ended and nondirective approach to moral education in the schools will help students develop a mature grasp of ethics. Schools should go no further than stimulating and eliciting an awareness of values; they should not teach students any set of rules and values.

NO: Edward Wynne, a professor of education, makes the case for schools to return to their traditional role of deliberately transmitting moral values to students, and he argues that the best method for doing so is by indoctrination.

In all societies, human beings become fully human by learning the culture that surrounds them—the great collection of beliefs and behavior patterns that people continuously observe and absorb from birth to death. In their study of cultures, sociologists emphasize the importance of how the young are socialized to the basic values of the society.

Western tradition has always been deeply ambivalent about what we today call values education. On the one hand, there has always been a concern that, without a firm and early grounding in morality, young people will grow up to be lawless and dissolute. On the other hand, there has been a recognition that moral behavior must consist of more than puppet-like obedience; it must proceed from some sort of interior principles that are not merely memorized but grasped by the mind and the heart. "The letter kills," said St. Paul during the early years of Christianity, "but the spirit gives life." Paul was a very stern moralist, yet he insisted that written rules of behavior ("the letter") must be subordinated to the spirit underlying them. Paul would surely agree that the spirit cannot be transferred mechanically into people's consciousness. People must be inspired.

Inspiration can take several forms; in the Judeo-Christian tradition, miracles and other forms of divine intervention play a prominent role. In Western philosophy, human cognition has always been emphasized: the rules of moral behavior must pass the test of reason. "The unexamined life is not worth living," said Socrates at his trial in Athens in 399 B.C. Socrates was accused of corrupting the youth of Athens by teaching them to question the conventional moral wisdom of the city. In his defense, Socrates proudly characterized himself as a "gadfly," one who proposed no final answers but only a stinging series of questions about the rules of morality. Yet even here there is ambivalence. Plato, who was Socrates' greatest pupil, wrote down Socrates' famous defense and certainly must have approved of it, but he also drew up a pedagogical scheme that emphasized indoctrination and even "noble lies" in the education of the young. Such an education would leave little or no room for extended Socratic questioning.

The ambivalence runs throughout Western history. Should moral education raise questions or teach answers? During the Middle Ages, trained theologians were allowed to debate disputed questions on religion and morality, but ordinary people were given the answers and told to obey. In more recent times, attempts have been made to work out systems of moral reasoning that can be taught to young people. In America at the end of the eighteenth century, Benjamin Franklin said that the young should be taught that it was in "everyone's interest to be virtuous who wished to be happy even in this world." Temperance was considered to be good for health; hard work and patience would produce wealth; and so on. Franklin's contemporary in Germany was the philosopher Immanuel Kant. He wrote that morality could be grounded on a "categorical imperative": act as if you would wish the maxim of your conduct were universal. If you want people to be honest, Kant suggested, you yourself must be honest; otherwise, you would be logically inconsistent.

It is questionable whether either logic or self-interest can be used to teach morality to the young. Every youngster today can see that many corrupt people prosper and lead pleasurable lives. As for logical consistency, why is that sufficient to keep young people in line? What is so great about logic? But perhaps there are other ways to help the young work out meaningful moral codes. Some educators think that values clarification—showing students the implications of various moral choices—will lead them to make the right ones. Others worry that this will produce even greater confusion in the minds of the young.

In the following selections, Lawrence Kohlberg suggests that an open-ended and nondirective approach to values education will help students develop a mature grasp of ethics, while Edward A. Wynne makes the case for moral indoctrination of young people.

YES

Lawrence Kohlberg

MORAL GROWTH STAGES

The cognitive-developmental approach was fully stated for the first time by John Dewey. The approach is called *cognitive* because it recognizes that moral education, like intellectual education, has its basis in stimulating the *active thinking* of the child about moral issues and decisions. It is called developmental because it sees the aims of moral education as movement through moral stages. According to Dewey:

> The aim of education is growth or *development*, both intellectual and moral. Ethical and psychological principles can aid the school in the *greatest of all constructions—the building of a free and powerful character*. Only knowledge of the *order and connection of the stages in psychological development can insure this*. Education is the work of *supplying the conditions* which will enable the psychological functions to mature in the freest and fullest manner.

Dewey postulated three levels of moral development: 1) the *pre-moral* or *preconventional* level "of behavior motivated by biological and social impulses with results for morals," 2) the *conventional* level of behavior "in which the individual accepts with little critical reflection the standards of his group," and 3) the *autonomous* level of behavior in which "conduct is guided by the individual thinking and judging for himself whether a purpose is good, and does not accept the standard of his group without reflection."[1]

Dewey's thinking about moral stages was theoretical. Building upon his prior studies of cognitive stages, Jean Piaget made the first effort to define stages of moral reasoning in children through actual interviews and through observations of children (in games with rules). Using this interview material, Piaget defined the pre-moral, the conventional, and the autonomous levels as follows: 1) the *pre-moral stage*, where there is no sense of obligation to rules; 2) the *heteronomous stage*, where the right was literal obedience to rules and an equation of obligation with submission to power and punishment (roughly ages 4–8); and 3) the *autonomous stage*, where the purpose and consequences of following rules are considered and obligation is based on reciprocity and exchange (roughly ages 8–12).[2]

In 1955 I started to redefine and validate (through longitudinal and cross-cultural study) the Dewey-Piaget levels and stages. The resulting stages are presented in Table 1.

We claim to have validated the stages defined in Table 1. The notion that stages can be *validated* by longitudinal study implies that stages have definite empirical characteristics. The concept of stages (as used by Piaget and myself) implies the following characteristics:

1. Stages are "structured wholes," or organized systems of thought. Individuals are *consistent* in level of moral judgment.

2. Stages form an *invariant sequence*. Under all conditions except extreme trauma, movement is always forward, never backward. Individuals never skip stages; movement is always to the next stage up.

3. Stages are "hierarchical integrations." Thinking at a higher stage includes or comprehends within it lower-stage thinking. There is a tendency to function at or prefer the highest stage available.

Each of these characteristics has been demonstrated for moral stages. Stages are defined by responses to a set of verbal moral dilemmas classified according to an elaborate scoring scheme. Validating studies include:

1. A 20-year study of 50 Chicago-area boys, middle- and working-class. Initially interviewed at ages 10–16, they have been reinterviewed at three-year intervals thereafter.

2. A small, six-year longitudinal study of Turkish villages and city boys of the same age.

3. A variety of other cross-sectional studies in Canada, Britain, Israel, Taiwan, Yucatán, Honduras, and India.

With regard to the structured whole or consistency criterion, we have found that more than 50% of an individual's thinking is always at one stage, with the remainder at the next adjacent stage (which he is leaving or which he is moving into).

With regard to invariant sequence, our longitudinal results have been presented in the *American Journal of Orthopsychiatry*, and indicate that on every retest individuals were either at the same stage as three years earlier or had moved up. This was true in Turkey as well as in the United States.

With regard to the hierarchical integration criterion, it has been demonstrated that adolescents exposed to written statements at each of the six stages comprehend or correctly put in their own words all statements at or below their own stage but fail to comprehend any statements more than one stage above their own. Some individuals comprehend the next stage above their own; some do not. Adolescents prefer (or rank as best) the highest stage they can comprehend.

To understand moral stages, it is important to clarify their relations to stage of logic or intelligence, on the one hand, and to moral behavior on the other. Maturity of moral judgment is not highly correlated with IQ or verbal intelligence (correlations are only in the 30s, accounting for 10% of the variance). Cognitive development, in the stage sense, however, is more important for moral development than such correlations suggest. Piaget has found that after the child learns to speak there are three major stages of reasoning: the intuitive, the concrete operational, and the formal operational. At around age 7, the child enters the stage of concrete logical

Table 1

Definition of Moral Stages

I. Preconventional level

At this level, the child is responsive to cultural rules and labels of good and bad, right or wrong, but interprets these labels either in terms of the physical or the hedonistic consequences of action (punishment, reward, exchange of favors) or in terms of the physical power of those who enunciate the rules and labels. The level is divided into the following two stages:

Stage 1: *The punishment-and-obedience orientation.* The physical consequences of action determine its goodness or badness, regardless of the human meaning or value of these consequences. Avoidance of punishment and unquestioning deference to power are valued in their own right, not in terms of respect for an underlying moral order supported by punishment and authority (the latter being Stage 4).

Stage 2: *The instrumental-relativist orientation.* Right action consists of that which instrumentally satisfies one's own needs and occasionally the needs of others. Human relations are viewed in terms like those of the marketplace. Elements of fairness, of reciprocity, and of equal sharing are present, but they are always interpreted in a physical, pragmatic way. Reciprocity is a matter of "you scratch my back and I'll scratch yours," not of loyalty, gratitude, or justice.

II. Conventional level

At this level, maintaining the expectations of the individual's family, group; or nation is perceived as valuable in its own right, regardless of immediate and obvious consequences. The attitude is not only one of *conformity* to personal expectations and social order, but of loyalty to it, of actively *maintaining*, supporting, and justifying the order, and of identifying with the person or group involved in it. At this level, there are the following two stages:

Stage 3: *The interpersonal concordance or "good boy-nice girl" orientation.* Good behavior is that which pleases or helps others and is approved by them. There is much conformity to stereotypical images of what is majority or "natural" behavior. Behavior is frequently judged by intention—"he means well" becomes important for the first time. One earns approval by being "nice."

Stage 4: *The "law and order" orientation.* There is orientation toward authority, fixed rules, and the maintenance of the social order. Right behavior consists of doing one's duty, showing respect for authority, and maintaining the given social order for its own sake.

III. Postconventional, autonomous, or principled level

At this level, there is a clear effort to define moral values and principles that have validity and application apart from the authority of the groups or persons holding these principles and apart from the individual's own identification with these groups. This level also has two stages:

Stage 5: *The social-contract, legalistic orientation*, generally with utilitarian overtones. Right action tends to be defined in terms of general individual rights and standards which have been critically examined and agreed upon by the whole society. There is a clear awareness of the relativism of personal values and opinions and a corresponding emphasis upon procedural rules for reaching consensus. Aside from what is constitutionally and democratically agreed upon, the right is a matter of personal "values" and "opinion." The result is an emphasis upon the "legal point of view," but with an emphasis upon the possibility of changing law in terms of rational considerations of social utility (rather than freezing it in terms of Stage 4 "law and order"). Outside the legal realm, free agreement and contract is the binding element of obligation. This is the "official" morality of the American government and constitution.

Stage 6: *The universal-ethical-principle orientation.* Right is defined by the decision of conscience in accord with self-chosen *ethical principles* appealing to logical comprehensiveness, universality, and consistency. These principles are abstract and ethical (the Golden Rule, the categorical imperative); they are not concrete moral rules like the Ten Commandments. At heart, these are universal principles of *justice*, of the *reciprocity* and *equality* of human *rights*, and of respect for the dignity of human beings as *individual persons*. ("From Is to Ought," pp. 164, 165)

—Reprinted from *The Journal of Philosophy*, October 25, 1973.

thought: he can make logical inferences, classify, and handle quantitative relations about concrete things. In adolescence individuals usually enter the stage of formal operations. At this stage they can reason abstractly, i.e., consider all possibilities, form hypotheses, deduce implications from hypotheses, and test them against reality.[3]

Since moral reasoning clearly is reasoning, advanced moral reasoning depends upon advanced logical reasoning: a person's logical stage puts a certain ceiling on the moral stage he can attain. A person whose logical stage is only concrete operational is limited to the preconventional moral stages (Stages 1 and 2). A person whose logical stage is only partially formal operational is limited to the conventional moral stages (Stages 3 and 4). While logical development is necessary for moral development and sets limits to it, most individuals are higher in logical stage than they are in moral stage. As an example, over 50% of late adolescents and adults are capable of full formal reasoning, but only 10% of these adults (all formal operational) display principled (Stages 5 and 6) moral reasoning.

The moral stages are *structures of moral judgment* or *moral reasoning*. *Structures* of moral judgment must be distinguished from the *content* of moral judgment. As an example, we cite responses to a dilemma used in our various studies to identify moral stage. The dilemma raises the issue of stealing a drug to save a dying woman. The inventor of the drug is selling it for 10 times what it costs him to make it. The woman's husband cannot raise the money, and the seller refuses to lower the price or wait for payment. What should the husband do?

The choice endorsed by a subject (steal, don't steal) is called the *content* of his moral judgment in the situation. His reasoning about the choice defines the structure of his moral judgment. This reasoning centers on the following 10 universal moral values or issues of concern to persons in these moral dilemmas:

1. Punishment
2. Property
3. Roles and concerns of affection
4. Roles and concerns of authority
5. Law
6. Life
7. Liberty
8. Distributive justice
9. Truth
10. Sex

A moral choice involves choosing between two (or more) of these values as they *conflict* in concrete situations of choice.

The stage or structure of a person's moral judgment defines; 1) *what* he finds valuable in each of these moral issues (life, law), i.e., how he defines the value, and 2) *why* he finds it valuable, i.e., the reasons he gives for valuing it. As an example, at Stage 1 life is valued in terms of the power or possessions of the person involved; at Stage 2, for its usefulness in satisfying the needs of the individual in question or others; at Stage 3, in terms of the individual's relations with others and their valuation of him; at Stage 4, in terms of social or religious law. Only at Stages 5 and 6 is each life seen as inherently worthwhile, aside from other consideration.

MORAL JUDGMENT VS. MORAL ACTION

Having clarified the nature of stages of moral *judgment*, we must consider the relation of moral judgment to moral *action*. If logical reasoning is a necessary but not sufficient condition for mature moral judgment, mature moral judgment is a necessary but not sufficient condition for mature moral action. One cannot follow moral principles if one does not understand (or believe in) moral principles. However, one can reason in terms of principles and not live up to these principles. As an example, Richard Krebs and I found that only 15% of students showing some principled thinking cheated as compared to 55% of conventional subjects and 70% of preconventional subjects. Nevertheless, 15% of the principled subjects did cheat, suggesting that factors additional to moral judgment are necessary for principled moral reasoning to be translated into "moral action." Partly, these factors include the situation and its pressures. Partly, what happens depends upon the individual's motives and emotions. Partly, what the individual does depends upon a general sense of will, purpose, or "ego strength." As an example of the role of will or ego strength in moral behavior, we may cite the study of Krebs: Slightly more than half of his conventional subjects cheated. These subjects were also divided by a measure of attention/will. Only 26% of the "strong-willed" conventional subjects cheated; however, 74% of the "weak-willed" subjects cheated.

If maturity of moral reasoning is only one factor in moral behavior, why does the cognitive-developmental approach to moral education focus so heavily upon moral reasoning? For the following reasons:

1. Moral judgment, while only one factor in moral behavior, is the single most important or influential factor yet discovered in moral behavior.

2. While other factors influence moral behavior, moral judgment is the only distinctively *moral* factor in moral behavior. To illustrate, we noted that the Krebs study indicated that "strong-willed" conventional stage subjects resisted cheating more than "weak-willed" subjects. For those at a preconventional level of moral reasoning, however, "will" had an opposite effect. "Strong-willed" Stages 1 and 2 subjects cheated more, not less, than "weak-willed" subjects, i.e., they had the "courage of their (amoral) convictions" that it was worthwhile to cheat. "Will," then, is an important factor in moral behavior, but it is not distinctively moral; it becomes moral only when informed by mature moral judgment.

3. Moral judgment change is long-range or irreversible; a higher stage is never lost. Moral behavior as such is largely situational and reversible or "lose-able" in new situations.

AIMS OF MORAL AND CIVIC EDUCATION

Moral psychology describes what moral development is, as studied empirically. Moral education must also consider moral philosophy, which strives to tell us what moral development ideally *ought to be*. Psychology finds an invariant sequence of moral stages; moral philosophy must be invoked to answer whether a later stage is a better stage. The "stage" of senescence and death follows the "stage" of adulthood, but that does not mean that senescence and death are better. Our claim that the latest or principled stages of moral reasoning are morally better stages, then, must rest on considerations of moral philosophy.

The tradition of moral philosophy to which we appeal is the liberal and rational tradition, in particular the "formalistic" or "deonotological" tradition running from Immanuel Kant to John Rawls. Central to this tradition is the claim that an adequate morality is *principled*, i.e., that it makes judgments in terms of *universal* principles applicable to all mankind. *Principles* are to be distinguished from *rules*. Conventional morality is grounded on rules, primarily "thou shalt nots" such as are represented by the Ten Commandments, prescriptions of kinds of actions. Principles are, rather, universal guides to making a moral decision. An example is Kant's "categorical imperative," formulated in two ways. The first is the maxim of respect for human personality, "Act always toward the other as an end, not as a means." The second is the maxim of universalization, "Choose only as you would be willing to have everyone choose in your situation." Principles like that of Kant's state the formal conditions of a moral choice or action. In the dilemma in which a woman is dying because a druggist refuses to release his drug for less than the stated price, the druggist is not acting morally, though he is not violating the ordinary moral rules (he is not actually stealing or murdering). But he is violating principles: He is treating the woman simply as a means to his ends of profit, and he is not choosing as he would wish anyone to choose (if the druggist were in the dying woman's place, he would not want a druggist to choose as he is choosing). Under most circumstances, choice in terms of conventional moral rules and choice in terms of principles coincide. Ordinarily, principles dictate not stealing (avoiding stealing is implied by acting in terms of a regard for others as ends and in terms of what one would want everyone to do). In a situation where stealing is the only means to save a life, however, principles contradict the ordinary rules and would dictate stealing. Unlike rules which are supported by social authority, principles are freely chosen by the individual because of their intrinsic moral validity.[4]

The conception that a moral choice is a choice made in terms of moral principles is related to the claim of liberal moral philosophy that moral principles are ultimately principles of justice. In essence, moral conflicts are conflicts between the claims of persons, and principles for resolving these claims are principles of justice, "for giving each his due." Central to justice are the demands of *liberty, equality*, and *reciprocity*. At every moral stage, there is a concern for justice. The most damning statement a school child can make about a teacher is that "he's not fair." At each higher stage, however, the conception of justice is reorganized. At Stage 1, justice is punishing the bad in terms of "an eye for an eye and a tooth for a tooth." At Stage 2, it is exchanging favors and goods in an equal manner. At Stages 3 and 4, it is treating people as they desire in terms of the conventional rules. At Stage 5, it is recognized that all rules and laws flow from justice, from a social contract between the governors and the governed designed to protect the equal rights of all. At Stage 6, personally chosen moral principles are also principles of justice, the principles any member of a society would choose for that society if he did not know what his position was to be in the society and in which he might be the least advantaged. Principles chosen from this point of view are, first, the maximum liberty compatible with the like liberty of others and, second, no inequalities of goods and respect which are not to the benefit of all, including the least advantaged.

As an example of stage progression in the orientation of justice, we may take judgments about capital punishment. Capital punishment is only firmly rejected at the two principled stages, when the notion of justice as vengeance or retribution is abandoned. At the sixth stage, capital punishment is not condoned even if it may have some useful deterrent effect in promoting law and order. This is because it is not a punishment we would choose for a society if we assumed we had as much chance of being born into the position of a criminal or murderer as being born into the position of a law abider.

Why are decisions based on universal principles of justice better decisions? Because they are decisions on which all moral men could agree. When decisions are based on conventional moral rules, men will disagree, since they adhere to conflicting systems of rules dependent on culture and social position. Throughout history men have killed one another in the name of conflicting moral rules and values, most recently in Vietnam and the Middle East. Truly moral or just resolutions of conflicts require principles which are, or can be, universalizable.

ALTERNATIVE APPROACHES

We have given a philosophic rationale for stage advance as the aim of moral education. Given this rationale, the developmental approach to moral education can avoid the problems inherent in the other two major approaches to moral education. The first alternative approach is that of indoctrinative moral education, the preaching and imposition of the rules and values of the teacher and his culture on the child. In America, when this indoctrinative approach has been developed in a systematic manner, it has usually been termed "character education."

Moral values, in the character education approach, are preached or taught in terms of what may be called the "bag of virtues." In the classic studies of character by Hugh Hartshorne and Mark May, the virtues chosen were honesty, service, and self-control. It is easy to get superficial consensus on such a bag of virtues—until one examines in detail the list of virtues involved and the details of their definition. Is the Hartshorne and May bag more adequate than the Boy Scout bag (a Scout should be honest, loyal, reverent, clean, brave, etc.)? When one turns to the details of defining each virtue, one finds equal uncertainty or difficulty in reaching consensus. Does honesty mean one should not steal to save a life? Does it mean that a student should not help another student with his homework?

Character education and other forms of indoctrinative moral education have aimed at teaching universal values (it is assumed that honesty or service are desirable traits for all men in all societies), but the detailed definitions used are relative; they are defined by the opinions of the teacher and the conventional culture and rest on the authority of the teacher for their justification. In this sense character education is close to the unreflective valuings by teachers which constitute the hidden curriculum of the school.[5] Because of the current unpopularity of indoctrinative approaches to moral education, a family of approaches called "values clarification" has become appealing to teachers. Values clarification takes the first step implied by a rational approach to moral education: the eliciting of the child's own judgment or opinion about issues or situations in which values conflict, rather than imposing the teacher's opinion on him. Values clarification, however, does not attempt to go further than eliciting awareness of values; it is assumed that becoming more self-aware about one's values is an end in itself. Fundamentally, the definition of the end of values education as self-awareness derives form a belief in ethical relativity held by many value-clarifiers. As stated by Peter Engel, "One must contrast value clarification and value inculcation. Value clarification implies the principle that in the consideration of values there is no single correct answer." Within these premises of "no correct answer," children are to discuss moral dilemmas in such a way as to reveal different values and discuss their value differences with each other. The teacher is to stress that "our values are different," not that one value is more adequate than others. If this program is systematically followed, students will themselves become relativists, believing there is no "right" moral answer. For instance, a student caught cheating might argue that he did nothing wrong, since his own hierarchy of values, which may be different from that of the teacher, made it right for him to cheat.

Like values clarification, the cognitive-developmental approach to moral education stresses open or Socratic peer discussion of value dilemmas. Such discussion, however, has an aim: stimulation of movement to the next stage of moral reasoning. Like values clarification, the developmental approach opposes indoctrination. Stimulation of movement to the next stage of reasoning is not indoctrinative, for the following reasons:

1. Change is in the way of reasoning rather than in the particular beliefs involved.

2. Students in a class are at different stages; the aim is to aid movement at each to the next stage, not convergence on a common pattern.

3. The teacher's own opinion is neither stressed nor invoked as authoritative. It enters in only as one of many opinions, hopefully one of those at a next higher stage.

4. The notion that some judgments are more adequate than others is communicated. Fundamentally, however, this means that the student is encouraged to articulate a position which seems most adequate to him and to judge the adequacy of the reasoning of others.

In addition to having more definite aims than values clarification, the moral development approach restricts value education to that which is moral or, more specifically, to justice. This is for two reasons. First, it is not clear that the whole realm of personal, political, and religious values is a realm which is non-relative, i.e., in which there are universals and a direction of development. Second, it is not clear that the public school has a right or mandate to develop values in general.[6] In our view, value education in the public schools should be restricted to that which the school has the right and mandate to develop: an awareness of justice, or of the rights of others in our constitutional system. While the Bill of Rights prohibits the teaching of religious beliefs, or of specific value systems, it does not prohibit the teaching of the awareness of rights and principles of justice fundamental to the Constitution itself.

When moral education is recognized as centered in justice and differentiated from value education or affective education, it becomes apparent that moral and civic education are much the same thing. This equation, taken for granted by the classic philosophers of education from Plato and Aristotle to Dewey, is basic to our claim that a concern for moral education is central to the educational objectives of social studies.

NOTES

1. These levels correspond roughly to our three major levels: the preconventional, the conventional, and the principled. Similar levels were propounded by William McDougall, Leonard Hobhouse, and James Mark Baldwin.

2. Piaget's stages correspond to our first three stages; Stage 0 (pre-moral), Stage 1 (heteronomous), and Stage 2 (instrumental reciprocity).

3. Many adolescents and adults only partially attain the stage of formal operations. They do consider all the actual relations of one thing to another at the same time, but they do not consider all possibilities and form abstract hypoth-eses. A few do not advance this far, remaining "concrete operational."

4. Not all freely chosen values or rules are principles, however. Hitler chose the "rule," "exterminate the enemies of the Aryan race," but such a rule is not a universalizable principle.

5. As an example of the "hidden curriculum," we may cite a second-grade classroom. My son came home from this classroom one day saying he did not want to be "one of the bad boys." Asked "Who are the bad boys?" he replied, "The ones who don't put their books back and get yelled at."

6. Restriction of deliberate value education to the moral may be clarified by our example of the second-grade teacher who made tidying up of books a matter of moral indoctrination. Tidiness is a value, but it is not a moral value. Cheating is a moral issue, intrinsically one of fairness. It involves issues of violation of trust and taking advantage. Failing to tidy the room may under certain conditions be an issue of fairness, when it puts an undue burden on others. If it is handled by the teacher as a matter of cooperation among the group in this sense, it is a legitimate focus of deliberate moral education. If it is not, it simply represents the arbitrary imposition of the teacher's values on the child.

NO

Edward A. Wynne

THE GREAT TRADITION IN EDUCATION: TRANSMITTING MORAL VALUES

Within the recent past, American education substantially disassociated itself from what may be called the great tradition in education: the deliberate transmission of moral values to students. Despite this separation, many education reforms are being considered or are under way to increase the academic demands made on students. These reforms can be generally helpful; however, unless they are sensitive to the implications of our break with the great tradition, their effect on student conduct and morality may be transitory or even harmful. To understand the significance of the great tradition, we must engage in a form of consciousness-raising by enriching our understanding of the past and by understanding the misperceptions that pervade contemporary education.

The transmission of moral values has been the dominant educational concern of most cultures throughout history. Most educational systems have been simultaneously concerned with the transmission of cognitive knowledge—skills, information, and techniques of intellectual analysis—but these admittedly important educational aims, have rarely been given priority over moral education. The current policies in American education that give secondary priority to transmitting morality represent a sharp fracture with the great tradition.

Our break with the past is especially significant in view of the increase since the early 1950s of youth disorder: suicide, homicide, and out-of-wedlock births. Patterns revealed by statistics coincide with popular conceptions about these behaviors. For instance, in 16 of the past 17 Gallup Polls on education, pupil discipline has been the most frequent criticism leveled against public schools. One may wonder if better discipline codes and more homework are adequate remedies for our current school problems, or whether these dysfunctions are more profound and should be treated with more sensitive and complex remedies. Although literacy and student diligence are unquestionably worthy of pursuit, they are only a part of the process of communicating serious morality. If we want to improve the ways

From Edward A. Wynne, "The Great Tradition in Education: Transmitting Moral Values," *Educational Leadership*, vol. 43, no. 4, (December 1985/January 1986). Copyright © 1985 by the Association for Supervision and Curriculum Development. All rights reserved. Reprinted by permission.

we are now transmitting morality, it makes sense to recall the way morality was transmitted before youth disorder became such a distressing issue.

SOME DEFINITIONS

The term "moral values" is ambiguous and requires some definition. It signifies the specific values that particular cultures generally hold in regard. Such values vary among cultures; during World War II, a Japanese who loved his homeland was likely to be hostile to Americans, and vice versa. Value conflicts along national or ethnic lines are common, although most cultures treat the characteristic we call "patriotism" as a moral value, and treat "treason" with opprobrium. Comparable patterns of value govern interpersonal relations in cultures: beliefs about proper family conduct or the nature of reciprocal relationships. Such beliefs are laden with strong moral components.

In sum, common "moral values" are the vital common beliefs that shape human relations in each culture. Often these values—as in the Ten Commandments—have what is popularly called a religious base. Whether their base is religious, traditional, or secular, however, such values are expected to be widely affirmed under most circumstances.

The term "educational systems" also is somewhat obscure. Contemporary Americans naturally think in terms of formal public or private schools and colleges. But for most history, and all prehistory, formal agencies were a minute part of children's and adolescents' education. In traditional cultures, education was largely transmitted by various formal and informal nonschool agencies: nuclear and extended families; religious institutions; "societies" for the young organized and monitored by adults. In addition, the complex incidental life of preindustrial rural and urban societies, and the demands of work in and out of the family socialized young persons into adult life. Many of these agencies still play important educational roles in contemporary America; nonetheless, in the modern period, the gradual replacement of such agencies by schools has been a strong trend.

TRANSMITTING MORAL VALUES

Whether the dominant educational system has been formal or informal, the transmission of moral values has persistently played a central role. This role has been necessary and universal for two reasons.

1. Human beings are uniquely adaptable animals and live in nearly all climates and in diverse cultural systems. But, as the anthropologist Yehudi Cohen (1964) put it, "No society allows for the random and promiscuous expression of emotions to just anyone. Rather, one may communicate those feelings, either verbally, physically, or materially, to certain people." Because our means of communicating emotions are socially specific, slow maturing young persons must be socialized gradually to the right—or moral—practices appropriate to their special environment.

2. Without effective moral formation, the human propensity for selfishness—or simply the advancement of self-interest—can destructively affect adult institutions. Thus, moral formation is necessary to cultivate our inherent, but moderate, propensity for disinterested sacrifice. The institutions of any persisting society must be organized to ensure

that people's "unselfish genes" are adequately reinforced.

The general modes of moral formation have remained relatively stable throughout all cultures. To be sure, social class and sex-related differences have influenced the quantity and nature of moral formation delivered to the young; for instance, in many environments, limited resources have restricted the extent and intensity of the education provided to lower-class youths. Furthermore, the substance of the moral training transmitted to older youths has varied among cultures: according to Plato, Socrates was put to death because the Athenians disapproved of the moral training he was offering to Athenian young men. But such variations do not lessen the strength of the general model. Despite his affection for Socrates, Plato, in *The Republic* (circa 390 B.C.) emphasized the importance of constraining the learning influences on children and youths, to ensure appropriate moral outcomes.

Although secular and church-related educators have disputed the *means* of moral formation since the nineteenth century both, until comparatively recently, have agreed on their programs' behavioral *ends*. Children should be moral: honest, diligent, obedient, and patriotic. Thus, after the American Revolution, deists and secularists such as Thomas Jefferson and John Adams felt democracy would fail unless citizens acquired an unusually high degree of self-discipline and public spiritedness. They termed this medley of values "republican virtue." After the revolution, many of the original 13 states framed constitutions with provisions such as " . . . no government can be preserved to any people, but by a firm adherence to justice, moderation, temperance, frugality,

and virtue."[1] The founders believed that popular education would be a means of developing such precious traits. As the social historians David J. and Sheila Rothman have written, "The business of schools [in our early history] was not reading and writing but citizenship, not education but social control." The term "social control" may have a pejorative sound to our modern ears, but it simply and correctly means that schools were concerned with affecting conduct, rather than transmitting information or affecting states of mind.

CHARACTERISTICS OF THE GREAT TRADITION

Although issues in moral formation posed some conflicts in traditional societies, there were great areas of congruence around the great tradition of transmitting moral values. Documents generated in historical societies as well as ethnographic studies of many ancient and primitive cultures reveal through anecdote and insight the principles that characterize the tradition. Since the principles are too often ignored in contemporary education, we should consider them in some detail.

• *The tradition was concerned with good habits of conduct as contrasted with moral concepts or moral rationales.* Thus, the tradition emphasized visible courtesy and deference. In the moral mandate, "Honor thy father and mother," the act of *honoring* can be seen. It is easier to observe people *honoring* their parents than *loving* them. Loving, a state of mind, usually must be inferred.

• *The tradition focused on day-to-day moral issues: telling the truth in the face of evident temptation, being polite, or obeying legitimate authority.* It assumed that most moral challenges arose in mundane situations, and that people were often prone to act improperly.

• *The great tradition assumed that no single agency in society had the sole responsibility for moral education.* The varieties of moral problems confronting adults and youths were innumerable. Thus, youths had to be taught to practice morality in many environments. One agency, for example, the nuclear family or the neighborhood, might be deficient, so considerable redundancy was needed. In other words, there could be no neutrality about educating the young in morality: youth-serving agencies were either actively promoral or indifferent.

• *The tradition assumed that moral conduct, especially of the young, needed persistent and pervasive reinforcement.* To advance this end, literature, proverbs, legends, drama, ritual, and folk tales were used for cautionary purposes. Systems of symbolic and real rewards were developed and sustained: schools used ribbons, awards, and other signs of moral merit; noneducational agencies used praise and criticism as well as many symbolic forms of recognition.

• *The tradition saw an important relationship between the advancement of moral learning and the suppression of wrong conduct.* Wrong acts, especially in the presence of the young, were to be aggressively punished, as punishment not only suppressed bad examples, but also corrected particular wrongdoers. The tradition also developed concepts such as "scandal," a public, immoral act that also lowered the prestige of a person or institution. Conversely, since secret immoral acts were less likely to confuse or misdirect innocent persons, they received less disapproval.

• *The tradition was not hostile to the intellectual analysis of moral problems.* Adults recognized that life occasionally generates moral dilemmas. In the Jewish religious tradition, learned men were expected to analyze and debate Talmudic moral issues. Other cultures have displayed similar patterns. But such analyses typically relied on a strong foundation of habit-oriented, mundane moral instruction and practice. Instruction in exegetical analysis commenced only after the selected neophyte had undergone long periods of testing, memorized large portions of semididactic classics, and displayed appropriate deference to exegetical experts.

• *The great tradition assumed that the most important and complex moral values were transmitted through persistent and intimate person-to-person interaction.* In many cases, adult mentors were assigned to develop close and significant relationship with particular youths. The youths might serve as apprentices to such persons, or the mentors might accept significant responsibilities for a young relative. In either case, constructive moral shaping required a comparatively high level of engagement.

• *The tradition usually treated "learners," who were sometimes students, as members of vital groups, such as teams, classes, or clubs.* These groups were important reference points for communicating values, among them, group loyalty, and the diverse incidents of group life provided occasions for object lessons. The emphasis on collective life contrasts sharply with the individualism that pervades contemporary American education, and which is often mistaken for "humanism."

• *The tradition had a pessimistic opinion about the perfectibility of human beings, and about the feasibility or value of breaking with previous socialization patterns.* The tradition did not contend that whatever "is" is necessarily right, but it did assume that the persistence of certain conduct over hundreds of years suggested that careful deliberation should precede any modification or rejection.

As schooling spread, the tendency was to present the formal curriculum in a manner consistent with the tradition, and thus to focus on the transmission of correct habits and values. We should not assume that the interjection of moral concern was necessarily cumbersome. The famous *McGuffey's Reader* series featured stories and essays by substantial writers, such as Walter Scott and Charles Dickens. The literary quality of such writings was appropriate to the age of the student. Significantly, both the materials and their authors supported the development of certain desired traits.

CHARACTER EDUCATION

The most recent efflorescence of the great tradition in America can be found in the "character education" movement in our public schools between 1880 and about 1930. That movement attempted to make public schools more efficient transmitters of appropriate moral values.

The efforts to foster character education assumed schools had to operate from a purely secular basis, which posed special challenges for moral formation. Whereas some earlier education reformers had semisecular sympathies, in previous eras their impact had been tempered by the proreligious forces concurrently affecting schools. Before 1900, for example, probably 15–25 percent of American elementary and secondary school pupils attended either private or public schools that were explicitly religious; an-

other 25–50 percent attended public schools that were tacitly religious. For example, they used readings from the *King James Bible.*

The character education movement articulated numerous traditional moral aims: promptness, truthfulness, courtesy, and obedience. The movement strove to develop elementary and secondary school programs to foster such conduct. It emphasized techniques such as appropriately structured materials in history and literature; school clubs and other extracurricular activities; rigorous pupil discipline codes; and daily flag salutes and frequent assemblies. Many relatively elaborate character education plans were designed and disseminated to schools and school districts. Often the plans were adopted through the mandate of state legislatures or state boards of education. Some modern authorities, such as James Q. Wilson (1973), have perceived a strong relationship between the character education movement and the relatively high levels of youth order in America during the nineteenth century.

AN UNFAVORABLE EVALUATION

From the first, the supporters of character education emphasized rational organization and research. Despite such attempts, much of the research was superficial. Nonetheless, the research persisted because of the importance attributed to character, and gradually its quality improved. During the mid-1920s, researchers led by Hugh Hartschorne and Mark A. May concluded that the relationship between pupil good conduct and the application of formal character education approach was slight. Good conduct appeared to be relatively situation-specific: a person might routinely act correctly in one situation and incorrectly in another slightly different one. A person could cheat on exams, for example, but not steal money from the class fund. This situational specificity meant that good character was not a unified trait that could be cultivated by any single approach.

Despite this research, character education was never formally abandoned. Few educators or researchers have ever said publicly that schools should *not* be concerned with the morality or character of their pupils. Indeed, recent research and statistical reanalysis of earlier data has contended that Hartschorne and May's findings were excessively negative. Still, their research was a turning point in the relationship between American public education and the great tradition of moral values. Before the research many schools were fully concerned with carrying forward that tradition, and the intellectual forces affecting schools were in sympathy with such efforts. Even after the 1930s, many schools still reflexively maintained their former commitment to moral formation; the prevailing intellectual climate among researchers and academics, however, was indifferent or hostile to such efforts. Gradually, a disjunction arose between what some educators and many parents thought was appropriate (and what some of them applied), and what was favored by a smaller, more formally trained group of experts.

Ironically, the research findings of Hartschorne and May did not refute conflict with the major intellectual themes of the great tradition. The tradition emphasized that moral formation was complex. To be effective, it had to be incremental, diverse, pervasive, persistent, and rig-

orous. Essentially, it relied on probalistic principles: the more frequent and more diverse techniques applied, the more likely that more youths would be properly formed; but even if all techniques were applied, some youths would be "missed." Given such principles, it logically follows that the measured long-term effect of any limited program of "moral instruction" would be minute.

The Hartschorne and May findings demonstrated that American expectations for character education were unrealistic, a proposition not inconsistent with expectations we seem to have for *any* education technique. This does not mean that education's effects are inconsequential, but that Americans often approach education from a semi-utopian perspective. We have trouble realizing that many things happen slowly, and that not all problems are solvable.

NEW APPROACHES TO MORAL INSTRUCTION

During the 1930s, 1940s, and 1950s, there was little intellectual or research concern with moral formation in America. Schools continued to be engaged in moral instruction, both deliberately or incidentally, but the in-school process relied on momentum stimulated by earlier perspectives. In other words, moral instruction went on, but without substantial intellectual underpinning.

Since the 1960s, a number of different—perhaps more scientific—approaches to moral instruction have evolved. Many of these approaches have been described by the term "moral education." Among these have been values clarification, identified with Louis L. Raths and Sidney B. Simon, and the moral development approach identified with Lawrence Kohlberg and his colleagues. Despite the variations among contemporary approaches, almost all the more recent techniques have had certain common elements. Their developers were not school teachers, ministers, or education administrators, but college professors who sought to emphasize the scientific base for their efforts. But, most important, the approaches disavowed the great tradition's persistent concern with affecting *conduct*. The moral dilemmas used in some exercises were highly abstract and probably would never arise in real life. Their aim was to cause students to feel or reason in particular ways rather than to practice right conduct immediately.

The developers of the new systems were conscious of Hartschorne and May's research. They recognized the difficulty of shaping conduct and presumably felt that shaping patterns of reasoning was more feasible. Furthermore, many of the moral education approaches were designed as curriculum materials that could be taught through lectures and class discussion. Such designs facilitated their adoption by teachers and schools. Had the approaches aimed to pervasively affect pupil day-to-day conduct, they would have been more difficult to disseminate. Finally, both the researchers and the proponents of the new approaches felt it was morally unjustifiable to apply the vital pressures needed to actually shape pupil's conduct, feeling such pressures would constitute "indoctrination." On the other hand, methods of moral reasoning apparently might be taught as routine school subjects with the tacit consent of the pupils involved.

The anti-indoctrination stance central to the new approaches invites amplification. Obviously, the great tradition regarded the issue of indoctrination as a specious question. Proponents of the great tradition say, "Of course indoctrination happens. It is ridiculous to believe children are capable of objectively assessing most of the beliefs and values they must absorb to be effective adults. They must learn a certain body of 'doctrine' to function on a day-to-day basis in society. There is good and bad doctrine, and thus things must be weighed and assessed. But such assessment is largely the responsibility of parents and other appropriate adults."

It is hard to articulate fairly the position of the anti-indoctrinators. Although they are against indoctrination, they provide no clear answer as to how children are given many real choices in a relatively immutable world necessarily maintained by adults. The anti-indoctrinators also do not say what adults are to do when children's value choices and resulting potential conduct are clearly harmful to them or others. After all, punishments for bad value choices are, in effect, forms of indoctrination. And the idea of presenting pupils with any particular approach to moral education in a school is inherently indoctrinative: the pupils are not allowed to refuse to come to school, or to hear seriously the pros and cons articulated by sympathetic spokespersons (or critics) for moral education or to freely choose among various approaches to them. Providing such choices is antithetical to the operation of any school.

To consider another perspective, the secular nature of the typical public school obviously indoctrinates pupils against practicing religion in that environment, although most religions contend that some religious practices of a public nature are inextricably related to day-to-day life. This "reality" of separating religion and public education is understandable.

However, it is disingenuous to call this policy nonindoctrinative. Thus, it is specious to talk about student choices. The point is that, *on the whole, school is and should and must be inherently indoctrinative.* The only significant questions are: Will the indoctrination be overt or covert, and what will be indoctrinated?

The great tradition has never died. Many administrators and teachers in public and private schools have continued practices consistent with its principles. Given the increased support from academics and intellectuals, . . . these principles deserve widespread professional support.

NOTE

1. The Virginia Constitution.

REFERENCES

Cohen, Y. *The Transition from Childhood to Adolescence.* Chicago: Aldine, 1964.

Hartschorne, H., and May, M. A. *Studies in Deceit, Studies in Service and Self-Control,* and *Studies in the Organization of Character.* New York: Macmillan, 1928, 1929, 1930.

Klapp. O. *The Collective Search for Identity.* New York: Holt, Rinehart, and Winston, 1969.

Meyers, E. *Education in the Perspective of History.* New York: Harper & Row, 1960.

Rothman, D. J., and Rothman, S. M. *Sources of American Social Tradition.* New York: Basic, 1975.

Wilkinson, R. *Governing Elites.* New York: Oxford University Press, 1969.

Wilson, J. Q. "Crime and American Culture." *The Public Interest* 70 (Winter 1973): 22–48.

Wynne, E. A. *Looking at Schools.* Lexington, MA.: Heath/Lexington, 1980.

Yulish, S. M. *The Search for a Civic Religion,* Lanham, Md.: University Press of America, 1980.

POSTSCRIPT

Teaching Moral Values in the Schools: Is Indoctrination the Wrong Approach?

Wynne may not be quite accurate to characterize "the tradition" of moral education as indoctrination. In Western Judeo-Christian societies, there has always been some place for questioning and debate in moral education. Nevertheless, it is true that Western tradition has emphasized firm moral guidance of the young—giving them answers more than questions, and reinforcing the answers at every turn. Has the erosion of this tradition cleared the way for a more mature approach to values education, or has it produced moral confusion and nihilism?

How should moral values be instilled in the young? In his *Republic*, written some time after 380 B.C., Plato proposed a regimen of mathematics, metaphysics, and moral philosophy; even music for young people would be regulated. The eminent behavioral psychologist B. F. Skinner (b. 1904) envisaged a society using various kinds of psychological and material incentives to build good social habits in the young. See his influential *Walden Two* (Macmillan, 1948). Many writers, however, reject indoctrination. In the early 1960s, social critic Paul Goodman worried that American education was putting social conformity ahead of creativity. See Goodman's *Growing Up Absurd* (Random House, 1962). Times have changed since then, and many agree with Wynne that, today, the young need more, not less, normative socialization. See the essays in John H. Bunzel, ed., *Challenge to American Schools: The Case for Standards and Values* (Oxford, 1985).

ISSUE 2

Are Liberal Values Propagated by the News Media?

YES: William Rusher, from *The Coming Battle for the Media* (Morrow, 1988)

NO: Edward S. Herman and Noam Chomsky, from "Propaganda Mill," *The Progressive* (June 1988)

ISSUE SUMMARY

YES: William Rusher, a media analyst and publisher of the *National Review,* argues that the media are biased against conservatives and that news coverage promotes liberal opinions.
NO: Professors Edward Herman and Noam Chomsky critique the mass media from the perspective of the left and find the media to be a "propaganda mill" in the service of the wealthy and powerful.

"A small group of men, numbering perhaps no more than a dozen 'anchormen,' commentators, and executive producers . . . decide what forty to fifty million Americans will learn of the day's events in the nation and the world." The speaker was Spiro Agnew, vice president of the United States during the Nixon administration. The thesis of Agnew's speech, delivered to an audience of midwestern Republicans in 1969, was that the television news media are controlled by a small group of liberals who foist their liberal opinions on viewers under the guise of "news." The upshot of this control, said Agnew, "is that a narrow and distorted picture of America often emerges from the televised news." Many Americans, even many of those who were later shocked by revelations that Agnew took bribes while serving in public office, agreed with Agnew's critique of the "liberal media."

Politicians' complaints about unfair news coverage go back much further than Spiro Agnew and the Nixon administration. The third president of the United States, Thomas Jefferson, was an eloquent champion of the press, but after six years as president, he could hardly contain his bitterness. "The man who never looks into a newspaper," he wrote, "is better informed than he who reads them, inasmuch as he who knows nothing is nearer to truth than he whose mind is filled with falsehoods and errors."

The press today is much different than it was in Jefferson's day. The press then was a mom-and-pop operation. Newspapers were pressed in hand-operated frames in many little printing shops around the country; everything was local and decentralized, and each paper averaged a few hundred subscribers. Today, newspaper chains have taken over most of the once independent local newspapers. The remaining independents rely heavily on national and international wire services. Almost all major magazines have national circulations; some newspapers, like *USA Today* and the *Wall Street Journal,* do too. Other newspapers, like the *New York Times* and the *Washington Post,* enjoy nationwide prestige and help set the nation's news agenda. In the case of television, about 70 percent of national news on television comes from three networks whose programming originates in New York City.

A second important difference between the media of the eighteenth century and the media today has to do with the ideal of objectivity. In past eras, newspapers were frankly partisan sheets, full of nasty barbs at the politicians and parties they didn't like. The ideal of objective journalism is a relatively recent development. It traces back to the early years of the twentieth century. Disgusted with the sensationalist journalism of the time, intellectual leaders urged that newspapers cultivate a core of professionals who would concentrate on accurate reporting and who would leave their opinions to the editorial page. Journalism schools cropped up around the country, helping to promote the ideal of objectivity.

The two historical developments, news centralization and news professionalism, play off against one another in the current debate over news bias. The question of bias was irrelevant when the press was a scatter of little independent newspapers. If you didn't like the bias of one paper, you picked another one—or you started your own, which could be done with modest capital outlay. Bias started to become an important question when newspapers became dominated by chains and airwaves by networks, and when a few national press leaders (e.g., the *New York Times* and the *Washington Post*) began to emerge. When one news anchor can address a nightly audience of 25 million people, the question of bias is no longer irrelevant.

But *is* there bias? If so, *whose* bias? The media constitute a major socializing institution, so these are important questions. Defenders of the press usually concede that journalists, like all human beings, have biases, but they deny that they carry their biases into their writing. Journalists, they say, are professionals, trained to bring us news unembellished by personal opinion. They conclude that bias is in the eye of the beholder: left-wingers think the press is conservative, right-wingers call it liberal; both are unhappy that the press isn't biased in *their* direction.

Both the left and the right disagree. The left considers the press conservative because it is tied in with big business, indeed *is* a big business. The right insists that the bias of the press is overwhelmingly liberal because most reporters are liberal. In the following selections, professors Noam Chomsky and Edward Herman develop a critique of the media from a "left" perspective, and *National Review* editor William Rusher argues that the media are biased against conservatives.

YES
William Rusher

THE COMING BATTLE FOR THE MEDIA

It is the conviction of a great many people, not all of them conservative by any means, that news presentation by the media elite is heavily biased in favor of liberal views and attitudes.

It is important, right at the outset, to specify precisely what is being objected to. This is a free country, and journalists are every bit as entitled to their private political opinions as the rest of us. But the average newspaper or television news program, and certainly those we have categorized as the "media elite," purport to be offering us something more than the personal opinions of the reporter, or the chief editor, or even the collective opinions of the journalistic staff. In one way or another, to one extent or another, they all profess to be offering us the "news"—which is to say, an account of as many relevant events and developments, in the period in question, as can be given in the space or time available. Moreover, in offering this account, the media we are discussing implicitly claim to be acting with a reasonable degree of objectivity. Their critics sharply challenge that claim.

But just how much objectivity is it reasonable to expect? The question is more complicated than it may at first appear. There is a school of thought—popular, perhaps naturally, among a certain subcategory of journalists themselves—that a journalist is, or at least ought to be, a sort of vestal virgin: a chalice of total and incorruptible objectivity. But this, of course, is nonsense, and is certainly not expected by any reasonable person.

Journalists too are, after all, sons and daughters of Adam. Their conception was far from immaculate; they share our taint of Original Sin. They were born into our common society, received the same general education we all received, and had roughly the same formative experiences. How likely is it that, simply by choosing to pursue a career in journalism, they underwent some sort of miraculous transformation, to emerge shriven and pure, purged of all bias and dedicated henceforth solely to the pursuit of the unvarnished Truth? . . . Just how does one go about demonstrating that the media elite are, in the matter of their private opinions, overwhelmingly partial to liberal policies and liberal political personalities? A general impression, based on

From William Rusher, *The Coming Battle for the Media* (William Morrow & Co., 1988). Copyright © 1988 by William Rusher. Reprinted by permission of William Morrow & Company, Inc.

familiarity with their work-product as on display in the *New York Times* or the *Washington Post*, in *Time* or *Newsweek*, or on the evening news programs of one or another of the major networks, is absolutely worthless. You will be told that your perception is distorted by your own partiality to conservative policies and personalities. You will be assured that the liberals complain just as loudly as conservatives about maltreatment by the media (though on inspection it turns out to be the harder left—e.g., Alexander Cockburn—that complains; liberals typically, and understandably, complain very little about distortion by the media elite). You will be referred to news stories in which there was no liberal bias, and to news presentations well and truly balanced—shining exceptions that merely emphasize the rule.

There is, in fact, only one way to ascertain with precision anyone's political leaning, inclination, or prejudice, and that is to interview him or her in depth. Moreover, if the intention is to evaluate the opinions of an entire group, the sample interviewed must be large enough to be dependably representative. Fortunately there have recently been several conscientious surveys of the political views of America's media elite, and the results are thoroughly unambiguous. . . .

[A] remarkable survey, whose results were published in 1981 . . . was conducted in 1979 and 1980 by two professors of political science—S. Robert Lichter of George Washington University and Stanley Rothman of Smith College— as part of a larger inquiry into the attitudes of various elites, under the auspices of the Research Institute on International Change at Columbia University. The survey itself was supervised by Response Analysis, a survey research organization.

Lichter and Rothman began by defining the following organizations as America's "most influential media outlets": three daily newspapers—the *New York Times*, the *Washington Post*, and the *Wall Street Journal;* three weekly newsmagazines—*Time, Newsweek*, and *U.S. News and World Report;* the news departments of four networks— CBS, NBC, ABC, and PBS; and the news departments of certain major independent broadcasting stations.

Within these organizations they then selected at random, from among those responsible for news content, individuals to be approached for interviews. In the print media, these included "reporters, columnists, department heads, bureau chiefs, editors and executives responsible for news content." In the electronic media, those selected included "correspondents, anchormen, producers, film editors and news executives." . . .

It transpires that, of those who voted in these elections at all (and this was 82 percent in 1976, when all but the youngest among those interviewed in 1979–80 would have qualified), *never less than 80 percent of the media elite voted for the Democratic candidate.* . . .

Like many American liberals, the media elite accept the essential free-enterprise basis of the United States economy, but they are devoted to welfarism. Over two thirds (68 percent) believe "the government should substantially reduce the income gap between the rich and the poor," and nearly half (48 percent) think the government should guarantee a job to anyone who wants one.

On sociocultural issues, the media elite's support for liberal positions is overwhelming. Ninety percent believe it is a woman's right to decide whether or not to have an abortion. A solid majority (53 percent) can't even bring itself to affirm that adultery is wrong.

There is far more to the Lichter-Rothman survey than the above brief sample of its findings, but the basic thrust of the study is unmistakable: America's media elite are far to the left of American public opinion in general on the great majority of topics. . . .

THE EFFECT ON THE "NEWS"

Proving statistically that the media's demonstrated liberalism influences their handling of the news is no simple matter. The media clearly aren't going to do us the favor of admitting it, and the formidable human capacity for self-delusion makes it likely that many members of the media don't even realize it, at least not fully. A good many of them undoubtedly think their selection and treatment of stories is governed solely by their acute "news sense," where any objective observer would detect bias. And even when a member of the media knows full well that his handling of news stories is influenced by his biases, he is naturally prone to minimize that influence and make excuses for the residue.

Adding to the difficulty is the fact that evidence of bias, liberal or otherwise, is almost inevitably somewhat subjective. One man's "bias" is another man's "robust journalism," etc. Obvious as the bias may be to many thoughtful people, how can one nail it down?

One of the earliest and still one of the best efforts to do so was made by Edith Efron in her book *The News Twisters* (Nash, 1971). It is said that medieval philosophers had a high old time arguing

over how many teeth a horse has, until some spoilsport ended the game by going out and actually counting them. That was essentially Efron's solution, too. . . .

[Rusher quotes extensively from Efron's discussion of her methodology. She counted the number of words used in prime-time TV news programs that could be classified "for" and "against" the three major candidates for president in 1968: Alabama governor George Wallace (running as an independent), Democrat Hubert Humphrey, and Republican Richard Nixon. —Eds.]

Efron then sets forth, in bar-graph form, the total number of words spoken for and against the three presidential candidates on the three major networks during the period under study. In the case of George Wallace, the result was as follows:

THE EFFECT ON THE "NEWS"

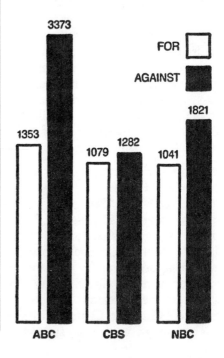

In the case of Hubert Humphrey, the graph looked like this:

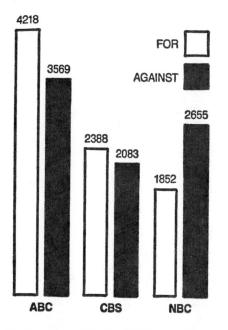

In the case of Richard Nixon, this was the result:

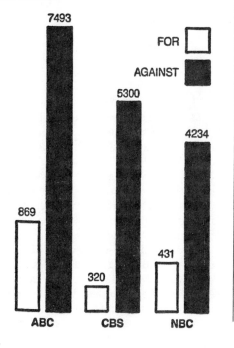

Now, how can the statistics regarding Nixon be interpreted, save as a product of bias? Bear in mind that this was long before Watergate—indeed, that in the next election (1972) Nixon would be re-elected by a landslide. Yet in 1968 the words spoken *against* Nixon on ABC (the network with the smallest imbalance in this respect) outnumbered the words spoken *for* him by nearly nine to one. At NBC the negative proportion was almost ten to one. At CBS it actually exceeded sixteen to one. . . .

Maura Clancey and Michael Robinson conducted another comprehensive study of the media's bias in reporting the "news," in connection with the 1984 presidential election, under the auspices of George Washington University and the American Enterprise Institute. . . .

Clancey and Robinson summed up their findings as follows:

There may be some questions about the validity of our measure, but there can be no question about the lopsidedness of what is uncovered. Assuming that a piece with a positive spin equals "good press," and assuming that negative spin equals "bad press," Ronald Reagan and George Bush proved over-whelmingly to be the "bad press" ticket of 1984. Figure 1 [see next page] contains the number of news seconds we scored as good press or bad press for each of the candidates. Ronald Reagan's bad press total was *ten times greater* than his good press total. (7,230 seconds vs. 730). In other words, his "spin ratio" was ten-to-one negative.

George Bush had a spin ratio that defied computation—1,500 seconds of "bad press" pieces and zero seconds of good press.

Walter Mondale and Geraldine Ferraro, on the other hand, had slightly *positive* spin ratios—1,970 seconds of

Figure 1

News seconds

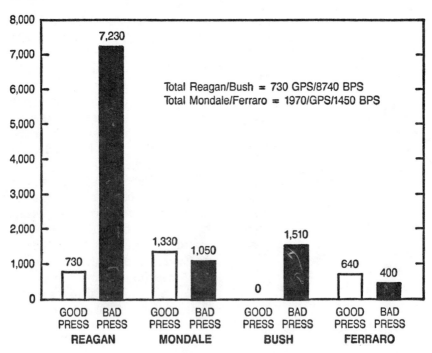

Total Reagan/Bush = 730 GPS/8740 BPS
Total Mondale/Ferraro = 1970/GPS/1450 BPS

good press about themselves as people or potential leaders, and 1,450 seconds of bad press. Given what we know about the bad news bias of television, the fact that anyone, let alone any ticket, got more positive spin than negative is news indeed.

But Clancey and Robinson are not even prepared to concede that their own lopsided results in 1984 conclusively demonstrated a liberal bias on the part of the media. On the contrary, they suggest, "liberal bias is not the only explanation, or even the best."

Instead, they posit the existence of what they call "the four I's"—non-ideological reasons for the bad press admittedly accorded Reagan and Bush in 1984. These are:

"Impishness"—a human tendency to want to turn a walkaway into a horse race "to keep one's own work interesting."

"Irritation"—annoyance at what the media perceived as Reagan's glib one-liners and his alleged "Teflon coating" (i.e., his seeming invulnerability to criticism).

"Incumbency"—a sense that the media have "a special mission to warn Americans about the advantages any incumbent has," especially when he is winning big.

"Irrevocability"—the feeling that a double standard is justified because 1984 was the last time Reagan would ever face the electorate. Under those circumstances, giving him a bad press became "a near-messianic mission."

Defenders of the media may well wonder whether pleading them guilty to the above unpleasant set of impulses would actually constitute much of an improvement over admitting that they have a liberal bias. But they can be spared that painful decision, because "the four I's" simply don't survive careful inspection. In pure theory they might explain the media's astonishing bias against Reagan in 1984, but not one of them applies to the equally well-established instance of bias discussed earlier: the media's treatment of Nixon in the 1968 campaign.

That campaign was no "walkaway" for Nixon; it was one of the closest presidential elections in United States history—43.4 percent for Nixon, 42.7 for Humphrey, and 13.5 for Wallace. And Nixon was certainly no Reagan, either in his mastery of glib one-liners or in possessing a "Teflon coating." Moreover, he was not the incumbent, or even the nominee of the incumbent's party. And 1968 was *not* the last time Nixon could or would face the electorate. Yet the media gave him the same biased treatment that Reagan received in 1984. The conclusion is unavoidable that the media's conduct had the same basis in both cases: a liberal bias neatly congruent with the demonstrated liberal preferences of the overwhelming majority of the media elite.

NO

Edward S. Herman
and Noam Chomsky

PROPAGANDA MILL

It is a primary function of the mass media in the United States to mobilize public support for the special interests that dominate the Government and the private sector.

This is our conclusion after years of studying the media. Perhaps it is an obvious point—but the common assumption seems to be that the media are independent and committed to discovering and reporting the truth. Leaders of the media claim that their news judgments rest on unbiased, objective criteria. We contend, on the other hand, that the powerful are able to fix the premises of discourse, decide what the general populace will be allowed to see, hear, and think about, and "manage" public opinion by mounting regular propaganda campaigns.

We do not claim this is all the mass media do, but we believe the propaganda function to be a very important aspect of their overall service.

In countries where the levers of power are in the hands of a state bureaucracy, monopolistic control of the media, often supplemented by official censorship, makes it clear that media serve the ends of the dominant elite. It is much more difficult to see a propaganda system at work where the media are private and formal censorship is absent.

This is especially true where the media actively compete, periodically attack and expose corporate and governmental malfeasance, and aggressively portray themselves as spokesmen for free speech and the general community interest. What is not evident (and remains undiscussed in the media) is the severely limited access to the private media system and the effect of money and power on the system's performance.

Critiques of this kind are often dismissed by Establishment commentators as "conspiracy theories," but this is merely an evasion. We don't rely on any kind of conspiracy hypothesis to explain the performance of the media; in fact, our treatment is much closer to a "free-market" analysis.

From Edward S. Herman and Noam Chomsky, "Propaganda Mill," *The Progressive* (June 1988). Adapted from *Manufacturing Consent: The Political Economy of the Mass Media* by Edward Herman and Noam Chomsky (Pantheon Books, 1988). Copyright © 1988 by Edward Herman and Noam Chomsky. Reprinted by permission of Pantheon Books, a division of Random House, Inc.

Most of the bias in the media arises from the selection of right-thinking people, the internalization of preconceptions until they are taken as self-evident truths, and the practical adaptation of employees to the constraints of ownership, organization, market, and political power.

The censorship practiced within the media is largely self-censorship, by reporters and commentators who adjust to the "realities" as they perceive them. But there are important actors who do take positive initiatives to define and shape the news and to keep the media in line. This kind of guidance is provided by the Government, the leaders of the corporate community, the top media owners and executives, and assorted individuals and groups who are allowed to take the initiative.

The media are not a solid monolith on all issues. Where the powerful are in disagreement, the media will reflect a certain diversity of tactical judgments on how to attain generally shared aims. But views that challenge fundamental premises or suggest that systemic factors govern the exercise of State power will be excluded.

The pattern is pervasive. Consider the coverage from and about Nicaragua. The mass media rarely allow their news columns—or, for that matter, their opinion pages—to present materials suggesting that Nicaragua is more democratic than El Salvador and Guatemala; that its government does not murder ordinary citizens, as the governments of El Salvador and Guatemala do on a routine basis; that it has carried out socioeconomic reforms important to the majority that the other two governments somehow cannot attempt; that Nicaragua poses no military threat to its neighbors but has, in fact, been subjected to continuous attack by the United States and its clients and surrogates, and that the U.S. fear of the Nicaraguan government is based more on its virtues than on its alleged defects.

The mass media also steer clear of discussing the background and results of the closely analogous attempt of the United States to bring "democracy" to Guatemala in 1954 by means of a CIA-supported invasion, which terminated Guatemalan democracy for an indefinite period. Although the United States supported elite rule and organized terror in Guatemala (among many other countries) for decades, actually subverted or approved the subversion of democracy in Brazil, Chile, and the Philippines (again, among others), is now "constructively engaged" with terror regimes around the world, and had no concern about democracy in Nicaragua so long as the brutal Somoza regime was firmly in power, the media take U.S. Government claims of a concern for "democracy" in Nicaragua at face value.

In contrast, El Salvador and Guatemala, with far worse records, are presented as struggling toward democracy under "moderate" leaders, thus meriting sympathetic approval.

IN CRITICIZING MEDIA BIASES, WE OFTEN draw on the media themselves for at least some of the "facts." That the media provide some information about an issue, however, proves absolutely nothing about the adequacy or accuracy of media coverage. The media do, in fact, suppress a great deal of information, but even more important is the way they present a particular fact—its placement, tone, and frequency of repetition—and the framework of analysis in which it is placed. That a careful reader looking for a fact can sometimes find it, with diligence and a skeptical eye, tells us nothing about whether that fact received the attention and context it deserved, whether it was intelligible to most readers, or whether it was effectively distorted or suppressed.

The standard media pattern of indignant campaigns and suppressions, of shading and emphasis, of carefully selected context, premises, and general agenda, is highly useful to those who wield power. If, for example, they are able to channel public concern and outrage to the abuses of enemy states, they can mobilize the population for an ideological crusade.

Thus, a constant focus on the victims of communism helps persuade the public that the enemy is evil, while setting the stage for intervention, subversion, support for terrorist regimes, an endless arms race, and constant military conflict—all in a noble cause. At the same time, the devotion of our leaders—and our media—to this narrow set of victims raises public patriotism and self-esteem, demonstrating the essential humanity of our nation and our people.

The public does not notice media silence about victims of America's client states, which is as important as the media's concentration on victims of America's enemies. It would have been difficult for the Guatemalan government to murder tens of thousands over the past decade if the U.S. press had provided the kind of coverage it gave to the difficulties of Andrei Sakharov in the Soviet Union or the murder of Jerzy Popieluszko in Poland. It would have been impossible to wage a brutal war against South Vietnam and the rest of Indochina, leaving a legacy of misery and destruction that may never be overcome, if the media had not rallied to the cause,

portraying murderous aggression as a defense of freedom.

Propaganda campaigns may be instituted either by the Government or by one or more of the top media firms. The campaigns to discredit the government of Nicaragua, to support the Salvadoran elections as an exercise in legitimizing democracy, and to use the Soviet shooting down of the Korean airliner KAL 007 as a means of mobilizing support for the arms buildup were instituted and propelled by the Government. The campaigns to publicize the crimes of Pol Pot in Cambodia and the allegations of a KGB plot to assassinate the Pope were initiated by the *Reader's Digest*, with strong follow-up support from NBC television, *The New York Times*, and other major media companies.

Some propaganda campaigns are jointly initiated by the Government and the media; all of them require the media's cooperation.

THE MASS MEDIA ARE DRAWN INTO A SYMbiotic relationship with powerful sources of information by economic necessity and reciprocity of interest. The media need a steady, reliable flow of the raw material of news. They have daily news demands and imperative news schedules. They cannot afford to have reporters and cameras at all places where important stories may break, so they must concentrate their resources where significant news often occurs, where important rumors and leaks abound, and where regular press conferences are held.

The White House, the Pentagon, and the State Department are central nodes of such news activity at the national level. On a local basis, city hall and the police department are regular news beats for reporters. Corporations and trade groups are also regular and credible purveyors of stories deemed newsworthy. These bureaucracies turn out a large volume of material that meets the demands of news organizations for reliable, scheduled flows. They also have the great merit of being recognizable and credible because of their status and prestige.

Another reason for the heavy weight given to official sources is that the mass media claim to be "objective" dispensers of the news. Partly to maintain the image of objectivity, but also to protect themselves from criticism of bias and the threat of libel suits, they need material that can be portrayed as presumptively accurate. This also reduces cost: Taking information from sources that may be presumed credible reduces investigative expense, whereas material from sources that are not *prima facie* credible, or that will draw criticism and threats, requires careful checking and costly research.

The Government and corporate bureaucracies that constitute primary news sources maintain vast public-relations operations that ensure special access to the media. The Pentagon, for example, has a public-information service that involves many thousands of employees, spending hundreds of millions of dollars every year and dwarfing not only the public-information resources of any dissenting individual or group but the aggregate of *all* dissenters.

During a brief interlude of relative openness in 1979 and 1980, the U.S. Air Force revealed that its public-information outreach included 140 newspapers with a weekly total circulation of 690,000; *Airman* magazine with a monthly circulation of 125,000; thirty-four radio and seventeen television stations, primarily overseas; 45,000 headquarters and unit news releases; 615,000 hometown news releases; 6,600 news media interviews; 3,200 news conferences; 500 news media orientation flights; fifty meetings with editorial boards, and 11,000 speeches. Note that this is just the Air Force. In 1982, *Air Force Journal International* indicated that the Pentagon was publishing 1,203 periodicals.

To put this into perspective, consider the scope of public information activities of the American Friends Service Committee and the National Council of the Churches of Christ, two of the largest nonprofit organizations that consistently challenge the views of the Pentagon. The Friends' main office had an information services budget of less than $500,000 and a staff of eleven in 1984–1985. It issued about 200 press releases a year, held thirty press conferences, and produced one film and two or three slide shows. The Council of Churches office of information has an annual budget of about $350,000, issues about 100 news releases, and holds four press conferences a year.

Only the corporate sector has the resources to produce public information and propaganda on the scale of the Pentagon and other Government bodies. These large actors provide the media with facilities and with advance copies of speeches and reports. They schedule news conferences at hours geared to news deadlines. They write press releases in usable language. They carefully organize "photo-opportunity" sessions.

In effect, the large bureaucracies of the powerful subsidize the mass media, and thereby gain special access. They become "routine" news sources, while non-routine sources must struggle for access and may be ignored.

Because of the services they provide, the continuous contact they sustain, and the mutual dependency they foster, the powerful can use personal relationships, threats, and rewards to extend their influence over the news media. The media may feel obligated to carry extremely dubious stories, or to mute criticism, to avoid offending sources and disturbing a close relationship. When one depends on authorities for daily news, it is difficult to call them liars even if they tell whoppers.

Powerful sources may also use their prestige and importance as a lever to deny critics access to the media. The Defense Department, for example, refused to participate in discussions of military issues on National Public Radio if experts from the Center for Defense Information were invited to appear on the same program. Assistant Secretary of State Elliott Abrams would not appear on a Harvard University program dealing with human rights in Central America unless former Ambassador Robert White were excluded. Claire Sterling, a principal propagandist for the "Bulgarian connection" to the plot to assassinate the Pope, refused to take part in television programs on which her critics would appear.

The relation between power and sourcing extends beyond official and corporate provision of news to shaping the supply of "experts." The dominance of official sources is undermined when highly respectable unofficial sources give dissident views. This problem is alleviated by "coopting the experts"—that is, putting them on the payroll as consultants, funding their research, and organizing think tanks that will hire them directly and help disseminate their messages.

The process of creating a body of experts who will confirm and distribute the opinions favored by the Government

and "the market" has been carried out on a deliberate basis and a massive scale. In 1972, Judge Lewis Powell, later elevated to the Supreme Court, wrote a memo to the U.S. Chamber of Commerce in which he urged business "to buy the top academic reputations in the country to add credibility to corporate studies and give business a stronger voice on the campuses."

During the 1970s and early 1980s, new institutions were established and old ones reactivated to help propagandize the corporate viewpoint. Hundreds of intellectuals were brought to these institutions, their work funded, and their output disseminated to the media by a sophisticated propaganda effort.

The media themselves also provide "experts" who regularly echo the official view. John Barron and Claire Sterling are household names as authorities on the KGB and terrorism because the *Reader's Digest* has funded, published, and publicized their work. The Soviet defector Arkady Shevchenko became an expert on Soviet arms and intelligence because *Time*, ABC television, and *The New York Times* chose to feature him despite his badly tarnished credentials. By giving these vehicles of the preferred view much exposure, the media confer status and make them the obvious candidates for opinion and analysis.

Another class of experts whose prominence is largely a function of their serviceability to power consists of former radicals who have "come to see the light." The motives that induce these individuals to switch gods, from Stalin (or Mao) and communism to Reagan and free enterprise, may vary, but so far as the media are concerned, the ex-radicals have simply seen the error of their ways. The former sinners, whose previous work was ignored or ridiculed by the mass media, are suddenly elevated to prominence and anointed as experts.

MEDIA PROPAGANDA CAMPAIGNS HAVE generally been useful to elite interests. The Red Scare of 1919–1920 helped abort the postwar union-organizing drive in steel and other major industries. The Truman-McCarthy Red Scare of the early 1950s helped inaugurate the Cold War and the permanent war economy, and also weakened the progressive coalition that had taken shape during the New Deal years.

The chronic focus on the plight of Soviet dissidents, on enemy killings in Cambodia, and on the Bulgarian Connection helped weaken the Vietnam Syndrome, justify a huge arms buildup and a more aggressive foreign policy, and divert attention from the upward distribution of income that was the heart of the Reagan Administration's domestic economic program. The recent propaganda attacks on Nicaragua have averted eyes from the savageries of the war in El Salvador and helped justify the escalating U.S. investment in counterrevolution in Central America.

Conversely, propaganda campaigns are *not* mobilized where coverage of victimization, though it may be massive, sustained, and dramatic, fails to serve the interests of the elite.

The focus on Cambodia in the Pol Pot era was serviceable, for example, because Cambodia had fallen to the communists and useful lessons could be drawn from the experience of their victims. But the many Cambodian victims of U.S. bombing *before* the communists came to power were scrupulously ignored by the U.S. press. After Pol Pot was ousted by the Vietnamese, the United States quietly shifted its support to this "worse than Hitler" villain, with little or no notice in the press, which once again adjusted to the official political agenda.

Attention to the Indonesian massacres of 1965–1966, or to the victims of the Indonesian invasion of East Timor since 1975, would also be distinctly unhelpful as bases of media campaigns, because Indonesia is a U.S. ally and client that maintains an open door to Western investment. The same is true of the victims of state terror in Chile and Guatemala—U.S. clients whose basic institutional structure, including the state terror system, were put in place by, or with crucial assistance from, the United States.

No propaganda campaigns are mounted in the mass media on behalf of such victims. To publicize their plight would, after all, conflict with the interests of the wealthy and powerful.

POSTSCRIPT

Are Liberal Values Propagated by the News Media?

As the opposing arguments in this section indicate, we can find critics on both the left and the right who agree that the media are biased. What divides such critics is the question of whether the bias is "left-wing" or "right-wing." Defenders of the news media may seize upon this disagreement to bolster their own claim that "bias is in the eye of the beholder." But it could also mean that the news media are unfair to both sides. If that were true, however, it would seem to take some of the force out of the argument that the news media have a distinct ideological tilt.

Though published in 1973, Edward Jay Epstein's *News From Nowhere* (Random House, 1973) remains one of the great studies of the factors that influence television news shows. A study by S. Robert Lichter et al., *The Media Elite* (Adler and Adler, 1986) tends to support Rusher's contention that the media slant leftward, while Ben Bagdikian's *The Media Monopoly* (Beacon Press, 1983) lends support to Chomsky and Herman. David Halberstam's *The Powers That Be* (Knopf, 1979), a historical study of CBS, the *Washington Post,*

Time magazine, and the *Los Angeles Times,* describes some of the political and ideological struggles that have taken place within major media organizations.

Edward Jay Epstein's book, cited above, uses as an epigraph a statement by Richard Salant, president of CBS News in the 1970s: "Our reporters do not cover stories from *their* point of view. They are presenting them from *nobody's* point of view." Most probably, Salant had not intended to be facetious or ironic, but the statement so amused Epstein that he parodied it in the title of his book: *News From Nowhere*!

PART 2

Sex Roles and the Family

The modern feminist movement has advanced the cause for the well-being of women to the point where there are now more women in the work force in the United States than ever before. Professions and trades that were traditionally regarded as the province of men have opened up to women, and women have easier access to the education and training necessary to excell in these new areas. But does feminism as a universal philosophy continue to serve women well in all respects as we move through the 1990s? What are the experiences of women who are balancing careers and families? What is happening to sex roles, and what are the effects of changing sex roles? The issues in this part address these sorts of questions.

Is the Feminist Agenda Right for American Women?

———————

Can Women Combine Careers and Families?

ISSUE 3

Is the Feminist Agenda Right for American Women?

YES: Marilyn French, from *Beyond Power* (Summit Books, 1985)

NO: Nicholas Davidson, from *The Failure of Feminism* (Prometheus Books, 1988)

ISSUE SUMMARY

YES: Novelist and essayist Marilyn French argues that feminism offers a serious and coherent alternative to patriarchal thinking and structures.
NO: Writer Nicholas Davidson contends that the feminist perspective imposes a one-dimensional interpretation on human life and devalues the real life of women. He declares that the "Feminist Era is over."

The publication of Betty Friedan's *The Feminine Mystique* in 1963 is generally used to mark the beginning of the modern women's movement, and since that time significant changes have occurred in American society: Occupations and professions, schools, clubs, associations, and governmental position that were by tradition or law previously reserved for men only are now open to women. Women are found in increasing numbers among lawyers, judges, physicians, and elected officials. In 1981, then president Ronald Reagan appointed the first woman, Sandra Day O'Connor, to the Supreme Court. In 1983, the first American woman astronaut was included in the crew of a space shuttle (Sally Ride), and women have been on more recent space shuttle missions as well. The service academies have accepted women since 1976, and women in the military participated in the U.S. invasion of Panama in December 1989. There are ongoing debates in Congress and among the armed services themselves about whether or not to lift restrictions on women serving in combat. Elizabeth Watson became the first woman to head a big city police department when the mayor of Houston appointed her chief of police in January 1990.

These sorts of changes—quantifiable and highly publicized—may signal a change in women's roles, at least to this extent: women now engage in occupations that were previously exlcusive tc men, and women can pursue the necessary training and education required to do so. But as we enter the decade of the 1990s, to what extent is the United States a society in which females and males have equal standing? Are femininity and femaleness prized or valued the same as maleness or masculinity? What is happening to our concepts of both? Even as changes are occurring in the public world, what is happening on a personal level to the roles of men and women? How do we value the domestic sphere? What is happening to child care? To our concept of the family?

Feminism—an ideology that, in its most basic form, directly opposes sexism by supporting gender equality and portraying women and men as equals—has been a driving force in shaping the modern women's movement. However, because sex differences are at once anatomical and physiological, the significance and implications of these differences are hotly disputed. Among men and women, among feminists and antifeminists, it is hard to arrive at a definition of terms on this issue of sex roles. On the subject of feminism, there is great ambivalence throughout American society. The Equal Rights Amendment to the Constitution (ERA), which would have made gender an irrelevant distinction under the law, and which passed both houses of Congress by overwhelming margins in 1972, failed to win ratification of the required three-fourths of the state legislatures in 1978. Although Congress extended the ratification date to 1982, the amendment—which Betty Friedan had termed "both the symbol and substance of women's rights"—failed to be ratified. That the amendment was not ratified was due in part to the efforts of a coalition of groups, composed overwhelmingly of women, who went to battle against it. In the readings that follow, novelist and critic Marilyn French argues that the feminist agenda is a sound one and that it needs to be pushed further. In contrast, writer Nicholas Davidson, although he acknowledges past accomplishemtns of feminism, argues that its agenda is not relevant in today's society and that it does not benefit American women.

YES

Marilyn French

FEMINISM

Feminism is the only serious, coherent, and universal philosophy that offers an alternative to patriarchal thinking and structures. Feminists believe in a few simple tenets. They believe that women are human beings, that the two sexes are (at least) equal in all significant ways, and that this equality must be publicly recognized. They believe that qualities traditionally associated with women—the feminine principle—are (at least) equal in value to those traditionally associated with men—the masculine principle—and that this equality must be publicly recognized. (I modify these statements with *at least* because some feminists believe in the superiority of women and "feminine" qualities. Indeed, it is difficult not to stress the value of the "feminine" in our culture because it is so pervasively debased and diminished.) Finally, feminists believe the personal is the political—that is, that the value structure of a culture is identical in both public and private areas, that what happens in the bedroom has everything to do with what happens in the boardroom, and vice versa, and that, mythology notwithstanding, at present the same sex is in control in both places.

There are also those who believe they consider women equal to men, but see women as fettered by their traditional socialization and by the expectations of the larger world. These people see women as large children who have talent and energy, but who need training in male modes, male language, and an area of expertise in order to "fit in" in the male world. One philosopher, for example, has commented that women are *not yet ready* for top government posts. This is not just patronizing; it shows a lack of comprehension of feminism. For although feminists do indeed want women to become part of the structure, participants in public institutions; although they want access for women to decision-making posts, and a voice in how society is managed, *they do not want women to assimilate to society as it presently exists but to change it*. Feminism is not yet one more of a series of political movements demanding for their adherents access to existing structures and their rewards. This is how many people see it, however: as a strictly political movement through which women demand entry into the "male" world, a share of male prerogatives, and the chance to be like men. This perception of feminism alienates many nonfeminist women.

Feminism is a political movement demanding access to the rewards and responsibilities of the "male" world, but it is more: it is a revolutionary moral movement, intending to use political power to transform society, to "feminize" it. For such a movement, assimilation is death. The assimilation of women to society as it presently exists would lead simply to the inclusion of certain women (not all, because society as it presently exists is highly stratified) along with certain men in its higher echelons. It would mean continued stratification and continued contempt for "feminine" values. Assimilation would be the cooption of feminism. Yet it must be admitted that the major success of the movement in the past twenty years has been to increase the assimilation of women into the existing structure. This is not to be deplored, but it is only a necessary first step.

There have been many revolutions against various patriarchal forms over the past three or four thousand years, but in each case, what has succeeded an oppressive structure is another oppressive structure. This is inevitable because, regardless of the initial ideas and ideals of rebellious groups, they come to worship power above all: only power, they believe, can overwhelm power; only their greater power can bring them victory over an "enemy" that is the Father. But each victory has increased the power of the *idea* of power, thus each victory has increased human oppression. . . .

If women and men were seen as equal, if male self-definition no longer depended upon an inferior group, other stratifications would also become unnec-

essary. Legitimacy (which has no meaning without the idea of illegitimacy) would no longer be a useful concept, and its disappearance from human minds would lead to the establishment of new structures for social organization. These structures would blur the distinction between public and private spheres, a distinction that was originally created not only to exclude women from a male (public) arena, but to permit discourse which ignored and effectively eliminated from existence the parts of all lives that are bound to nature, that are necessary and nonvolitional. If public and private life were integrated, it would no longer seem incongruous to discuss procreation and weapons systems in the same paragraph. Since pleasure would be the primary value of both personal and public life, harmony (which produces pleasure) would be a universal societal goal, and would no longer have to be manufactured in the ersatz form of coerced uniformity, conformity. Love too would regain its innocence, since it would not be coerced into playing a role within a power structure and thus functioning as an oppression—as it often does in our world.

The foregoing is a sketch of feminist beliefs. It is difficult at present to provide more than a sketch, for to create truly feminist programs we must rid our heads of the power notions that fill them, and that cannot be done in a generation, or even several generations. The sketch may sound utopian: I think it is not. That is, I believe such a world is possible for humans to maintain, to live within, once it is achieved. What may be utopian is the idea that we can achieve it. For to displace power as the highest human value means to supersede patriarchal modes while eschewing traditional power maneuvers as a means. But it is impossible to function in the public world without using power maneuvers; and revolution does imply overthrow of current systems.

Two elements cast a friendly light on feminist goals. One is that the movement is not aimed at overthrow of any particular government or structure, but at the displacement of one way of thinking by another. The other is that feminism offers desirable goals. The first means that the tools of feminism are naturally nonviolent: it moves and will continue to move by influencing people, by offering a vision, by providing an alternative to the cul-de-sacs of patriarchy. The second means that feminism is in a state I call blessed: its ends and its means are identical. Feminism increases the well-being of its adherents, and so can appeal to others on grounds of the possibility of greater felicity. Integration of the self, which means using the full range of one's gifts, increases one's sense of well-being; if integration of one's entire life is not always possible because of the nature of the public world, it is a desirable goal. Patriarchy, which in all its forms requires some kind of self-sacrifice, denial, or repression in the name of some higher good which is rarely (if ever) achieved on earth, stresses nobility, superiority, and victory, the satisfaction of a final triumph. Feminism requires use of the entire self in the name of present well-being, and stresses integrity, community, and the *jouissance* of present experience. . . .

It was probably Betty Friedan's *The Feminine Mystique*, published in 1963, that first galvanized American women into action. Women legislators had seen to it that laws passed to redress wrongs done to blacks were expanded to include women. The Equal Pay Act was passed in 1963; the Civil Rights Act in 1965. Title VII of the latter prohibited discrimination on grounds of sex, race, color, religion, or national origin. The word *sex* was included as a result of maneuvers by Representative Martha Griffiths, Senator Margaret Chase Smith, and a reporter, Mae Craig. In 1965 the Supreme Court held that laws banning contraceptives were unconstitutional, and in 1966 a federal court declared that an Alabama law barring women from juries violated the Fourteenth Amendment (guaranteeing equal protection under the law). In that year too, the National Organization for Woman was founded. . . .

The decade that followed was enormously fertile; the seeds planted then are still bearing fruit. Women scholars began to delve into women's history, to break away from male interpretations and lay the groundwork for an alternative view of anthropology, psychology, sociology, philosophy, and language. Politically oriented groups pressed for legislation granting women equality in education, housing, credit, and promotion and hiring. Other women established feminist magazines, journals, publishing houses, and bookstores. Some strove for political office; some entered the newly open "male" world of business and industry. In the exhilaration of that period, women who had felt crippled found limbs, women who had felt marginal found a center, women who had felt alone found sisters.

It is now less than twenty years since the rising of the "second wave." The difference is astonishing. Women are now working in hundreds of jobs that were closed to them in the past. Women can sign leases, buy cars and houses, obtain credit; they cannot be denied telephone service because they are divorced.

They can be seated in restaurants although they are dining without a man. Although some women's fashions still inhibit mobility, they are no longer *de riguer*. Women are no longer expected to produce elaborate entertainments: life can be easier, more leisurely, for both sexes.

Most important of all, women now possess reproductive freedom. Although men have long had access to condoms, which were and are sold over the counter in every drugstore, women needed doctors' prescriptions to purchase diaphragms and, later, the birth control pill. This is still true, but such prescriptions are widely available now, and women do not have to be married to obtain them. (In France, where men an also obtain condoms easily, women could not purchase contraceptive devices in drugstores until 1967, and such purchases still require the authorization of the minister of social affairs.) Clearly, it is not birth control—or, more accurately, the prevention of conception—per se that is offensive to patriarchal culture, but the placing of that control in the hands of women. Despite continuing attempts to wrest it from them, American women are likely to hold on to this right over their own bodies. But in some Western nations—Ireland, for example—they still do not possess it.

The difference is great for a huge number of women, and because the difference permeates their lives, change may seem complete. But in the scale of things, the change is minimal. Capitalism, under great pressure for almost a hundred and fifty years, has yielded women about what socialism yielded them immediately. But it has managed—as has socialism—to retain its essential character. Capitalism has assimilated women, it has not broadened itself; it has swallowed women rather than alter itself. And it has done this in accordance with its traditional structures. Thus the women who have benefited most from the changes are well-educated, white, middle-class women, often without children. Thus the divisiveness of racism has pervaded the women's movement itself. Thus women have by and large been kept out of the most sensitive and powerful areas of business and government, so that they have not achieved a voice in the running of our society. And thus women who have not managed to live like men, or with them, have been condemned to the lowest rank in our society: women are the new poor. It is not an exaggeration to say that although feminism in capitalist states has freed many women and improved the lives of others, it has had little effect on the patriarchy, which has simply absorbed a few women who appear acceptable to its purposes, and barred the door for the rest. . . .

. . . [T]he gap between male and female earnings has increased. According to the last census, the mean income of white females was $10,244 (59 cents of a white male dollar), of black females $9,476 (54 cents of a white male dollar), and of Hispanic females $8,466 (49 cents of a white male dollar). Despite differences in the concerns and approaches of women of color and white women, in the realm of economics, women as a caste comprise a lower class.

The poor of America are women: the poor of the world are women. In 1980, in America, the median adjusted income for men was $12,530, for women it was $4,920. In 1980 the poverty level was $8,414 for a nonfarm family of four, and nearly thirty million Americans live beneath it. Seventy percent of these are white, 30 percent black—and we may note that only 12 percent of the population is black—two thirds of them women and children. If we limit these figures to adults, two out of every three poor adults are female. If present trends continue, by the year 2000 the poor of America will be entirely its women.

There are a number of reasons for this. A presidential report published in 1981 claims that women are "systematically underpaid," that "women's work" pays about four thousand dollars a year less than men's work, and that occupational segregation is more pronounced by sex than by race: 70 percent of men and 54 percent of women are concentrated in jobs done only by those of their own sex.

Because women are still held responsible—by themselves and by men—for raising the children, they are forced to take jobs that are close to home, that offer flexible hours (like waitressing), or are part-time; jobs that do not require extended traveling or long hours. They are not able to "compete" in a job market that demands single-minded devotion to work, fast running on a narrow track. For some this is a tolerable situation: some women are not notably ambitious, prefer a balanced life, and have working husbands. But this is not the case for all, or even most, women.

More women than ever in the period covered by American record keeping on this point are living without men: they are single mothers, divorced mothers, and widows, as well as single working women. The reasons for this are complex. Two major reasons, however, are the movement for "sexual liberation" and the feminist movement.

The movement for "sexual liberation" begun in the 1950s was a male campaign, rooted in ideas that seem for the most part honest and beneficial: that sex was good, the body was good; that trading sexual access for financial support degraded sex and the body; that virginity was a questionable good in women and not at all necessary in men; and that the requirement of sexual fidelity in marriage was an oppression. However, the campaign was also extremely self-serving: it was not based on a philosophy that saw a joyous sex life as one element in a life concerned with the pleasure and the good of self and others. It was not a responsible movement: in fact it "masculinized" sex by making it a commodity and by isolating sex from other elements intrinsic to it—affection, connection, and the potential for procreation. To speak lightly, what the sexual revolution accomplished was to change the price of sexual access to a woman from marriage to a dinner.

At the same time, the ties of marriage lost their force—for men. As of 1963, almost all divorces sought in America were initiated (whether openly or not) by men. Divorce—like marriage—is morally neutral. Insofar as it ends a relationship of misery, it is a good; insofar as it ends a long-term intimacy, it is to be lamented. Even when a marriage involves children, it cannot be pre-judged: divorce may be better for the children than the marriage was. It seems reasonable to assume that if one party to a marriage wants a divorce, divorce should occur. But marriage and divorce are both tied to responsibility, and it was this tie that was broken by the "sexual liberation" movement.

If a man—and society in general—requires a woman to set aside ideas of an individual life, and to accept the role of functionary—wife, mother, housekeeper—without payment, then that role must be structured to guarantee that women a secure life despite her unpaid labor. In cognizance of this contract, traditional divorce laws stipulated alimony. Laws did not, of course prevent men from abandoning their families completely, or failing in alimony payments. But the new sexual morality was growing in the sixties, a period when feminists were struggling to gain the right to paid employment above the national level, and when many women who had gained such work were initiating divorce themselves. The thinking of legislators and judges underwent an amazing swift change. The new assumption was that women worked, that they earned as much as men, and thus that they did not require alimony—which is rarely granted now, and even more rarely paid. In 1979, only 14 percent of all divorced or separated women were granted alimony or child support, and of those at least 30 percent did not receive what they were awarded.

This situation is unjust to women who have accepted lesser jobs to help their husbands through school, or given up fellowships or promotions to accompany a husband to his new job. It is appallingly unjust to women who have neglected their own potential careers to care for husbands and children. But it become outrageous when we consider the statistics (if we need statistics, many women are too well acquainted with the reality behind them) on men's support of their children after divorce.

Although some very rich men use the power of their wealth to take the children away from their mothers after divorce, most men who divorce leave not just a marriage but a family. Men father children; although the degree to which they participate in childraising varies, it seems likely that they have some love and concern for those children. Nevertheless, after divorce they often disappear: they contribute neither emotion, time, nor money to the care of their own children. More than 90 percent of children who live with one parent live with their mothers; in 1978 there were 7.1 million single mothers with custody of their children in the United States. The number of men raising children on their own declined in the decade of the seventies. "The result of divorce, in an overwhelming number of cases, is that men become singles and women become single mothers." Women's incomes decline by 73 percent in the first year after divorce; men's incomes *increase* by 42 percent. The father is better off, the children are often hungry.

In recent years judges have tended not to award child support to mothers with custody; they have denied it to 41 percent of such mothers. Studies of the amounts awarded vary, ranging from as low as an average of $539 per year to an average of $2,110. But over 50 percent of custodial mothers never receive the amounts due them. Lenore Weitzman's research in California shows that only 13 percent of women with custody of preschool children receive alimony; child support payments (even when they are made) are almost never enough to cover the cost of raising small children. . . .

The women's movement under capitalism has worked almost unbelievably hard and made large gains. Those gains are changes in law and custom, and they affect all women, although they have their greatest effect on middle-class educated women. But feminism has not been able to budge an intransigent establishment bent on destroying the globe; it has not moved us one inch closer to the feminization of society. Indeed, it seems to lose ground with every decade, as the nourishing, procreative, communal, emotional dimensions of experience are increasingly ground into dust, as high technology and more intense pursuit of power are increasingly exalted.

This situation constitutes a quandary for feminists. Only by bringing great numbers of women with feminist values into the institutional structure of the nation can women achieve a voice in the way this country is run. Only by unified political action can women influence the course of the future. But at present, and for the foreseeable future, women are carefully screened, hired in small numbers, and watched for deviance. Women hired by institutions are far more likely to be coopted by institutional policy than to change it; they will assimilate or be fired or quit. Some feminist groups oppose women's efforts to enter the establishment on the ground that women should not contribute to a structure that is sexist, racist, and dedicated to profit and power. On the other hand, to refuse to enter the establishment is to refuse even to try to change it from within and thus to accept the marginal position women have traditionally held. To refuse to enter American institutions may also be to doom oneself to poverty, and poverty is silent and invisible. It has no voice and no face.

For this problem, as for so many others, there is no clear right answer.

NO
Nicholas Davidson

THE FAILURE OF FEMINISM

It is very tempting to take a positive view of the accomplishments of this feminism, to continue to believe it was the "most humane revolution of all," a pure net gain for all concerned. Can such a view be sustained?

Feminism has real and significant achievements to its credit. Feminists have played a major role in opening doors to women in employment, education, and sports. Feminism has provided a guiding philosophy to many women in their prolonged and bruising penetration of the corporate and academic worlds. Feminism has provided enough of a supporting framework to sustain many women through a difficult period of complete uncertainty about their sex roles. Feminists formed an important part of the constituency for abortion rights at the start of the seventies. They were responsible for desperately needed attention given to the crime of rape. They have thrown the spotlight on the syndrome of battered women. Feminists have played a highly effective role in the grass roots attempt to introduce humanity and common sense to medical practice in America. They have relentlessly hammered home the inadequacy of all intellectual disciplines that fail to take into account a female point of view. History, anthropology, sociology, psychology, sociobiology, primatology, and literary criticism will never be quite the same. Feminists have destroyed the plausibility of oversimple explanations for our partly arbitrary sex roles. Perhaps above all, feminism has helped to tear open the deceptively uniform surface presented by the mystique of femininity to reveal the cornucopia of needs, talents, and aspirations within. . . .

These positive changes of the Feminist Era have had a generally beneficial effect on women's perceptions of themselves and the possibilities open to them. In the first place, the sense is now widespread that what women do is significant: women feel important. In the second place, women no longer feel significantly constrained in their life choices. They readily imagine themselves in any occupation, and can reasonably aspire to practically any ambition open to men (as well as to some that are not).

It would be highly unwise to reject these accomplishments. Indeed, it is probably not possible to do so. Future generations will be in part the children

From Nicholas Davidson, *The Failure of Feminism* (Prometheus Books, 1988). Reprinted by permission of Prometheus Books, Buffalo, New York.

of feminism. Feminism has advanced the cause of humanity in important ways. However, we cannot afford to spend all our time eulogizing past accomplishments. We must also cope with the new problems facing us today, which have been brought about in great measure by feminism's very successes. Beside its real accomplishments we must place the failures of feminism.

The first of these lies in the ambiguous nature of all its successes. When one rereads *The Feminine Mystique* a generation later, one realizes how thoroughly feminism replaced the feminine mystique with its own mystique in all the areas Friedan examined: education, psychology, advertising, journalism, and so forth. Feminism successfully took over the cultural loci that were its main targets. It is now ensconced as the official philosophy of America's leading women's colleges, such as Smith, Radcliffe, and Barnard. Universities, corporations, professional associations, and departments of government are committed to enforcing its worldview. In place of the feminine mystique, it supplied its own warnings against men, marriage, spontaneity in love, and femininity. Young women in the eighties received a message as uncompromising as any the fifties had devised.

It was not worth opening the door of the workplace to women at the cost of shutting the door of the home. The message against marriage contributed heavily to the formation of an entire cohort of single women. Statisticians concluded in the middle of the eighties that many of them would be unable to marry unless they drastically lowered their standards for husbands (which, moved by the biological imperative to mate with a dominant male, they were not about to do).

No amount of ideological apology can undo the fact that many women were marooned in the public arena, some for years and some forever, and denied the equal or greater fulfillments of home and family. Too, as Greer had at one point predicted, women were granted "admission to the world of the ulcer and the coronary" as, along with their increased participation in the work force, women's rates of cancer, heart disease, and the other great scourges of male occupational stress rose to rival those of men. The feminist attention to rape does not validate the analysis responsible for that attention, that rape is a political crime, or the destructive model of sexuality from which that analysis arises. Nor can the push to include women's points of view in the social sciences conceal that most of the resulting efforts were dogmatic and unimaginative, resulting in at best a marginal advance to human understanding.

As a guiding philosophy for women, feminism makes all relations with men difficult, and good relations virtually impossible. In the words of one disillusioned feminist, a leading exponent of Women's Studies, "For a long time, I thought feminism explained everything. It taught me how to analyze what was going on between me and the men I lived and worked with. But now it's left me out on a limb, feeling angry with nowhere to go and no way to turn back."

Feminism is a failure as an explanation for male psychology and behavior. It is totally unworkable as a guiding philosophy for men, as shown by the rapid fizzling of the men's "consciousness-raising groups" of the early seventies. Feminists claimed to have the real goods on women. If men wanted to learn about women—how to please them sexually, for instance—they would have to passively accept the feminist insights. Men who believed this claim put themselves in the false position of the "New Man." The demands of feminism destroyed authenticity of emotion and behavior in the men who tried to comply with them. Unable to please either himself or women, the New Man, like the New Woman, was left to the cold comfort of envisioning himself as a pioneer of human progress. Feminism's inhibition of relations between the sexes leached joy from the lives of millions of young people whose youth would not come again. It was not at all clear that the thrill of having imagined oneself to be a pioneer of human progress could compensate for this permanent loss.

Feminism is a failure as an intellectual approach. The feminist perspective imposes a one-dimensional interpretation on all aspects of human life, namely, that the evils of the world can all be traced to men oppressing women. This view forces its scientifically minded acolytes into denying the most obvious facts of human biology and psychology. It generates female chauvinism and the sex-hate mongering seen in *The Color Purple*, in which tearing a newborn baby from its mother's arms is presented as typical, everyday male behavior. Not only is the feminist perspective anti-male, it also devalues female experience by denying the authenticity of women's experience under "patriarchy," that is, before the Feminist Era. After her consciousness is raised, the feminist looks at her mother and sees a victim instead of a person.

Feminism exploits women in a particularly insidious way. Many is the feminist mother today who imposes feminist goals on her feminine daughter, who tries to accept them out of deference toward a perceived cultural consensus.

Feminist teachers, employers and counselors all pressure young women to live by their tenets. Olive Chancellor is engaged in a ceaseless struggle to remake Verena in her own image. Why a movement so hostile to the feminine should have become known as "feminism" is far from clear.

The feminist revolution never took into account the fact that millions of American women would continue to choose to be housewives. In consequence, feminist policies ignored or, more often, worked against the needs of these millions of American women. Feminists could not help to stabilize "traditional" marriage while they were calling for its destruction. . . .

The assault on the misogynist trivialization of women was in some ways a success. Yet like the other works of feminism, this accomplishment was not to be the end of the road. The misogyny of the Feminist Era was of a different sort. Where before wifedom and motherhood had been presented as the only route to female fulfillment, now they were disparaged as obstacles to progress or more subtly denigrated by redefining them as "spousehood" and "parenthood." Where before women had sometimes been limited to the role of sex objects, now they were denied validation as sex objects. Where before the main actors in devaluing the feminine had been men, now they were women. If the old enemy was sexism, the new one was unisexism. . . .

As a universal philosophy, feminism is a dismal failure. Feminism cannot supply a reason why an abstraction called "freedom of the press" should be allowed to stand in the way of censoring the "sexual subordination of women." It is unable to acknowledge the psychological damage being inflicted on defenseless children in

Sara Bonnett Stein's horror stories of nonsexist child rearing, for their parents are acting according to the best feminist principles, which are by definition the most advanced that exist. Indeed, such is the strength of their messianic belief that feminists frequently claim their principles are right in a pure, universal sense.

Even the idea of "liberating" women implies that they must be enslaved: enslaved by men and by masculinity in all its pernicious guises. The very words "Women's Liberation" thus represent an assault on the necessary relational bases of human existence. Contemporary feminism is a philosophy based on resentment, and while one certainly wishes the situation were different, the conclusion is inescapable that feminism as it exists is one of the most negative world-views to have emerged in recent years.

For all these reasons, it is impossible to sustain the 1970s characterization of feminism as a universal philosophy with a messianic mission. A better future will come from men and women, not from women alone; and will come from men and women practicing the traditional virtues of masculinity and femininity, albeit sometimes in new contexts, not from a neutered New Woman and New Man whose gender is limited to their genitals. Feminism is not the end of the road. . . .

One of the unanticipated results of the feminist revolution was to threaten the social democratization of American family life. Motherhood was disparaged as "merely biological" by Friedan, Millett, Greer, and every other major feminist writer. Traditional feminine roles were condemned as "soulless and degrading." Professional careers were glamorized to an extent fully as extreme as the fifties' admiration for motherhood and femininity. It is extraordinary that in a coun-

try with the egalitarian tradition of America "nannies" suddenly became chic in the early 1980s after a lapse of half a century. The practical result of the Feminist Era's skewed beliefs on the relative worth of the private and public worlds in women's lives is that, in many circles, upper class women now pay lower class women to perform the "soulless and degrading" tasks of home and child care that the fifties, in their retrograde innocence, had thought worthy the attention of all women. Motherhood becomes a nuisance from which society must relieve women. So long as feminism remains our consensus philosophy of gender, women will be obliged to flee from or apologize for the pleasure they take in domesticity. In the meantime, home and child care will be "professionalized" by paying the poor to perform them.

The fifties went too far. Men, women, and children alike were expected to become so involved in family life that their scope for individuation was limited. This was one common impulse behind the divorce, countercultural, and feminist revolutions, which came in rapid fire succession at the end of the sixties. The first was in part a cry for autonomy by men; the second by adolescents; the third by women. Yet though it is possible to sympathize to an extent with the motivations for these revolts, it is far more difficult to sympathize with their result, the cult of singleness and independence aptly described as "the culture of narcissism" of the late seventies.

In the eighties it became obvious that the flight from the family had reached extreme lengths. It is now easier to see that the original impulse behind the fifties celebration of domesticity was sound, even though its expression was too constraining. It is time to strike a balance. To do so we must consult our own needs. Those needs will take most of us back to the family, not away from it. . . .

Feminism took a wrong turn at the very beginning, with Betty Friedan's anti-feminine complaint in *The Feminine Mystique*, and went completely off course just as it emerged from sixties radicalism as a national movement. What should have been a movement to uplift women, and men, bogged down in a fever swamp of dogma and intolerance.

The "women's movement" based its strategy to uplift women on severely flawed analyses. It took its conception of women from the simplistic tenets of cultural determinism, the facile abstractions of unisexism, and the implicit misogyny of psychologies which assumed that women's patterns of development would simply follow those of men. Its notions of social justice were based on the reductionism of the feminist perspective, which defined human society as the product of male oppression of females. It planned to "liberate" women from some of the most important constants in life: home, family, love.

As the eighties advanced and feminists nationally continued to hew to the same fundamental line, it came to seem less and less likely that this movement, which had set out to reform society, would be able to successfully reform itself. Could the many issues of family and gender be safely left to the initiative of a movement so dogmatic, uncompromising, and out of sympathy with the reality of Americans' everyday lives?

The real achievements of feminism must be admired and preserved, yet the ideology which has brought us this far can take us no farther. It is equally inca-pable of serving as a constructive guide to women or to men, to intellectual inquiry, social policy, or individual choice. Feminist ideology in any of its current forms is demonstrably misleading as a guide to the human condition. It is true that men have individually and collectively oppressed women at times, but women have also on their own initiative oppressed men and in any case this is not the central force in the human dynamic. The hallmark of the sexes' relations has always been cooperation more than conflict. The form of society is not and has never been determined by men oppressing women. The problems of the human race consequently cannot be solved by homogenizing sexual temperament or eliminating sex roles. Men and women are equally important to the future of humanity; the feminist hypothesis that masculine values are now obsolete because there are "no bears to kill" is not just vindictive but naive. Feminism is a disaster as a universal philosophy, for even if feminism is able to reform itself to better reflect women's points of view, it will still fail to reflect men's points of view.

Because humanity cannot be understood in terms of either sex alone, even the most enlightened feminism is inherently incapable of providing a balanced understanding of gender issues. This is nowhere more glaringly apparent than in feminists' treatment of the issues surrounding divorce.

DIVORCE

Recent feminist writings describe divorce as a "golden parachute" for men, overlooking the enormous price paid by divorced men, who usually lose child custody and who commit suicide at a rate five times higher than divorced women.

Even a Sylvia Hewlett has yet to escape the feminist perspective when it comes to men and divorce. Hewlett writes that *"49 percent of children in the custody of their mothers do not see their fathers at all"* (her emphasis), while glossing over the fact that women are awarded custody in the vast majority of cases. She piles up mounds of additional statistics, which have all the seemingly irrefutable weight of Millett's or Greer's "science," to prove "the low priority . . . divorced men attach to their children."

Feminists routinely paint men as the heavies in divorce, emphasizing how few divorced men continue to see their children on a regular basis, presenting the figures at their most damaging to men without bothering to ask whether any mitigating factors might be at work. For instance, some women do not *allow* their ex-husbands access to the children—whose custody the courts usually leave to their mothers. Yet one recent poll suggests that most divorced fathers not living with their kids would like to see them more but can't because of custody arrangements or because they live too far away.

Even if the man does care for his children he cannot win, for he is then accused by feminists of "buying" the children away from their mother (who is presumably the only one to really care). It is considered outrageous that children may elect "to spend most of their vacation time with their dad." The male is always guilty, the villain of history, the villain of divorce. Now of course this is sometimes true; but equally often it is not.

Feminists picture divorce as a tragedy for women and a triumph for men. Syl-

via Hewlett presents as typical a woman who says that "My ex-husband is going to get richer and richer and will spend his middle age in comfort surrounded by a growing family. I, on the other hand, am going to get poorer and more lonely. I've lost my partner, my house, my friends, my status, and even my children. . . . I guess I feel cheated."

The picture of divorce feminists paint is true, though it is largely their own creation: the problem of divorce for women has been severely exacerbated by the cult of singleness, and by the reduction in alimony caused by feminists' promotion of "no-fault" divorce laws. . . .

Disregarding the pleas of homemakers, feminists in the seventies forced through "no-fault" divorce laws that trampled on homemakers' hard-earned rights to share in the fruit of marriages on which they had long worked. The actions of feminists led to real suffering for hundreds of thousands of women with little or no compensating benefit. Today, feminists stand ready to punish men for their movement's own errors. The net result, if they succeed, will be to distance men further from marriage, leading to further breakdown of the family. The divorce rate will actually *rise*; divorced fathers will evade their families more; and families, consisting increasingly of single mothers with children, will be thrown more and more on the mercy of government—as will the resulting single men, who, devoid of family emotional support or impoverished by alimony and child payments, will be forced to turn to the state for counseling, detoxification, and other services. Single mothers will increasingly become normative, as they already are among the black urban poor; and single mothers are inherently needy. This will then redouble feminists' cries to institute universal day care and open-ended maternity leave, and to increase welfare payments to single mothers.

It can readily be seen that every feminist "solution" generates in turn worse problems than those it was supposed to solve, requiring yet more socially costly "reforms" to make it work. The immediate result for society will be severe, and the end result catastrophic, if feminists are allowed to propound their fantasies unchecked. This is the inevitable result of trying to apply any philosophy that is radically false. The old saw turns out to be true after all: you can't change human nature. . . .

THE END OF THE FEMINIST ERA

The arguments presented in this book are directed to contemporary American feminism, which is in some respects a phenomenon of a particular place and time, but they also point to the limitations of any feminism as a universal philosophy. Either a feminism or a virism may be justified as a short-term response to particular historical conditions, but no feminism or virism can supply a long-term philosophy adequate to guide human thought and action. "Feminism" cannot possibly cover the spectrum of needs and abilities that must be addressed and reconciled in the coming era, some of which are male, some female, while others are common to both sexes; in addition, the needs of some women conflict with the needs of other women.

For once we discard unisexism, female chauvinism, feminist messianism, and the feminist perspective, what is left of feminism? The answer is, very little. Feminism becomes simply a commitment to the well-being of women. And here a national consensus may be possible in many areas. However, such a new, open-ended meaning is incompatible with the dogmatic movement we have known; and it may well be simpler to let the term "feminism" fall by the wayside along with the movement to which it currently refers.

Neither "feminism" nor "virism" can supply an adequate guide to matters human. If our society's discourse on gender is to progress further, men must reenter the discussion on an equal basis with women. It is time to move beyond feminism.

POSTSCRIPT

Is the Feminist Agenda Right for American Women?

Davidson may not be fair to characterize feminism as "unisexism." As we can see, French struggles to combine a demand for full sexual equality with an identifiably "feminine" perspective, one that stresses nurturing and nonviolence while discouraging power-seeking. Yet, as French seems to acknowledge, it is difficult to put all this together coherently. If immunity to the lust for power is a specifically feminine trait, can it be sustained in a movement that must engage in fierce power struggles to gain and protect feminist victories? Can people "empower" themselves without acquiring a strong attachment to power? Perhaps, in French's words, "there is no clear right answer."

Over the past twenty years, there has been a deluge of books, articles, and periodicals devoted to expounding feminist positions. The first in this flood was Betty Friedan's book *The Feminine Mystique* (Norton, 1962). Friedan later wrote *The Second State* (Summit, 1980), seeking to chart a more ambitious course for the future of the feminist movement. A sympathetic analysis of the development and direction of the woman's movement is presented by Myre Mara Ferre and Beth B. Hess in *Controversy and Coalition: The New Feminist Movement* (Twayne Publishers, 1985). Pamela Johnson

Conover and Virginia Gray provide a political analysis of the success and failure of the women's movement to achieve its political objectives in *Feminism and the New Right: Conflict Over the American Family* (Praeger, 1983). A clear summary of many aspects of feminism is Hester Eisenstein's *Contemporary Feminist Thought* (G. K. Hall, 1983).

Antifeminist works are rarer. (Davidson charges that it is "extremely difficult to find a publisher for a work critical of feminism.") Still, anyone seeking antifeminist arguments should not have much trouble finding them. Midge Decter's *The New Chastity and Other Arguments Against Women's Liberation* (Putnam, 1974) has enjoyed fairly wide circulation, as have George Gilder's *Sexual Suicide* (Times Books, 1973) and Phyllis Schlafly's *The Power of Positive Woman* (Arlington House, 1977). Among the more recent critiques, besides Davidson's *The Failure of Feminism* (Prometheus, 1988), which is excerpted here, there is Michael Levin, *Feminism and Freedom* (Transaction Books, 1987).

ISSUE 4

Can Women Combine Careers and Families?

YES: Shirley Wilkins and Thomas A. W. Miller, from "Working Women: How It's Working Out," *Public Opinion* (October/November 1985)

NO: George Gilder, from "Women in the Work Force" *Atlantic Monthly* (September 1986)

ISSUE SUMMARY

YES: Shirley Wilkins and Thomas Miller, professionals in polling and surveying, use a national survey to show that most women want to combine work and family even though it may be difficult.
NO: Social critic George Gilder points out that only slightly more than one-third of working-age women held full-time year-round jobs, and he argues that women are much less committed to careers than men.

Women have come a long way, but there seems to be much confusion about where they are now. It is well known that most working-age women are in the paid labor force, but it is not clear what women have gained and lost thereby, particularly women with families. Are women happy to be leaving the home? Surveys show that most women want both family and career. On the other hand, Betty Friedan, who launched the modern women's movement with her book *The Feminine Mystique* (Norton, 1963), has more recently acknowledged the strong natural desire of some women for children and motherhood. Can a woman handle both career and family even when she wants to? The numbers suggest that they are doing both, but the literature currently highlights the many problems of doing so.

What problems are women with families having? According to Barbara Berg, who interviewed nearly 1,000 working women, "guilt was their greatest emotional problem." In "The Guilt That Drives Working Mothers Crazy" (*Ms.*, May 1987), she writes about her own experience: "But as soon as I reached for my briefcase, they [her two toddlers] would burst into inconsolable tears. 'Please don't go. Please don't leave us,' they would chorus pitifully, sometimes wrapping their little bodies around my legs in an effort to keep me home." These women also felt guilty for working late and missing dinner, for having little interest in sex, for being short-tempered with their children, for not disciplining more, and for not earning more. They also felt guilty for taking time off from work to attend school plays or to meet other family needs.

Guilt heads a long and painful list of problems for working mothers. The list obviously includes overwork, exhaustion, and inattention to personal needs. Sylvia Ann Hewlett describes many of these problems in her controversial book, *A Lesser Life: The Myth of Women's Liberation in America* (Morrow, 1986). She argues that working mothers are forced to carry an impossible double burden of a job plus the bulk of the housework and child caring. "It is now possible to become a successful career woman, provided one has the right educational credentials, has stayed on track, and has been sensible enough not to have children. But putting these roles together is an invitation for failure." Her message is that society does not support working mothers, and maternity leaves, child care, and early childhood education programs are necessary. The controversial aspect of her message is her criticism of the women's movement for failing to advocate and obtain these supports.

So where are women today? In the selections that follow, Shirley Wilkins and Thomas Miller argue that not only are the majority of women working, but the majority are committed to their work. George Gilder, on the other hand, argues that women work less and are less committed to work.

YES

Shirley Wilkins and
Thomas A. W. Miller

WORKING WOMEN:
HOW IT'S WORKING OUT

Lynn and John are in their early thirties, married, and both lawyers. They are about to have their first child—and their first big marital problem.

How are they to raise their child? Which of these talented individuals will be called upon to make the greater professional sacrifice? Whose career will be at least temporarily, if not permanently, derailed in order to have a family?

The couple does have some options. Lynn is eligible for several months of maternity leave, but she worries that she will be taken off the interesting and important cases. John can take a more limited amount of paternity leave, but, frankly, it would be frowned upon. They certainly have the combined income to be able to afford a full-time nanny, but they are not anxious to entrust their child's early education to a professional—no matter how sensitive and intelligent that person may be. Day-care centers are available, but there the problem of paying an outsider to do their child-rearing is compounded by an environment that, however well managed, is in no sense a home.

In brief, Lynn and John do not want to be absentee parents—and yet both of them derive enormous personal satisfaction from their work.

This couple's problem is by no means an isolated one. Writ large, it exemplifies a growing challenge for a rapidly increasing number of American women and men: how to combine careers and families when both spouses work. Time is of the essence—and for working couples, their time is particularly pressed. How can all of the things that people want for themselves—children, a happy marriage, a job—be fit into a twenty-four-hour day?

The 1985 Virginia Slims American Women's Opinion Poll, conducted by the Roper Organization, has monitored and tracked Americans' opinions on social, familial, and personal issues since 1970. The fifth in a series of polls sponsored by Virginia Slims, this one is based on a representative nation-wide sample of 3,000 adult women and 1,000 adult men. The results of this

From Shirley Wilkins and Thomas A. W. Miller, "Working Women: How It's Working Out," *Public Opinion* (October/November 1985), pp. 44-48. Reprinted by permission of American Enterprise Institute for Public Policy Research.

year's survey suggest that changing attitudes toward women's role in society, toward marriage, and toward the essential components of a full and satisfying personal life portend major social changes in the future. The traditional organization of family life, and the very nature of work itself, may never be the same.

ONCE A BREAD BAKER, NOW A BREAD WINNER

If one word could sum up the vast progress made by women in the past fifteen years, it would be "choice." The freedom to choose a fulfilling individual lifestyle—and, simultaneously, tolerance of others' choices—has been the essential force underlying the social transformations of this period.

And a key element in this ongoing social evolution has been, and undoubtedly will continue to be, women's move into the workplace. Over the past fifteen years, the percentage of women employed full time has doubled; combined with part-time workers, this brings the total percentage of working women to more than half (52 percent) of the adult female population.

It is not simply out of economic necessity, moreover, that this fast-rising number of women choose to work. When asked whether they would continue to work even if financially secure, an identical proportion of employed women and employed men (66 percent) reply that they would. Perhaps more to the point, for the first time ever a majority of women (51 percent) would prefer to have a job rather than stay at home and take care of a family, if that were their only choice. In 1970, six out of ten women chose home over the workplace.

In the opinion of a growing majority of women, the most personally satisfying and interesting life is one that combines marriage, a career, and children (see Table 1). Particularly among younger women and better-educated ones, this preference for a full professional *and* family life is pronounced (see Table 2). This result leads to two conclusions. First, as younger women mature, they may be more likely to stay in the workforce even as they attempt to raise a family. Second, as more women enroll in colleges and universities, so too will they tend to seek the best of both these worlds. It appears that the desire for a "working marriage"—in which career, marriage, and a family all contribute to a woman's personal satisfaction—is bound to spread in the future.

Table 1

Question: Now let me ask you a somewhat different question. Considering the possibilities for combining or not combining marriage, children, and a career, and assuming you had a choice, which *one* of these possibilities do you think would offer *you* the most satisfying and interesting life? (card shown respondent)

| | Women | |
	1974	1985
Combining marriage, career, and children	52%	63%
Marrying, having children, but not having career	38	26
Having career and marrying, but not having children	4	4
Having career, but not marrying or having children	2	3
Marrying, but not having children or career	1	1
Don't know	3	2

Source: Surveys by the Roper Organization for Virginia Slims, latest that of March 1985.

Table 2

Preferences for Marriage, Children, and Career by Demographic Groups, 1985

	Combining marriage, career, and children	Marrying, having children, but not having career	Having career and marrying, but not having children	Having career, but not marrying or having children	Marrying, but not having children or career
All women	63%	26%	4%	3%	1%
White	63	26	5	3	1
Black	63	26	3	7	1
18–29 years	70	19	6	3	1
30–39 years	66	21	6	5	1
40–49 years	66	22	4	5	1
50 years and over	54	37	3	2	*
Non-high school graduate	53	37	3	4	1
High school graduate	63	28	3	3	*
College graduate	70	17	7	4	1

Note: * = less than .5%.

Source: Survey by the Roper Organization for Virginia Slims, March 1985.

Table 3

Efforts to Strengthen Women's Status

Question: Do you favor or oppose most of the efforts to strengthen and change women's status in society today?

	Women		Men	
	Favor	Oppose	Favor	Oppose
1970	40%	42%	44%	39%
1972	48	36	49	36
1974	57	25	63	19
1980	64	24	64	23
1985	73	17	69	17

Source: Surveys by the Roper Organization for Virginia Slims, latest that of March 1985.

This move of women into a traditionally male domain—the workplace—has enormous social consequences. In the first place, it is clearly linked to women's improving status in our society—and to women's increasing self-confidence as their own, ardent advocates. According to three-quarters of women and men, women's role in society will continue to change, and larger majorities today (69 percent of women, 67 percent of men) than in 1980 think those roles *should* continue to change.

What is more, overwhelming majorities favor efforts to improve the status of women, and for the first time ever, more women than men support such efforts (see Table 3). This is indeed a dramatic shift in opinion from fifteen years ago, when a slight plurality of women *opposed* efforts to improve their status. They were fearful of the unknown and were much more comfortable with the status quo. Men, not being the object of such efforts, either could afford to be more objective or were reluctant to appear too self-interested. Now, however, women have observed what has happened to many other women as a result of these efforts and have, apparently, decided that the result is good.

In step with women's changing roles, furthermore, has come greater respect for women as individuals, which helps to explain why growing majorities favor efforts to improve women's status. Today, 60 percent of women and 61 percent of men believe that women are more respected now than they were ten years ago. This, too, represents quite a change from the attitudes of 1970, when only 38 percent of women and 40 percent of men thought that women were more respected compared to ten years previously. And, once again, the young and college-educated are among the most optimistic women.

Despite such growing respect for women, however, working women have encountered difficulties in the professional world. Sexual discrimination does persist, and the consensus of both women and men is that, all things considered, there are more advantages in being a man in today's world. Yet it is heartening that majorities of working women say they stand an equal chance with men in three vital areas concerning their jobs: salary, responsibility, and promotion possibilities. The major barrier that remains, according to a plurality of these women (45 percent), is being promoted to a top management position (see Table 4).

Nevertheless, women with actual work experience think that things are generally better now than they were five years ago. But men do not agree. Men are *less* inclined today than they were in 1980 to think that women have equal chances in the workplace. Thus, those who are allegedly discriminated against believe that the situation is improving; those who are supposed to be doing the discriminating think it is getting worse. What explains this fascinating contradiction?

It would seem that men's attitudes toward this problem have been influenced, at least to some extent, by the increasing amount of information on sexual discrimination in general. That is, men have become more aware that there is a problem, and this is influencing their opinions about possible unfairness in the workplace. Men are now more sensitive, and perhaps even more defensive, about equal professional opportunities, even though the attitudes of working women suggest that real progress is being made.

Of course, it would be premature to declare that battle for equal economic

Table 4

Equal Opportunity on the Job, 1985

Question: Do you feel you stand an equal chance with the men you work with in the following areas?

	Working women say they have:			Men say working women have:		
	Equal chance	Not equal	Don't know	Equal chance	Not equal	Don't know
Salary	57%	33%	10%	48%	46%	6 %
Responsibility	73	18	9	61	33	6
Promotion	53	35	12	45	49	7
Becoming an executive	38	45	17	37	54	9

Source: Survey by the Roper Organization for Virginia Slims, March 1985.

opportunity, for completely nondiscriminatory treatment at work, over. Certain issues, such as the complex and emotional one of comparable worth, are still on the public agenda. Yet, women *have* come far in seeking and obtaining meaningful jobs for themselves. They *are* moving into occupations once considered the sole preserves of men, as Sally Ride's space flight in 1983 and Geraldine Ferraro's vice presidential nomination in 1984 symbolize. There *is* a widespread feeling today that a talented and capable woman can succeed in whatever profession she chooses.

More and more, women's professional potential is obstructed not by discrimination *in* the workplace but rather by obligations *outside* it. Women may increasingly enjoy equal opportunities at work, but, compared to men, they have relatively little time to capitalize on those opportunities. The major challenges for the future—challenges created by women's very success in moving into the workplace over the past fifteen years—concern the organization of *domestic* life. The problem is to find a new balance between work and home for both women and men—and, further down the road, perhaps to alter the structure of work in order to have a fuller and more satisfying family life.

MARRIAGES OF MUTUAL RESPONSIBILITY

Marriage these days is enjoying something of a comeback, despite all the attention typically paid to the divorce rate in this country. Although fewer men and women today are married and living with their spouses than in 1980—in part, it must be said, because the baby boom generation is still in its marrying years and tends to marry later—other signs indicate that attitudes about marriages may be changing.

Nine out of ten women and men say, for instance, that marriage is their preferred lifestyle. Substantially fewer people today than in 1970 believe that marriage as an institution is weaker now than ten years ago.

The fact is that marriage and the nuclear family have always been, and will long continue to be, the core of American society. True, large majorities say that people can be happy without being married. And they also think that a happy marriage does not require children. Yet, there has been virtually no increase since 1972 in the number of Americans who have or plan to have no children, and the extremely high proportion (90 percent) saying that marriage is their preferred lifestyle has remained remarkably constant. Instead, these attitudes toward the role of marriage and children in personal happiness demonstrates Americans' growing tolerance of alternative lifestyles—of those minorities who choose to remain single or childless.

Yet by far the most significant change in Americans' views of marriage concerns the *kind* of marriage that people want. Today, majorities of men and women desire a marriage of shared responsibility—one in which both spouses work and divide housekeeping and childrearing equally. Merely a decade ago, a majority of women and a plurality of men opted for a traditional marriage, in which he was the financial provider and she ran the house and took care of the children (see Table 5).

Once again, enthusiasm for this new type of marriage is most pronounced among younger women and men, which suggests that it will increasingly become the norm. But more indicative of the challenges ahead, and the problems obstructing such shared-responsibility marriages, is that women have more eagerly embraced this concept than men.

The main reasons for this divergence in attitudes of women and men is that, while women have moved quickly into the "male" domain of the workplace, men have been much slower to help out with "female" tasks in the home. For instance, 30 percent of married women who are employed full time assert they do nearly all of the household chores, and another 44 percent claim they do a lot but their husbands help out some. Merely 24 percent say these tasks are evenly divided between the spouses. Men with working wives tend to be more charitable toward themselves—28 percent claim that the chores are evenly divided—but even so, the imbalance is evident.

Another factor that helps to explain men's relative reluctance about the shared-responsibility marriage is that they, much more than women, derive a greater sense of their personal identity from their work. For many men, their careers are the key element defining their place in society and even their concept of self-worth. Women, however, have long relied on other sources—particularly, perhaps their children—to establish their sense of identity, precisely because customarily they have spent so much time with kids in the home. One indication of this major difference between the sexes can be found in attitudes toward work. A majority of employed men (56 percent) consider their work to be a career, while a majority of employed women (58 percent) say their work is "just a job."

Yet what exactly do these figures mean? Is work just a stopgap measure or a kind of pastime for many women? This is hardly the appropriate conclusion, given that a majority of women consider work to be an essential ingredient of a full and satisfying life, that two-thirds of employed women would continue to work even if financially secure, that more employed women than employed men derive a great deal of personal satisfaction from their work, and that a majority of *all* women would choose a job instead of staying home. Instead, the proper conclusion would appear to be that women place a different *degree* of importance on their work—that, in the grand scheme of life, work may be somewhat less important than it is to many men.

Table 5

Question: In today's society, there are different lifestyles, and some that are acceptable today that weren't in the past. Regardless of what you may have done or plan to do with your life, and thinking just of what would give *you personally* the most satisfying and interesting life, which one of these different ways of life do you think would be the best as a way of life? (Card shown respondent)

	1974		1985					
	Total women	Total men	Total women	18–29 years	30–39 years	40–49 years	50 years and over	Total men
Marriage where husband and wife share responsibilities more—both work, share housekeeping and child responsibilites	46%	44%	57%	69%	65%	58%	42%	50%
Traditional marriage with husband assuming responsibility for family and wife running house and taking care of children	50	48	37	24	30	34	52	43
Living with someone of opposite sex, but not marrying	3	3	2	3	1	2	1	3
Remaining single and living alone	1	1	2	1	1	4	2	3
Remaining single and living with others of the same sex	—	—	—	—	—	—	—	1
Living in large family of people with similar interests in which some are married and some are not	1	1	1	1	1	—	1	1

Source: Surveys by the Roper Organization for Virginia Slims, latest that of March 1985.

WORKING TOWARD
A MORE BALANCED FUTURE

It may sound rather radical to suggest that the very nature of the work may change as a result of these evolving attitudes, but that may be the case—someday. If so, what will be the most obviously affected?

First, a larger number of employed women will probably consider their work to be a career rather than "just a job." Already the opinions of college-educated women on this issue are identical to the beliefs of college-educated men: more than six in ten say they are pursuing a career, not working a job. The very meaning of a career, however, could well be transformed. Career paths in most professions were established when men overwhelmingly dominated them. That is no longer the case. Some better mechanism will have to be found to accommodate these career-minded women—and their aspirations for a happy family life as well.

Second, working couples will face more difficult decisions about whose career should take priority. Right now, large majorities of women and men think a woman should quit her job if her husband is offered a very good one elsewhere; at the same time, majorities also believe that a wife should turn down a very good job offer in another city so that her husband can continue his present career. In part this can be explained by the probability that the man has a higher salary and hence is the main source of income for the family. It may simply reflect the public's acceptance of economic reality. But as the earnings of both spouses draw closer together, issues concerning career advancement will become more complex—and Americans' attitudes toward them more ambivalent.

There may also be greater pressure from such two-income families for employers to allow more flexibility in work schedules. Staggering the hours that the parents are at work or shortening the work week could help alleviate some of the problems associated with day care. Or shared jobs, half-time jobs, and other forms of part-time work may take on even greater significance in the future, allowing at least one parent to spend more time with the family.

In the same vein, the provision of day-care services by employers—and perhaps better policies on maternity and paternity leave—may eventually come to be seen as more valuable employee benefits. Employers who provide these kinds of options will be better placed to attract talented individuals from two-income households.

These general attitudes also indicate that the trend toward smaller families is firmly established and will, in all likelihood, continue. It is one thing to hold down a job while attempting to care for two children, quite another if the parents have to look after five.

And even the nature of relationships between women and men undergo some fundamental changes. Hackneyed as the cliché may be, there is power in the purse—psychological as well as economic. Among other things, men's habit of paying for things may fade, in part out of deference to the more independent status of women and in part, perhaps, out of necessity. Plus, they will undoubtedly have to help out a lot more around the home, or the couple will have to learn to tolerate a less clean, orderly environment. But offsetting this, men may get to know their children a little bit better, because they spend more time with them. In fact, children who are raised more equally by both parents may well turn out to be different in many respects from previous generations.

These are just some of the adjustments, it seems, that Americans will be making in coming years. In many respects, this will be a period of consolidation, of sorting out how best to cope with the changing responsibilities of women and men. As Walt Whitman once wrote to Ralph Waldo Emerson: "Women in these States approach the day of that organic equality with men, without which, I see, men cannot have organic equality among themselves." The poet was simply a century and a half before his time.

NO

George Gilder

WOMEN IN THE WORK FORCE

Drastic shifts in sex roles seem to be sweeping through America. From 1890 to 1985 the participation in the work force of women between the ages of twenty-five and forty-four soared from 15 to 71 percent, with the pace of change tripling after 1950. At the end of the Second World War only 10 percent of married women with children under the age of six held jobs or were seeking them. Since then mothers of preschool children have thronged the job market: by 1985 the census had classified more than half of these young mothers as participants in the work force.

Women seem to be crowding into sectors of the work force traditionally occupied by men. From 1972 to 1985 women's share of professional jobs increased from 44 to 49 percent and their share of "management" jobs nearly doubled—growing from 20 to 36 percent. The sociologist Andrew Hacker reported in *The New York Times Magazine* in 1984 that from 1960 to 1983 the percentage of lawyers who are women had risen from 2 to 15 and the percentage of jobs in banking and financial management held by women had risen from 9 to 39.

According to Hacker, a similar shift had occurred in blue-collar work. He cited as examples the fact that from 1970 to 1984 the number of female butchers in packinghouses had risen by more than a third and that by 1984 nearly 80 percent of new bartending jobs were going to women. Moreover, Hacker pointed out, the number of male flight attendants rose by 10,000 during the 1970s. In a poll conducted in 1983 by *The New York Times*, 21 percent of married men declared that they would prefer to stay home and care for the children if they could.

The future apparently promises yet more blurring of traditional sex roles in the work force. Half of all 1985 college graduates were women, and women are earning a steadily rising share of all advanced degrees, including close to one third of all degrees in law, business, accounting, and computer and information sciences.

Every year seems to bring new evidence of radical change in the masculine and feminine roles around which most Americans have oriented their lives

From George Gilder, "Women in the Work Force," *The Atlantic Monthly* (September 1986), pp. 20, 22, 24. Copyright © 1986 by George Gilder. Reprinted by permission of George Borchardt, Inc., and the author.

and expectations. Yet this "revolution"—for all its numerical weight and anecdotal pervasiveness—is largely a statistical illusion.

Many of the statistics that have been cited in the stories of sexual revolution are reflections instead of the Industrial Revolution. The entrance of women into the work force has accompanied, at a slower pace, their departure from farms. As recently as eighty years ago 36 percent of American families were engaged in agriculture; today fewer than three percent are. This shift is truly a revolution, and it has transformed the official labor statistics for women. Although these statistics show women entering the work force in record numbers, the fact is that women have always worked. Their labor on farms, however—in an array of arduous jobs beyond the hearth and cribside—was never monitored by statisticians.

Some 80 percent of single (that is, never married) women between the ages of twenty-five and forty-four now work for pay, and this percentage has not changed significantly since 1950. (The rest presumably include welfare recipients and women of independent means.) Although work-force participation by married women in this age group has increased dramatically—from 26 percent in 1950 to some 67 percent in the mid-1980s—the vast majority of married women, like their grandmothers on the farm, seek part-time or seasonal work convenient to their homes.

As of 1984—the most recent year for which detailed figures are available—only 37 percent of all women between the ages of twenty and sixty-four and 41 percent of all women between the ages of twenty-five and forty-four held full-time year-round jobs (including teaching jobs). Also as of 1984 only 29 percent of married women held full-time year-round jobs. That same year married women contributed an average of only 18.6 percent of the total incomes of their families. From 1960 to 1980 the incomes of working wives actually fell in relation to the incomes of working husbands: from 40 percent to 38 percent.

Statistics such as these are generally interpreted as evidence of tenacious discrimination against women. Such discrimination unquestionably exists, but one can argue that it is only a small part of what the statistics reflect.

It is possible that the data also reflect choices that women themselves are making. A study conducted in the mid-1970s by the Institute for Research on Poverty at the University of Wisconsin, with the assistance of the U.S. Department of Health, Education, and Welfare, lends support to the hypothesis that the job priorities of married women are not the same as those of married men. The study uncovered a sharp difference between wives and husbands in the extent to which they exploit what the researchers termed their "earnings capacity," or potential, as defined by a complex formula that includes such variables as age, location, education, experience, training, and physical health. For women the researchers considered one other variable: discrimination. Because the researchers allowed for discrimination in their calculation of the extent to which women exploit their earnings capacity, discrimination alone cannot explain the differences they found.

The study showed that single men and single women are about equally successful in the extent to which they exploit their earnings capacity (68 percent for single men, 64 percent for single women). However, whereas married men of working age exploit 87 percent of their earnings capacity, married women exploit only 33 percent. Thus, according to the study, married men are more than twice as successful in realizing their financial potential as married women are.

More significant still is the difference that the institute found between the most highly educated married women and men. The women with the best credentials and qualifications—the top 10 percent in earnings capacity—exploited one quarter as much of their financial potential as did similarly qualified men. In direct contrast with the pattern exhibited by married men, the more earnings capacity commanded by married women the less they used it—that is, the less likely they were to work full-time all year at a demanding and highly remunerative job. The inadequacies of day care cannot account for this discrepancy; these women presumably have a potential income high enough to cover an array of options in child care.

The institute based its study on data from the early 1970s, but more recent data are compatible with its findings. The gap in earnings between married men and women still widens dramatically as age and schooling increase. As of 1983 married women with a graduate education earned 11 percent less than married men with a high school education. However, single women who work full-time year-round have long earned about as much as their single male peers. Therefore, the pattern of low earnings by highly qualified wives seems a reflection more of personal choice than of discrimination against women.

A Louis Harris poll conducted in 1980 revealed basic differences between the sexes in attitudes toward work. Unlike the working men surveyed, who overwhelmingly preferred full-time jobs, working women expressed a preference for part-time over full-time work by a 41 to 17 percent margin. The women with the highest earnings capacity—managerial, professional, and executive women—preferred part-time work by a 51 to 19 percent margin.

Large numbers of women are using entrepreneurial activity to satisfy their apparent preference for work in the home. From knitting mittens to selling real estate and writing software packages for personal computers, more and more women are working for themselves, launching small businesses in their homes. From 1972 to 1982 the percentage of self-employed workers in nonagricultural industries who are women rose from 26 to 32. For the past two years women have actually formed sole proprietorships at a faster rate than men.

The more education and the better credentials women have, the more freedom they have to choose the extent to which they will work outside their homes. Female physicians, for example, see 38 percent fewer patients per hour and work fewer hours than male physicians; female professors write fewer books and research papers than male professors.

A study in 1979 by the Brookings Institution showed that women in the prime earning years were eleven times more likely to leave the work force voluntarily—if often temporarily—than men were. Current data from the Bureau of Labor Statistics indicate that women work only 70 percent as long for a given employer as men do. According to a study of census data done for the Civil Rights Commission by Solomon Polachek in 1984, the differences in the number of years of continuous service in the work force—and resulting differences in training and experience—explain "close to 100 percent of the wage gap" between men and women in the job market.

Although polls show an increasing desire for jobs on the part of women, in a 1985 Roper survey only 10 percent of women declared that a husband should turn down a very good job in another city "so the wife can continue her job." This percentage has not increased since 1980 and offers a reason, beyond maternity, why women leave their jobs so often: they still rate their own employment as less important than their husband's.

The most recent data on occupational trends, released by the Bureau of Labor Statistics for 1985, show little sign that sex roles in the work force are disappearing. The percentage of women in such blue-collar jobs as plumbing, electrical work, and carpentry has scarcely changed. Federal contractors and private firms, including Sears, Roebuck and Co., that have attempted to hire women for jobs traditionally held by men have consistently failed to meet their own goals, for lack of applicants.

Regardless of the evidence of polls and of labor-force-participation rates that include part-time workers, women do not seem to be behaving like men in the labor market. While the government is pressuring private firms to employ and promote more women, the government itself fails to show employment patterns much different from those in the private sector. Even in November of 1980—the final year of a Democratic Administration that made equal rights for women a prime goal—only seven percent of the employees in the top five GS ratings were women, while more than three quarters in the bottom grades were.

In fact, the pattern of employment in the federal government would suffice to justify an anti-discrimination suit if the government were a private institution. Yet the government may not be discriminating against women, and private companies may not be either. Let us at least consider the possibility that many women, deliberately rejecting the values of male careerists, are discriminating against the job "rat race" and in favor of their families.

POSTSCRIPT

Can Women Combine Careers and Families?

Gilder is not at all impressed by the types of statistics that are presented by Wilkins and Miller. "Every year seems to bring new evidence of radical change in the masculine and feminine roles around which most Americans have oriented their lives and expectations. Yet this 'revolution'—for all its numerical weight and anecdotal pervasiveness—is largely a statistical illusion." Single women have always worked and "the vast majority of married women, like their grandmothers on the farms, seek part-time or seasonal work convenient to their homes." So where is the revolution? Furthermore, according to his reading of the evidence most mothers are not trying to combine career with family but rather are trying to find part-time work to fit around their family life.

Gilder's analysis suggests that women's lives could be significantly improved if much more part-time work were available in all lines of work. Wilkins and Miller's analysis suggests that working mothers are more interested in institutional supports (i.e., job protection, leave policies, quality child care centers, preschools, flexible work schedules, and flexible career ladders than) in shorter hours at work.

Much of the literature on career and family are articles in magazines, but two key books are Sylvia Ann Hewlett's *A Lesser Life: The Myth of Women's Liberation in America* (Morrow, 1986) and Barbara Berg's *The Crisis of the Working Mother* (Summit, 1986). See also Berg's article, "The Guilt That Drives Working Mothers Crazy" (*Ms.*, May 1987; Kathleen Gerson's "Briefcase, Baby or Both?" (*Psychology Today*, November 1986); Karl Zinsmeister's

"Family's Tie to the American Dream" (*Public Opinion*, September/October 1986); and Cheryl Russell's "The New Homemakers" (*American Demographics*, October 1985). For germane time-use studies see F. Thomas Juster et al., *Time, Goods, and Well-Being* (University of Michigan Press, 1985) and William Michelson, *From Sun to Sun—Daily Obligations and Community Structure in the Lives of Employed Women and Their Families* (Rowman and Allanheld, 1985). Two books in addition to Hewlett's that are trying to redirect the women's movement to focus more on family-related issues are Betty Friedan's *The Second Stage* (Summit, 1981) and Ruth Sidel's *Women and Children Last* (Viking, 1986). Three articles address these issues in response to Hewlett's book: "What Now?" by Dorothy Wickenden (*The New Republic*, May 5, 1986); "Family Ties: Feminism's Next Frontier," by Joan Walsh (*The Progressive*, September 1986); and "Feminism, Stage Three," by Michael Levin (*Commentary*, August 1986). For an important study of the problems of women in the corporate world see Liz Roman Gallese's *Women Like Us* (Morrow, 1985).

PART 3

Stratification and Inequality

Have all societies at all times in all places been patriarchies (that is, structured so that the father is supreme, the male dominant)? What is the significance of what the research may or may not tell us in this regard? For sociologists, these questions are central to the debate over patriarchy.

Although the ideal of equal opportunity for all is strong in the United States, many charge that inequities in the U.S. political and economic system do exist. Various affirmative action programs have been implemented to remedy inequalities, but some argue that this is discrimination in reverse. Does poverty continue to exist in the United States despite public assistance programs because it has become a deeply ingrained way of life? Or is poverty a result of the failure of policymakers to live up to U.S. egalitarian principles? Social scientists debate these questions in this part.

Is Patriarchy Universal and Genetically Determined?

Is Economic Inequality Beneficial to Society?

Does "Lower-Class" Culture Perpetuate Poverty?

Is Racial Oppression Declining in America?

Is Affirmative Action Reverse Discrimination?

ISSUE 5

Is Patriarchy Universal and Genetically Determined?

YES: Steven Goldberg, from "Reaffirming the Obvious," *Society* (September/October 1986)

NO: Cynthia Fuchs Epstein, from "Inevitabilities of Prejudice," *Society* (September/October 1986)

ISSUE SUMMARY

YES: Sociologist Steven Goldberg argues his thesis that there are inherent, unchangeable differences between men and women and that these differences have made male dominance "inevitable."

NO: Sociologist Cynthia Fuchs Epstein is critical of Goldberg's research methods and findings, his conclusions, and what they imply for the structure of society and for women's roles.

"Nature versus nurture" is one of the thorniest issues in social science. To what extent is human behavior the result of natural, biological forces over which we have no control, and to what extent is it a result of "nurture," that is, our socialization from the cradle to the grave? The issue is tremendously important, especially for reformers. If, say, undesirable behavior is the result of our humanly-constructed environment, then, in theory at least, the solution is simple: change the environment; reconstruct it. But if a behavioral trait is purely natural—the result of genes or hormones or some other biological given—then changing society will not necessarily bring about any fundamental change.

The nature-nurture issue runs through a number of social science disputes, from debates over intelligence to the question of whether or not there is a criminal personality. But where the issue seems to be most sharply drawn is in the dispute over male dominance.

About certain facts there is little dispute. For at least 2,500 years, men have dominated the chief social, ecclesiastical, political, and military institutions of the West. From the churches to the war rooms, from the boardrooms to the schoolrooms, men have occupied the command posts. Even modern Western democracies have been dominated by men: until well into the twentieth century, women were largely barred from voting and holding public office. True, more recently, there has been a handful of women leaders, such as

Margaret Thatcher in England, Benazir Bhutto in Pakistan, Golda Meir (1898–1978) in Israel, and Corazón Aquino in the Philippines, but these women are the exceptions. There has never been a female-dominated leadership cadre in the Western world.

The issue is whether this tendency toward patriarchy—rule by men—is the result of purely historical and social forces or whether there is some natural human tendency toward male dominance. Feminists readily agree that Western society *has* been dominated by men; what they dispute is that the dominance has been the result of some inherent biological traits. Biology is *not* destiny," they argue.

In 1973 Steven Goldberg published a book devoted to proving the theses that there are inherent, unchangeable differences between men and women that have made male dominance "inevitable" in history. Entitled *The Inevitability of Patriarchy*, Goldberg's book was praised as cogent, well-researched sociology. It was also condemned as simplistic pseudoscience. Thirteen years later, *Society* magazine invited Goldberg to defend his thesis against some of its critics. The following selections are excerpts from the arguments of Goldberg and one of his critics, Cynthia Fuchs Epstein.

YES   Steven Goldberg

REAFFIRMING THE OBVIOUS

That anyone doubted it, was astonishing from the start. All experience and observation seemed to attest to the presence of core-deep differences between men and women, differences of temperament and emotion we call masculinity and femininity. All analyses of such differences were, it seemed obvious, empty or incoherent unless they saw the differences as related to substrative differences between men and women, differences that gave masculine and feminine direction to the emotions and behavior of men and women. The question to be answered, it seemed, was how these substrative differences manifest themselves on a social and institutional level—not whether the differences exist.

Yet there it was. A generation of educated people was jettisoning the evidence of both experience and intellect in order to propound a clearly indefensible hypothesis: emotional and behavioral differences between men and women, and the social expectations associated with them, are primarily the result of environmental factors to which physiology is of little relevance. Proponents supported this view with arguments ranging from the confused to the misrepresentative. Individuals who are exceptions were invoked as somehow refuting the possibility of physiological roots of behavior, a maneuver that makes about as much sense as arguing that a six-foot-tall woman somehow demonstrates the social causation of height. Myths about matriarchies were introduced as historical evidence, an approach that would justify a belief in cyclopses. The primary argument supporting this view, an argument accepted even in college textbooks, was the argument that emotional and behavioral differences between men and women were caused primarily by socialization.

The central problem with this approach is that it does not explain anything; it merely begs the question: Why does not one of the thousands of disparate societies on which we have evidence reverse male and female expectations? Why does every society from that of the Pygmy to that of the

Swede associate dominance and attainment with males? To say that males are more aggressive because they have been socialized that way is like saying that men can grow moustaches because boys have been socialized toward that end. There is no outside experimenter for society, setting up whatever rules seem desirable. Possible social values are limited by observation of reality; if male physiology is such that males have a lower threshold for the elicitation of dominance behavior, then social expectations denying this cannot develop.

Ten years ago it was not clear to all that there had never been a society reversing the sexual expectations I discuss. Social science texts, out of ignorance or tendentiousness, misrepresented ethnographic studies and asserted the existence of societies that reversed the sexual expectations. Recourse to the original ethnography on every alleged exception demonstrated beyond the possibility of reasonable dispute that not one of the thousands of societies (past and present) on which we have any sort of evidence lacks any of three institutions: patriarchy, male attainment, and male dominance.

All societies that have ever existed have associated political dominance with males and have been ruled by hierarchies overwhelmingly dominated by men. A society may have a titular queen or a powerful queen when no royal male is available; there were more female heads of state in the first two-thirds of the sixteenth century than the first two-thirds of the twentieth. An occasional woman may gain the highest position in a modern state; the other eighteen ministers in Golda Meir's cabinet, and all other Israeli prime ministers, were male. In every society from the most primitive to the most modern—whatever the yardstick—it is the case that political dominance, in particular, and hierarchical dominance, in general, are overwhelmingly in the hands of men.

Whatever the nonmaternal roles that are given highest status—whichever these are and whatever the reasons they are given high status in any given society—these roles are associated with males. A modern example describes the situation that obtains in every society: if being a medical doctor is given high status (as in the United States), most doctors are male; if being an engineer is given high status and being a doctor relatively low status (as in the Soviet Union), then most engineers are male and most nonhierarchical doctors may be female. There are societies—although modern societies, by their nature, could not be among them—in which women perform objectively far more important economic functions while working harder and longer outside the home than do men. Indeed, save for political and hierarchical leadership, internal and external security, and nurturance of the young, every task is seen as male in some societies and female in others. However, in every society that which is given highest status is associated with men. It is tempting to explain this as a residue of male political dominance, but this view gets things backwards. Male roles do not have high status because they are male; nor do high-status roles have high status because they are male. Many male roles have low status and many low-status roles are male. High-status roles are male because they have (for different reasons in different societies) high status; this high-status motivates males to attain the roles—for psychophysiological reasons—more strongly than it does females (statistically-speaking). Social expectations conform to limits set by this reality.

The emotions of both males and females of all societies associate dominance with the male in male-female relationships and encounters. The existence of this reality is evidenced by the ethnographies of every society; the observations and statements of the members of every society; the values, songs, and proverbs of every society; and, in our own society, also by feminists who abhor this reality and incorrectly attribute it primarily to social and environmental causes. We might argue that in the family the women of some or all societies have greater power, attributable to either a male abdication or a female psychological acuity that enables women to get around men. But the question relevant to universality is why both the men and women have the emotional expectation of a male dominance that must be gotten around.

The social sciences have discovered precious few nontrivial institutions that are both universal and sufficiently explicable with direct physiological evidence. The three institutions I discuss require explanation and this explanation must be simple. I mention this in anticipation of the inevitable, however wrongheaded, criticism that any physiologically-rooted theory is simplistic, determinist, or reductionist. Were we to attempt to explain variation in the forms of these institutions in physiological terms, an explanation would, in all likelihood, be simplistic. Physiology is in all likelihood irrelevant to differences between, say, American patriarchy and Arabic patriarchy. An explanation sufficient to explain the universal limits within which all variation takes place, if it is to be at all persuasive, requires a single factor common to, and imposing limits on, all societies that have ever existed. Indeed, the very extensiveness of the cross-cultural variation in most institutions emphasizes the need to explain why the institutions we discuss always work in the same direction. No reality is inevitable simply because it is universal, but when an institution is universal we must ask why. If the reason for universality is a physiological factor giving direction to the motivations that make us what we are, then we must entertain the possibility that the institution is an inevitable social resolution of the psychophysiological reality. . . .

Differences between the male and female endocrine/central nervous systems are such that—statistically speaking—males have a greater tendency to exhibit whatever behavior is necessary in any environment to attain dominance in hierarchies and male-female encounters and relationships, and a greater tendency to exhibit whatever behavior is necessary for attainment of nonmaternal status. Using somewhat unrigorous terms, we might say that males are more strongly motivated by the environmental presence of hierarchy, by a member of the other sex, or by status to do what is necessary to attain dominance. It is irrelevant whether we conceptualize this as a lower male threshold for the release of dominance behavior, a greater male drive for dominance, a greater male need for dominance, or a weaker male ego that needs shoring up by attainment of dominance and status. It is the reality of the male-female difference that matters, not the model used to explain the difference that any model must explain. Likewise, it is irrelevant why our species (and those from which we are descended) evolved the psychophysiological differentiation;

all that matters for an explanation of universality is that the differentiation exists. . . .

Physiology does not determine the actual behavior required for dominance and attainment in any given society: that is socially determined. What physiology accounts for is the male's greater willingness to sacrifice the rewards of other motivations—the desire for affection, health, family life, safety, relaxation, vacation and the like—in order to attain dominance and status. This model makes clear why physiology need not be considered in a causal analysis of the behavior of a given individual exception. At the same time physiology is necessary for an analysis of the existence on a societal level of the universal institutions I discuss. Even the effects of virtually pure physiology expect many exceptions (as the six-foot-tall woman demonstrates). Dominance motivation no doubt has other causes—experiential and familial—in addition to the physiological causes and, for the exception, these may counteract the physiological factors.

When we speak of an entire society, the law of large numbers becomes determinative. The statistical, continuous, and quantitative reality of the male's greater dominance tendency becomes concretized on the social level in absolute, discrete, and qualitative terms. The statistical reality of the male's greater aggression becomes in its pure and exaggerated form: "men are aggressive (or dominant); women are passive (or submissive)." This leads to discrimination, often for the woman who is an exception and occasionally for every woman. Discrimination is possible precisely because the statistical reality makes the exception an exception, exposed to the possibility of discrimination. The six-foot-tall girl who wishes she were short lives in a world of boys who are praised for being six feet tall.

As long as societies have hierarchies, differentiated statuses, and intermixing of men and women, they will possess the only environmental cues necessary to elicit greater dominance and attainment behavior from males. In utopian fantasy a society lacking hierarchy, status, and male-female relationships may be possible, but in the real world it is not. In the real world, societies have cultures. These cultures will value some things more than others and—particularly in the modern, bureaucratic society—some positions more than others. If male physiology is such that males are willing to sacrifice more for these things and positions, they will learn what is necessary and do what is necessary—whatever that may be in any given society—for dominance and attainment. There are other necessary conditions: it is not only gender that keeps a black woman from ruling the Republic of South Africa. Nevertheless, within any group possessing the other necessary conditions, dominance will go to those most willing to sacrifice for dominance and status (and social values will lead to such expectations). . . .

The male-female differentiation that I have discussed is the one for which the evidence is by far the most overwhelming. There are other differences that may well be functions of endocrine-central nervous system differentiation. The stereotype that sees logically abstract thinking as "thinking like a man" and psychological perception as "woman's intuition" without question reflect empirical realities; it is only the cause of these realities that is open to question. A score on the SAT mathematics aptitude section that puts a girl in the ninetieth percentile among girls places a boy in only the sixty-eighth percentile among boys; among mathematically-precocious students (thirteen years old), a score of 700 is thirteen times more likely to be attained by a boy than by a girl (with equal numbers of boys and girls with similar mathematical backgrounds taking the test). There also seems to be a linear relationship between the importance of logical abstraction to an area and the percentage of those at the highest levels who are men; there has never been a woman at the highest level of mathematics, chess, or composing music (which is not thought of as a macho enterprise), while there have been many women of genius in literature and the performing arts. . . .

Nothing I have written about patriarchy, male attainment, or male dominance im-plies (or precludes) males' better performing roles once they attain them. Whether the male tendencies increase performance or retard it is another issue (save for the fact that a position must be attained before it can be performed). Similarly, nothing I have written implies the desirability of any particular social or political program. "Is cannot imply ought," and no scientific analysis of how the world works can entail a subjective decision on which of two programs is preferable. We might accept all that I have written and see this as demonstrating the need for an equal rights law limiting the male physiological advantage for attainment. Or we might see the same evidence as justifying a socialization system that provides clear role models by emphasizing the sex differences I discuss. Science is silent on such a choice.

NO

Cynthia Fuchs Epstein

INEVITABILITIES OF PREJUDICE

Is there any reason to believe that patriarchy is more inevitable than anti-Semitism, child abuse, or any other mode of oppression that has been around for as long as anyone can remember? On the basis of his own experience, Aristotle believed that slavery was inevitable; and although it is still around in some countries, few reasonable people now believe it must be inevitable. Unfortunately, people with credentials for reasonableness, such as a new school of sociobiologists and their popularizers—among them Steven Goldberg—feel comfortable believing that the subordination of women is inevitable, programmed into human nature.

Many forms of oppression seem inevitable because they are so difficult to dislodge. History shows us that. It is easier to maintain oppression than to overthrow it. This is because when a group has a power advantage (which may emerge by chance, or historical accident), even if it is small, it may escalate rapidly if those in power can monopolize not only material resources but the avenues of communication as well. The Nazis did so effectively. Karl Marx cautioned that the owners of production were also the owners of the production of ideas. This means that the values and knowledge of a society usually reflect the views of those who rule, often by convincing those in subordinate statuses that they deserve what they get. The Nazis argued that they belonged to the "master race" and tried to build a science to prove it. They were less subtle than other rulers, but their case is instructive: beware the thesis of any powerful group that claims its power is derived solely from "divine right" or from its genes.

If anything is inevitable, it is change. Change in history is characteristic of human experience and reflects the human capacity to order and reorder it, to understand the processes of its ordering, and to sweep away old superstitions. As Robert K. Merton pointed out in the *American Journal of Sociology* in 1984: "What everyone should know from the history of thought is that what everyone knows turns out not to be so at all."

Some twelve years have passed since Steven Goldberg published his book, *The Inevitability of Patriarchy*, more than a decade which has produced thousands of studies of gender differences and similarities, an extensive reanalysis of the relationship and applicability of primate behavior to human behavior, and debate and analysis of sociobiological interpretation. Goldberg has offered us once again, a view of women's subordination as inevitable simply because it has always existed. The thesis, unchanged from his formulation of a decade ago, is uninformed about the rich body of scholarship that has been published—much of it disproving his assumptions about significant differences in men's and women's emotions, cognitive capacities, and situation in the structure of the social hierarchy. In these intervening years, there have also been changes in the statuses and roles of women in the United States and in other parts of the world—these also invalidate Goldberg's perspective on the constancy and universality of his observations about the subordination of women.

Women in the United States, as elsewhere, have been elected and appointed to positions of power. They have joined the ranks of the prestigious and the powerful in the domains of law and medicine, and are entering specialties and practices to which they were denied admission and discouraged from pursuing only a decade ago. Women are now judges at every level of the judiciary in the United States, as well as prosecutors in the courts engaging in adversarial and assertive behavior, exhibiting what may be termed as "dominant behavior." There is considerable evidence that women perform well, sometimes even better than do men, in examinations that determine admission to all fields in professional and graduate schools, where women constitute from a third to half of all students. Each year sees an increase in the number of women admitted to schools of engineering and science in spite of men's supposed greater social orientation toward careers in these fields.

Women have also become university professors and researchers and have thus been empowered to challenge many biased views about human nature and to fill gaps left by male scholars who have characteristically had little interest or inclination to do research in this field. Therefore, a revised view of what is "natural" or "inevitable" is part of the contemporary intellectual agenda.

Women are also making inroads in blue-collar technical work, heretofore denied them because of restrictions in apprenticeship programs made yet more difficult because of personal harassment. Women have experienced the same exclusionary mechanisms exercised against all minority groups who have had the audacity to compete with white males for the privileged positions guarded by "covenants" instituted by unions and ethnic clusters. According to a 1985 Rand Corporation research study by Linda Waite and Sue Berryman, *Women in Non-Traditional Occupations: Choice and Turnover,* women behave similarly to men in that they exhibit similar work force commitment and turnover rates once involved in nontraditional jobs such as those of the blue-collar crafts or in the army. These researchers emphasize that policies equalizing work conditions for men and women also equalize commitment to the job.

Increasing convergence of gender role behavior is also seen in studies of crime. Girls' crime rates show increasing similarity to that of boys. Girls and boys both commit violent crimes and exhibit increasingly similar criminal histories.

Certainly much of the challenge and change is due to the women's movement and the insistence of women on their rights to equality. Sizable numbers of women in every sphere of society have taken an aggressive role in contesting the domination of men in personal, political, and intellectual life. Given the short period of time in which women have been active on their own behalf and in which they have succeeded in engaging the support of sympathetic men, their strides have been great both with regard to social rank and intellectual accomplishment.

This movement has evolved within the historical context still affected by centuries of oppression that have created and perpetuated the sense that women's inequality is natural. Yet no society, no social group, and especially no ruling group, has ever left gender hierarchy (nor any other form of hierarchy) to nature. It has not been women's incompetence or inability to read a legal brief, to perform brain surgery, to predict a bull market, or to make an intonation to the gods that has kept them from interesting and highly paid jobs. The root of discrimination against women, preventing their access to a variety of fields, has been a rule system replete with severe punishments for those who deviate from "traditional" roles. Access is now achieved through political and social action, and not at all through genetic engineering.

Sociobiologists, on the other hand, argue that the division of labor by sex is a biological rather than a social response. If this were so, sex-role assignments would not have to be coercive. Social groups do not actually depend on instinct or physiology ·to enforce social arrangements because they cannot reliably do so. Societies assign groups to be responsible for such social needs as food, shelter, and child care; nowhere do they depend on nature to meet these requirements. The types of work that men and women perform in each society are stipulated by society, allowing few individuals to make choices outside the prescribed range. The assignments are justified on the basis of ideologies claiming that they are just and reflect popular, cultural opinions that the arrangement is good (or that, if not, little can be done about it).

Such ideologies and popular views suppose that a fit exists between the job and worker—a fit that makes sense. This argument relies on the maintenance of gender differences. Division according to sex is reinforced by requirements that men and women dress differently (whether it is to don the veil or a skirt if female; and trousers or a *doti* if male), learn different skills (women's literacy rates are considerably lower than those of males in the Third World; in the Western world males and females still are "encouraged" to choose "sex-appropriate" subjects) and engage in different forms of activity. Violators are punished for infractions. Sometimes a raised eyebrow will keep a woman in line; in the extreme she may even face being stoned to death or burned alive (as in the recent outbreak of deaths over dowries in India).

The literal binding of women's feet or the constraint of their minds by law and social custom is part of the process by which the gender division of human beings perpetuates a two-class system. The hierarchy is kept in place subtly by the insistence that people behave in the way society's opinion molders say they should. Thus, "ideal" roles mask real behavior. If we look at what men and women actually do—or *can* do without the distorting mirror of "ideal" gender roles—there is a fundamental similarity in personalities, behavior, and competence, given equal opportunity and social conditions. This is what the vast array of scholarship in psychology, sociology, and physiology has revealed in the last decade.

The research has been so extensive that it is impossible to summarize it here, although I shall review it in my forthcoming book, *Deceptive Distinctions*. By now, reviewers have reanalyzed thousands of articles on gender differences in every attribution and behavior imaginable. Despite what everyone believes, the similarities far outweigh the differences, even in considering aggression. As for the differences that census takers count —frequencies of women and men in different jobs and leisure activities—these clearly seem to be a result of social rules and habits. . . .

SEX HORMONES

. . . The question relevant to gender in society is the meaning of differences. For Goldberg, there is an unbroken line between "androgen binding sites in the brain, rough and tumble play in infants, and the male domination of state, industry and the nuclear family." E. O. Wilson is more cautious: "we can go against it if we wish, but only at the cost of some efficiency." If the hormone testosterone is supposed to make men aggressive and thus fit for public office, "female" hormones and the cycles attached to them are seen as detrimental to women's participation in public life. Edgar Berman, medical adviser to the late Senator (and Vice President) Hubert Humphrey, warned against women's participation in public affairs because of their "raging hor-

mones." (Berman later published a book, *The Compleat Chauvinist*, in which he provided "biological evidence" for his views that menopausal women might create havoc if they held public office. Chapter titles from his book are: "The Brain That's Tame Lies Mainly in the Dame," "Testosterone, Hormone of Champions," and "Meno: The Pause that Depresses.") More recently, United Nations Ambassador Jeane Kirkpatrick reported that White House critics resisted her advancement into a higher political post because of the "temperament" she exhibited as a woman. No similar attributions of hormonal barriers to decision-making posts have been offered for men, although they have been excused from infidelity that is explained in popular culture by "male menopause," or by the sociobiologists who see it as an evolutionary response of men.

Many sociobiologists of the Wilson school have been committed to a model of inequity as a product of the natural order, arguing that male domination (patriarchy) is the most adaptive form of society, one that has conferred an advantage on individuals who operate according to its precepts. This thesis—put forth by E. O. Wilson, Lionel Tiger, Robin Fox, and Steven Goldberg—maintains that the near universality of male dominance arose because of the long dependence of the human infant and as a result of hunting and gathering, the early modes of obtaining food. Male-based cooperation was expressed through dominance relations. Men guarded the bands and thus ensured survival. There was pressure on men to perfect hunting skills and on women to stay home and mind the children. Each sex would have developed cognitive abilities attached to these activities. A socially imposed hierarchical division of labor between the sexes gradually became genetically fixed. . . .

MAN THE HUNTER; WOMAN THE GATHERER

In recent years, anthropologists have reevaluated the perspective of "man the hunter," which long served as a model of the origins of human society. . . . Using this model, primatologists and anthropologists such as Sherwood Washburn and Irven De Vore in *The Social Life of Early Man* and Desmond Morris in *The Naked Ape* had reasoned that hunting, a male activity, was a creative turning point in human evolution—that it required intelligence to plan and to stalk game, and to make hunting and other tools. It also required social bonding of men, the use of language to cooperate in the hunt, and then the distribution of meat and the development of tools for hunting and cutting the meat. According to Washburn and Lancaster in Lee and De Vore's *Man the Hunter,* "In a very real sense our intellect, interests, emotions and basic social life—all are evolutionary products of the success of the hunting adaptation." . . . The question is, what merit is there to the model and the explanations derived from it?

Among others, Frances Dahlbert in *Woman the Gatherer* suggests the account can only be considered a "just-so story" in the light of new scholarship. Beginning in the 1960s, research on primates, on hunter-gatherer societies, and archaeological and fossil records made this story obsolete. For example, the paleoanthropological myth of man the hunter was deflated when the "killer ape" of Robert Ardrey's *The Hunting Hypothesis,* the presumed australopithecine forebear of humans, turned out to be predominantly vegetarian. . . . A greater challenge to the man the hunter model came from Sally Linton in Sue Ellen Jacobs's *Women in Cross-Cultural Perspective.* Linton attacked the validity of theories of evolution that excluded or diminished women's contributions to human culture and society. She noted that women contribute the bulk of the diet in contemporary hunting and gathering societies, that small-game hunting practiced by both sexes preceded large-game hunting practiced by men, and that females as well as males probably devised tools for their hunting and gathering and some sort of carrying sling or net to carry babies. According to this view, the collaboration and cooperation of women was probably as important to the development of culture as that of men. . . .

People persist in wanting to view the world in terms of sex differences. They insist that individuals conform to ideal roles and turn away from their real roles, common interests, and goals, and from their mutual fate. These people disregard the obvious truth that most things that most people do most of the time can be performed equally well by either sex. The persistence of the view, as well as the persistence of physical and symbolic sex segregation, is created and maintained for a purpose, which is to maintain the privileges of men who predictably resist claims to the contrary. I suspect that the debates will continue and may do so as long as one group derives advantage from suppressing another. But evidence is mounting that supports equality between the sexes and which no truly reasonable people can continue to deny.

POSTSCRIPT

Is Patriarchy Universal and Genetically Determined?

Epstein suggests that the passage of time has destroyed whatever plausibility Goldberg's thesis might once have had. She cites recent studies by feminist scholars and points to the rise of women's power in the United States. Goldberg would find such scholarship tendentious and self-serving, but no one can ignore the political developments since 1973. If Epstein is right that women "have joined the ranks of the prestigious and powerful" in the United States, then perhaps this country will provide the ultimate test of whether there are inherent behavioral differences between males and females that result in male dominance.

For another treatment of this topic, see Edward O. Wilson, *Sociobiology: The New Synthesis* (Harvard, 1975). (And, of course, see Goldberg's *The Inevitability of Patriarchy*, Morrow, 1973). In recent years a large body of writing has been devoted specifically to disproving the thesis. Most has been done by feminist scholars, who tend to regard scholarship in such areas an essential instrument of women's liberation. Gerda Lerner states at the outset of her book *The Creation of Patriarchy* (Oxford, 1986) that "Women's history is indispensable and essential to the emancipation of women." The notion that there might be "detached" or "objective" scholarship in this area tends to be regarded with suspicion. See, for example, the essays in Marion Lowe and Ruth Hubbard, eds., *Woman's Nature: Rationalizations of Inequality* (Pergamon Press, 1983), especially Elizabeth Fee's "Women's Nature and Scientific Objectivity" (pp. 9–27). See also, Cannie Stark-Adamec, ed., *Sex Roles: Origins, Influences, and Implications for Women* (Eden Press, 1980), which begins with the statement that "science is not pure."

ISSUE 6

Is Economic Inequality Beneficial To Society?

YES: George Gilder, from *Wealth and Poverty* (Basic Books, 1981)

NO: William Ryan, from *Equality* (Pantheon Books, 1981)

ISSUE SUMMARY

YES: Social critic George Gilder praises the American political economy that provides so many incentives for people to get ahead and make money. He maintains that the economy is dynamic and all classes benefit.
NO: Psychologist William Ryan contends that income inequalities in America are excessive and immoral because they vastly exceed differences of merit and result in tremendous hardships for the poor.

No one thinks that the president of the United States should be paid the same salary as a professor of sociology or a teaching assistant. Everyone benefits when the financial rewards for being president are large enough to motivate the most capable members of society to compete for the job. A society is better off with income inequality than with income equality as long as everyone has an equal opportunity to compete for the high paying jobs. Pay differentials are needed to get the best possible fit between people and jobs. But how much income inequality is desirable? On this issue, people strongly disagree, and they carry their disagreement into the political arena.

Income inequality, however, should be viewed as only one type of inequality. Four other essential dimensions of equality/inequality are the degree of equality of opportunity, legal rights, political power, and social status. The American creed is fully committed to equality of opportunity and equality of legal and political rights. We believe everyone should have an equal opportunity to compete for jobs and awards. Laws forbidding discrimination and free public school education are the major means for providing equal opportunities to U.S. citizens. Whether society should also compensate for handicaps such as disadvantaged family backgrounds or the ravages of past discrimination, however, is a knotty issue, which has divided the country. Policies such as Head Start, income-based scholarships, quotas, and affirmative action are hotly debated. Equality of legal rights has been promoted by the civil rights and women's movements. A major debate in this area, of course, is the Equal Rights Amendment (ERA). However, the disagreement is not over the principle of equality but over whether ERA is good or bad for women. America's commitment to political equality is strong in principle, though less strong in practice. Everyone over eighteen gets one vote, and all votes are counted equally, but the political system tilts in the direction of special interest groups; those who belong to no such groups are seldom heard. Furthermore, money plays an increasingly important role in political campaigns. Clearly, there is room for improvement here. The final dimension of equality/inequality is status. Inequality of status involves differences in prestige, and it is arguable as to whether or not it can or should be eliminated. Ideally, the people who contribute the most to society are the most highly esteemed. The reader can judge the extent to which this principle holds true in the United States.

The Declaration of Independence proclaims that "all men are created equal," and the Founding Fathers who wrote the Declaration of Independence went on to base the laws of the land on the principle of equality. The equality they were referring to was equality of opportunity and legal and political rights for white, property-owning males. They did not mean equality of income or status, though they recognized that too much inequality of income would jeopardize democratic institutions. In the two centuries following the signing of the Declaration, non-whites and women struggled for and won considerable equality of opportunity and rights. Meanwhile, income gaps have been widening (except from 1929 to 1945 when the crash harmed the wealthy and wartime full employment favored the poor).

Should America now move toward greater income equality? Must this dimension of inequality be rectified in order for society to be just? George Gilder strongly believes that people must try hard, work hard, innovate, compete, aspire and accept risks, and be rewarded for their efforts. He maintains that welfare, public enterprise, highly progressive taxes, and many other egalitarian measures are sapping American initiative, crippling American enterprise, slowing the American economy, and perpetuating the poverty of the poor. According to Gilder, the free enterprise system, with all of its inequalities, stimulates individual effort and enterprise, and this is what makes America great and prosperous. On the other hand, William Ryan makes the case that the existing income inequalities are obscene and offensive to moral sensibilities. He believes some reduction of inequalities is essential to social justice. Ryan contends that the rich and their propagandists justify existing inequalities by claiming that the system is fair and the inequalities result largely from differential effort, skill, and achievement. He makes his case for establishing that this justification is weak.

YES

George Gilder

THE DIRGE OF TRIUMPH

The most important event in the recent history of ideas is the demise of the socialist dream. Dreams always die when they come true, and fifty years of socialist reality, in every partial and plenary form, leave little room for idealistic reverie. In the United States socialism chiefly rules in auditoria and parish parlors, among encounter groups of leftist intellectuals retreating from the real world outside, where socialist ideals have withered in the shadows of Stalin and Mao, Sweden and Tanzania, gulag and bureaucracy.

The second most important event of the recent era is the failure of capitalism to win a corresponding triumph. For within the colleges and councils, governments and churches where issue the nebulous but nonetheless identifiable airs and movements of new opinion, the manifest achievements of free enterprise still seem less comely than the promise of socialism betrayed. . . .

A prominent source of trouble is the profession of economics. Smith entitled Book One of *The Wealth of Nations*, "Of the Causes of Improvement in the productive Powers of Labour and the Order according to which its Produce is naturally distributed among the different Ranks of the people." He himself stressed the productive powers, but his followers, beginning with David Ricardo, quickly became bogged down in a static and mechanical concern with distribution. They all were forever counting the ranks of rich and poor and assaying the defects of capitalism that keep the poor always with us in such great numbers. The focus on distribution continues in economics today, as economists pore balefully over the perennial inequalities and speculate on brisk "redistributions" to rectify them.

This mode of thinking, prominent in foundation-funded reports, best-selling economics texts, newspaper columns, and political platforms, is harmless enough on the surface. But its deeper effect is to challenge the golden rule of capitalism, to pervert the relation between rich and poor, and to depict the system as "a zero-sum game" in which every gain for someone implies a loss for someone else, and wealth is seen once again to create poverty. As Kristol has said, a free society in which the distributions are

From George Gilder, *Wealth and Poverty* (Basic Books, 1981). Copyright © 1981 by George Gilder. Reprinted by permission of Basic Books, Inc., Publishers, New York.

widely seen as unfair cannot long survive. The distributionist mentality thus strikes at the living heart of democratic capitalism.

Whether of wealth, income, property, or government benefits, distributions always, unfortunately, turn out bad: highly skewed, hugely unequal, presumptively unfair, and changing little, or getting worse. Typical conclusions are that "the top 2 percent of all families own 44 percent of all family wealth, and the bottom 25 percent own none at all"; or the "the top 5 percent get 15.3 percent of the pretax income and the bottom 20 percent get 5.4 percent." . . .

Statistical distributions, though, can misrepresent the economy in serious ways. They are implicitly static, like a picture of a corporate headquarters, towering high above a city, that leaves out all the staircases, escalators, and elevators, and the Librium® on the executive's desk as he contemplates the annual report. The distribution appears permanent, and indeed, like the building, it will remain much the same year after year. But new companies will move in and out, executives will come and go, people at the bottom will move up, and some at the top will leave their Librium® and jump. For example, the share of the tobacco industry commanded by the leading four firms has held steady for nearly thirty years, but the leader of the 1950s is now nearly bankrupt. The static distributions also miss the simple matter of age; many of the people at the bottom of the charts are either old, and thus beyond their major earning years, or young, and yet to enter them. Although the young and the old will always be with us, their low earnings signify little about the pattern of opportunity in a capitalist system.

Because blacks have been at the bottom for centuries now, economists often miss the dynamism within the American system. The Japanese, for example, were interned in concentration camps during World War II, but thirty years later they had higher per capita earnings than any other ethnic group in America except the Jews. Three and one-half million Jewish immigrants arrived on our shores around the turn of the century with an average of nine dollars per person in their pockets, less than almost any other immigrant group. Six decades later the mean family income of Jews was almost double the national average. Meanwhile the once supreme British Protestants (WASPs) were passed in per capita earnings after World War II not only by Jews and Orientals but also by Irish, Italians, Germans, and Poles (which must have been the final Polish joke), and the latest generation of black West Indians.

It is a real miracle that learned social scientists can live in the midst of these continuing eruptions and convulsions, these cascades and cataracts of change, and declare in a tone of grim indignation that "Over the last fifty years there has been no shift in the distribution of wealth and income in this country." . . .

The income distribution tables also propagate a statistical illusion with regard to the American rich. While the patterns of annual income changed rather little in the 1970s, there was a radical shift in the distribution of wealth. In order to understand this development, it is crucial to have a clear-eyed view of the facts and effects of inflation, free of the pieties of the Left and the Right: the familiar rhetoric of the "cruelest tax," in which all the victims seem to be widows and orphans. In fact, widows and orphans—at least the ones who qualified for full social security and welfare benefits—did rather well under inflation. Between 1972 and 1977, for example, the median household income of the elderly rose from 80 to 85 percent of the entire population's. As Christopher Jencks of Harvard University and Joseph Minarek of the Brookings Institution, both men of the Left, discovered in the late 1970s, inflation hit hardest at savers and investors, largely the rich. . . .

Wealth consists of assets that promise a future stream of income. The flows of oil money do not become an enduring asset of the nation until they can be converted into a stock of remunerative capital—industries, ports, roads, schools, and working skills—that offer a future flow of support when the oil runs out. Four hundred years ago, Spain was rich like Saudi Arabia, swamped by a similar flood of money in the form of silver from the mines of Potosi in its Latin American colonies. But Spain failed to achieve wealth and soon fell back into its previous doldrums, while industry triumphed in apparently poorer parts of Europe.

A wealthy country must be able to save as well as to consume. Saving is often defined as deferred consumption. But it depends on investment: the ability to produce consumable goods at that future date to which consumption has been deferred. Saving depends on having something to buy when the deposit is withdrawn. For an individual it sounds easy; there must always be *something* to buy after all. But for a nation, with many savers, real wealth is hard work, requiring prolonged and profitable production of goods. . . .

Work, indeed, is the root of wealth, even of the genius that mostly resides in sweat. But without a conception of goals and purposes, well-paid workers consume or waste all that they earn. Pop singers rocking and rolling in money, rich basketball stars who symbolize wealth to millions, often end up deep in debt with nothing solid to show for their efforts, while the poorest families can often succeed in saving enough to launch profitable businesses. The old adages on the importance of thrift are true not only because they signify a quantitative rise in investible funds, but because they betoken imagination and purpose, which make wealth. Few businesses begin with bank loans, and small businesses almost never do. Instead they capitalize labor.

For example, ten years ago a Lebanese family arrived in Lee, Massachusetts, with a few dollars and fewer words of English. The family invested the dollars in buying a woebegone and abandoned shop beside the road at the edge of town, and they started marketing vegetables. The man rose at five every morning to drive slowly a ramshackle truck a hundred miles to farms in the Connecticut Valley, where he purchased the best goods he could find as cheaply as possible to sell that morning in Lee. It was a classic entrepreneurial performance, arbitrage, identifying price differentials in different markets, and exploiting them by labor. But because both the labor and the insight was little compensated, it was in a sense invisibly saved and invested in the store. All six children were sources of accumulating capital as they busily bustled about the place. The store remained open long hours, cashed checks of locals, and began to build a clientele. A few years later one had to fight through the crowds around it in summer, when the choice asparagus or new potted plants went on sale. Through the year it sold flowers and Christmas trees, gas and dry goods, maple syrup and blackberry jam, cider and candies, and wines and liquors, in the teeth of several supermarkets, innumerable gas stations, and other shops of every description, all better situated, all struggling in an overtaxed and declining Massachusetts economy.

The secret was partly in the six children (who placed the family deep in the statistics of per capita poverty for long after its arrival) and in the entrepreneurial vision of the owner, which eluded all the charts. Mr. Michael Zabian is the man's name, and he recently bought the biggest office building in the town, a three-story structure made of the same Lee marble as the national capitol building. He owns a large men's clothing store at street level and what amounts to a small shopping center at his original site; and he preens in three-piece suits in the publicity photos at the Chamber of Commerce.

As extraordinary as may seem his decade of achievement, though, two other Lebanese have performed similar marvels in the Berkshires and have opened competing shops in the area. Other immigrants in every American city—Cubans in Miami, Portuguese in Providence and Newark, Filipinos in Seattle, Koreans in Washington, D.C., and New York, Vietnamese in Los Angeles, to mention the more recent crop—have performed comparable feats of commerce, with little help from banks or government or the profession of economics.

Small firms, begun by enterprising men, can rise quickly to play important roles in the national economy. Berkshire Paper Company, for example, was started by Whitmore (Nick) Kelley of Glendale, Massachusetts, as a maker of scratch pads in the rural town of Great Barrington. One of the array of paper manufacturers along the Housatonic River, the firm endured repeated setbacks, which turned into benefits, and, by 1980, it was providing important capital and consumer goods to some of the nation's largest and fastest growing corporations, though Kelley himself had no inherited wealth or outside support.

From the onset, the company's capital consisted mostly of refuse. Like the copper and steel companies thriving on the contents of slag heaps, Berkshire Paper Company employed paper, machinery, and factory space rejected as useless by other companies. Berkshire Paper, in fact, was launched and grew with almost no recourse to resources or capital that was accorded by any value at all in any national economic accounts. Yet the company has now entered the semiconductor industry and holds virtual monopolies in three sophisticated products. The story of its rise from scratch pads to semiconductor products shows the irrelevance of nearly all the indices of economic value and national wealth employed by the statisticians of our economy.

As a sophomore in college, Nick Kelley used to visit his stepfather at Clark-Aiken, a manufacturer of papermaking machine tools in Lee, Massachusetts. Within and around the factory, he noticed random piles of paper and asked his stepfather what was done with them. He was told they were leftovers from machinery tests and would be loaded into a truck and taken to the Lee dump. Kelley asked whether he could have them instead.

He took a handful of paper to an office-supply store, Gowdy's in Pittsfield, and asked the proprietor what such paper was good for. Scratch pads, he was told. After long trial and error, and several visits to a scratch pad factory in the guise of a student, he figured out how to make the pads. With the help of his stepfather he purchased and repaired a broken paper-cutting machine, and he even found a new method of applying glue, replacing the usual paintbrush with a paint roller. He then scoured much of the Northeast for markets and created a thriving scratch pad business that, again with his stepfather's help, even survived Kelley's stint in Southeast Asia during the Vietnam War.

In every case, setbacks led to innovation and renewed achievement. Deprived of paper from Clark-Aiken, he learned how to purchase it from jobbers in New York. Discovering that it cost two cents a pound more in sheets than in rolls (nine cents rather than seven cents), he computed that the two pennies represented a nearly 30 percent hike in cost and determined to contrive a sheeter out of old equipment. Finally, his worst setback drove him out of the scratch pad business altogether and allowed him to greatly expand his company.

Attempting to extend his marketing effort to Boston, Kelley approached the buyer for a large office-supply firm. The buyer said he doubted that Kelley could meet the competition. Kelley demanded to know how anyone could sell them for less, when the raw materials alone cost some fourteen cents a pound, and he sold the pads for eighteen cents. He went off to investigate his rival, a family firm run by Italians in Somerville. Kelley found a factory in an old warehouse, also filled with old equipment, but organized even more ingeniously than Kelley's own. He had to acknowledge that the owner was "the best." "He had me beat." Kelley said, "I decided then and there to go out of scratch pad manufacturing." Instead he resolved to buy pads from the Somerville factory and use his own marketing skills to sell them. He also purchased printing equipment and began adding value to the pads by printing specified lines and emblems on them.

This effort led to a request from Schweitzer, a large paper firm in the Berkshires, that Kelley print up legal pads, and then later, in a major breakthrough, that he cut up some tea bag paper that the Schweitzer machines could not handle. Although Kelley had only the most crude cutting machinery, he said sure, he could process tea bags. He took a pile of thin paper and spent several days and nights at work on it, destroying a fourth of the sheets before his machine completely jammed and pressed several of the layers together so tightly that he found he could easily cut them. This accident gave Kelley a reputation as a worker of small miracles with difficult and specialized papermaking tasks, and the large companies in the area began channeling their most difficult production problems to him.

These new assignments eventually led to three significant monopolies for the small Berkshire firm. One was in making women's fingernail mending tissue (paper with long fibers that adhere to the nail when it is polished) for cosmetic firms from Avon to Revlon. Another was in manufacturing facial blotting tissue (paper that cleans up dirt and makeup without rubbing) for such companies as Mary Kaye and Bonne Belle. His third and perhaps most important project, though—a task that impelled Kelley to pore endlessly through the literature of semiconductor electronics, trafficking in such concepts as microns (one-thousandth of a centimeter) and angstroms (one thousandth of a micron)—was production of papers for use in the manufacture of microprocessors and other semiconductor devices. This required not only the creation of papers sufficiently lint free to wrap a silicon wafer in (without dislodging an electron), but also a research effort to define for the companies precisely what impurities and "glitches" might remain. Kelley now provides this paper, along with the needed information, to all leading semiconductor companies, from National Semiconductor to Intel and Motorola, and he continues research to perfect his product.

Throughout his career, Kelley had demonstrated that faith and imagination are the most important capital goods in the American economy, that wealth is a product less of money than of mind.

The official measures miss all such sources of wealth. When Heilbroner and Thurow claim that 25 percent of American households owned zero net wealth in 1969, they are speaking of families that held above 5 billion dollars' worth of automobiles, 16 billion dollars of other consumer durables, such as washers and television sets, 11 billion dollars' worth of housing (about one-third had cars and 90 percent TVs), as well as rights in Medicaid, social security, housing, education, and other governmental benefits. They commanded many billions of dollars' worth of human capital, some of it rather depreciated by age and some by youthful irresponsibilities (most of these poor households consisted either of single people or abandoned mothers and their offspring). Their net worth was zero, because their debts exceeded their calculable worth. Yet some 80 percent of these people who were poor in 1969 escaped poverty within two years, only to be replaced in the distributions by others too young, too old, too improvident, or too beset with children to manage a positive balance in their asset accounts.

Now it may be appropriate to exclude from the accounting such items as rights in government welfare and transfer programs, which often destroy as much human worth as they create. But the distribution tables also miss the assets of the greatest ultimate value. For example, they treated as an increment of poverty, bereft of net worth, the explosive infusion of human capital that arrived on our shores from Lebanon in the guise of an unlettered family.

Families of zero wealth built America. Many of the unincorporated businesses that have gained some 500 billion dollars in net value since World II (six times more than all the biggest corporations combined) were started in households of zero assets according to the usual accounts. The conception of a huge and unnegotiable gap between poverty and wealth is a myth. In the Berkshires, Zabian moving up passed many scions of wealth on their way down. . . .

In the second tier of wealth-holders, in which each member would average nearly 2 million dollars net worth in 1970 dollars, 71 percent reported no inherited assets at all, and only 14 percent reported substantial inheritance. Even in the top group of multimillionaires, 31 percent received no inherited assets, and 9 percent only small legacies. Other studies indicate that among the far larger and collectively more important group of wealth-holders of more than $60,000 in 1969, 85 percent of the families had emerged since 1953. With a few notable exceptions, which are always in the news, fast movement up or down in two generations has been the fate of the American rich. . . .

In attacking the rich, tax authorities make great use of the concept of "unearned income," which means the returns from money earned earlier, heavily taxed, then saved or invested. Inheritances receive special attention, since they represent undemocratic transfers and concentrations of power. But they also extend the time horizons of the economy (that is, business), and retard the destruction of capital. That inheritance taxes are too high is obvious from the low level of revenue they collect and the huge industry of tax avoidance they sustain. But politically these levies have long been regarded as too attractive to forgo at a time of hostility toward the rich.

Nonetheless, some of the most catalytic wealth in America is "unearned." A few years before Michael Zabian arrived on our shores, Peter Sprague, now his Berkshire neighbor, inherited 400,000 dollars, largely from the sale of Sprague Electric Company stock. Many heirs of similar legacies have managed to lose most of it in a decade or so. But Sprague set out on a course that could lose it much faster. He decided on a career in venture capital. To raise the odds against him still further, he eventually chose to specialize in companies that faced bankruptcy and lacked other sources of funds.

His first venture was a chicken hatchery in Iran, which taught him the key principles of entrepreneurship—chiefly that nothing happens as one envisions it in theory. The project had been based on the use of advanced Ralston-Purina technology, widely tested in Latin America, to tap the rapidly growing poultry markets of the Middle East. The first unexpected discovery was two or three feet of snow; no one had told him that it *snowed* in Iran. Snow ruined most of the Ralston-Purina equipment. A second surprise was chicanery (and sand) in the chicken

feed business. "You end up buying two hundred pounds of stone for every hundred pounds of grain." But after some seven years of similar setbacks, and a growing capital of knowledge, Sprague began to make money in Iran; growing a million trees fertilized with chicken manure, cultivating mushrooms in abandoned ice houses, and winding up with the largest cold storage facilities in the country. The company has made a profit through most of the seventies.

In 1964, three years after starting his Iranian operations, Sprague moved in on a failing electronics company called National Semiconductor. Sprague considered the situation for a week, bought a substantial stake, and became its chairman. The firm is now in the vanguard of the world-wide revolution in semiconductor technology and has been one of America's fastest growing firms, rising from 300 employees when Sprague joined it to 34,000 in 1980.

Also in the mid-sixties Sprague bought several other companies, including the now fashionable Energy Resources, and rescued Design Research from near bankruptcy (the firm finally folded in 1976). In 1969, he helped found Auton Computing Company, a firm still thriving in the business of detecting and analyzing stress in piping systems in nuclear and other power plants, and in 1970 he conducted a memorably resourceful and inventive but finally unsuccessful Republican campaign for the New York City congressional seat then held by Edward Koch (who is now mayor).

He then entered the latest phase of his career rescuing collapsing companies. A sports car buff, he indicated to some friends an interest in reviving Aston-Martin, which had gone out of business six months earlier, in mid-1974. Arriving in England early in 1975 with a tentative plan to investigate the possibilities, he was besieged by reporters and TV cameras. Headlines blared: MYSTERY YANK FINANCIER TO SAVE ASTON MARTIN. Eventually he did, and the company is now securely profitable. . . .

A government counterpart of Sprague's investment activity was Wedgewood Benn's National Enterprise Board in England, which spent some 8 billion dollars attempting to save various British companies by drowning them in money. Before Sprague arrived in England Benn had adamantly refused to invest in Aston-Martin—dismissing the venerable firm as a hopeless case—and instead subsidized a large number of other companies, most of which, unlike Aston, still lose money, and some of which ended up bankrupt. The British, however, did find 104 million dollars—fifty times more than Sprague had to invest in Aston-Martin—to use in luring John DeLorean's American luxury car project to Northern Ireland and poured 47.8 million dollars into the effort to create Ininos, a British nationalized semiconductor firm that has yet to earn any money and technologically remains well in the wake of Sprague's concern. With 400,000 dollars inheritance and his charismatic skills, Sprague has revived many times more companies than Wedgewood Benn with the British Treasury. One entrepreneur with energy, resolution, and charisma could turn 400,000 dollars into a small fortune for himself and a bonanza for the economy, accomplishing more than any number of committee-bound foundations, while a government agency usually requires at least 400,000 dollars to so much as open an office.

Nonetheless, considering the sometimes unedifying spectacle of the humpty-dump-

ty heirs of wealth—and often focusing on the most flamboyant and newsworthy consumers of cocaine and spouses—it is all too easy to forget that the crucial role of the rich in a capitalist economy is not to entertain and titillate the classes below, but to invest: to provide unencumbered and unbureaucratized cash. The broad class of rich does, in fact, perform this role. Only a small portion of their money is consumed. Most of it goes to productive facilities that employ labor and supply goods to consumers. The rich remain the chief source of discretionary capital in the economy.

These are the funds available for investment outside the largely sterile channels of institutional spending. This is the money that escapes the Keynesian trap of compounded risk, created by the fact that a bank, like an entrepreneur, may lose most of its investment if an enterprise fails, but only the entrepreneur can win the large possible payoff that renders the risk worthwhile. Individuals with cash comprise the wild card—the mutagenic germ—in capitalism, and it is relatively risky investments that ultimately both reseed the economy and unseat the rich. . . .

The risk-bearing role of the rich cannot be performed so well by anyone else. The benefits of capitalism still depend on capitalists. The other groups on the pyramid of wealth should occasionally turn from the spectacles of consumption long enough to see the adventure on the frontiers of the economy above them—an adventure not without its note of nobility, since its protagonist families will almost all eventually fail and fall in the redeeming struggle of the free economy.

In America the rich should not be compared to the Saudi Arabians or be seen in the image of Midas in his barred cage of gold. . . . Under capitalism, when it is working, the rich have the anti-Midas touch, transforming timorous liquidity and unused savings into factories and office towers, farms and laboratories, orchestras and museums—turning gold into goods and jobs and art. That is the function of the rich: fostering opportunities for the classes below them in the continuing drama of the creation of wealth and progress. . . .

THE NATURE OF POVERTY

To get a grip in the problems of poverty, one should also forget the idea of overcoming inequality by redistribution. Inequality may even grow at first as poverty declines. To lift the incomes of the poor, it will be necessary to increase the rates of investment, which in turn will tend to enlarge the wealth, if not the consumption, of the rich. The poor, as they move into the work force and acquire promotions, will raise their incomes by a greater percentage than the rich; but the upper classes will gain by greater absolute amounts, and the gap between the rich and the poor may grow. All such analyses are deceptive in the long run, however, because they imply a static economy in which the *numbers* of the rich and the middle class are not growing.

In addition, inequality may be favored by the structure of a modern economy as it interacts with demographic changes. When the division of labor becomes more complex and refined, jobs grow more specialized; and the increasingly specialized workers may win greater rents for their rare expertise, causing their incomes to rise relative to common labor. This tendency could be height-

ened by a decline in new educated entrants to the work force, predictable through the 1990s, and by an enlarged flow of immigration, legal and illegal. Whatever the outcome of these developments, an effort to take income from the rich, thus diminishing their investment, and to give it to the poor, thus reducing their work incentives, is sure to cut American productivity, limit job opportunities, and perpetuate poverty.

Among the beneficiaries of inequality will be the formerly poor. Most students of the problems of poverty consider the statistics of success of previous immigrant groups and see a steady incremental rise over the years, accompanied by the progressive acquisition of educational credentials and skills. Therefore, programs are proposed that foster a similar slow and incremental ascent by the currently poor. But the incremental vision of the escape from poverty is mostly false, based on a simple illusion of statistical aggregates that conceals everything important about upward mobility. Previous immigrants earned money first by working hard; their children got the education.

The rising average incomes of previous groups signify not the smooth progress of hundreds of thousands of civil-service or bureaucratic careers, but the rapid business and professional successes of a relative few, who brought their families along and inspired others to follow. Poor people tend to rise up rapidly and will be damaged by a policy of redistribution that will always hit new and unsheltered income and wealth much harder than the elaborately concealed and fortified winnings of the established rich. The poor benefit from a dynamic economy full of unpredictable capital gains (they have few capital losses!) more than from a stratified system governed by educational and other credentials that the rich can buy.

The only dependable route from poverty is always work, family, and faith. The first principle is that in order to move up, the poor must not only work, they must work harder than the classes above them. Every previous generation of the lower class has made such efforts. But the current poor, white even more than black, are refusing to work hard. Irwin Garfinkel and Robert Haveman, authors of an ingenious and sophisticated study of what they call *Earning Capacity Utilization Rates*, have calculated the degree to which various income groups use their opportunities—how hard they work outside the home. This study shows that, for several understandable reasons, the current poor work substantially less, for fewer hours and weeks a year, and earn less in proportion to their age, education, and other credentials (even *after* correcting the figures for unemployment, disability, and presumed discrimination) than either their predecessors in American cities or those now above them on the income scale (the study was made at the federally funded institute for Research on Poverty at the University of Wisconsin and used data from the census and the Michigan longitudinal survey). The findings lend important confirmation to the growing body of evidence that work effort is the crucial unmeasured variable in American productivity and income distribution, and that current welfare and other subsidy programs substantially reduce work. The poor choose leisure not because of moral weakness, but because they are paid to do so.

A program to lift by transfers and preferences the incomes of less diligent groups is politically divisive—and very unlikely—because it incurs the bitter resistance of the real working class. In addition, such an effort breaks the psychological link between effort and reward, which is crucial to long-run upward mobility. Because effective work consists not in merely fulfilling the requirements of labor contracts but "in putting out" with alertness and emotional commitment, workers have to understand and feel deeply that what they are given depends on what they give—that they must supply work in order to demand goods. Parents and schools must inculcate this idea in their children both by instruction and example. Nothing is more deadly to achievement than the belief that effort will not be rewarded, that the world is a bleak and discriminatory place in which only the predatory and the specially preferred can get ahead. Such a view in the home discourages the work effort in school that shapes earnings capacity afterward. As with so many aspects of human performance, work effort begins in family experiences, and its sources can be best explored through an examination of family structure.

Indeed, after work the second principle of upward mobility is the maintenance of monogamous marriage and family. Adjusting for discrimination against women and for child-care responsibilities, the Wisconsin study indicates that married men work between two and one-third and four times harder than married women, and more than twice as hard as female family heads. The work effort of married men increases with their age, credentials, education, job experience, and birth of children, while the work effort of married women steadily declines. Most important in judging the impact of marriage, husbands work 50 percent harder than bachelors of comparable age, education, and skills.

The effect of marriage, thus, is to increase the work effort of men by about half. Since men have higher earnings capacity to begin with, and since the female capacity-utilization figures would be even lower without an adjustment for discrimination, it is manifest that the maintenance of families is the key factor in reducing poverty.

Once a family is headed by a woman, it is almost impossible for it to greatly raise its income even if the woman is highly educated and trained and she hires day-care or domestic help. Her family responsibilities and distractions tend to prevent her from the kind of all-out commitment that is necessary for the full use of earning power. Fewer women with children make earning money the top priority in their lives.

A married man, on the other hand, is spurred by the claims of family to channel his otherwise disruptive male aggressions into his performance as a provider for a wife and children. These sexual differences alone, which manifest themselves in all societies known to anthropology, dictate that the first priority of any serious program against poverty is to strengthen the male role in poor families.

These narrow measures of work effort touch on just part of the manifold interplay between family and poverty. Edward Banfield's *The Unheavenly City* defines the lower class largely by its lack of an orientation to the future. Living from day to day and from hand to mouth, lower class individuals are unable to plan or save or keep a job. Banfield gives the impression that short-time horizons are a deep-seated psychological defect afflicting hundreds of thousands of the poor.

There is no question that Banfield puts his finger on a crucial problem of the poor and that he develops and documents his theme in an unrivaled classic of disciplined social science. But he fails to show how millions of men, equally present oriented, equally buffeted by impulse and blind to the future, have managed to become farseeing members of the middle classes. He also fails to explain how millions of apparently future-oriented men can become dissolute followers of the sensuous moment, neglecting their jobs, dissipating their income and wealth, pursuing a horizon no longer than the most time-bound of the poor.

What Banfield is in fact describing in his lower-class category is largely the temperament of single, divorced, and separated men. The key to lower-class life in contemporary America is that unrelated individuals, as the census calls them, are so numerous and conspicuous that they set the tone for the entire community. Their congregation in ghettos, moreover, magnifies greatly their impact on the black poor, male and female (though, as Banfield rightly observes, this style of instant gratification is chiefly a male trait).

The short-sighted outlook of poverty stems largely from the breakdown of family responsibilities among fathers. The lives of the poor, all too often, are governed by the rhythms of tension and release that characterize the sexual experience of young single men. Because female sexuality, as it evolved over the millennia, is psychologically rooted in the bearing and nurturing of children, women have long horizons within their very bodies, glimpses of eternity within their wombs. Civilized society is dependent upon the submission of the short-term sexuality of young men to the extended maternal horizons of women. This is what happens in monogamous marriage; the man disciplines his sexuality and extends it into the future through the womb of a woman. The woman gives him access to his children, otherwise forever denied him; and he gives her the product of his labor, otherwise dissipated on temporary pleasures. The woman gives him a unique link to the future and a vision of it; he gives her faithfulness and a commitment to a lifetime of hard work. If work effort is the first principle of overcoming poverty, marriage is the prime source of upwardly mobile work.

It is love that changes the short horizons of youth and poverty into the long horizons of marriage and career. When marriages fail, the man often returns to the more primitive rhythms of singleness. On the average, his income drops by one-third and he shows a far higher propensity for drink, drugs, and crime. But when marriages in general hold firm and men in general love and support their children, Banfield's lower-class style changes into middle-class futurity. . . .

Adolph A. Berle, contemplating the contrast between prosperous and dominantly Mormon Utah and indigent, chiefly secular Nevada next door, concluded his study of the American economy with the rather uneconomic notion of a "transcendental margin," possibly kin to Leibenstein's less glamorous X-efficiency and Christopher Jencks's timid "luck." Lionel Tiger identifies this source of unexplained motion as "evolutionary optimism—the biology of hope," and finds it in the human genes. Ivan Light, in his fascinating exploration of the sources of difference between entrepreneurial Orientals and less venturesome blacks,

resolved on "the spirit of moral community." Irving Kristol, ruminating on the problems of capitalism, sees the need for a "transcendental justification." They are all addressing, in one way or another, the third principle of upward mobility, and that is faith.

Faith in man, faith in the future, faith in the rising returns of giving, faith in the mutual benefits of trade, faith in the providence of God are all essential to successful capitalism. All are necessary to sustain the spirit of work and enterprise against the setbacks and frustrations it inevitably meets in a fallen world; to inspire trust and cooperation in an economy where they will often be betrayed; to encourage the forgoing of present pleasures in the name of a future that may well go up in smoke; to promote risk and initiative in a world where the rewards all vanish unless others join the game. In order to give without the assurance of return, in order to save without the certainty of future value, in order to work beyond the requirements of the job, one has to have confidence in a higher morality: a law of compensations beyond the immediate and distracting struggles of existence.

NO   William Ryan

EQUALITY

It should not surprise us [that] the clause "all men are created equal" can be interpreted in quite different ways. Today, I would like to suggest, there are two major lines of interpretation: one, which I will call the "Fair Play" perspective, stresses the individual's right to pursue happiness and obtain resources; the other, which I will call the "Fair Shares" viewpoint, emphasizes the right of access to resources as a necessary condition for equal rights to life, liberty and happiness.

Almost from the beginning, and most apparently during the past century or so, the Fair Play viewpoint has been dominant in America. This way of looking at the problem of equality stresses that each person should be equally free from all but the most minimal necessary interferences with his right to "pursue happiness." . . . Given significant differences of interest, of talents, and of personalities, it is assumed that individuals will be variably successful in their pursuits and that society will consequently propel to its surface what Jefferson called a "natural aristocracy of talent," men who because of their skills, intellect, judgment, character, will assume the leading positions in society that had formerly been occupied by the hereditary aristocracy—that is, by men who had simply been born into positions of wealth and power. In contemporary discussions, the emphasis on the individual's unencumbered pursuit of his own goals is summed up in the phrase "equality of opportunity." Given at least an approximation of this particular version of equality, Jefferson's principle of a natural aristocracy—spoken of most commonly today as the idea of "meritocracy"—will insure that the ablest, most meritorious, ambitious, hardworking, and talented individuals will acquire the most, achieve the most, and become the leaders of society. The relative inequality that this implies is seen not only as tolerable, but as fair and just. Any effort to achieve what proponents of Fair Play refer to as "equality of results" is seen as unjust, artificial, and incompatible with the more basic principle of equal opportunity.

The Fair Shares perspective, as compared with the Fair Play idea, concerns itself much more with equality of rights and of access, particularly the implicit rights to a reasonable share of society's resources, sufficient to sustain life at a decent standard of humanity and to preserve liberty and freedom from compulsion. Rather than focusing on the individual's pursuit of his own happiness, the advocate of Fair Shares is more committed to the principle that all members of the society obtain a reasonable portion of the goods that society produces. From his vantage point, the overzealous pursuits of private goals on the part of some individuals might even have to be bridled. From this it follows, too, that the proponent of Fair Shares has a different view of what constitutes fairness and justice, namely, an appropriate distribution throughout society of sufficient means for sustaining life and preserving liberty.

So the equality dilemma is built into everyday life and thought in America; it comes with the territory. Rights, equality of rights—or at least interpretations of them—clash. The conflict between Fair Play and Fair Shares is real, deep, and serious, and it cannot be easily resolved. Some calculus of priorities must be established. Rules must be agreed upon. It is possible to imagine an almost endless number of such rules:

• Fair Shares until everyone has enough; Fair Play for the surplus

• Fair Play until the end of a specified "round," then "divvy up" Fair Shares, and start Fair Play all over again (like a series of Monopoly games)

• Fair Play all the way, except that no one may actually be allowed to starve to death.

The last rule is, I would argue, a perhaps bitter parody of the prevailing one in the United States. Equality of opportunity and the principle of meritocracy are the clearly dominant interpretation of

"all men are created equal," mitigated by the principle (usually defined as charity rather than equality) that the weak, the helpless, the deficient will be more or less guaranteed a sufficient share to meet their minimal requirements for sustaining life.

FAIR PLAY AND UNEQUAL SHARES

The Fair Play concept is dominant in America partly because it puts forth two most compelling ideas: the time-honored principle of distributive justice and the cherished image of America as the land of opportunity. At least since Aristotle, the principle that rewards should accrue to each person in proportion of his worth or merit has seemed to many persons one that warrants intuitive acceptance. The more meritorious person—merit being some combination of ability and constructive effort—*deserves* a greater reward. From this perspective it is perfectly consistent to suppose that *unequal* shares could well be *fair* shares; moreover, within such a framework, it is very unlikely indeed that equal shares could be fair shares, since individuals are not equally meritorious.

The picture of America as the land of opportunity is also very appealing. The idea of a completely open society, where each person is entirely free to advance in his or her particular fashion, to become whatever he or she is inherently capable of becoming, with the sky the limit, is a universally inspiring one. This is a picture that makes most Americans proud.

But is it an accurate picture? Are these two connected ideas—unlimited opportunity and differential rewards fairly distributed according to differences in individual merit—congruent with the facts of life? The answer, of course, is yes and no. Yes, we see some vague congruence here and there—some evidence of upward mobility, some kinds of inequalities that can appear to be justifiable. But looking at the larger picture, we must answer with an unequivocal "No!" The fairness of unequal shares and the reality of equal opportunity are wishes and dreams, resting on a mushy, floating, purely imaginary foundation. Let us look first at the question of unequal shares.

Fair Players and Fair Sharers disagree about the meaning, but not about the fact, of unequal shares and of the significant degree of inequality of wealth and income and of everything that goes along with wealth and income—general life conditions, health, education, power, access to services and to cultural and recreational amenities, and so forth. Fair Sharers say that this fact is the very *essence* of inequality, while Fair Players define the inequalities of condition that Fair Sharers decry as obvious and necessary *consequences* of equality of opportunity. Fair Players argue, furthermore, that such inequalities are for the most part roughly proportional to inequalities of merit. . . .

There [are] some patterns of ownership that are reasonably consistent with the Fair Play paradigm. In the distribution of such items as automobiles, televisions, appliances, even homes, there are significant inequalities, but they are not extreme. And if the Fair Player is willing to concede that many inequities remain to be rectified—and most Fair Players are quite willing, even eager, to do so—these inequalities can, perhaps, be swallowed.

It is only when we begin to look at larger aspects of wealth and income—aspects that lie beyond our personal vision—that the extreme and, I believe, gross inequalities of condition that pre-

vail in America become evident. Let us begin with income. How do we divide up the shares of what we produce annually? In 1977 about one American family in ten had an income of less than $5,000 and about one in ten had an income of $35,000 a year and up ("up" going all the way to some unknown number of millions). It is difficult to see how anyone could view such a dramatic disparity as fair and justified. One struggles to imagine any measure of merit, any sign of membership in a "natural aristocracy," that would manifest itself in nature in such a way that one sizable group of persons would "have" eight or ten or twenty times more of it—whatever "it" might be—than another sizeable group has.

Income in the United States is concentrated in the hands of a few: one-fifth of the population gets close to half of all the income, and the top 5 percent of this segment get almost one-fifth of it. The bottom three-fifths of the population—that is, the majority of us—receive not much more than one-third of all income. . . .

As we move [to] the reality of living standards, the pertinent questions are: How much do people spend and on what? How do the groups at the different tables, that is, different income groups in America, live? Each year the Bureau of Labor Statistics publishes detailed information on the costs of maintaining three different living standards, which it labels "lower," "intermediate," and "higher"; in less discreet days it used to call the budgets "minimum," "adequate," and "comfortable." The adequate, intermediate budget is generally considered to be an index of a reasonably decent standard of living. It is on this budget, for example, that newspapers focus when they write their annual stories on the BLS budgets.

To give some sense of what is considered an "intermediate" standard of living, let me provide some details about this budget as it is calculated for a family of four—mother, father, eight-year-old boy, and thirteen-year-old girl. As of the autumn of 1978, for such a family the budget allows $335 a month for housing, which includes rent or mortgage, heat and utilities, household furnishings, and all household operations. It allows $79 a week for groceries, which extends to cleaning supplies, toothpaste, and the like. It allows $123 a month for transportation, including car payments. It allows $130 a month for clothing, clothing care or cleaning, and all personal-care items.

In his book *The Working Class Majority*, Andrew Levinson cites further details about this budget from a study made by the UAW:

A United Auto Workers study shows just how "modest" that budget is: The budget assumes, for example, that a family will own a toaster that will last for thirty-three years, a refrigerator and a range that will each last for seventeen years, a vacuum cleaner that will last for fourteen years, and a television set that will last for ten years. The budget assumes that a family will buy a two-year-old car and keep it for four years, and will pay for a tune-up once a year, a brake realignment every three years, and front-end alignment every four years. . . . The budget assumes that the husband will buy one year-round suit every four years . . . and one topcoat every eight and a half years. . . . It assumes that the husband will take his wife to the movies once every three months and that one of them will go to the movies alone once a year. The average family's two children are each al-

lowed one movie every four weeks. A total of two dollars and fifty-four cents per person per year is allowed for admission to all other events, from football and baseball games to plays or concerts. . . . The budget allows nothing whatever for savings.

This budget, whether labeled intermediate, modest, or adequate, is perhaps more accurately described by those who call it "shabby but respectable." . . .

In 1978 the income needs by an urban family of four in order to meet even this modest standard of living was $18,622. This is a national average; for some cities the figure was much higher: in Boston, it was $22,117, in metropolitan New York, $21,587, in San Francisco, $19,427. More than *half* of all Americans lived *below* this standard. As for the "minimum" budget (which, by contrast with the "intermediate" budget, allows only $62 rather than $79 for groceries, $174 rather than $335 for housing, $67 rather than $123 for transportation, and $93 rather than $130 for clothing and personal care), the national average cost for an urban family in 1978 was $11,546. Three families out of ten could not afford even *that* standard, and one family in ten had an income below $5,000 which is *less than half enough* to meet minimum standards.

These dramatically *unequal* shares are —it seems to me—clearly *unfair* shares. Twenty million people are desperately poor, an additional forty million don't get enough income to meet the minimal requirements for a decent life, the great majority are just scraping by, a small minority are at least temporarily comfortable, and a tiny handful of persons live at levels of affluence and luxury that most persons cannot even imagine.

The myth that America's income is symmetrically distributed—an outstanding few at the top getting a lot, an inadequate few at the bottom living in poverty, and the rest clustered around the middle—could hardly be more false. The grotesquely lopsided distribution of our yearly production of goods and services is well illustrated by Paul Samuelson's famous image:

A glance at the income distribution in the United States shows how pointed is the income pyramid and how broad its base. "There's always room at the top" is certainly true; this is so because it is hard to get there, not easy. If we make an income pyramid out of a child's blocks, with each layer portraying $1000 of income, the peak would be far higher than the Eiffel Tower, but almost all of us would be within a yard of the ground.

When we move from income to wealth—from what you *get* to what you *own*—the *degree* of concentration makes the income distribution look almost fair by comparison. About one out of every four Americans owns *nothing*. Nothing! In fact, many of them *owe* more than they have. Their "wealth" is actually negative. The persons in the next quarter own about 5 percent of all personal assets. In other words, half of us own 5 percent, the other half own 95 percent. But it gets worse as you go up the scale. Those in the top 6 percent own half of all the wealth. Those in the top 1 percent own one-fourth of all the wealth. Those in the top 1/2 percent own one-fifth of all the wealth. That's one-half of 1 percent— about one million persons, or roughly 300,000 families.

And even this fantastic picture doesn't tell the whole story, because "assets" include homes, cars, savings accounts, cash value of life insurance policies—the kinds of assets that the very rich don't bother with very much. The very rich put their wealth into the ownership of things that produce more wealth—corporate stocks and bonds, mortgages, notes, and the like. Two-thirds of their wealth is in this form and the top 1 percent owns 60 percent of all that valuable paper. The rest of it is owned by only an additional 10 percent, which means that nine people out of ten own none of it—and, if they're like me, they probably have never seen a real stock certificate in their lives.

America, we are sometimes told, is a nation of capitalists, and it is true that an appreciable minority of its citizens have a bank account here, a piece of land there, along with a few shares of stock. But quantitative differences become indisputably qualitative as one moves from the ownership of ten shares of General Motors to the ownership of ten thousand. There are capitalists, and then there are capitalists. . . .

Another way of grasping the extreme concentration of wealth in our society is to try to imagine what the ordinary person would have if that wealth were evenly distributed rather than clumped and clotted together in huge piles. Assuming that all the personal wealth was divided equally among all the people in the nation, we would find that every one of us, man, woman, and child, would *own* free and clear almost $22,000 worth of goods: $7,500 worth of real estate, $3,500 in cash, and about $5,000 worth of stocks and bonds. For a family of four that would add up to almost $90,000 in assets, including $30,000 equity in a house, about $14,000 in the bank, and about $20,000 worth of stocks and bonds. That much wealth would also bring in an extra $3,000 or $4,000 a year in income.

If you have any doubts about the reality of grossly unequal shares, compare the utopian situation of that imaginary "average" family with your own actual situation. For most of us, the former goes beyond our most optimistic fantasies of competing and achieving and getting ahead. Actually only about ten million persons in the country own as much as that, and, as I suggested before, the majority of us have an *average* of less than $5,000 per family including whatever equity we have in a home, our car and other tangible assets, and perhaps $500 in the bank.

Still another way of thinking about this is to remark that the fortunate few at the top, and their children, are more or less guaranteed an opulent standard of living because of what they own, while the majority of American families are no more than four months' pay away from complete destitution.

All of this, of course, takes place in the wealthiest society the world has ever known. If we extended our horizons further and began to compare the handful of developed, industrial nations with the scores of underdeveloped, not to say "over-exploited," nations, we would find inequalities that are even more glaring and appalling. . . .

THE VULNERABLE MAJORITY

Stripped down to its essentials, the rule of equal opportunity and Fair Play requires only that the best man win. It doesn't necessarily specify the margin of victory, merely the absence of unfair barriers. The practical test of equal opportunity is *social mobility*—do talented and hardworking persons, whatever their backgrounds, actually succeed in rising to higher social and economic positions?

The answer to that of course, is that they do. Remaining barriers of discrimination notwithstanding, it is plain that many persons climb up the social and economic ladder and reach much higher rungs than those their parents attained and than those from which they started. Fair Players prize these fortunate levitations as the ultimate justification of their own perspective and as phenomena that must be protected against any erosion caused by excessive emphasis upon Fair Shares.

It is necessary, then, to look seriously at the question of mobility. Among the questions to be asked are the following:

• How much mobility can we observe? No matter how rigidly hierarchical it might be, every society permits some mobility. How much movement up and down the scale is there in ours?

• How far do the mobile persons move?

• Is mobility evident across the whole social and economic range? Do the very poor stay poor, or do they, too, have an equal chance to rise? Are the very rich likely to slide *down* the ladder very often?

Given our great trove of rags-to-riches mythology, our creed that any child (well, any man-child) can grow up to be president—if not of General Motors, at least of the United States—we clearly assume that our society is an extraordinarily open one. And everyone knows, or has a friend who knows, a millionaire or someone on the way to that envied position: the patient, plodding peddler who transformed his enterprise into a great department store; the eccentric tinkerer in his garage whose sudden insight produced the great invention that everyone had been saving his pennies to buy.

At lesser levels of grandeur, we all know about the son of the illiterate cobbler who is now a wealthy neurosurgeon, the daughter of impoverished immigrants who sits in a professional chair at Vassar or Smith—or even Princeton. In America social mobility is an unquestioned fact.

But how many sons of illiterate cobblers become physicians, on the other hand, and how many become, at best, literate cobblers? And how many settle for a job on the assembly line or in the sanitation department? And all of those daughters of impoverished immigrants— how many went on to get Ph.D.'s and become professors? Very few. A somewhat larger number may have gone to college and gotten a job teaching sixth grade. But many just finished high school and went to work for an insurance company for a while, until they married the sons of other impoverished immigrants, most of them also tugging at their bootstraps without much result.

About all of these facts there can be little dispute. For most people, there is essentially no social mobility—for them, life consists of rags to rags and riches to riches. Moreover, for the relatively small minority who do rise significantly in the social hierarchy, the *distance* of ascent is relatively short. Such a person may start life operating a drill press and eventually become a foreman or even move into the white-collar world by becoming a payroll clerk or perhaps an accountant. Or he may learn from his father to be a cobbler, save his money, and open a little cobbler shop of his own. He hardly ever starts up a shoe factory. It is the son of the owner of the shoe factory who gets to do that. So there is mobility—it is rather common, but also rather modest, with only an occasional dramatic rise from rags to riches.

To provide some specific numbers, it has been calculated that for a young man born into a family in which the father does unskilled, low-wage manual work, the odds against his rising merely to the point of his becoming a nonmanual white-collar worker are at least three or four to one; the odds against his rising to the highest level and joining the wealthy upper class are almost incalculable. For the son of a middle-level white-collar worker, the odds against his rising to a higher-level professional or managerial occupation are two or three to one. On the other hand, the odds are better than fifty to one that the son of a father with such a high-level occupation will not descend the ladder to a position as an unskilled or semiskilled manual worker. Upward mobility is very limited and usually involves moving only one or two levels up the hierachy. . . .

Finally, we have to look carefully to see that, for all our social mobility, the very rich almost all stay at the top and welcome only a select handful to their ranks. The rich of one generation are almost all children of the rich of the previous generation, partly because more than half of significant wealth is inherited, partly because all the other prerogatives of the wealthy are sufficient to assure a comfortable future for Rockefeller and Du Pont toddlers. It may well take more energy, ingenuity, persistence, and single-mindedness for a rich youngster to achieve poverty than for a poor one to gain wealth.

The dark side of the social-mobility machine is that it is, so to speak, a reciprocating engine—when some parts go up, others must come *down*. Downward mobility is an experience set aside almost exclusively for the nonrich, and it is grossly destructive of the quality of life. The majority of American families are constantly vulnerable to economic disaster—to downward mobility to the point where they lack sufficient income to meet their most basic needs—food, shelter, clothing, heat, and medical care. Included in this vulnerable majority, who have at least an even chance of spending some portion of their lives in economic distress, are perhaps three out of four Americans.

This does to accord with the common view of poverty. We have been given to understand that "the poor" form a fairly permanent group in our society and that those who are above the poverty line are safe and perhaps even on their way up. This thought is comforting but false. A number of small studies have raised serious questions about this static picture; recently we have received massive evidence from one of the most comprehensive social and economic investigations ever mounted. This study, under the direction of James Morgan, has traced the life trajectories of five thousand American families over a period, to date, of eight years, concentrating on the nature of and possible explanations for economic progress or the lack of it.

Five Thousand American Families indicates that over a period of eight years, although only one in ten families is poor during *every one* of the eight years, over one-third of American families are poor for *at least one* of those eight years.

From the Michigan study, the census data, and other sources, we can readily estimate that a few are permanently protected against poverty because they *own things*—property, stocks, bonds—that provide them with income sufficient to meet their needs whether or not they work or have any other source of income. Another small minority of Americans own only *rights*—virtual job tenure, a guaranteed pension—but these rights also give

effective protection against poverty. At the bottom of the pyramid, there are a few who might be called permanently poor. Between these extremes come persons whose income is primarily or wholly dependent on salaries or wages. This is the core of the vulnerable majority—not poor now, but in jeopardy. In any given year one family out of six in that vulnerable majority will suffer income deficit, will go through a year of poverty. Over a five-year period nearly half of them will be poor for at least one year. If we project this over ten or fifteen years, we find that well over half will be poor for at least one year. On adding this group to the permanently poor, we arrive at the startling fact that a *substantial majority* of American families will experience poverty at some point during a relatively short span of time.

Several elements in our socioeconomic structure help account for income deficiency. Let us consider, for example, those who are more or less permanently poor. Why do they stay mired in poverty? The answer in most cases is simple: they remain poor because it has been deliberately *decided* that they should remain poor. They are, for the most part, dependent on what we impersonally call transfer payments—mostly Social Security, some private pensions, some welfare. To put it as simply as possible, these transfer payments are not enough to live on, not enough to meet basic needs. Countrywide, public assistance payments provide income that is only 75 percent of what is required to pay for sufficient food, adequate shelter, clothing, and fuel; the percentage decreases as the size of the family increases. For very large families, welfare provides only half of what is needed to live on. The poverty of the permanently poor is thus easily explained by the fact that the income assistance that we provide them is simply too small.

For the vulnerables, however, economic hills and valleys are created by the job situation. Economic status, progress, and deficit are determined by what social scientists call "family composition and participation in the labor force." In plain English that means they depend on the number of mouths to be fed and on the number of people working—that is, on how many children there are, on whether both wife and husband are working, and so forth. But this, of course, is only synonymous with the natural ebb and flow in the life of almost any family. It should not be an economic catastrophe, after all, when people get married and have children. . . . So, children are born and they grow up, sometimes work awhile, and then leave home. One parent, usually the mother, is tied to the home during some periods, free to work during others. A family member finds a job, loses a job, gets sick or injured, sometimes dies tragically young. All of these events are the landmarks in the life of a family, most of them are common enough, and some are inevitable sources of joy or sorrow. Yet these ordinary occurrences have a drastic impact on families, because they lead to greater changes in one or both sides of the ratio of income and needs. In most cases they are direct causes of most of the economic progress or distress that a family experiences. . . .

WHY NOT FAIR SHARES?

I have been trying to show, in a preliminary way, that the beliefs and assumptions associated with the Fair Play rendering of equality are quite inconsistent with the facts of life as we know them, although its principles are paraded as a version—in fact, the correct version—of equality and are widely accepted as quite plausible, indeed obvious. To the extent that there is any competition between Fair Players and Fair Sharers for the mind of the public, the former usually win hands down. Yet, as we have seen, the Fair Play idea appears to condone and often to endorse conditions of inequality that are blatant and, I would say, quite indefensible. Such equal opportunities for advancing in life as do exist are darkly overshadowed by the many head starts and advantages provided to the families of wealth and privilege. As for the workings out of the solemnly revered principles of meritocracy, they are—like many objects of reverence—invisible to most persons and rarely discernible in the lives of the vulnerable majority of us. Barely two centuries after its most persuasive formulation, the Fair Play concept of equality has shriveled to little more than the assertion that a few thousand individuals are fully licensed to gather and retain wealth at the cost of the wasteful, shameful, and fraudulent impoverishment of many millions. . . .

A Fair Shares egalitarian would hold that all persons have a *right* to a reasonable share of material necessities, a right to do constructive work, and a right of unhindered access to education, to gratifying social memberships, to participation in the life and decisions of the community, and to all the major amenities of society. This principle doesn't lend itself to the calculation of "equal results," and it certainly doesn't imply a demand for uniformity of resources. No one in his right mind would entertain some cockeyed scheme in which everyone went to school for precisely thirteen years; consumed each year 19,800 grams of protein and 820,000 calories; read four works of fiction and six of non-fiction; attended two concerts, one opera, and four basketball games, and voted in 54 percent of the elections. . . . Unfortunately, many persons who are upset about the present state of inequality tend to talk vaguely about the need "to redistribute income" or even "to redistribute wealth." When such ideas are tossed out without consideration of the fact that they will then be discussed within the framework of Fair Play, we have a surefire prescription for disaster. From that viewpoint, which is, after all, the dominant one in America, such ideas appear both extremely inpracticable and not particularly desirable. For example, are we to take redistribution of income to mean that every individual will somehow receive the same compensation, no matter what work he or she does or whether he works at all? And would we try to redistribute wealth by giving every person, say, a share of stock in GM, Exxon, IBM, and the local paperbag factory? Hardly. Fair Players can make mincemeat of such silly ideas, and they love to pretend that that's what Fair Share egalitarians are proposing. I don't think many of us have strong objections to inequality of monetary income as such. A modest range, even as much as three or four to one, could, I suspect, be tolerable to almost everybody. (And one would suppose that, given some time for adjustment and perhaps some counseling and training in homemaking and budgeting skills, those who now get a lot more could learn to scrape by on something like eight or nine hundred dollars a week.) The current range in annual incomes—from perhaps $3,000 to some unknown number of *millions*—is, however, excessive and intolerable, impossible to justify rationally, and plain inhuman.

The problem of wealth is more fundamental. Most of the evils of inequality derive from the reality that a few thousand families control almost all the necessities and amenities of life, indeed the very conditions of life. The rest of us, some 200 million, have to pay tribute to them if we want even a slight illusion of life, liberty, and the pursuit of happiness. But the solution to this problem is certainly not simply the fragmentation of ownership into tiny units of individual property. This naive solution has been well criticized by serious proponents of equality, perhaps most gracefully by R. H. Tawney:

> It is not the division of the nation's income into eleven million fragments, to be distributed, without further ado, like cake as a school treat, among its eleven million families. It is, on the contrary, the pooling of its surplus resources by means of taxation, and use of the funds thus obtained to make accessible to all, irrespective of their income, occupation, or social position, the conditions of civilization which, in the absence of such measures, can only be enjoyed by the rich. . . .
>
> It can generalize, by collective action, advantages associated in the past with ownership of property. . . . It can secure that, in addition to the payments made to them for their labour, its citizens enjoy a social income, which is provided from the surplus remaining after the necessary cost of production and expansion have been met, and is available on equal terms for all its members. . . .

The central problem of inequality in America—the concentration of wealth and power in the hands of a tiny minority—cannot, then, be solved, as Tawney makes clear, by any schemes that rest on the process of long division. We need, rather, to accustom ourselves to a different method of holding resources, namely, holding them in common, to be *shared* amongst us all—not divided up and parceled out, but shared. That is the basic principle of Fair Shares, and it is not at all foreign to our daily experience. To cite a banal example, we share the air we breathe, although some breathe in penthouses or sparsely settled suburbs and others in crowded slums. In a similar fashion, we share such resources as public parks and beaches, although, again, we cannot overlook the gross contrast between the size of vast private waterfront holdings and the tiny outlets to the oceans that are available to the public. No one in command of his senses would go to a public beach, count the number of people there, and suggest subdividing the beach into thirty-two-by-twenty-six-foot lots, one for each person. Such division would not only be unnecessary, it would ruin our enjoyment. If I were assigned to Lot No. 123, instead of enjoying the sun and going for a swim, I might sit and watch that sneaky little kid with the tin shovel to make sure he did not extend the sand castle onto my beach. We own it in common; it's *public*; and we just plain *share* it.

We use this mode of owning and sharing all the time and never give it a second thought. We share public schools, streets, libraries, sewers, and other public property and services, and we even think of them as being "free" (many libraries even have the word in their names). Nor do we need the "There's no such thing as a free lunch" folks reminding us that they're not really free; everyone is quite aware that taxes support them. We don't feel any need to divide up all the books in the library among all the citizens. And there's no sensible way of looking at the use of libraries in terms of "equal opportunity" as opposed to "equal results." Looking at the public library as a tiny example of what Fair Shares equality is all about, we note that it satisfies the principle of equal access if no one is *excluded* from the library on the irrelevant grounds of not owning enough or of having spent twelve years in school learning how not to read. And "equal results" is clearly quite meaningless. Some will withdraw many books; some, only a few; some will be so unwise as to never even use the facility.

The *idea* of sharing, then, which is the basic idea of equality, and the *practice* of sharing, which is the basic methodology of Fair Shares equality, are obviously quite familiar and acceptable to the American people in many areas of life. There are many institutions, activities, and services that the great majority believe should be located in the public sector, collectively owned and paid for, and equally accessible to everyone. We run into trouble when we start proposing the same system of ownership for the resources that the wealthy have corralled for themselves. . . .

Most of the good things of life have either been provided free by God (nature, if you prefer) or have been produced by the combined efforts of many persons, sometimes many generations. As all share in the making, so all should share in the use and the enjoyment. This may help convey a bit of what the Fair Shares idea of equality is all about.

POSTSCRIPT

Is Economic Inequality Beneficial to Society?

The spirit of personal initiative seems to be alive in the hearts of Michael Zabian, the vegetable stand owner, Nick Kelley, the scratch paper dealer, and Peter Sprague, the venture capitalist, whose success stories are related by George Gilder. But how typical are their experiences? What about the government's bail-outs of Lockheed and Chrysler and the trials of U.S. Steel, General Motors, and many other corporations? What about the limitation of individual initiative in countless corporations guided by decisions made by committees and teams of experts? And what about the issues of fairness raised by William Ryan? Perhaps the basic question is: "Can the system be made more just, fair and humane without squelching enterprise and drive?"

Stratification and social mobility are two of the central concerns of sociology, and much literature has been produced discussing these issues. Two major publications of research on census statistics are Peter M. Blau and Otis Dudley Duncan's *The American Occupational Structure* (John Wiley & Sons, 1967), and Robert M. Hauser and David L. Featherman's *The Process of Social Stratification* (Academic Press, 1972). For general works, see Gerhard Lenski's *Power and Privilege* (McGraw-Hill, 1966) and Leonard Beeghley's *Social Stratification in the United States* (Goodyear, 1978). Many have written about the rich and their power, including Ferdinand Lundberg in *The Rich and the Super Rich* (Lyle Stuart, 1968); E. Digby Baltzell, *The Protestant Establishment* (Random House, 1964); and G. William Dornhoff in *Who Rules America?* (Prentice Hall, 1967) and *The Higher Circles* (Random House, 1970). For a journalistic account of the process of climbing up the ladder of success, see Vance Packard's *The Pyramid Climbers* (McGraw-Hill, 1962). A number of important works look at the poor and their disadvantages, including Joe Feagin's *Subordinating the Poor* (Prentice Hall, 1975); Richard Sennett and Jonathan Cobbs's, *The Hidden Injuries of Class* (Alfred A. Knopf, 1973); Michael Harrington's *The Other America* (Macmillan, 1962) and *The New American Poverty* (Holt, Rinehart and Winston, 1984); William Wilson's *The Truly Disadvantaged* (University of Chicago Press, 1987); and Elliot Liebow's *Tally's Corner* (Little, Brown, 1967).

Some studies of the social origins of elites include Suzanne Keller's *Beyond the Ruling Class* (Random House, 1963), and Floyd Warner and James Abegglen's *Big Business Leaders in America* (Harper, 1955). An interesting study of how the rich view themselves and the poor and income inequalities is *Equality in America: The View from the Top*, by Sidney Verber and Gary Orren (Harvard University Press, 1985).

ISSUE 7

Does "Lower-Class" Culture Perpetuate Poverty?

YES: Edward Banfield, from *The Unheavenly City* (Little, Brown, 1970)

NO: William Ryan, from *Blaming the Victim* (Pantheon, 1971)

ISSUE SUMMARY

YES: Sociologist Edward Banfield suggests that it is the cultural outlook of the poor that tends to keep them in poverty.
NO: Psychologist William Ryan responds that this is a form of "blaming the victim" for the conditions that surround him.

The Declaration of Independence proclaims the right of every human being to "life, liberty, and the pursuit of happiness." It never defines happiness, but Americans have put their own gloss on the term. Whatever else happiness means, Americans tend to agree that it includes doing well, getting ahead in life, and a comfortable standard of living.

The fact, of course, is that millions of Americans do not do well and do not get ahead. They are mired in poverty and seem unable to get out of it. On the face of it, this fact poses no contradiction to America's commitment to the pursuit of happiness. To pursue is not necessarily to catch; it certainly does not mean that everyone should feel entitled to a life of material prosperity. "Equality of opportunity," the prototypical American slogan, is vastly different from the socialist dream of "equality of condition," which perhaps is one reason socialism has so few adherents in America.

The real difficulty in reconciling the American ideal with American reality is not the problem of income differentials but of the *persistence* of poverty from generation to generation. Often, parent, child, and grandchild seem to be locked into a hopeless cycle of destitution and dependence. One explanation is that a large segment of the poor do not really try to get out of poverty. In its more vicious form this view portrays these poor as lazy, stupid, or base. Their poverty is not to be blamed on defects of American society but on their own defects. After all, this account of poverty continues, many successful Americans have worked their way up from humble beginnings, and many immigrant groups have made progress in one generation. Therefore, the United States provides opportunities for all who will work hard and make something of themselves. Another explanation, however, could be that the poor have few opportunities and many obstacles to overcome to climb out of poverty. If so, then America is not the land of opportunity for the poor and the American dream is reserved for the more fortunate.

That first explanation above of the persistence of poverty holds that among some groups there is a *culture* that breeds poverty because it is antithetical to the self-discipline and hard work that enable others to climb out of their poverty. In other words, the poor have a culture all their own that is at variance with middle-class culture and hinders their success. While it may keep people locked into what seems to be an intolerable life, this culture nevertheless has its own compensations and pleasures: It is full of "action" and it does not demand that people postpone pleasure, save money, or work hard. It is, for the most part, tolerable to those who live in it. Furthermore, according to this argument, not all poor people embrace the culture of poverty, and those who embrace middle-class values should be given every workable form of encouragement—material and spiritual—for escaping poverty. But for those poor who embrace lower-class culture, very little can be done. These poor will always be with us.

According to the second explanation of poverty, most of the poor will become self-supporting if they are given a decent chance. Their most important need is for decent jobs that can go somewhere. But often they cannot find jobs, and when they do, the jobs are dead-end or degrading. Some need job training or counseling to give them more self-confidence before navigating the job market. Others need temporary help through programs such as rent supplements, inexpensive housing, income supplements, protection from crime, medical services, or better education to help them help themselves.

The culture of poverty thesis shields the economic system from blame for poverty and honors better-off Americans. But it is a lie. Most of the poor are as committed to taking care of themselves and their families through hard work as the middle class, and a sense of dignity is common to all classes. Critics judge the culture of poverty thesis to be a smug, self-righteous justification by spokesmen for the middle and upper classes for the economic system that rewards them so handsomely while subjecting the poor to an intolerable existence. The culture of the poor is similar to the culture of the middle class. Where they do differ, however, the difference is because the culture of the poor is materially different. Change their material conditions and their culture will change rather quickly.

Proponents of the culture of poverty thesis maintain that it is not the material that controls the culture but the other way around; only the abandonment of lower-class culture will get the poor out of poverty. This is Harvard sociologist Edward Banfield's argument. On the other side is William Ryan, a psychologist and social activist, who says that the Banfield approach is a typical case of "blaming the victim."

YES   Edward Banfield

THE FUTURE OF THE LOWER CLASS

So long as the city contains a sizable lower class, nothing basic can be done about its most serious problems. Good jobs may be offered to all, but some will remain chronically unemployed. Slums may be demolished, but if the housing that replaces them is occupied by the lower class it will shortly be turned into new slums. Welfare payments may be doubled or tripled and a negative income tax instituted, but some persons will continue to live in squalor and misery. New schools may be built, new curricula devised, and the teacher-pupil ratio cut in half, but if the children who attend these schools come from lower-class homes, they will be turned into blackboard jungles, and those who graduate or drop out from them will, in most cases, be functionally illiterate. The streets may be filled with armies of policemen, but violent crime and civil disorder will decrease very little. If, however, the lower class were to disappear—if, say, its members were overnight to acquire the attitudes, motivations, and habits of the working class—the most serious and intractable problems of the city would all disappear with it.

[The] serious problems of the city all exist in two forms—a normal-class and a lower-class form—which are fundamentally different from each other. In its normal-class form, the employment problem, for example, consists mainly of young people who are just entering the labor market and who must make a certain number of trials and errors before finding suitable jobs; in its lower-class form, it consists of people who prefer the "action" of the street to any steady job. The poverty problem in its normal-class form consists of people (especially the aged, the physically handicapped, and mothers with dependent children) whose only need in order to live decently is money; in its lower-class form it consists of people who live in squalor and misery even if their incomes were doubled or tripled. The same is true with the other problems—slum housing, schools, crime, rioting; each is really two quite different problems.

The lower-class forms of all problems are at bottom a single problem: the existence of an outlook and style of life which is radically present-oriented and which therefore attaches no value to work, sacrifice, self-improvement, or service to family, friends, or community. Social workers, teachers, and law-enforcement officials—all those whom Gans calls "caretakers"—cannot achieve their goals because they can neither change nor circumvent this cultural obstacle. . . .

Robert Hunter described it in 1904:

They lived in God only knows what misery. They ate when there were things to eat; they starved when there was lack of food. But, on the whole, although they swore and beat each other and got drunk, they were more contented than any other class I have happened to know. It took a long time to understand them. Our Committees were busy from morning until night in giving them opportunities to take up the fight again, and to become independent of relief. They always took what we gave them; they always promised to try; but as soon as we expected them to fulfill any promises, they gave up in despair, and either wept or looked ashamed, and took to misery and drink again,—almost, so it seemed to me at times, with a sense of relief.

In Hunter's day these were the "undeserving," "unworthy," "depraved," "debased," or "disreputable" poor; today, they are the "troubled," "culturally deprived," "hard to reach," or "multiproblem." In the opinion of anthropologist Oscar Lewis, their kind of poverty "is a way of life, remarkably stable and persistent, passed down from generation to generation among family lines." This "culture of poverty," as he calls it, exists in city slums in many parts of the world, and is, he says, an adaptation made by the poor in order to defend themselves against the harsh realities of slum life.

The view that is to be taken here [is that] there is indeed such a culture, but that poverty is its effect rather than its cause. (There are societies even poorer than the ones Lewis has described—primitive ones, for example—in which nothing remotely resembling the pattern of behavior here under discussion exists.) Extreme present-orientedness, not lack of income or wealth, is the principal cause of poverty in the sense of "the culture of poverty." Most of those caught up in this culture are unable or unwilling to plan for the future, to sacrifice immediate gratifications in favor of future ones, or to accept the disciplines that are required in order to get and to spend. Their inabilities are probably culturally given in most cases—"multi-problem" families being normal representatives of a class culture that is itself abnormal. No doubt there are also people whose present-orientedness is rationally adaptive rather than cultural, but these probably comprise only a small part of the "hard core" poor.

Outside the lower class, poverty (in the sense of hardship, want, or destitution) is today almost always the result of external circumstances—involuntary unemployment, prolonged illness, the death of a breadwinner, or some other misfortune. Even when severe, such poverty is not squalid or degrading. Moreover, it ends quickly once the (external) cause of it no longer exists. Public or private assistance can sometimes remove or alleviate the cause—for example, by job retraining or remedial surgery. Even when the cause cannot be removed, simply providing the nonlower-class poor with sufficient income is enough to enable them to live "decently."

Lower-class poverty, by contrast, is "inwardly" caused (by psychological inability to provide for the future, and all that this inability implies). Improvements in external circumstances can affect this poverty only superficially: One problem of a "multiproblem" family is no sooner solved than another arises. In principle, it is possible to eliminate the poverty (material lack) of such a family, but only at great expense, since the capacity of the radically improvident to waste money is almost unlimited. Raising such a family's income would not necessarily improve its way of life, moreover, and could conceivably even make things worse. Consider, for example, the H. family:

> Mrs. H. seemed overwhelmed with the simple mechanics of dressing her six children and washing their clothes. The younger ones were running around in their underwear; the older ones were unaccounted for, but presumably were around the neighborhood. Mrs. H. had not been out of the house for several months; evidently her husband did the shopping. The apartment was filthy and it smelled. Mrs. H. was dressed in a bathrobe, although it was mid-afternoon. She seemed to have no plan or expectations with regard to her children; she did not know the names of their teachers and she did not seem to worry about their school work, although one child had been retained one year and another two years. Mrs. H. did seem to be somewhat concerned about her husband's lack of activity over the weekend—his continuous drinking and watching baseball on television. Apparently he and she never went out socially together nor did the family ever go anywhere as a unit.

If this family had a very high income— say, $50,000 a year—it would not be considered a "culture of poverty" case. Mrs. H. would hire maids to look after the small children, send the others to boarding schools, and spend her time at fashion shows while her husband drank and watched TV at his club. But with an income of only moderate size—say 100 percent above the poverty line—they would probably be about as badly off as they are now. They might be even worse off, for Mrs. H. would be able to go to the dog races, leaving the children alone, and Mr. H. could devote more time to his bottle and TV set. . . .

Welfare agencies, recognizing the difference between "internally" and "externally" caused poverty, have long been trying first by one means and then another to improve the characters or, as it is now put, to "bring about personal adjustment" of the poor. In the nineteenth century, the view was widely held that what the lower class individual needed was to be brought into a right relation with God or (the secular version of the same thing) with the respectable (that is, middle- and upper-class) elements of the community. The missionary who distributed tracts door to door in the slums was the first caseworker; his—more often, her—task was to minister to what today would be called "feelings of alienation."

> The stranger, coming on a stranger's errand, becomes a friend, discharging the offices and exerting the influence of a friend. . . .

Secularized, this approach became the "friendly visitor" system under which "certain persons, under the direction of a central board, pledge themselves to take one or more families who need counsel, if not material help, on their visiting list, and maintain personal friendly relations with them." The system did not work; middle- and upper-class people might be "friendly," but they could not sympathize, let alone communicate, with the lower class. By the beginning of the twentieth century the friendly visitor had been replaced by the "expert." The idea now was that the authority of "the facts" would bring about desired changes of attitude, motive, and habit. As it happened, however, the lower class did not recognize the authority of the facts. The expert then became a supervisor, using his (or her) power to confer or withhold material benefits in order to force the poor to do the things that were supposed to lead to "rehabilitation" (that is, to a middle-class style of life). This method did not work either; the lower class could always find ways to defeat and exploit the system. They seldom changed their ways very much and they never changed them for long. Besides, there was really no body of expertise to tell caseworkers how to produce the changes desired. As one caseworker remarked recently in a book addressed to fellow social service professionals:

> Despite years of experience in providing public aid to poor families precious little is yet known about how to help truly inadequate parents make long term improvements in child care, personal maturity, social relations, or work stability.

Some people understood that if the individual's style of life was to be changed at all, it would be necessary to change that of the group that produced, motivated, and constrained him. Thus, the settlement house. As Robert A. Woods explained:

> The settlements are able to take neighborhoods in cities, and by patience bring back to them much of the healthy village life, so that the people shall again know and care for one another. . . .

When it became clear that settlement houses would not change the culture of slum neighborhoods, the group approach was broadened into what is called "community action." In one type of community action ("community development"), a community organizer tries to persuade a neighborhood's informal leaders to support measures (for instance, measures for delinquency control) that he advances. In another form of it ("community organization"), the organizer tries to promote self-confidence, self-respect, and attachment to the group (and, hopefully, to normal society) among lower-class people. He attempts to do this by encouraging them in efforts at joint action, or by showing them how to conduct meetings, carry on discussions, pass resolutions, present requests to politicians, and the like. In still another form ("community mobilization"), the organizer endeavors to arouse the anger of lower-class persons against the local "power structure," to teach them the techniques of mass action—strikes, sit-ins, picketing, and so on—and to show them how they may capture power. The theory of community organization attributes the malaise of the poor to their lack of self-confidence (which is held to derive largely from their "inexperience"); community mobilization theory, by contrast, attributes it to their feelings of "powerlessness." According to this doctrine, the best cure for poverty is to give the poor power. But since power is not "given," it must be seized.

The success of the group approach has been no greater than that of the caseworker approach. Reviewing five years of effort on the part of various community action programs, Marris and Rein conclude:

> . . . the reforms had not evolved any reliable solutions to the intractable problems with which they struggled. They had not discovered how in general to override the intransigent autonomy of public and private agencies, at

any level of government; nor how to use the social sciences practically to formulate and evaluate policy; nor how, under the sponsorship of government, to raise the power of the poor. Given the talent and money they had brought to bear, they had not even reopened very many opportunities.

If the war on poverty is judged by its ability "to generate major, meaningful and lasting social and economic reforms in conformity with the expressed wishes of poor people," writes Thomas Gladwin, " . . . it is extremely difficult to find even scattered evidence of success." . . .

Although city agencies have sent community organizers by the score into slum neighborhoods, the lower-class poor cannot be organized. In East Harlem in 1948, five social workers were assigned to organize a five-block area and to initiate a program of social action based on housing, recreation, and other neighborhood needs. After three years of effort, the organizers had failed to attract a significant number of participants, and those they did attract were upwardly mobile persons who were unrepresentative of the neighborhood. In Boston a "total community" delinquency control project was found to have had "negligible impact," an outcome strikingly like that of the Cambridge-Somerville experiment—a "total caseworker" project—a decade earlier. Even community mobilization, despite the advantages of a rhetoric of hate and an emphasis on "action," failed to involve lower-class persons to a significant extent. Gangsters and leaders of youth gangs were co-opted on occasion, but they did not suffer from feelings of powerlessness and were not representative of the class for which mobilization was to provide therapy. No matter how hard they have tried to appeal to people

at the very bottom of the scale, community organizers have rarely succeeded. Where they have appeared to succeed, as, for example, in the National Welfare Rights Organization, it has been by recruiting people who had some of the *outward* attributes of the lower class—poverty, for example—but whose outlook and values were not lower class; the lower-class person (as defined here) is incapable of being organized. Although it tried strenuously to avoid it, what the Mobilization for Youth described as the general experience proved to be its own experience as well:

> Most efforts to organize lower-class people attract individuals on their way up the social-class ladder. Persons who are relatively responsible about participation, articulate and successful at managing organizational "forms" are identified as lower-class leaders, rather than individuals who actually reflect the values of the lower-class groups. Ordinarily the slum's network of informal group associations is not reached.

NO   William Ryan

BLAMING THE VICTIM

Twenty years ago, Zero Mostel used to do a sketch in which he impersonated a Dixiecrat Senator conducting an investigation of the origins of World War II. At the climax of the sketch, the Senator boomed out, in an excruciating mixture of triumph and suspicion, "What was Pearl Harbor *doing* in the Pacific?" This is an extreme example of Blaming the Victim.

Twenty years ago, we could laugh at Zero Mostel's caricature. In recent years, however, the same process has been going on every day in the arena of social problems, public health, anti-poverty programs, and social welfare. A philosopher might analyze this process and prove that, technically, it is comic. But it is hardly every funny.

Consider some victims. One is the miseducated child in the slum school. He is blamed for his own miseducation. He is said to contain within himself the causes of his inability to read and write well. The shorthand phrase is "cultural deprivation," which, to those in the know, conveys what they allege to be inside information: that the poor child carries a scanty pack of cultural baggage as he enters school. He doesn't know about books and magazines and newspapers, they say. (No books in the home: the mother fails to subscribe to *Reader's Digest*.) They say that if he talks at all—an unlikely event since slum parents don't talk to their children—he certainly doesn't talk correctly. Lower-class dialect spoken here, or even—God forbid!—Southern Negro. *(Ici on parle nigra.)* If you can manage to get him to sit in a chair, they say, he squirms and looks out the window. (Impulse-ridden, these kids, motoric rather than verbal.) In a word he is "disadvantaged" and "socially deprived," they say, and this, of course, accounts for his failure (*his* failure, they say) to learn much in school.

Note the similarity to the logic of Zero Mostel's Dixiecrat Senator. What is the culturally deprived child *doing* in the school? What is wrong with the victim? In pursuing this logic, no one remembers to ask questions about the collapsing buildings and torn textbooks, the frightened, insensitive teachers, the six additional desks in the room, the blustering, frightened principals, the relentless segregation, the callous administrator, the irrelevant curriculum, the bigoted or cowardly members of the school board, the insulting

From William Ryan, *Blaming the Victim* (Pantheon Books, 1971), pp. 3-9, 121-125, 236-237. Copyright © 1971 by William Ryan. Reprinted by permission of Pantheon Books, a division of Random House, Inc.

history book, the stingy taxpayers, the fairy-tale readers, or the self-serving faculty of the local teachers' college. We are encouraged to confine our attention to the child and to dwell on all his alleged defects. Cultural deprivation becomes an omnibus explanation for the educational disaster area known as the inner-city school. This is Blaming the Victim.

Pointing to the supposedly deviant Negro family as the "fundamental weakness of the Negro community" is another way to blame the victim. Like "cultural deprivation," "Negro family" has become a shorthand phrase with stereotyped connotations of matriarchy, fatherlessness, and pervasive illegitimacy. Growing up in the "crumbling" Negro family is supposed to account for most of the racial evils in America. Insiders have the word, of course, and know that this phrase is supposed to evoke images of growing up with a long-absent or never-present father (replaced from time to time perhaps by a series of transient lovers) and with bossy women ruling the roost, so that the children are irreparably damaged. This refers particularly to the poor, bewildered male children, whose psyches are fatally wounded and who are never, alas, to learn the trick of becoming upright, downright, forthright all-American boys. Is it any wonder the Negroes cannot achieve equality? From such families! And, again, by focusing our attention on the Negro family as the apparent *cause* of racial inequality, our eye is diverted. Racism, discrimination, segregation, and the powerlessness of the ghetto are subtly, but thoroughly, downgraded in importance.

The generic process of Blaming the Victim is applied to almost every American problem. The miserable health care of the poor is explained away on the grounds that the victim has poor motivation and lacks health information. The problems of slum housing are traced to the characteristics of tenants who are labeled as "Southern rural migrants" not yet "acculturated" to life in the big city. The "multiproblem" poor, it is claimed, suffer the psychological effects of impoverishment, the "culture of poverty," and the deviant value system of the lower classes; consequently, though unwittingly, they cause their own troubles. From such a viewpoint, the obvious fact that poverty is primarily an absence of money is easily overlooked or set aside.

The growing number of families receiving welfare are fallaciously linked together with the increased number of illegitimate children as twin results of promiscuity and sexual abandon among members of the lower orders. Every important social problem—crime, mental illness, civil disorder, unemployment—has been analyzed within the framework of the victim-blaming ideology. In the following pages, I shall present in detail nine examples that relate to social problems and human services in urban areas.

It would be possible for me to venture into other areas—one finds a perfect example in literature about the underdeveloped countries of the Third World, in which the lack of prosperity and technological progress is attributed to some aspect of the national character of the people, such as lack of "achievement motivation"—but I plan to stay within the confines of my own personal and professional experience, which is, generally, with racial injustice, social welfare, and human services in the city.

I have been listening to the victim-blamers and pondering their thought processes for a number of years. That process is often very subtle. Victim-blaming is cloaked in kindness and concern, and bears all the trappings and statistical furbelows of scientism; it is obscured by a perfumed haze of humanitarianism. In observing the process of Blaming the Victim, one tends to be confused and disoriented because those who practice this art display a deep concern for the victims that is quite genuine. In this way, the new ideology is very different from the open prejudice and reactionary tactics of the old days. Its adherents include sympathetic social scientists with social consciences in good working order, and liberal politicians with a genuine commitment to reform. They are very careful to dissociate themselves from vulgar Calvinism or crude racism; they indignantly condemn any notions of innate wickedness or genetic defect. "The Negro is *not born* inferior," they shout apoplectically. "Force of circumstance," they explain in reasonable tones, "has *made* him inferior." And they dismiss with self-righteous contempt any claims that the poor man in America is plainly unworthy or shiftless or enamored of idleness. No, they say, he is "caught in the cycle of poverty." He is trained to be poor by his culture and his family life, endowed by his environment (perhaps by his ignorant mother's outdated style of toilet training) with those unfortunately unpleasant characteristics that make him ineligible for a passport into the affluent society.

Blaming the Victim is, of course, quite different from old-fashioned conservative ideologies. The latter simply dismissed victims as inferior, genetically defective, or morally unfit; the emphasis is on the intrinsic, even hereditary, defect. The former shifts its emphasis to the environmental causation. The old-fashioned conservative could hold firmly to the belief that the oppressed and the victimized were born that way—that way being defective or inadequate in character or ability. The new ideology attributes defect and inadequacy to the malignant nature of poverty, injustice, slum life, and racial difficulties. The stigma that marks the victim and accounts for his victimization is an acquired stigma, a stigma of social, rather than genetic, origin. But the stigma, the defect, the fatal difference—though derived in the past from environmental forces—is still located *within* the victim, inside his skin. With such an elegant formulation, the humanitarian can have it both ways. He can, all at the same time, concentrate his charitable interest on the defects of the victim, condemn the vague social and environmental stresses that produced the defect (some time ago), and ignore the continuing effect of victimizing social forces (right now). It is a brilliant ideology for justifying a perverse form of social action designed to change, not society, as one might expect, but rather society's victim.

As a result, there is a terrifying sameness in the programs that arise from this kind of analysis. In education, we have programs of "compensatory education" to build up the skills and attitudes of the ghetto child, rather than structural changes in the schools. In race relations, we have social engineers who think up ways of "strengthening" the Negro family, rather than methods of eradicating racism. In health care, we develop new programs to provide health information (to correct the supposed ignorance of the poor) and to reach out and discover cases of untreated illness and disability (to compensate for their supposed unwillingness to seek treatment). Meanwhile, the gross inequities of our medical care delivery systems are left completely unchanged. As we might expect, the logical outcome of analyzing social problems in terms of the deficiencies of the victim is the development of programs aimed at correcting those deficiencies. The formula for action becomes extraordinarily simple: change the victim.

All of this happens so smoothly that it seems downright rational. First, identify a social problem. Second, study those affected by the problem and discover in what ways they are different from the rest of us as a consequence of deprivation and injustice. Third, define the differences as the cause of the social problem itself. Finally, of course, assign a government bureaucrat to invent a humanitarian action program to correct the differences.

Now no one in his right mind would quarrel with the assertion that social problems are present in abundance and are readily identifiable. God knows it is true that when hundreds of thousands of poor children drop out of school—or even graduate from school—they are barely literate. After spending some ten thousand hours in the company of professional educators, these children appear to have learned very little. The fact of failure in their education is undisputed. And the racial situation in America is usually acknowledged to be a number one item on the nation's agenda. Despite years of marches, commissions, judicial decisions, and endless legislative remedies, we are confronted with unchanging or even widening racial differences in achievement. In addition, despite our assertions that Americans get the best health care in the world, the poor stubbornly remain unhealthy. They lose more work because of illness, have more carious teeth, lose more babies as a result of both miscarriage and infant death, and die considerably younger than the well-to-do.

The problems are there, and there in great quantities. They make us uneasy. Added together, these disturbing signs reflect inequality and a puzzlingly high level of unalleviated distress in America totally inconsistent with our proclaimed ideals and our enormous wealth. This thread—this rope—of inconsistency stands out so visibly in the fabric of American life, that it is jarring to the eye. And this must be explained, to the satisfaction of our conscience as well as our patriotism. Blaming the Victim is an ideal, almost painless, evasion.

The second step in applying this explanation is to look sympathetically at those who "have" the problem in question, to separate them out and define them in some way as a special group, a group that is *different* from the population in general. This is a crucial and essential step in the process, for that difference is in itself hampering and maladaptive. The Different Ones are seen as less competent, less skilled, less knowing—in short, less human. . . .

The ultimate effect is always to distract attention from the basic causes and to leave the primary social injustice untouched. And, most telling, the proposed remedy for the problem is, of course, to work on the victim himself. Prescriptions for cure, [are] invariably conceived to revamp and revise the victim, never to change the surrounding circumstances. They want to change his attitudes, alter his values, fill up his cultural deficits, energize his apathetic soul, cure his character defects, train him and polish him and woo him from his savage ways.

. . . The old, reactionary exceptionalistic formulations are replaced by new progressive, humanitarian exceptionalistic formulations. In education, the outmoded and unacceptable concept of racial or class differences in basic inherited intellectual ability simply gives way to the new notion of cultural deprivation: there is very little functional difference between these two ideas. In taking a look at the phenomenon of poverty, the old concept of unfitness or idleness or laziness is replaced by the newfangled theory of the culture of poverty. In race relations, plain Negro inferiority—which was good enough for old-fashioned conservatives—is pushed aside by fancy conceits about the crumbling Negro family. With regard to illegitimacy, we are not so crass as to concern ourselves with immorality and vice, as in the old days; we settle benignly on the explanation of the "lower-class pattern of sexual behavior," which no one condemns as evil, but which is, in fact, simply a variation of the old explanatory idea. Mental illness is no longer defined as the result of hereditary taint or congenital character flaw; now we have new causal hypotheses regarding the ego-damaging emotional experiences that are supposed to be the inevitable consequence of the deplorable child-rearing practices of the poor.

In each case, of course, we are persuaded to ignore the obvious: the continued blatant discrimination against the Negro, the gross deprivation of contraceptive and adoption services to the poor, the heavy stresses endemic in the life of the poor. And almost all our make-believe liberal programs aimed at correcting our urban problems are off target; they are designed either to change the poor man or to cool him out. . . .

But, in any case, are the poor really all that different from the middle class? Take a common type of study, showing that ninety-one percent of the upper class, compared to only sixty-eight percent of the poor, prefer college education for their children. What does that tell us about the difference in values between classes?

First, if almost seventy percent of the poor want their children to go to college, it doesn't make much sense to say that the poor, as a group, do not value education. Only a minority of them—somewhat less than one-third—fail to express a *wish* that their children attend college. A smaller minority—one in ten—of the middle class give similar responses. One might well wonder why this small group of the better-off citizens of our achieving society reject higher education. They have the money; many of them have the direct experience of education; and most of them are aware of the monetary value of a college degree. I would suggest that the thirty percent of the poor who are unwilling to express a wish that their children go to college are easier to understand. They know the barriers—financial, social, and for black parents, racial—that make it very difficult for the children of the poor to get a college education. That seven out of ten of them nevertheless persist in a desire to see their children in a cap and gown is, in a very real sense, remarkable. Most important, if we are concerned with cultural or subcultural differences, it seems highly illogical to emphasize the values of a small minority of one group and then to attribute these values to the whole group. I simply cannot accept the evidence. If seventy percent of a group values education, then it is completely illogical to say that the group as a whole does *not* value education.

A useful formulation is to be found in Hyman Rodman's conception of the "lower class value stretch" which, to give a highly oversimplified version, proposes that members of the lower class *share* the dominant value system but *stretch* it to include as much as possible of the variations that circumstances force upon them. Rodman says:

> Lower class persons in close interaction with each other and faced with similar problems do not long remain in a state of mutual ignorance. They do not maintain a strong commitment to middle class values that they cannot attain, and they do not continue to respond to others in a rewarding or punishing way simply on the basis of whether these others are living up to the middle class values. A change takes place. They come to tolerate and eventually to evaluate favorably certain deviations from the middle class values. In this way they need not be continually frustrated by their failure to live up to unattainable values. The resultant is a stretched value system with a low degree of commitment to all the values within the range, including the dominant, middle class values.

In Rodman's terms, then, differences in range of values and commitments to specific elements within that range occur primarily as an *adaptive* rather than as a *cultural* response. . . .

The most recent, and in many ways the best information on [the related issue of child rearing] comes to us from the Hylan Lewis child-rearing studies, which I have mentioned before. Lewis has demonstrated (finally, one hopes) that there really *is* no "lower class child-rearing pattern." There are a number of such patterns—ranging from strict and over-controlled parenting, to permissiveness, to down-right neglect—just as in Lewis' sample there are a variety of different kinds of families—ranging from those with rigid, old-fashioned standards of hard work, thrift, morality and obsessive cleanliness, to the disorganized and disturbed families that he calls the "clinical poor." Lewis says:

> . . . it appears as a broad spectrum of pragmatic adjustments to external and internal stresses and deprivation. . . . Many low income families appear here as, in fact, the frustrated victims of what are thought of as middle class values, behavior and aspirations.

We return, finally, to where we began: the concept of Deferred Need Gratification. The simple idea that lower class folk have, as a character trait, a built-in deficiency in ability to delay need gratification has been explored, analyzed and more or less blown apart by Miller, Riessman, and Seagull. They point out that the supposed commitment of the middle classes to the virtues of thrift and hard work, to the practices of planning and saving for every painfully-chosen expenditure is, at this point in time, at best a surviving myth reflecting past conditions of dubious prevalence. The middle classes of today are clearly consumption-minded and debt-addicted. So the comparison group against which the poor are judged exists largely as a theoretical category with a theoretical behavior pattern. They go on to raise critical questions, similar to those I have raised earlier in this chapter. For example, on the question of what one would do with a two thousand dollar windfall, there was a difference between class groups of only five percent—about seventy percent of the middle class said they would save most of it, compared with about sixty-five percent of the lower class. On the basis of this small difference (which was statistically, but not practically, significant), the researchers, you will remember, had concluded that working-class people had less ability to defer need gratification. This conclusion may reflect elegant research methodology, but it fails the test of common sense. . . .

As for the idea that the poor share a culture in the sense that they subscribe to and follow a particular, deviant prescription for living—a poor man's blueprint for choosing and decision-making which accounts for the way he lives—this does not deserve much comment. Every study—with the exception of the egregious productions of Walter Miller—shows that, at the very least, overwhelming numbers of the poor give allegiance to the values and principles of the dominant American culture.

A related point—often the most overlooked point in any discussion of the culture of poverty—is that there is not, to my knowledge, *any evidence whatever* that the poor perceive their way of life as good and preferable to that of other ways of life. To make such an assertion is to talk pure nonsense. . . .

Perhaps the most fundamental question to ask of those who are enamored of the idea that the poor have one culture and the rich another is to ask, simply, "So what?" Suppose the mythical oil millionaire behaves in an unrefined "lower class" manner, for example. What difference does that make as long as he owns the oil wells? Is the power of the Chairman of the Ways and Means Committee in the state legislature diminished or enhanced in any way by his taste in clothing or music? And suppose every single poor family in America set as its long-range goal that its sons and daughters would get a Ph.D.—who would pay the tuition?

The effect of tastes, child-rearing practices, speech patterns, reading habits, and other cultural factors is relatively small in comparison to the effect of wealth and influence. What I am trying to suggest is that the inclusion in the analytic process of the elements of social stratification that are usually omitted—particularly economic class and power—would produce more significant insights into the circumstances of the poor and the pressures and deprivations with which they live. The simplest—and at the same time, the most significant—proposition in understanding poverty is that it is caused by lack of money. The overwhelming majority of the poor are poor because they have, first: insufficient income; and second: no access to methods of increasing that income—that is, no power. They are to young, too old, too sick; they are bound to the task of caring for small children, or they are simply discriminated against. The facts are clear, and the solution seems rather obvious—raise their income and let their "culture," whatever it might be, take care of itself.

The need to avoid facing this obvious solution—which is very uncomfortable since it requires some substantial changes and redistribution of income—provides the motivation for developing the stabilizing ideology of the culture of poverty which acts to sustain the *status quo* and delay change. The function of the ideology of lower class culture, then, is plainly to maintain inequality in American life.

The millionaire, freshly risen from the lower class, whose crude tongue and appalling table manners betray the newness of his affluence, is a staple of American literature and folklore. He comes on stage over and over, and we have been taught exactly what to expect with each entrance. He will walk into the parlor in his undershirt, gulp tea from a saucer, spit into the Limoges flower pot, and, when finally invited to the society garden party, disgrace his wife by saying "bullshit" to the president of the bank. When I was growing up, we had daily lessons in this legend from Jiggs and Maggie in the comic strip.

This discrepancy between *class* and *status*, between possession of economic resources and life style, has been a source of ready humour and guaranteed fascination for generations. The centrality of this mythical strain in American thought is reflected again in the strange and perverse ideas emerging from the mouths of many professional Pauper Watchers and Victim Blamers.

In real life, of course, Jiggs' character and behavior would never remain so constant and unchanging over the decades. The strain between wealth and style is one that usually tends to be quickly resolved. Within a fairly short time, Jiggs would be coming into the parlor first with a shirt, then with a tie on, and, finally, in one of his many custom-made suits. He would soon be drinking tea from a Limoges cup, and for a time he would spit in an antique cuspidor, until he learned not to spit at all. At the garden party, he would confine his mention of animal feces to a discussion of the best fertilizer for the rhododendron. In real life, style tends to follow close on money, and money tends to be magnetized and attracted to power. Those who try to persuade us that the process can be reversed, that a change in style of life can lead backward to increased wealth and greater power, are preaching nonsense. To promise that improved table manners can produce a salary increase; that more elegant taste in clothes will lead to the acquisition of stock in IBM; that an expanded vocabulary will automatically generate an enlargement of community influence—these are pernicious as well as foolish. There is no record in history of any *group* having accomplished this wondrous task. (There may be a few clever individuals who have followed such artful routes to money and power, but they are relatively rare.) The whole idea is an illusion of fatuous social scientists and welfare bureaucrats blinded by the ideology I have painstakingly tried to dissect in the previous chapters.

POSTSCRIPT

Does "Lower-Class" Culture Perpetuate Poverty?

The debate over the culture of poverty thesis is as strong today as it was fifteen years ago when Banfield and Ryan were debating. In 1981 George Gilder incorporated the culture of poverty thesis in his book *Wealth and Poverty* (Basic Books) and argued that hard work is the tried and true path from poverty to wealth (see Issue 7). He also agrees that many welfare programs perpetuate poverty by breeding dependence and supporting the culture of poverty. This criticism of welfare has been forcefully argued with ample statistics by Charles Murray in *Losing Ground* (Basic Books, 1984) (see Issue 13). Both Gilder and Murray view the welfare system as an important contributor to the culture of poverty, whereas Banfield sees the culture of poverty as virulent long before welfare became a major fact in the lives of poor people.

There are countless works that describe the crushing and numbing conditions of the poor. The nineteenth-century English novelist Charles Dickens was a crusader for the poor, and many of his novels, still in print and certainly considered classics, graphically depict the wretchedness of poverty. Michael Harrington (1929–1989), a prominent political theorist and socialist, is one example of a more contemporary writer whose works call attention to the poor in our society. He described poverty in America in his influential nonfiction book *The Other America* (Macmillan, 1963) at a time when most of the country was increasingly affluent. He helped launch the War on Poverty of the Kennedy-Johnson administrations. Thomas Gladwin in *Poverty USA* (Little, Brown, 1967) and Nick Katz in *Let Them Eat Promises* (Prentice Hall, 1969) sought to maintain national concern about poverty in the late 1960s by documenting its prevalence even though the poverty rate dropped from 30 percent in 1950 to 13 percent in 1970. In 1968, however, the administration changed and the crusade against poverty died down. Nevertheless, public welfare expenditures rose mainly because Social Security, Medicare, and Medicaid kept expanding.

The anti-poverty crusaders have new concerns with more recent developments such as the increase in the number of female-headed single-parent families living below the poverty line and the increase throughout the 1980s in the number of homeless. Michael Harrington chronicled these changes in the condition of the poor in *The New American Poverty* (Holt, Rinehart and Winston, 1984). More recently, William Julius Wilson has written about the macroeconomic forces at work on the poor in *The Truly Disadvantaged* (University of Chicago Press, 1987).

ISSUE 8

Is Racial Oppression Declining in America?

YES: William Julius Wilson, from *The Declining Significance of Race* (University of Chicago Press, 1978)

NO: Charles V. Willie, from "The Inclining Significance of Race," *Society* (July/August 1978)

ISSUE SUMMARY

YES: University of Chicago sociologist William Julius Wilson argues that class, rather than race, is now the dominant factor in determining a person's life chances.
NO: Educator and sociologist Charles V. Willie counters that race remains the primary consideration.

"We didn't land on Plymouth Rock, my brothers and sisters—Plymouth Rock landed on *us*." This observation by Malcom X, the founder of the Organization of Afro-American Unity and symbol for the black nationalist impulses of the 1960s, is borne out by the facts of American history. Snatched from their native land, transported thousands of miles, and sold into slavery, blacks were reduced to the legal status of cattle. The *Dred Scott* decision of the Supreme Court in 1857 declared them to be "private property." The Civil War and the subsequent Reconstruction period gave many the hope that slavery and its vestiges would be abolished forever. But even before the last federal troops were withdrawn from the South in 1877, the bourbons had begun to regain control of the legislatures of the South. Before long, the gains made by blacks at the close of the war were wiped out. There was little public outcry and only one dissent on the bench when the Supreme Court in 1883 declared unconstitutional a Reconstruction statute that had prohibited segregation in public accommodations. In 1896, in the case of *Plessy v. Ferguson*, the Supreme Court sealed the fate of civil rights by upholding state-imposed segregation.

Not for another half-century was there any relief from the deliberate and systematic oppression of blacks. In 1954, in *Brown v. Board of Education*, the Supreme Court in effect reversed the *Plessy* decision of 1896 by outlawing state-imposed racial segregation. As a result of the civil rights movement in the 1960s, more improvements were won: Congress passed a series of statutes protecting voting rights and prohibiting discrimination in employment, housing, and public accommodations. It also created offices within the executive branch to enforce and administer its new laws. By any fair estimation, these are remarkable gains, but there still remains a legacy of three hundred years of oppression. Blacks had been confined to the most menial jobs. In addition, they had first been forbidden, then denied, education. Later they were given only the most rudimentary schooling and found the doors to advancement were closed everywhere. As a result, by practically every index—employment, income, education, and even health and longevity—blacks have trailed whites by large margins.

In economic terms, the past thirty years have been years of both progress and retrogression for blacks. During the 1960s, black family income increased steadily. By 1969, it was 61 percent of white income (compared to 53 percent in 1961). By 1977, however, the ratio had fallen to 57 percent and it was still at that level in 1985. Why? According to some observers, it was related to the erosion of liberal policies in the 1970s combined with an economic downturn. Yet, that explanation seems to be belied by the fact that for some black families the gap between black and white incomes *continued* to narrow during the 1970s. In that category were black married couples with both spouses working and younger educated blacks. (In the latter case, black income was essentially equal to that of whites.) The more likely explanation for the overall slippage is the fact that the number of female-headed single-parent families among blacks increased dramatically—from 8 percent in 1950 to 54 percent in 1986. Only 18 percent of white families fell into that category in 1986—up from 3 percent in 1950.

Though the picture is complex, one fact is starkly clear: Overall, a wide disparity in income and in general well-being still exists between blacks and whites in America. The question is whether this social inequality is still related, in any meaningful sense, to American racism. To put it simply: Are blacks still being oppressed in America simply because they are black?

The question has been hotly debated for over a decade. In the following selections William Julius Wilson, a black sociologist, argues that race is much less significant than class in explaining the gap between black and white income, while another black social scientist, Charles V. Willie, considers it premature to conclude that oppression has become color-blind in America.

YES

William Julius Wilson

THE DECLINING SIGNIFICANCE OF RACE

Race relations in the United States have undergone fundamental changes in recent years, so much so that now the life chances of individual blacks have more to do with their economic class position than with their day-to-day encounters with whites. In earlier years the systematic efforts of whites to suppress blacks were obvious to even the most insensitive observer. Blacks were denied access to valued and scarce resources through various ingenious schemes of racial exploitation, discrimination, and segregation, schemes that were reinforced by elaborate ideologies of racism.

But the situation has changed. However determinative such practices were in the previous efforts of the black population to achieve racial equality, and however significant they were in the creation of poverty-stricken ghettoes and a vast underclass of black proletarians—that massive population at the bottom of the social class ladder plagued by poor education and low-paying unstable jobs—they do not provide a meaningful explanation of the life chances of black Americans today. The traditional patterns of interaction between blacks and whites, particularly in the labor market, have been fundamentally altered.

NEW AND TRADITIONAL BARRIERS

In the pre–Civil War period, and in the latter half of the nineteenth through the first half of the twentieth century, the continuous and explicit efforts of whites to construct racial barriers profoundly affected the lives of black Americans. Racial oppression was designed, overt, and easily documented. As the nation has entered the latter half of the twentieth century, however, many of the traditional barriers have crumbled under the weight of the political, social, and economic changes of the civil rights era. A new set of obstacles has emerged from basic structural shifts in the economy.

These obstacles are therefore impersonal, but may prove to be even more formidable for certain segments of the black population. Specifically, whereas the previous barriers were usually designed to control and restrict

From William J. Wilson, *The Declining Significance of Race* (University of Chicago Press, 1979), pp. 1, 2, 146-154. Copyright © 1978 by William Julius Wilson. Reprinted by permission of The University of Chicago Press.

the entire black population, the new barriers create hardships essentially for the black underclass; whereas the old barriers were based explicitly on racial motivations derived from intergroup contact, the new barriers have racial significance only in their consequences, not in their origins. In short, whereas the old barriers portrayed the pervasive features of racial oppression, the new barriers indicate an important and emerging form of class subordination.

It would be shortsighted to view the traditional forms of racial segregation and discrimination as having essentially disappeared in contemporary America; the presence of blacks is still firmly resisted in various institutions and social clubs. However, in the economic sphere class has become more important than race in determining black access to privilege and power. It is clearly evident in this connection that many talented and educated blacks are now entering positions of prestige and influence at a rate comparable to or, in some situations, exceeding that of whites with equivalent qualifications. It is equally clear that the black underclass is in a hopeless state of economic stagnation, falling further and further behind the rest of society. . . .

CLASS AND RACE RELATIONS

Except for the brief period of fluid race relations in the North between 1870 and 1890 and in the South during the Reconstruction era, racial oppression is the single best term to characterize the black experience prior to the twentieth century. In the antebellum South both slaves and free blacks occupied what could best be described as a caste position, in the sense that realistic changes for occupational mobility simply did not exist. In the antebellum North a few free blacks were able to acquire some property and improve their socioeconomic position, and a few were even able to make use of educational opportunities. However, the overwhelming majority of free northern Negroes were trapped in menial positions and were victimized by lower-class white antagonism, including the racial hostilities of European immigrant ethnics (who successfully curbed the black economic competition). In the postbellum South the system of Jim Crow segregation wiped out the small gains blacks had achieved during Reconstruction, and blacks were rapidly pushed out of the more skilled jobs they had held since slavery. Accordingly, there was very little black occupational differentiation in the South at the turn of the century.

Just as the shift from a plantation economy to an industrializing economy transformed the class and race relations in the postbellum South, so too did industrialization in the North change the context for race-class interaction and confrontation there. On the one hand, the conflicts associated with the increased black-white contacts in the early twentieth century North resembled the forms of antagonism that soured the relations between the races in the postbellum South. Racial conflicts between blacks and whites in both situations were closely tied to class conflicts among whites. On the other hand, there were some fundamental differences. The collapse of the paternalistic bond between the blacks and the southern business elite cleared the path for the almost total subjugation of blacks in the South and resulted in what amounted to a white racial movement that solidified in the system of Jim Crow segregation. However, a united white movement against blacks never really developed in the North. In the first quarter of the twentieth century, management attempted to undercut white labor by using blacks as strikebreakers and, in some situations, as permanent replacements for white workers who periodically demanded higher wages and more fringe benefits. Indeed, the determination of industrialists to ignore racial norms of exclusion and to hire black workers was one of the main reasons why the industry-wide unions reversed their racial policies and actively recruited black workers during the New Deal era. Prior to this period the overwhelming majority of unskilled and semiskilled blacks were nonunionized and were available as lower-paid labor or as strikebreakers. The more management used blacks to undercut white labor, the greater were the racial antagonisms between white and black labor.

Moreover, racial tension in the industrial sector often reinforced and sometimes produced racial tension in the social order. The growth of the black urban population created a housing shortage during the early twentieth century which frequently produced black "invasions" or ghetto "spillovers" into adjacent poor white neighborhoods. The racial tensions emanating from labor strife seemed to heighten the added pressures of racial competition for housing, neighborhoods, and recreational areas. Indeed, it was this combination of racial friction in both the economic sector and the social order that produced the bloody riots in East Saint Louis in 1917 and in Chicago and several other cities in 1919.

In addition to the fact that a united white movement against blacks never really developed in the North during the industrial period, it was also the case that the state's role in shaping race relations was much more autonomous, much less directly related to developments in the economic sector. Thus, in the brief period of fluid race relations in the North from 1870 to 1890, civil rights laws were passed barring discrimination in public places and in public institutions. This legislation did not have any real significance to the white masses at that time because, unlike in the pre–Civil War North and the post–Civil War South, white workers did not perceive blacks as major economic competitors. Blacks constituted only a small percentage of the total population in northern cities; they had not yet been used in any significant numbers as cheap labor in industry or as strikebreakers; and their earlier antebellum competitors in low-status jobs (the Irish and German immigrants) had improved their economic status in the trades and municipal employment.

POLITY AND RACIAL OPPRESSION

For all these reasons liberal whites and black professionals, urged on by the spirit of racial reform that had developed during the Civil War and Reconstruction, could pursue civil rights programs without firm resistance; for all these reasons racial developments on the political front were not directly related to the economic motivations and interests of workers and management. In the early twentieth century the independent effect of the political system was displayed in an entirely different way. The process of industrialization had significantly altered the pattern of racial interaction, giving rise to various manifestations of racial antagonism.

Although discrimination and lack of training prevented blacks from seeking higher-paying jobs, they did compete with lower-class whites for unskilled and semiskilled factory jobs, and they were used by management to undercut the white workers' union movement. Despite the growing importance of race in the dynamics of the labor market, the political system did not intervene either or mediate the racial conflicts or to reinforce the pattern of labor-market racial interaction generated by the system of production. This was the case despite the salience of a racial ideology system that justified and prescribed unequal treatment for Afro-Americans. (Industrialists will more likely challenge societal racial norms in situations where adherence to them results in economic losses.)

If nothing else, the absence of political influence on the labor market probably reflected the power struggles between management and workers. Thus legislation to protect the rights of black workers to compete openly for jobs would have conflicted with the interests of management. To repeat, unlike the South, a united white movement resulting in the almost total segregation of the work force never really developed in the North.

But the state's lack of influence in the industrial sector of private industries did not mean that it had no significant impact on racial stratification in the early twentieth century North. The urban political machines, controlled in large measure by working-class ethnics who were often in direct competition with blacks in the private industrial sector, systematically gerrymandered black neighborhoods and excluded the urban black masses from meaningful political participation throughout the early twentieth century. Control by the white ethnics of the various urban political machines was so complete that blacks were never really in a position to compete for the more important municipal political rewards, such as patronage jobs or government contracts and services. Thus the lack of racial competition for municipal political rewards did not provide the basis for racial tension and conflict in the urban political system. This political racial oppression had no direct connection with or influence on race relations in the private industrial sector.

In sum, whether one focuses on the way race relations were structured by the system of production or the polity or both, racial oppression (ranging from the exploitation of black labor by the business class to the elimination of black competition for economic, social, and political resources by the white masses) was a characteristic and important phenomenon in both the preindustrial and industrial periods of American race relations. Nonetheless, and despite the prevalence of various forms of racial oppression, the change from a preindustrial to an industrial system of production did enable blacks to increase their political and economic resources. The proliferation of jobs created by industrial expansion helped generate and sustain the continuous mass migration of blacks from the rural South to the cities of the North and West. As the black urban population grew and became more segregated, institutions and organizations in the black community also developed, together with a business and a professional class affiliated with these institutions. Still, it was not until after World War II (the modern industrial period) that the black class structure started to take on some of the characteristics of the white class structure.

CLASS AND BLACK LIFE CHANCES

Class has also become more important than race in determining black life chances in the modern industrial period. Moreover, the center of racial conflict has shifted from the industrial sector to the sociopolitical order. Although these changes can be related to the more fundamental changes in the system of production and in the laws and policies of the state, the relations between the economy and the polity in the modern industrial period have differed from those in previous periods. In the preindustrial and industrial periods the basis of structured racial inequality was primarily economic, and in most situations the state was merely an instrument to reinforce patterns of race relations that grew directly out of the social relations of production.

Except for the brief period of fluid race relations in the North from 1870 to 1890 the state was a major instrument of racial oppression. State intervention in the modern industrial period has been designed to promote racial equality, and the relationship between the polity and the economy has been much more reciprocal, so much so that it is difficult to determine which one has been more important in shaping race relations since World War II. It was the expansion of the economy that facilitated black movement from the rural areas to the industrial centers and that created job opportunities leading to greater occupational differentiation in the black community (in the sense that an increasing percentage of blacks moved into white-collar positions); and it was the intervention of the state (responding to the pressures of increased black political resources and to the racial protest movement that removed many artificial discrimination barriers by municipal, state, and federal civil rights legislation, and that contributed to the more liberal racial policies of the nation's labor unions by protective union legislation. And these combined political and eco-

nomic changes created a pattern of black occupational upgrading that resulted, for example, in a substantial drop in the percentage of black males in the low-paying service, unskilled labor, and farm jobs.

However, despite the greater occupational differentiation within the black community, there are now signs that the effect of some aspects of structural economic change has been the closer association between black occupational mobility and class affiliation. Access to the means of production is increasingly based on educational criteria (a situation which distinguishes the modern industrial from the earlier industrial system of production) and thus threatens to solidify the position of the black underclass. In other words, a consequence of the rapid growth of the corporate and government sectors has been the gradual creation of a segmented labor market that currently provides vastly different mobility opportunities for segments of the black population.

On the one hand, poorly trained and educationally limited blacks of the inner city, including that growing number of black teenagers and young adults, see their job prospects increasingly restricted to the low-wage sector, their unemployment rates soaring to record levels (which remain high despite swings in the business cycle), their labor force participation rates declining, their movement out of poverty slowing, and their welfare roles increasing. On the other hand, talented and educated blacks are experiencing unprecedented job opportunities in the growing government and corporate sectors, opportunities that are at least comparable to those of whites with equivalent qualifications. The improved job situation for the more privileged blacks in the corporate and government sectors is related both to the expansion of salaried white-collar positions and to the pressures of state affirmative action programs.

In view of these developments, it would be difficult to argue that the plight of the black underclass is solely a consequence of racial oppression, that is, the explicit and overt efforts of whites to keep blacks subjugated, in the same way that it would be difficult to explain the rapid economic improvement of the more privileged blacks by arguing that the traditional forms of racial segregation and discrimination still characterize the labor market in American industries. The recent mobility patterns of blacks lend strong support to the view that economic class is clearly more important than race in predetermining job placement and occupational mobility. In the economic realm, then, the black experience has moved historically from economic racial oppression experienced by virtually all blacks to economic subordination for the back underclass. And as we begin the last quarter of the twentieth century, a deepening economic schism seems to be developing in the black community, with the black poor falling further and further behind middle and upper-income blacks.

SHIFT OF RACIAL CONFLICT

If race is declining in significance in the economic sector, explanations of racial antagonism based on labor-market conflicts, such as those advanced by economic class theories of race, also have less significance in the period of modern industrial race relations. Neither the low-wage sector nor the corporate and government sectors provide the basis for the kind of interracial job competition and conflict that plagued the economic order in previous periods. With the absorption of blacks into industrywide labor unions, protective union legislation, and equal employment legislation, it is no longer feasible for management to undercut white labor by using black workers. The traditional racial struggles for power and privilege have shifted away from the economic sector and are now concentrated in the sociopolitical order. Although poor blacks and poor whites are still the main actors in the present manifestations of racial strife, the immediate source of the tension has more to do with racial competition for public schools, municipal political systems, and residential areas than with the competition for jobs.

To say that race is declining in significance, therefore, is not only to argue that the life chances of blacks have less to do with race than with economic class affiliation, but also to maintain that racial conflict and competition in the economic sector—the most important historical factors in the subjugation of blacks—have been substantially reduced. However, it could be argued that the firm white resistance to public school desegregation, residential integration, and black control of central cities all indicate the unyielding importance of race in the United States. The argument could even be entertained that the impressive occupational gains of the black middle class are only temporary, and that as soon as affirmative action pressures are relieved, or as soon as the economy experiences a prolonged recession, industries will return to their old racial practices.

Both of these arguments are compelling if not altogether persuasive. Taking the latter contention first, there is little available evidence to suggest that the economic gains of privileged blacks will be reversed. Despite the fact that the recession of the early 1970s decreased job prospects for all educated workers, the more educated blacks continued to experience a faster rate of job advancement than their white counterparts. And although it is always possible that an economic disaster could produce racial competition for higher-paying jobs and white efforts to exclude talented blacks, it is difficult to entertain this idea as a real possibility in the face of the powerful political and social movement against job discrimination. At this point there is every reason to believe that talented and educated blacks, like talented and educated whites, will continue to enjoy the advantages and privileges of their class status.

My response to the first argument is not to deny the current racial antagonism in the sociopolitical order, but to suggest that such antagonism has far less effect on individual or group access to those opportunities and resources that are centrally important for life survival than antagonism in the economic sector. The factors that most severely affected black life chances in previous years were the racial oppression and antagonism in the economic sector. As race declined in importance in the economic sector, the Negro class structure became more differentiated and black life chances became increasingly a consequence of class affiliation.

Furthermore, it is even difficult to identify the form of racial contact in the sociopolitical order as the source of the current manifestations of conflict between lower-income blacks and whites, because neither the degree of racial competition between the have-nots, nor their structural relations in urban communities, nor their patterns of interaction constitute the ultimate source of present racial antagonism. The ultimate basis for current racial tension is the deleterious effect of basic structural changes in the modern American economy on black and white lower-income groups, changes that include uneven economic growth, increasing technology and automation, industry relocation, and labor market segmentation.

FIGHTING CLASS SUBORDINATION

The situation of marginality and redundancy created by the modern industrial society deleteriously affects all the poor, regardless of race. Underclass whites, Hispanic Americans, and Native Americans are all victims, to a greater or lesser degree, of class subordination under advanced capitalism. It is true that blacks are disproportionately represented in the underclass population and that about one-third of the entire black population is in the underclass. But the significance of these facts has more to do with the historical consequences of racial oppression than with the current effects of race.

Although the percentage of blacks below the low-income level dropped steadily throughout the 1960s, one of the legacies of the racial oppression in previous years is the continued disproportionate black representation in the underclass. And since 1970 both poor whites and non-whites have evidenced very little progress in their elevation from the ranks of the underclass. In the final analysis, therefore, the challenge of economic dislocation in the modern industrial society calls for public policy programs to attack inequality on a broad class front, policy programs—in other words—that go beyond the limits of ethnic and racial discrimination by directly confronting the pervasive and destructive features of class subordination.

NO

Charles V. Willie

THE INCLINING SIGNIFICANCE OF RACE

It is all a matter of perspective. From the perspective of the dominant people of power, inequality exists because of the personal inadequacies of those who are less fortunate. Varying degrees of fortune is the essence of the social stratification system in this nation. In America, it is the affluent rather than the poor who use social class theory to explain poverty. Moreover, they assert that poverty is not a function of institutional arrangements but a matter of individual capacities. From the perspective of the dominant people of power, the social stratification system in the United States is open and any who has the capacity can rise within it. This orientation toward individual mobility tends to mask the presence of opportunities that are institutionally based such as attending the "right" school, seeking employment with the "right" company or firm, and being of the "right" race. Also this orientation toward individual mobility tends to deny the presence of opposition and oppression that are connected with institutions. According to the perspective of the dominant people of power, opportunity and especially educational and economic opportunity is a function of merit.

William Julius Wilson has used the perspective of the dominant people of power in his article on "The Declining Significance of Race" that appeared in the January/February edition of *Society*. An individual, including a scholar in the social sciences, is free to use any perspective that he or she wishes to use. The tradition of friendly criticism in this field, however, supports the effort which I shall undertake in this commentary. My purpose is to make explicit that which is implicit so that others may assess the conclusions of Professor Wilson on the basis of the premises and the perspective of his analysis . . .

INCOME

First, let us look at income. As recently as 1975, the median income for white families was $14,268 compared with a median of $9,321 for blacks and other minority races. This means that blacks and other racial minorities received only two-thirds as much income as whites. At both ends of the income scale, the ratio of black to white income was about the same. Under $5,000 a year there was only 10.2 percent of the white families and individuals compared with 26.3 percent of the population of black families and individuals. Earning $25,000 a year and over in 1975, was 15.1 percent of the white population compared with 6.4 percent of the black population. The proportion of blacks who were very poor was two and one-half times greater than the proportion of whites who were very poor; and the proportion of whites who were most affluent was two and one-third times greater than the proportion of blacks with high incomes. There is not much of a difference in these income ratios by race for the poor and the affluent. In general, the proportion of high-income blacks is far less than what it would be if there was no racial discrimination. The 1977 report, *All Our Children*, by the Carnegie Council on Children of which Kenneth Keniston was senior author states that "90 percent of the income gap between blacks and whites is the result . . . of lower pay for blacks with comparable levels of education and experience." Despite this and other findings such as those presented by economist Herman Miller in his book *Rich Man, Poor Man*, Professor Wilson states that "many talented and educated blacks are now entering positions of prestige and influence at a rate comparable to or, in some situations, exceeding that of whites with equal qualifications.

In 1974, 15 percent of the white male population was of the professional or technical workers category compared with 9 percent of the male population of blacks and other minority races. This appeared to be a notable change relative to whites but it represented only an increase of 3 percentage points over the 6 percent of black and other minority males who were professionals 10 years earlier. Moreover, only 5 percent of the black and other racial minority males were managers and administrators in 1974 compared with 15 percent of all white employed males. In summary, 42 percent of the white male population was white collar in 1974 compared with 24 percent of the racial minority males in this nation. These data indicate that blacks have a long way to go before they catch up with whites in high-level occupations.

Moreover, a study by the Survey Research Center of the University of Michigan that was published in the *New York Times* February 26, 1978, reported that 61 percent of all blacks in a nationwide poll believed that whites either don't care whether or not blacks "get a break" or were actively trying to keep blacks down. It would appear that neither the sentiment of blacks nor the facts of the situation are in accord with the analysis of Professor Wilson and his claim that "class has become more important than race in determining black life chances."

The University of Michigan study also found that one out of every two white persons believed that "few blacks . . . miss out on jobs and promotions because of racial discrimination." This response is similar to the conclusion of Professor Wilson and is the reason why I stated earlier that his analysis was from the perspective of the dominant people of power.

EDUCATION

Second, let us look at what is happening to poor blacks to determine whether their circumstances are more a function of social class than of race. This analysis,

I believe, reveals a fundamental error in the analysis of Professor Wilson—an error no less serious than that committed by Daniel Patrick Moynihan and Christopher Jencks who made observations on whites and projected these upon blacks . . .

It is obvious that Professor Wilson has analyzed the job situation for affluent blacks. The census data that I reported earlier indicated that blacks were catching up with whites, relatively, so far as employment in the professions is concerned. While the proportion of white male professionals a decade ago was twice as great as the proportion of black and other minority male professionals, the proportion as late as 1974 was only two-thirds greater. On the basis of data like these, Professor Wilson states that "talented and educated blacks are experiencing unprecedented job opportunities in the growing government and corporate sectors." After analyzing the "job situation for the more privileged blacks," Professor Wilson projects these findings upon the poor and says "it would be difficult to argue that the plight of the black underclass is solely the consequence of racial oppression, that is, the explicit and overt efforts of whites to keep blacks subjugated. . . ."

While the facts cited earlier cast doubt upon the conclusion that talented blacks are experiencing "unprecedented job opportunities," even if one accepts the modest improvement for "talented blacks" as fact, it is inappropriate to project middle-class experience upon the underclass of blacks. This is precisely what Professor Wilson has done.

His assertion that "the black experience has moved historically from economic racial oppression experienced by virtually all blacks to economic subordination for the black underclass" cancels out racial discrimination as a key cause of poverty among blacks. If one assumes that there are not extraordinary biological differences between blacks and whites in the United States, then it is difficult to explain why the proportion of poor blacks with an annual income under $5,000 is two and one-half times greater than the proportion of poor whites. Among poor white youth and young adults the unemployment rate is higher for high school dropouts than for persons who graduated from high school but did not receive more education. Among blacks, however, the unemployment rate is high and is the same for high school dropouts and for those who graduated from high school but did not receive more education. Staying in high school seems not to make a difference for blacks so far as the risk of unemployment is concerned.

Among whites with only an elementary school education or less, 50 percent are likely to have jobs as service workers or laborers at the bottom of the occupational heap but 80 percent of black workers with this limited education are likely to find work only in these kinds of jobs. This was what Herman Miller found in his analysis of 1960 census data. These facts indicate that education alone cannot explain the disproportionate number of blacks in low-paying jobs. If the absence of education is the basis for limited upward mobility in the stratification system, why do whites with little education get better jobs than blacks?

Using 1968 data, Miller analyzed difference in median income for whites and blacks and other nonwhite minorities. He found that the difference for the races ranged from $880 for those who had completed grade school only to $2,469 for those who had attended or graduated from college. Median income by schooling not only differed by race but tended to widen between the racial groups with increase in education. On the bases of these findings, Miller said that "there is some justification for the feeling by Puerto Ricans, Negroes, and other minority groups that education does not do as much for them financially as it does for others." These findings Miller reported in the 1971 edition of his book, *Rich Man, Poor Man*, and they indicated that racial discrimination is a contributing factor to the occupational opportunities and income received by poor as well as affluent blacks.

RESIDENTIAL SEGREGATION

With reference to residential segregation which Professor Wilson wants to ignore as irrelevant, he has received modest support from the findings of Albert Simkus that were reported in the February 1978 edition of the *American Sociological Review* in an article entitled "Residential Segregation by Occupation and Race in Ten Urbanized Areas, 1950–1970," Simkus said that "historically, blacks with high incomes have been as highly or more highly segregated from whites with similar incomes than have low-income blacks." This fact became "slightly less true . . . by 1970." However, Simkus attributes the slight change to political rather than economic factors. Particularly singled out for credit is civil rights and housing legislation of the 1960s.

Simkus points out that the decrease in residential segregation of affluent blacks is beginning to catch up with the integrated residential areas that characterized lower-income blacks and whites in the past. Specifically, he said that "apart from the comparisons involving nonwhite professionals, nonwhites and whites in the lowest occupational categories were still slightly less segregated than those in the higher categories."

Finally, I call attention to the fact that Professor Wilson's data are at variance with the clinical observations of other blacks. The unprecedented job opportunities simply have not been experienced by some talented and educated blacks. During the summer of 1977, the *New York Times* published an interview with Sanford Allen, a black violinist with the New York Philharmonic Orchestra. Allen announced his intention to resign from his position. He said that he was "simply tired of being a symbol." At that time, Allen was the only black who had been a member of the 133-year-old musical organization. He charged the more prestigious symphony orchestras of this nation, such as the Boston Symphony, the Chicago Symphony, and two or three others, with running a closed shop that excluded blacks. Allen joined the New York Philharmonic in 1962. During a decade and a half, no other blacks had been hired. A story like this one, of course, is clinical evidence and does not carry the same weight as research evidence systematically gathered. But such clinical evidence has been accumulated recently and deserves to be looked at carefully.

The response of white professionals to admissions policies by colleges and universities that are designed to reserve space for members of previously excluded racial populations in the first-year classes of professional schools is a case in point. The opposition to such practices indicates that talented and educated blacks are not being given access to privilege and power "at a rate comparable to or, in some situations, exceeding that of whites with equivalent qualifications" as

Professor Wilson claims. The opposition to special minority admissions programs is led by white professionals, not white hard-hat or blue-collar workers. This is further clinical evidence that race is not irrelevant and has not declined in significance for talented and educated blacks.

COUNTERHYPOTHESIS

Actually, I would like to introduce a counterhypothesis that the significance of race is increasing especially for middle-class blacks who, because of school desegregation and affirmative action and other integration programs, are coming into direct contact with whites for the first time for extended interaction.

My case studies of black families who have moved into racially integrated neighborhoods and racially integrated work situations indicate that race for some of these pioneers is a consuming experience. They seldom can get away from it. When special opportunities are created, such as in the admissions programs, the minorities who take advantage of them must constantly prove themselves. When a middle-class black has been accepted as Sanford Allen was in the Philharmonic, the issue then shifts to whether or not one is being used as a symbol. Try as hard as they may, middle-class blacks, especially middle-class blacks in racially integrated situations at this period in American history, are almost obsessed with race. Many have experienced this adaptation especially in residential and work situations.

Any obsession, including obsession with race, is painful. Freedom is circumscribed and options are delimited not because of physical segregation but because of the psychological situation. So painful is the experience of racial obses-

sion that two extreme reactions are likely to occur. Middle-class blacks may attempt to deal with the obsession by capitulation—that is, by assuming everything is race-related, that all whites are racists, and that all events and circumstances must be evaluated first in terms of their racial implications. The other adaptation is denial, believing that race is irrelevant and insignificant even when there is clear and present evidence that is not. This is one of the personal consequences of a racist society for the oppressed as the old separatist system begins to crumble. The people who most severely experience the pain of dislocation due to the changing times are the racial minorities who are talented and educated and integrated, not those who are impoverished and isolated.

POSTSCRIPT

Is Racial Oppression Declining in America?

One theme running through Charles V. Willie's argument is that of black emotional suffering. He cites evidence that suggests that blacks *perceive* themselves as victims of white oppression. A logician would pounce on that. A *perception* of oppression does not by itself prove the *existence* of oppression. Whatever its logical difficulties, however, Willie's argument is buttressed by reports that "racism is on the rise" (*Time*, February 2, 1987). On the other hand, Wilson presents a strong argument that the trends in race relations are moving in the right direction.

The debate over the basic causes of inequalities between blacks and whites continues among black scholars and leaders. In 1978 William Julius Wilson wrote *The Declining Significance of Race* (University of Chicago Press), which launched the debate. Somewhat earlier, Nathan Glazer argued that the problems faced by blacks and other minorities were due to the effects of past not present discrimination (*Affirmative Discrimination: Ethnic Inequality and Public Policy*, Basic Books, 1975). The black whose works most challenge civil rights leaders is Thomas Sowell. In *Markets and Minorities* (Basic Books, 1981) he argued that blacks should take responsibility for their own success. In *Civil Rights: Rhetoric or Reality?* (Morrow 1984) he chides the civil rights movement. He calls on black leaders to stop asking for special treatment and instead challenge blacks to fight for basic rights, not entitlements. For a contrary view, look at Charles V. Willie's *Race, Ethnicity, and Socioeconomic Status: A Theoretical Analysis of Their Interrelationship* (General Hall, 1983).

For a dialogue that reveals the gulf between the perceptions of blacks and whites—or, between some blacks and some whites—see Margaret Mead and James Baldwin in *A Rap on Race* (Lippincott, 1971). At one point Mead accuses Baldwin of "going back into the past." Baldwin answers: "When I go downstairs out of this building I can be murdered for trying to get a cab. That is not the past. That's the present." For a black perspective that is sharply opposed to Baldwin's, see Thomas Sowell's *Ethnic America: A History* (Basic Books, 1981). A thoughtful exchange appeared in the *New York Times Magazine* on October 9, 1980; see "The Black Plight: Race or Class? A Debate Between Kenneth B. Clark and Carl Gershman," p. 22. For a history of racial oppression, see *Oppression: A Socio-History of Black-White Relations in America* (Nelson-Hall, 1984), by Jonathan H. Turner et al.

ISSUE 9

Is Affirmative Action Reverse Discrimination?

YES: Glenn C. Loury, from "Beyond Civil Rights," *The New Republic* (October 7, 1985)

NO: Herman Schwartz, from "In Defense of Affirmative Action," *Dissent* (Fall 1984)

ISSUE SUMMARY

YES: Harvard professor Glenn C. Loury contends that insistence on "ill-suited" civil rights strategies makes it impossible for blacks to achieve full equality in American society.
NO: Law professor Herman Schwartz argues that we must somehow undo the cruel consequences of racism that still plague our society and its victims.

In America, equality is a political principle as basic as liberty. "All men are created equal" is the most famous phrase in the Declaration of Independence. More than half a century later, Alexis de Tocqueville examined democracy in America and concluded that its most essential ingredient was the equality of condition. Today we know that the "equality of condition" that de Tocqueville perceived did not exist for women, blacks, American Indians, and other racial minorities, nor for other disadvantaged social classes. Nevertheless, the ideal persisted. When slavery was abolished after the Civil War, the Constitution's newly ratified Fourteenth Amendment proclaimed: "No State shall . . . deny to any person within its jurisdiction the equal protection of the laws."

Equality has been a long time coming. For nearly a century after the abolition of slavery, American blacks were denied equal protection by law in some states and by social practice nearly everywhere. One-third of the states and the nation's capital either permitted or compelled racially segregated schools, and segregation was achieved elsewhere through housing policy and social behavior. In 1954 the Supreme Court reversed a fifty-eight-year-old standard that had found "separate but equal" schools compatible with equal protection of the law. A unanimous Court in *Brown v. Board of Education* held that separate is *not* equal for the members of the discriminated-against group when the segregation "generates a feeling of inferiority as to their status in the community that may affect their hearts and minds in a way unlikely ever to be undone." The 1954 ruling on public elementary education has been extended to other areas of both governmental and private conduct, including housing and employment.

Even if judicial decisions and congressional statutes could end all segregation and racial discrimination, would we have achieved equality—or simply perpetuated the *status quo?* The black unemployment rate today is more than twice that of whites. Disproportionately higher numbers of blacks experience poverty, brutality, broken homes, physical and mental illness, and early death, while disproportionately lower numbers of them have reached positions of affluence and prestige. It seems likely that much of this *de facto* inequality results from three hundred years of slavery and segregation. If we do no more than to cease this ill-treatment, have we done enough to end the injustices? No, say the proponents of "affirmative action."

The Supreme Court has considered the merits of affirmative action in four major cases: *Regents of the University of California v. Bakke* (1978), *United Steelworkers of America v. Weber* (1979), *Fullilove v. Klutznik* (1980), and *Firefighters v. Stotts* (1984). In the *Bakke* decision, a five-to-four majority agreed that Bakke, the white applicant to the medical school, had been wrongly excluded due to the school's affirmative action policy, but the majority did not agree that admission policies must be completely "color-blind." Indeed, Justice Lewis Powell, whose opinion seemed to hold the balance in the case, specifically affirmed that race may be taken into account in considering a candidate's qualifications. In the *Weber* case, a five-to-two majority upheld an agreement between an aluminum plant and a union to establish a quota for blacks in admitting applicants to a special training program. In *Fullilove v. Klutznik,* a six-to-three majority upheld the constitutionality of a federal public works program that required ten percent of spending be reserved for minority contractors.

The above decisions gave Supreme Court endorsement to the principle of race-conscious remedies. But in *Memphis Firefighters v. Stotts* (1984) and *Wygant v. Jackson Board of Education* (1986) the Court seemed to retreat from that view. In *Stotts* it ruled that federal courts may not order the firing of white employees who have more seniority than blacks simply for the purpose of saving the jobs of newly hired blacks during a period of layoffs. In *Wygant* it ruled that a Michigan school board's policy of laying off white teachers before minority-group teachers was unconstitutional.

But in July of 1986 the Court twice again endorsed affirmative action policies. In *Local 93 v. City of Cleveland*, it held that local courts can approve settlements that involve the preferential hiring of blacks, and in *Local 28 v. Equal Employment Opportunity Commission*, it approved a lower court order requiring a union local to hire a fixed quota of blacks by 1987.

In the following selections, Professor Loury and Professor Schwartz debate the merits of affirmative action. In Loury's view, affirmative action only ends up demoralizing the people it was meant to serve, depriving them of a sense of accomplishment, while Schwartz maintains that it is an essential means of undoing the effects of racism in America.

YES

Glenn C. Loury

BEYOND CIVIL RIGHTS

There is today a great deal of serious discussion among black Americans concerning the problems confronting them. Many, if not most, people now concede that not all problems of blacks are due to discrimination, and that they cannot be remedied through civil rights strategies or racial politics. I would go even further: using civil rights strategies to address problems to which they are ill-suited thwarts more direct and effective action. Indeed, the broad application of these strategies to every case of differential achievement between blacks and whites threatens to make it impossible for blacks to achieve full equality in American society.

The civil rights approach has two essential aspects: first, the cause of a particular socioeconomic disparity is identified as a racial discrimination; and second, advocates seek such remedies for the disparity as the courts and administrative agencies provide under the law.

There are fundamental limitations on this approach deriving from our liberal political heritage. What can this strategy do about those important contractual relationships that profoundly affect one's social and economic status but in which racial discrimination is routinely practiced? Choice of marital partner is an obvious example. People discriminate here by race with a vengeance. A black woman does not have an opportunity equal to that of a white woman to become the wife of a given white man. Since white men are on the whole better off financially than black men, this racial inequality of opportunity has substantial monetary costs to black women. Yet surely it is to be hoped that the choice of husband or wife will always be beyond the reach of the law.

The example is not facetious. All sorts of voluntary associations—neighborhoods, friends, business partnerships—are the result of choices often influenced by racial criteria, but which lie beyond the reach of civil rights laws. A fair housing law cannot prevent a disgruntled white resident from moving away if his neighborhood becomes predominantly or even partly black. Busing for desegregation cannot prevent unhappy parents from sending their children to private schools. Withdrawal of university support

From Glenn C. Loury, "Beyond Civil Rights," *The New Republic* (October 7, 1985). Copyright © 1985 by The New Republic, Inc. Reprinted by permission of *The New Republic*.

for student clubs with discriminatory selection rules cannot prevent student cliques from forming along racial lines. And a vast majority of Americans would have it no other way.

As a result, the nondiscrimination mandate has not been allowed to interfere much with personal, private, and intimately social intercourse. Yet such exclusive social connections along group lines have important economic consequences. An extensive literature in economics and sociology documents the crucial importance of family and community background in determining a child's later success in life. Lacking the right "networks," blacks with the same innate abilities as whites wind up less successful. And the elimination of racial discrimination in the economic sphere—but not in patterns of social attachment—will probably not be enough to make up the difference. There are thus elemental limits on what one can hope to achieve through the application of civil rights strategies to what must of necessity be a restricted domain of personal interactions.

The civil rights strategy has generally been restricted to the domain of impersonal, public, and economic transactions such as jobs, credit, and housing. Even in these areas, the efficacy of this strategy can be questioned. The lagging economic condition of blacks is due in significant part to the nature of social life *within* poor black communities. After two decades of civil rights efforts, more than three-fourths of children in some inner-city ghettos are born out of wedlock; black high school dropout rates hover near 50 percent in Chicago and Detroit; two-fifths of murder victims in the country are blacks killed by other blacks; fewer black women graduate from college than give birth while in high school; more than two in five black children are dependent on public assistance. White America's lack of respect for blacks' civil rights cannot be blamed for all these sorry facts. This is not to deny that, in some basic sense, most of these difficulties are related to our history of racial oppression, but only to say that these problems have taken on a life of their own, and cannot be effectively reversed by civil rights policies.

Higher education is a case in point. In the not too distant past, blacks, Asians, and women faced severe obstacles to attending or teaching at American colleges and universities, especially at the most prestigious institutions. Even after black scholars studied at the great institutions, their only possibilities for employment were at the historically black colleges, where they faced large teaching loads and burdensome administrative duties. Their accomplishments were often acknowledged by their white peers only grudgingly, if at all.

Today opportunities for advanced education and academic careers for blacks abound. Major universities throughout the country are constantly searching for qualified black candidates to hire as professors, or to admit to study. Most state colleges and universities near black population centers have made a concerted effort to reach those in the inner city. Almost all institutions of higher learning admit blacks with lower grades or test scores than white students. There are special programs funded by private foundations to help blacks prepare for advanced study in medicine, economics, engineering, public policy, law, and other fields.

Yet, with all these opportunities (and despite improvement in some areas), the number of blacks advancing in the academic world is distressingly low. The percentage of college students who are black, after rising throughout the 1970s, has actually begun to decline. And though the proportion of doctorates granted to blacks has risen slightly over the last decade, a majority of black doctorates are still earned in the field of education. Despite constant pressure to hire black professors and strenuous efforts to recruit them, the percentage of blacks on elite university faculties has remained constant or fallen in the past decade.

Meanwhile, other groups traditionally excluded are making impressive gains. Asian-Americans, though less than two percent of the population, make up 6.6 percent of U.S. scientists with doctorates; they constitute 7.5 percent of the students at Yale, and nine percent at Stanford. The proportion of doctorates going to women has risen from less than one-seventh to nearly one-third in the last decade. Less than two percent of Harvard professors at all ranks are black, but more than 25 percent are women.

Now, it is entirely possible that blacks experience discrimination at these institutions. But as anyone who has spent time in an elite university community knows, these institutions are not racist in character, nor do they deny opportunities to blacks with outstanding qualifications. The case can be made that just the opposite is true—that these institutions are so anxious to raise the number of blacks in their ranks that they overlook deficiencies when making admissions or appointment decisions involving blacks.

One obvious reason for skepticism about discrimination as the cause of the problem here is the relatively poor academic performance of black high school and college students. Black performance on standardized college admissions test, though improving, still lags far behind whites. In 1982 there were only 205 blacks in the entire country who scored above 700 on the math component of the SAT. And, as Robert Klitgaard shows convincingly in his book *Choosing Elites*, post-admissions college performance by black students is less than that of whites, even when controlling for differences in high school grades and SAT scores. These differences in academic performance are not just limited to poor blacks, or to high school students. On the SAT exam, blacks from families with incomes in excess of $50,000 per year still scored 60 to 80 points below comparable whites. On the 1982 Graduate Record Exam, the gap between black and white students' average scores on the mathematics component of this test was 171 points. According to Klitgaard, black students entering law school in the late 1970s had median scores on the LSAT at the eighth percentile of all students' scores.

Such substantial differences in educational results are clearly a matter of great concern. Arguably, the government should be actively seeking to attenuate them. But it seems equally clear that this is not a civil rights matter that can be reversed by seeking out and changing someone's discriminatory behavior. Moreover, it is possible that great harm will be done if the problem is defined and pursued in those terms.

Take the controversy over the racial quotas at the Boston Latin School, the pride and joy of the city's public school system. It was founded before Harvard, in 1635, and it has been recognized ever since as a center of academic excellence. Boston Latin maintains its very high standards through a grueling program of study, including Latin, Greek, calculus, history, science, and the arts. Three hours of homework per night are typical. College admissions personnel acknowledge the excellence of this program; 95 percent of the class of 1985 will go to college.

The institution admits its students on the basis of their marks in primary school and performance on the Secondary School Admissions Test. In 1974, when Boston's public schools became subject to court-ordered desegregation, Judge Arthur Garrity considered closing Boston Latin, because the student population at the time was more than 90 percent white. In the end, a racial admissions quota was employed, requiring that 35 percent of the entering classes be black and Hispanic. Of the 2,245 students last year, over half were female, 57 percent white, 23 percent black, 14 percent Asian, and six percent Hispanic.

Historically the school has maintained standards through a policy of academic "survival of the fittest." Those who were unable to make it through the academic rigors simply transferred to another school. Thus, there has always been a high rate of attrition; it is now in the range of 30 percent to 40 percent. But today, unlike the pre-desegregation era, most of those who do not succeed at Boston Latin are minority students. Indeed, though approximately 35 percent of each entering class is black and Hispanic, only 16 percent of last year's senior class was. That is, for each non-Asian minority student who graduates from Latin, there is one who did not. The failure rate for whites is about half that. Some advocates of minority student interest have complained of discrimination, saying in effect that the school is not doing enough to assist those in academic difficulty. Yet surely one reason for

the poor performance of the black and Hispanic students is Judge Garrity's admissions quota. To be considered for admission, whites must score at the 70th percentile or higher on the admissions exam, while blacks and Hispanics need only score above the 50th percentile.

Recently Thomas Atkins, former general counsel of the NAACP, who has been representing the black plaintiffs in the Boston school desegregation lawsuit, which has been going on for ten years, proposed that the quota at Boston Latin be raised to roughly 50 percent black, 20 percent Hispanic and Asian, and 30 percent white—a reflection of the racial composition of the rest of Boston's public schools. Unless there were a significant increase in the size of the school, this could only be accomplished by doubling the number of blacks admitted while cutting white enrollment in half. This in turn, under plausible distributional assumptions, would require that the current difference of 20 points in the minimum test scores required of black and white students accepted be approximately doubled. Since the additional black students admitted would be less prepared than those admitted under the current quota, one could expect an even higher failure rate among minorities were this plan to be accepted. The likely consequence would be that more than three-fourths of those leaving Boston Latin without a degree would be blacks and Hispanics. It is also plausible to infer that such an action would profoundly alter, if not destroy, the academic climate in the school.

This is not simply an inappropriate use of civil rights methods, though it is surely that. It is an almost wanton moral surrender. By what logic of pedagogy can these students' difficulties be attributed to racism in view of the fact that the school system has been run by court order for over a decade? By what calculus of fairness can those claiming to be fighting for justice argue that outstanding white students, many from poor homes themselves (80 percent of Latin graduates require financial aid in college), should be denied the opportunity for this special education so that minority students who are not prepared for it may nonetheless enroll? Is there so little faith in the aptitude of the minority young people that the highest standards should not be held out for them? It would seem that the real problem here—a dearth of academically outstanding black high school students in Boston—is not amendable to rectification by court order.

Another example from the field of education illustrates the "opportunity costs" of the civil rights strategy. In 1977 the Ann Arbor public school system was sued by public interest lawyers on behalf of a group of black parents with children in the primary grades. The school system was accused of denying equal educational opportunity to these children. The problem was that the black students were not learning how to read at an acceptable rate, though the white youngsters were. The suit alleged that by failing to take into account in the teaching of reading to these children the fact that they spoke an identifiable, distinct dialect of the English language—Black English—the black students were denied equal educational opportunity. The lawsuit was successful.

As a result, in 1979 the court ordered that reading teachers in Ann Arbor be given special "sensitivity" training so that, while teaching standard English to these children, they might take into account the youngsters' culturally distinct patterns of speech. Ann Arbor's public school system has dutifully complied. A recent discussion of this case with local educators revealed that, as of six years after the initial court order, the disparity in reading achievement between blacks and whites in Ann Arbor persists at a level comparable to the one before the lawsuit was brought. It was their opinion that, though of enormous symbolic importance, the entire process had produced little in the way of positive educational impact on the students.

This is not intended as a condemnation of those who brought the suit, nor do I offer here any opinion on whether promotion of Black English is a good idea. What is of interest is the process by which the problem was defined, and out of which a remedy was sought. In effect, the parents of these children were approached by lawyers and educators active in civil rights, and urged to help their children learn to read by bringing this action. Literally thousands of hours went into conceiving and trying this case. Yet, in the end only a hollow, symbolic victory was won.

But it is quite possible that this line of attack on the problem caused other more viable strategies not to be pursued. For example, a campaign to tutor the first and second graders might have made an impact, giving them special attention and extra hours of study through the voluntary participation of those in Ann Arbor possessing the relevant skills. With roughly 35,000 students at the University of Michigan's Ann Arbor campus (a fair number of whom are black), it would have required that only a fraction of one percent of them spare an afternoon or evening once a week for there to be sufficient numbers to provide the needed services. There were at most only a few hundred poor black students in the primary grades experiencing reading difficulties. And, more than providing this needed aid for specific kids, such an undertaking would have helped to cultivate a more healthy relationship between the university and the town. It could have contributed to building a tradition of direct services that would be of more general value. But none of this happened, in part because the civil rights approach was almost reflexively embraced by the advocating parties concerned.

The danger to blacks of too broad a reliance on civil rights strategies can be subtle. It has become quite clear that affirmative action creates uncertain perceptions about the qualifications of those minorities who benefit from it. In an employment situation, for example, if it is known that different selection criteria are used for different races, and that the quality of performance on the job depends on how one did on the criteria of selection, then in the absence of other information, it is rational to expect lower performance from persons of the race that was preferentially favored in selection. Using race as a criterion of selection in employment, in other words, creates objective incentives for customers, coworkers, and others to take race into account after the employment decision has been made.

The broad use of race preference to treat all instances of "underrepresentation" also introduces uncertainty among the beneficiaries themselves. It undermines the ability of people confidently to assert, if only to themselves, that they are as good as their achievements would seem to suggest. It therefore undermines the extent to which the personal success of any one black can become the basis of guiding the behavior of other blacks. Fewer individuals in a group subject to such preferences return to their communities of origin to say, "I made it on my own, through hard work, self-application, and native ability, and so can you!" Moreover, it puts even the "best and brightest" of the favored group in the position of being supplicants of benevolent whites.

And this is not the end of the story. In order to defend such programs in the political arena—especially at the elite institutions—it becomes necessary to argue that almost no blacks could reach these heights without special favors. When there is internal disagreement among black intellectuals, for example, about the merits of affirmative action, critics of the policy are often attacked as being disingenuous, since (it is said) they clearly owe their own prominence to the very policy they criticize. The specific circumstances of the individual do not matter in this, for it is presumed that *all* blacks, whether directly or indirectly, are indebted to civil rights activity for their achievements. The consequence is a kind of "socialization" of the individual's success. The individual's effort to claim achievement for himself (and thus to secure the autonomy and legitimacy needed to deviate from group consensus, should that seem appropriate) is perceived as a kind of betrayal. There is nothing wrong, of course, with acknowledging the debt all blacks owe to those who fought and beat Jim Crow. There is everything wrong with a group's most accomplished persons feeling that the celebration of their personal attainment represents betrayal of their fellows.

In his recent, highly esteemed comparative history of slavery, *Slavery and Social Death*, sociologist Orlando Patterson defines slavery as the "permanent, violent domination of natally alienated and generally dishonored persons." Today's policy debates frequently focus on (or perhaps more accurately, appropriate) the American slave experience, especially the violent character of the institution, its brutalization of the Africans, and its destructive effects on social life among the slaves. Less attention is paid nowadays to the *dishonored* condition of the slave, and by extension, of the freedman. For Patterson this dishonoring was crucial. He sees as a common feature of slavery wherever it has occurred the parasitic phenomenon whereby masters derive honor and standing from their power over slaves, and the slaves suffer an extreme marginality by virtue of having no social existence except that mediated by their masters. Patterson rejects the "property in people" definition of slavery, arguing that relations of respect and standing among persons are also crucial. But if this is so, it follows that emancipation—the ending of the master's property claim—is not of itself sufficient to convert a slave (or his descendant) into a genuinely equal citizen. There remains the intractable problem of overcoming the historically generated "lack of honor" of the freedman.

This problem, in my judgment, remains with us. Its eventual resolution is made less likely by blacks' broad, permanent reliance on racial preferences as remedies for academic or occupational under-performance. A central theme in Afro-American political and intellectual history is the demand for respect—the struggle to gain inclusion within the civic community, to become coequal participants in the national enterprise. This is, of course, a problem that all immigrant groups also faced, and that most have overcome. But here, unlike some other areas of social life, it seems that the black population's slave origins, subsequent racist exclusion, and continued dependence on special favors from the majority uniquely exacerbates the problem.

Blacks continue to seek the respect of their fellow Americans. And yet it becomes increasingly clear that, to do so, black Americans cannot substitute judicial and legislative decree for what is to be won through the outstanding achievements of individual black persons. That is, neither the pity, nor the guilt, nor the coerced acquiescence in one's demands—all of which have been amply available to blacks over the last two decades—is sufficient. *For what ultimately is being sought is the freely conveyed respect of one's peers.* Assigning prestigious positions so as to secure a proper racial balance—this is a permanent, broadly practiced policy—seems fundamentally inconsistent with the attainment of this goal. It is a truth worth noting that not everything of value can be redistributed.

If in the psychological calculus by which people determine their satisfaction such status considerations of honor, dignity, and respect are important, then this observation places basic limits on the extent to which public policy can bring about genuine equality. This is especially so with respect to the policy of racially preferential treatment, because its use to "equalize" can actually destroy the good that is being sought on behalf of those initially unequal. It would seem that, where the high regard of others is being sought, there is no substitute for what is to be won through the unaided accomplishments of individual persons.

NO

Herman Schwartz

IN DEFENSE OF AFFIRMATIVE ACTION

The Reagan administration's assault on the rights of minorities and women has focused on the existing policy of affirmative action. This strategy may be shrewd politics but it is mean-spirited morally and insupportable legally. . . .

Affirmative action has been defined as "a public or private program designed to equalize hiring and admission opportunities for historically disadvantaged groups by taking into consideration those very characteristics which have been used to deny them equal treatment." The controversy swirls primarily around the use of numerical goals and timetables for hiring or promotion, for university admissions, and for other benefits. It is fueled by the powerful strain of individualism that runs through American history and belief.

It is a hard issue, about which reasonable people can differ. Insofar as affirmative action is designed to compensate the disadvantaged for past racism, sexism, and other discrimination, many understandably believe that today's society should not have to pay for their ancestors' sins. But somehow we must undo the cruel consequences of the racism and sexism that still plague us, both for the sake of the victims and to end the enormous human waste that costs society so much. Civil Rights Commission Chairman Pendleton has conceded that discrimination is not only still with us but is, as he put it, "rampant." As recently as January 1984, the dean of faculty at Amherst College wrote in the *New York Times:*

> In my contacts with a considerable range of academic institutions, I have become aware of pervasive residues of racism and sexism, even among those whose intentions and conscious beliefs are entirely nondiscriminatory. Indeed, I believe most of us are afflicted with such residues. Beyond the wrongs of the past are the wrongs of the present. Most discriminatory habits in academia are nonactionable; affirmative action goals are our only instrument for focusing sustained attention.

The plight of black America not only remains grave, but in many respects, it is getting worse. The black unemployment rate—21 percent in early 1983— is double that for whites and the gap continues to increase. For black

From *Dissent* (Fall 1984). Excerpt from Herman Schwartz, "In Defense of Affirmative Action," *Minority Report*, ed. Leslie Dunbar (Pantheon Books, 1984). Copyright © 1984 by Herman Schwartz. Reprinted by permission of Pantheon Books, a division of Random House, Inc

20- to 24-year-old males, the rate—an awful 30 percent—is almost triple that for whites; for black teenagers the rate approaches 50 percent. More than half of all black children under three years of age live in homes below the poverty line. The gap between white and black family income, which prior to the '70s had narrowed a bit, has steadily edged wider, so that black-family income is now only 55 percent of that of whites. Only 3 percent of the nation's lawyers and doctors are black and only 4 percent of its managers, but over 50 percent of its maids and garbage collectors. Black life expectancy is about six years less than that of whites; the black infant mortality rate is nearly double.

Although the situation for women, of all races, is not as bad, the average earnings of women still, at most, are only two-thirds of those of their male counterparts. And the economic condition of black women, who now head 41 percent of the 6.4 million black families, is particularly bad; a recent Wellesley study found that black women are not only suffering in the labor market, but they receive substantially less public assistance and child support than white women. The economic condition of female household heads of any race is just as deplorable: 90 percent of the 4 million single-parent homes are headed by women, and more than half are below the poverty line. Bureau of Labor Statistics data reveal that in 1983 women actually earned *less* than two-thirds of their male counterparts' salaries, and black women earned only 84 percent of the white female incomes. In his 1984 State of the Union address, President Reagan claimed dramatic gains for women during the 1983 recovery. A *Washington Post* analysis the next day charitably described his claims as "overstated," noting that the Bureau of Labor Statistics reports (on which the president relied) showed that "there was no breakthrough. The new jobs which the president cited included many in sales and office work, where women have always found work" and are paid little.

We must close these gaps so that we do not remain two nations, divided by race and gender. Although no one strategy can overcome the results of centuries of inequity, the use of goals and timetables in hiring and other benefit distribution programs has helped to make modest improvements. Studies in 1983 show, for example, that from 1974 to 1980 minority employment with employers subject to federal affirmative action requirements rose 20 percent, almost twice the increase elsewhere. Employment of women by covered contractors rose 15 percent, but only 2 percent among others. The number of black police officers nationwide rose from 24,000 in 1970 to 43,500 in 1980; that kind of increase in Detroit produced a sharp decline in citizen hostility toward the police and a concomitant increase in police efficiency. There were also large jumps in minority and female employment among firefighters, and sheet metal and electrical workers.

Few other remedies work as well or as quickly. As the New York City Corporation Counsel told the Supreme Court in the *Fullilove* case about the construction industry (before Mayor Edward Koch decided that affirmative action was an "abomination"), "less drastic means of attempting to eradicate and remedy discrimination have been attempted repeatedly and continuously over the past decade and a half. They have all failed."

What, then, is the basis for the assault on affirmative action?

Apart from the obvious political expediency and ideological reflex of this administration's unvarying conclusion that the "haves" deserve government help and the "have-nots" don't, President Reagan and his allies present two related arguments: (1) hiring and other distributional decisions should be made solely on the basis of individual merit; (2) racial preferences are always evil and will take us back to *Plessy vs. Ferguson* and worse.

Quoting Dr. Martin Luther King Jr., Thurgood Marshall, and Roy Wilkins to support the claim that anything other than total race neutrality is "discriminatory," Assistant Attorney General Reynolds warns that race consciousness will "creat[e] . . . a racial spoils system in America," "stifle the creative spirit," erect artificial barriers, and divide the society. It is, he says, unconstitutional, unlawful, and immoral.

Midge Decter, writing in the *Wall Street Journal* a few years ago, sympathized with black and female beneficiaries of affirmative action programs for the "self-doubts" and loss of "self-regard" that she is sure they suffer, "spiritually speaking," for their "unearned special privileges."

Whenever we take race into account to hand out benefits, declares Linda Chavez, the new executive director of the Reagan Civil Rights Commission, we "discriminate," "destroy[ing] the sense of self."

The legal position was stated by Morris Abram, in explaining why the reshaped Commission hastened to do Reagan's bidding at its very first meeting by withdrawing prior Commission approval of goals and timetables:

> I do not need any further study of a principle that comes from the basic bedrock of the Constitution, in which the words say that every person in the land shall be entitled to the equal protection of the law. Equal means equal. Equal does not mean you have separate lists of blacks and whites for promotion, any more than you have separate accommodations for blacks and whites for eating. Nothing will ultimately divide a society more than this kind of preference and this kind of reverse discrimination.

In short, any form of race preference is equivalent to racism.

All of this represents a nadir of "Newspeak," all too appropriate for this administration in Orwell's year. For it has not only persistently fought to curtail minority and women's rights in many contexts, but it has used "separate lists" based on color, sex, and ethnic origin whenever politically or otherwise useful.

For example, does anyone believe that blacks like Civil Rights Commission Chairman Clarence Pendleton or Equal Employment Opportunities Commission Chairman Clarence Thomas were picked because of the color of their eyes? Or that Linda Chavez Gersten was made the new executive director for reasons having nothing to do with the fact that her maiden and professional surname is Chavez?

Perhaps the most prominent recent example of affirmative action is President Reagan's selection of Sandra Day O'Connor for the Supreme Court. Obviously, she was on a "separate list," because on any unitary list this obscure lower-court state judge, with no federal experience and no national reputation, would never have come to mind as a plausible choice for the highest court. (Incidentally, despite Ms. Decter's, Mr. Reynolds's, and Ms. Chavez's concern about the loss of "self-regard" suffered by beneficiaries of such preferences, "spiritually speaking" Justice O'Connor seems to be bearing her loss and spiritual pain quite easily.) And, like so many other beneficiaries of affirmative action given an opportunity that would otherwise be unavailable, she may perform well.

This is not to say that Reagan should not have chosen a woman. The appointment ended decades of shameful discrimination against women lawyers, discrimination still practiced by Reagan where the lower courts are concerned, since he has appointed very few female federal judges apart from Justice O'Connor—of 123 judgeships, Reagan has appointed no women to the courts of appeals and only 10 to the district benches. Of these judgeships, 86 percent went to white males. But the choice of Sandra O'Connor can be explained and justified only by the use of affirmative action and a separate list, not by some notion of neutral "individual merit" on a single list.

But is affirmative action constitutional and legal? Is its legal status, as Mr. Abram claims, so clear by virtue of principles drawn from the "basic bedrock of the Constitution" that no "further study" is necessary?

Yes, but not in the direction that he and this administration want to go. Affirmative action is indisputably constitutional. Not once but many times the Supreme Court has upheld the legality of considering race to remedy the wrongs of prejudice and discrimination. In 1977, for example, in *United Jewish Organizations vs. Carey*, the Supreme Court upheld a New York statute that "deliberately increased the nonwhite majorities in certain districts in order to enhance the opportunity for election of nonwhite representatives from those districts," even if it disadvan-

taged certain white Jewish communities. Three members of the Court including Justice Rehnquist explained that "no racial slur or stigma with respect to whites or any other race" was involved. In the *Bakke* case, five members of the Court upheld the constitutionality of a state's favorable consideration of race as a factor in university admissions, four members would have sustained a fixed 16 percent quota. In *United Steelworkers of America vs. Weber*, a 5:2 majority held that private employers could set up a quota system with separate lists for selecting trainees for a newly created craft program. In *Fullilove vs. Klutznick*, six members of the Court led by Chief Justice Burger unequivocally upheld a congressional setaside of 10 percent for minority contractors on federal public works programs.

All members of the present Court except for Justice O'Connor have passed on affirmative action in one or more of these four cases, and each has upheld it at one time or another. Although the decisions have been based on varying grounds, with many differing opinions, the legal consequence is clear: affirmative action is lawful under both the Constitution and the statutes. To nail the point home, the Court in January 1984 not once but *twice* rejected the Justice Department's effort to get it to reconsider the issue where affirmative action hiring plans are adopted by governmental bodies (the Detroit Police Department and the New York State Corrections system), an issue left open in *Weber*, which had involved a private employer.

The same result obtains on the lower-court levels. Despite the persistent efforts of Reagan's Justice Department, all the courts of appeals have unanimously and repeatedly continued to sustain hiring quotas.

Nor is this anything new. Mr. Reynolds told an audience of prelaw students in January 1984 that the Fourteenth Amendment was intended to bar taking race into account for any purpose at all, and to ensure race neutrality. "That was why we fought the Civil War," he once told the *New York Times*. If so, he knows something that the members of the 1865–66 Congress, who adopted that amendment and fought the war, did not.

Less than a month after Congress approved the Fourteenth Amendment in 1866 the very same Congress enacted eight laws exclusively for the freedman, granting preferential benefits regarding land, education, banking facilities, hospitals, and more. No comparable programs existed or were established for whites. And that Congress knew what it was doing. The racial preferences involved in those programs were vigorously debated with a vocal minority led by President Andrew Johnson, who argued that the preferences wrongly discriminated against whites.

All these governmental actions reflect the obvious point that, as Justice Harry Blackmun has said, "in order to get beyond racism, we must first take account of race. There is no other way." Warren Burger, our very conservative chief justice, had made the point even clearer in the prophetic commentary on this administration's efforts to get the courts to ignore race when trying to remedy the ravages of past discrimination. Striking down in 1971 a North Carolina statute that barred considerations of race in school assignments, the chief justice said:

> The statute exploits an apparently neutral form to control school assignments' plans by directing that they be "color blind"; *that requirement, against the background of segregation, would render illusory the promise of Brown.* Just as the race of students must be considered in determining whether a constitutional violation has occurred so also must race be considered in formulating a remedy... *[color blindness] would deprive school authorities of the one tool [race consideration] absolutely essential to fulfillment of their constitutional obligation to eliminate existing dual school systems. . . .* [Emphasis added.]

But what of the morality of affirmative action? Does it amount to discrimination? Is it true, as Brian Weber's lawyer argued before the Supreme Court, that "you can't avoid discrimination by discriminating"? Will racially influenced hiring take us back to *Plessy vs. Ferguson*, as Pendleton and Reynolds assert? Were Martin Luther King, Jr., Thurgood Marshall, Roy Wilkins, and other black leaders against it?

Hardly. Indeed, it is hard to contain one's outrage at this perversion of what Dr. King, Justice Marshall, and others have said, at this manipulation of their often sorrow-laden eloquence, in order to deny a handful of jobs, school admissions, and other necessities for a decent life to a few disadvantaged blacks out of the many who still suffer from discrimination and would have few opportunities otherwise.

No one can honestly equate a remedial preference for a disadvantaged (and qualified) minority member with the brutality inflicted on blacks and other minorities by Jim Crow laws and practices. The preference may take away some benefits from some white men, but none of them is being beaten, lynched, denied the right to use a bathroom, a place to sleep or eat, being forced to take the dirtiest jobs or denied any work at all, forced to attend dilapidated and mind-killing schools, subjected to brutally unequal justice, or stigmatized as an inferior being.

Setting aside, after proof of discrimination, a few places a year for qualified minorities out of hundreds and perhaps thousands of employees, as in the Kaiser plant in the *Weber* case, or 16 medical-school places out of 100 as in *Bakke*, or 10 percent of federal public work contracts as in *Fullilove*, or even 50 percent of new hires for a few years as in some employment cases—this has nothing in common with the racism that was inflicted on helpless minorities, and it is a shameful insult to the memory of the tragic victims to lump together the two.

This administration claims that it does favor "affirmative action" of a kind: "employers should seek out and train minorities," Linda Chavez told a *Washington Post* interviewer. Apart from the preference involved in setting aside money for "seeking out" and "training" minorities (would this include preference in training programs like the *Weber* plan, whose legality Mr. Reynolds said was "wrongly decided"?), the proposed remedy is ineffectual—it just doesn't work. As the "old" Civil Rights Commission had reported, "By the end of the 1960s, enforcement officials realized that discernible indicators of progress were needed." Consequently, "goals and timetables" came into use. . . .

There are indeed problems with affirmative action, but not of the kind or magnitude that Messrs. Reynolds and Abram claim: problems about whether these programs work, whether they impose heavy burdens, how these burdens can be lightened, and the like. They are not the basis for charges that affirmative action is equivalent to racism and for perverting the words of Dr. King and others.

"Equal is equal" proclaims Morris Abram, and that's certainly true. But it is just as true that equal treatment of unequals perpetuates and aggravates inequality. And gross inequality is what we still have today. As William Coleman, secretary of transportation in the Ford administration, put it,

> For black Americans, racial equality is a tradition without a past. Perhaps, one day America will be color-blind. It takes an extraordinary ignorance of actual life in America today to believe that day has come. . . . [For blacks], there is another American "tradition"—one of slavery, segregation, bigotry, and injustice.

POSTSCRIPT

Is Affirmative Action Reverse Discrimination?

Much of the argument between Loury and Schwartz turns on the question of color blindness. To what extent should our laws be color-blind? During the 1950s and early 1960s, civil rights leaders were virtually unanimous on this point. "I have a dream," said Martin Luther King, "[that white and black people] will not be judged by the color of their skin but on the content of their character." This was the consensus view in 1963, but today Schwartz seems to be suggesting that the statement needs to be qualified. In order to *bring about* color blindness, it may be necessary to become temporarily color-conscious. But for how long? And is there a danger that this temporary color-consciousness may become a permanent policy?

Robert M. O'Neil, in *Discriminating Against Discrimination* (Indiana, 1975), studied preferential admission to universities and supported preferential treatment without racial quotas. Those critical of this distinction hold that preferential treatment necessarily implies racial quotas, or at least race-consciousness. Another area that requires officials to focus upon race is that of busing, a policy of which Lina A. Gragli's *Disaster by Decree* (Cornell, 1976) is highly critical. The focus of Allan P. Sindler's *Bakke, DeFunis, and Minority Admissions* (Longman, 1978) is on affirmative action in higher education. Thomas N. Dayment estimates that the differences between black and white earnings will require half a century to decrease substantially (see "Racial Equity or Racial Equality," *Demography*, vol. 17, 1980, pp. 379–393).

Whatever the Supreme Court says today or in the future, it will not be easy to lay to rest the issue of affirmative action. There are few issues on which opposing sides are more intransigent. It appears as if there is no satisfactory solution, and, at the moment, no compromise that can satisfy the passionate convictions on both issues.

PART 4

Political Economy

Are political power and economic power merged within a "power elite" that dominates the U.S. political system? The first issue in this part explores that debate. There are also two debates concerning public policy: Is the size of the American government creating problems? How should we assess the impact and efficacy of welfare programs? Finally, in the last issue in this part, we examine the political economy from a global perspective: Have the core capitalist countries developed by exploiting Third World countries, and thereby slowing their growth?

Is the U.S. Political System Dominated by Big Business?

Has American Government Become Too Big?

Does Welfare Do More Harm Than Good?

Do Capitalist Powers Hinder the Development of Third World Countries?

ISSUE 10

Is the U.S. Political System Dominated by Big Business?

YES: Charles E. Lindblom, from *Politics and Markets: The World's Political-Economic Systems* (Basic Books, 1977)

NO: David Vogel, from "The New Political Science of Corporate Power," *The Public Interest* (Spring 1987)

ISSUE SUMMARY

YES: Economist and political scientist Charles Lindblom claims that large business corporations exercise disproportionate sway over government, in violation of democracy.
NO: Professor David Vogel rejects the view that big business occupies a dominating position, and he sees big business as one interest among many that influence political decisions in the U.S. system.

Since the framing of the U.S. Constitution in 1787, there have been periodic charges that America is unduly influenced by wealthy financial interests. Richard Henry Lee, a signer of the Declaration of Independence, spoke for many Anti-Federalists, those who opposed ratification of the Constitution, when he warned that the proposed charter shifted power away from the people and into the hands of the "aristocrats" and "moneyites," those who "avariciously grasp at all power and property." Before the Civil War, Jacksonian Democrats denounced the eastern merchants and bankers who, they charged, were usurping the power of the people. After the Civil War, a number of radical parties and movements revived this theme of antielitism. The ferment—which was brought about by the rise of industrial monopolies, government corruption, and economic hardship for western farmers—culminated in the founding of the People's party at the beginning of the 1890s. The Populists, as they were more commonly called, wanted economic and political reforms aimed at transferring power away from the rich and back to "the plain people."

By the early 1900s the People's party had disintegrated, but many writers and activists have continued to echo the Populists' central thesis: that the U.S. democratic political system is in fact dominated by business elites. Socialists, communists, those on the political left, some on the political right, have all argued it or made it the premise of other arguments.

Yet the thesis has not gone unchallenged. During the 1950s and the early 1960s, many social scientists subscribed to the *pluralist* view of America. Pluralists admit that there are many influential elites in our society, and that is precisely their point: Because America contains so many groups, the pluralists argue, each group has a tendency to counterbalance the power of the others. Labor groups are often opposed to business groups; conservative interests challenge liberal interests, and vice versa; organized civil libertarians sometimes fight with groups that seek government-imposed bans on pornography or groups that demand tougher criminal laws. No single group can dominate the political system, or have a monopoly on power in our pluralist system. Pluralists were not comfortable with calling America a *democracy*, a word that has become invested with emotional connotations, but they did think that rule in America emanates from many centers, so they favored the word *polyarchy* (literally, "rule by many") to describe the operation of our system.

Among the leading pluralists of the 1950s was Charles E. Lindblom, an economist and political scientist. But Lindblom altered his views considerably over the course of the years, and in *Politics and Markets,* published in 1977 to considerable attention, Lindblom contends that corporate influence in all capitalist countries is so disproportionate that the political and social systems in those countries are *not* truly pluralist. Sections from that book are excerpted here. David Vogel, a business school professor, argues against Lindblom's contentions, and he maintains that the U.S. system is indeed pluralist.

YES

Charles E. Lindblom

POLITICS AND MARKETS

A key element of much democratic theory is the informed, active, rational participant, a point on which democratic theory can be suspected of being a form of wishful thinking. To John Stuart Mill, the first merit of ideal representative government is its contribution to the citizen's "advancement in intellect, in virtue, and in practical activity and efficiency." The second is that it ideally organized "the moral, intellectual, and active worth already existing, so as to operate with the greatest effect on public affairs."

Whether democracy, real or imaginable, has all or any of these virtues is problematic. Whether in any real-world instance popular control is in fact made highly effective is also problematic. All that we know about these systems to begin with is that their social machinery for the control of authority is of a particular and distinctive kind. To analyze this family of systems without begging the question by calling them what they may not be, we had better make use of another name for them and keep our wits about us. Following recent precedent, we shall call the controls "polyarchic," meaning rule by many, and a system that incorporates them a polyarchy rather than a democracy.*

POLYARCHY AS AN AUTHORITY SYSTEM

The core of polyarchy is a specific new pattern of behavior called for by a particular complex set of authoritative rules. Polyarchy is not a social system. Nor, strictly speaking, is it a political system. It is only part of a political system: a set of authoritative rules, together with certain patterns of political behavior that follow directly and indirectly from the existence of rules.

Just what are the core authoritative rules of polyarchy? They are rules that limit the struggle for authority, specifying a particular orderly and peaceful

*For convenience we will call the United States, the nations of Western Europe, and certain others polyarchies, just as many people call them democracies. Strictly speaking, however, polyarchy is no more than one system of social controls embedded in these nations. Strictly speaking, therefore, they contain polyarchy, they are not polyarchies.

From Charles E. Lindblom, *Politics and Markets* (Basic Books, 1977). Copyright © 1977 by Basic Books, Inc. Reprinted by permission of Basic Books, Inc., Publishers, New York. Notes omitted.

process to replace armed conflict, threat of force, and other crude contests. But, in that respect, they are like the rules of any other constitutional system, however undemocratic it may be. What is distinctive about a contest for authority* designed by polyarchal rules is that top authority is assigned in response to a minimized indication of citizens' wishes—that is, an election—an indication, moreover, in which any one citizen's vote is by some formula counted as equal to any other's. It is hard to imagine how the struggle for authority could be made simpler, more peaceful, or more egalitarian.

In all polyarchies citizens are authorized not only to choose their top leaders in government, but also to inform and misinform themselves, express themselves wisely or foolishly, and organize into political groups in order to decide how best to cast their votes and to influence others. They are also authorized to communicate their wishes to political leaders and in other ways influence them. In all polyarchies, these authorizations are to a significant degree effective. They are worth a great deal more than the paper they are written on. They are, however, not effective for all, nor equally effective, nor always effective. . . .

THE BUSINESSMAN AS PUBLIC OFFICIAL IN GOVERNMENT AND POLITICS

. . . Businessmen generally and corporate executives in particular take on a privileged role in government that is, it seems reasonable to say, unmatched by any leadership group other than government officials themselves.* Let us see, step by step, how this comes about. Every step in the analysis will refer to a familiar aspect of these systems, the im-

plications of which, taken together, have been overlooked by most of us.

Because public functions in the market system rest in the hands of businessmen, it follows that jobs, prices, production, growth, the standard of living, and the economic security of everyone all rest in their hands. Consequently, government officials cannot be indifferent to how well business performs its functions. Depression, inflation, or other economic distress can bring down a government. A major function of government, therefore, is to see to it that businessmen perform their tasks.

Every day about us we see abundant evidence of governmental concern with business performance. In the polyarchies, government responsibility for avoiding inflation and unemployment is a common issue in elections. In all market-oriented systems, a major concern of tax and monetary policy is their effects on business activity. In subsidies and other help to water, rail, highway, and air transport; in patent protection; in fair trade regulation; in tariff policy; in overseas trade promotion through foreign ministries; in subsidized research and development (recently conspicuous, the Concorde in the United Kingdom and France, the aerospace industry in the United States)—in countless ways governments in these systems recognize that businessmen need to be encouraged to perform.

*In contemporary thought, especially democratic thought, "privilege" often connotes something improper. That is not my intention in using the term. Webster says privilege is "a right or immunity granted as a peculiar benefit, advantage, or favor; esp.: one attached specif. to a position or an office," and something that is privileged is "not subject to the usual rules and penalties because of some special circumstance" (Webster's Seventh New Collegiate Dictionary [Springfield, Mass.: G. & C. Merriam]).

But take particular note of another familiar feature of these systems. Constitutional rules—especially the law of private property—specify that, although governments can forbid certain kinds of activity, they cannot command business to perform. They must induce rather than command. They must therefore offer benefits to businessmen in order to stimulate the required performance. The examples above are all examples of benefits offered, not of commands issued. . . .

What, then, is the list of necessary inducements? They are whatever businessmen need as a condition for performing the tasks that fall to them in a market system: income and wealth, deference, prestige, influence, power, and authority, among others. Every government in these systems accepts a responsibility to do what is necessary to assure profits high enough to maintain as a minimum employment and growth. If businessmen say, as they do, that they need tax offsets to induce investment, governments in all these systems seriously weigh the request, acknowledging that the tax concessions may indeed be necessary. In these systems such concessions are in fact granted. If corporation executives say that the chemical industries need help for research and development, governments will again acknowledge the probability that indeed they do and will commonly provide it. If corporate executives want to consult with government officials, including president or prime minister, they will be accommodated. Given the responsibilities of businessmen in these societies, it would be a foolish chief executive who would deny them consultation. If corporate executives ask, as they frequently do, for veto power over government appointments to regulatory positions, it will again be ac-

knowledged that such a concession may be necessary to induce business performance. All this is familiar. And we shall see below that governments sometimes offer to share their formal authority with corporate officials as a benefit offered to induce business performance.

In the eyes of government officials, therefore, businessmen do not appear simply as the representatives of a special interest, as representatives of interest groups do. They appear as functionaries performing functions that government officials regard as indispensable. When a government official asks himself whether business needs a tax reduction, he knows he is asking a question about the welfare of the whole society and not simply about a favor to a segment of the population, which is what is typically at stake when he asks himself whether he should respond to an interest group.

Any government official who understands the requirements of his position and the responsibilities that market-oriented systems throw on businessmen will therefore grant them a privileged position. He does not have to be bribed, duped, or pressured to do so. Nor does he have to be an uncritical admirer of businessmen to do so. He simply understands, as is plain to see, that public affairs in market-oriented systems are in the hands of two groups of leaders, government and business, who must collaborate and that, to make the system work government leadership must often defer to business leadership. Collaboration and deference between the two are at the heart of politics in such systems. Businessmen cannot be left knocking at the doors of the political systems, they must be invited in. . . .

Thus politics in market-oriented systems takes a peculiar turn, one largely ignored in conventional political science. To understand the peculiar character of politics in market-oriented systems requires, however, no conspiracy theory of politics, no theory of common social origins uniting government and business officials, no crude allegation of a power elite established by clandestine forces. Business simply needs inducements, hence a privileged position in government and politics, if it is to do its job.

Other Privileged Positions?

How might the thesis that businessmen occupy a privileged position—that they constitute a second set of major leaders in government and politics—be challenged? It can hardly be denied that business performance is required in market-oriented systems. Nor that it has to be induced rather than commanded. Nor that, consequently, government officials have to be solicitous in finding and offering appropriate inducements. Perhaps, however, other groups enjoy similar privilege for similar reason? It seems reasonable to suggest that labor leaders, who might be thought the most likely occupants of a similar privileged position, do not occupy one. They and their unions do not provide, we have already noted, essential services. Their function is instead to advance the segmental interests of workers. But workers themselves provide essential services, it might be replied. If they do not work, the whole productive system halts.

The plain fact, however, is that workers do work—without special inducement from government. Their livelihoods depend on it. Their position is quite different from that of the businessman, who has a dimension of choice. He will not risk capital, reputation, or the solvency of an enterprise in order to

undertake an entrepreneurial venture unless the conditions are favorable. The test of the difference is an obvious one. All over the world men work at ordinary jobs because they have no choice but to do so. But in many parts of the world the conditions that call forth entrepreneurial energy and venturesomeness are still lacking, and the energy and venturesomeness are therefore not forthcoming. The particular roles that businessmen are required to play in market-oriented systems they play well only when sufficiently indulged. . . .

Changing Privileges

The level and character of privilege that businessmen require as a condition of their satisfactory performance vary from time to time and place to place. All about us is conspicuous evidence that some older privileges have been withdrawn, even to the point of nationalizing some firms and industries. In many of the market-oriented systems, business enterprise is more heavily taxed than before. It is also subjected to increasing regulation on some scores—for example, regulation of industrial relations, monopoly, and now environmental pollution. Clearly businessmen have commonly demanded of government more indulgences than are actually necessary to motivate their required performances. As some of these indulgences have been taken away, their performance has not faltered.

On the other hand, the removal of some privileges appears to require the institution of offsetting new ones—for example, tax credits. Forty percent of net investments in manufacturing equipment in the United States in 1963 was estimated to be attributable to the investment tax credit of 1962. In the market-oriented systems, governments underwrite much of the cost of research and development for business. They also provide security to business enterprises through a variety of protections for monopoly, like fair trade legislation. In some industries, government shares or bears the risk of new plant construction by renting facilities to firms that do not want to construct their own. Half of the plant facilities of U.S. defense plants are provided by government. Governments also bail out failing enterprises with loans. . . .

Many of the new privileges, which offset some taken away, are not widely recognized to be such. Urban renewal, for example, comes to the aid of retailers, banks, theaters, public utilities, brokers, and builders. Highway development promotes a long list of industries including cement, automobiles, construction, petroleum, construction equipment, and trucking. But the ostensible purpose of urban renewal and highway development is not aid to business.

Conflicts Among Businessmen

On some demands—those pertaining to enterprise autonomy, private property, limited business taxation, and tax incentives, for example—business volitions are relatively homogeneous. On other demands, some businessmen want one kind of benefit; others want another. That businessmen disagree on such demands is not usually a barrier to their occupying a privileged position, for to give one kind of business a benefit is not necessarily to deprive another. On some issues, of course, privilege granted to one segment of the business community represents the withdrawal of a privilege from another. Large meat packers, for example, may press for inspection laws that, by raising the costs of small packers, give the large ones a competitive advantage. But it is possible for government officials to find an offsetting benefit to the small packers to compensate for the injury, if officials understand that redress is necessary.

MUTUAL ADJUSTMENT BETWEEN THE TWO GROUPS

So far we have stressed controls by businessmen over government. But of course controls go in both directions. In briefest outline the reciprocal controls look like the following:

Government exercises broad authority over business activities.

But the exercise of that authority is curbed and shaped by the concern of government officials for its possible adverse effects of business, since adverse effects can cause unemployment and other consequences that government officials are unwilling to accept.

In other areas of public policy, the authority of government is again curbed and shaped by concern for possible adverse effects on business.

Hence even the unspoken possibility of adversity for business operates as an all-pervasive constraint on government authority.

Mindful of government concern for business performance, businessmen, especially corporate executives, actively voice and negotiate demands on government, with both implicit threat of poor performance if their demands are not met.

For all these reasons, business officials are privileged not only with respect to the care with which government satisfies business needs in general but also in privileged roles as participants in policy deliberations in government.

At least hypothetically, government always has the option, if dissatisfied with business performance, of refusing further privilege and simply terminating private enterprise in a firm, industry or the entire system. Short of taking that course, however, government has to meet business needs as a condition of inducing business performance. . . .

In addition, business executives come to be admitted to circles of explicit negotiation, bargaining, and reciprocal persuasion, from which ordinary citizens are excluded. Other leaders are admitted—union and farm leaders and other interest-group representatives. In these consultations, however, corporate executives occupy a privileged position, since they and not the interest-group leaders are there mainly in their capacity as "public" officials.

It follows that evidence, which is abundant, of conflict between business and government—and of business defeats—is not evidence of lack of privilege. Knowing that they must have some privileges and knowing that government officials fully understand that simple fact, businessmen ask for a great deal. They also routinely protest any proposal to reduce any of their privileges. They are not highly motivated to try to understand their own needs. It might weaken them in governmental negotiations to do so. Hence they often predict dire consequences when a new regulation is imposed on them, yet thereafter quickly find ways to perform under it.

It appears that disputes between government and business are intense because of—not in spite of—their sharing the major leadership roles in the politico-economic order. Inevitably two separate yet cooperating groups of leaders will show hostility to each other. They will also invest some of their energies in outwitting each other, each trying to gain the upper hand. Conflict will always lie, however, within a range of dispute constrained by their understanding that they together constitute the necessary leadership for the system. They do not wish to destroy or seriously undermine the function of each other. . . .

BUSINESS AUTHORITY IN GOVERNMENT

The far edge of the privileged position of business is represented by actual grants of government authority to businessmen. Decades ago in the United States the right of eminent domain was granted to private utility corporations, conferring on them compulsory authority to acquire land for their operations. In this and other ways governments respond to demands with a formal or informal grant of authority to businessmen, cementing their privileged position in government.

Business groups that become established as clients of specific U.S. government agencies often win grants of informal authority. Examples are the civil contractors dealing with the Army Corps of Engineers, the Rural Electrification Administration, and the Small Business Administration, respectively. Their collaborations have been characterized as "joint government by public and private bodies."

Some of these grants are relatively explicit. The president of the United States grants authority to executives of regulated industries to veto appointments to regulatory agencies. Some are formal. Since 1933, the president, Cabinet members, and other high officials have met with the Business Council, composed of leading corporate executives. The federal government has also established between 1,000 and 2,000 business councils to consult with agencies on common policies—this in addition to about 4,000 particular to the Department of Agriculture. In addition, it invites corporation executives, while still active in and salaried by their own corporations, to serve as unpaid government officials.

In 1953, that practice was given a more permanent peacetime basis when the Business and Defense Services Administration was established. Of it, a congressional committee said:

> In operation, the organization arrangements of BDSA have effected a virtual abdication of administrative responsibility on the part of the Government officials in charge of the Department of Commerce in that their actions in many instances are but the automatic approval of decisions already made outside the Government in business and industry.

For less formal grants, the line between granting a rule of obedience, thus establishing an acceptance of authority, and yielding to the offers or threats of exchange is often a thin one. This is made by a report on consultations on New York city and state finance:

> One stumbling block to the [absorption of] $3 billion of New York City's short-term debt was resolved yesterday. . . . The one agreement reached . . . was on a demand from the investment community that the city sales tax be converted to a state sales tax. . . .

Under these circumstances, the "For years I thought what was good for our country was good for General Motors, and vice versa," spoken by a president of GM is easy to understand. However partisan they may be in fact, however un-critical about the coincidence of their own interests with broader public interests, businessmen do understand that they carry a public responsibility for discharging necessary public functions that other nongovernmental leaders do not carry. If they are, on the one hand, capable of gross abuse of that responsibility, they are, on the other hand, at least dimly aware of their special role as one of two groups that constitute a dual leadership in the market-oriented systems.

In a passage that could be taken as a summary comment on the line of analysis so far, Woodrow Wilson once wrote:

> The government of the United States at present is a foster-child of the special interests. It is not allowed to have a will of its own. It is told at every move: "Don't do that; you will interfere with our prosperity."

In these comments, Wilson is angry. He sees these characteristics of government as inexcusable. On that, opinions will differ. My point has been only to explain the fundamental mechanism by which a great degree of business control, unmatched by similar control exercised by any other group of citizens, comes to be exercised over government and to indicate why this is inevitable in all private enterprise systems if they are to be viable.

Again; businessmen do not get everything they want. But they get a great deal. And when they do not get enough, recession or stagnation is a consequence.

RIVAL CONTROLS

For all the reasons of the preceding chapter, privileged business controls are largely independent of the electoral controls of polyarchy. To be sure, the electorate in a polyarchy wants a high level of employment and other satisfying performance from businessmen. Its frequent passivity might be taken to imply an approval for many of the privileges of businessmen so long as business goes on producing. But the particular demands that businessmen make on government are communicated to government officials in ways other than through the electoral process and are largely independent of and often in conflict with the demands that the electorate makes. Many business demands represent a condition of business performance whether the electorate knows it or not, whether it cares or not, whether it approves or not. In their voting citizens may or may not give careful consideration to business demands. Nothing in the polyarchal process requires that they do. . . .

Another kind of evidence now appears to be emerging from the history of American reform efforts. A new group of historians believe they are finding evidence of a common pattern. Policy is changed in response to business controls and is then paraded as democratic reform. Meat inspection legislation, once thought the consequence of popular revulsion against the conditions revealed in Upton Sinclair's The Jungle, is now found in large part to be a consequence of the packing industry's desire for universally enforced standards to improve the quality reputation of American meat exports. Food and drug regulation was sought by pharmaceutical companies to limit the excesses of some manufacturers whose products and claims damaged the pharmaceutical industry as a whole. Forest conservation was sought by processors of lumber who wished to engage the U.S. government in the expenses of reforestation. Municipal reform was pushed by

businessmen who required improved municipal services. The Clayton Act and the Federal Trade Commission Act were urged on Congress by big businesses wishing to regulate their smaller competitors. Insurance of bank deposits, a reform of the depression of the 1930s, was inaugurated to draw deposits into the banks in order to make funds more easily available to business. To none of these reforms was popular demand an important contributor.

Whatever the sources of such reforms as these, there is for the United States an impressive record of reforms being turned sharply away from their ostensible polyarchically chosen purposes. The Fourteenth Amendment to the Constitution, intended for the protection of freed slaves, was for that purpose rendered ineffective for many years by judicial interpretation. Simultaneously it was made the foundation for corporate autonomy, based on the doctrine that the corporation is a "fictitious person" and therefore entitled to the protection specified in the amendment. The Sherman Act, ostensibly enacted to regulate industrial monopoly, was used to constrain unions rather than enterprises. It continued to be so used even after the Clayton Act explicitly exempted unions from its provisions. Regulatory policies generally are diverted from their ostensible purposes in order to meet many of the demands that businessmen can place upon government.

An oft-quoted statement from an earlier U.S. attorney general shows how business controls can work even when reforms are popularly demanded. Commenting on the new Interstate Commerce Commission, he said in a nice demonstration of his understanding of the political system:

It satisfies the popular clamor for a governmental supervision of railroads, at the same time that that supervision is almost entirely nominal. Further, the older such a Commission gets to be, the more inclined it will be found to take the business and railroad view of things. It thus becomes a sort of barrier between the railroad corporations and the people and a sort of protection against hasty and crude legislation hostile to railroad interests. . . . The part of wisdom is not to destroy the Commission but to utilize it.

As acknowledged [previously], businessmen do not win all they ask for. The point here is that business and polyarchal controls are largely independent of each other and are in conflict. The scope of polyarchy is consequently restricted.

COORDINATION OF THE RIVAL CONTROLS

The implications for polyarchy of this rivalry go much further. Conflict between electoral and privileged business controls seems much less apparent than would be expected if the two controls were wholly independent. Why do we not see more frequent electoral demands for, say, corporate reform, curbs on monopoly, income redistribution, or even central planning? The answer must be that the two controls are not genuinely independent of each other. They are coordinated in large degree.

I suggest that the coordination is accomplished largely by controls that bend polyarchy to accommodate business controls. The controls are exercised through interest-group, party, and electoral activity of businessmen, about which we have so far said almost nothing. We recognize these activities now not as the chief instruments of business influence over government but as processes for adapting polyarchal controls to privileged controls by businessmen. The proposition puts interest-group and electoral activity in a new light.

One of the conventional insensitivities of contemporary social science is revealed in scholarly works on interest groups. By some unthinking habit, many such works treat all interest groups as though on the same plane, and, in particular, they treat labor, business and farm groups as though operating at some parity with each other. Business interest-group activity, along with its other electoral activity, is only a supplement to its privileged position. And it is, we shall see, greatly more effective than any other interest-group and electoral activity of its ostensible rivals. It is a special case. That is not to say, however, that businessmen always win or even that they are unified in electoral and interest-group activity.

It is difficult to offer such propositions as we have been developing without appearing to allege conspiracy or subversion. I mean to do neither. Both the privileged controls in the hands of business and the additional controls businessmen exercise through their energetic participation in polyarchal politics are established, stable, and fundamental parts of government and politics in the systems called market-oriented polyarchy. Although these controls challenge and limit the effectiveness of popular control, they cannot on that account be deprecated as peripheral or as aberrations. Only in the light of democratic aspiration are these controls subversive; but these systems never have been highly democratic; and their polyarchal processes, which approximate democracy, are only a part of these systems.

BUSINESS PARTICIPATION IN POLYARCHY

It is not necessary to detail business activity in electoral politics: the frequency and intimacy of business consultation with government officials from prime minister or president down to lesser officials, the organization of business interest groups, business financing of political parties, and business public relations and propaganda. All of this is familiar and has often been described. Let us instead look for certain key phenomena.

The activities that businessmen undertake to capture polyarchal politics cannot always be distinguished from their privileged activities which are not dependent on polyarchal channels. But an analytic distinction is possible, and an empirically observable distinction is often easy. Corporate financing of political parties is clearly part of businessmen's participation in polyarchal processes. So, for example is the participation of business interest groups in legislative hearings.

No other group of citizens can compare with businessmen, even roughly, in effectiveness in the polyarchal process. How so? Because, unlike any other group of citizens, they can draw on the resources they command as public "officials" to support their activities in polyarchal politics.

To some degree, every public official inevitably uses his public position to advance his private or his partisan objectives in politics. Yet the law draws a distinction between a public official in his governmental role and the same man as candidate, interest-groups activist, or citizen. In the United States the president is expected to raise his campaign funds from private contributions and not from the government's treasury. Neither he nor other government officials freely use government funds and personnel for partisan objectives, even though they often find ways to evade constraints.

Not so with corporation executives. The funds that pass through their hands in their official capacities—that is, the proceeds from corporate sales—can, with little constraint, be thrown into party, interest-group, and electoral activity in pursuit of whatever objectives the corporate executives themselves choose. The ease with which executives can bring corporate assets to the support of these activities is a remarkable feature of politics in market-oriented polyarchies. It has no rationale in democratic theory. . . .

Funds for Businessmen in Polyarchal Politics

Corporate funds go to political campaigns and to parties, to lobbying and other forms of corporate communication with governmental officials, to entertainment and other factors for government officials, to political and institutional advertising in the mass media, to educational materials for the public schools, and to litigation designed to influence governmental policy or its enforcements.

We have no adequate figures on how much of their funds they allocate for these political activities, all of which overwhelm those of ordinary citizens. But there are a million corporations in the United States, 40,000 with at least 100 employees. Each of the largest of them takes in more receipts than most national governments. We also know that American businesses allocate roughly $60 billion per year to sales promotion, a large part of which is institutional advertising with a political content, like Exxon's "Energy for a strong America." On top of that are additional amounts available explicitly for politics. Hence the scale of corporate spending dwarfs political spending by all other groups. Something of the discrepancy is suggested by the fact that all campaign expenditures in 1972, a presidential election year, totaled only a half billion dollars.

In the 1972 presidential election, unions spent $8.5 million on activities on which organizations are required by law to report. In addition, they spent $4 million or $5 million on nonpartisan "get out the vote" activities. Thus, the total was roughly $13 million. Business groups reported spending only about $6 million. But since corporate contributions of most kinds were illegal, business contributions took the form of legal and illegal expenditures, often routed personally though corporate executives. One can only guess at their total. But we have to account for a grand total of campaign expenditures that year of nearly $500 million, of which the union contribution was only about $13.5 million. We have other clues. Some members of the President's Business Council are known to have contributed jointly over $1 million, officers and directors of five oil companies $1.5 million, officers and directors of the 25 largest defense contractors over $2 million, and NASA contractors over $1 million. On hundreds of other major business contributors, we have no record.

In 1964 union committees made contributions of less than $4 million, while a total of no more than 10,000 individuals, mostly from business, contributed $13.5 million. And in 1956, a year for which direct union-business comparisons are possible, it took the contributions of only 742 businessmen to match in amount the contribution of unions representing 17 million workers. If these figures begin to scratch the surface, they are enough to indicate the enormous discrepancy between business spending in politics and that of any other group, including labor.

Some years ago a House of Representatives committee estimated expenses of various interest groups to influence legislation. The queried a sample of 173 corporations, the principal national farmers organizations, the AFL-CIO, and the major independent national unions (but not the national unions affiliated with AFL-CIO). These organizations reported expenditures for a three-year period in the following gross disproportions:

173 corporations	$32.1 million
Farm organizations	0.9 million
Labor unions	0.55 million

. . . The executive of the large corporation is, on many counts, the contemporary counterpart to the landed gentry of an earlier era, his voice amplified by the technology of mass communication. A single corporate voice on television, it has been estimated, can reach more minds in one evening than were reached from all the platforms of all the world's meetings in the course of several centuries preceding broadcasting. More than class, the major specific institutional barrier to fuller democracy may therefore be the autonomy of the private corporation.

It has been a curious feature of democratic thought that it has not faced up to the private corporation as a peculiar organization in an ostensible democracy. Enormously large, rich in resources, the big corporations, we have seen, command more resources than do most government units. They can also, over a broad range, insist that government meet their demands, even if these demands run counter to those of citizens expressed through their polyarchal controls. Moreover, they do not disqualify themselves from playing the partisan role of a citizen—for the corporation is legally a person. And they exercise un-usual veto powers. They are on all these counts disproportionately powerful, we have seen. The large private corporation fits oddly into democratic theory and vision. Indeed, it does not fit.

NO

David Vogel

THE NEW POLITICAL SCIENCE OF CORPORATE POWER

The amount of political power exercised by business has been the subject of considerable debate among political scientists. Their views have fallen roughly into two camps. One perspective views business primarily as an interest group, actively competing with a plurality of other political constituencies to both define the political agenda and influence specific public policies. In the political marketplace, business is not regarded as enjoying any particular advantages that cannot be matched by other interest groups. As a result, its power varies depending on such factors as the climate of public opinion, the performance of the economy, the political skills and resources of particular companies or industries, and the relative strength of other interest groups. This perspective is commonly identified with pluralism. Another approach regards business not as another interest group but as a kind of private government, which enjoys a privileged position in American politics. Its ability to define the terms of public debate and its superior access to government officials is seen as overshadowing that of any other political constituency, thus making a mockery of the principles of pluralist democracy.

The study of American politics was dominated by pluralists from the early 1940s through the late 1960s. The most influential studies of American politics—such as David Truman's *The Governmental Process*, published in 1951, V. O. Key's *Politics, Parties and Pressure Groups*, which went through five editions and more than twenty-five printings between 1942 and 1964, and Robert Dahl's *Who Governs?*, published in 1961, argued that the American political system was both fluid and accessible. They documented the inability of any one interest group, including business, to dominate it. Their point of view was reflected in virtually every textbook on American government published during these decades and in all but a few scholarly books and articles on the subject.

Over the last fifteen years, however, the pluralist view of American politics has been increasingly challenged. Since 1970, a steady stream of monographs

From David Vogel, "The New Political Science of Corporate Power," *The Public Interest*, no. 87 (Spring 1987), pp. 63-79. Copyright © 1987 by National Affairs, Inc. Reprinted with permission of the author. Notes omitted.

and textbooks has been published arguing that American democracy is fundamentally flawed, largely on the ground that business exercises disproportionate political and social power. Significantly, two of the discipline's most prominent pluralists—Yale political scientists Robert Dahl and Charles Lindblom— have publicly repudiated their earlier position. In a preface they wrote for a new edition of *Politics, Economics and Welfare*, published in 1976, they confessed that

> in our discussion of pluralism we made another error—and it is a continuing error in social science—in regarding business groups as playing the same interest-group role as other groups in polyarchal systems, though more powerfully. Businessmen play a distinctive role in polyarchal politics that is qualitatively different from that of any interest group. It is also much more powerful than an interest group role.

They added,

> . . . common interpretations that depict the American or any other market-oriented system as a competition among interest groups are seriously in error for their failure to take account of the distinctive privileged position of businessmen in politics.

Lindblom's *Politics and Markets* (1977) presents a wide-ranging analysis of what he calls "the world's political-economic systems." But it is best known for its last two sentences: "The large private corporation fits oddly into democratic theory and vision. Indeed, it does not fit." Today the book is the most widely known and influential study of American business-government relations by an academic to appear in the last quarter-century. It has sold more than sixty thousand copies since its publication and is widely used as a college text. . . .

THE PRIVILEGED POSITION OF BUSINESS

Charles Lindblom . . . argues that the probusiness slant of public policy is not merely the result of business's superior economic and political resources, but rather that business enjoys a privileged position in a capitalist system because of its unique relationship to the public welfare. This relationship sets it apart from other interests that compete for influence on public policy. Corporate leaders hold a privileged position because, according to Lindblom, society has placed in their hands the responsibility for mobilizing and organizing its economic resources. In this capacity, corporate executives "decide a nation's industrial technology, the pattern of work organization, location of industry, market structure, resource allocation, and, of course, executive compensation status." Lindblom contends that this broad category of major decisions has been removed from the political agenda and thus from democratic control. To compound the problem, constitutional rules, especially those protecting private-property rights, prevent public control over corporate decision making from being exercised directly.

As a result, corporate executives must be induced *to perform their primary social functions*; they cannot be commanded to do so. These inducements may take the form of delegated monopoly rights, limited liability, rights of way, subsidies, tax incentives, infrastructural services such as public works and education, insurance, military protection of investments, rights to transfer costs of pollution or other externalities to third parties, and so on. All of these inducements impose costs, in the form of taxes, eminent domain, uncompensated damages, extracted consumer surplus, and the like, on the rest of society. According to Lindblom, this analysis of corporate power requires "no conspiracy theory of politics, no theory of common social origins uniting government and business officials, no crime allegation of a power elite established by clandestine forces." Rather, "simply minding one's own business is the formula for an extraordinary system for repressing change." The result is that "pluralism at most operates only in an imprisoned zone of policy making." He adds that escape from the "prison of the marketplace" is undermined by corporate attempts to mold the desires of individual citizens:

> Consider the possibility that businessmen achieve an indoctrination of citizens so that citizens' volitions serve not their own interests but the interests of businessmen. Citizens then become allies of businessmen. The privileged position of business comes to be widely accepted.

Thus, what is often seen as the quasi-democratic give-and-take of interest-group politics should be understood, in Lindblom's view, to apply only to secondary issues. These are issues for which a broad consensus does not exist within the business community. As these issues reach the political agenda, the public is subjected to competing messages from various business interests. A divided business community is forced to join coalitions and compromise with other societal interests. According to Lindblom, this then can be conveniently cited as evidence of the limits on corporate power, and further reinforces the myth that democratic pluralism is alive and well.

The essence of Lindblom's argument is that businessmen are uniquely powerful because the government relies upon them to organize the nation's production and distribution of wealth. But while this makes the government dependent on the decisions of businessmen, it also makes business at least as dependent on the decisions of government. In the real world, neither business nor government gets all they want from each other: Government officials are usually dissatisfied with the economy's rate of growth while businessmen invariably argue that their profits would be higher if the government were more responsive to their needs. . . .

DOES BUSINESS MAKE POLICY?

Lindblom's analysis of corporate power also tends to reify "business." Even though the government has to provide inducements to business to enable the economy to grow, it does not follow that it has to provide inducements to any particular company or industry. After all, segments of the economy can perform poorly even when the economy as a whole is doing relatively well; the reverse is also true. The government can—and in fact does—discriminate among businesses. Government spending, tax, trade, industrial and regulatory policies invariably favor particular sectors, industries, regions, products, and even some plants over others. (Indeed, competing to increase their share of benefits from government is among the most important corporate political activities.) This in turn gives government an important source of leverage over business: It can play off different segments of business against each other. And it also tends to increase the power of nonbusiness constituencies, since their support may be critical in enabling certain segments of business to increase their share of governmental favors. . . .

The fact that there are so many different businesses significantly increases the flexibility of public policy. There are scarcely any tasks that the government might wish to undertake that it cannot find some businessman willing to perform in the expectation of making money. Do we wish to reduce pollution? Such a policy will certainly reduce the profits of those firms that pollute. But the money they are forced to spend on combating pollution represents, in turn, a source of profit for the manufacturers of pollution-control equipment. Do we wish drug and cosmetic companies to do more testing on their products before they market them? The costs imposed on these firms, in turn, represent a business opportunity for companies that specialize in running laboratory tests. Do we wish to divert resources from the production of weaponry to health care? The result will be that the profits of defense contractors will decline and those of the health-care industry will increase.

If one surveys the public policies of the democratic-capitalist nations in the postwar period, one is struck not by how narrowly constrained they have been by the imperatives of a privately owned economy, but how varied they have been. Capitalist economies have prospered with virtually no government ownership of the means of production and with an extremely large public sector, with market-based capital markets and with politically directed ones, with very weak labor unions and with very strong ones, with virtually no environmental protection laws and with extremely strict ones, with extremely generous welfare states and with very limited ones, with regressive tax policies and pro-gressive ones. And, of course, capitalist economies have done poorly under all these varied public policies as well. In short, the relationship between any particular set of policies and economic growth or corporate profitability is by no means as clear-cut as Lindblom implies.

THE LIMITS OF INFLUENCE

Even if politicians are persuaded by businessmen that a particular set of policies is necessary to increase economic growth, they can still refuse to enact them. Democratic governments can and do choose to accept lower growth rates in order to achieve other public policy objectives. These range from protecting the livelihood of small, inefficient farmers, as in Japan and France, maintaining the income levels of the elderly, as in Western Europe and the United States, or spending a significant share of GNP on the military as in the United States, Great Britain, and Sweden. There are literally hundreds of policy changes the American government could enact that would likely increase the rate of corporate investment—and thus presumably enhance corporate profits, improve economic growth rates, and reduce unemployment. We do not choose to enact them for a simple reason: Influential segments of the American public are not interested in making the tradeoffs that they would entail. The rate of return to capital does not constitute a fixed point in the social universe around which politicians must structure their economic and social policies. On the contrary, the governments of democratic societies can and do exercise considerable discretion in determining how they wish to allocate their nation's limited resources. . . .

Because we live in a highly specialized society, different social tasks are entrusted to different groups of individuals. Government, for example, is held responsible for safeguarding the public's health. This, in turn, makes government officials dependent on the skills and commitment of a certain category of medical person; if the latter cannot be induced to perform their tasks—such as, for example, finding a cure for AIDS—tens of thousands of citizens will find their lives endangered. Similarly, if the government wishes to develop more advanced nuclear weapons, put a man on the moon, or design a strategic defense, it makes itself dependent on the relative handful of individuals who possess the appropriate scientific and technical skills. Indeed, since the number of each of these is far smaller than the number of businessmen, each of them is even proportionately more powerful than is each businessman. And unlike those who currently occupy the role of businessman, they cannot be readily replaced.

It is not simply businessmen who warn us that unless they are given additional resources, dire consequences will follow. The head of every single governmental agency and nonprofit institution makes the identical argument. Thus, educators inform us that unless they are given more funds, the next generation of Americans will be inadequately educated. Similarly, military officials tell Congress each year that unless they are given more advanced and expensive weaponry, the sovereignty of the Untied States will be endangered. Their threats are no more—or no less—credible than those of business executives. Nor are the potential consequences of ignoring their demands necessarily any less severe. Indeed, on balance, the adverse social consequences of not giving certain categories of government employees sufficient incentives or resources to discharge their various responsibilities are often much more immediate—and potentially catastrophic—than depriving businessmen of sufficient incentives with which to make additional investments. . . .

THE POWER STRUCTURE

Some political scientists who study the political power of business have focused on the business system itself as a structure of power. This perspective owes much to Marxism, but it is also reflected in the writings of political economists such as John Kenneth Galbraith. The literature in this genre describes a system of economic production in which the distribution of power and privilege is both stable and secure—akin in important ways to that of an authoritarian government. It depicts a "corporate state," dominated by a relatively small number of giant corporations, each of whose managers has achieved a substantial degree of freedom from the restraints imposed by the marketplace.

Until fifteen years ago, this vision was, in many respects, an accurate one. The managerial revolution, first noted by Berle and Means in 1932, appeared to have finally triumphed. American companies were governed by what was essentially a self-perpetuating elite with "stockholder democracy" amounting to nothing more than a legal fiction. Nor were large companies vulnerable to the pressures of marketplace competition: Companies rarely competed on price, and consumer tastes and preferences were both stable and relatively predictable. Moreover, the fruits of technological innovation were usually captured by existing firms. As a result, with only a handful of exceptions, both the industries and the individual companies that dominated the American economic system during the 1920s continued to dominate it throughout the 1960s. And thanks to the steady, and relatively uninterrupted, growth of the economy in the quarter-century following World War II, large companies, regardless of how well or poorly they were managed, were invariably profitable.

A detailed discussion of the changes in American business that have taken place since the early 1970s is beyond the scope of this article, but they include these developments:

• The managerial revolution has been followed by a counter-revolution of stockholders, inspired by investment bankers and supported by institutional investors. Now virtually every American corporation is vulnerable to a hostile takeover, many of which are initiated and backed by investors from well outside the "business establishment."

• Economic conditions are increasingly unpredictable and unstable. Since the early 1970s we have witnessed two major recessions, a prolonged period of inflation as well as both a major increase and then an equally unexpected decrease in the price of agricultural products and raw materials, most notably energy. Each of these developments has wreaked havoc on corporate balance sheets; large corporations no longer automatically make money.

• The deregulation of financial markets, airlines, railroads, and trucking have forced a substantial segment of the American business community to engage in actual price competition for the first time in decades. The market shares of companies in each of these industries now changes constantly and a number of firms have either been forced to merge or become bankrupt.

• The northeast quadrant of the United States, which dominated American manufacturing and finance for more than a century, has lost a significant share of its wealth and power to the Sun Belt.

• The United States is in the midst of an entrepreneurial revolution. Since 1980, new businesses have been formed at the rate of approximately five hundred thousand a year. Many of these firms are in industries that did not exist a decade ago, while others have successfully challenged the market positions of previously established companies. As a result, virtually no American companies—even the very largest—remain unthreatened by marketplace competition.

• American industry has become vulnerable to foreign competition: Approximately 70 percent of the products manufactured in the United States now face competition from imports—up from 20 percent fifteen years ago. The increase in the extent of international trade among the established industrial nations, coupled with the aggressive export strategies of the newly industrializing nations—primarily from the Pacific—has meant that the world marketplace is much more competitive than at any time in recent history.

• Finally, the control and ownership of capital within the world economy as a whole has begun to change significantly. The historic dominance of the global economy by Western Europe and the United States has been steadily eroding. The world's economic center of gravity is moving from the Atlantic basin—where it has been concentrated for nearly five hundred years—to the Pacific.

Each of these developments challenges the notion that business constitutes a stable system of power; on the contrary, those who currently control and own capital can no longer be assured of maintaining their wealth or power into the future. They are, in fact, no more or less vulnerable to changing economic conditions than politicians are to changing political currents.

Of all of these developments, among the most important concerns is the changing role of the large business corporation. Both Dahl and Lindblom explicitly single out the "large" business corporation. Dahl considers worker self-management to be particularly important for large corporations, while Lindblom specifically mentions the large firm in the oft-quoted final two sentences of *Politics and Markets*. The "business as a system of power" perspective also assumes that the large corporation is the prototypical form of capitalist enterprise. But is it? There is growing evidence that suggests that the large business corporation is becoming an increasingly *less* important form of wealth creation in advanced capitalist societies. Each year a smaller proportion of Americans work for large firms; virtually all of the recent growth in private-sector employment in the American economy has taken place in smaller companies. More importantly, many of the most dynamic and innovative sectors of the American economy tend not to be dominated by large companies; this is particularly true of the rapidly growing service sector. If these trends continue—and many students of management believe that they are even likely to accelerate—then one of the central assumptions of critics of corporate power may no longer be valid.

Clearly businessmen exercise political power. But that is hardly the issue. In a democratic society, *all* citizens, in principle, have the opportunity to exercise power. Presumably, none of the critics of pluralism believes that a businessman should have *less* power than anyone else. The issue is: Do they wield power out of proportion to their numerical representation in our society? Given that a significant portion of Americans either own or manage business, it is by no means clear that they do. Moreover businessmen are not in a position to influence equally all kinds of decisions. Their opinion, for example, as to whether or not we should permit abortions or provide hand-held missile launchers to the rebels in Afghanistan presumably carries no more weight than that of any other group of citizens. On the other hand, they might well be able to affect disproportionately tax or regulatory policies. But what is the relative importance of the issues whose resolution they are in a unique position to affect as compared to those which they are not?

If political scientists are to advance our understanding of the extent and scope of corporate political power, they need to express their arguments in terms that can be tested and falsified. Just how successful, in fact, is business in getting what it wants from government and how does its influence vary from industry to industry, from issue to issue, and over time? Of course individual companies, trade associations, and inter-industry coalitions wield significant political power. In many respects, the power of business is now clearly greater than it was a decade ago. Between the 1960s and 1970s, however, business found its power and influence effectively challenged by other political constituencies, most notably the public interest groups. There is nothing about the nature of power exercised by business that cannot be accounted for within the framework of interest-group politics. Nor is the challenge posed to democratic thought or practice by the large corporation any different than that of any other large bureaucracy—whether private or public. We need not abandon pluralism in order to understand the political power of business in capitalist democracies.

POSTSCRIPT

Is the U.S. Political System Dominated by Big Business?

Having read both Lindblom and Vogel, consider these questions: Does Lindblom really mean to suggest that big business always gets its way in the American system, even when other interests fight against it? How would he explain those instances where business interests have lost—for example, businesses attempted to kill a revision to the tax code in 1986 and they lobbied to get a reduction in the capital gains tax in 1989, and, in both instances, they were defeated. Yet Vogel, too, is puzzling in some respects. Can he deny that wealthy business interests enjoy easy access to public officials, an access that is not usually available to those interests that do not command great wealth? If so—if there are great asymmetries of access to power in the U.S. political system—then in what sense can our system be called pluralist?

Social science literature contains a number of works discussing the issues of pluralism and corporate power. As Vogel notes, Lindblom himself once took the pluralist view. See Lindblom and Robert A. Dahl's *Politics, Economics, and Welfare* (Harper & Brothers, 1953). Dahl, like Lindblom, has changed his view since that time, but he was a vigorous exponent of the pluralist thesis during the 1950s and early 1960s. See Dahl's *A Preface to Democratic Theory* (University of Chicago, 1956) and *Who Governs* (Yale, 1961). By the late 1960s, pluralism had come under increasing critical scrutiny. See, for example, Peter Bachrach, *The Theory of Democratic Elitism* (Little, Brown, 1967) and Theodore Lowi, *The End of Liberalism* (Norton, 1969).

A collection of articles by current researchers of corporate power is *The Structure of Power in America: The Corporate Elite as a Ruling Class,* edited by Michael Schwartz (Holmes and Meier, 1987). Other important studies of corporate elite dominance are: G. William Domhoff, *Who Rules America Now?* (Prentice-Hall, 1983); Michael Useem, *The Inner Circle* (Oxford University Press, 1984); Beth Mintz and Michael Schwartz, *The Power Structure of American Business* (University of Chicago Press, 1985); and Robert R. Alford and Roger Friedland, *Powers of Theory: Capitalism, the State, and Democracy* (Cambridge University Press, 1985).

Today, pluralism has few defenders, though Vogel's essay may help it gain back some of the ground it has lost.

ISSUE 11

Has American Government Become Too Big?

YES: William Simon, from *A Time for Truth* (McGraw-Hill, 1978)

NO: John Kenneth Galbraith, from "The Social Consensus and the Conservative Onslaught," *The Millenium Journal of International Studies* (Spring 1982)

ISSUE SUMMARY

Yes: Former Treasury Secretary William Simon argues that excessive government involvement in the economy abridges basic liberties and hurts the nation's productivity.

No: Economist John Kenneth Galbraith says that since public services are essential to those Americans who can't afford private services, the attack on "big government" is really an attack on the poor.

What is the purpose of government? The question has been asked and answered since ancient times. The answers have varied with the times. For the ancient Greeks and Romans, government was an instrument of glory, the means of making immortal the great words and deeds of statesmen. In the Middle Ages, government was supposed to be a servant of Christianity, a protecter of the faith against foreign and domestic enemies. By the seventeenth century, government was largely a vehicle of kingly ambition; through regulations, taxes, licenses, armies, swarms of officials, and a wide array of punishments, government was used to increase the power of kings and intimidate potential challengers.

Then came the eighteenth century, the Age of Enlightenment. For many of the leading thinkers of the time—from Adam Smith to Thomas Paine, from the Physiocrats in France to Thomas Jefferson in America—government was not the solution but the problem, and the stronger the government, the greater the problem. "I own I am no friend of energetic government," Jefferson said, "it is always oppressive." Admittedly, government is necessary to keep people from killing and robbing each other. Thomas Paine said, "Government, like clothes, is the badge of lost innocence." But it is at best a necessary evil and should be kept as small as possible. Thus the famous maxim: "That government is best which governs least." Those who entertained such views were called liberals, because they were committed to liberty as opposed to what they considered excessive government restraint.

Their philosophy of government was summed up in the French expression *laissez-faire*, meaning "leave to be," or "leave alone." Government, they thought, should stay out of our lives as much as possible. Today, their philosophy is often called classical liberalism, or libertarianism, to distinguish it from modern liberalism.

Modern liberalism arrived in the 1930s. When Franklin Roosevelt was nominated for president by the Democratic party in 1932, the nation was caught up in the worst depression of its history. A quarter of the nation's work force was unemployed; everywhere there was idleness and despair and, in some places, outright starvation. In accepting the nomination, Roosevelt said: "I pledge you, I pledge myself, to a new deal for the American people." The New Deal was meant to fight the Depression by regulating business, stimulating the economy, and bringing welfare to the needy.

This new strain of liberalism opposed some forms of government regulation, especially the attempt to regulate speech, press, and religion. But in the economic sphere, it openly supported government activism. Regulation of business, supervision of the economic sphere, public assistance to the poor: these were the hallmarks of New Deal liberalism, a liberalism that rejected *laissez-faire* economics in favor of a more activist role of the state. Modern liberalism builds upon that tradition, expanding still further the size and scope of government.

The question is whether the activist role has gone too far. After all, the original insight of liberalism was that big government stifles freedom and creativity. Those who still cherish that insight (the libertarians or classical liberals, sometimes called conservatives) say that modern liberalism is bringing us back to the bad old days of excessive government. True, the big government of the eighteenth century was much different than today's democratic government. It was government by kings and bishops and court intriguers, and it was motivated more by lust for power than by public spirit. Modern democratic government rests upon popular suffrage, so it cannot totally ignore people's needs. Moreover, our economic system has changed drastically since the eighteenth century. We are no longer a nation of small farms but of giant industrial firms wielding enormous power. The whole modern economy is complex and interdependent.

Even so, libertarians argue that government intervention must be kept to a minimum. In their view, *laissez-faire* is still the best way to ensure economic growth and preserve liberty. In the following selections, former Treasury Secretary William Simon develops that view, while economist John Kenneth Galbraith argues that it is unrealistic and out-of-date.

YES

William Simon

THE ROAD TO LIBERTY

Normally in life, if one finds oneself in a situation where *all* known courses of action are destructive, one reassesses the premises which led to that situation. The premise to be questioned here is the degree of government intervention itself—the very competence of the state to function as a significant economic ruler. But to question that premise is to hurl oneself intellectually into a free market universe. And that the social democratic leaders will not do. A few may actually understand—as did the brilliant Chancellor Erhard in postwar Germany—that the solution to shortages, recession and unemployment, and an ominous decline in technological innovation is to dispense with most intervention and regulation and allow men to produce competitively in freedom. But they know that if they proposed this, they would be destroyed by the political intellectuals of their countries. . . .

What we need today in America is adherence to a set of broad guiding principles, not a thousand more technocratic adjustments. [I] shall not waste my time or yours with a set of legislative proposals. Instead, I will suggest a few of the most important general principles which I would like to see placed on the public agenda. They are actually the conclusions I have reached in the course of working on this book.

- The overriding principle to be revived in American political life is that which sets individual liberty as the highest political value—that value to which all other values are subordinate and that which, at all times, is to be given the highest "priority" in policy discussions.

- By the same token, there must be a conscious philosophical prejudice against any intervention by the state into our lives, for by definition such intervention abridges liberty. Whatever form it may take, state intervention in the private and productive lives of the citizenry must be presumed to be a negative, uncreative, and dangerous act, to be adopted only when its proponents provide overwhelming and incontrovertible evidence that the benefits to society of such intervention far outweigh the costs.

• The principle of "no taxation without representation" must again become a rallying cry of Americans. Only Congress represents American voters, and the process of transferring regulatory powers—which are a hidden power to tax—to unelected, uncontrollable, and unfireable bureaucrats must stop. The American voters, who pay the bills, must be in a position to know what is being economically inflicted on them and in a position to vote men out of office who assault their interests, as *the voters* define those interests. Which means that Congress should not pass bills creating programs that it cannot effectively oversee. The drive to demand scrupulous legislative oversight of our policing agencies, such as the CIA, is valid; it should be extended to *all* agencies of the government which are also, directly or indirectly, exercising police power.

• A critical principle which must be communicated forcefully to the American public is the inexorable interdependence of economic wealth and political liberty. Our citizens must learn that what keeps them prosperous is production and technological innovation. Their wealth emerges, not from government offices or politician's edicts, but only from that portion of the marketplace which is *free.* They must also be taught to understand the relationship among collectivism, centralized planning, and poverty so that every new generation of Americans need not naively receive the Marxist revelations afresh.

• Bureaucracies themselves should be assumed to be noxious, authoritarian parasites on society, with a tendency to augment their own size and power and to cultivate a parasitical clientele in all classes of society. Area after area of American life should be set free from their blind power drive. We commonly hear people call for a rollback of prices, often unaware that they are actually calling for the destruction of marginal businesses and the jobs they furnish. People must be taught to start calling for a rollback of the bureaucracy, where nothing will be lost but strangling regulation and where the gains will always take the form of liberty, productivity, and jobs.

• Productivity and the growth of productivity must be the *first* economic consideration at all times, not the last. That is the source of technological innovation, jobs and wealth. This means that profits needed for investment must be respected as a great social blessing, not as a social evil, and that the envy of the "rich" cannot be allowed to destroy a powerful economic system.

• The concept that "wealth is theft" must be repudiated. It now lurks, implicitly, in most of the political statements we hear. Wealth can indeed be stolen, but only *after* it has been produced, and the difference between stolen wealth and produced wealth is critical. If a man obtains money by fraud or by force, he is simply a criminal to be handled by the police and the courts. But if he has earned his income honorably, by the voluntary exchange of goods and services, he is not a criminal or a second-class citizen and should not be treated as such. A society taught to perceive producers as criminals will end up by destroying its productive processes.

• Conversely, the concept that the absence of money implies some sort of virtue should be repudiated. Poverty may result from honest misfortune, but it also may result from sloth, incompetence, and dishonesty. Again the distinction between deserving and undeserving poor is important. It is a virtue to assist those who are in acute need through no fault of their own, but it is folly to glamorize men simply because they are penniless. The crude linkage between wealth and evil, poverty and virtue is false, stupid, and of value only to demagogues, parasites, and criminals—indeed, the three groups that alone have profited from the linkage.

• Similarly, the view that government is virtuous and producers are evil is a piece of folly, and a nation which allows itself to be tacitly guided by these illusions must lose both its liberty and its wealth. Government has its proper functions, and consequently, there can be both good and bad governments. Producers as well can be honest and dishonest. Our political discourse can be rendered rational only when people are taught to make such discriminations.

• The "ethics" of egalitarianism must be repudiated. Achievers must not be penalized or parasites rewarded if we aspire to a healthy, productive, and ethical society. Able-bodied citizens must work to sustain their lives, and in a healthy economic system they should be enabled and encouraged to save for their old age. Clearly, so long as the government's irrational fiscal policies make this impossible, present commitments to pensions and Social Security must be maintained at all cost, for the bulk of the population has no other recourse. But as soon as is politically feasible—meaning, as soon as *production* becomes the nation's highest economic value—the con-

tributions of able-bodied citizens to their own future pensions should be invested by them in far safer commercial institutions, where the sums can earn high interest without being squandered by politicians and bureaucrats. American citizens must be taught to wrest their life savings from the politicians if they are to know the comfort of genuine security.

• The American citizen must be made aware that today a relatively small group of people is proclaiming its purposes to be the will of the People. That elitist approach to government must be repudiated. There is no such thing as the People; it is a collectivist myth. There are only individual citizens with individual wills and individual purposes. There is only one social system that reflects this sovereignty of the individual: the free market, or capitalist, system, which means the sovereignty of the individual "vote" in the marketplace and the sovereignty of the individual vote in the political realm. That individual sovereignty is being destroyed in this country by our current political trends, and it is scarcely astonishing that individuals now feel "alienated" from their government. They are not just alienated from it; they have virtually been expelled from the governmental process, where only organized mobs prevail.

• The growing cynicism about democracy must be combated by explaining why it has become corrupted. People have been taught that if they can get together big enough gangs, they have the legal power to hijack other citizens' wealth, which means the power to hijack other people's efforts, energies, and lives. No decent society can function when men are given such power. A state does need funds, but a clear cutoff line must be established beyond which no political group or institution can confiscate a citizen's honorably earned property. The notion that one can differentiate between "property rights." and "human rights" is ignoble. One need merely see the appalling condition of "human rights" in nations where there are no "property rights" to understand why. This is just a manifestation of the socialist myth which imagines that one can keep men's minds free while enslaving their bodies.

These are some of the broad conclusions I have reached after four years in office. Essentially they are a set of guiding principles. America is foundering for the lack of principles; it is now guided by the belief that *unprincipled* action—for which the respectable name is "pragmatism"—is somehow superior. Such principles as I have listed do not represent dogma. There is, as I said, nothing arbitrary or dogmatic about the interlocking relationship between political and economic liberty. The history of every nation on earth demonstrates that relationship, and no economist known to me, including the theoreticians of interventionism and totalitarianism, denies this. If liberty is to be our highest political value, this set of broad principles follows consistently. . . .

It is often said by people who receive warnings about declining freedom in America that such a charge is preposterous, that there is no freer society on earth. That is true in one sense, but it is immensely deceptive. There has never been such freedom before in America to speak freely, indeed, to wag one's tongue in the hearing of an entire nation; to publish anything and everything, including the most scurrilous gossip; to take drugs and to prate to children about

their alleged pleasures; to propagandize for bizarre sexual practices; to watch bloody and obscene entertainment. Conversely, compulsion rules the world of work. There has never been so little freedom before in America to plan, to save, to invest, to build, to produce, to invent, to hire, to fire, to resist coercive unionization, to exchange goods and services, to risk, to profit, to grow.

The strange fact is that Americans are constitutionally free today to do almost everything that our cultural tradition has previously held to be immoral and obscene, while the police powers of the state are being invoked against almost every aspect of the productive process. Even more precisely, Americans today are left free by the state to engage in activities that could, for the most part, be carried on just as readily in prisons, insane asylums, and zoos. They are not left free by the state to pursue those activities which will give them *independence*.

That is not a coincidence. It is characteristic, in fact, of the contemporary collectivist, in both America and Europe, to clamor that freedom pertains exclusively to the verbal and emotional realms. It allows the egalitarian socialist the illusion that he is not trying to weave a noose for the throats of free men, and it renders him all the more dangerous to the credulous. It is difficult, indeed, to identify as a potential tyrant someone who is raising a righteous uproar over your right to fornicate in the streets. But in this as well, our contemporary "liberators" are not original. I transmit to you a warning by Professor Nisbet, professor of humanities at Columbia University, included in his essay "The New Despotism." He says something I consider vital for the contemporary citizen to know because it is the final reason for the invisibility surrounding the destruction of some of our most crucial liberties:

> [M]ore often than not in history, license has been the prelude to exercises of extreme political coercion, which shortly reach all areas of a culture. . . . [V]ery commonly in ages when civil rights of one kind are in evidence—those pertaining to freedom of speech and thought in, say, theater, press and forum, with obscenity and libel laws correspondingly loosened—very real constrictions of individual liberty take place in other, more vital areas; political organization, voluntary association, property and the right to hold jobs, for example. . . .
>
> There are, after all, certain freedoms that are like circuses. Their very existence, so long as they are individual and enjoyed chiefly individually as by spectators, diverts men's minds from the loss of other, more fundamental social and economic and political rights.
>
> A century ago, the liberties that now exist routinely on stage and screen, on printed page and canvas would have been unthinkable in America—and elsewhere in the West, for that matter, save in the most clandestine and limited of settings. But so would the limitations upon economic, professional, education and local liberties, to which we have by now become accustomed, have seemed equally unthinkable half a century ago. We enjoy the feeling of great freedom, of protection of our civil liberties, when we attend the theater, watch television, buy paperbacks. But all the while, we find ourselves living in circumstances of a spread of military, police and bureaucratic power that cannot help but have, that manifestly does have, profoundly erosive effect upon those economic, local and associative liberties that are by far the most vital to any free society.
>
> From the point of view of any contemporary strategist or tactician of political power indulgence in the one kind of

liberties must seem a very requisite to dimunition of the other kind. We know it seemed that way to the Caesars and Napoleons of history. Such indulgence is but one more way of softening the impact of political power and of creating the illusion of individual freedom in a society grown steadily more centralized, collectivized and destructive of the diversity of allegiance, the autonomy of enterprise in all spheres and the spirit of spontaneous association that any genuinely free civilization requires.

I cite this for another reason. Like others whom I have quoted at length at several points in this book, Mr. Nisbet stands as a living illustration of what I mean by a counterintellectual. It is only the scholar with a profound understanding of the nature of liberty and the institutions on which it rests who can stand ultimate guard over American cultural life. It is only he who can offer the American citizen the authentic and profound choices that our political system and our press no longer offer him.

I do not mean to imply here that it is only on a lofty, scholarly level that the fight can be conducted, although it unquestionably must begin at that level. At any time and on any social level the individual can and should take action. I have done so in my realm, and you, too, can work for your liberty, immediately and with impact. . . .

Stop asking the government for "free" goods and services, however desirable and necessary they may seem to be. They are not free. They are simply extracted from the hide of your neighbors—and can be extracted only by force. If you would not confront your neighbor and demand his money at the point of a gun to solve every new problem that may appear in your life, you should not allow the government to do it for you. Be prepared to identify any politician who simultaneously demands your "sacrifices" and offers you "free services" for exactly what he is: an egalitarian demagogue. This one insight understood, this one discipline acted upon and taught by millions of Americans to others could do more to further freedom in American life than any other.

There is, of course, a minimum of government intervention needed to protect a society, particularly from all forms of physical aggression and from economic fraud and, more generally, to protect the citizen's liberty and constitutional rights. What that precise minimum is in terms of a percentage of the GNP I am not prepared to say, but I do know this: that a clear cutoff line, beyond which the government may not confiscate our property, must be sought and established if the government is not to invade every nook and cranny of our lives and if we are to be free and productive. It is with *our* money that the state destroys our freedom. It is not too soon to start the process of tightening the leash on the state on the individual level, above all, by refusing to be a parasite. In the lowest-income groups in our nation there are men and women too proud, too independent to accept welfare, even though it is higher than the wages they can earn. Surely such pride can be stimulated on the more affluent levels of our society. . . .

It is with a certain weariness that I anticipate the charge that I am one of those "unrealistic" conservatives who wishes to "turn back the clock." There is a good deal less to this criticism than meets the eye. History is not a determinist carpet rolling inexorably in the direction of collectivism, although an extraordinary number of people believe this to be the case. The truth is that it has unrolled gloriously in the opposite direction many

times. Above all, the United States was born. There is nothing "historically inevitable" about the situation we are in. There is also nothing "realistic" in counseling people to adjust to that situation. That is equivalent to counseling them to adjust to financial collapse and the loss of freedom. Realism, in fact, requires the capacity to see beyond the tip of one's nose, to face intolerably unpleasant problems and to take the necessary steps to dominate future trends, not to be crushed passively beneath them.

The time plainly has come to act. And I would advise the socially nervous that if our contemporary "New Despots" prefer to conceive of themselves as "progressive" and denounce those of us who would fight for liberty as "reactionary," let them. Words do not determine reality. Indeed, if language and history are to be taken seriously, coercion is clearly reactionary, and liberty clearly progressive. In a world where 80 percent of all human beings still live under harrowing tyranny, a tyranny always rationalized in terms of the alleged benefits to a collectivist construct called the People, the American who chooses to fight for the sanctity of the individual has nothing for which to apologize.

One of the clearest measures of the disastrous change that has taken place in this country is the fact that today one must intellectually justify a passion for individual liberty and for limited government, as though it were some bizarre new idea. Yet angry as I get when I reflect on this, I know there is a reason for it. Seen in the full context of human history, individual liberty *is* a bizarre new idea. And an even more bizarre new idea is the free market—the discovery that allowing millions upon millions of individuals to pursue their material interests as they choose, with a minimum of interference by the state, will unleash an incredible and orderly outpouring of inventiveness and wealth. These twin ideas appeared like a dizzying flare of light in the long night of tyranny that has been the history of the human race. That light has begun to fade because the short span of 200 years has not been long enough for most of our citizens to understand the extraordinary nature of freedom. I say this with genuine humility. I came to understand this late in life myself, inspired by a very special perspective: I was flying high over the land of one of the bloodiest tyrants on earth. But having understood it, I cannot let that light die out without a battle.

NO

John Kenneth Galbraith

THE SOCIAL CONSENSUS AND THE CONSERVATIVE ONSLAUGHT

THE ECONOMIC AND SOCIAL CONSENSUS

In economic and social affairs we value controversy and take it for granted; it is both the essence of politics and its principal attraction as a modern spectator sport. This emphasis on controversy regularly keeps us from seeing how substantial, on occasion, can be the agreement on the broad framework of ideas and policies within which the political debate proceeds.

This has been the case with economic and social policy in the industrial countries since the Second World War. There has been a broad consensus which has extended to most Republicans and most Democrats in the United States, to both Christian Democrats and Social Democrats in Germany and Austria, to the Labour and Tory Parties in Britain, and to Liberals and Progressive Conservatives in Canada. In France, Italy, Switzerland and Scandinavia also, policies have generally been based on a consensus. Although the rhetoric in all countries has been diverse, the practical action has been broadly similar.

All governments in all of the industrial countries, although differing in individual emphasis, have agreed on three essential points. First, there must be macroeconomic management of the economy to minimise unemployment and inflation. This, particularly in the English-speaking countries, was the legacy of Keynes. Second, there must be action by governments to provide those services which, by their nature, are not available from the private sector, or on which, like moderate-cost housing, health care and urban transportation, the private economy defaults. Finally, there must be measures—unemployment insurance, old age pensions, medical insurance, environmental protection, job-safety and produce-safety regulation, and special welfare payments—to protect the individual from circumstances with which he or she, as an individual, cannot contend, and which may be seen as a smoothing and softening of the harsh edges of capitalism.

There is no accepted term for the consensus which these policies compromise. 'Keynesian' policy refers too narrowly to macroeconomic action;

From John Kenneth Galbraith, "The Social Consensus and the Conservative Onslaught," *The Millennium Journal of International Studies* (Spring 1982). Copyright © 1982 by John Kenneth Galbraith. Reprinted by permission.

'liberal' or 'social democratic' policy has too strong a political connotation for what has been embraced in practice by Dwight E. Eisenhower, Gerald Ford, Charles de Gaulle, Konrad Adenauer, Winston Churchill and Edward Heath. I will not try to devise a new term; instead I will refer to the broad macroeconomic, public-service and social welfare commitment as the economic and social consensus, or just "the consensus." It is the present attack on this consensus—notably in Mrs. Thatcher's government in Britain and by Ronald Reagan's government in the United States—that I wish to examine.

THE CONSERVATIVE CHALLENGE TO THE CONSENSUS

The ideas supporting the economic and social consensus have never been without challenge. Keynesian macroeconomic management of the economy, the first pillar of the consensus, was powerfully conservative in intent. It sought only to correct the most self-destructive feature of capitalism (the one Marx thought decisive), namely its tendency to produce recurrent and progressively more severe crisis or depression, while leaving the role of the market, the current distribution of income and all property rights unchallenged. Despite this, numerous conservatives, especially in the United States, for a long time equated Keynesian economics with subversion. There was discomfort among conservatives when, thirty years after Keynes's *General Theory*[1] was published and the policy it prescribed was tending visibly towards obsolescence, Richard Nixon, in an aberrant moment, was led to say that all Americans, including Republicans, were Keynesians now. A reference to the welfare policies of the consensus—'the welfare state'—has always encountered a slightly disapproving mood; something expensive or debilitating, it was felt, was being done for George Bernard Shaw's undeserving poor. The need to compensate for the failures of capitalism through the provision of lower-cost housing, lower-income health care and mass transportation has been accepted in all countries; but, in the United States at least, not many have wanted to admit that this is an unavoidable form of socialism. In contrast, in all countries at all times there has been much mention of the cost of government, the level of taxes, the constraints of business regulation and the effect of these on economic incentives.

There has always been a likelihood, moreover, that an attack on the economic and social consensus would be taken to reflect the views of a larger section of the population than was actually the case, because a large share of all public comment comes from people of relatively high income, while the consensus is of greatest importance to those of lowest income. High social business and academic position gives access to television, radio, and the press, and those who are professionally engaged in the media are, themselves, relatively well off. It follows that the voice of economic advantage, being louder, regularly gets mistaken for the voice of the masses. Furthermore, since it is so interpreted by politicians, it has much the same effect on legislatures and legislation as a genuine shift of opinion.

In the last thirty-five years we have had many such shifts of opinion—all drastically to the right. Professor Friedrich Hayek with his *Road to Serfdom;*[2] Senator Goldwater in 1964; the unpoor, non-black, distinctly unradical Dayton, Ohio housewife, the supposed archetype discovered by two American scholars; Vice President Spiro Agnew; George Wallace; and Enoch Powell in Britain—they were all, in their turn, seen to represent a growing new conservative mood, before being, each in his turn, rejected.

However, even if proper allowance is made for the dismal success, in the past, of conservative revival, it seems certain that there is now not only in the United States but in other industrial countries as well, an attack on the economic and social consensus that has a deeper sub-stance. Mrs. Thatcher and Mr. Reagan have both won elections. Of course, much, if not most, of Mr. Reagan's success in 1980 must be attributed to President Carter's economists—to the macroeconomic management that combined a severe recession with severe inflation with a drastic slump in the housing industry with particular economic distress in the traditional Democratic industrial states, and all these in the year of the election. (Economists do some things with precision.) But *effective* macroeconomic management was one part of the consensus and, obviously, there is nothing wrong with the way it now functions.

THE CONSERVATIVE ONSLAUGHT

There is, indeed, substance to the conservative attack on the economic and social consensus, especially in Britain and the United States. It strikes at genuine points of vulnerability. This, however, is not true of all of the attack; some of it is merely a rejection of reality—or of compassion. The conservative onslaught we now witness needs careful dissection and differentiation. . . .

THE SIMPLISTIC ATTACK

The *simplistic* attack, which is currently powerful in the United States, consists in a generalised assault on all the civilian services of modern government. Education, urban services and other conventional functions of government; government help to the unemployed, unemployable or otherwise economically incapable; public housing and health care; and the regulatory functions of government are all in the line of fire. People, in a now famous phrase, must be left free to choose.

In its elementary form this attack on the consensus holds that the services of government are the peculiar malignity of those who perform them; they are a burden foisted on the unwilling taxpayer by bureaucrats. One eloquent American spokesman for this view, Mr. William Simon, the former Secretary of the Treasury, has said that,

> Bureaucrats should be assumed to be noxious, authoritarian parasites on society, with a tendency to augment their own size and power and to cultivate a parasitical clientele in all classes of society.[3]

There must, he has urged, "be a conscious, philosophical prejudice against any intervention by the state into our lives."[4] If public services are a foisted malignancy—if they are unrelated to need or function—it follows that they can be reduced more or less without limit and without significant social cost or suffering. This is implicit, even explicit, in the simplistic attack.

Other participants in this line of attack are, superficially at least, more sophisticated. Professor Arthur Laffer of the University of Southern California has supported the case with his now famous curve, which shows that when no taxes are levied, no revenue is raised, and that when taxes absorb all income, their yield, not surprisingly, is also zero. Taxes that are too high, as shown by a curve connecting these two points, have at some point a reduced aggregate yield. The Laffer Curve—which in its operative ranges is of purely freehand origin—has become, in turn, a general case against all taxes. Let there be large horizontal reductions, it is argued, and the resulting expansion of private output and income—for those who will believe anything—can be great enough to sustain public revenues at more or less the previous level. For the less gullible, the Laffer Curve still argues for a large reduction in the cost and role of the government.[5]

Another stronger attack on the public services comes from Professor Milton Friedman and his disciples. It holds that these services are relentlessly in conflict with liberty: the market accords to the individual the sovereignty of choice; the state, as it enlarges its services, curtails or impairs that choice—a cumulative and apocalyptic process. By its acceptance of a large service and protective role for the state, democracy commits itself to an irreversible descent into totalitarianism and to Communism. Professor Friedman is firm as to the prospect. He argues that,

If we continue our present trend, and our free society is replaced by a collectivist society, the intellectuals who have done so much to drive us down this path will not be the ones who run the society; the prison, insane asylum, or the graveyard would be their fate.[6]

Against this trend he asks,

shall we have the wisdom and the courage to change our course, to learn from experience, and to benefit from a 'rebirth of freedom'?[7]

I have called this attack on the social consensus simplistic: it could also be called rhetorical and, by the untactful, vacuous, because it depends almost wholly on passionate assertion and emotional response. No one, after reflection, can conclude that publicly rendered services are less urgently a part of the living standard than privately purchased ones—that clean water from the public sector is less needed than clean houses from the private sector, that good schools for the young are less important than good television sets. In most countries public services are not rendered with high efficiency, a point worthy of real concern. But no way has ever been found for seriously reducing outlays for either efficiently or inefficiently rendered services without affecting performance. Public bureaucracy has a dynamic of its own, but so does private bureaucracy. As road builders promote public highways and public educators promote public education, so private weapons firms promote weapons and other corporate bureaucracies promote tobacco, alcohol, toothpaste and cosmetics. This is the common tendency of organisation, as we have known since Max Weber. Good education, health care and law enforcement do not impair liberty or foretell authoritarianism. On the contrary, the entire experience of civilised societies is that these services are consistent with liberty and enlarge it. Professor Friedman's belief that liberty is measured, as currently in New York City, by the depth of the uncollected garbage is, as I have previously observed, deeply questionable.

Taxes on the affluent do reduce the freedom of those so taxed to spend their own money. "An essential part of economic freedom is freedom to choose how to use our income."[8] But, unemployment compensation, old-age pensions and other welfare payments serve even more specifically to increase the liberty of their recipients. That is because the difference for liberty between considerable income and a little less income can be slight; in contrast, the effect on liberty of the difference between *no* income and *some* income is always very, very great. It is the unfortunate habit of those who speak of the effect of government on freedom that they confine their concern to the loss of freedom for the affluent. All but invariably they omit to consider the way income creates freedom for the indigent.

The differential effect of taxes and public services on people of different income is something we must not disguise. Taxes in industrial countries are intended to be moderately progressive; in any case, they are paid in greatest absolute amount by people of middle income and above. Public services, in contrast, are most used by the poor. The affluent have access to private schools, while the poor must rely on public education. The rich have private golf courses and swimming pools; the poor depend on public parks and public recreation. Public transportation is most important for the least affluent, as are public hospitals, public libraries and public housing, the services of the police and other municipal services. Unemployment and welfare benefits are important for those who have no other income, while they have no similar urgency for those who are otherwise provided.

We sometimes hesitate in these careful days to suggest an apposition of interest between the rich and the poor. One should not, it is felt, stir the embers of the class struggle. To encourage envy is uncouth, possibly even un-American or un-British. However, any general assault on the public services must be understood for what it is; it is an attack on the living standard of the poor.

NOTES

1. John Maynard Keynes, *The General Theory of Employment Interest and Money* (London: Macmillan, 1936).

2. Fredrich von Hayek, *Road to Serfdom* (London: Routledge and Kegan Paul, 1944).

3. William Simon, *A Time for Truth* (New York: McGraw-Hill, 1978), p. 219.

4. *Ibid.*, p. 218.

5. Professor Laffer's inspired use of purely fortuitous hypotheses, it is only fair to note, has been a source of some discomfort to some of his more scrupulous academic colleagues.

6. Professor Friedman's foreword in William Simon, *op. cit.*, p. xiii.

7. Milton and Rose Friedman, *Free to Choose* (New York: Harcourt Brace Jovanovich, 1979), p. 7.

8. *Ibid.*, p. 65.

POSTSCRIPT

Has American Government Become Too Big?

"There is no such thing as the People," Simon insists, "it is a collectivist myth." Yet the U.S. Constitution begins, "We the People of the United States . . . " Does Simon think that our Constitution is based on a "collectivist myth"? Perhaps the question is unfair, because at the time the Constitution was written, the national government had little to do directly with the economy. Commercial activity was largely, to use Simon's words, the work of "individual citizens with individual wills and individual purposes." On the other hand, the Constitution left room for the growth of government, and a few of the Founding Fathers, such as Alexander Hamilton, actively promoted it. It is hard to say whether they would like the kind of big government we have today.

One of the best systematic treatments of the thesis argued by Simon is Milton Friedman's short classic, *Capitalism and Freedom* (University of Chicago, 1962). For another discussion of the theme, see Michael Novak, ed., *The Denigration of Capitalism: Six Points of View* (American Enterprise Institute, 1979). Galbraith develops his thesis at length in a number of works, especially *Economics and the Public Purpose* (Houghton Mifflin, 1973) and *The New Industrial State* (Houghton Mifflin, 1967).

Whether or not government has become too big may become a moot question. It is already clear that huge budget deficits, coupled with citizens' aversion to tax increases, are going to force cutbacks in government programs. The argument is starting to shift from *whether* to reduce government involvement to *where* to reduce it: in the military sphere or in the area of domestic welfare programs? With the demise of the Soviet empire, Galbraith would cut the military, and Simon would undoubtedly make some of his cuts in domestic spending. Their economic arguments are thus closely tied to their political assumptions and priorities.

ISSUE 12

Does Welfare Do More Harm Than Good?

YES: Charles Murray, from *Losing Ground* (Basic Books, 1984)

NO: Christopher Jencks, from "How Poor Are the Poor?" *The New York Review of Books* (May 9, 1985)

ISSUE SUMMARY

YES: Social researcher and writer Charles Murray outlines his contention that welfare programs can result in long-term dependency on the part of the poor.
NO: Sociologist Christopher Jencks argues that government aid programs are vital to meeting the needs of the poor.

Long before Ronald Reagan's campaign for the presidency in 1980, "the welfare mess" had become a national issue. As far back as the Nixon administration, plans had been made to reform the system by various means, including the substitution of modest cash payments based upon a negative income tax for the crazy quilt pattern of services, commodities, checks, and in-kind payments provided by the existing welfare system. The Carter administration also tried to interest Congress in a reform plan that would simplify, though probably not reduce, welfare.

There is a backlash against welfare, often voiced in mean-spirited jibes such as "make the loafers work" and "I'm tired of paying them to breed." Such slogans ignore the fact that most people on welfare are not professional loafers, but women with dependent children or old or disabled persons. Petty fraud may not be uncommon, but "welfare queens" who cheat the system for spectacular sums are extremely rare. The overwhelming majority of people on welfare are those whose condition would become desperate if payments were cut off. Finally, to reassure those who worry about "breeding for dollars," there is no conclusive evidence that child support payments have anything to do with conception; the costs of raising childen far exceed the payments.

This does not mean that all objections to welfare can be dismissed as Scrooge-like grumblings. There does seem to be evidence that welfare can in some cases promote work disincentives (i.e., make it possible for a recipient to stay home instead of looking for a job). Benefits available in some states exceed what some recipients would earn after taxes, and the high rate at which welfare benefits are reduced as other income increases—the so-called notches in the payment scale—may mean that an additional dollar in earnings can result in more than a dollar loss in total income. Nor is it only in the economic sphere that the welfare system produces unintended effects. Of particular concern to sociologists were the experiments conducted during the 1970s in Seattle and Denver, in which poor families were supplied with guaranteed annual incomes. Family breakups then began to increase. The reasons for this phenomenon were not clear from the experiments, but some critics of welfare have hypothesized that guaranteed income may undermine the traditional "provider role" of husbands. There are also some severe social costs of welfare that must be borne by the recipients themselves. In addition to the stigma of being on welfare, there is the constant threat of intrusion by government agents. The social workers charged with administering the program have a great deal of power over those who receive the benefits, and some of the provisions of the program can add more strain to an already shaky family situation.

What is to be done about welfare? Broadly speaking, the suggestions fall into three categories: (a) some say to *trim down* the program; (b) others advocate *monitoring* it carefully to make sure the truly needy are receiving a fair share of it. That may mean trimming the program in some areas while expanding it in others; (c) others favor outright *abolition* of welfare, except for the aged and the physically handicapped.

The trim it approach was a central tenet in the philosophy of the Reagan administration. When Ronald Reagan first campaigned for the presidency in 1980, he promised to "get government off our backs." His contention was that government welfare programs tend to stifle initiative, depress the economy, and do the poor more harm than good. After eight years in office, the President's conservative critics claimed that he had not really fulfilled his promises to trim welfare; his liberal critics claimed that he had indeed carried out his promises, with disastrous results.

The radical approach of abolishing welfare is advocated by writer Charles Murray. In the excerpt from his book *Losing Ground*, which we present here, Murray provides some of the reasons why he thinks welfare has deepened the problem of poverty rather than alleviated it. Professor Christopher Jencks, whose critique of Murray is presented here, agrees that the welfare system is flawed, but he points out that it has greatly reduced poverty, so he favors a more careful monitoring of the system.

YES   Charles Murray

LOSING GROUND

The complex story we shall unravel comes down to this:

Basic indicators of well-being took a turn for the worse in the 1960s, most consistently and most drastically for the poor. In some cases, earlier progress slowed; in other cases mild deterioration accelerated; in a few instances advance turned into retreat. The trendlines on many of the indicators are—literally—unbelievable to people who do not make a profession of following them.

The question is why. Why at that moment in history did so many basic trends in the quality of life *for the poor* go sour? Why did progress slow, stop, reverse?

The easy hypotheses—the economy, changes in demographics, the effects of Vietnam or Watergate or racism—fail as explanations. As often as not, taking them into account only increases the mystery.

Nor does the explanation lie in idiosyncratic failures of craft. It is not just that we sometimes administered good programs improperly, or that sound concepts sometimes were converted to operations incorrectly. It is not that a specific program, or a specific court ruling or act of Congress, was especially destructive. The error was strategic.

A government's social policy helps set the rules of the game—the stakes, the risks, the payoffs, the tradeoffs, and the strategies for making a living, raising a family, have fun, defining what "winning" and "success" mean. The more vulnerable a population and the fewer its independent resources, the more decisive is the effect of the rules imposed from above. The most compelling explanation for the marked shift in the fortunes of the poor is that they continued to respond, as they always had, to the world as they found it, but that we—meaning the not-poor and un-disadvantaged—had changed the rules of their world. Not of our world, just of theirs. The first effect of the new rules was to make it profitable for the poor to behave in the short term in ways that were destructive in the long term. Their second effect was to mask these long-term losses—to subsidize irretrievable mistakes. We tried to provide more for the poor and produced more poor instead. We tried to remove the barriers to escape from poverty, and inadvertently built a trap. . . .

POVERTY

Reducing poverty was the central objective of federal social programs during the reform period. Policymakers and legislators hoped for a variety of good things from the War on Poverty and OEO, the entitlements, and the widening population of eligible recipients. But, whatever else the programs were to accomplish, they were to put more money in the hands of poor people. They were to reduce poverty. . . .

The popular conception about poverty is that, at least on this one fundamental goal, the Great Society brought progress. The most widely shared view of history has it that the United States entered the 1960s with a large population of poor people—Harrington's "other America"—who had been bypassed by the prosperity of the Eisenhower years. The rich and the middle class had gained, but the poor had not. Then, after fits and starts during the Kennedy years, came the explosion of programs under Johnson. These programs were perhaps too ambitious, it is widely conceded, and perhaps the efforts were too helter-skelter. But most people seem to envision a plot in which dramatic improvement did not really get started until the programs of the Great Society took effect. . . .

The reality is that improvement was stopping, not starting, during that time. . . . Poverty did fall during the five Johnson years, from 18 percent of the population in 1964 to 13 percent in 1968, his last year in office, and the slope of the decrease was the steepest during this period. . . .

[The] Great Society reforms had very limited budgets through the Johnson administration. The real annual expenditures of the 1970s were far larger—by many orders of magnitude, for some of the programs—than expenditures in the sixties. Yet progress against poverty stopped in the seventies. The steep declines in poverty from 1964 to 1968 cannot glibly be linked with government antipoverty dollar expenditures. . . .

MAXIMIZING SHORT-TERM GAINS

When large numbers of people begin to behave differently from ways they behaved before, my first assumption is that they do so for good reason. [I] will apply this assumption to the trends of the 1960s and 1970s and suggest that it fits the facts.

Specifically, I will suggest that changes in incentives that occurred between 1960 and 1970 may be used to explain many of the trends we have been discussing. It is not necessary to invoke the *Zeitgeist* of the 1960s, or changes in the work ethic, or racial differences, or the complexities of postindustrial economies, in order to explain increasing unemployment among the young, increased dropout from the labor force, or higher rates of illegitimacy and welfare dependency. All were results that could have been predicted (indeed, in some instances were predicted) from the changes that social policy made in the rewards and penalties, carrots and sticks, that govern human behavior. All were rational responses to changes in the rules of the game of surviving and getting ahead. I will not argue that the responses were the right ones, only that they were rational. Even of our mistakes, we say: It seemed like a good idea at the time.

I begin with the proposition that all, poor and not-poor alike, use the same general calculus in arriving at decisions; only the exigencies are different. Poor people play with fewer chips and cannot wait as long for results. Therefore they tend to reach decisions that a more affluent person would not reach. The reformers of the 1960s were especially myopic about this, tending not only to assume that the poor and not-poor were alike in trying to maximize the goods in their lives (with which I agree), but also that, given the same package of benefits, the decision that seem reasonable to one would seem reasonable to the other. They failed to recognize that the behaviors that are "rational" are different at different economic levels. . . .

In the exercise we are about to conduct, it is important to suspend thoughts about how the world ought to work, about what the incentives should be. The objective is to establish what the incentives *are* (or were), and how they are likely to affect the calculations of a person who has few chips and little time. It is also important to put aside the distant view of long-term rewards that we, surveying the scene from above, know to be part of the ultimate truth of self-interest, and instead to examine the truth as it appears at ground level at the time decisions must be made.

Dramatis Personae

Our guides are a young couple—call them Harold and Phyllis. I deliberately make them unremarkable except for the bare fact of being poor. They are not of a special lower-class culture. They have no socialized propensities for "serial monogamy." They are not people we think of as "the type who are on welfare." They have just graduated from an average public school in an average American city. Neither of them is particularly industrious or indolent or dull. They are the children of low-income parents, are not motivated to go to college, and have no special vocational skills. Harold and Phyllis went together during their last year in high school and find themselves in a familiar predicament. She is pregnant.

They will have a child together. They will face the kinds of painful decisions that many young people have had to face. What will they decide? What will seem to them to be "rational" behavior?

We shall examine the options twice—first, as they were in 1960, then as they were only ten years later, in 1970. We shall ignore the turbulent social history of the intervening decade. We shall ignore our couple's whiteness or blackness. We simply shall ask: Given the extant system of rewards and punishments, what course of action makes sense?

Options in 1960

Harold's Calculations, Pre-Reform. Harold's parents have no money. Phyllis has no money. If Harold remains within the law, he has two choices: He can get a job, or he can try to get Phyllis to help support him.

Getting Phyllis to support him is intrinsically more attractive, but the possibilities are not promising. If Phyllis has the baby, she will qualify for $23 a week in AFDC ($63 in 1980 purchasing power). This is not enough to support the three of them. And, under the rules of AFDC, Phyllis will not be able to contribute more to the budget. If she gets a job, she will lose benefits on a dollar-for-dollar basis. There is in 1960 no way to make the AFDC payment part of a larger package

Also, Harold and Phyllis will not be able to live together. AFDC regulations in 1960 prohibit benefits if there is "a man in the house." Apart from its psychic and sexual disadvantages, this regulation also means that Harold cannot benefit from Phyllis's weekly check. The amount cannot possibly be stretched across two households.

It follows that, completely apart from the moral stance of Harold, his parents, or society, it is not possible to use Phyllis for support. Whether or not he decides to stay with her, he will have to find a job.

The only job he can find is working the presses in a dry cleaning shop. It pays the rock-bottom minimum wage—$40 for a forty-hour week, or about $111 in the purchasing power of the 1980 dollar. It is not much of a living, not much of a job. There is no future in it, no career path. But it pays for food and shelter. And Harold has no choice.

The job turns out to be as tedious as he expected. It is hot in the laundry, and Harold in on his feet all day; he would much rather not stay there. But the consequences of leaving the job are intolerable. Unemployment Insurance will pay him only $20 ($56 in 1980 purchasing power). He stays at the laundry and vaguely hopes that something better will come along.

Phyllis's Calculations, Pre-Reform. Phyllis has three (legal) options: to support herself (either keeping the baby or giving it up for adoption); to go on AFDC (which means keeping the baby); or to marry Harold.

Other things being equal, supporting herself is the least attractive of these options. Like Harold, she can expect to find only menial minimum-wage employment. There is no intrinsic reason to take such a job.

The AFDC option is worth considering. The advantage is that it will enable her to keep the baby without having to work. The disadvantages are the ones that Harold perceives. The money is too little, and she is not permitted to supplement it. And Harold would not be permitted to be a live-in husband or father. If she tries to circumvent the rules and gets caught, she faces being cut off from any benefits for the foreseeable future.

If Phyllis thinks ahead, the economic attraction of AFDC might appear more enticing. The total benefits she will receive if she has several children may seem fairly large. If she were already on AFDC it might make sense to have more children. But, right now, setting up a household with Harold is by far the most sensible choice, even given the miserable wage he is making at the laundry.

Being married (as opposed to just living together) has no short-term economic implications. This is shown in the following table:

Harold employed?

| | Living Together | |
	Unmarried	Married
Yes	$111	$111
No	0	0

The choice of whether to get married is dependent primarily on noneconomic motivations, plus the economic advantages to Phyllis of having Harold legally responsible for the support of her and the baby.

Once the decision not to go on AFDC is made, a new option opens up. As long as Phyllis is not on AFDC, no penalty is attached to getting a part-time or full-time job.

Options in 1970

Harold's and Phyllis's namesakes just ten years later find themselves in the identical situation. Their parents have no money; he doesn't want to go to school any longer; she is pregnant; the only job he can get is in the back room of a dry cleaners. That much is unchanged from 1960.

Harold's Calculations, Post-Reform. Harold's options have changed considerably. If he were more clever or less honest (or, perhaps, just more aggressive), he would have even more new options. But since he is none of those things, the major changes in his calculations are limited to these:

First, the AFDC option. In 1960, he had three objections to letting Phyllis go on welfare: too little money, no way to supplement it, and having to live separately from his family. By 1970, all three objections have been removed.

Economically, the total package of AFDC and other welfare benefits has become comparable to working. Phyllis will get about $50 a week in cash ($106 in 1980 dollars) and another $11 in Food Stamps ($23 in 1980 dollars). She is eligible for substantial rent subsidies under the many federal housing programs, but only a minority of AFDC recipients use them, so we will omit housing from the package. She will get Medicaid. We assume that a year's worth of doctor's bills and medication for a mother and infant is likely to be more than $250 (many times that if there is even one major illness), and we therefore add $5 a week (1980 dollars) onto the package. Without bending or even being imaginative about the new regulations, without tapping nearly all the possible sources of public support, and using conservative estimates in reaching a dollar total, the package of benefits available to Phyllis in a typical northern state has a purchasing power of about $134. This minimal package adds up to $23 more than the purchasing power of forty hours of work at a minimum-wage job ten years earlier, in 1960.

Also, the money can be supplemented. If Phyllis works, she can keep the first thirty dollars she makes. After that, her benefits are reduced by two dollars for every three additional dollars of income.

Harold has even greater flexibility. *As long as he is not legally responsible for the care of the child*—a crucial proviso—his income will not count against her eligibility for benefits. He is free to work when they need a little extra money to supplement their basic (welfare) income.

The third objection, being separated from Phyllis, has become irrelevant. By Supreme Court ruling, the presence of a man in the house of a single woman cannot be used as a reason to deny her benefits.

The old-fashioned solution of getting married and living off their earned income has become markedly inferior. Working a full forty-hour week in the dry-cleaning shop will pay Harold $64 ($136 in 1980 dollars) *before* Social Security and taxes are taken out. The bottom line is this: Harold can get married and work forty hours a week in a hot, tiresome job; or he can live with Phyllis and their baby without getting married, not work, and have more disposable income. From an economic point of view, getting married is dumb. From a noneconomic point of view, it involves him in a legal relationship that has no payoff for him. If he thinks he may sometime tire of Phyllis and fatherhood, the 1970 rules thus provide a further incentive for keeping the relationship off the books.

Phyllis's Calculations, Post-Reform. To keep the baby or give it up? To get married or not? What are the pros and cons?

Phyllis come from a poor family. They want her out of the house, just as she wants to get out of the house. If she gives up the baby for adoption (or, in some states by 1970, has a legal abortion), she will be expected to support herself; and, as in 1960, the only job she will be able to find is likely to be unattractive, with no security and a paycheck no larger than her baby would provide. *The only circumstance under which giving up the baby is rational is if she prefers any sort of job to having and caring for a baby.* It is commonly written that poor teenaged girls have babies so they will have someone to love them. This may be true for some. But one *need* not look for psychological explanations. Under the rules of 1970, it was rational on grounds of dollars and cents for a poor, unmarried woman who found herself to be pregnant to have and keep the baby even if she did not particularly want a child.

In Phyllis's case, the balance favors having the baby. What about getting married?

If Phyllis and Harold marry and he is employed, she will lose her AFDC benefits. His minimum wage job at the laundry will produce no more income than she can make, and, not insignificantly, he, not she, will have control of the check. In exchange for giving up this degree of independence, she gains no real security. Harold's job is not nearly as stable as the welfare system. And, should her marriage break up, she will not be able to count on residual benefits. Enforcement of payment of child sup-

port has fallen to near-zero in poor communities. In sum, marriage buys Phyllis nothing—not companionship she couldn't have otherwise, not financial security, not even increased income. In 1970, her child provides her with the economic insurance that a husband used to represent.

Against these penalties for getting married is the powerful positive inducement to remain single: Any money that Harold makes is added to their income without affecting her benefits as long as they remain unmarried. It is difficult to think of a good economic reason from Phyllis's viewpoint why marriage might be attractive.

Let us pause and update the table of economic choices, plugging in the values for 1970. Again, we assume that the two want to live together. Their maximum weekly incomes (ignoring payroll deductions and Harold's means-tested benefits) are:

Harold employed?

| | Living Together | |
	Unmarried	Married
Yes	$270	$136
No	$134	$134

The dominant cell for maximizing income is clearly "living together unmarried, Harold employed." If they for some reason do decide to get married and they live in a state that permits AFDC for families with unemployed fathers (as most of the industrial states do), they are about equally well off whether or not Harold is employed. Or, more precisely, they are about equally well off, in the short run, if Harold moves in and out of the labor market to conform to whatever local rules apply to maintaining eligibility. This is a distinction worth emphasizing, . . . the changed rules do not encourage permanent unemployment so much as they encourage periodic unemployment.

Harold and Phyllis take the economically logical step—she has the baby, they live together without getting married, and Harold looks for a job to make some extra money. He finds the job at the laundry. It is just as unpleasant a job as it was in 1960, but the implications of persevering are different. In 1970, unlike 1960, Harold's job is *not* his basic source of income. Thus, when the back room of the laundry has been too hot for too long, it becomes economically feasible and indeed reasonable to move in and out of the labor market. In 1980 dollars, Unemployment Insurance pays him $68 per week. As the sole means of support it is not an attractive sum. But added to Phyllis's package, the total is $202, which beats the heat of the presses. And, if it comes to it, Harold can survive even without the Unemployment payment. In 1970, Phyllis's welfare package is bringing in more real income than did a minimum-wage job in 1960.

Such is the story of Harold and Phyllis. They were put in a characteristically working-class situation. In 1960, the logic of their world led them to behave in traditional working-class ways. Ten years later, the logic of their world had changed and, lo and behold, they behaved indistinguishably from "welfare types." What if we had hypothesized a more typical example—or ar least one that fits the stereotype? What if we had posited the lower-class and black cultural influences that are said to foster high illegitimacy rates and welfare dependency? The answer is that the same general logic would apply, but with even

more power. When economic incentives are buttressed by social norms, the effects on behavior are multiplied. But the main point is that the social factors are not necessary to explain behavior. There is no "breakdown of the work ethic" in this account of rational choices among alternatives. There is no shiftless irresponsibility. It makes no difference whether Harold is white or black. There is no need to invoke the spectres of cultural pathologies or inferior upbringing. The choices may be seen much more simply, much more naturally, as the behavior of people responding to the reality of the world around them and making the decisions—the legal, approved, and even encouraged decisions—that maximize their quality of life. . . .

A PROPOSAL
FOR PUBLIC WELFARE

I begin with the proposition that it is within our resources to do enormous good for some people quickly. We have available to us a program that would convert a large proportion of the younger generation of hardcore unemployed into steady workers making a living wage. The same program would drastically reduce births to single teenage girls. It would reverse the trendline in the breakup of poor families. It would measurably increase the upward socioeconomic mobility of poor families. These improvements would affect some millions of persons.

All these are results that have eluded the efforts of the social programs installed since 1965, yet, from everything we know, there is no real question about whether they would occur under the program I propose. A wide variety of persuasive evidence from our own culture and around the world, from experimental data and longitudinal studies, from theory and practice, suggests that the program would achieve such results.

The proposed program, our final and most ambitious thought experiment, consists of scrapping the entire federal welfare and income-support structure for working-aged persons, including AFDC, Medicaid, Food Stamps, Unemployment Insurance, Worker's Compensation, subsidized housing, disability insurance, and the rest. I would leave the working-aged person with no recourse whatsoever except the job market, family members, friends, and public or private locally funded services. It is the Alexandrian solution: cut the knot, for there is no way to untie it.

It is difficult to examine such a proposal dispassionately. Those who dislike paying for welfare are for it without thinking. Others reflexively imagine bread lines and people starving in the streets. But as a means of gaining fresh perspective on the problem of effective reform, let us consider what this hypothetical society might look like.

A large majority of the population is unaffected. A surprising number of the huge American middle and working classes go from birth to grave without using any social welfare benefits until they receive their first Social Security check. Another portion of the population is technically affected, but the change in income is so small or so sporadic that it makes no difference in quality of life. A third group comprises persons who have to make new arrangements and behave in different ways. Sons and daughters who fail to find work continue to live with their parents or relatives or friends. Teenaged mothers have to rely on support from their parents or the father of the child and perhaps work as well. People laid off from work have to use their own savings or borrow from others to make do until the next job is found. All these changes involve great disruption in expectations and accustomed roles.

Along with the disruptions go other changes in behavior. Some parents do not want their young adult children continuing to live off their income, and become quite insistent about their children learning skills and getting jobs. This attitude is most prevalent among single mothers who have to depend most critically on the earning power of their offspring.

Parents tend to become upset at the prospect of a daughter's bringing home a baby that must be entirely supported on an already inadequate income. Some become so upset that they spend considerable parental energy avoiding such an eventuality. Potential fathers of such babies find themselves under more pressure not to cause such a problem, or to help with its solution if it occurs.

Adolescents who were not job-ready find they are job-ready after all. It turns out that they can work for low wages and accept the discipline of the workplace if the alternative is grim enough. After a few years, many—not all, but many—find that they have acquired salable skills, or that they are at the right place at the right time, or otherwise find that the original entry-level job has gradually been transformed into a secure job paying a decent wage. A few—not a lot, but a few—find that the process leads to affluence.

Perhaps the most rightful, deserved benefit goes to the much larger population of low-income families who have been doing things right all along and have been punished for it: the young man who has taken responsibility for his wife and child even though his friends with the same choice have called him a fool; the single mother who has worked full time and forfeited her right to welfare for very little extra money; the parents who have set an example for their children even as the rules of the game have taught their children that the example is outmoded. For these millions of people, the instantaneous result is that no one makes fun of them any longer. The longer-term result will be that they regain the status that is properly theirs. They will not only be the bedrock upon which the community is founded (which they always have been), they will be recognized as such. The process whereby they regain their position is not magical, but a matter of logic. When it becomes highly dysfunctional for a person to be dependent, status will accrue to being independent, and in fairly short order. Noneconomic rewards will once again reinforce the economic rewards of being a good parent and provider.

The prospective advantages are real and extremely plausible. In fact, if a government program of the traditional sort (one that would "do" something rather than simply get out of the way) could *as plausibly* promise these advantages, its passage would be a foregone conclusion. Congress, yearning for programs that are not retreads of failures, would be prepared to spend billions. Negative side-effects (as long as they were the traditionally acceptable negative side-effects) would be brushed aside as trivial in return for the benefits. For let me be quite clear: I am not suggesting that we dismantle income support for the working-aged to balance the budget or punish welfare cheats. I am hypothesizing, with

the advantage of powerful collateral evidence, that the lives of large numbers of poor people would be radically changed for the better.

There is, however, a fourth segment of the population yet to be considered, those who are pauperized by the withdrawal of government supports and unable to make alternate arrangements: the teenaged mother who has no one to turn to; the incapacitated or the inept who are thrown out of the house; those to whom economic conditions have brought long periods in which there is no work to be had; those with illnesses not covered by insurance. What of these situations?

The first resort if the network of local services. Poor communities in our hypothetical society are still dotted with storefront health clinics, emergency relief agencies, employment services, legal services. They depend for support on local taxes or local philanthropy, and the local taxpayers and philanthropists tend to scrutinize them rather closely. But, by the same token, they also receive considerably more resources than they formerly did. The dismantling of the federal services has poured tens of billions of dollars back into the private economy. Some of that money no doubt has been spent on Mercedes and summer homes on the Cape. But some has been spent on capital investments that generate new jobs. And some has been spent on increased local services to the poor, voluntarily or as decreed by the municipality. In many cities, the coverage provided by this network of agencies is more generous, more humane, more wisely distributed, and more effective in its results than the services formerly subsidized by the federal government.

But we must expect that a large number of people will fall between the cracks.

How might we go about trying to retain the advantages of a zero-level welfare system and still address the residual needs?

As we think about the nature of the population still in need, it becomes apparent that their basic problem in the vast majority of the cases is the lack of a job, and this problem is temporary. What they need is something to tide them over while finding a new place in the economy. So our first step is to re-install the Unemployment Insurance program in more or less its previous form. Properly administered, unemployment insurance makes sense. Even if it is restored with all the defects of current practice, the negative effects of Unemployment Insurance *alone* are relatively minor. Our objective is not to wipe out chicanery or to construct a theoretically unblemished system, but to meet legitimate human needs without doing more harm than good. Unemployment Insurance is one of the least harmful ways of contributing to such ends. Thus the system has been amended to take care of the victims of short-term swings in the economy.

Who is left? We are now down to the hardest of the hard core of the welfare-dependent. They have no jobs. They have been unable to find jobs (or have not tried to find jobs) for a longer period of time than the unemployment benefits cover. They have no families who will help. They have no friends who will help. For some reason, they cannot get help from local services or private charities except for the soup kitchen and a bed in the Salvation Army hall.

What will be the size of this population? We have never tried a zero-level federal welfare system under conditions of late-twentieth-century national wealth, so we cannot do more than speculate.

But we may speculate. Let us ask of whom the population might consist and how they might fare.

For any category of "needy" we may name, we find ourselves driven to one of two lines of thought. Either the person is in a category that is going to be at the top of the list of services that localities vote for themselves, and at the top of the list of private services, or the person is in a category where help really is not all that essential or desirable. The burden of the conclusion is not that every single person will be taken care of, but that the extent of resources to deal with needs is likely to be very great—not based on wishful thinking, but on extrapolations from reality.

NO

Christopher Jencks

HOW POOR ARE THE POOR?

From 1946 until 1964 the conservative politicians who dominated Congress thought that the federal government might be capable of transforming American society, but they saw this as a danger to be avoided at almost any cost. For the following twelve years the liberals who dominated Congress thought that the federal government should try to cure almost every ill Americans were heir to. After 1976 the political climate in Congress changed again. The idea that government action could solve—or even ameliorate—social problems became unfashionable, and federal spending was increasingly seen as waste. As a result, federal social-welfare spending, which had grown from 5 percent of the nation's gross national product in 1964 to 11 percent in 1976, has remained stuck at 11 percent since 1976.

Conservative politicians and writers are now trying to shift the prevailing view again, by arguing that federal programs are not just ineffective but positively harmful. The "problem," in this emerging view, is not only that federal programs cost a great deal of money that the citizenry would rather spend on video recorders and Caribbean vacations, but that such programs hurt the very people they are intended to help.

Losing Ground, by Charles Murray, is the most persuasive statement so far of this new variation on Social Darwinism. Murray is a former journalist who has also done contract research for the government and is now associated with the Manhattan Institute, which raises corporate money to support conservative authors such as George Gilder and Thomas Sowell. His name has been invoked repeatedly in Washington's current debates over the budget—not because he has provided new evidence on the effects of particular government programs, but because he is widely presumed to have proven that federal social policy as a whole made the poor worse off over the past twenty years. Murray's popularity is easy to understand. He writes clearly and eloquently. He cites many statistics, and he makes his statistics seem easy to understand. Most important of all, his argument provides moral legitimacy for budget cuts that many politicians want to make in order to reduce the federal deficit. . . .

In appraising this argument, we must, I believe, draw a sharp distinction between the material condition of the poor and their social, cultural, and moral condition. If we look at material conditions we find that, Murray notwithstanding, the position of poor people showed marked improvement after 1965, which is the year Murray selects as his "turning point." If we look at social, cultural, and moral indicators, the picture is far less encouraging. But since most federal programs are aimed at improving the material conditions of life, it is best to start with them. . . .

1

. . . Murray is right that, apart from health, the material condition of the poor improved faster from 1950 to 1965 than from 1965 to 1980. The most obvious explanation is that the economy turned sour after 1970. Inflation was rampant, output per worker increased very little, and unemployment began to edge upward. The real income of the median American family, which had risen by an average of 2.9 percent a year between 1950 and 1965, rose only 1.7 percent a year between 1965 and 1980. From 1950 to 1965 it took a 4.0 percent increase in median family income to lower net poverty by one percentage point. From 1965 to 1980, because of expanding social welfare spending, a 4.0 percent increase in median income lowered net poverty by 1.2 percent. Nonetheless, median income grew so much more slowly after 1965 that the decline in net poverty also slowed.

Murray rejects this argument. In his version of economic history the nation as a whole continued to prosper during the 1970s. The only problem, he claims, was that "the benefits of economic growth stopped trickling down to the poor." He supports this version of economic history with statistics showing that gross national product grew by 3.2 percent a year during the 1970s compared to 2.7 percent a year between 1953 and 1959. This is true, but irrelevant. The economy grew during the 1950s because output per worker was growing. It grew during the 1970s because the labor force was growing. The growth of the labor force reflected a rapid rise in the number of families dividing up the nation's economic output. GNP per household hardly grew at all after 1970.

But a question remains. [T]otal government spending on "social welfare" programs grew from 11.2 to 18.7 percent of GNP between 1965 and 1980. If all this money had been spent on the poor, poverty should have fallen to virtually zero. But "social welfare" spending is not mostly for the poor. It includes programs aimed primarily at the poor, like Medicaid and food stamps, but it also includes programs aimed primarily at the middle classes, like college loans and military pensions, and programs aimed at almost everybody, like medical research, public schools, and Social Security. In 1980, only a fifth of all "social welfare" spending was explicitly aimed at low-income families, and only a tenth was for programs providing cash, food, or housing to such families. [C]ash, food, and housing for the poor grew from 1.0 percent of GNP in 1965 to 2.0 percent in 1980. This was a large increase in absolute terms. But redistributing an extra 1.0 percent of GNP could hardly be expected to reduce poverty to zero.

A realistic assessment of what social policy accomplished between 1965 and 1980 must also take account of the fact that if all else had remained equal, demographic changes would have pushed the poverty rate up during these years, not down. [B]oth the number of people over sixty-five and the number living in families headed by women grew steadily from 1950 to 1980. We do not have poverty rates for these groups in 1950, but in 1960 the official rates were roughly 33 percent for the elderly and 45 percent of families headed by women. Since neither group includes many jobholders, economic growth does not move either group out of poverty fast. From 1960 to 1965, for example, economic growth lowered official poverty from 22 to 17 percent for the nation as a whole, but only lowered it from 33 to 31 percent among the elderly and from 45 to 42 percent among households headed by women.

When poverty became a major social issue during the mid-1960s, government assistance to both these groups was quite modest. In 1965 the typical retired person got only $184 a month from Social Security in 1980 dollars, and a large minority got nothing whatever. Only about a quarter of all families headed by women got benefits from Aid to Families with Dependent Children (AFDC), and benefits for a family of four averaged only $388 a month in 1980 dollars.

From 1965 to 1970 the AFDC system changed drastically. Welfare offices had to drop a wide range of restrictive regulations that had kept many women and children off the rolls. It became much easier to combine AFDC with employment, and benefit levels rose appreciably. As a result of these changes something like half of all persons in families headed by women appear to have been receiving AFDC by 1970.

But as the economy floundered in the 1970s legislators began to draw an increasingly sharp distinction between the "deserving" and the "undeserving" poor. The "deserving" poor were those whom legislators judged incapable of working, namely the elderly and the disabled. Despite their growing numbers, they got more and more help. By 1980 the average Social Security retirement check bought 50 percent more than it had in 1970, and official poverty among the elderly had fallen from 25 percent to 16 percent. Taking noncash benefits into account, the net poverty rate was lower for those over 65 than for those under 65 in 1980.

We have less precise data on the disabled, but we know their monthly benefits grew at the same rate as benefits for the elderly, and the percentage of the population receiving disability benefits also grew rapidly during the 1970s. Since we have no reason to suppose that the percentage of workers actually suffering from serious disabilities grew, it seems reasonable to suppose that a larger fraction of the disabled were getting benefits, and that poverty among the disabled fell as a result.

While legislators were increasingly generous to the "deserving" poor during the 1970s, they showed no such concern for the "undeserving poor." The undeserving poor were those who "ought" to work but were not doing so. They were mainly single mothers and marginally employable men whose unemployment benefits had run out—or who had never been eligible in the first place. Men whose unemployment benefits have run out usually get no federal benefits. Most states offer them token "general assistance," but it is seldom enough to live on. Data on this group is scanty.

Single mothers do better than unemployable men, because legislators are reluctant to let the children starve and cannot find a way of cutting benefits for mothers without cutting them for children as well. Nonetheless, the purchasing power (in 1980 dollars) of AFDC benefits for a family of four rose from $388 a month in 1965 to $435 in 1970. In addition, Congress made food stamps available to all low-income families after 1971. These were worth another $150 to a typical family of four. By 1972, the AFDC-food stamp "package" for a family of four was worth about $577 a month. Benefits did not keep up with inflation after 1972, however, and by 1980 the AFDC-food stamp package was worth only $495 a month. As a result, the welfare rolls grew no faster than the population after 1975, though the number of families headed by women continued to increase.

According to Murray, keeping women off the welfare tolls should have raised their incomes in the long run, since it should have pushed them into jobs where they would acquire the skills they need to better themselves. This did not happen. The official poverty rate in households headed by women remained essentially constant throughout the 1970s, at around 37 percent. Since the group at risk was growing, families headed by women accounted for a rising fraction of the poor.

Taken together, these data tell a story very different from the one Murray tells in *Losing Ground*. First, contrary to what Murray claims, "net" poverty declined almost as fast after 1965 as it had before. Second, the decline in poverty after 1965, unlike the decline before 1965, occurred despite unfavorable economic conditions, and depended to a great extent on government efforts to help the poor. Third, the groups that benefited from this "generous revolution," as Murray

rightly calls it, were precisely the groups that legislators hoped would benefit, notably the aged and the disabled. The groups that did not benefit were the ones that legislators did not especially want to help. Fourth, these improvements took place despite demographic changes that would ordinarily have made things worse. Given the difficulties, legislators should, I think, look back on their efforts to improve the material conditions of poor people's lives with some pride.

2

Up to this point I have treated demographic change as if it were entirely beyond human control, like the weather. According to Murray, however, what I have labeled "demographic change" was a predictable byproduct of government policy. Murray does not, it is true, address the role of government in keeping old people alive longer. But he does argue that changes in social policy, particularly the welfare system, were responsible for the increase in families headed by women after 1965. Since this argument recurs in all conservative attacks on the welfare system, and since scholarly research supports it in certain respects, it deserves a fair hearing.

Murray illustrates his argument with an imaginary Pennsylvania couple named Harold and Phyllis. They are young, poorly educated, and unmarried. Phyllis is also pregnant. The question is whether she should marry Harold. Murray first examines her situation in 1960. If Phyllis does not marry Harold, she can get the equivalent of about $70 a week in 1984 money from AFDC. She cannot supplement her welfare benefits by working, and on $70 a week she cannot live by herself. Nor can she live with Harold, since the welfare agency checks up on her living arrangements, and if she is living with a man she is no longer eligible for AFDC. Thus if Phyllis doesn't marry Harold she will have to live with her parents or put her baby up for adoption. If Phyllis does marry Harold, and he gets a minimum-wage job, they will have the equivalent of $124 a week today. This isn't much, but it is more than $70. Furthermore, if Phyllis is not on AFDC she may be able to work herself, particularly if her mother will help look after her baby. Unless Harold is a complete loser, Phyllis is likely to marry Harold if he asks.

Now the scene shifts to 1970. The Supreme Court has struck down the "man in the house" rule, so Phyllis no longer has to choose between Harold and AFDC. She can have both. According to Murray, if Phyllis does not marry Harold and he does not acknowledge that he is the father of their child, Harold's income will not "count" when the local welfare department decides whether Phyllis is eligible for AFDC, food stamps, and Medicaid. This means she can get paid to stay home with her child while Harold goes out to work, but only so long as she doesn't marry Harold. Furthermore, the value of her welfare "package" is now roughly the same as what Harold or she could earn at a minimum-wage job. Remaining eligible for welfare is thus more important than it was in 1960, as well as being easier. From Phyllis's viewpoint marrying Harold is now quite costly.

While the story of Harold and Phyllis makes persuasive reading, it is misleading in several respects. First, it is not quite true, as Murray claims, that "any money that Harold makes is added to their income without affecting her benefits as long as they remain unmarried." If Phyllis is living with Harold, and Harold

is helping to support her and her child, the law requires her to report Harold's contributions when she fills out her "need assessment" form. What has changed since 1960 is not Phyllis's legal obligation to report Harold's contribution but the likelihood that she will be caught if she lies. Federal guidelines issued in 1965 now prohibit "midnight raids" to determine whether Phyllis is living with Harold. Furthermore, even if Phyllis concedes that she lives with Harold, she can deny that he pays the bills and the welfare department must then prove her a liar. Still, Phyllis must perjure herself, and there is always some chance she will be caught.

The second problem with the Harold and Phyllis story is that Murray's account of Harold's motives is not plausible. In 1960, according to Murray, Harold marries Phyllis and takes a job paying the minimum wage because he "has no choice." But the Harolds of this world have always had a choice. Harold can announce that Phyllis is a slut and that the baby is not his. He can tell Phyllis to get an illegal abortion. He can join the army. Harold's parents may insist that he do his duty by Phyllis, but then again they may blame her for leading him astray. If Harold cared only about improving his standard of living, as Murray suggests, he would not have married Phyllis in 1960.

According to Murray, Harold is less likely to marry Phyllis in 1970 than in 1960 because, with the demise of the "man in the house" rule and with higher benefits, Harold can get Phyllis to support him. But unless Harold works, Phyllis has no incentive either to marry him or to let him live off her meager check, even if she shares her bed with him occasionally. If Harold *does* work, and all he cares about is having money in his pocket, he is better off on his own than he is sharing his check with Phyllis and their baby. From an economic viewpoint, in short, Harold's calculations are much the same in 1970 as in 1960. Marrying Phyllis will still lower his standard of living. The main thing that has changed since 1960 is that Harold's friends and relatives are less likely to think he "ought" to marry Phyllis.

This brings us to the central difficulty in Murray's story. Since Harold is unlikely to want to support Phyllis and their child, and since Phyllis is equally unlikely to want to support Harold, the usual outcome is that they go their separate ways. At this point Phyllis has three choices: get rid of the baby (through adoption or abortion), keep the baby and continue to live with her parents, or keep the baby and set up housekeeping on her own. If she keeps the baby she usually decides to stay with her parents. In 1975 three-quarters of all first-time unwed mothers lived with their parents during the first year after the birth of their baby. (No room for Harold here.) Indeed, half of all unmarried mothers under twenty-four lived with their parents in 1975—and this included divorced and separated mothers as well as those who had never been married.

If Phyllis expects to go on living with her parents, she is not likely to worry much about how big her AFDC check will be. Phyllis has never had a child and she has never had any money. She is used to her mother's paying the rent and putting food on the table. Like most children she is likely to assume that this arrangement can continue until she finds an arrangement she prefers. In the short run, having a child will allow her to leave school (if she has not done so already)

without having to work. It will also mean changing a lot of diapers, but Phyllis may well expect her mother to help with that. Indeed, from Phyllis's viewpoint having a child may look rather like having another little brother or sister. If it brings in some money, so much the better, but if she expects to live with her parents money is likely to be far less important to her than her parents' attitude toward illegitimacy. That is the main thing that changed for her between 1960 and 1970.

Systematic efforts at assessing the impact of AFDC benefits on illegitimacy rates support my version of the Harold and Phyllis story rather than Murray's. The level of a state's AFDC benefits has no measurable effect on its rate of illegitimacy. In 1984, AFDC benefits for a family of four ranged from $120 a month in Mississippi to $676 a month in New York. David Ellwood and Mary Jo Bane recently completed a meticulous analysis of the way such variation affects illegitimate births. In general, states with high benefits have *less* illegitimacy than states with low ones, even after we adjust for differences in race, region, education, income, urbanization, and the like. This may be because high illegitimacy rates make legislators reluctant to raise welfare benefits.

To get around this difficulty, Ellwood and Bane asked whether a change in a state's AFDC benefits led to a change in its illegitimacy rate. They found no consistent effect. Nor did high benefits widen the disparity in illegitimate births between women with a high probability of getting AFDC—teen-agers, nonwhites, high school dropouts—and women with a low probability of getting AFDC.

What about the fact that Phyllis can now live with Harold (or at least sleep with him) without losing her benefits?

Doesn't this discourage marriage and thus increase illegitimacy? Perhaps. [Data show] that illegitimacy has risen at a steadily accelerating rate since 1950. There is no special "blip" in the late 1960s, when midnight raids stopped and the "man in the house" rules passed into history. Nor is there consistent evidence that illegitimacy increased faster among probable AFDC recipients than among women in general.

Murray's explanation of the rise in illegitimacy thus seems to have at least three flaws. First, most mothers of illegitimate children initially live with their parents, not their lovers, so AFDC rules are not very relevant. Second, the trend in illegitimacy is not well correlated with the trend in AFDC benefits or with rule changes. Third, illegitimacy rose among movie stars and college graduates as well as welfare mothers. All this suggests that both the rise of illegitimacy and the liberalization of AFDC reflect broader changes in attitudes toward sex, law, and privacy, and that they had little direct effect on each other.

But while AFDC does not seem to affect the number of unwed mothers, as Murray claims, it does affect family arrangements in other ways. Ellwood and Bane found, for example, that benefit levels had a dramatic effect on the living arrangements of single mothers. If benefits are low, single mothers have trouble maintaining a separate household and are likely to live with their relatives—usually their parents. If benefits rise, single mothers are more likely to maintain their own households.

Higher AFDC benefits also appear to increase the divorce rate. Ellwood and Bane's work suggests, for example, that if the typical state had paid a family of four only $180 a month in 1980 instead of $350, the number of divorced women would have fallen by a tenth. This might be partly because divorced women remarry more hastily in states with very low benefits. But if AFDC pays enough for a woman to live on, she is also more likely to leave her husband. The Seattle-Denver "income maintenance" experiments, which Murray discusses at length, found the same pattern. . . .

Shorn of rhetoric, then, the "empirical" case against the welfare system comes to this. First, high AFDC benefits allow single mothers to set up their own households. Second, high AFDC benefits allow mothers to end bad marriages. Third, high benefits may make divorced mothers more cautious about remarrying. All these "costs" strike me as benefits. . . .

3

. . . Murray's conviction that getting checks from the government is always bad for people is complemented by his conviction that working is always good for them, at least in the long run. Since many people do not recognize that working is in their long-run interest, Murray assumes such people must be forced to do what is good for them. Harold, for example, would rather loaf than take an exhausting, poorly paid job in a laundry. To prevent Harold from indulging his self-destructive preference for loafing, we must make loafing financially impossible. America did this quite effectively until the 1960s. Then we allegedly made it easier for him to qualify for unemployment compensation, so he was more likely to quit his job whenever he got fed up. We also made it easier for him to live off Phyllis's AFDC check. Once Harold had tasted the pleasures of indolence, he found them addictive, like smoking, so he never acquired either the skills or the self-discipline he would have needed to hold a decent job and support a family. By trying to help we therefore did him irreparable harm.

While I share Murray's enthusiasm for work, I cannot see much evidence that changes in government programs significantly affected men's willingness to work during the 1960s. When we look at the unemployed, for example, we find that about half of all unemployed workers were getting unemployment benefits in 1960. The figure was virtually identical in both 1970 and 1980. Thus while the rules governing unemployment compensation did change, the changes did not make joblessness more attractive economically. Murray is quite right that dropping the man-in-the-house rule made it easier for Harold to live off Phyllis's AFDC check. But there is no evidence that this contributed to rising unemployment. Since black women receive about half of all AFDC money, Murray's argument implies that as AFDC rules became more liberal and benefits rose in the late 1960s, unemployment should have risen among young black men. Yet Murray's own data show that such men's unemployment rates fell during the late 1960s. Murray's argument also implies that young black men's unemployment rate should have fallen in the 1970s, when the purchasing power of AFDC benefits was falling. In fact, their unemployment rates rose. . . .

4

While Murray's claim that helping the poor is really bad for them is indefensible, his criticism of the ways in which government tried to help the poor from 1965 to 1980 still raises a number of issues that defenders of these programs need to face. Any successful social policy must strike a balance between collective compassion and individual responsibility. The social policies of the late 1960s and 1970s did not strike this balance very well. They vacillated unpredictably between the two ideals in ways that neither Americans nor any other people could live with over the long run. This vacillation played a major role in the backlash against government efforts to "do good." Murray's rhetoric of individual responsibility and self-sufficiency is not the basis for a social policy that would be politically acceptable over the long run either, but it provides a useful starting point for rethinking where we went wrong.

One chapter of *Losing Ground* is titled "The Destruction of Status Rewards"—not a happy phrase, but a descriptive one. The message is simple. If we want to promote virtue, we have to reward it. The social policies that prevailed from 1964 to 1980 often seemed to reward vice instead. They did not, of course, reward vice for its own sake. But if you set out to help people who are in trouble, you almost inevitably find that most of them are to some extent responsible for their present troubles. Few victims are completely innocent. Helping those who are not doing their best to help themselves poses extraordinarily difficult moral and political problems.

Phyllis, for example, turns to AFDC after she has left Harold. Her cousin Sharon, whose husband has left her, works forty hours a week in the same laundry where Harold worked. If we help Phyllis very much, she will end up better off than Sharon. This will not do. Almost all of us believe it is "better" for people to work than not to work. This means we also believe those who work should end up "better off" then those who do not work. . . .

The AFDC revolution of the 1960s sometimes left Sharon worse off than Phyllis. In 1970, for example, Sharon's minimum-wage job paid $275 a month if she worked forty hours every week and was never laid off. Once her employer deducted Social Security and taxes she was unlikely to take home more than $250 a month. Meanwhile, the median state (Oregon) paid Phyllis and her three children $225 a month, and nine states paid her more than $300 a month. This comparison is somewhat misleading in one respect, however. By 1970 Sharon could also get AFDC benefits to supplement her earnings in the laundry. Under the "thirty and a third" rule, adopted in 1967, local welfare agencies had to ignore the first $30 of Sharon's monthly earnings plus a third of what she earned beyond $30 when they computed her need for AFDC. . . .

Yet while Murray claims to be concerned about rewarding virtue, he seems only interested in doing this if it does not cost the taxpayer anything. Instead of endorsing the "thirty and a third" rule, for example, on the grounds that it rewarded work, he lumps it with all the other undesirable changes that contributed to the growth of the AFDC rolls during the late 1960s. . . .

The difficulty of helping the needy without rewarding indolence or folly recurs when we try to provide "second chances." America was a "second chance" for many of our ancestors, and it remains more committed to the idea that people can change their ways than any other society I know. But we cannot give too many second chances without under-

mining people's motivation to do well the first time around. In most countries, for example, students work hard in secondary school because they must do well on the exams given at the end of secondary school in order to get a desirable job or go on to a university. In America, plenty of colleges accept students who have learned nothing whatever in high school, including those who score near the bottom on the SAT. Is it any wonder that Americans learn less in high school than their counterparts in other industrial countries? . . .

The problem of "second chances" is intimately related to the larger problem of maintaining respect for the rules governing rewards and punishments in American society. As Murray rightly emphasizes, no society can survive if it allows people to violate its rules with impunity on the grounds that the system is at fault.

POSTSCRIPT

Does Welfare Do More Harm Than Good?

The welfare debate in this issue has been argued in rational terms. In the public arena, however, it is entangled in emotional language, and rational discussion seems impossible. One side accuses the other of being heartless. The other side responds with anecdotes about "welfare queens." The only way a genuine public dialogue can begin is to de-escalate the rhetoric.

A little candor on both sides might help. Surely all rational Americans accept the fact that there are genuinely needy people. In many cases, these people do not have families to help them, and private charity is limited. They need public assistance. At the same time, we have to recognize that public assistance carries with it a cost—not merely the immediate dollar cost of the programs, but cost in terms of its effect on self-respect and work incentives. This, according to Murray, is the central defect of the U.S. welfare system. Jencks defends the record of achievement of welfare against Murray's attack even while fully agreeing with Murray's point that welfare should not undermine work incentives.

The American welfare system is often criticized for being both stingy and too free with tax monies. Socialist Michael Harrington's opinion in *The Other America* (Macmillan, 1962) is that the system is ungenerous. Harrington continues his criticism of what he considers the heartless treatment of the poor in America in *The New American Poverty* (Holt, 1984). After analyzing its history and structure, Sar A. Levitan and Clifford M. Johnson conclude that the current welfare system is a fairly rational and necessary response to emerging societal needs: *Beyond the Safety Net: Reviving the Promise of Opportunity in America* (Ballinger, 1984).

Writers who criticize the welfare program for going too far include Martin Anderson, *Welfare* (Hoover Institution, 1977), and Charles Hobbs, *The Welfare Industry* (Heritage Foundation, 1978). Neil Gilbert acknowledges in *Capitalism and the Welfare State* (Yale, 1983) that the welfare system is overextended, but he points out that this is largely because much of the money goes into the pockets of middle-class service providers and middle-class recipients. An excellent review of some of the debates on the welfare system from several viewpoints is presented in the January/February 1986 issue of *Society*. A work that should be examined to understand the psychology of the recipients of welfare is Leonard Goodwin's *Causes and Cures of Welfare: New Evidence on the Social Psychology of the Poor* (Lexington, 1983). He explodes the myth that welfare recipients do not want to work and argues that welfare creates less dependency than is commonly supposed.

ISSUE 13

Do Capitalist Powers Hinder the Development of Third World Countries?

YES: Gerald J. Kruijer, from *Development Through Liberation* (Humanities Press, 1987)

NO: Peter L. Berger, from *The Capitalist Revolution: Fifty Propositions About Prosperity, Equality, and Liberty* (Basic Books, 1986)

ISSUE SUMMARY

YES: Dutch sociologist Gerald J. Kruijer describes the exploitation of Third World countries by capitalist powers and the harm that the capitalist powers inflict.

NO: Sociologist Peter L. Berger argues that the world capitalist system benefits the Third World and that multinational corporations more effectively contribute to the development of these countries than their own governments, many of which are obstacles to development.

In the early 1960s, social scientists were optimistic that the development of North America from a primitive economy to a modern industrial economy could be replicated throughout the Third World. The method for achieving economic development was clearly understood. Capital investments had to increase, modern technologies had to be adopted, modern education had to become widespread, and the country's organizations and institutions had to become more rational and effective. With help from the West, the Third World would modernize rapidly once it set out on the path of progress. After all, the United States had poured capital into Western Europe after World War II, and Europe had rapidly recovered from the devastation of the war. U.S. aid to the Third World, it was thought, should produce similarly dramatic effects.

This optimism was tempered, however, by the knowledge that some countries faced serious obstacles to development, which would have to be overcome before the developmental miracle could take place. Traditional elites and hindering cultural patterns had to be replaced, and tribal discord had to wane. Nevertheless, it was predicted that with capital, technology, and technical assistance from the West, Third World countries would modernize.

In 1957, Paul Baran proclaimed that underdevelopment in the Third World is a direct result of the development of capitalism in the West (*The Political*

Economy of Growth). At that time, his was a minority voice. This theme was repeated in 1969 by Andre Gunder Frank, who attacked modernization theory and argued that the Third World has subsidized the development of Western capitalist countries through net outflows of capital, profits, and skilled labor (*Latin America: Underdevelopment or Revolution?*). Underdevelopment and development, therefore, are both aspects of the world capitalist system. If Third World countries are to develop, Frank argued, they must weaken their links to the world capitalist system, as Argentina, Brazil, Chile, and Mexico did during the two world wars, and as Japan did in its drive to develop during the half century before World War II. According to dependency theory, dependent countries in the world capitalist system remain underdeveloped.

During the 1970s, dependency theory won out over modernization theory in sociology. Critical to its victory was Immanuel Wallerstein's painstaking analysis of the development and characteristics of the world capitalist system. He gave life to world systems theory by describing how the capitalist world economy, having a single division of labor but multiple polities and cultures, emerged in sixteenth-century Europe (*The Modern World System*). Now, all agree that the economic development of each country is deeply affected by its relation to the world economic system. Debate does remain, however, over whether the economic linkage of poor countries to core capitalist countries has positive or negative overall effects. In the selections that follow, Gerald J. Kruijer tallies up the negative side, and Peter L. Berger stresses the positive contributions of Western capitalism.

YES

Gerald J. Kruijer

DEVELOPMENT THROUGH LIBERATION

THE INTERNATIONAL POVERTY-AND-WEALTH SYSTEM

International relationships do not do the poor in the world much good. Thus the Chinese textile industry was destroyed by the import of cloth from Great Britain. Only occasionally do poor peasants profit from international trade. . . .

Production in the poor countries by small, medium-sized and large producers is usually linked to production by companies in the rich countries, and generally in a way that is disadvantageous to the producers. Organisations in the rich countries usually have the upper hand and can dictate terms (financially, technically, and also militarily). People in the Third World are weighed down by a multifarious power bloc. They are oppressed.

Domination on an international scale is just one aspect of the capitalist world economy which comprises the rich and the poor countries and which is characterised by a division of labour and by exchange relations from which the economically powerful profit and the poor suffer. The exercise of power by capitalist enterprises established in the rich countries and supported by their governments is usually referred to as imperialism. Imperialism is based on the old principle that the (neo)colonies are there to be exploited for the benefit of the mother country.

It is therefore understandable that the wealthy capitalist countries should wish to maintain their hold on the Third World and that they should be opposed to those countries disposed to align themselves with the Soviet Union. Below, we shall be examining the draining of capital from the poor countries through commerce with the rich countries and the exodus of skilled workers (the brain drain). Since all these developments favour the rich countries, those countries have little interest in incisive change. . . .

The Drain of Capital

From the poor countries large amounts of money flow to the rich countries in the form of profits, technology payments and interest. In Indonesia, for instance, 2.71 US dollars are siphoned off for every US dollar's worth of direct foreign capital investment made during the period 1970–77. And in 1979, North American companies alone made 12.7 thousand million dollars profit in the Third World and shifted it to the United States. In addition, many of the local rich transfer their money to banks in the prosperous countries.

If an underdeveloped country grants favourable terms to foreign countries, it can count on a generous slice of development aid, mostly in the form of credits. Now, it is partly as result of such credits that the poor countries are so badly in debt, and these debts are growing. Between 1970 and 1984, the outstanding medium and long-term debt expanded almost tenfold to 686,000 million US dollars. Ten years earlier the debt was still a mere 119,000 million. Such an increase is not necessarily a bad thing. If the economy is growing quickly, then the foreign debt may safely be allowed to grow as well, but this is not what has been happening: compared with the growth of the gross national product and of exports, there has been a clear increase in the burden of debt.

There has been a marked increase in indebtedness to such private creditors as foreign banks, which has meant a higher interest rate and shorter loans. It does not have to be stressed that banks only lend money to those regimes they consider credit-worthy, such as Chile, where the government spends little on the welfare of the masses. Governments that try to help their poor and become financially embarrassed as a result are too great a risk for the banks. These governments can then appeal to the International Monetary Fund, a bank in which all countries of the world are represented but in which the rich capitalist countries have the final say. And these make high demands. To obtain help from the IMF, a government must first arrange its finances in such a way as to make sure that it can pay off its debts and is able to contract new loans and to order goods from the rich countries, all of which greatly benefits foreign banks and foreign business. The great majority of the population is made to suffer in the wake of these arrangements inasmuch as their wages are frozen, there is less money for social services and food subsidies are reduced or abolished. . . .

Unequal Exchanges
Poor countries hold an unfavourable position in international trade. One handicap they suffer is that the rich countries have no wish to buy finished or even semi-finished goods from them. Their system of import regulations is governed by an 'anti-finishing policy,' by a kind of value added tax. That means that levies on imported goods are the higher the more finished are the goods: for example, 0 per cent on skins, 4.8 per cent on leather, 11.9 per cent on shoes. The rich countries give preference to unfinished products lest their own industries suffer, and as a result the development of industries in the Third World is gravely impeded. Moreover, the industrial countries are increasingly adding further impediments, quite apart from non-official protectionism. In the European Community, for instance, whole industries or industrial sectors enjoy large-scale state subsidies. In return, it is usually understood that a state-supported industry will not order materials or goods abroad that can be obtained at home, say cheaper steel from a poor country. One good turn deserves another.

Even so, some poor countries have been able to step up their industrial exports. Industrialisation in the Third World has made great headway during the last two decades; indeed in the period from 1960 to 1968 the increase was more rapid than in highly developed capitalist countries. But this increase is insignificant if it is related to per capita income. A number of industrial products flow out from the poor countries; the proportion of manufactured goods in the total exports rose from about 15 per cent in the early 1960s to nearly 50 per cent in the early 1980s. The countries with the lowest incomes, by contrast, produced much less favourable figures. More than half the exports from Third World countries come from just five countries. The newcomers among the countries exporting manufactured goods specialise in less sophisticated, labour-intensive products.

It is clear that the export of finished goods has risen in a small number of poor countries, but the figures do not tell us who profits. It may well be that the chief beneficiaries are foreign companies.

Among the relatively unfinished products that leave the poor countries, minerals rank first. They come from the so-called extractive sector of the economy, siphoning off raw materials and energy mainly intended for the processing industries of the rich countries.

As for imports, many poor countries are forced to buy expensive machinery, tools and the like, abroad. In addition, several are dependent upon oil imports. Remarkably enough, large amounts of foodstuffs that could easily be produced at home are also imported. Cereals, soya beans, cotton, sugar and similar products travel from the rich countries to the poor. Of the total amount of agricultural produce exported by 'Western' countries, about 20 per cent goes to the poor countries. The peasants in these countries are unwilling to grow these products because a horde of profiteers has seen to it that they are grossly underpaid; and in some cases the peasants find it more attractive to concentrate on cash crops for export.

A remarkable phenomenon is the import of luxury articles for the privileged social classes. The Dutch journalist Jan van der Putten gives the example of French wines to be seen freely on sale in Santiago de Chile (while Chile itself produces excellent wines). Caviar, too, and other luxuries are available for the refined taste of a small but well-funded upper stratum. No one needs to be told that the foreign currency required for the import of these delicacies is earned by the work of those for whom French wine and caviar will always belong to a remote and unattainable world.

In addition to food, the means of death, too, travel in the direction of the Third World. We know what happens to them. It was with North American arms that the Nicaraguan National Guard inflicted massacres in defence of a social system that favoured those in power.

The poor countries are an attractive market for the rich countries. They absorb some of the rich countries' overproduction, and shoddy or faulty goods may be disposed of in them. This applies, for instance, to medicines prohibited in North America and Western Europe, and to insecticides that the rich countries do not allow on their fields.

For every country without its own supply, oil is an essential import. An increase in its price is unwelcome to every consumer, but for the poor countries it is a disaster. Towards the end of

1973, they were delivered a staggering blow when the price of oil almost quadrupled; oil imports in the poor countries rose from 8,000 million US dollars in 1973 to 24,000 million in 1974. In addition, the cost of their other imports also rose, since the industrial countries were having to pay more for their energy. At the end of 1978 there was another energy crisis and the price of oil in the poor countries doubled again, almost overnight. To make things still worse, their chances of exporting goods to the rich countries were severely curtailed by economic stagnation in the latter.

In exports no less than in imports, the rich countries make more money than the poor countries. According to some authors this is the most important cause of the growing poverty gap between rich and poor countries. There is a constant siphoning of labour value from the poor countries to the rich. Samir Amin, an Egyptian specialist on economic development, has calculated that in the middle of the sixties the loss to the poor countries from unequal exchanges amounted to about 22,000 million US dollars a year. That was twice as much as the 'aid' and private capital received by the Third World. . . .

The Brain Drain

One ghastly consequence of imperialism is the literal sucking out of human beings. This happened, among other places, in Haiti where companies from the United States collected blood for use in luxury hospitals in North America. On a much larger scale, the Third World suffers a brain drain, although that term does not, of course, have to be taken literally.

Between 1961 and 1972, some 300,000 highly skilled workers left the under-developed for the developed countries. Most of them went to the United States (90,000), Great Britain (84,000) and Canada (56,000). The largest number of immigrants came from Asia (more than 50 per cent), above all from the Philippines and India. Most of these were engineers (25 per cent), followed by doctors and surgeons (20 per cent) and scientists (10 per cent). It has been computed that the educational value of the qualified labour force that left the Third World for the United States, Great Britain and Canada between 1960 and 1972 was 50,900 million dollars, vastly more than all development aid put together.

Had the West had to pay for this brain drain there would, according to an UNCTAD report, have been a 50 per cent reduction in the foreign debt of the Third World in 1972.

The Capitalist World Economy

We saw in the last section that a great deal of wealth is pumped from the poor countries into the rich. Why does this happen and who is responsible for it? To find the answers we must examine the origins of the domination of the poor countries by the rich.

Capitalism emerged in Western Europe when the bourgeoisie acquired possession of the means of production created by the work of others.

The members of this social class seized the surplus value of the work performed by people who did not own the means of production. With the capital acquired as a result, the entrepreneurs were either able to step up production very considerably in Europe, or else—if higher profits could be made that way—they tried their luck in the colonies.

In the sixteenth century, ships sailed to what is now called the Third World ostensibly to trade, but what went by that term was often little better than robbery. At a later stage, Europeans founded colonies for the express purpose of encouraging the cultivation of crops whose export to Europe promised large profits. By contrast, simple industrial products, for instance textiles, were exported to the colonies. This was the beginning of a division of labour on a world scale introduced for the benefit of the ruling class in Western Europe. Later, from the end of the nineteenth century, an increasing amount of ore and oil was removed from the Third World, having been extracted with capital supplied by the rich countries.

European penetration did a great deal of damage to autochthonous production in the poor countries. In his book *How Europe Underdeveloped Africa*, the Guyanese historian, Walter R. Rodney, has shown to just what extent colonisation by the European powers has had a negative effect on the development of Africa. That continent was in the process of developing its own productive resources when the Europeans arrived and brought such development to an end. Africa, thus doomed to impotence, fell further and further behind Europe.

Other continents experienced other developments, but none brought improvements for the native population. Asia, Africa and Latin America, before being introduced to the capitalist division of labour on an international scale, were quite unfamiliar with such phenomena as landless peasants, slums and massive unemployment or underemployment, as Samir Amin has observed. The European bourgeoisie must bear full responsibility for these.

During the colonial period, the exploitation of the colonies served European interests above all. However, after the Second World War, the balance shifted in favour of North American business. . . .

The favourable position of the rich countries is not exclusively due to such spontaneous processes as unequal exchanges—the protectionist policy of rich countries must also be taken into consideration. Thus 32 per cent of all animal products, 31 per cent of all textiles, 29 per cent of all vegetable products, and 28 per cent of all prepared food and tobacco products are subject to import restrictions in the wealthy countries. In addition, the governments of the rich countries assist ailing exporters with elaborate schemes. European agriculture, in particular, is so heavily subsidised that imports of food (*inter alia* from poor countries) is only possible in those areas where European production falls short. Moreover, if subsidised farmers produce more than the inhabitants of the European Community can consume, the surpluses are reduced with the help of export subsidies and dumped on to what is often an oversaturated world market, so that prices drop further and it becomes increasingly difficult for anyone in the poor countries to make money from crops.

If we reflect on the structure of the capitalist world economy, we shall find that it is largely in the hands of three great power groups: the big international corporations, the big international banks and the dependent bourgeoisie of the poor countries. The latter, who are hand in glove with those who run the political machine in their countries, render considerable services to the other two power groups. In her *Third World in Global Development*, Ankie Hoogvelt speaks of a tripartite collaboration between international finance capital, the multinationals and Third World governments in the exploitation of the Third World. The resulting power structure bears a great deal of similarity to that of the colonial period. Then, too, the governments in the poor countries saw to it that foreign capital could exploit resources and labour under the most favourable conditions.

The big multinational corporations are the leading actors on the international stage. One cannot help admiring them. To set them up and to keep them going requires a great deal of energy and intelligence. They are among capitalism's greatest achievements: in 1978, the four largest multinationals between them had an annual turnover greater than the total GNP of the whole continent of Africa.

The importance of the multinationals is reflected in the scope of their commercial activities, mainly conducted by affiliated companies. Statistical tables give the impression that world trade takes place between countries, but this is far from being the case. There are divisions of multinationals that supply goods to other divisions of the same corporations. Moreover, many of these goods are also manufactured by the multinationals to whom international production is more important than international trade. In one of her books, Hoogvelt points out that as early as 1971 the combined production of all multinational corporations outside their countries of origin was greater than the total value of goods and services that make up the trade between countries (outside the Socialist bloc).

It is partly because of investments by the multinationals that the Third World, too, has experienced a considerable degree of industrialisation. The multinationals do this because production costs in the poor countries (including wages)

are low. Their power is great enough to stop developments that might lead to wage increases, and they can count on the support of the local economic ruling class whose interests in this area are the same as those of the multinationals. As a result the unequal exchange mentioned [earlier in this reading] can be maintained.

There is no question but that the activities of multinational corporations are disadvantageous to the great majority in the Third World. True, a small number of privileged people in the poor countries profit from their presence, albeit in a very limited way. Local employees are assigned the less highly paid jobs, the senior staff being recruited in the rich countries. Nor is local production boosted to any great extent. Thus Philips-Chile imported 81.7 per cent of the raw materials it needed in 1968, 87.2 per cent of its spare parts and 94 per cent of its machinery. The multinationals, moreover, do very little to hand on advanced knowledge and skills, and they are masters at avoiding taxation. If they do well, the subsidiaries of the multinationals in the poor countries minimise their declared profits with various kinds of bookkeeping tricks (by increasing the ostensible costs of products and other materials obtained from the mother company). The biggest local beneficiaries of foreign industries are found among local businessmen and government officials who supply different services and labour to the foreigners. In addition, when it suits them, members of the bourgeoisie are only too happy to dispose of their businesses to foreign interests. Thus statistics show that a large part of the investment of foreign companies is devoted to buying up viable local businesses. By the end of the 1960s, 65 per cent of 2,904 subsidiaries of

396 North American and other multinationals in underdeveloped countries had been bought in that way.

Capitalism is of little benefit to the great majority in the Third World. Indeed, it is no exaggeration to say that it causes a great deal of suffering. But perhaps that is not the whole story, since after a period of social misery in Europe and North America it brought prosperity to a good many people. That, at least, is how it looks to my solidarity groups; in the rich countries themselves there are many who complain about the results of the capitalist system. Still, the poor in the Third World would gladly change places with them, a fact that has persuaded quite a few writers that capitalism has not exploited the Third World as much as it might have done. If the capitalists were only allowed to have their way, these writers continue, they would bring prosperity to the Third World as well. This way of thinking is quite absurd. . . . Samir . . . argues that capitalist production in the underdeveloped countries is based on cheap labour and does not greatly stimulate internal demand, with the result that few industries geared to the national market can develop. The economy of the poor country has been distorted by an export bias, which may suit a small minority. For this group, luxury goods are imported freely, as anyone can see in, say, large cities in many parts of Africa. However poor that continent may be, the stores are full of consumer goods for the better-off.

The economy of the rich capitalist countries is much healthier than that. Here, high wages and salaries have helped to boost purchasing power and hence mass production of consumer goods. Despite the high labour cost, industry has been able to make good profits and to acquire what capital equipment was needed to step up output dramatically. The combination of the mass production of consumer goods with the large-scale production of capital goods is the true explanation of the favourable economic position of the rich capitalist countries. That position was largely created by trade unions who managed to keep wage rises roughly in tune with increases in productivity. The workers were able, as Amin puts it, to wring a social contract from the employers in which it is laid down that consumers must be paid enough to spend freely, and employers must be able to retain enough to make sizeable investments. The social contract reflects a balance of power between organised workers and organised employers, with the state acting as a kind of referee: it makes sure that both parties keep the 'contract.'

Amin calls development in the North Atlantic countries autocentric: it generates its own expansion, at least in general, for without some profits in the Third World, Western Europe and North America would not fare nearly so well.

Some Third World countries, too, seem to show signs of autocentric development, for instance South Korea and Brazil, but such signs are misleading. From about 1966, the Republic of Korea has been the scene of labour-intensive developments focused on the export of industrial goods. The consequent increase in the gross national product did not, however, lead to a significant increase in internal buying power. True, social provisions were made for large groups of the population and there were also—especially in the seventies—some wage increases, but real wages rose less than GNP and productivity. A low wage level is and remains the basis of South Korean industrial development. It helps to make South Korean products considerably cheaper than similar products from other countries. Foreign enterprises, too, profit from the low wages for, as the South Korean expert Sun-Hwan Jo explains, they are able to swamp their home markets with highly competitive imports. The peasants in South Korea are forced to make a contribution to this process by growing cheap food for the factory workers. That spells poverty for the rural areas and explains why millions of people have moved to the slums of the cities, where they swell the labour supply and thus help to keep the wages of the factory workers low.

The low wages of the workers and the low incomes of the peasants mean that the buying power of South Koreans is low, but this is not considered a serious complaint by the rulers, writes Phyllis Kim, because the production is mainly geared at foreign markets. And here we come up against the central flaw of the South Korean development model: the economy is *not* being guided towards an autocentric system. Because the country has no trade unions with enough influence to impose a different policy, improvements in the lot of the masses can only come about if a scarcity of labour forces the employers to pay decent wages. The resulting increase in purchasing power would lead to increased production for the internal market, which would bring further wages increases, and so on. This, at least, is the view of Dieter Senghaas, though I doubt whether spontaneous economic processes will ever bring the desired result; without a powerful labour movement no substantial wage increases can be expected.

According to Senghaas, there is no sign that the labour factor in South Korea will ever grow scarce and hence expensive. This is prevented by demographic factors, by a surplus of labour in agriculture and by the acquisition of labour-saving machinery. Nor should the political influence of the employers be overlooked. They know how to make sure that further mechanisation does not go hand in hand with a shorter working week, something that did happen in Western Europe. In South Korea the workers still put in long hours. In 1982, for instance, women still worked an average of 52.9 hours per week.

In Brazil, the future of the poor looks no rosier. Here, too, production is strongly geared to exports. There is a great deal of development by foreigners in the interest of foreign countries, which leads to great social contrasts. *Time* magazine has called it a social scandal: while the Brazilian economy is growing spectacularly, more than two million children have been deserted by their desperate parents to roam about the streets. Another fourteen million children live in such poor circumstances that they would probably be better off if their parents deserted them as well. Altogether one Brazilian child in three is destitute. . . .

According to Johan Galtung, the capitalist world is made up of elements that rob one another of wealth. This is also true of every individual country. The capital city drains wealth from the provincial towns, the provincial towns from the villages, the villages (the merchants) from the peasants, the peasants from the farm labourers, and the men from the women. The main losers are the poverty-stricken women and children in rural areas of the Third World. . . .

The consolidation of inequality in economic power.

The creaming off of wealth, discussed in the previous paragraph, is the main system-maintaining factor. The crux of the inequalities between various countries or between urban and rural groups is that the rulers siphon off wealth from the ruled, from the oppressed. If the system works 'well', the poor countries keep growing poorer and so do the poorer regions of a country. And the system works quite well. It is based on a division of labour and an unequal exchange that is disadvantageous to those who are badly placed in the system.

Development aid is often based on the maintenance of the status quo. It is a kind of umbilical cord, writes A. M. Babu, that ties the underdeveloped countries to the economies of the rich. A major part of the so-called aid is used by Third World governments to service loans from banks in the rich countries. Another part is given by the donor countries to help their own exports and to enable their own businesses to invest in the Third World. Thus the development aid given to Surinam was largely directed at the improvement of the infrastructure for the benefit of international capital, for what is so euphemistically called the improvement of the investment climate. . . .

Violent oppression.

When the imperialist world system functions smoothly in the economic, cultural and political sphere, the big capitalist powers do not have to use violence to defend their interests. But if other mechanisms prove inadequate, the use of arms is first threatened, and if that does not have the required effect, weapons are then brought out. Notorious is the enormous devastation wrought in Vietnam for the sole purpose of maintaining a regime favourable to the North Americans in Saigon.

NO
Peter L. Berger

THE CAPITALIST REVOLUTION: FIFTY PROPOSITIONS ABOUT PROSPERITY, EQUALITY, AND LIBERTY

CAPITALISM AND DEVELOPMENT

Capitalism has become a global phenomenon. From the enclaves of capitalist enterprise, superimposed on the centuries-old feudal and subsistence economies of Europe, it first conquered those economies and then thrust out beyond them—through trade, imperial expansion, and cultural penetration—until today it has reached virtually every part of the world not ruled by Communist regimes (and even there its outposts are to be found). Capitalism has been one of the most dynamic forces in human history, transforming one society after another, and today it has become established as an international system determining the economic fate of most of mankind and, at least indirectly, its social, political, and cultural fate, as well. . . .

A theory of capitalism must necessarily address the question whether and to what extent capitalism as an economic system favors development in the contemporary world. Put simply, the question is whether capitalism can realize the expectations contained in the notion of development. As soon as one asks this question, one must recall that, of course, all the countries that today constitute the "metropolis" of advanced industrial capitalism were once poor, "underdeveloped." In terms of all the obvious indicators of poverty—infant mortality, life expectancy, caloric intake, housing conditions, standards of education and health care, and, last not least, cash income—every single country of Europe and North America was a "Third World" country two hundred years ago, and several were very poor indeed much more recently. Capitalist history in these countries, as discussed in earlier chapters of this book [which is not part of this reading], has been a story of development in precisely the sense just suggested. If so, the question about capitalism and development can be further refined: *Is it plausible to assume*

From Peter L. Berger, *The Capitalist Revolution: Fifty Propositions About Prosperity, Equality, and Liberty* (Basic Books, 1986). Copyright © 1986 by Peter L. Berger. Reprinted by permission of Basic Books, Inc., Publishers, New York. Notes omitted.

that the story of development as it took place in Europe and North America will repeat itself in the poor countries of the Third World? If the assumption holds, the outlook, of course, is optimistic. It makes sense then to look at, say, India today through the eyes of England in the earlier days of the Industrial Revolution, with the prospect being that India farther down the road will increasingly resemble contemporary England in its material standards of life (if not also in other ways). One will then ask what stage of development any particular country is in at any given point in time, with the implication that underdevelopment, however painful at the moment, is a temporary and even necessary condition in a predictably upswing process.

It is fair to say that the optimistic assumption generally prevailed when social scientists first turned their attention to the issue of Third World development in the years following World War II, especially in the 1950s and early 1960s. A paradigmatic and at the time very influential statement of this position was that by W. W. Rostow. Britain is here presented as the first society experiencing modern economic growth (no one, of course, will question that), but it is also presented as the exemplar that other societies will have to follow. These other societies will pass through the same stages (though, of course, within different time spans). It would be wrong to read into Rostow the notion that this sequence of stages is rigidly determined, or that it cannot be modified by policies or events. All the same, in his view it makes very good sense indeed to look at any given Third World society today and place it on a trajectory corresponding to the history of modern Britain. . . .

Beginning with the late 1960s, this approach to development came under increasing fire and was increasingly replaced by viewpoints much less optimistic about the prospects of the Third World within the international capitalist system. Both within Western academia and within the portion of the Western policy community concerned with these issues, not to mention Third World intellectual and political elites, an outlook much farther to the "left" came to dominance in a surprisingly short period of time. Today it has become the conventional position in sizable parts of the intellectual world, and it requires close attention. It should be pointed out, though, that the optimistic outlook sketched above was subjected to earlier criticisms, most of them precisely caused by skepticism about its optimistic forecasts.

The new position, when confronted with the question of whether contemporary Third World societies can be expected to run through the "stages" experienced by England and other Western capitalist economies, supplies a clear reply: *No.* Today this position is often designated as "dependency theory." . . .

Whatever may have been the driving forces and the results of imperial expansion in the countries of advanced capitalism in the West, what have been the consequences in the Third World societies which have been the targets of this expansion? This has been the focus of so-called dependency theory. Its central thesis has been that the development of the periphery has been distorted or even prevented by this penetration ("dominance") by the forces of international capitalism. In exploring this thesis, it is important to distinguish the *facts* of "dependency" from the *alleged nefarious consequences* of this condition. Few observers would question that something reasonably called "dependency" comes about when very powerful economies impinge on much weaker ones: When, say, United States corporations powerfully intrude into a small Central American country, it is plausible to say that the latter comes to be "dependent" on the United States economy. But is this dependent condition necessarily bad for the people of the Central American country and specifically for their chances of development?

Dependency theorists have answered this question affirmatively, for several reasons: Decisions on national economic policy are now made outside the country and for the benefit of others. The national economy is "distorted," because its course is dictated by external needs and not by its indigenous logic. National enterprise is smothered, often to the point of "industrial infanticide"—that is, domestic industrial development is arrested in the interest of the foreign enterprises dominating the national economy. Last not least, the indigenous population is pauperized (immiserated), with the exception of the so-called comprador class—the local groups who become agents of foreign enterprise. This view of the effects of capitalist penetration has been brilliantly summed up in a phrase coined by Andre Gunder Frank, himself an important dependency theorist—the "development of underdevelopment." In other words, the underdevelopment of the Third World is not a condition preceding the advent of international capitalism in those countries but rather is a condition *brought about* by this international capitalism, and necessarily so. . . .

Yet, even limiting oneself to the past, the presupposition [that capitalist penetration is responsible for underdevelopment] is dubious. It may be stipulated that in some specific cases the effects of capitalist penetration on the "periphery" have indeed been nefarious. For example, there is a good case to be made that it was deliberate British policy to throttle the Indian textiles industry because the Indian market was desired for British textiles. And even in the postcolonial situation, similar cases can be made, for example for the operation of some United States corporations in Central America or for the role of French capital in West Africa. But to argue that, *in the aggregate*, capitalist penetration has done economic harm to Third World countries is very difficult indeed. Taking Africa as an important test area, countries *least* affected by colonialism (such as Ethiopia) are in the worst economic condition, while countries *most* affected by it (such as Kenya) are in a much better state. Even in cases where one might plausibly speak of colonial "exploitation," the colonial regimes left behind physical infrastructures (such as railroads and highways) and social institutions (such as a modern bureaucracy and an educational system) that can only be regarded as assets for development in the postcolonial period. And even if the argument could be made (which it probably cannot) that the wealth of the erstwhile colonial powers (notably Britain, France, and the Netherlands) can be explained, at least in part, by "exploitation" of the colonies, such explanation fails completely for some of the major industrial countries whose colonial history is comparatively insignificant (notably the United States, Germany, and Japan). Finally, one should observe that, even if dependency were an economically debilitating condition, this would not be in itself an indictment of capitalism: If the international capitalist system contains all sorts of "inequalities," there is no reason whatever to believe that an international socialist system would be any more egalitarian; indeed, this point need not be made speculatively, since the Soviet Union and its industrialized allies in Europe have indeed established such an international socialist system, in which both "inequality" and "dependency" are important features.

In the manner in which dependency theory is used today, there are two major actors to whom reference is frequently made—the multinational corporations and Third World governments. The overall bias is that the actions of the former are inimical to development, while the latter are to be fostered as agents of development. Again, one should not be one-sided or doctrinaire on this subject: There *are* multinational corporations whose actions inhibit development, and there *are* Third World governments whose policies are conducive to development. In the aggregate, however, the reverse formulation is more persuasive. Multinational corporations, whatever sins they may have committed here and there, are the most important vehicles for the transfer of capital and technology to Third World countries, for training of indigenous personnel in modern economic occupations, and, last not least, for reliable tax revenues into Third World treasuries. On the other hand, a much better argument can be made that a large number of Third World governments are *obstacles* to development. Often their policies have the direct effect of perpetuating underdevelopment—such as economically destructive socialist experiments, regulations that favor urban populations by artificially depressing farm prices and thus discourage agricultural develop-

ment, persecution of economically productive minorities (such as the Indians in East Africa or the Chinese in Southeast Asia), and policies that discourage enterprise and international trade through excessive regulation and licensing. At other times, even if government policies are not directly inimical to development, the latter is hindered by widespread government ineffectiveness (what Gunnar Myrdal has aptly termed the "soft state") and by pervasive corruption (P. T. Bauer has coined the word "kleptocracy" for this, alas, common feature of many Third World governments). Thus both the anti-multinational and the statist biases of dependency theory as currently used have very little empirical justification. . . .

But back to the presupposition that capitalism has been bad for development in the Third World: The empirical basis for this allegation is generally very shaky. There is one very important case, though, which undermines the presupposition in a decisive manner. *The development of the capitalist societies of East Asia is the most important empirical falsification of dependency theory.*

These societies, which constitute a "second case" of modern industrial capitalism, will be looked at in greater detail in the next chapter [which is not part of this reading]. But their place in the present argument should be stated now. Here are the preeminent "success stories" of development since World War II—Japan, of course, as the most significant case, but followed now by the so-called Four Little Dragons (South Korea, Taiwan, Hong Kong, and Singapore) and now possibly being followed by at least some of the other Southeast Asian countries (notably Thailand, Malaysia, and Indonesia). These are not only "success stories" in terms of economic growth (which, of course, has been phenomenal over a sustained period of time) but also in terms of development precisely in the aforementioned sense-with masses of people being lifted from poverty into a comfortable and in places highly affluent standard of life, with the virtual eradication of the common indicators of Third World underdevelopment, and with comparatively egalitarian income and wealth distributions. None of this makes any sense whatever in terms of dependency theory. Japan alone makes this point. If ever there was a victim of imperialism, it was Japan. Its first great miracle of development took place during the Meiji period—the direct result of an act of naked imperialist aggression, when Commodore Perry of the United States Navy steamed into Tokyo Bay in 1853 and, at gunpoint, forced the opening of Japan to Western capitalist penetration. The second miracle, of course, took place after World War II—following devastating military defeat at the hands of the Western powers, after two atomic bombs had been dropped on the country, and (an epitome of "neocolonialism") under American military occupation. The dramatic development of the Four Little Dragons is equally inexplicable in dependency-theory terms. All four could be cited as textbook cases of "neocolonial" dominance, by the United States and Britain—and one, Hong Kong, remains under colonial rule to this day.

If these were some small countries with little international importance, one might dismiss them as special cases of no theoretical significance. This is not feasible here. Together they contain large populations and they have made a great difference in the world economy. And one, Japan, has become one of the major industrial powers in the contemporary world, directly competing in many ares with the old "metropolitan" countries of the West.The theoretical significance of East Asia for the immediate argument can be simply stated: One cannot go on doing dependency theory while ignoring this region of the world, but its development cannot be explained from within the theory.

If the explanations of the relation between capitalism and development of both the older and the more recent imperialism theorists must be rejected, a general counterproposition should now be formulated. Its empirical plausibility will be argued for the rest of this chapter.

Proposition: *The inclusion of a Third World country within the international capitalist system tends to favor its development. . . .*

There is widespread agreement today, from Chile to China, that an economy allowing market forces the fullest feasible sway will perform better than one in which all decisions are centrally administered. . . .

Proposition: *The superior productive power of capitalism, as manifested in the advanced industrial countries of the West, continues to manifest itself today wherever the global capitalist system has intruded.*

Some words of caution are necessary here. It would be a serious error to understand this proposition as implying that *only* capitalism can generate economic growth. In recent decades the overall world economy has grown phenomenally and virtually *all* countries have registered positive economic growth. The latter statement definitely includes the less developed countries (LDCs) as a group. Thus between 1955 and 1970 the aggregate of these LDCs experienced 5.4 percent growth in Gross National Product and 3.1 percent in GNP per capita;

between 1970 and 1980 the LDCs registered 5.3 percent growth in GNP and, once again, 3.1 percent growth in GNP per capita (the major reason for the difference between GNP growth and growth in GNP per capita, of course, is population growth). Economic growth of similar proportions continued in the early 1980s, despite a worldwide recession, and the growth of the LDCs was, in many individual countries, greater than the growth of Western economies. From 1955 to 1980 world output (that is, the sum total of all countries' GNPs) tripled in real terms (that is, measured in constant dollars, so as to control for inflation). In the same quarter-century world GNP per capita doubled, despite the fact that the world population rose from about 2.8 to about 4.4 billion.

This is an awesome spectacle. There is no way in which capitalism alone can be credited with it. Modern technology as such, operating in virtually any economic system, will result in a vast increase in productive power and thus necessarily in increased economic growth. Indeed, one may argue that any country that has access even to a modicum of modern technology and nevertheless *fails* to grow must strain considerably to do so: Nongrowth represents a sort of political achievement. The argument, then, is *not* that only capitalism can provide economic growth. Rather, it is that capitalism provides economic growth on a more secure and sustained basis and also that the economic performance of capitalism has a much more dynamic quality in terms of innovation and versatility. And the reasons for this, again, are not mysterious at all. They all go back to the unique capacity of the market in stimulating and rationalizing economic activity. . . .

Nick Eberstadt, a demographer, has suggested that a study of the poor ought to focus on the "physiology" of development—that is, on basic demographic changes derived from census data rather than on the usual economic data. The reason is that demographic census data are at least *relatively* reliable if compared with, for example, data on the average income of the poor. Specifically, data on life expectancy and infant mortality allow some reasonably confident deductions on the condition of the people to whom the data refer. . . .

Eberstadt compared capitalist and socialist societies in the Third World in terms of these basic demographic data. As far as life expectancy and infant mortality are concerned (the latter typically determining the former), the main fact is these have improved virtually everywhere. The reason for this, again, lies with modernization as such rather than with any particular socioeconomic system. Elementary hygiene, better nutrition, access to even rudimentary methods of modern child care and medicine, water purification—these factors can have a dramatic impact on demographic data even in the very short run, and this has indeed been the case in most less developed countries. If, however, one wishes to explore how the poor fare under different socioeconomic systems, one must see whether a particular system falls above or below the general rising curve of demographic improvement. As to life expectancy (the demographic measure par excellence), there is no evidence that the socialist countries do better. For example, life expectancy in Cuba *declined* in the immediate postrevolutionary period, 1960–69; since then, there has been improvement but less so than in other Caribbean countries.

Eberstadt believes that postrevolutionary improvement in life expectancy could have been projected from the prerevolutionary data: Cuba was one of the healthiest countries in the region in the 1950s; the revolution retarded its health development briefly (for whatever reasons), and then allowed the curve to continue its upward secular trend. This is not in itself a bad record, but it hardly substantiates the extravagant claims for what the revolution is supposed to have done for the health of the poor. For another (and much more important example), China clearly suffered terrible demographic costs in the wake of the so-called Great Leap after 1958; since then, life expectancy has improved—in a development very similar to that of India (not to mention the vastly superior performance of Taiwan and the other capitalist societies of East Asia). For a final example, if one compares the two Koreas, the record on life expectancy in the South is better, despite the better starting point of the North at the time the country was divided.

In any discussion of the condition of the poor in the Third World, the question of hunger looms very large indeed. Eberstadt argues plausibly that infant mortality is the best available indicator of the presence of hunger, since young children are its most immediate and numerous victims. There has been a sharp decline in infant mortality in some less developed countries (for example, Mexico, the Philippines, and Thailand). Even India and Indonesia (hardly top performers in demographic improvement) have experienced a drop of more than half since the 1950s. The data for Cuba, not surprisingly, reflect the above-mentioned data on life expectancy—after a hiatus in the immediate aftermath of the revolution, Cuba continued to improve its record—but no more so than a number of other countries in the Caribbean (for instance, Jamaica) and no more so than could have been projected from prerevolutionary trends. China, as is now known (and admitted by the Chinese government), suffered massive famines in the early 1960s, as a direct consequence of the follies of Maoist agrarian policy. As against this, there has been an agricultural miracle in India, which can be directly related not only to the so-called Green Revolution (a technological event not necessarily linked to any particular socioeconomic system) but to the fact that Indian agriculture has remained organized as an almost purely capitalist enterprise in sharp distinction to the industrial sectors on the Indian economy. One of the most dramatic changes in China in recent years has been the freeing of agriculture from the constraints of the socialist system. The result has been a rapid and enormous increase in agricultural productivity, from which, by all available accounts, the rural poor have profited directly and substantially.

To sum up, the performance of socialist Third World societies in improving the material condition of its peoples (most of whom, of course, were poor to begin with) is hardly remarkable and certainly does not substantiate the extravagant ideological claims made in this regard. It is no better than the performance of many Third World societies with capitalist systems. Even more important is that all the socialist societies have been dramatically out-performed by a number of successful capitalist countries, especially in Asia. Finally, as particularly shown by the agricultural developments in India and China, the move from socialist to capitalist agrarian strategies dramatically improves the condition of the rural poor. This is all the more important in view of the widespread agreement (including development experts on the "left") that agriculture is the key to development and thus to the fate of the urban as well as the rural poor.

The following hypothesis may then be formulated: *Capitalist development is more likely than socialist development to improve the material standards of life of people in the contemporary Third World, including the poorest groups.*

(Needless to say, this proposition does *not* imply that capitalist development has this effect automatically and in all places; the proposition is phrased in probabilistic language.)

It is safe to say that most poor people are much more interested in the improvement of their condition than in comparing themselves with other groups. It is the intellectuals rather than the poor who tend to have an interest in "equality." This is why, given the yardstick for development supplied by the "preferential option for the poor," it is much more important to look at absolute standards of material life than at the relativities of income distribution. Still, the latter issue must also be addressed, not only because it looms large in the contemporary debates but also because extreme inequalities of income, even if these do not necessarily preclude an improvement in the condition of the poor, tend to generate social and political tensions inimical to development. There is a widespread assumption that, in the choice between capitalist and socialist development models, there is a trade-off between growth and equality. In other words, it is conceded, even by socialist theorists, that capitalism is better for the achievement of economic growth, but it is then maintained that the cost of this greater economic efficiency is a high degree of inequality. Let the question be put aside here whether, in view of the effects of economic growth on material standards of life, the price of inequality may not be well worth paying. Rather, the question at the moment is whether the trade-off does indeed prevail. . . .

Among economists there is a very widespread (though not completely undisputed) belief that the Kuznets effect . . . holds in the Third World today. . . . In other words, the majority of economists believe that their data show that inequality in income increases in the earlier stages of economic growth and then levels off at a later stage. Belief in the Kuznets effect has led to the argument that redistributionist government interventions are necessary to offset the inequalities that would otherwise occur "naturally." An important question, then, is that of the basic mechanisms of equalization and their susceptibility to government intervention: What economic processes make for a more equitable income distribution and to what extent can these processes be influenced by government policies?

Gustav Papanek, an economist who has spent many years in cross-national studies of income distribution, argues for the primacy of the wages of unskilled labor in any process of equalization. The assumption here is that, as these wages rise, income distribution becomes more equal. If one is interested in "equality," one ought then to focus on how different development strategies affect the wages of unskilled labor. Statistically, the question is whether unskilled labor income improves more rapidly than per capita income nationwide (a sort of neat statistical correlate of the "preferential option for the poor").

Unlike Eberstadt, Papanek disregards the fully socialist societies. Instead, he differentiates between three strategies in other Third World societies: a growth-oriented private-enterprise strategy or, if one prefers, a capitalist strategy *tout court* (for example, the "Four Little Dragons" of East Asia, and Indonesia and Pakistan in the 1960s); "modified capitalism"— that is, heavy government interference through wage and price controls (for example, Indonesia and Pakistan in the 1970s and many African countries); "populist strategies"—even heavier government interference, both through nationalization and regulation (for example, India and Tanzania). The result of Papanek's investigations is quite unambiguous: In terms of the income of the poor, as measured by the wages of unskilled labor, the "populist" strategies are worst; "modified capitalism" is better; an all-out growth strategy is best.

Papanek is not satisfied with nothing these effects; he is also interested in explaining them. He argues that redistributionist government policies tend (unintentionally, of course) to make for inequality, not only because they inhibit growth but because they introduce political distortions into the economic process. Specifically, they tend to create a "protected sector" (mostly consisting of urban skilled labor), which benefits from the policies, and then ipso facto tends to generate economic hardships in the other sectors of the society. The same government policies tend to set artificially low prices for agricultural products, thus depressing the income of the rural population (which, of course, is the large majority in most Third World countries). When government intervention takes the heavier "populist" course, there tend to be the additional aggravating factors of unprofitable nationalized industries and heavy investment in capital-intensive "big projects"—with negative results for the income of unskilled labor.

It should be stressed that this analysis by no means leads to the conclusion that government can do nothing to improve income distribution. Among equality-inducing policies cited by Papanek are education, improving asset ownership among the poor (this means, above all, land ownership), fostering investment in labor-intensive projects, moving away from primary exports only (that is, fostering industrialization), and removing legal or social barriers to opportunity (this applies, very importantly, to the status of women, also to discrimination against groups on the basis of race, caste, or religion). But the general point here is that government policies designed to control economic growth in the pursuit of equality typically produce the opposite effect from the intended one. "Populist" strategies slow down economic growth, which in turn reduces the number of jobs. The impact of this is heaviest on the poor, *both* in terms of absolute living standards *and* of relative income. And, while Papanek does not do this, the same argument can be applied a fortiori to full-blown socialist strategies. The "preferential option for the poor" here translates itself to an option for capitalist development strategies.

Proposition: *Capitalist development leading to rapid and labor-intensive economic growth is more likely to equalize income distribution than strategies of deliberate, government-induced income redistribution.*

Once again, this is a hypothesis, carefully put in probabilistic terms. Capitalism can no more *guarantee* greater equality than material prosperity. Every development strategy is uncertain, threatened by unforeseen disasters of every kind, and liable to have severe unintended consequences. What this means is that the probabilistic character of all social-scientific prognoses has its logical correlate in the situation of the policymaker, who is constrained to gamble. Every development strategy is a gamble. What the considerations of this chapter suggest is that capitalism is generally the better bet. There is some reason to think that this insight is spreading in the Third World today.

POSTSCRIPT

Do Capitalist Powers Hinder the Development of Third World Countries?

It is clear from Gerald J. Kruijer's arguments and descriptions that the poor countries have much to complain about. Their relations with core countries are not equal and, he argues, the poor countries are exploited. Could they nevertheless also gain from these relationships? Peter L. Berger concedes that relations between core and periphery countries are unequal and create dependency. Nevertheless, he claims that the relations on average are beneficial to the poor country's development. Dependency theorists recognize that relations with core countries create benefits for some people in poor countries, but they argue that most of these benefits go to a small elite cadre who cooperate with the capitalists, while the poor are left no better off than before. Berger, however, does not concede this point.

As we write, the communist world seems to be disintegrating: Many communist countries are experimenting with markets and capitalist incentives without adopting full-scale capitalism. Clearly, capitalism is not seen by many communist countries as the great evil it once was. Francis Fukuyama, deputy director of the U.S. State Department's policy planning staff, even goes so far as to announce in "The End of History?" (*The National Interest*, Summer 1989) the "unabashed victory of economic and political liberalism" (capitalism and democracy) over all alternative systems as viable ideals. The celebration, however, may be premature. Sociologists must look beyond capitalism's economic benefits and examine its social costs, principal among which are the inequality it creates, the needy that it ignores, and the exploitation in which it engages.

Among the major works expounding dependency theory are Paul Baran, *The Political Economy of Growth* (Monthly Review Press, 1957); Andre Gunder Frank, *Latin America: Underdevelopment or Revolution?* (Monthly Review Press, 1969); and Immanuel Wallerstein, *The Modern World System: Capitalist Agriculture and the Origins of the European World-Economy in the Sixteenth Century* (Academic Press, 1974). For an opposing view, see David H. Blake and Robert S. Walters, *The Politics of Global Economic Relations* (Prentice-Hall, 1987). They write: "To the extent that the global economy as a whole, and individual states' policies, conform to classical liberal economic principles, *all* states' growth and economic efficiency will be maximized." Michael Novak's *The Spirit of Democratic Capitalism* (American Enterprise/Simon & Schuster, 1982) is even more sharply critical of dependency theory. See particularly chapter 16, entitled "Guilt for Third World Poverty." See also, Charles Krauthammer, "Rich Nations, Poor Nations," *The New Republic* (April 11, 1981).

PART 5

Crime and Social Control

The social costs of crime are often weighed against the public funds expended for crime prevention. Inevitably, this leads to debates over degrees of crime, as society struggles to match funds and punishment with the severity of the transgressions that occur. Does street crime pose more of a threat to the public well-being than white-collar crime? Billions of dollars have been spent in the "War on Drugs," but who is winning? Would legalizing some drugs free up money that could be directed to other types of social welfare programs, such as rehabilitation of addicts? Does incapacitation serve as an effective means of reducing crime by removing criminals from the streets? Or is it, in the long run, costly and inhumane?

Is Street Crime More Harmful Than
    White-Collar Crime?
    _____

Should Drugs Be Legalized?
    _____

Is Incapacitation the Answer to the
    Crime Problem?

ISSUE 14

Is Street Crime More Harmful Than White-Collar Crime?

YES: John J. DiIulio, Jr., from "The Impact of Inner-City Crime," *The Public Interest* (Summer 1989)

NO: Jeffrey H. Reiman, from *The Rich Get Richer and the Poor Get Prison* (Macmillan, 1984)

ISSUE SUMMARY

YES: Professor John J. DiIulio, Jr., describes and analyzes the enormous harm done—especially to the urban poor and, by extension, to all of society—by street criminals and their activities.
NO: Professor Jeffrey H. Reiman suggests that the dangers visited on society by corporations and white-collar criminals are a great menace, and he reviews some of those dangers and how they threaten society.

The word *crime* entered the English language (from the Old French) in about A.D. 1250, when it was identified with "sinfulness." Later, the meaning of the word was modified: crime became the kind of sinfulness which was rightly punishable by law. Even medieval writers, who did not distinguish very sharply between church and state, recognized that there were some sins for which punishment was best left to God; the laws should punish only those that cause harm to the community. Of course, their concept of harm was a very broad one, embracing such offenses as witchcraft and blasphemy. Modern jurists, even those who deplore such practices, would say that the state has no business punishing the perpetrators of these types of offenses.

What, then, should the laws punish? The answer depends in part on our notion of harm. We usually limit the term to the kind of harm that is tangible and obvious: taking a life, causing bodily injury (or extreme psychological trauma, as in the case of rape, for example), and destruction or loss of property. For most Americans today, particularly those who live in cities, the word *crime* is practically synonymous with street crime. Anyone who has ever been robbed or beaten by street criminals will never forget the experience, and there are few people living in urban slums today who have not been victimized or threatened by street criminals. The harm that these criminals cause is tangible, and the connection between the harm and perpetrator is very direct, even intimate: A hits B on the head; A points a pistol at B and demands money; A rapes B.

But suppose the connection is not so intimate. Suppose, for example, that A hires B to shoot C. Is that any less a crime? B is the actual shooter, but is A any less guilty? Of course not, we say; he may even be more guilty, since he is the ultimate mover behind the crime. A would be guilty even if the chain of command were much longer, involving A's orders to B, and B's to C, then on to D, E, and F to kill G. We send organized crime kingpins to jail even when they are far removed from the people who carry out their orders. High officials of the Nixon administration, even though they were not directly involved in the burglary attempt at the Democratic National Committee headquarters at the Watergate Hotel complex in 1972, were imprisoned.

This brings us to the topic of white-collar crime. The actual burglars at the Watergate Hotel were acting on orders that trickled down from the highest reaches of power in the United States. Their orders were issued by men who wore well-tailored suits and did not carry burglar's tools. Other white-collar criminals are as varied as the occupations from which they come. They include stockbrokers who make millions, as Ivan Boesky did, through insider trading; members of Congress who take payoffs; and people who cheat on their income tax, like hotel owner and billionaire Leona Helmsley. Some, like Mrs. Helmsley, get stiff prison sentences when convicted, though many others (like most of the officials in the Watergate scandal) do little or no time in prison. Do they deserve stiffer punishment, or do their crimes seem less harmful than the crimes of street thugs?

White-collar criminals do not put guns to people's heads or beat them. They do not directly cause physical harm or relieve people of their wallets. You can walk to the bus stop tonight with the certain knowledge that you will not be assaulted by the likes of Leona Helmsley or Ivan Boesky. Still, white-collar crime can end up doing considerable harm. The harm done by Nixon's aides threatened the integrity of the U.S. electoral system. Every embezzler, bad check writer, corrupt politician, and tax cheat exacts a toll on our society. Individuals can also be hurt in more tangible ways by decisions made in corporate boardrooms. Auto executives have approved design features that have caused fatalities. Managers of chemical companies have given the go-ahead to practices that have polluted the environment with cancer-causing agents. Heads of corporations have presided over industries wherein workers have been needlessly killed and maimed.

Whether these decisions should be considered crimes is debatable. As we noted at the beginning, the English word *crime* originally meant sin, and there is some trace of that meaning left. A crime must always involve "malicious intent," what jurists call *mens rea*. This certainly applies to street crime—the mugger obviously has sinister designs—but does it apply to every decision made in a boardroom that ends up causing harm? And does that harm match or exceed the harm caused by street criminals? In the following selections, political scientist John DiIulio focuses on the enormous harm done—especially to the poor—by street criminals, while professor Jeffrey Reiman suggests that the white-collar criminals are a greater menace.

YES

John J. DiIulio, Jr.

THE IMPACT OF INNER-CITY CRIME

My grandmother, an Italian immigrant, lived in the same Philadelphia row house from 1921 till her death in 1986. When she moved there, and for the four decades thereafter, most of her neighbors were Irish and Italian. When she died, virtually all of her neighbors were black. Like the whites who fled, the first blacks who moved in were mostly working-class people living just above the poverty level.

Until around 1970, the neighborhood changed little. The houses were well-maintained. The children played in the streets and were polite. The teenagers hung out on the street corners in the evenings, sometimes doing mischief, but rarely—if ever—doing anything worse. The local grocers and other small businesspeople (both blacks and the few remaining whites) stayed open well past dark. Day or night, my grandmother journeyed the streets just as she had during the days of the Great Depression, taking the bus to visit her friends and relatives, going shopping, attending church, and so on.

She was a conspicuous and popular figure in this black community. She was conspicuous for her race, accent, and advanced age; she was popular for the homespun advice (and home-baked goods) she dispensed freely to the teenagers hanging out on the corners, to the youngsters playing ball in the street in front of her house, and to their parents (many of them mothers living without a husband).

Like the generations of ethnics who had lived there before them, these people were near the bottom of the socioeconomic ladder. I often heard my grandmother say that her new neighbors were "just like us," by which she meant that they were honest, decent, law-abiding people working hard to advance themselves and to make a better life for their children.

But in the early 1970s, the neighborhood began to change. Some, though by no means all, of the black families my grandmother had come to know moved out of the neighborhood. The new neighbors kept to themselves. The exteriors of the houses started to look ratty. The streets grew dirty. The grocery and variety stores closed or did business only during daylight hours. The children played in the schoolyard but not in front of their homes. The

From John J. DiIulio, Jr., "The Impact of Inner-City Crime," *The Public Interest*, no. 96 (Summer 1989), pp. 28-46. Copyright © 1989 by National Affairs, Inc. Reprinted with permission of the author.

teenagers on the corners were replaced by adult drug dealers and their "runners." Vandalism and graffiti became commonplace. My grandmother was mugged twice, both times by black teenagers; once she was severely beaten in broad daylight.

In the few years before she died at age eighty-four, and after years of pleading by her children and dozens of grandchildren, she stopped going out and kept her doors and windows locked at all times. On drives to visit her, when I got within four blocks of her home, I instinctively checked to make sure that my car doors were locked. Her house, where I myself had been raised, was in a "bad neighborhood," and it did not make sense to take any chances. I have not returned to the area since the day of her funeral.

My old ethnic and ghetto neighborhood had become an underclass neighborhood. Why is it that most readers of this article avoid, and advise their friends and relatives to avoid, walking or driving through such neighborhoods? Obviously we are not worried about being infected somehow by the extremely high levels of poverty, joblessness, illiteracy, welfare dependency, or drug abuse that characterize these places. Instead we shun these places because we suppose them to contain exceedingly high numbers of predatory street criminals, who hit, rape, rob, deal drugs, burglarize, and murder.

This supposition is absolutely correct. The underclass problem, contrary to the leading academic and journalistic understandings, is mainly a crime problem. It is a crime problem, moreover, that can be reduced dramatically (although not eliminated) with the human and financial resources already at hand.

Only two things are required: common sense and compassion. Once we understand the underclass problem as a crime problem, neither of those two qualities should be scarce. Until we understand the underclass problem as a crime problem, policymakers and others will continue to fiddle while the underclass ghettos of Philadelphia, Newark, Chicago, Los Angeles, Miami, Washington, D.C., and other cities burn. . . .

THE TRULY DEVIANT

Liberals . . . have understood the worsening of ghetto conditions mainly as the by-product of a complex process of economic and social change. One of the latest and most influential statements of this view is William Julius Wilson's *The Truly Disadvantaged: The Inner City, the Underclass, and Public Policy* (1987).

Wilson argues that over the last two decades a new and socially destructive class structure has emerged in the ghetto. As he sees it, the main culprit is deindustrialization. As plants have closed, urban areas, especially black urban areas, have lost entry-level jobs. To survive economically, or to enjoy their material success, ghetto residents in a position to do so have moved out, leaving behind them an immobilized "underclass." . . .

Wilson has focused our attention on the socioeconomic straits of the truly disadvantaged with an elegance and rhetorical force that is truly admirable.[1] But despite its many strengths, his often subtle analysis of the underclass problem wrongly deemphasizes one obvious possibility: "The truly disadvantaged" exist mainly because of the activities of "the truly deviant"—the large numbers of chronic and predatory street criminals—in their midst. One in every nine adult black males in this country is under some form of correctional supervision (prison, jail, probation, or parole).[2] Criminals come disproportionately from underclass neighborhoods. They victimize their neighbors directly through crime, and indirectly by creating or worsening the multiple social and economic ills that define the sad lot of today's ghetto dwellers.

PREDATORY GHETTO CRIMINALS

I propose [another] way of thinking about the underclass problem. The members of the underclass are, overwhelmingly, decent and law-abiding residents of America's most distressed inner cities. Fundamentally, what makes them different from the rest of us is not only their higher than normal levels of welfare dependency and the like, but their far higher than normal levels of victimization by predatory criminals.

This victimization by criminals takes several forms. There is *direct victimization*—being mugged, raped, or murdered; being threatened and extorted; living in fear about whether you can send your children to school or let them go out and play without their being bothered by dope dealers, pressured by gang members, or even struck by a stray bullet. And there is *indirect victimization*—dampened neighborhood economic development, loss of a sizable fraction of the neighborhood's male population to prison or jail, the undue influence on young people exercised by criminal "role models" like the cash-rich drug lords who rule the streets, and so on.

Baldly stated, my hypothesis is that this victimization causes and perpetuates the other ills of our underclass neighborhoods. Schools in these neighborhoods are unable to function effectively because of their disorderly atmosphere and because of the violent behavior of the criminals (especially gang members) who hang around their classrooms. The truly deviant are responsible for a high percentage of teen pregnancies, rapes, and sexual assaults. Similarly, many of the chronically welfare-dependent, female-headed households in these neighborhoods owe their plights to the fact that the men involved are either unable (because they are under some form of correctional supervision) or unwilling (because it does not jibe well with their criminal lifestyles) to seek and secure gainful employment and live with their families. And much of the poverty and joblessness in these neighborhoods can be laid at the door of criminals whose presence deters local business activity, including the development of residential real estate.

Blacks are victims of violent crimes at much higher rates than whites. Most lone-offender crime against blacks is committed by blacks, while most such crimes against whites are committed by whites; in 1986, for instance, 83.5 percent of violent crimes against blacks were committed by blacks, while 80.3 percent of violent crimes against whites were committed by whites. This monochrome picture of victim-offender relationships also holds for multiple-offender crimes. In 1986, for example, 79.6 percent of multiple-offender violent crimes against blacks were committed by blacks; the "white-on-white" figure was 59.4 percent.

Criminals are most likely to commit crimes against people of their own race. The main reason is presumably their physical proximity to potential victims. If so, then it is not hard to understand why underclass neighborhoods, which have more than their share of would-be criminals, have more than their share of crime.

Prison is the most costly form of correctional supervision, and it is normally reserved for the most dangerous felons—violent or repeat offenders. Most of my readers do not personally know anyone in prison; most ghetto dwellers of a decade or two ago probably would not have known anyone in prison either. But most of today's underclass citizens do; the convicted felons were their relatives and neighbors—and often their victimizers.

For example, in 1980 Newark was the street-crime capital of New Jersey. In the Newark area, there were more than 920 violent crimes (murders, non-negligent manslaughters, forcible rapes, robberies, and aggravated assaults) per 100,000 residents; in the rest of the state the figure was under 500, and in affluent towns like Princeton it was virtually nil. In the same year, New Jersey prisons held 5,866 criminals, 2,697 of them from the Newark area.[3] In virtually all of the most distressed parts of this distressed city, at least one of every two hundred residents was an imprisoned felon.[4] The same basic picture holds for other big cities.[5]

Correlation, however, is not causation, and we could extend and refine this sort of crude, exploratory analysis of the relationship between crime rates, concentrations of correctional supervisees, and the underclass neighborhoods from which they disproportionately come. But except to satisfy curiosity, I see no commanding need for such studies. For much the same picture emerges from the anecdotal accounts of people who have actually spent years wrestling with—as opposed to merely researching—the problem.

For example, in 1988 the nation's capital became its murder capital. Washington, D.C., had 372 killings, 82 percent of them committed on the streets by young black males against other young black males. The city vied with Detroit for the highest juvenile homicide rate in America. Here is part of the eloquent testimony on this development given by Isaac Fulwood, a native Washingtonian and the city's police-chief designate:

> The murder statistics don't capture what these people are doing. We've had in excess of 1,260 drug-related shootings. . . . People are scared of these kids. Someone can get shot in broad daylight, and nobody saw anything. . . . Nobody talks. And that's so different from the way it was in my childhood.

The same thing can be said about the underclass neighborhoods of other major cities. In Detroit, for instance, most of the hundreds of ghetto residents murdered over the last six years were killed within blocks of their homes by their truly deviant neighbors.

To devise meaningful law-enforcement and correctional responses to the underclass problem, we need to understand why concentrations of crime and criminals are so high in these neighborhoods, and to change our government's criminal-justice policies and practices accordingly.

UNDERSTANDING THE PROBLEM

We begin with a chicken-and-egg question: Does urban decay cause crime, or does crime cause urban decay?

In conventional criminology, which derives mainly from sociology, ghettos are portrayed as "breeding grounds" for predatory street crime. Poverty, joblessness, broken homes, single-parent families, and similar factors are identified as the "underlying causes" of crime.[6] These conditions cause crime, the argument goes; as they worsen—as the ghetto community becomes the underclass neighborhood—crime worsens. This remains the dominant academic perspective on the subject, one that is shared implicitly by most public officials who are close to the problem.

Beginning in the mid-1970s, however, a number of influential studies appeared that challenged this conventional criminological wisdom.[7] Almost without exception, these studies have cast grave doubts on the classic sociological explanation of crime, suggesting that the actual relationships between such variables as poverty, illiteracy, and unemployment, on the one hand, and criminality, on the other, are far more ambiguous than most analysts freely assumed only a decade or so ago. . . .

LOCKS, COPS, AND STUDIES

Camden, New Jersey, is directly across the bridge from Philadelphia. Once-decent areas have become just like my grandmother's old neighborhood: isolated, crime-torn urban war zones. In February 1989 a priest doing social work in Camden was ordered off the streets by drug dealers and threatened with death if he did not obey. The police chief of Camden sent some extra men into the area, but the violent drug dealers remained the real rulers of the city's streets.

The month before the incident in Camden, the Rockefeller Foundation announced that it was going to devote some of its annual budget (which exceeds $100 million) to researching the underclass problem. Other foundations, big and small, have already spent (or misspent) much money on the problem. But Rockefeller's president was quoted as follows: "Nobody knows who they are, what they do. . . . The underclass is not a topic to pursue from the library. You get out and look for them."

His statement was heartening, but it revealed a deep misunderstanding of the problem. Rather than intimating that the underclass was somehow hard to locate, he would have done better to declare that his charity would purchase deadbolt locks for the homes of ghetto dwellers in New York City who lacked them, and subsidize policing and private-security services in the easily identifiable neighborhoods where these poor people are concentrated.

More street-level research would be nice, especially for the networks of policy intellectuals (liberal and conservative) who benefit directly from such endeavors. But more locks, cops, and corrections officers would make a more positive, tangible, and lasting difference in the lives of today's ghetto dwellers.

NOTES

1. In addition, he has canvassed competing academic perspectives on the underclass; see William Julius Wilson, ed., "The Ghetto Underclass: Social Science Perspectives," *Annals of the American Academy of Political and Social Science* (January 1989). It should also be noted that he is directing a $2.7 million research project on poverty in Chicago that promises to be the most comprehensive study of its kind yet undertaken.

2. According to the Bureau of Justice Statistics, in 1986 there were 234,430 adult black males in prison, 101,000 in jail, an estimated 512,000 on probation, and 133,300 on parole. There were 8,985,000 adult black males in the national residential population. I am grateful to Larry Greenfeld for his assistance in compiling these figures.

3. I am grateful to Hank Pierre, Stan Repko, and Commissioner William H. Fauver of the New Jersey Department of Corrections for granting me access to these figures and to related data on

density of prisoner residence; to Andy Ripps for his heroic efforts in organizing them; and to my Princeton colleague Mark Alan Hughes for his expert help in analyzing the data.

4. Ten of the thirteen most distressed Newark census tracts were places where the density of prisoner residence was that high. In other words, 76.9 percent of the worst underclass areas of Newark had such extremely high concentrations of hardcore offenders. In most of the rest of Newark, and throughout the rest of the state, such concentrations were virtually nonexistent.

5. In 1980 in the Chicago area, for example, in 182 of the 1,521 census tracts at least one of every two hundred residents was an imprisoned felon.

Fully twenty of the thirty-five worst underclass tracts had such extraordinary concentrations of serious criminals; in several of them, more than one of every hundred residents was behind prison bars. I am grateful to Wayne Carroll and Commissioner Michael Lane of the Illinois Department of Corrections for helping me with these data.

6. For example, see the classic statement by Edwin H. Sutherland and Donald R. Cressey, *Principles of Criminology*, 7th rev. ed. (Philadelphia: J. P. Lippincott, 1966).

7. See, for example, James Q. Wilson, *Thinking About Crime* (New York: Basic Books, 1975), especially the third chapter.

NO

Jeffrey H. Reiman

A CRIME BY ANY OTHER NAME

WHAT'S IN A NAME?

If it takes you an hour to read this chapter, by the time you reach the last page, two of your fellow citizens will have been murdered. *During that same time, at least 4 Americans will die as a result of unhealthy or unsafe conditions in the workplace!* Although these work-related deaths could have been prevented, they are not called murders. Why not? Doesn't a crime by any other name still cause misery and suffering? What's in a name?

The fact is that the label "crime" is not used in America to name all or the worst of the actions that cause misery and suffering to Americans. It is primarily reserved for the dangerous actions of the poor.

In the March 14, 1976 edition of the *Washington Star*, a front-page article appeared with the headline: "Mine Is Closed 26 Deaths Late." The article read in part:

> *Why, the relatives [of the 26 dead miners] ask, did the mine ventilation fail and allow pockets of methane gas to build up in a shaft 2,300 feet below the surface? . . .*
>
> *[I]nvestigators of the Senate Labor and Welfare Committee . . . found that there have been 1,250 safety violations at the 13-year-old mine since 1970. Fifty-seven of those violations were serious enough for federal inspectors to order the mine closed and 21 of those were in cases where federal inspectors felt there was imminent danger to the lives of the miners working there. . . .*

Next to the continuation of this story was another, headlined: "Mass Murder Claims Six in Pennsylvania." It described the shooting death of a husband and wife, their three children, and a friend in a Philadelphia suburb. This was murder, maybe even mass murder. My only question is, why wasn't the deaths of the miners also murder?

Why do 26 dead miners amount to a "disaster" and 6 dead suburbanites a "mass murder"? "Murder" suggests a murderer, while "disaster" suggests the work of impersonal forces. But if over 1000 safety violations had been found in the mine—three the day before the first explosion—was no one responsible for failing to eliminate the hazards? Was no one responsible for preventing the hazards? And if someone could have prevented the hazards and did not, does that person not bear responsibility for the deaths of 26 men? Is he less evil because he did not want them to die although he chose to leave them in jeopardy? Is he not a murderer, perhaps even a mass murderer?

These questions are at this point rhetorical. My aim is not to discuss this case but rather to point to the blinders we wear when we look as such a "disaster." Perhaps there will be an investigation. Perhaps someone will be held responsible. Perhaps he will be fined. But will he be tried for *murder*? Will anyone think of him as a murderer? *And if not, why not?* Would the miners not be safer if such people were treated as murderers? Might they not still be alive? . . . didn't those miners have a right to protection from the violence that took their lives? *And if not, why not?*

Once we are ready to ask this question seriously, we are in a position to see that the reality of crime—that is, the acts we label crime, the acts we think of as crime, the actors and actions we treat as criminal—is *created*: It is an image shaped by decisions as to *what* will be called crime and *who* will be treated as a criminal.

THE CARNIVAL MIRROR

It is sometimes coyly observed that the quickest and cheapest way to eliminate crime would be to throw out all the criminal laws. There is a thin sliver of truth to this view. Without criminal laws, there would indeed be no "crimes." There would, however, still be dangerous acts. And this is why we cannot really solve our crime problem quite so simply. The criminal law *labels* some acts "crimes." In doing this, it identifies those acts as so dangerous that we must use the extreme methods of criminal justice to protect ourselves against them. But this does not mean that the criminal law *creates* crime—it simply "mirrors" real dangers that threaten us. And what is true of the criminal law is true of the whole justice system. If police did not arrest or prosecutors charge or juries convict, there would be no "criminals." But this does not mean that police or prosecutors or juries create criminals any more than legislators do. They *react* to real dangers in society. The criminal justice system—from lawmakers to law enforcers—is just a mirror of the real dangers that lurk in our midst. *Or so we are told.*

How accurate is this mirror? We need to answer this in order to know whether or how well the criminal justice system is protecting us against the real threats to our well-being. The more accurate a mirror, the more the image it shows is created by the reality it reflects. The more misshapen a mirror is, the more the distorted image it shows is created by the mirror, not by the reality reflected. It is in this sense that I will argue that the image of crime is created: The American criminal justice system is a mirror that shows a distorted image of the dangers that threaten us—an image created more by the shape of the mirror than by the reality reflected. What do we see when we look in the criminal justice mirror?

On the morning of September 16, 1975, the *Washington Post* carried an article in its local news section headlined "Arrest Data Reveals Profile of a Suspect." The article reported the results of a study of crime in Prince George's County, a suburb of Washington, D.C. It read in part that

The typical suspect in serious crime in Prince George's County is a black male, aged 14 to 19. . . .

This is the Typical Criminal feared by most law-abiding Americans. His crime, according to former Attorney General John Mitchell (who is by no means a typical criminal), is forcing us "to change the fabric of our society," "forcing us, a free people, to alter our pattern of life," "to withdraw from our neighbors, to fear all strangers and to limit our activities to 'safe' areas." These poor, young, urban (disproportionately) black males comprise the core of the enemy forces in the war against crime. They are the heart of a vicious, unorganized guerrilla army, threatening the lives, limbs, and possessions of the law-abiding members of society—necessitating recourse to the ultimate weapons of force and detention in our common defense. They are the "career criminals" President Reagan had in mind when he told the International Association of Chiefs of Police, assuring them of the tough stance that the Federal Government would take in the fight against crime, that "a small number of criminals are responsible for an enormous amount of the crime in American society." . . .

The acts of the Typical Criminal are not the only acts that endanger us, nor are they the acts that endanger us the most. We have a greater chance (as I show below) of being killed or disabled, for example, by an occupational injury or disease, by unnecessary surgery, by shoddy emergency medical services than by aggravated assault or even homicide! Yet even though these threats to our well being are graver than that posed by our

poor, young, urban, black males, they do not show up in the FBI's Index of serious crimes. And the individuals who are responsible for them do not turn up in arrest records or prison statistics. *They never become part of the reality reflected in the criminal justice mirror, although the danger they pose is at least as great and often greater than those who do!*

Similarly the general public loses more money *by far* . . . from price-fixing and monopolistic practices, and from consumer deception and embezzlement, than from all the property crimes in the FBI's Index combined. Yet these far more costly acts are either not criminal, or if technically criminal, not prosecuted, or if prosecuted, not punished, or if punished, only mildly. . . . *Their faces rarely appear in the criminal justice mirror, although the danger they pose is at least as great and often greater than those who do. . . .*

A CRIME BY ANY OTHER NAME . . .

Think of a crime, any crime. Picture the first "crime" that comes into your mind. What do you see? The odds are you are not imagining a mining company executive sitting at his desk, calculating the costs of proper safety precautions, and deciding not to invest in them. Probably what you see with your mind's eye is one person physically attacking another or robbing something from another on the threat of physical attack. Look more closely. What does the attacker look like? It's a safe bet he (and it is a *he*, of course) is not wearing a suit and tie. In fact, my hunch is that you—like me, like almost anyone in America—picture a young, tough, lower-class male when the thought of crime first pops into your head. You (we) picture someone like the Typical Criminal described above. And the crime itself is one in which the Typical Criminal sets out to attack or rob some specific person.

This last point is important. What it indicates is that we have a mental image not only of the Typical Criminal, but also of the Typical Crime. If the Typical Criminal is a young lower-class male, the Typical Crime is *one-on-one harm*—where harm means either physical injury or loss of something valuable or both. . . .

It is important to identify this model of the Typical Crime because it functions like a set of blinders. It keeps us from calling a mine disaster a mass murder even if 26 men are killed, even if someone is responsible for the unsafe conditions in which they worked and died. In fact, I argue that this particular piece of mental furniture so blocks our view that it keeps us from using the criminal justice system to protect ourselves from the greatest threats to our persons and possessions.

What keeps a mine disaster from being a mass murder in our eyes is the fact that it is not one-on-one harm. What is important here is not the numbers but the *intent to harm someone*. An attack by a gang on one or more persons or an attack by one individual on several fits the model of one-on-one harm. That is, for each person harmed there is a least one individual who wanted to harm that person. Once he selects his victim, the rapist, the mugger, the murderer, all want this person they have selected to suffer. A mine executive, on the other hand, does not want his employees to be harmed. He would truly prefer that there be no accident, no injured or dead miners. What he does want is something legitimate. It is what he has been hired to

get: maximum profits at minimum costs. If he cuts corners to save a buck, he is just doing his job. If 26 men die because he cut corners on safety, we may think him crude or callous but not a killer. He is, at most, responsible for an *indirect harm*, not a one-on-one harm. For this, he may even be criminally indictable for violating safety regulations—but not for murder. The 26 men are dead as an unwanted consequence of his (perhaps overzealous or undercautious) pursuit of a legitimate goal. And so, unlike the Typical Criminal, he has not committed the Typical Crime. Or so we generally believe. As a result, 26 men are dead who might be alive now if cutting corners of the kind that leads to loss of life, whether suffering is specifically intended or not, were treated as murder.

This is my point. Because we accept the belief . . . that the model for crime is one person specifically intending to harm another, we accept a legal system that leaves us unprotected against much greater dangers to our lives and well-being than those threatened by the Typical Criminal . . .

WORK MAY BE DANGEROUS TO YOUR HEALTH

Since the publication of *The President's Report on Occupational Safety and Health* in 1972, numerous studies have documented both the astounding incidence of disease, injury, and death due to hazards in the workplace *and* the fact that much or most of this carnage is the consequence of the refusal of management to pay for safety measures and of government to enforce safety standards.

In that 1972 report, the government estimated the number of job-related illnesses at 390,000 per year and the number of annual deaths from industrial disease at 100,000 In *The Report of the President to the Congress on Occupational Safety and Health* for 1980, these estimates were rather sharply reduced to 148,900 job-related illnesses and 4950 work-related deaths. Note that the latter figure is not limited to death from occupational disease but includes all work-related deaths including those resulting from accidents on the job.

Before considering the significance of these figures, it should be mentioned that all sources including the just-mentioned report as well the U.S. Department of Labor's *Interim Report to Congress on Occupational Diseases* indicate that occupational diseases are seriously underreported. *The Report of the President* states that "recording and reporting of illnesses continue to present measurement problems, since employers (and doctors) are often unable to recognize some illnesses as work-related. The annual survey includes data only on the visible illnesses of workers. To the extent that occupational illnesses are unrecognized and, therefore, not recorded or reported, the illness survey estimates may understate their occurrence. . . .

For these reasons, plus the fact that OSHA's* figures on work-related deaths are only for workplaces with 11 or more employees, we must supplement the OSHA figures with other reported figures. One study conservatively estimates the number of annual cancer deaths attributable to occupational factors at 17,000. Richard Schweiker, U.S. Secretary of Health and Human Services, states that "current estimates for overall workplace-associated cancer mortality

*[Occupational Health and Safety Administration.—ED.]

vary within a range of five to fifteen percent." With annual cancer deaths at 400,000, that translates into between 20,000 and 60,000 cancer deaths per year associated with the workplace. A report for the American Lung Association estimates 25,000 deaths a year from job caused respiratory diseases. None of these figures include deaths from heart disease, America's number one killer, a substantial portion of which are likely caused by stress and strain on the job. Thus even if we discount the OSHA's 1972 estimate of 100,000 deaths a year due to occupational disease, we would surely be erring in the other direction to accept the figure of 4950. We can hardly be overestimating the actual toll if we set it at 25,000 deaths a year resulting from occupational disease.

As for the OSHA estimate of 148,000 job-related illnesses, here too there is reason to assume that the figure considerably underestimates the real situation. One study suggests that it may represent no more than half of the actual number. However, since this figure is probably less inaccurate than the figure for job-related deaths, it will suffice for our purposes. Let us assume, then, that there are annually in the United States approximately 150,000 job-related illnesses and 25,000 deaths from occupational diseases. How does this compare to the threat posed by crime? Before jumping to any conclusions, note that the risk of occupational disease and death falls only on members of the labor force, while the risk of crime falls on the whole populations, from infants to the elderly. Since the labor force is less than half the total population (96,800,000 in 1980, out of a total population approaching 230,000,000), to get a true picture of the *relative* threat posed by occupational diseases compared to that posed by crime we should *halve* the crime statistics when comparing them to the figures for industrial disease and death. Using the 1980 statistics, this means that the *comparable* figures would be:

	Occupational Disease	Crime (halved)
Death	25,000	11,500
Other physical harm	150,000	325,000

. . . It should be noted further that the statistics given so far are *only* for occupational *diseases* and deaths from those diseases. They do not include death and disability from work-related injuries. Here too, the statistics are gruesome. The National Safety Council reported that in 1980, work-related accidents caused 13,000 deaths and 2.2 million disabling work injuries; 245 million man-days lost during that year because of work accidents, plus another 120 million man-days that will be lost in future years because of these accidents; and a total cost to the economy of $30 billion. This brings the number of occupation-related deaths to 38,000 a year. If, on the basis of these additional figures, we recalculated our chart comparing occupational to criminal dangers, it would look like this:

	Occupational Hazard	Crime (halved)
Death	38,000	11,500
Other physical harm	2,350,000	325,000

Can there be any doubt that workers are more likely to stay alive and healthy in the face of the danger from the under-

world than in the face of what their employers have in store for them on the job? . . .

To blame the workers for occupational disease and deaths is simply to ignore the history of governmental attempts to compel industrial firms to meet safety standards that would keep dangers (such as chemicals or fibers or dust particles in the air) that are outside of the worker's control down to a safe level. This has been a continual struggle, with firms using everything from their own "independent" research institutes to more direct and often questionable forms of political pressure to influence government in the direction of loose standards and lax enforcement. . . .

Over and over again, the same story appears. Workers begin to sicken and die at a plant. They call on their employer to lower the level of hazardous material in the air, and their employer responds first by denying that a hazard exists. As the corpses pile up, the firm's scientists "discover" that some danger does exist but that it can be removed by reducing the hazardous material to a "safe" level—which is still above what independent and government researchers think is really safe. At this point, government and industry spar about "safe" levels and usually compromise at a level in between—something less dangerous than industry wants but still dangerous. This does not mean that the new levels are met, even if written into the law. So government inspectors and compliance officers must come in, and when (and if) they do, their efforts are too little and too late:

• Federal officials cited the Beryllium Corporation for 26 safety violations and 5 "serious violations" for "excessive beryllium concentration in work place areas." Fine: $928. The corporation's net sales for 1970 were $61,400,000.

• On request from the Oil, Chemical and Atomic Workers Union, OSHA officials inspected the Mobil Oil plant at Plausboro, New Jersey. Result: citations for 354 violations of the Occupational Health and Safety Act of 1970. Fine: $7350 (about $20 a violation).

• In 1972, a fire and explosion at the same Mobil plant killed a worker. Fine: $1215. . . .

• "In 1981, a Labor Department study found nearly 2 million Americans were severely or partially disabled from an occupational disease; the lost income is estimated at $11.4 billion. Yet, the study found, only 5 percent of the severely disabled received workers' compensation." . . .

Is a person who kills another in a bar brawl a greater threat to society than a business executive who refuses to cut into his profits in order to make his plant a safe place to work? By any measure of death and suffering the latter is by far a greater danger than the former. But because he wishes his workers no harm, because he is only indirectly responsible for death and disability while pursuing legitimate economic goals, his acts are not called *crimes*. . . .

HEALTH CARE MAY BE DANGEROUS TO YOUR HEALTH

. . . On July 15, 1975, Dr. Sidney Wolfe of Ralph Nader's Public Interest Health Research Group testified before the House Commerce Oversight and Investigations Subcommittee that there "were 3.2 million cases of unnecessary surgery performed each year in the United States." These unneeded operations, Dr. Wolfe

added, "cost close to $5 billion a year and killed as many as 16,000 Americans." . . .

A congressional committee earlier this year [1976] estimated that more than 2 million of the elective operations performed in 1974 were not only unnecessary—but also killed about 12,000 patients and cost nearly $4 billion.

WAGING CHEMICAL WARFARE AGAINST AMERICA

. . . Based on the knowledge we have, there can be no doubt that air pollution, tobacco, and food additives amount to a chemical war that makes the crime wave look like a football scrimmage. Quite conservatively, I think we can estimate the death toll in this war as at least a quarter of a million lives a year—*more than ten times the number killed by criminal homicide!*

POVERTY KILLS

. . . We are prone to think that the consequences of poverty are fairly straightforward: Less money equals less things. And so poor people have fewer clothes or cars or appliances, go to the theater less often, and live in smaller homes with less or cheaper furniture. And this is true and sad, but perhaps not intolerable. I will argue that one of the things poor people have less of is *good health*. Less money means less nutritious food, less heat in the winter, less fresh air in summer, less distance from other sick people, less knowledge about illness or medicine, fewer doctor visits, fewer dental visits, less preventive health care, and above all, less first-quality medical attention when all these other deprivations take their toll and a poor person finds himself seriously ill. What this means is that the poor suffer more from poor health and die earlier than do those who are well off. Poverty robs them of their days while they are alive and then kills them before their time. A prosperous society that allows poverty in its midst is guilty of murder. . . .

ONCE AGAIN, OUR INVESTIGATION LEADS to the same result. The criminal justice system does not protect us against the gravest threats to life, limb, or possessions. Its definitions of crime are not simply a reflection of the objective dangers that threaten us. The workplace, the medical profession, the air we breathe, and the poverty we refuse to rectify lead to far more human suffering, far more death and disability, and take far more dollars from our pockets than the murders, aggravated assaults, and thefts reported annually by the FBI. And what is more, this human suffering is preventable. A government really intent on protecting our well-being could enforce work safety regulations, police the medical profession, require that clean air standards be met, and funnel sufficient money to the poor to alleviate the major disabilities of poverty. But it does not. Instead we hear a lot of cant about law and order and a lot of rant about crime in the streets. It is as if our leaders were not only refusing to protect us from the major threats to our well-being but trying to cover up this refusal by diverting our attention to crime—as if this were the only real threat. But as we have seen, the criminal justice system is a carnival mirror that presents a distorted image of what threatens us. . . . All the mechanisms by which the criminal justice system comes down more frequently and more harshly on the poor criminal than on the well-off criminal take place *after* most of the dangerous acts of the well-to-do have been excluded from the definition of crime itself.

POSTSCRIPT

Is Street Crime More Harmful Than White-Collar Crime?

John J. DiIulio, Jr., implies that much of the social misery of America, including the persistence of poverty, can be traced to the "truly depraved" street criminals in our central cities. Is this focus too narrow? Surely there are many other sources of the social crisis that afflicts our central cities. Reiman's focus, on the other hand, may be overly broad. He claims that more people are killed and injured by "occupational injury or disease, by unnecessary surgery, and by shoddy emergency medical services than by aggravated assault or even homicide!" Though we may say it rhetorically, can we really categorize shoddy medical services as a crime? And could Reiman ever convince residents of city ghettos, where most of the violent crime occurs, that they face a greater risk from occupational injury or disease than from street criminals?

A set of readings that support Reiman's viewpoint is *Corporate Violence: Injury and Death for Profit,* edited by Stuart L. Hills (Rowman & Littlefield, 1987). *White-Collar Crime,* edited by Gilbert Geis and Robert F. Meier (Free

Press, 1977) is a useful compilation of essays on corporate and political crime. Four other books that focus on crime in high places are J. Douglas and J. M. Johnson, *Official Deviance* (Lippincott, 1977); J. Anthony Lukas, *Nightmare: The Underside of the Nixon Years* (Viking Press, 1976); Marshall B. Clinard, *Corporate Elites and Crime* (Sage, 1983); and David R. Simon and Stanley Eitzen, *Elite Deviance* (Allyn and Bacon, 1982). A work that deals with the prevalence and fear of street crime is Elliott Currie, *Confronting Crime: An American Challenge* (Pantheon, 1985).

ISSUE 15

Should Drugs Be Legalized?

YES: Claudia Mills, from "The War on Drugs: Is It Time to Surrender?" *QQ: Report from the Institute for Philosophy and Public Policy* (Spring/Summer 1989)

NO: James Q. Wilson and John J. DiIulio, Jr., from "Crackdown," *The New Republic* (July 10, 1989)

ISSUE SUMMARY

YES: Claudia Mills, a writer and student of philosophy, concludes that the cost of fighting drugs—in financial and human terms—outweighs any benefits obtained from waging the battle against drugs, and she argues that they should therefore be legalized.

NO: Political scientists James Q. Wilson and John J. DiIulio, Jr., argue that drug legalization would vastly increase dangerous drug use and the social ills created by such usage.

A century ago, drugs of every kind were freely available to Americans. Laudanum, a mixture of opium and alcohol, was popularly used as a painkiller. One drug company even claimed that it was a very useful substance for calming hyperactive children, and they called it Mother's Helper. Morphine came into common use during the Civil War. Heroin, developed as a supposedly less addictive substitute for morphine, began to be marketed at the end of the nineteenth century. By that time, drug paraphernalia could be ordered through Sears and Roebuck catalogues, and Coca-Cola, which contained small quantities of cocaine, had become a popular drink.

Public concerns about addiction and dangerous patent medicines, and an active campaign for drug laws waged by Dr. Harvey Wiley, a chemist in the U.S. Department of Agriculture, led Congress to pass the first national drug regulation act in 1906. The Pure Food and Drug Act required that medicines containing certain drugs, such as opium, must say so on their labels. Later amendments to the Act required that the labels must also state the quantity of each drug and affirm that the drug met official standards of purity. The Harrison Narcotic Act of 1914 went much further and cut off completely the supply of legal opiates to addicts. Since then, ever stricter drug laws have been passed by Congress and by state legislatures.

Drug abuse in America again came to the forefront of public discourse during the 1960s, when heroin addiction started growing rapidly in inner-city neighborhoods. Also, by the end of the decade, drug experimentation had spread to the middle-class, affluent Baby Boomers who were then attending college. (The name "Baby Boom" generation has been given to Americans born during the late 1940s through 1960, whose cohort history has been widely analyzed and widely publicized because they are far more numerous than were older generations.) Indeed, certain types of drugs began to be celebrated by some of the leaders of the counterculture. Heroin was still taboo, but other drugs, notably marijuana and LSD (a psychedelic drug), were regarded as harmless and even spiritually transforming. At music festivals like Woodstock in 1969, marijuana and LSD were used openly and associated with love, peace, and heightened sensitivity. Much of this enthusiasm cooled over the next twenty years as Baby Boomers entered the work force full-time and began their careers. But even among the careerists, certain types of drugs enjoyed high status. Cocaine, noted for its highly stimulating effects, became the drug of choice for many hard-driving young lawyers, TV writers, and Wall Street bond traders.

The high price of cocaine put it out of reach for many people, but by the early 1980s, cheap substitutes began to appear on the streets and to overtake poor urban communities. Crack cocaine, a potent, highly addictive, smokable form of cocaine, came into widespread use. More recent reports indicate that "ice," or as it is called on the West Coast, "L.A. glass," a smokable form of amphetamine, is the newest drug to hit the streets. These stimulants tend to produce very violent, disorderly behavior. Moreover, the street gangs who sell it are frequently at war with one another and are well-armed. Not only gang members but also many innocent people have become victims of contract killings, street battles, and drive-by shootings.

This new drug epidemic has prompted President Bush to declare a "war on drugs." He appointed former Education Secretary William Bennett to the Cabinet-level post of "drug czar," and he has asked Congress to appropriate $10.6 billion for the fight. Reaction has been mixed. Some support it in its entirety; others think that more money is needed, or that spending priorities should be shifted more toward treatment than law enforcement. Still, the vast majority of Americans seem ready to support some version of a major national campaign to fight drugs. Others, however, see the whole effort as doomed to failure, and they argue that the best solution to the drug problem would be to legalize, tax, and control drugs, as has been done with alcohol.

The drug legalization issue is especially interesting to sociologists because it raises basic questions about what should be socially sanctioned or approved, what is illegal or legal, and what is immoral or moral. An aspect of the basic value system of America is under review. The process of value change may be taking place in front of our eyes. As part of this debate, Claudia Mills makes a case for the legalization of drugs, and political scientists James Q. Wilson and John DiIulio argue against it.

YES

Claudia Mills

THE WAR ON DRUGS:
IS IT TIME TO SURRENDER?

Two decades after the doomed and undeclared war in Vietnam, America has declared itself at war with drugs. Recent polls have blasted illegal drugs as public enemy number one; in an era of budget retrenchments and hands-off government, the crusade against drugs has become a central priority for federal action and funding. All told, expenditures on all aspects of drug enforcement, from drug eradication in foreign countries to imprisonment of drug users and dealers in the United States, totaled in 1987 over ten billion dollars. Convicted drug offenders crowd our prisons: nationwide in 1987, 75,000 people were arrested for violating drug laws, and many faced stiff mandatory sentences. Drug "czar" William Bennett has called for capital punishment for drug dealers and remarked that "morally" he doesn't "have any problem" with beheading as the method of execution. In unison schoolchildren shout "Just say no!" and everyone knows what it is they're saying no to. Even legal drug use—the consumption of alcohol and tobacco—is declining steadily, as we strive toward the goal of drug-free schools, drug-free neighborhoods, a drug-free America.

Yet few think this is a war we are winning. Despite accelerated enforcement efforts, the black market in cocaine has grown to record size. Crack, the most lethal cocaine derivative, was all but unheard of five years ago; today 15 percent of infants born in the nation's capitol suffer brain damage from exposure to crack in the womb. Drug-related murder rates soar; drug-related violence holds our inner cities hostage to fear; drug-related civil war rages in Colombia. Is the drug war one we can possibly win?

Indeed, the drug war itself has come to be more deadly than the enemy it is waged against. The greatest costs are incurred, it can be claimed, not by drugs per se, but as a direct or indirect by-product of their criminalization. While 90 percent of Americans appear to be opposed to the legalization of drugs, decriminalization measures are gaining support across the political spectrum; advocates of legalization range from conservative William F. Buckley to the liberal, black mayor of Baltimore, Kurt Schmoke.

From Claudia Mills, "The War on Drugs: Is It Time to Surrender?" *QQ: Report from the Institute for Philosophy and Public Policy* (Spring/Summer 1989), pp. 1-5. Copyright © 1989 by the Institute for Philosophy and Public Policy, School of Public Affairs, University of Maryland. Reprinted by permission.

Are there moral considerations that tell in favor of legalization? Can we draw parallels between how we treat legal drugs such as tobacco and alcohol and how we should treat illegal drugs such as heroin, marijuana, and cocaine? Should we legalize drugs as a way of respecting individual autonomy against government paternalism, or as a way of showing compassion to the victims of addiction? Most important, do the consequences of legalization promise to be less terrible than those we now face?

THE ARGUMENT FROM CONSISTENCY

A first argument offered for legalization is that currently illegal drugs are in no relevant way morally different from the most popular legal drugs—alcohol and tobacco—and so consistency demands that if beer and cigarettes are legal, marijuana, heroin, and cocaine should be legal as well. There is certainly nothing particularly distinctive, nothing inherently *worse*, about the drugs that through historical accident happen to find themselves on the "illegal" list. After all, narcotics were legal in this country only a century ago, with a wide choice of hypodermic kits available for purchase from the Sears, Roebuck Catalog. Many doctors at the turn of the century prescribed opium as a treatment for alcoholism, viewing opiate addiction as the lesser of two evils. And cocaine, of course, gave its name to Coca-Cola, of which it was long an ingredient.

If anything, illegal drugs are far less harmful than the legal ones. The federal data for 1985 documented 2177 deaths from the most popular illicit drugs: heroin, cocaine (including crack), PCP, and marijuana. Disease related to alcohol and tobacco, on the other hand, kill close to half a million Americans every year. No illegal drug is more clearly linked to drug-induced violence than alcohol; nicotine and alcohol are both powerfully addictive. Ethan A. Nadelman, assistant professor of politics and public affairs at Princeton University, suggests that "if degrees of immorality were measured by the levels of harm caused by one's products, the 'traffickers' in tobacco and alcohol would be vilified as the most evil of all substance purveyors."

But parallels between legal and illegal drugs can cut both ways. While Prohibition produced a level of crime and gang violence eerily prescient of today's drug-related crime and violence, it also slashed alcohol consumption in half, with all the attendant benefits to human health and family stability. Legal drugs may take a greater toll on health and happiness precisely as a result of their legality—and so of their widespread use and cultural entrenchment. Sue Rusche, director of the National Drug Information Center of Families in Action, claims that "illegal drugs kill fewer people only because fewer people use them." Why on earth, one might ask, would we want to encourage the use of cocaine and heroin on a par with today's levels of smoking and drinking?

But in any case, the argument from consistency is a weak one. Robert Fullinwider, research scholar at the Institute for Philosophy and Public Policy, regards the argument that if we tolerate alcohol and tobacco, we are somehow logically bound to tolerate crack in the same way, as the kind of foolish consistency that is the hobgoblin of small minds. We make our laws not only on the basis of logic, but of history; we have an entrenched cultural history with some drugs that we need not repeat with others. Thus Fullinwider, who is inclined toward drug legalization, notes that we could treat cocaine and heroin, if legalized, very differently from alcohol and tobacco. It would be insane, for example, to allow advertising of such drugs; we needn't permit a whole new array of billboards extolling their pleasures.

THE ARGUMENT AGAINST PATERNALISM

A second argument against criminal penalties for drug use is essentially an argument against the exercise of state power to coerce citizens' private and personal choices regarding what they do with their own "free" time. Steven Wisotsky, professor of law at Nova University, argues that "zero tolerance" of drug use is simply an inappropriate goal for a liberal society. "The overwhelming majority of incidents of drug use," Wisotsky claims, "are without lasting personal or societal consequence, just as the overwhelming majority of drinking causes no harm to the drinker or to society." For Wisotsky, "The . . . goal of a drug-free America, except for children, is both ridiculous—as absurd as a liquor-free America—and wrong in principle. This is not a fundamentalist Ayatollah land after all. A democratic society must respect the decisions made by its adult citizens, even those perceived to be foolish or risky."

David A. J. Richards, in his book *Sex, Drugs, Death, and the Law*, also argues that we must respect "the individual's ability to determine, evaluate, and revise the meaning of his or her own life." Drug experience, Richards suggests, "is merely one means by which the already existing interests of the person may be explored or realized." While it may seem strange to claim that the drug *addict* is voluntarily pursuing his or her own possibly quite reasonable goals, Richards sees the whole concept of addiction as complex and highly confused: talk of "addiction" conflates the *physiological* features of tolerance (the progressive need for higher doses of a drug to secure the same effect) and physical dependence (the incidence of withdrawal symptoms when drug use is stopped), with the *psychological* centrality of the drug in the user's system of ends, and, most important, with a *moral* judgment that drug use is intrinsically degrading or debasing. These features have no necessary connection to one another. Moreover, the moral condemnation of certain drug use as drug "abuse," according to Richards, involves importing middle-class values into judgments about others' lifestyle choices. He writes, "The psychological centrality of drug use for many young addicts in the United States may, from the perspective of their own circumstances, not unreasonably organize their lives and ends."

But it hardly takes a set of stuffy "middle-class values" to argue that involvement with a highly addictive drug such as crack counts as a form of slavery. The insatiable craving for crack leads people to neglect and abuse their children, to live in unspeakable filth and foulness, to commit any crime to service one all-encompassing obsession. No crack mother, it is safe to say, views crack addiction as a future she would choose for her children. John Kaplan, professor of law at Stanford University, observes that the anti-paternalistic principle of letting each person decide for himself "seems singularly inappropriate when it is applied to a habit-forming psychoactive drug that alters the user's perspective as to postponement of gratification and his desire for the drug itself." Kaplan cites research showing that cocaine scores by far the highest "pleasure" score in laboratory experiments on drug use and is also the most "reinforcing" of drugs known to man: in animal studies, monkeys, if permitted, will perform a given task again and again to gain a reward of cocaine, neglecting food or rest until they die of debilitation.

The anti-paternalistic argument for legalization of drugs is most persuasive for benign and non-addictive drugs like marijuana—but marijuana is the least of our drug problems today. When the drugs to be legalized are dangerous and highly addictive drugs like crack, the argument fails. If paternalism is justifiable anywhere, it is justifiable here. Paternalistic prohibitions against highly addictive drugs are legitimate in principle; the central issue, as we shall see shortly, is how they work in practice.

THE ARGUMENT FOR COMPASSION

By contrast, a third argument for the legalization of drugs starts from a very different assumption: that drug abuse is a serious health problem, a condition to be addressed with compassionate medical aid rather than stigmatizing criminal sanctions. While the argument against paternalism downplays the addictiveness of many drugs, the argument from compassion fastens on this as its starting point. As Baltimore's Mayor Schmoke, a leading advocate of this position, argues, "Addiction is a disease, and whether we want to admit it or not, addicts need medical care." Decriminalization, for Schmoke, is a means of reassigning responsibility for the epidemic of drug abuse away from the overburdened criminal justice system to the public health system, where it properly belongs.

Given the fundamental nature of drug addiction, Schmoke points out that "we cannot hope to solve addiction through punishment. . . . Even after prolonged periods of incarceration, during which they have no physical access to heroin, most addicts are still defeated by their physical dependence and return to drugs. . . . The sad truth is that heroin and morphine addiction is, for most users, a lifetime affliction that is impervious to any punishment that the criminal justice system could reasonably mete out."

While the anti-paternalism argument would justify a relatively free market in drugs on the analogy to current arrange-

Number of Americans Killed by Illegal Drugs
(Bars Represent Thousands of Users)

Number of Americans Killed by Legal Drugs
(Bars Represent Thousands of Users)

30,000   100,000   500,000

ALL ILLEGAL DRUGS

ALCOHOL

CIGARETTES

Source: Sue Rusche, Testimony before the House Select Committee on Narcotics Abuse

ments for alcohol and tobacco, the argument from addiction would point to a prescription system as we have today for tranquilizers and other drugs under the control of the medical establishment. A prescription system, however, would fail to eradicate the worst problems accompanying the criminalization of drug use, for it is likely we would continue to see a booming black market in the controlled substances.

THE ARGUMENT FROM CONSEQUENCES

However tolerant and compassionate our attitudes and policies may be toward drug users, we may take a very different and far dimmer view of drug pushers. How can we sanction the terrible harms wrought by those who purvey drugs such as crack and PCP to children and to other vulnerable groups? By taking steps toward legalizing drugs it seems that we implicitly condone and legitimate a market in misery.

But the most powerful and persuasive argument for the legalization of drugs is simply that however morally distasteful legalization of crack and PCP might intrinsically be, in practical terms the alternative is far worse. A sane policy analysis must consider not only the harm caused by using illegal drugs, but also the harm caused by the measures we take against them. The war on drugs is turning out to be a holocaust for our inner cities, and on these grounds it is unconscionable not to surrender.

In the first place, the war on drugs creates all-but irresistible financial incentives for drug dealers. Black market prices of heroin and cocaine are about a hundred times greater than their pharmaceutical prices: on one estimate, for example, $625 worth of coca leaves has a street value in the United States of $560,000. Such hyper-inflated prices mean hyper-inflated profits. As James Ostrowski, former chairman of the New York County Lawyers Association Committee on Law Reform, explains, "Failure [of the war on drugs] is guaranteed because the black market thrives on the war on drugs and benefits from any intensification of it. At best, increased enforcement simply boosts the black market price of drugs, encouraging more drug suppliers to supply more drugs. The publicized conviction of a drug dealer, by instantly creating a vacancy in the lucrative drug market, has the same effect as hanging up a help-wanted sign saying, 'Drug dealer needed—$5,000 a week to start—exciting work.' "

Given this kind of financial incentive to deal in illegal drugs (an industry boasting an estimated $200 billion in annual sales), Fullinwider suggests that no criminal sanction can work to dissuade the dealer. The necessary cost-benefit calculations are easily performed: given that the rewards are enormous and certain, no penalty, even Bennett's favorite beheading, can act as a countervailing consideration, unless the penalty can be made equally certain. And it cannot, even if all the resources of all our police forces and all our courts were to be devoted exclusively to the war on drugs.

Furthermore, the circumstances of criminalization worsen the consequences of the drugs themselves on users. As drug interdiction efforts have increased, drug traffickers have turned to smuggling purer forms of their product; for example, the average purity of cocaine has soared. More potent law enforcement leads to the development of more potent drugs. Schmoke is one who argues that "crack is almost entirely a result of prohibition." Illegal drugs keep getting stronger, even as legal drugs are becoming weaker, with health pressures for low-tar cigarettes, light beer, and wine coolers. There is no Food and Drug Administration regulating the content and purity of illegal drugs, so users buy drugs of uncertain strength, adulterated with various poisons. The illegal status of drugs hastens the spread of AIDS by posing obstacles to needle exchange programs; it inhibits drug users from seeking needed medical attention.

The most serious negative consequence threatened by decriminalization of drugs is a possible increase in use. Opponents of legalization argue that drug-prohibition laws succeed in deterring many people from trying drugs and reduce their availability. But while the lessons of Prohibition lend some support for worries about increased drug use following the repeal of drug laws, decriminalization of marijuana by about a dozen states in the 1970s did not lead to increases in marijuana consumption; in the Netherlands, which decriminalized pot during the 1970s, consumption has actually declined significantly. Culture seems more important than law in determining patterns of drug use. One may doubt that most Americans would inject cocaine or heroin into their veins even if given the chance to do so legally. And, finally, usage could double or triple without tipping the balance in favor of any escalation in the war on drugs, given the scale of the devastation from that war.

One last danger of the war on drugs, and in some ways the most troubling, is the threat that it poses to our civil rights. In a state of war, ordinary protections of civil liberties may give way to an all-out effort to combat the enemy. The same is true in the war on drugs. Wisotksy expresses concern about what he sees as two dangerous and related phenomena: "(1) the government's sustained attack, motivated by the imperatives of drug enforcement, on traditional protections afforded to criminal defendants under the Bill of Rights [such as more permissive use of illegally seized evidence, relaxation of search and seizure requirements, and draconian mandatory sentences], and (2) the gradual but perceptible rise of "Big Brotherism" against the public at large in the form of drug testing, investigative detention, eavesdropping, surveillance, monitoring, and other intrusive enforcement methods. "He concludes, "Since the early 1980s, the prevailing attitude, both within government and in the broader society, has been that the crackdown on drugs is so imperative that extraordinary measures are justified. The end has come to justify the means. The result is that Americans have significantly less freedom than they did only five or six years ago"—all in the waging of a war we cannot win.

CONCLUSION

Whatever the strength of any other arguments for the legalization of drugs, a sober cost-benefit analysis that pays heed to the terrible costs brought by our national war on drugs seems to support some degree of decriminalization. In the end, the best war on drugs may be to revive and overhaul our old war on poverty: to take the resources and energy marshaled in the war on drugs and direct them instead to programs designed to combat the entrenched hopelessness that makes drug use and abuse so tragically appealing.

The sources quoted in this article are: Ethan A. Nadelman, "The Case for Legalization" *The Pub-*

lic Interest, vol. 92 (1988); Sue Rusche, testimony before the House Select Committee on Narcotics Abuse and Control, September 29, 1988; Robert Fullinwider, interview; Steven Wisotsky, testimony before the House Select Committee; David A. J. Richards, *Sex, Drugs, Death, and the Law* (Totowa, N.J.: Rowman and Littlefield, 1982); John Kaplan, "Taking Drugs Seriously," *The Public Interest*, vol. 92 (1988); Kurt Schmoke, testimony before the House Select Committee; and James Ostrowski, "Thinking about Drug Legalization," *Cato Institute Policy Analysis*, No. 121 (May 25, 1989).

NO

James Q. Wilson
and John J. DiIulio, Jr.

CRACKDOWN

According to the projections, crime was supposed to be under control by now. The postwar baby-boom generation, which moved into its crime-prone years during the early 1960s, has grown up, yielding its place to the (proportionately) less numerous baby-bust generation. With relatively fewer 18-year-olds around, we should all be walking safer streets.

And in fact for most people crime *has* gone down. The Census Bureau's victimization surveys tell us that between 1980 and 1987 the burglary rate declined by 27 percent, the robbery rate by 21 percent. Despite what we hear, 3,000 fewer murders were committed in 1987 than in 1980. Even in some big cities that are in the news for the frequency with which their residents kill each other, the homicide rate has decreased. Take Los Angeles: despite freeway shootings and gang warfare, there were 261 fewer murders in 1987 than in 1980, a drop of more than 20 percent.

But in specific enclaves the horror stories are all too true. In south central Los Angeles, in much of Newark, in and around the housing projects of Chicago, in the South Bronx and Bedford-Stuyvesant sections of New York, and in parts of Washington, D.C., conditions are not much better than they are in Beirut on a bad day. Drugs, especially crack, are sold openly on street corners; rival gangs shoot at each other from moving automobiles; automatic weapons are carried by teenagers onto school playgrounds; innocent people hide behind double-locked doors and shuttered windows. In Los Angeles there is at least one gang murder every day, Sundays included. A ten-foot-high concrete wall is being built around the junior high school one of us attended, in order, the principal explained, to keep stray bullets from hitting children on the playground.

The problem is drugs and the brutal struggles among competing gangs for control of the lucrative drug markets. The drug of choice is crack (except in Washington, where it is PCP). The crack craze has led to conditions far worse than were found in these same neighborhoods a decade or so ago, when

From James Q. Wilson and John J. DiIulio, Jr., "Crackdown," *The New Republic* (July 10, 1989). Copyright © 1989 by The New Republic, Inc. Reprinted by permission of *The New Republic*.

heroin was the preferred drug. The reasons for the change are not reassuring.

Crack is a stimulant; heroin is a sedative. Crack produces exceptional euphoria; heroin produces, after a quick "rush," oblivion. Crack (and PCP) addicts are often stimulated to acts of violence and daring that make them dangerous to themselves as well as to others; heroin addicts are rarely violent when high—the drug even depresses the sexual drive.

Crack is marketed by competitive distribution systems, some of whose members are fighting—literally—to establish monopoly control. Heroin (at least on the East Coast) was marketed in a criminal environment dominated by established monopolies that were well equipped, in muscle and in political connections, to protect their market shares with a minimum of random violence.

Crack users have no attractive chemical alternative. The drug is far more rewarding than any substitute. Heroin users who had progressed to the point where they wanted nothing but relief from the pains of withdrawal and the disease caused by intravenous injection could take oral methadone. The heroin substitute, though addictive, required no injections, prevented withdrawal pains, and (in the correct dosages) produced little or no "high."

In short, certain neighborhoods of our larger cities are being ravaged by a drug that consumers find more alluring than heroin, that stimulates rather than sedates its users, that suppliers must use violence to sell, and that therapists are at a loss to manage by chemical means.

Attempting to suppress the use of drugs is very costly. Some people therefore conclude that we must eliminate all the costs of law enforcement by repealing the laws that are being enforced. The result would be less crime, fewer and weaker gangs, and an opportunity to address the public health problems in a straightforward manner.

But legalizing drugs would also entail costs. Those costs are hard to measure, in part because they are to a large degree moral and in part because we have so little experience with legalized drugs.

There is an obvious moral reason for attempting to discourage drug use: the heavy consumption of certain drugs ravages human character. These drugs—principally heroin, cocaine, and crack—are for many people powerfully reinforcing. The pleasure or oblivion they produce leads many users to devote their lives to seeking pleasure or oblivion, and to do so regardless of the cost in ordinary human virtues, such as temperance, duty, and sympathy. The dignity, autonomy, and productivity of users is at best impaired, at worst destroyed.

SOME PEOPLE THINK SOCIETY HAS NO obligation to form and sustain the character of individuals. Libertarians would leave all adults free to choose their own habits and seek their own destiny so long as their behavior did not cause any direct harm to others. But most people, however willing they may be to tolerate human eccentricities and support civil liberties, act as if they believe that government, as the agent for society, is responsible for helping to instill certain qualities in the citizenry. This was the original reason for mandatory schooling. We not only want to train children to be useful, we want to train them to be decent. It is also the reason that virtually every nation that has been confronted by a sharp increase in addiction to any psychoactive substance, including alcohol, has enacted laws designed to regulate or suppress its use.

Great Britain once allowed physicians to prescribe opiates for addicts. The system worked reasonably well so long as the addicts were middle-class people who had become hooked as a consequence of receiving pain-killers in hospitals. But when thrill-seeking youth discovered heroin, the number of addicts increased 40-*fold*, and so Britain ended the prescription system. It was replaced at first with a system of controlled dispensation from government clinics, and then with a system of substituting methadone for heroin coupled with the stringent enforcement of the laws against the latter.

Even if we were to decide that the government had no responsibility for character formation and should regulate only behavior that hurts other people, we would still have to figure out what to do about drug-dependent people—because such dependency does hurt other people. A heroin addict dreamily enjoying his euphoria, a crack smoker looking for the next high, a cocaine snorter eager for relief from his depression—these users are not likely to be healthy people, productive workers, good parents, reliable neighbors, attentive students, or safe drivers. Moreover, some people are harmed by drugs that they have not chosen to use. The babies of drug-dependent women suffer because of their mothers' habits. We all pay for drug abuse in lowered productivity, more accidents, higher insurance premiums, bigger welfare costs, and less effective classrooms.

The question is whether the costs of drug use are likely to be higher when the drug is illegal or when it is legal. In both cases society must pay the bill. When the drug is illegal, the cost consists of the law enforcement costs (crime, corruption, extensive and intrusive policing), the welfare costs (poorer health, lost wages, higher unemployment benefits, more aid to families with dependent children, and various treatment and prevention programs), and the moral costs (debased and degraded people). If the drug were legal, the bill would consist primarily of the welfare costs and the moral costs. And there would still be the law enforcement costs: the costs of enforcing tax collection if the drugs were sold, or of preventing diversion if the drugs were distributed through the health care system, and the costs in either case of keeping the drugs out of the hands, lungs, and veins of minors. Legalization without some form of regulation is inconceivable; the more stringent the regulation, the higher the law enforcement bill.

WHICH SCENARIO WILL BE COSTLIER? THE answer chiefly depends on how many people will use the drug. We have a rough idea of how many people regularly use heroin and cocaine despite its illegality. How many will regularly use it under the legal scenario?

No one really knows, but it will almost surely be many more than now. The free market price of cocaine is probably no more than five percent of its present black market price. Even allowing for heavy taxes, Stanford's John Kaplan has estimated that the free market price would be no more than 20 percent of what it now costs. The consumption of a widely desired, pleasure-inducing substance without question will increase dramatically if the price is cut by 80 percent to 95 percent.

Moreover, the true price of the drug is the monetary cost plus the difficulty and inconvenience of the search for it and the risk associated with consuming a product of unknown quality. Though drugs are sold openly on the streets of some communities, for most people—especially for novice, middle-class users—they are hard to come by and often found only in threatening surroundings. Legalization will make the drug more attractive, even if the price actually rises, by reducing the costs of searching for it, negotiating a transaction, and running the risk of ingesting a dangerous substance. The combined effect of lowered market prices and lowered transaction costs will be very great.

Just how great cannot be known without trying it. And one cannot try it experimentally, for there is no way to run a meaningful experiment. The increase in use that would occur if people in one neighborhood or patients at one clinic were allowed to buy the drug at its market cost can give us no reliable information on how many people would use the drug if it were generally available. And the experiment would have irreversible effects. Moreover, as the British experience showed, there is no such thing as "controlled distribution." Inevitably there will be massive leaks of government-supplied drugs into the black market.

We already have the "benefits" of one quasi-experiment. So long as cocaine was available only in its relatively expensive powdered form, its use was pretty much concentrated among more affluent people. But with the invention of crack, which can be sold in single low-priced doses rather than by the high-priced gram, cocaine use increased sharply.

We believe that the moral and welfare costs of heavy drug use are so large that society should continue to enforce the laws against its use for the sake of keeping the number of users as small as possible. But we recognize that by adopting this position, we are placing a heavy burden on those poor communities where drug use is endemic. We are allowing these neighborhoods to be more violent than they would be if the drug were legal. Since we do not live in such communities, we must ask ourselves whether our preferences can be justified to people who do.

The answer to that question is given by the testimony of those who live in the midst of the problem. They want drugs kept illegal. They say so and their representatives in Congress say so. We hope that our libertarian critics will not accuse the people of Watts, Anacostia, and the South Bronx of suffering from false consciousness on this matter. These people know what drug use is and they don't like it.

But if drugs are to be kept illegal, we have a special responsibility to prevent the streets of inner-city neighborhoods from being controlled by those who seek to profit from the trade. We have not done a very good job of this.

In some places there may not be enough police. In others the cops are just badly used, as when the focus is on making a case against "Mr. Big," the local drug kingpin. There are two things wrong with this. First, nothing is easier than replacing Mr. Big; indeed, often the police get evidence on him from tips supplied by his would-be replacement. Meanwhile the distribution of drugs goes on unabated. Second, arresting Mr. Big does nothing to improve the lives of the decent people in the neighborhood who want the drug dealers off the street.

MANY CITIES, NOTABLY NEW YORK, HAVE recognized this and are concentrating on street-level dealers. The NYPD has wrested control from the drug dealers in parts of the Lower East Side, all of Washington Square Park, much of West 107th Street, and other places. But they have done so at a cost, what Aric Press of *Newsweek* calls the criminal justice equivalent of bulimia. The police go on an arrest binge, and then, "overwhelmed and overfed, the rest of the system—prosecutors, defenders, judges, and jailers—has spent its days in an endless purge, desperately trying to find ways to move its population before it gets hit with another wave tomorrow." The purgatives included granting early release to some inmates and trying to shift other city prisoners to state penitentiaries; pressuring the governor to authorize the appointment of more judges while encouraging faster plea bargaining to clear the crowded dockets; and building "temporary" holding facilities for new arrestees.

The District of Columbia has begun to enter the bulimia phase. The number of people going through the criminal justice system on drug charges has exploded. Between 1983 and 1987 drug arrests increased by 45 percent, drug prosecutions by over 500 percent, drug convictions by over 700 percent. Clearly judges and prosecutors were starting to get tough. But until very recently, the toughness stopped at the jailhouse door. As recently as 1986, only seven percent of the adults arrested on drug charges—and only 20 percent of those convicted on such charges—were sent to the city's principal correctional facility at Lorton. Then, suddenly, the system lurched into overdrive. Between 1986 and 1987 the number of drug incarcerations more than doubled, so that by the end of the year an adult arrested on a drug charge had a one-in-five chance of going to jail, and one convicted on such a charge had a one-in-two chance of winding up at Lorton.

This means that, until very recently, the price of drug dealing in Washington has been quite low. Those who say that "law enforcement has failed" should remember that until the last two years it was barely tried. Police Chief-designate Isaac Fulwood says that the same dealer may be arrested eight or nine times in the space of a few weeks. The city has been operating a revolving-door criminal justice system.

One reason for the speed with which the door revolves is that in Washington, as in most parts of the country, the prisons are jammed full. Another factor is that professional drug dealers know they can get a favorable plea bargain if they threaten to make the system give them a full trial, replete with every conceivable motion. The mere threat of such a demand is ordinarily enough to ensure that an attractive bargain is offered.

HOW CAN AN OVERTAXED SYSTEM HELP protect people in the drug-ridden neighborhoods? Building more conventional prisons is part of the answer, but that takes a lot of time, and no one wants them in their back yard. The goal is to take drug dealers off the streets for a longer period than the time it takes to be booked and released. One step is to ensure that no good arrest is washed out for want of prosecution because of a shortage of judges, prosecutors, and public defenders. These are not cheap, but candidates for these posts are more readily available than vacant lots on which to build jails.

Nevertheless, prisons are still needed and can be had, provided we are willing to think of alternatives to conventional holding tanks. One is to reserve regular prison space for major traffickers and to use parts of present (or all of former) military camps as boot camps for lower-level dealers. At these minimum-security camps, inmates would receive physical training, military discipline, and drug-abuse treatment, all under the direction of military personnel and with the aim of preparing them for a life that would combine, to the extent possible, the requirement of regular drug tests and the opportunity for gainful employment.

Meanwhile, the chances of released inmates rejoining old gangs can perhaps be reduced by enforcing a law, such as the one recently passed in California, that makes mere membership in certain gangs illegal and attaches civil or criminal penalties to parents who knowingly allow their children to join them. . . .

AT THIS STAGE, WE ARE NOT TRYING TO deter drug sales or reduce drug use. All we wish to do is to reassert lawful public control over public spaces. Everything else we may wish to achieve—reducing the demand for drugs, curing the users of drugs, deterring the sale of drugs—can only be done after the public and the police, not the dealers and the gangs, are in charge of the neighborhoods. In the short run, this can be done by repeatedly arresting every suspected dealer and user and sending them through the revolving door. If we cannot increase the severity of the penalties they face, we can at least increase the frequency with which they bear them. In police terms, we want to roust the bad guys.

After the bad guys find they are making repeated trips to the same prison camps, the decent people of the neighborhood must form organizations willing and able to work with the police to keep the bad guys from regaining control of the streets. The Kenilworth-Parkside area of Washington shows what can be done. A few years ago this neighborhood, the site of a public housing project, was an open-air drug market that spawned all manner of crime. In 1982 a tenants' committee led by Kimi Gray formed a corporation and assumed control of the housing project. Though the residents were primarily unwed mothers living on welfare, over the next five years their association collected the rents, ran the buildings, enforced school attendance on the children, and got rid of the addicts. In 1988 the association signed a contract to purchase the project from the government. . . .

THE DRUGS-CRIME PROBLEM ULTIMATELY will be solved only when the demand for drugs is dramatically reduced. Though it is necessary to make major investments in overseas crop eradication, the interdiction of international drug shipments, and the control of our borders, there is scarcely an experienced law enforcement officer in the country who does not believe that controlling the sources of supply is much more than a holding operation.

How do we reduce demand? We do not know. Realizing that is the beginning of wisdom. The greatest mischief is to assume that the demand for drugs will decline only when there is less racism and poverty, better schools and more jobs, more religion, and better-quality television.

Recall how the heroin epidemic finally ended. At one time the number of new addicts seemed to be rising exponentially despite the ending of the Turkish supply of illicit opium and the breaking up of the French processing laboratories. Now we have a fairly stable number of confirmed addicts whose ranks seem not to be increasing and may be decreasing. This was accomplished by three things: death, testing, and methadone.

Youngsters who were ready to ignore the lectures of their teachers or the blandishments of public-service television commercials were not so ready to ignore the testimony of their everyday experiences. Heroin addicts were dying from drug overdoses, dirty needles, and personal neglect. Doing heroin no longer seemed as glamorous as it did when one first heard about it from jazz musicians and big-time crooks.

The military began a rigorous program of testing, which continues to this day. There were sanctions attached to being found out—often a delay in being returned home, possibly military punishment, and probably a dishonorable discharge. Drug use in the military dropped dramatically and has stayed low.

Heroin addicts who were burned out by their long and increasingly unsatisfying bout with the drug often turned to methadone as a way of easing the pain and stabilizing their lives. If they stayed with it, they had a good chance of benefiting from the counseling and training programs made available to them.

These three prevention measures were not likely to be as effective with cocaine and crack addicts. Some users were dying from these drugs, but smoking crack still seems to many users to be far more exciting and much less dangerous than injecting heroin. In time, enough people will ruin their lives so that even the fantastic high that crack produces will begin to seem unattractive to potential users. But that time is not here yet.

Testing works but only if it is done rigorously and with real consequences, ranging from immediate counseling to discharge or punishment. As yet few civilian institutions seem prepared (or able) to do what the armed forces did. It is hard enough for private employers to test, and they are not subject to the search-and-seizure provisions of the Fourth Amendment. Opposition from employee groups and civil libertarians shows little sign of abating. Some government agencies are testing, but they are doing so gingerly, usually by limiting tests to workers such as prison guards and customs agents who are in obviously sensitive positions. It is hard to imagine many schools adopting a testing program, though some are trying.

And there is no cocaine equivalent for methadone, though science may yet find one.

That doesn't leave much: some school-based drug-education programs that look promising but have not (as yet) proved their efficacy and many treatment programs that can have some success—provided the patient is willing to stay in them.

"WILLING": THAT IS THE KEY. HEAVY DRUG use is an addiction about which we have in other contexts already learned a great deal. Fifty years ago we knew as little about dealing with alcoholism as we now know about cocaine abuse. Today we know enough about alcoholism to realize the key steps to coping with it.

First and foremost: addicts will not get better until they first confront the fact that they are addicts. Alcoholics Anonymous knows this full well, making it the cornerstone of its Twelve Steps. The families of alcoholics are taught that they did not cause and can neither control nor cure the addictive behavior—the disease—of the alcoholic. The deaths of others and an inescapable testing program can help provoke among drug users what the destruction of the lives of alcoholics sometimes stimulates—a recognition that they are powerless in the face of the drug and that they need the help of others like themselves. . . .

We must begin with the facts, not with theories. The facts are these: some parts of our cities are being destroyed by gangs competing for the right to destroy lives by selling drugs. Those gangs have to be defeated, even if it means hiring more judges and building more correctional facilities. After that we can help communities reorganize themselves so that the good people control the streets and the teachers, doctors and scientists have a chance to find out what will prevent another addictive epidemic from breaking out when some chemist discovers a drug that is even cheaper and more euphoria-inducing than crack. And that last event, we can be certain, will happen.

POSTSCRIPT

Should Drugs Be Legalized?

The analogy often cited by proponents of drug legalization is the ill-fated attempt to ban the sale of liquor in the United States, which lasted from 1919 to 1933. Prohibition has been called "an experiment noble in purpose," but it was an experiment that greatly contributed to the rise of organized crime. The repeal of Prohibition brought about an increase in liquor consumption and alcoholism, but it also deprived organized crime of an important source of income. Would drug decriminalization similarly strike a blow at the drug dealers? Possibly, and such a prospect is obviously appealing. But would drug decriminalization also exacerbate some of the ills associated with drugs? Would there be more violence, more severe addiction, more crack babies born to addicted mothers? Here, there is clearly a choice between evils. How should society go about answering questions like these? What role should the social sciences play?

David F. Musto's *The American Disease* (Yale, 1973) is a classic discussion of the drug problem in America. Sidney Cohen reviews the problems of alcoholism in *The Alcoholism Problem* (Haworth, 1983). Erich Goode, *Drugs in American Society* (McGraw-Hill, 1988) provides a sociological perspective on drugs. H. Wayne Morgan's *Drugs in America: A Social History, 1800–1900* (Syracuse University, 1981) is also useful for anyone seeking a historical background on the drug problem. Larry Sloman's book *Reefer Madness: The History of Marijuana in America* (Grove Press, 1983) describes changing attitudes and laws regarding marijuana, while Lester Brinspoon and James B. Bakalar do the same for cocaine in *Cocaine: A Drug and Its Social Evolution* (Basic Books, 1985). James A. Inciardi, *The War on Drugs: Heroin, Cocaine, Crime and Public Policy* (Mayfield, 1986) gives a close-up look at the cocaine and crime scene. A book by Edward M. Brecher and the editors of *Consumer Reports*, entitled *Licit and Illicit Drugs* (Consumers Union, 1972), argues for the decriminalization of marijuana, heroin maintenance programs, and lenient treatment of other drug offenders. Thomas S. Szasz, *Ceremonial Chemistry: The Ritual Persecution of Drugs, Addicts, and Pushers*, revised ed. (Learning Publications, 1985) criticizes our current antidrug crusades. Numerous periodicals are devoted to discussion of drugs in America. For example, *The Drug Policy Letter*, published every two months by the Drug Policy Foundation in Washington, D.C., considers issues relating to the legal status of drugs. *The Drug Educator*, published quarterly by the American Council for Drug Education of Rockville, Maryland, stresses the health hazards associated even with "soft" drugs like marijuana.

ISSUE 16

Is Incapacitation the Answer to the Crime Problem?

YES: James Q. Wilson, from *Thinking About Crime* (Basic Books, 1975)

NO: David L. Bazelon, from "Solving the Nightmare of Street Crime" *USA Today Magazine*, a publication of the Society for the Advancement of Education (January 1982)

ISSUE SUMMARY

YES: Professor James Q. Wilson argues that imprisoning everyone convicted of a serious offense for several years would greatly reduce these crimes. He contends that incapacitation is the one policy that works.
NO: Judge David L. Bazelon discusses the moral and financial costs of the incapacitation approach and argues that society must attack the brutal social and economic conditions that are the root causes of street crime.

Not a day passes in America without reports of murders, rapes, or other violent crimes. As crime has increasingly captured the headlines, public indignation has intensified—particularly when spectacular cases have been brought to light about paroled convicts committing new felonies, light sentences being handed down for serious crimes, and cases being thrown out of court on legal technicalities. The perception that Michael Dukakis was soft on criminals seriously hurt his bid for the presidency in 1988. (As governor of Massachusetts, Dukakis approved a prison furlough program that released a convict named Willie Horton, who subsequently went on to commit a widely publicized, horribly violent crime in another state.) Over the past three decades, there has been a dramatic increase in the number of Americans who think that the authorities should be tougher on criminals. To take one prominent example: While a majority of Americans in the 1960s favored the abolition of the death penalty, today more than seventy percent favor its use in some cases.

Even in the intellectual community, there has been a turnaround. When George Wallace, the Southern Democrat and presidential candidate, and other politicians raised the issue of "law and order" at the end of the 1960s, the term was called "a code word for racism" in academic and literary circles. This is understandable because Wallace *had* previously identified himself with white racism. The attitude toward crime that was popular in academic circles during the 1960s might be briefly summarized under two headings, the prevention of crime and the treatment of criminals.

To prevent crime, some academics argued, government must do more than rely upon police, courts, and jails. It must do something about the underlying social roots of crime, especially poverty and racism. It was assumed that, once these roots were severed, crime would begin to fade away, or at least cease to be a major social problem.

The prescription for treating criminals followed much the same logic. The word *punishment* was avoided in favor of *treatment* or *rehabilitation*, for the purpose was not to inflict pain or to "pay back" the criminal but to bring about a change in his behavior. If that could be done by lenient treatment— by short prison terms, by education, counseling, and above all by under- standing—then so much the better.

By the late 1970s, the intellectual community itself showed signs that it was reassessing its outlook toward crime. Harvard professor James Q. Wilson's views on crime became widely respected in universities and in the mass media. Wilson stresses the need for "realism." It may be that some day all poverty and social injustice will cease to exist, says Wilson, but until that day arrives we had better keep criminals off the streets. He maintains that crime can be significantly reduced here and now simply by incapacitating (incar- cerating) dangerous offenders. Wilson also takes a dim view of the prospects for rehabilitating criminals in prison. In his view, statistics prove that the question of whether a criminal goes back to crime after release does not depend upon what kind of prison he has gone to but rather his own personal characteristics. In other words, Wilson believes, it is unlikely that even the most enlightened prison system can rehabilitate a hardened criminal.

David L. Bazelon admits that incapacitation is a short-term solution to street crime that delivers some results. He points out, however, that it has high financial and moral costs, explaining that the United States already imprisons a larger proportion of its citizens than all other developed nations except the U.S.S.R. A three-fold increase in the prison population will not make a significant dent in the rate of serious crimes, maintains Bazelon, and the new prisons needed to house those increased numbers will cost many billions of dollars. More importantly, he says, the incapacitation approach assumes that convicted offenders will continue to commit crimes and in effect punishes them for future misdeeds. Bazelon's approach raises serious questions concerning individual justice. He believes the only satisfactory answer is to attack the social and economic conditions that are the root causes of street crime; others, such as Wilson, argue for more immediate action. These two competing approaches are illustrated in the following selections.

YES

James Q. Wilson

THINKING ABOUT CRIME

I argue for a sober view of man and his institutions that would permit reasonable things to be accomplished, foolish things abandoned, and utopian things forgotten. A sober view of man requires a modest definition of progress. A 20 percent reduction in robbery would still leave us with the highest robbery rate of almost any Western nation but would prevent about sixty thousand robberies. A small gain for society, a large one for the would-be victims. Yet a 20 percent reduction is unlikely if we concentrate our efforts on dealing with the causes of crime or even if we concentrate on improving police efficiency. Were we to devote those resources to a strategy that is well within our abilities—namely, to incapacitating a larger fraction of the convicted serious robbers—than not only is a 20 percent reduction possible, but even larger ones are conceivable.

Most serious crime is committed by repeaters. What we do with first offenders is probably far less important than what we do with habitual offenders. A genuine first offender (and not merely a habitual offender caught for the first time) is in all likelihood a young person who, in the majority of cases, will stop stealing when he gets older. This is not to say we should forgive first offenses, for that would be to license the offense and erode the moral judgments that must underlie any society's attitude toward crime. The gravity of the offense must be appropriately impressed on the first offender, but the effort to devise ways of reeducating or uplifting him in order to insure that he does not steal again is likely to be wasted—both because we do not know how to reeducate or uplift and because most young delinquents seem to reeducate themselves no matter what society does.

After tracing the history of nearly ten thousand Philadelphia boys born in 1945, Marvin Wolfgang and his colleagues at the University of Pennsylvania found that over one-third were picked up by the police for something more serious than a traffic offense, but that 46 percent of these delinquents had no further police contact after their first offense. Though a third started on crime, nearly half seemed to stop spontaneously—a good thing, because the criminal justice system in that city, already sorely taxed, would in all

From James Q. Wilson, *Thinking About Crime* (Basic Books, 1975). Copyright © 1975 by Basic Books, Inc. Reprinted by permission of Basic Books, Inc., Publishers, New York.

likelihood have collapsed. Out of the ten thousand boys, however, there were six hundred twenty-seven—only 6 percent—who committed five or more offenses before they were eighteen. Yet these few chronic offenders accounted for *over half* of these recorded delinquencies and about *two-thirds* of all the violent crimes committed by the entire cohort.

Only a tiny fraction of all serious crimes lead immediately to an arrest, and only a slightly larger fraction are ultimately "cleared" by an arrest, but this does not mean that the police function is meaningless. Because most serious crime is committed by repeaters, most criminals eventually get arrested. The Wolfgang findings and other studies suggest that the chances of a persistent burglar or robber living out his life, or even going a year, with no arrest are quite small. Yet a large proportion of repeat offenders suffer little or no loss of freedom. Whether or not one believes that such penalties, if inflicted, would act as a deterrent, it is obvious that they could serve to incapacitate these offenders and thus, for the period of the incapacitation, prevent them from committing additional crimes.

We have a limited (and declining) supply of detention facilities, and many of those that exist are decrepit, unsafe, and overcrowded. But as important as expanding the supply and improving the decency of the facilities is the need to think seriously about how we wish to allocate those spaces that exist. At present, that allocation is hit or miss. A 1966 survey of over fifteen juvenile correctional institutions revealed that about 30 percent of the inmates were young persons who had been committed for conduct that would not have been judged criminal were it committed by adults. They were runaways, "stubborn children," or chronic truants—problem children, to be sure, but scarcely major threats to society. Using scarce detention space for them when in Los Angeles over 90 percent of burglars with a major prior record receive no state prison sentence seems, to put it mildly, anomalous.

Shlomo and Reuel Shinnar have estimated the effect on crime rates in New York State of a judicial policy other than that followed during the last decade or so. Given the present level of police efficiency and making some assumptions about how many crimes each offender commits per year, they conclude that the rate of serious crime would be only *one-third* what it is today if every person convicted of a serious offense were imprisoned for three years. This reduction would be less if it turned out (as seems unlikely) that most serious crime is committed by first time offenders, and it would be much greater if the proportion of crimes resulting in an arrest and conviction were increased (as also seems unlikely). The reduction, it should be noted, would be solely the result of incapacitation, making no allowance for such additional reductions as might result from enhanced deterrence or rehabilitation.

The Shinnar estimates are based on uncertain data and involve assumptions that can be challenged. But even assuming they are overly optimistic by a factor of two, a sizable reduction in crime would still ensue. In other countries such a policy of greater incapacitation is in fact followed. A robber arrested in England, for example, is more than three times as likely as one arrested in New York to go to prison. That difference in sentencing does not account for all the difference between English and American crime rates, but it may well account for a substantial fraction of it.

That these gains are possible does not mean that society should adopt such a policy. One would first want to know the costs, in additional prison space and judicial resources, of greater use of incapacitation. One would want to debate the propriety and humanity of a mandatory three-year term; perhaps, in order to accommodate differences in the character of criminals and their crimes, one would want to have a range of sentences from, say, one to five years. One would want to know what is likely to happen to the process of charging and pleading if every person arrested for a serious crime faced a mandatory minimum sentence, however mild. These and other difficult and important questions must first be confronted. But the central fact is that *these are reasonable questions* around which facts can be gathered and intelligent arguments mustered. To discuss them requires us to make few optimistic assumptions about the malleability of human nature, the skills of officials who operate complex institutions, or the capacity of society to improve the fundamental aspects of familial and communal life.

Persons who criticize an emphasis on changing the police and courts to cope with crime are fond of saying that such measures cannot work so long as unemployment and poverty exist. We must acknowledge that we have not done very well at inducting young persons, especially but not only blacks, into the work force. Teenage unemployment rates continue to exceed 20 percent; though the rate of growth in the youthful component of the population has slowed, their unemployment shows little sign of abating. To a degree, anticrime policies may be frustrated by the failure of employment policies, but it would be equally correct to say that so long as the criminal justice system does not impede crime, efforts to reduce unemployment will not work. If legitimate opportunities for work are unavailable, many young persons will turn to crime; but if criminal opportunities are profitable, many young persons will not take those legitimate jobs that exist. The benefits of work and the costs of crime must be increased simultaneously; to increase one but not the other makes sense only if one assumes that young people are irrational.

One rejoinder to this view is the argument that if legitimate jobs are made absolutely more attractive than stealing, stealing will decline even without any increase in penalties for it. That may be true provided there is no practical limit on the amount that can be paid in wages. Since the average "take" from a burglary or mugging is quite small, it would seem easy to make the income from a job exceed the income from crime. But this neglects the advantages of a criminal income: One works at crime at one's convenience, enjoys the esteem of colleagues who think a "straight" job is stupid and skill at stealing is commendable, looks forward to the occasional "big score" that may make further work unnecessary for weeks, and relishes the risk and adventure associated with theft. The money value of all these benefits—that is, what one who is not shocked by crime would want in cash to forego crime—is hard to estimate, but is almost certainly far larger than what either public or private employers could offer to unskilled or semiskilled young workers. The only alternative for society is to so increase the risks of theft that its value is depreciated below what society can afford to pay in legal wages, and then take whatever steps are necessary to insure that those legal wages are available.

Another rejoinder to the "attack poverty" approach to crime is this: The desire to reduce crime is the worst possible reason for reducing poverty. Most poor persons are not criminals; many are either retired or have regular jobs and lead conventional family lives. The elderly, the working poor, and the willing-to-work poor could benefit greatly from economic conditions and government programs that enhance their incomes without there being the slightest reduction in crime—indeed, if the experience of the 1960s is any guide, there might well be, through no fault of most beneficiaries, an increase in crime. Reducing poverty and breaking up the ghettoes are desirable policies in their own right, whatever their effects on crime. It is the duty of government to devise other measures to cope with crime, not only to permit antipoverty programs to succeed without unfair competition from criminal opportunities, but also to insure that such programs do not inadvertently shift the costs of progress, in terms of higher crime rates, onto innocent parties, not the least of whom are the poor themselves.

One cannot press this economic reasoning too far. Some persons will commit crimes whatever the risks; indeed, for some, the greater the risk the greater the thrill, while others—the alcoholic wife beater, for example—are only dimly aware that there are any risks. But more important than the insensitivity of certain criminal activities to changes in risks and benefits is the impropriety of casting the crime problem wholly in terms of a utilitarian calculus. The most serious offenses are crimes not simply because society finds them inconvenient, but because it regards them with moral horror. To steal, to rape, to rob, to assault—these acts are destructive of the very possibility of society and affronts to the humanity of their victims. It is my experience that parents do not instruct their children to be law abiding merely by pointing to the risks of being caught, but by explaining that these acts are wrong whether or not one is caught. I conjecture that those parents who simply warn their offspring about the risks of crime produce a disproportionate number of young persons willing to take those risks.

Even the deterrent capacity of the criminal justice system depends in no small part on its ability to evoke sentiments of shame in the accused. If all it evoked were a sense of being unlucky, crime rates would be even higher. James Fitzjames Stephens makes the point by analogy. To what extent, he asks, would a man be deterred from theft by the knowledge that by committing it he was exposing himself to one chance in fifty of catching a serious but not fatal illness—say, a bad fever? Rather little, we would imagine—indeed, all of us regularly take risks as great or greater than that; when we drive after drinking, when we smoke cigarettes, when we go hunting in the woods. The criminal sanction, Stephens concludes, "operates not only on the fears of criminals, but upon the habitual sentiments of those who are not criminals. [A] great part of the general detestation of crime . . . arises from the fact that the commission of offenses is associated . . . with the solemn and deliberate infliction of punishment wherever crime is proved."

Much is made today of the fact that the criminal justice system "stigmatizes" those caught up in it, and thus unfairly marks such persons and perhaps even furthers their criminal careers by having "labeled" them as criminals. Whether the labeling process operates in this way is as yet unproved, but it would indeed be unfortunate if society treated a convicted offender in such a way that he had no reasonable alternative but to make crime a career. To prevent this, society ought to insure that one can "pay one's debt" without suffering permanent loss of civil rights, the continuing and pointless indignity of parole supervision, and frustration in being unable to find a job. But doing these things is very different from eliminating the "stigma" from crime. To destigmatize crime would be to lift from it the weight of moral judgment and to make crime simply a particular occupation or avocation which society has chosen to reward less (or perhaps more!) than other pursuits. If there is not stigma attached to an activity, then society has no business making it a crime. Indeed, before the invention of the prison in the late eighteenth and early nineteenth centuries, the stigma attached to criminals was the major deterrent to and principal form of protection from criminal activity. The purpose of the criminal justice system is not to expose would-be criminals to a lottery in which they either win or lose, but to expose them in addition and more importantly to the solemn condemnation of the community should they yield to temptation. . . .

One wonders whether the stigma properly associated with crime retains much deterrent or educative value. My strong inclination is to resist explanations for rising crime that are based on the alleged moral breakdown of society, the community, or the family. I resist in part because most of the families and communities I know have not broken down, and in part because, had they broken down, I cannot imagine any collective action we could take consistent with our civil liberties that would restore a moral consensus, and yet the facts are hard to ignore. Take the family: Over one-third of all black children and one in fourteen of all white children live in single-parent families. Over two million children live in single-parent (usually father absent) households, almost *double* the number of ten years ago. In 1950, 18 percent of black families were female-headed; in 1969 the proportion had risen to 27 percent; by 1973 it exceeded 35 percent. The average income for a single-parent family with children under six years of age was, in 1970, only $3,100, well below the official "poverty line."

Studies done in the late 1950s and the early 1960s showed that children from broken homes were more likely than others to become delinquent. In New York State, 58 percent of the variation in pupil achievement in three hundred schools could be predicted by but three variables—broken homes, overcrowded housing, and parental educational level. Family disorganization, writes Urie Bronfenbrenner, has been shown in thousands of studies to be an "omnipresent overriding factor" in behavior disorders and social pathology. And that disorganization is increasing.

These facts may explain some elements of the rising crime rate that cannot be attributed to the increased number of young persons, high teenage unemployment, or changed judicial policies. The age of persons arrested has been declining for more than fifteen years and the median age of convicted defendants (in jurisdictions for which data are available) has been declining for the last six years. Apparently, the age at which persons begin to commit serious crime has been falling. For some young people, thus, whatever forces weaken their resistance to criminal activity have been increasing in magnitude, and these forces may well include the continued disorganization of the family and the continued deterioration of the social structure of inner city communities.

One wants to be objective, if not optimistic. Perhaps single-parent families today are less disorganized or have a different significance than such families in the past. Perhaps the relationship between family structure and social pathology will change. After all, there now seem to be good grounds for believing that, at least on the East Coast, the heroin epidemic of the 1960s has run its course; though there are still thousands of addicts, the rate of formation of new addicts has slowed and the rate of heroin use by older addicts has dropped. Perhaps other aspects of the relationship among family, personality, and crime will change. Perhaps.

No one can say how much of crime results from its increased profitability and how much from its decreased shamefulness. But one or both factors must be at work, for population changes alone simply cannot account for the increases. Crime in our cities has increased far faster than the number of young people, or poor people, or black people, or just plain people who live in those cities. In short, objective conditions alone, whether demographic or economic, cannot account for the crime increases, though they no doubt contributed to it. Subjective forces—ideas, attitudes, values—played a great part, though in ways hard to define and impossible to measure. An assessment of the effect of these changes on crime would provide a partial understanding of changes in the moral structure of our society.

But to understand is not to change. If few of the demographic factors contributing to crime are subject to planned change, virtually none of the subjective ones are. Though intellectually rewarding, from a practical point of view it is a mistake to think about crime in terms of its "causes" and then to search for ways to alleviate those causes. We must think instead of what it is feasible for a government or a community to do, and then try to discover, by experimentation and observation, which of those things will produce, at acceptable costs, desirable changes in the level of criminal victimization.

There are, we now know, certain things we can change in accordance with our intentions, and certain ones we cannot. We cannot alter the number of juveniles who first experiment with minor crimes. We cannot lower the recidivism rate, though within reason we should keep trying. We are not yet certain whether we can increase significantly the police apprehension rate. We may be able to change the teenage unemployment rate, though we have learned by painful trial and error that doing this is much more difficult than once supposed. We can probably reduce the time it takes to bring an arrested person to trial, even though we have as yet made few serious efforts to do so. We can certainly reduce the arbitrary and socially irrational exercise of prosecutorial discretion over whom to charge and whom to release, and we can most definitely stop pretending that judges know, any better than the rest of us, how to provide "individualized justice." We can confine a larger proportion of the serious and repeat offenders and fewer of the common drunks and truant children. We know that confining criminals prevents them from harming society, and we have grounds for suspecting that some would-be criminals can be deterred by the confinement of others.

Above all, we can try to learn more about what works, and in the process abandon our ideological preconceptions about what *ought* to work. Nearly ten years ago I wrote that the billions of dollars the federal government was then preparing to spend on crime control would be wasted, and indeed might even make matters worse if they were merely pumped into the existing criminal justice system. They were, and they have. In the next ten years I hope we can learn to experiment rather than simply spend, to test our theories rather than fund our fears. This is advice, not simply or even primarily to government—for governments are run by men and women who are under irresistible pressures to pretend they know more than they do—but to my colleagues: academics, theoreticians, writers, advisers. We may feel ourselves under pressure to pretend we know things, but we are also under a positive obligation to admit what we do not know and to avoid cant and sloganizing. The government agency, the Law Enforcement Assistance Administration, that has futilely spent those billions was created in consequence of an act passed by Congress on the advice of a presidential commission staffed by academics, myself included.

It is easy and popular to criticize yesterday's empty hopes and mistaken beliefs, especially if they seemed supportive of law enforcement. It is harder, and certainly most unpopular, to criticize today's pieties and pretensions, especially if they are uttered in the name of progress and humanity. But if we were wrong in thinking that more money spent on the police would bring down crime rates, we are equally wrong in supposing that closing our prisons, emptying our jails, and supporting "community-based" programs will do any better. Indeed, there is some evidence that these steps will make matters worse, and we ignore it at our peril.

Since the days of the crime commission we have learned a great deal, more than we are prepared to admit. Perhaps we fear to admit it because of a new-found modesty about the foundations of our knowledge, but perhaps also because the implications of that knowledge suggest an unflattering view of man. Intellectuals, although they often dislike the common person as an individual, do not wish to be caught saying uncomplimentary things about humankind. Nevertheless, some persons will shun crime even if we do nothing to deter them, while others will seek it out even if we do everything to reform them. Wicked people exist. Nothing avails except to set them apart from innocent people. And many people neither wicked nor innocent, but watchful, dissembling, and calculating of their opportunities, ponder our reaction to wickedness as a cue to what they might profitably do. We have trifled with the wicked, made sport of the innocent, and encouraged the calculators. Justice suffers, and so do we all.

NO
David L. Bazelon

SOLVING THE NIGHTMARE
OF STREET CRIME

The nightmare of street crime is slowly paralyzing American society. Across the nation, terrified people have altered their lifestyles, purchasing guns and doubling locks to protect their families against the rampant violence outside their doors. After seething for years, public anxiety is now boiling over in a desperate search for answers. Our leaders are reacting to these public demands. In New York, Gov. Hugh Carey proposed the hiring of more police officers and prosecutors; in California, Attorney General Deukmejian has asked the legislature for immediate adoption of a package of new law enforcement bills.

A recent address by the Chief Justice of the United States has helped to place this crisis high on the public agenda. Speaking before the American Bar Association in February, Chief Justice Warren Burger described ours as an "impotent society," suffering a "reign of terror" in its streets and homes. The time has come, he declared, to commit vast social resources to the attack on crime—a priority comparable to the national defense.

Some have questioned whether a sitting Chief Justice should advocate sweeping changes in the criminal justice system and others have challenged his particular prescriptions, but I believe the prestige of his office has focused the nation's attention on issues critical to our future. We should welcome this opportunity to begin a thoughtful and constructive debate about our national nightmare.

In this debate, public concern is sure to generate facile sloganeering by politicians and professionals alike. It would be easy to convert this new urgency into a mandate for a "quick fix." The far-harder task is to marshall that energy toward examining the painful realities and agonizing choices we face. Criminologists can help make our choices the product of an informed, rational, and morally sensitive strategy. As citizens and as human beings, they have a special responsibility to contribute their skills, experience, and knowledge to keep the debate about crime as free of polemics and unexamined assumptions as possible.

I would like to outline some avenues of inquiry worthy of exploration. I offer no programs, no answers. After 31 years on the bench, I can say with

From David Bazelon, "Solving the Nightmare of Street Crime," *USA Today Magazine*, a publication of the Society for the Advancement of Education (January 1982). Copyright © 1982 by the Society for the Advancement of Education. Reprinted by permission.

confidence that we can never deal intelligently and humanely with crime until we face the realities behind it. First, we must carefully identify the problem that so terrorizes America. Second, we should seek to understand the conditions that breed those crimes of violence. Finally, we should take a close look at both the short- and long-term alternatives for dealing with the problem.

TYPES OF CRIMES AND WHO COMMITS THEM

A reasoned analysis must begin by asking: What is it that has our society in such a state of fear? Politicians, journalists, and criminal justice professionals who should know better speak rather generally about "crime in America" without specifying exactly what they mean. There are, in fact several distinct types of crimes and people who commit them.

Consider white-collar crime. This category embraces activities ranging from shoplifting to tax fraud to political corruption. It is undoubtedly a phenomenon of the gravest concern, costing society untold billions of dollars—far more than street crime. To the extent that such crimes appear to go unpunished, they breed disrespect for law and cynicism about our criminal justice institutions. Yet, as costly and corrosive as such crimes are, they do not instill the kind of fear reflected in the recent explosion of public concern. White-collar crimes, after all, are committed by the middle and upper classes, by "[p]eople who look like one's next-door neighbor," as sociologist Charles Silberman puts it. These people do not, by and large, threaten our physical safety or the sanctity of our homes.

Nor do the perpetrators of organized crime. After all, hired guns largely kill each other. The average citizen need not lock his doors in fear that he may be the object of gang warfare. Organized crime unquestionably does contribute to street crime—the most obvious connection is drugs—but organized crime has certainly not produced the recent hysteria.

Nor do crimes of passion cause us to bolt our doors so firmly at night. That would be like locking the fox *inside* the chicken coop. Clearly, it is the random assault of *street* crime—the muggings, rapes, purse snatchings, and knifings that plague city life—which puts us all in such mortal fear for our property and lives.

Once we focus on the kind of crime we fear, the second step in a constructive analysis is to identify those people who commit it. This is no pleasant task. The real roots of crime are associated with a constellation of suffering so hideous that, as a society, we can not bear to look it in the face. Yet, we can never hope to understand street crime unless we summon the courage to look as the ugly realities behind it. Nobody questions that street criminals typically come from the bottom of the socioeconomic ladder —from among the ignorant, the ill-educated, and the unemployed, and the unemployable. A recent National Institute of Justice study confirms that our prison population is disproportionately black and young. The offenders that give city dwellers nightmares come from an underclass of brutal social and economic deprivation. Urban League president Vernon Jordan calls them America's "boat people without boats."

It is no great mystery why some of these people turn to crime. They are born into families struggling to survive, if they have families at all. They are raised in deteriorating, overcrowded housing. They lack adequate nutrition and health care. They are subjected to prejudice and educated in unresponsive schools. They are denied the sense of order, purpose, and self-esteem that makes law-abiding citizens. With nothing to preserve and nothing to lose, they turn to crime for economic survival, a sense of excitement and accomplishment, and an outlet for frustration, desperation, and rage.

Listen to the words of a 15-year-old ghetto youth:

> In Brooklyn you fall into one of two categories when you start growing up.... First, there's the minority of the minority, the "ducks" or suckers. These are the kids who go to school every day. They even want to go to college. Imagine that! School after high school! . . . They're wasting their lives waiting for a dream that won't come true.
>
> The ducks are usually the ones getting beat up on by the majority group—the "hard rocks." If you're a real hard rock you have no worries, no cares. Getting high is as easy as breathing. You just rip off some duck. You don't bother going to school, it's not necessary. You just live with your mom until you get a job—that should be any time a job comes looking for you. Why should you bother to go looking for it? Even your parents can't find work.
>
> Hard rocks do what they want to do when they want to do it. When a hard rock goes to prison it builds up his reputation. He develops a bravado that's like a long sad joke. But it's all lies and excuses. It's a hustle to keep ahead of the fact that he's going nowhere. . . .

This, then, is the face behind the mask we call "the crime problem."

Having identified the kind of crime that causes public anxiety and the kind of people who commit it, we can now consider some alternative responses. For purpose of analysis, we can divide the alternatives into two types. The first set, which enjoys the greatest currency in the political arena today, consists of short-term proposals. They proceed from our universally acknowledged need to protect ourselves *immediately* from the menace of crime. These kinds of prescriptions are endorsed by many good people in high places, including the Chief Justice of the United States and the Mayor of New York. The short-term proposals rely principally on deterrence and incapacitation as means of controlling the symptoms of our national disease. The second, more long-term proposals seek to attack the root causes of crime. Both of these approaches have great costs as well as benefits that must be carefully understood and weighed before we set our course.

DETERRENCE

Let us first examine the short-run proposals. Deterrence has always been intuitively attractive. The recent spate of prescriptions underscores the popularity of this theory and have taken many forms. The Chief Justice says we must provide "swift and certain consequences" for criminal behavior. The California Attorney General advocates mandatory prison terms for certain kinds of crimes. New York Mayor Edward Koch favors harsher sentences including the death penalty. Former U.S. Attorney Whitney North Seymour, Jr., contends that tougher prosecution is necessary. Each of these proposals is premised on Harvard University Prof. James Q. Wilson's theory that, "if the expected cost of crime goes up without a corresponding increase in the expected benefits, then the would-be criminal—unless he or she is among that small fraction of criminals who are utterly irrational—engages in less crime." To the same effect, Wayne State Prof. Ralph Slovenko wrote in a letter to the editor of *The New York Times* that, since "[p]rofits are tax-free and penalties are minimal," those who violate the law are "criminals by choice."

This "rational man" theory of crime is quite plausible with respect to certain kinds of criminals. I can believe that those who have alternatives to crime can indeed be dissuaded from choosing the lawless path if the price is made high enough. If the Abscam episode accomplished nothing else, it induced some potentially corrupt politicians to forbear from taking bribes—at least where there might be cameras around. In fact, white-collar offenders may be so susceptible to deterrence that punishment is superfluous. The fellow country-club members of a corporate embezzler whose life is ruined in a storm of publicity may not need to actually see him go to jail in order to be deterred.

However, the white-collar criminal is *not* the object of these deterrence proposals. Seymour says his proposals are aimed at "the hoodlums and ruffians who are making life in our cit[ies] a nightmare for many citizens"; in other words, at the "hard rocks." Can *these* kinds of criminals be effectively deterred? Diana Gordon, Executive Vice Pres. of the National Council on Crime and Delinquency, points out that the threat of prison may be a meaningless deterrent to one whose urban environment is itself a prison; and as our 15-year-old ghetto resident informs us, "[w]hen a hard rock goes to prison it builds up his reputation."

Common sense is confirmed by experience. New York's highly touted Rockefeller drug law did not produce a decrease in heroin use. In fact, it was actually followed by an increase in property crimes associated with heroin users. Nor is the New York situation unique. Since 1965, the average time served in Federal prison has *risen* from 18 to 30 months. Yet, crime continues to rise unabated.

Even the high priest of deterrence, Prof. Wilson, recognizes the limits of this theory. Although many bandy about his name in support of get-tough proposals, Wilson suggests that the *severity* of punishment has little deterrent effect. Indeed, "the more severe the penalty, the more unlikely that it will be imposed." The benefits of deterrence, according to Wilson, lie only in *certainty* of punishment.

How can we increase that certainty? The *Miranda* rule, the right to seek collateral review, and even the time to prepare for trial have all come under attack in the name of "swift and certain" punishment. These trial and appellate safeguards reflect our fundamental commitment to the presumption of innocence. Before we trade them away, we must know what we are getting in return. From an exhaustive review of the evidence, Silberman concluded that "criminal courts generally *do* an effective job of separating the innocent from the guilty; most of those who should be convicted are convicted, and most of those who should be punished are punished." Today, we prosecute, convict, and incarcerate a larger proportion of those arrested for felonies than we did 50 years ago; yet, the crime rate continues to rise. Clearly, the uncertainty about punishment derives from the great unlikelihood of *arrest*. For every 100 crimes committed, only six persons will be arrested. Thus, sacrificing the constitutional protections of those charged with crime will do little to deter the "hard rocks."

What must we do to achieve certainty of arrest sufficient to have an impact on crime? I asked my good friend, Maurice Cullinane, the former Chief of Police of the District of Columbia, about this. He presided over a force with far more policemen per capita than any other in the country, and that is aside from the several thousand park, Capitol, and other Federal police visible all over Washington. Chief Cullinane told me that, in order to deter street crime to any significant degree, he would have to amass an enormous concentration of patrolmen in one particular area. Only then might the physical presence of a policemen on virtually every block possibly keep crime under control. Of course, crime suppressed in one neighborhood would burgeon in other, unguarded parts of the city. Before we can endorse certainty of arrest as an effective deterrent, we must consider whether we could tolerate the kind of police state it might require.

We need to know much more about the precise costs of an effective program of deterrence before we can dismiss the recent proposals. At the present time, however, the case for deterrence has not been convincingly made. After a comprehensive review of the literature, a panel of the National Academy of Sciences concluded:

> Despite the intensity of the research effort, the empirical evidence is still not sufficient for providing a rigorous confirmation of the existence of a deterrent effect. . . . Policy makers in the criminal justice system are done a disservice if they are left with the impression that the empirical evidence, which they themselves are frequently unable to evaluate, strongly supports the deterrence hypothesis.

INCAPACITATION

A more realistic rationale put forth for short-term proposals, in my opinion, is incapacitation. This politely named theory has become the new aim of corrections. No one who has been in an American prison can seriously adhere to the ideal of rehabilitation, and more and more of us have come to suspect the futility of deterrence. The new theory of incapacitation essentially translates as lock the bastards up. At least then they will pose no threat to us while incarcerated. Incapacitation takes many forms: preventive detention, isolation of "career criminals," and stricter parole release requirements.

This notion has something to be said for it. We *must* do something to protect ourselves immediately so that we may "live to fight another day." Thus, the swift and tough route is appealing—get the attackers off the street forthwith; put them away fast and long so that the threat they pose to our daily lives can be neutralized.

A thorough commitment to this policy might indeed make our streets somewhat safer, but at what price? Consider first the cost in dollars. Today, even without an avowed commitment to incapacitation, we already imprison a larger proportion of our citizens than any other industrialized nation in the world, except Russia and South Africa. This dubious honor has cost us dearly. A soon-to-be published survey by the Department of Justice's National Institute of Justice reports that the 1972-78 period saw a 54 percent increase in the population of state prisons. The survey predicts that demand for prison space will continue to outstrip capacity. It has been conservatively estimated that we need

$8–10,000,000,000 immediately for construction just to close the gap that exists *now*.

Embarking on a national policy of incapacitation would require much more than closing the gap. One study has estimated that, in New York, a 264 percent increase in state imprisonment would be required to reduce serious crime by only 10 percent! Diana Gordon has worked out the financial requirements for this kind of incapacitation program. In New York alone, it would cost about $3,000,000,000 just to construct the additional cells necessary and probably another $1,000,000,000 each year to operate them. The public must be made aware of the extraordinary financial costs of a genuine incapacitation policy.

In addition, there are significant non-monetary costs. Incapacitation rests on the assumption that convicted offenders would continue to commit crimes if not kept in prison, but can we determine in advance which offenders would in fact repeat and which would not? We simply do not know enough about the "hard rocks" to decide who to warehouse, and for how long. It has been estimated that, to be sure of identifying one potential criminal, we would have to include as many as eight people who would not offend. Thus, to obtain the benefits of incapacitation, we might have to incarcerate a substantial number of people who would have led a blameless life if released. A policy of sentencing individuals based on crimes not yet committed would therefore raise serious doubts about our dedication to the presumption of innocence. The thought of having to choose between immediate safety and sacred constitutional values is frightening.

Nor can there be any comfort that the grave moral and financial costs of incapacitation will only be temporary. Even as we put one generation of offenders behind bars, another set of "hard rocks" will emerge from the hopeless subculture of our ghettos, ready to follow the model set by their fathers and brothers. Unless we intend to keep every criminal and potential criminal in prison *forever*, we must acknowledge the futility of expecting them to behave when they get out. As journalist Tom Wicker recently observed, "to send them to the overcrowded, underfunded, inadequately staffed and policed prisons of America would negate [the] purpose; because more, and more frightening, criminals come out of these schools of crime and violence than go into them." Merely providing inmates with educational and counseling services would do little good "when they return to a society largely unwilling to hire them." We should not fool ourselves that the "hard rocks" will emerge from the cesspools of American prisons willing or able to conduct law-abiding lives.

Incapacitation, then, must be recognized as an extraordinarily costly and risky policy. To meaningfully affect crime, it might require a garrison state. This is not to deny that our "clear and present danger" must be addressed immediately. Still, reason and good faith require us to consider alternatives to a program of endlessly warehousing succeeding generations of human beings.

ATTACKING THE ROOT CAUSES OF CRIME

A more long-term response to crime is to attack its root causes. This approach also offers no decisive balance of costs and benefits. The unique advantage of a successful attack on the roots of crime would be the promise of *enduring* social tranquility. If we can first break the cycle of suffering which breeds crime, we could turn it to our advantage. We would achieve more than "damage control." Our nation could begin to tap the resources of those we now fear. Instead of a police or garrison state, ours would then be a social order rooted in the will and hearts of our people. We would achieve criminal justice by pursuing social justice.

However, like the short-term solutions, this path would involve substantial risks and uncertainties. The root causes of crime are, of course, far more complex and insidious than simple poverty. After all, the vast majority of the poor commit no crime. Our existing knowledge suggests that the roots of street crime lie in poverty *plus*—plus prejudice, plus poor housing, plus inadequate education, plus insufficient food and medical care, and, perhaps most importantly, plus a bad family environment or no family at all.

Accepting the full implications of what we know about street crime might require us to provide every family with the means to create the kind of home all human beings need. It might require us to afford the job opportunities that pose for some the only meaningful alternatives to violence. It would assure all children a constructive education, a decent place to live, and proper pre- and postnatal nutrition. It would seek to provide those children of inadequate family environments with proper day care or foster care. More fundamentally, it would seek to eradicate racism and prejudice.

Such an attack on the roots of crime would obviously be an extremely long and expensive process. Before we can determine which programs offer the greatest promise, we must face what we know about the crime and build on previous efforts to attack its root causes.

More importantly, a genuine commitment to attacking the roots of crime might force us to reconsider our entire social and economic structure. Like the short-term approach, this might conflict with other deeply held values. Can we break the cycle at crime's roots without invading the social sphere of the ghetto? Would this require the state to impose its values on the young? If we really want a lasting solution to crime, can we afford not to?

In short, any approach we take to crime presents attractive benefits and frightening risks. None of our choices offers a cheap or easy solution. Analysis takes us this far. As I have repeatedly emphasized, we can not choose which difficult path to take without facing the realities of street crime. Obviously, we can not deter those whom we do not understand. Nor can we make a rational assessment of incapacitation without knowing how many we will have to incapacitate and for how long. Finally, of course, we can not evaluate the long-term approach without some idea of its specific strategies and their various costs.

A constructive and fruitful debate about the best means of solving the nightmare of street crime is long overdue. The public's fear of crime cries out for a response and our leaders have made it a national priority, but we can never hope to achieve a just and lasting solution to crime without first facing the realities that underlie it. Emerson said, "God offers to every mind its choice between truth and repose." Truth will not come easy. It will take patience and the strength to put aside emotional reactions. If we do not strive for truth, this nation and all it stands for is bound to enjoy only a brief, false, and dangerous repose.

POSTSCRIPT

Is Incapacitation the Answer to the Crime Problem?

If realism is the criterion for choosing policy options, Wilson's case is the stronger. Bazelon himself allows that incapacitation is a realistic short-term solution, though he argues that it is too costly and produces unsatisfactory long-term results. Bazelon's major argument is a moral one. He criticizes the incapacitation approach as inhumane, dangerous to civil liberties, and hypocritical. Criminals may be errant humans, he says, but they are humans and should be treated with compassion. He sees the incapacitation approach as expressing a revengeful attitude of "lock the low-lifes up," and believes this attitude is unbecoming to a civilized society. The rehabilitation of criminals—not their punishment—should be our goal, even if its accomplishment is very difficult, maintains Bazelon, adding that the incapacitation approach also threatens the civil liberties upon which this society stands. He believes that it is unfortunate that our civil liberties, which are among our proudest possessions, increase the difficulty of putting criminals behind bars. But he emphasizes that we must not weaken these rights in trying to solve the crime problem. Finally, Bazelon contends that the incapacitation approach treats the criminal as the only guilty party and that a more enlightened view recognizes the contributions of blocked opportunities, slum environments, broken families, and social pressures that are in conflict with legitimate values.

It should be pointed out that Wilson shares many of Bazelon's concerns but still sees the incapacitation approach as necessary under present circumstances. On this issue, as on many other issues, hard choices must be made between conflicting values.

In *Crime in America* (Simon and Schuster, 1971) former Attorney General Ramsey Clark takes a position in many ways similar to Bazelon's. Hans Zeisel in *The Limits of Law Enforcement* (University of Chicago Press, 1983) argues that the criminal justice system can do little to effectively reduce crime. His emphasis is on increasing protection from crime and attacking its root causes in the conditions of poverty. On the other side, Andrew Von Hirsch's *Doing Justice* (Hill and Wang, 1976) is critical of the Bazelon philosophy.

The issue of deterrence is hotly debated by authors Ernest van den Haag and John P. Conrad in their book on the ultimate in deterrence punishment, *The Death Penalty: A Debate* (Plenum Press, 1983). Graeme Newman presents an extreme position on punishment in advocating electric shocks and whippings in *Just and Painful: A Case for the Corporal Punishment of Criminals* (Macmillan, 1983).

A revival of biological explanations of crime is occurring along with some shocking proposals such as sterilization and abortion when the wrong genes are detected in adults or fetuses (see Lawrence Taylor, *Born to Crime: The Genetic Causes of Criminal Behavior*, Greenwood Press, 1984). A more sophisticated and less shocking discussion is presented by James Q. Wilson and Richard Harstein in *Crime and Human Nature* (Simon and Schuster, 1985).

PART 6

The Future: Population/ Environment/Society

Can a world with limited resources support an unlimited population? This question has taken on new dimensions as we approach the start of a new century. Technology has increased enormously in the last 100 years, as have new forms of pollution that threaten to undermine the world's fragile ecological support system. Will technology itself be the key to improving our environment? All nations have a stake in the health of the planet and the world economy. Is America in a position to meet these global challenges?

Is Overpopulation a Major Problem?
_____

Is the Environment Improving?
_____

Is America Declining?

ISSUE 17

Is Overpopulation a Major Problem?

YES: Hal Burdett, Werner Fornos, Sheila Kinkade, and David Meyer, from "A Continent in Crisis: Building a Future for Africa in the 21st Century" (a special report by the Population Institute to the 101st Congress), *Toward the 21st Century*

NO: Ray Percival, from "Malthus and His Ghost," *National Review* (August 18, 1989)

ISSUE SUMMARY

YES: Hal Burdett, Werner Fornos, Sheila Kinkade, and David Meyer, all from the Population Institute in Washington, D.C., submit in this report to Congress that overpopulation is a destructive force and is causing major problems in Africa.
NO: Ray Percival, a doctoral student in philosophy, makes the case that population problems are lessening, not getting worse.

In 1968 Paul Ehrlich wrote *The Population Bomb* (Ballantine), which stated that overpopulation was the major problem facing mankind and that population had to be controlled or the human race might cause the collapse of the global ecosystem and its own destruction. Since 1968, many voices have joined Ehrlich's, and many have joined the organization that he founded, Zero Population Growth (ZPG). Back in 1970, Ehrlich explained why he thought the death of the world was imminent.

> Because the human population of the planet is about five times too large, and we're managing to support all these people—at today's level of misery—only by spending our capital, burning our fossil fuels, dispersing our mineral resources and turning our fresh water into salt water. We have not only overpopulated but overstretched our environment. We are poisoning the ecological systems of the earth—systems upon which we are ultimately dependent for all of our food, for all of our oxygen and for all of our waste disposal.

Let us review the population growth rates past, present, and future. At about A.D. 0, the world had about one-quarter billion people. It took about 1,650 years to double this number to one-half billion and two hundred years to double the world population again to one billion by 1850. The next doubling took only about eighty years, and the last doubling time about forty-five years (from two billion in 1930 to about four billion in 1975). The world population may double again to eight billion some time between 2010 and 2020. It is easy to keep multiplying by twos until one gets to standing-room-only densities, but obviously population must stop growing in the next century or two. As calculated in 1989 and reported in the *World Almanac,* the population of the world is 5 billion, 192 million.

When and at what level will population stop growing? The ZPG (zero population growth) advocates say population must stop growing now or we may overshoot the carrying capacity of the earth's ecosystem and cause the death of much of the human race. In the 1970 article cited above, Ehrlich stated that the world population should eventually be reduced "to an absolute maximum of 500,000,000." The research team headed by Dennis Meadows, which produced the "Limits to Growth" study on the basis of a complicated world systems model, estimated a population/environment long-term equilibrium at around three billion people. *The Global 2000 Report to the President* (Government Printing Office, 1980) came to roughly the same conclusion as the National Academy of Sciences study eleven years earlier: that without ecosystem collapse, about ten billion people could live on this earth in a measure of comfort, or thirty billion could be provided for, but at the barest of subsistence and without freedoms. Herman Kahn sees no reason why fifteen billion could not live on this planet in luxury forever (Herman Kahn et al., *The Next 200 Years,* Morrow, 1976). He predicts, however, that the environmental movement will lead to changes that will level population growth off at ten billion (*World Economic Development,* Morrow, 1979). Robert Katz (*A Giant in the Earth,* 1973) thinks that fifteen billion is too small to get the full benefits of the economic and synergistic effects of high population. He says that one hundred billion is a more ideal population because the additional geniuses, scientists, and engineers would improve the world's science and technology many-fold and life would be on a much higher plane. So what is the ideal population size? Ehrlich says one half billion, and Katz says one hundred billion. Ehrlich looks at the effect of population on the environment; Katz looks at what people contribute to their society.

In the first selection that follows, Hal Burdett and his colleagues outline and assess the population crisis in Africa in a report they submitted to Congress in an effort to influence legislation on population control programs abroad. Their views are challenged by Ray Percival, who argues that population problems are exaggerated by environmentalists and that there are fewer starving people now than a century ago.

YES

Hal Burdett et al.

A CONTINENT IN CRISIS: BUILDING A FUTURE FOR AFRICA IN THE 21ST CENTURY

The airlifts are underway again in Africa, this time to the Sudan. On December 4, [1987] Red Cross cargo planes carried desperately needed food to two starving Sudanese villages as the start of a new international effort to check the spreading famine there. The shipments were delayed by months of negotiations among the factions in Sudan's bloody civil war, and by the time relief workers reached the villages, they found that most of the young children had already perished from hunger and disease. Such is sadly the stuff of daily headlines from Africa. They are now buried on the bottom of inside pages of newspapers and are usually bumped altogether off network news programs. The "emergency" in Ethiopia that mobilized hundreds of millions of dollars in aid from Western governments and private donors has become a permanent pattern of suffering in the region. Although the heat of global public attention has faded almost as quickly as it began, and the aid flow has dwindled to its usual trickle, the tragedy has today, if anything, become entrenched on an even wider scale; the hunger and pain has settled into a grim routine. In the eyes of the industrialized world, however, Africa's plight has returned to its usual place on the inside pages, back in the shadows, mostly out of sight. . . .

That state of affairs will soon change. Africa, so long brushed aside in the hustle of global relations, will step to the fore in the years immediately ahead. It will be put under the global spotlight because of the tragedy developing there—a crisis cutting across its social structure, economy, and environment—but the spotlight this time will not quickly fade, because how effectively we deal with this crisis will, in a very real sense, determine the kind of world we inhabit in the 21st Century. That crisis is not simply an unfortunate flash in the pan, as we assumed in 1985 when we responded to the famine in Ethiopia. We are learning in stark ways that this is not a crisis we can "solve" with one-time donations and special rock concerts, and then

From Hal Burdett, Werner Fornos, Sheila Kinkade, and David Meyer, "A Continent in Crisis: Building a Future for Africa in the 21st Century," *Toward the 21st Century*, a publication by The Population Institute, no. 8 (1988). Copyright © 1988 by The Population Institute. Reprinted by permission.

move on without looking back. Africa's problems are structural, deeply rooted in demographic trends and human institutions. They are only a more concentrated and severe reflection of problems slowly developing throughout the Third World. And if we have learned anything in the past 25 years, it is that America's future, and that of our industrialized-world allies, is not secure unless we can help build a secure future for the nations of the Third World, where three-quarters of the earth's inhabitants live.

A brief overview of Africa's situation makes clear why it cannot be ignored. Africa's population is now 630 million, and it is growing faster than any other region in the world. If its present growth is not altered, its population would triple by the year 2028. But while Africa's population grows by 3.1 percent annually, the continent's food supply increases by only 1.1 percent per year. That means that every year Africa's dependence on uncertain food imports grows more acute. And, in painfully practical terms, it means that each year more Africans will starve. The suffering that was triggered in Ethiopia by severe drought is becoming built into the demographic structure of the entire continent.

There is no simple explanation for why Africa's economic development has been stunted and why Africans today remain so grievously poor. Lack of capital and highly skilled personnel is a factor. As is ongoing civil strife, which, besides its human toll, tends to be disruptive and costly to long-term development schemes. Staggering external debts act as drags on many African economies. Historical policies of colonial exploitation (so often pointed to by Africans themselves) have surely played a role, as have the present-day mistakes and mismanagement by some African governments (so often pointed to by Western donors). Finally, the accelerating degradation of one of Africa's greatest economic assets—its natural resource base—has had a clear and ominous impact on the continent's hopes for a self-sufficient future. Somewhere in the mix of these factors is the wellspring of Africa's woes. But it is the added element of runaway population growth that aggravates each of these factors and makes the mix so very difficult to overcome.

Despite wide-ranging economic reforms by African governments and key initiatives by the international community to support African recovery efforts, the continent's critical economic situation is still deteriorating. There can be no doubt whatsoever that this deterioration will continue unless reducing rampant population growth becomes a priority with all relevant government agencies, private organizations and with the nations of that beleaguered region of the world.

The United Nations Population Fund, the multi-lateral agency that has worked longest and most extensively in Africa, reported in its Mid-Term Review of the United Nations Programme of Action for African Economic Recovery and Development, that "half of Africa's people are under 14 years, and 70 percent are under 25. Many African countries are [doubling] their populations in 20 years or less. Their cities are growing even faster; some will double in size by the end of the century.

"The needs of these increasing numbers give added urgency to Africa's efforts for economic recovery," according to the report. "But the rate at which numbers increase will be one of the factors which will determine their success.

"In many countries, infant mortality has been cut by half in the past thirty years. Twenty years have been added to the average expectation of life. But while death rates have fallen over much of Africa, birth rates have hardly changed."

Before proceeding with a closer look at the prospects for individual African nations, it is important to take note of the large, sweeping, and dangerous ways in which population growth is reshaping Africa's future. We have already noted the growing food insecurity in Africa. Over the past 10 years, per capita food production in Africa has fallen by 11 percent, and the United Nations Food and Agriculture Organization (FAO) predicts that by the dawn of the 21st Century, 29 African nations will be unable to feed their populations. It should surprise no one that UNICEF has found that childhood malnutrition is already on the rise in 10 African countries. During the first half of 1988, FAO provided emergency food assistance to 17 African nations, far more than to any other world region. The widening scarcity cannot be explained away simply by unfavorable weather cycles or crop failures. To keep up with its population growth, Africa would need to more than double its yearly gains in agricultural productivity. Recent history makes clear that that kind of rapid expansion is not possible. Meanwhile, next year Africa will need to feed an additional 20 million people, and the year after than an even larger increment.

A second way in which population growth ensures that Africa will not be able to feed its people is by ravaging the environment, converting cropland to desert and robbing remaining arable land of its productive capacity. Wood remains the primary source of fuel in Africa. As the continent's population grows, demand for wood increases faster than it can be replaced through new planting, a fact which has both economic and environmental consequences. First, it means that Africa must devote ever increasing shares of human labor toward the effort to find wood and transport it to where it is needed. Already, according to World Bank figures, households in Gambia and Tanzania must devote between 250 and 300 working days each year simply to finding and collecting the wood they need for fuel. These costs are also great in Africa's swelling urban centers. In Addis Ababa, Ethiopia, for example, the cost of fuelwood consumes about 20 percent of the average household income. This diverts energies and investments from more constructive development efforts.

Second, the growing demand for fuelwood is resulting in large-scale deforestation of the African continent. The example of Ethiopia is instructive. In 1900, 40 percent of Ethiopia was covered by trees and brush. The excessive human demand for fuelwood has taken its toll, however, so that today less than 4 percent of the country has forest cover. Similar losses across Africa are adding up to a grand-scale environmental disaster. Across the continent, 29 trees are cut down for every new tree planted. Between 1850 and 1980, Africa lost 60 percent of its forest cover, and the pace of destruction is rapidly escalating. Without the forest and plantlife cover to hold the soil, absorb rainfall, and provide for transpiration back into the atmosphere, rainfall declines. With less rain, it is harder to grow new trees and plants to replace those taken for fuel, and the harmful cycle repeats itself that much faster. One result is that once deprived of its capacity to sustain vegetation, many African lands are being converted to desert. Already, ecologists have determined that the Sahara Desert is expanding by six miles each year, leaving Africa with even less arable land with which to support its growing population. Forty percent of Africa's arable land is vulnerable to desertification.

Africa's startling environmental losses and its steady declines in agricultural productivity do not bode well for a continent whose economy is so heavily based on agriculture. Rapid population growth is making Africa's economic problems dramatically worse by diluting the salving effect of foreign development assistance. With 32 out of 54 African countries doubling their populations within the next 25 years, foreign aid simply cannot keep up. Instead of paying for meaningful and lasting improvements in the African quality of life, our aid dollars right now are, in effect, subsidizing the rapid expansion of these populations. As population grows faster than national economies, quality of life declines for each person. In the last year, despite relatively favorable agricultural conditions, per capita income was stagnant or declined in 24 African nations.

Africa's economic quicksand has implications beyond the immediately obvious consequence of crippling development plans. American hopes for fostering stable democratic rule in African nations are directly dependent upon the ability of democracy to make good on the promise of a better future. Observers like former U.S. Secretary of Defense Robert McNamara have long warned that economic hopelessness, spawned by rapid population growth, is a primary cause behind civil strife and the rise of authoritarian governments. That warning has been sternly validated by events in Argentina, where President Raúl Alfonsin's tentative democracy recently survived a military challenge inspired largely by dissatisfaction with Argentina's economic straits. That should serve as a sobering caution to some key U.S. allies in Africa, such as Egypt and Kenya, which have been suffering acute economic problems closely related to runaway population growth.

AN EMERGING AFRICAN CONSENSUS

Yet the African story is not exclusively one of despair by any means. In fact, it is the story of the remarkable convergence of great need with great opportunity. This is because leaders across Africa have increasingly come to recognize in recent years the direct links between population growth and their problems related to development, the economy, and the environment. Robert I. Rothberg, academic vice president at Tufts University and the author of *Africa in the 1990s: U.S. Policy Opportunities and Choices*, observes that there have been "steady indigenous responses to well targeted local campaigns to limit family size in Africa. "Reducing population growth in Africa is in our interest as a superpower," he says. "Africa's well-being increases our own."

As the needs of Africa have grown more acute with surging population growth, an emerging majority of African governments is now prepared for the first time to deal directly and humanely with the population issue. Their arrival at this consensus is no incidental achievement, for only 15 years ago most African leaders agreed that rapid population growth was a *spur* to economic development rather than a hindrance. In fact, in 1974 at the first U.N. World Population Conference, African delegates were virtually unanimous in their rejection of Western calls for reductions in population growth; some even suspected racist motivations for the sudden Western concern with African overpopulation.

That resistance has been steadily washed away, however, in the years that followed the 1974 Bucharest conference by the increasingly unmistakable impact of population growth on Third World societies. As populations swelled, schools overflowed, homelessness and unemployment soared, cities spilled out into the countryside in haphazard, unplanned growth, and per capita productivity and national wealth shrank. By the time the delegates met again 10 years later in Mexico City for the International Conference on Population, it was the Third World participants who spoke loudest about the need for an easing of population pressures. The African delegates reflected that new perspective, and throughout the 1980s more and more African governments have agreed that lasting development is possible only if population growth subsides. That emerging African consensus was formalized at the Second African Population Conference, held in Arusha, Tanzania, in early 1984. At that conference, delegates from 44 African nations hammered out the Kilimanjaro Program of Action for African Population and Self-Reliant Development, which acknowledged the wide-scale harm caused by rapid population growth and called on all African nations to make population a central concern in development planning. That view was reaffirmed at the African Conference of Parliamentarians on Population and Development, held two years later at Harare, Zimbabwe.

In the words of Under Secretary General Nafis Sadik, Executive Director of the United Nations Population Fund, "There is a growing consensus among African leaders that part of the cure for Africa's economic problems will be slower population growth and well-spaced, healthier families. This is the message they are bringing to their people. The evidence is that they are being heard.

"Family size is a personal decision. Women in Africa still want large families, compared with women in the rest of the world. Men still take pride in the size of their families. But more and more ordinary people are seeing that having many children means costs as well as benefits, and they are making their own decisions."

Ironically, however, just as the African nations have come to agree with the "Western" view taken at the 1974 Bucharest Conference, the leading Western promoter of population policies has shown troubling hesitation to help. United States funding for population assistance has been slashed over the past eight years and U.S. contributions to the two leading international population aid programs—the United Nations Population Fund (UNFPA) and the International Planned Parenthood Federation (IPPF)—have been indefinitely suspended. Thus, just when the nations of Africa and the industrialized donor community should be working together at last to make their most important strides toward population stabilization and lasting development, U.S. equivocation is holding everyone back. That will have to change. The need is too urgent and the opportunities for a constructive partnership with the African leadership are too great to ignore.

NO

Ray Percival

MALTHUS AND HIS GHOST

IF THERE IS A SURE WAY TO INVITE RIDICULE IT IS TO DENY THAT POPULATION growth is dangerous. Malthus still carries authority, and his illustrious specter is invoked by what we might call the "neo-Malthusians" to silence impertinent doubt. But Malthus should not be confused with his ghost, and the confusion should not obscure the fact that both Malthus and his ghost are wrong in asserting that population growth rules out a rising standard of living.

Here is the ghost of Malthus in a book for children, *The Golden Stamp Book of Earth and Ecology:*

> When man first began to farm, there were fewer than five million people on earth, and it took more than a million years for the population to reach that figure. But populations increase geometrically—that is, they double (2, 4, 8, 16, 32, etc.). Food supplies, in contrast, increase only arithmetically, a much slower process (2, 4, 6, 8, 10, 12, etc.). . . . If the population continues to explode, many people will starve. About half of the world's population is underfed now, with many approaching starvation.

The general confusion will not save either Malthus or his ghost from refutation. Unfortunately, refutation is not persuasion, and, though weakening, the ghostly orthodoxy still stalks the land. Paul Ehrlich, one of its principal exponents, had a penchant for picking figures out of thin air: " . . . a minimum of ten million people, most of them children, will starve to death during each year of the 1970s." The Club of Rome at least packaged its scaremongering in a scientific-looking computer study done at MIT, which dutifully declared: "The limits to growth on our planet will be reached sometime within the next one hundred years." Fittingly, Ehrlich and the Club of Rome shared the axioms and confusions of the book meant for children: ultimate, catastrophic physical limits; geometric growth; explosive, senseless reproduction; and permanent starvation—a four-fold contradiction of Malthus. Malthus was right to deny these now-fashionable axioms of polite conversation.

Malthus's argument was not based on the premise of an *ultimate* limit to the earth's resources: "No limits whatever are placed to the productions of the earth; they may increase forever and be greater than any assignable quantity." Rather he was concerned with a disparity in the maximum possible *rates* of population growth and food production. Compare the arithmetical and geometrical series in the quotation from the children's book: 2, 4, 6, 8, 10; 2, 4, 8, 16, 32. Note the divergence at the third term, before which population grows unconstrained. In the children's book this point is placed in the future, but Malthus placed it in prehistoric times. Beyond this point population growth could be no higher than the ceiling set by the growth of food, and hence populations grows *at most* arithmetically. To Malthus geometric growth was a utopian dream, something man left behind in Eden.

FROM MALTHUS'S POINT OF VIEW, IF HALF of mankind had been underfed for a significant time, far from exploding, the population "would not grow at all." The misery of inadequate food prevented the population exceeding the food supply. Talk of a senseless explosion of population contradicts Malthus's emphasis on the individual's rational judgment, in which care for the welfare of potential offspring, fear of being reduced in rank, and the thought of the extra work and trouble to support additional offspring all play a role. Anthropologists have shown that all societies practice some form of contraception. The notion that most babies in less-developed countries must be unwanted because their parents do not connect birth with sex or because they cannot control their primitive urges is nonsense. The neo-Malthusians' appeal to the authority of Malthus has the unintended but charming consequence of undermining their case.

However, Malthus's theory itself is wrong. Its implications are: a) the theoretical maximum growth rate of population is greater than the theoretical maximum growth rate of food production; b) the long-term growth rate of food and population must be equal. But since plants and most animals have more numerous offspring and shorter gestation periods, they are capable with man's help of multiplying at a higher rate than mankind. Both jayhawks and men eat chickens, but whilst more jayhawks means fewer chickens, more men means more chickens. Malthus's picture of man the parasite just does not fit the facts; man produces more than he consumes.

Between the end of the seventeenth century and the outbreak of the First World War, per-capita income in England increased six-fold despite a six-fold increase in population (the absolute increase in production was thirty- to fifty-fold, far outstripping the rate of growth of the population). Data published by the U.S. Department of Agriculture and by the United Nations show that in the four decades since World War II, world per-capita food production has risen. In these facts we see the most thorough demolition of the Malthusian edifice. The neo-Malthusian ghost fares no better.

Hands up, those who watched on TV: Ten million children starve to death during each year of the Seventies. Ehrlich's prophecy resembled the mumblings of a clairvoyant. It was completely obscure how the predicted minimum figure of ten million deaths per year was derived from theory and data. We can only surmise that the figure was discerned in the cloudy crystal ball that is Ehrlich's head.

Nevertheless, it was a good gamble. If one prophesies a disaster and it occurs, one becomes famous. Yet if the disaster does not occur, the prophet is saved from infamy as another among thousands of flopped prophecies falls into oblivion.

BUT WE WILL NOT ALLOW EHRLICH'S mistake the luxury of oblivion this time. Gale D. Johnson argues that during the last quarter of the nineteenth century perhaps twenty to 25 million people died from famine. If Ehrlich's glib formula—more people = more famine—were correct, we could have expected at least fifty million famine deaths in the third quarter of this century. But for the entire twentieth century to the present, there have been at most 15 million famine deaths. And many, if not the majority, of these were due to deliberate government policy, official mismanagement, or war—not to serious crop failure. The Ethiopian famine, occurring in one of the least densely populated regions of the world, is a problem not of population but of repressive government.

But do actual data interest Ehrlich? After all, who wants to be reminded of reality when you're telling your favorite horror story? Ehrlich made much of the time it takes a population to double in size, calculated from the annual rate of growth. He chose doubling time because, as he says in *The Population Bomb*, it is "the best way to impress you with numbers." The magic formula is to pick a doubling time and—as if people bred like flies—simply project it and conclude that within a startlingly short time the earth will be completely carpeted by a two-thousand-story building packed with people. But as any demographer worth his salt will tell you, using the annual rate of growth to project from will exaggerate the prospects for population growth if the birth rate has fallen in the recent past. This is because it takes some decades for a decline in birth rate to show itself in slower population growth. Ehrlich ignored the fact that the birth rate in America had been falling for 13 years before his book was published. By 1975 the *total* number of births was no higher than in 1909.

The falling birth rate was part of the global demographic transition, a process in which first the death rate and then the birth rate fell from a high to a low level. Even Ehrlich could not completely ignore this most important event in the history of world population. With industrialization, children "became a financial drag—expensive to raise and educate . . . people just wanted to have fewer children." But this means that, contrary to Ehrlich's own argument, population growth is neither explosive nor reckless—ideas he uses to make population growth appear chaotic and frightening and thus set the stage for the state to act as the sole embodiment of rational planning.

In the last decade, the growth rate of the world population has shrunk from 2 per cent to 1.7 per cent. . . . The UN, whose authority Ehrlich accepts, now expects world population to stabilize at about ten billion near the end of the twenty-first century, and this given *only* the behavior of the population and not external physical constraints. But still the anti-baby crusade continues with the same old refrain about geometric growth leading to disaster. To Ehrlich the macromathematics of growth are everything, and he loses sight of the people behind the arithmetic.

When the human population is seen as a sort of mathematical monster, developments that would strike the nonmathematical as magnificent improvements in man's lot are instead seen as food for the beast. Ehrlich pointed in horror to the dramatic reduction in mortality in less-developed countries (LDCs) as merely an omen of higher growth. But exorcised of the rarfied mathematics of population growth, the dramatic reduction of the death rate in LDCs can be seen for what it really is: the triumph of medicine. It in turn was made possible by the economic development of more-developed countries (MDCs), a process that Ehrlich rejected as "unfair exploitation" of LDCs and as leading eventually to increased death rates through pollution.

It took the seventy years between 1830 and 1900 for average life expectancy in Europe to increase from forty years to fifty years. Thanks largely to the development of insecticides and drugs in MDCs during the 1940s, the same increase in LDCs took only the 15 years between 1950 and 1965. Peter Bauer of the London School of Economics points out that increases in life expectancy in LDCs began first in those places, such as India and Latin America, that had the most contact and commerce with MDCs. This is hardly exploitation in Ehrlich's sense. And if it were, who is exploiting whom? In addition, Ehrlich's prophecy of increased death rates owing to pollution sits uneasily with the fact that people worldwide now live longer.

Besides Ehrlich, the neo-Malthusian ghost also chose to appear in the form of that self-styled "independent college," the Club of Rome. The point of its book, *The Limits to Growth*, published in 1972, was an urgent call for "a non-growing state for society." It went to great lengths to make the message palatable, and even chose the rather exciting term "Global Equilibrium" to replace the grey and boring "no growth." . . .

For the most telling criticism of *The Limits to Growth* we need look no further than the Club's second technical report, available only a few months after the first, which asserted that with reasonable technological progress continuous growth is feasible, although the Club inconsistently retained the earlier gloomy public stance. One of the crucial defects of the Club's predictions was its neglect of historical price data for minerals. Julian Simon, the author of *The Ultimate Resource*, points out that if mineral resources had indeed become more scarce their prices would have increased. But their real prices on average have been sinking for as long as we can ascertain, indicating that they are now less scarce than they were. If one goes by the long trend, one can expect minerals to become cheaper and cheaper. Furthermore, any shortages on a free market will be accompanied by a rise in the price of the mineral, inducing suppliers to find new sources and substitutes for the mineral, and inducing customers to economize on its use.

Ehrlich and the Club of Rome represent the mistaken ideology of catastrophe. Is there not something to be said for a more modest though still pessimistic position on population growth? The current standard model of population is that of Coale and Hoover. Through Philander Claxton (at one time the highest-ranking U.S. State Department official involved with population matters), the Coale and Hoover model made birth control an important part of U.S. foreign-aid policy. The Coale-Hoover theory focused on economic trends: an increase in the number of consumers and a decrease in saving due to population growth.

Their conclusion was that in India income over the period 1956–86 could have been expected to rise 2.5 times as fast with declining fertility as with continued high fertility. Julian Simon points out that this result is obtained by a) ignoring that in the long run a faster-growing population produces a larger labor supply, which implies a larger output, and b) assuming that capital—land, machines, etc.—does not increase in proportion with the labor force, so that there are diminishing returns to labor. Coale and Hoover simply *assumed* a constant GNP and divided it by more consumers! Subsequent models have given more weight to the effect of an increased labor force, but they still hold on to the "capital dilution" assumption. The main Coale-Hoover prediction: more children = slower growth.

But as early as 1967, studies by Simon Kuznets had shown that even rapid population growth was no impediment to rapid economic development, as Thailand, Mexico, Panama, Ecuador, and Jordan illustrate. Blaming poverty on population density will not work either: Julian Simon found high density to be associated with high living standards.

THE INADEQUACIES OF THE COALE AND Hoover model stand out starkly next to the more complex model developed by Simon. His basic idea is that, in the long run, man produces more than he consumes.

A larger population makes for greater division of labor, economies of scale, and a more extensive market, supporting even very specialized services with minority appeal—how many metaphysical poets or ear specialists could a village support? (And remember, everyone is in a minority for some of his needs and tastes.)

With a larger population, there are more Edisons and Einsteins to contribute to production. In countries at the same level of income, scientific output is proportional to population size; the U.S. is much larger than Sweden, and it produces much more scientific knowledge. How come India and China are not world firsts in the scientific league, then? Well, since they are poor they cannot afford to educate as many people. But their poverty must be attributed to the bumbling brutality of their governments' economic interventions, not to a high proportion of children. There are many countries, such as Costa Rica, Thailand, and Jordan, that have both a high proportion of children in their populations and high levels of education.

What about the argument that a larger population merely consumes capital? Coale and Hoover naively assumed that usable land is a fixed resource. Rises in demand, however, spur people to increase the stock of land and to work the old land more intensively. New crops and methods of cultivation raise output even further, so that output per person is greater than it would have been if there had been no increase in demand. With human beings, scarcity is the mother of abundance. When people want more land, they just go out and create it. In India between 1951 and 1971, cultivated land was increased by 20 per cent. Even now, India is not densely populated. Measured by the number of persons per acre of arable land, Japan and Taiwan—hardly examples of starving populations—are about five times as densely populated. Everyone has heard of Holland's reclamation of land from the sea, and Israel furnished an instructive example for those who face the barren desert: the Israelis are reclaiming the Negev through the use of hydroponics, an agricultural technique that recycles all water and nutrients, is non-polluting, and needs little land and no soil at all. A desert-tolerant but tasty kind of livestock is also on the menu. One step in this direction is the goabex, a cross between a goat and a camel.

But have we not already stretched our use of land nearly to the limit? No. The Food and Agriculture Organization estimates that there are in the world nearly eight billion acres of arable land lying idle—four times that now being cultivated. Tropical lands allow multiple cropping. If this is taken into account, that fourfold potential increase becomes a tenfold increase. But as Israel and Holland show, even these untapped potentials do not set an upper limit on how much food could be produced. Imagination is the only limit, and more people means more minds and therefore more imagination.

Julian Simon's research has shown that there is no such thing as an ideal population growth rate. Whether a low, moderate, or high growth rate will maximize future income depends on the economic conditions of the country and the age structure of its population. Two conclusions, however, are unconditional: a) in economic terms, a declining population always does badly in the long run; b) all birth rates above the replacement level raise future income.

The possibility of a declining population, which is showing signs of becoming the next population scare, raises an important question. If we are faced with a declining birth rate, need the state intrude and attempt to boost it by, say, imposing a 5 percent cent surtax on per-sons who are not married before they are 25 years old (as is done in Rumania)? No. A declining birth rate means that people (on average) prefer fewer children and more of the goods—pecuniary and non-pecuniary—that they would have had to sacrifice if they had had more children. In any case, the Eastern European attempts to mold family life do not seem to be working. If there is any planning to be done, each family will manage on its own, thank you.

Both the prophets of doom and the sober pessimists have foundered on the rocks of scientific research. It is now time to lay to rest both Malthus and his troubled ghost, in the knowledge that population growth does not impede but actually contributes to man's rise from poverty and hardship. The more people there are, free to exploit their own and the earth's resources, the easier it is to feed them.

POSTSCRIPT

Is Overpopulation a Major Problem?

Each side in this debate on population highlights certain facts and downplays others. The report of Hal Burdett and his colleagues says nothing about what Ray Percival believes is an essential fact: there are eight billion acres of arable land that can still be cultivated. However, Percival is also selective. He ignores the destruction of the rain forests and other environmental crises that have occurred in recent years. Statistics, then, are used by each side, but each side keeps its eye on different indicators and interprets study results quite differently.

For an optimistic assessment of the world population situation, see Julian L. Simon, "World Food Supplies," *The Atlantic Monthly* (July 1981), and *The Ultimate Resource* (Princeton University, 1981), as well as Marylin Chou and David P. Harman, Jr., eds., *Critical Food Issues of the Eighties* (Pergamon, 1979). For a pessimistic assessment see Erik P. Eckholm, *Losing Ground: Environmental Stress and World Food Prospects* (Norton, 1976) and Paul R. Ehrlich et al., *Ecoscience: Population, Resources, Environment* (Freeman, 1977). For a middle-of-the-road assessment, see Philip M. Hauser, ed., *World Population and Development* (Syracuse University Press, 1979), and National Academy of Sciences, *Supporting Papers: World Food and Nutrition Study* (Washington, D.C., 1977).

On a more personal level, you might be interested in the brief paperback book *Fifty Simple Things You Can Do to Save the Earth* (Earthworks Press, 1989).

ISSUE 18

Is the Environment Improving?

YES: Julian L. Simon, from "Life on Earth Is Getting Better, Not Worse," *The Futurist* (August 1983)

NO: Lester R. Brown, Christopher Flavin, and Edward C. Wolf, from "Earth's Vital Signs," *The Futurist* (July/August 1988)

ISSUE SUMMARY

YES: Economist Julian Simon reviews several indicators of improving environmental conditions for human life.

NO: Lester R. Brown, Christopher Flavin, and Edward C. Wolf, president and senior researchers, respectively, at the Worldwatch Institute, argue that many of the earth's natural systems have become seriously destabilized in environmentally destructive ways. The earth is sick, and they prescribe strong medicine to cure it.

The literature on socioeconomic development in the 1960s was based on the belief in material progress for everyone. It largely ignored the environment and presumed that raw materials would not be a problem. All societies would get richer because all societies were investing in new machinery and technology that would improve productivity and increase wealth. Some poor countries were having trouble developing because their values were not supportive of modernization and they lacked the social, political, and economic organization or psychological attitudes conducive to growth. It was believed that, if certain social and psychological defects could be overcome by a modernizing elite, and ten percent of the gross national product devoted to capital formation for at least three decades, then poor countries would take off into self-sustained growth, just as industrial societies had done decades earlier (see Walt W. Rostow, *The Stages of Economic Growth*, Cambridge University Press, 1960). After take-off, growth would be self-sustaining—i.e., would continue for the foreseeable future.

In the 1970s an intellectual revolution occurred. Suddenly, the deeply entrenched idea of progress came under attack by environmentalists. By the end of the 1960s, Rachel Carson's *Silent Spring* (Alfred A. Knopf, 1962) had worked its way into the public's consciousness. Carson's book traced the noticeable loss of birds to the use of pesticides. Her book made the middle and upper classes in the United States realize that pollution affected complex ecological systems in ways that put even the wealthy at risk—deteriorating ecosystems affect everyone.

Many of the environmentalists sounded apocalyptic. Paul Ehrlich wrote *Population Bomb* (Ballantine Books, 1968), which pointed out all of the possible evils and problems that further population pressures on the environment might cause. In 1967 William and Paul Paddock wrote *Famine 1975* (Little, Brown) to warn of coming food shortages in many of the poor regions of the world. Increasing numbers of people became aware of the gloomy predictions, but most people trusted that technological developments and numerous private and government responses would prevent catastrophes and continue the growth of prosperity.

In 1973 the Arab members of OPEC (Organization of Petroleum Exporting Countries) cut off oil supplies to the United States and Western Europe because of their relationships with Israel. Quickly, gas lines formed and conservation policies were passed. The major U.S. policy was the national fifty-five miles per hour speed limit, which conserved very little oil. Europe instituted more stringent measures and confronted serious scarcities for the first time since World War II. The lesson of the oil embargo was that scarcity lies close at hand and that industrial societies are vulnerable to cut-offs of vital resources.

Currently, the major proponent of the optimistic view of further economic development without serious environmental consequences is Julian Simon. In the article that follows, he argues that the environment is becoming more beneficent for man because pollution is decreasing, resources are becoming more available, average food consumption levels are improving, few species are becoming extinct, and people are living longer. The picture that Simon presents suggests that the concerns of environmentalists are largely fanciful fears and that current environmental trends are healthy. Environmentalists Lester R. Brown, Christopher Flavin, and Edward C. Wolf are leading spokespersons for the pessimistic view. They argue for the need to radically change the mode of agricultural and industrial production and the wasteful life-styles of consumers in order to save the world from very real dangers of ecocatastrophes.

YES

Julian L. Simon

LIFE ON EARTH
IS GETTING BETTER, NOT WORSE

If we lift our gaze from the frightening daily headlines and look instead at wide-ranging scientific data as well as the evidence of our senses, we shall see that economic life in the United States and the rest of the world has been getting better rather than worse during recent centuries and decades. There is, moreover, no persuasive reason to believe that these trends will not continue indefinitely.

But first: I am *not* saying that all is well everywhere, and I do not predict that all will be rosy in the future. Children are hungry and sick; people live out lives of physical or intellectual poverty, with little opportunity for improvement; war or some new pollution may finish us. What I *am* saying is that for most relevant economic matters I have checked, aggregate trends are improving rather than deteriorating. Also, I do not say that a better future will happen automatically or without effort. It will happen because men and women will use muscle and mind to struggle with problems that they will probably overcome, as they have in the past.

LONGER AND HEALTHIER LIVES

Life cannot be good unless you are alive. Plentiful resources and a clean environment have little value unless we and others are alive to enjoy them. The fact that your chances of living through any given age now are much better than in earlier times must therefore mean that life has gotten better. In France, for example, female life expectancy at birth rose from under 30 years in the 1740s to 75 years in the 1960s. And this trend has not yet run its course. The increases have been rapid in recent years in the United States: a 2.1-year gain between 1970 and 1976 versus a 0.8-year gain in the entire decade of the 1960s. This pattern is now being repeated in the poorer countries of the world as they improve their economic lot. Life expectancy at birth in low-income countries rose from an average of 35.2 years in 1950 to 49.9 years in

From Julian L. Simon, "Life on Earth Is Getting Better, Not Worse," *The Futurist* (August 1983). Reprinted with permission from *The Futurist*, published by the World Future Society, 4916 St. Elmo Avenue, Bethesda, MD 20814.

1978, a much bigger jump than the rise from 66.0 to 73.5 years in the industrialized countries.

The threat of our loved ones dying greatly affects our assessment of the quality of our lives. Infant mortality is a reasonable measure of child mortality generally. In Europe in the eighteenth and nineteenth centuries, 200 or more children of each thousand died during their first year. As late as 1900, infant mortality was 200 per 1000 or higher in Spain, Russia, Hungary, and even Germany. Now it is about 15 per 1000 or less in a great many countries.

Health has improved, too. The incidence of both chronic and acute conditions has declined. While a perceived "epidemic" of cancer indicates to some a drop in the quality of life, the data show no increase in cancer except for deaths due to smoking-caused lung cancer. As Philip Handler, president of the National Academy of Sciences, said:

> The United States is not suffering an "epidemic of cancer," it is experiencing an "epidemic of life"—in that an even greater fraction of the population survives to the advanced ages at which cancer has always been prevalent. The overall, age-corrected incidence of cancer has not been increasing; it has been declining slowly for some years.

ABATING POLLUTION

About pollution now: The main air pollutants—particulates and sulfur dioxide—have declined since 1960 and 1970 respectively, the periods for which there is data in the U.S. The Environmental Protection Agency's Pollutant Standard Index, which takes into account all the most important air pollutants, shows that the number of days rated "unhealthful" has declined steadily since the index's inauguration in 1974. And the proportion of monitoring sites in the U.S. having good drinking water has greatly increased since record-keeping began in 1961.

Pollution in the less-developed countries is a different, though not necessarily discouraging, story. No worldwide pollution data are available. Nevertheless, it is reasonable to assume that pollution of various kinds has increased as poor countries have gotten somewhat less poor. Industrial pollution rises along with new factories. The same is true of consumer pollution—junked cars, plastic wrappers, and such oddments as the hundreds of discarded antibiotics vials I saw on the ground in an isolated Iranian village. Such industrial wastes do not exist in the poorest preindustrial countries. And in the early stages of development, countries and people are not ready to pay for clean-up operations. But further increases in income almost surely will bring about pollution abatement, just as increases in income in the United States have provided the wherewithal for better garbage collection and cleaner air and water.

THE MYTH OF FINITE RESOURCES

Though natural resources are a smaller part of the economy with every succeeding year, they are still important, and their availability causes grave concern to many. Yet, measured by cost or price, the scarcity of all raw materials except lumber and oil has been *decreasing* rather than increasing over the long run. . . .

Perhaps surprisingly, oil also shows downward cost trend in the long run. The price rise in the 1970s was purely political; the cost of producing a barrel of oil in the Persian Gulf is still only perhaps 15 to 25 cents.

There is no reason to believe that the supply of energy is finite, or that the price will not continue its long-run decrease. This statement may sound less preposterous if you consider that for a quantity to be finite it must be measurable. The future supply of oil includes what we usually think of as oil, plus the oil that can be produced from shale, tar sands, and coal. It also includes the oil from plants that we grow, whose key input is sunlight. So the measure of the future oil supply must therefore be at least as large as the sun's 7 billion or so years of future life. And it may include other suns whose energy might be exploited in the future. Even if you believe that one can in principle measure the energy from suns that will be available in the future—a belief that requires a lot of confidence that the knowledge of the physical world we have developed in the past century will not be superseded in the next 7 billion years, plus the belief that the universe is not expanding—this measurement would hardly be relevant for any practical contemporary decision making.

Energy provides a good example of the process by which resources become more abundant and hence cheaper. Seventeenth-century England was full of alarm at an impending energy shortage due to the country's deforestation for firewood. People feared a scarcity of fuel for both heating and the vital iron industry. This impending scarcity led inventors and businessmen to develop coal.

Then, in the mid-1800s, the English came to worry about an impending coal crisis. The great English economist William Stanley Jevons calculated then that a shortage of coal would surely bring England's industry to a standstill by 1900; he carefully assessed that oil could never make a decisive difference. But spurred by the impending scarcity of coal (and of whale oil, whose story comes next), ingenious and profit-minded people developed oil into a more desirable fuel than coal ever was. And today England exports both coal and oil.

Another strand in the story: Because of increased demand due to population growth and increased income, the price of whale oil used in lamps jumped in the 1840s. Then the Civil War pushed it even higher, leading to a whale oil "crisis." The resulting high price provided an incentive for imaginative and enterprising people to discover and produce substitutes. First came oil from rapeseed, olives, linseed, and pine trees. Then inventors learned how to get coal oil from coal, which became a flourishing industry. Other ingenious persons produced kerosene from the rock oil that seeped to the surface. Kerosene was so desirable a product that its price rose from 75 cents to $2 a gallon, which stimulated enterprisers to increase its supply. Finally, Edwin L. Drake sunk his famous oil well in Titusville, Pennsylvania. Learning how to refine the oil took a while, but in a few years there were hundreds of small refiners in the U.S. Soon the bottom dropped out of the whale oil market: the price fell from $2.50 or more a gallon at its peak around 1866 to well below a dollar.

Lumber has been cited as an exception to the general resource story of falling costs. For decades in the U.S., farmers clearing land disposed of trees as a nuisance. As lumber came to be more a commercial crop and a good for builders and railroad men, its price rose. For some time, resource economists expected the price to hit a plateau and then follow the course of other raw materials as the transition to a commercial crop would be completed. There was evidence consistent with this view in the increase, rather than the popularly supposed decrease, in the tree stock in the U.S., yet for some time the price did not fall. But now that expectation seems finally to have been realized as prices of lumber have fallen to a fourth of their peak in the late 1970s.

MORE FOOD FOR MORE PEOPLE

Food is an especially important resource, and the evidence indicates that its supply is increasing despite rising population. The long-run prices of food relative to wages, and even relative to consumer goods, are down. Famine deaths have decreased in the past century even in absolute terms, let alone relative to the much larger population, a special boon for poor countries. Per person food production in the world is up over the last 30 years and more. And there are no data showing that the people at the bottom of the income distribution have fared worse, or have failed to share in the general improvement, as the average has improved. Africa's food production per capita is down, but that clearly stems from governmental blunders with price controls, subsidies, farm collectivization, and other institutional problems.

There is, of course a food-production problem in the U.S. today: too much production. Prices are falling due to high productivity, falling consumer demand for meat in the U.S., and increased foreign competition in such crops as soybeans. In response to the farmers' complaints, the government will now foot an unprecedentedly heavy bill for keeping vast amounts of acreage out of production.

THE DISAPPEARING-SPECIES SCARE

Many are alarmed that the earth is losing large numbers of its species. For example, the *Global 2000 Report to the President* says: "Extinctions of plant and animal species will increase dramatically. Hundreds of thousands of species—perhaps as many as 20 percent of all species on earth—will be irretrievably lost as their habitats vanish, especially in tropical forests," by the year 2000.

The available facts, however, are not consistent with the level of concern expressed in *Global 2000*, nor do they warrant the various policies suggested to deal with the purported dangers.

The *Global 2000* projection is based upon a report by contributor Thomas Lovejoy, who estimates that between 437,000 and 1,875,000 extinctions will occur out of a present estimated total of 3 to 10 million species. Lovejoy's estimate is based on a linear relationship running from 0% species extinguished at 0% tropical forest cleared, to about 95% extinguished at 100% tropical forest cleared. (The main source of differences in the range of estimated losses is the range of 3 to 10 million species in the overall estimate.)

The basis of any useful projection must be a body of experience collected under a range of conditions that encompass the expected conditions, or that can reasonably be extrapolated to the expected conditions. But none of Lovejoy's references seems to contain any scientifically impressive body of experience.

A projected drop in the amount of tropical forests underlines Lovejoy's projection of species losses in the future. Yet to connect these two events as Lovejoy has done requires systematic evidence relating an amount of tropical forest removed to a rate of species reduction. Neither *Global 2000* nor any of the other sources I checked give such empirical evidence. If there is not better evidence for Lovejoy's projected rates, one could extrapolate almost any rate one chooses for the year 2000. Until more of the facts are in, we need not undertake alarmist protection policies. Rather, we need other sorts of data to estimate extinction rates and decide on policy. None of this is to say that we need not worry about endangered species. The planet's flora and fauna constitute a valuable natural endowment; we must guard them as we do our other physical and social assets. But we should also strive for a clear, unbiased view of this set of assets in order to make the best possible judgments about how much time and money to spend guarding them, in a world where this valuable activity must compete with other valuable activities, including the preservation of other assets and human life.

MORE WEALTH FROM LESS WORK

One of the great trends of economic history is the shortening of the workweek coupled with increasing income. A shorter workweek represents an increase in one's freedom to dispose of that most treasured possession—time—as one wishes. In the U.S., the decline was from about 60 hours per week in 1870 to less than 40 hours at present. This benign trend is true for an array of countries in which the length of the workweek shows an inverse relationship with income.

With respect to progress in income generally, the most straightforward and meaningful index is the proportion of persons in the labor force working in agriculture. In 1800, the percentage in the U.S. was 73.6%, whereas in 1980 the proportion was 2.7%. That is, relative to population size, only $1/25$ as many persons today are working in agriculture as in 1800. This suggests that the effort that produced one bushel of grain or one loaf of bread in 1800 will now produce the bushel of grain plus what 24 other bushels will buy in other goods, which is equivalent to an increase in income by a factor of 25.

Income in less-developed countries has not reached nearly so high a level as in the more-developed countries, by definition. But it would be utterly wrong to think that income in less-developed countries has stagnated rather than risen. In fact, income per person has increased at a proportional rate at least as fast, or faster, in less-developed than in more-developed countries since World War II.

THE ULTIMATE RESOURCE

What explains the enhancement of our material life in the face of supposed limits to growth? I offer an extended answer in my recent book, *The Ultimate Resource* (1981). In short, the source of our increased economic blessings is the human mind, and, all other things being equal, when there are more people, there are more productive minds. Productivity increases come directly from the additional minds that develop productive new ideas, as well as indirectly from the impact upon industrial productivity of the additional demand for goods. That is, population growth in the form of babies or immigrants helps in the long run to raise the standard of living because it brings increased productivity. Immigrants are the best deal of all because they usually migrate when they are young and strong; in the U.S., they contribute more in taxes to the public coffers than they take out in welfare services.

In the short run, of course, additional people mean lower income for other people because children must be fed and housed by their parents, and educated and equipped partly by the community. Even immigrants are a burden for a brief time until they find jobs. But after the children grow up and enter the work force, and contribute to the support of others as well as increasing productivity, their net effect upon others becomes positive. Over their lifetimes they are a boon to others.

I hope you will now agree that the long-run outlook is for a more abundant material life rather than for increased scarcity, in the U.S. and in the world as a whole. Of course, such progress does not come about automatically. And my message certainly is not one of complacency. In this I agree with the doomsayers—that our world needs the best efforts of all humanity to improve our lot. I part company with them in that they expect us to come to a bad end despite the efforts we make, whereas I expect a continuation of successful efforts. Their message is self-fulfilling because if you expect inexorable natural limits to stymie your efforts you are likely to feel resigned and give up. But if you recognize the possibility—indeed, the probability—of success, you can tap large reserves of energy and enthusiasm. Energy and enthusiasm, together with the human mind and spirit, constitute our solid hope for the economic future, just as they have been our salvation in ages past. With these forces at work, we will leave a richer, safer, and more beautiful world to our descendants, just as our ancestors improved the world that they bestowed upon us.

NO
Lester R. Brown, Christopher Flavin, and Edward C. Wolf

EARTH'S VITAL SIGNS

In giving the earth a physical examination, checking its vital signs, we find that the readings are not reassuring: The planet's forests are shrinking, its deserts expanding, and its soils eroding—all at record rates.

Each year, thousands of plant and animal species disappear, many before they are named or cataloged. The ozone layer in the upper atmosphere that protects us from ultraviolet radiation is thinning. The temperature of the earth appears to be rising, posing a threat of unknown dimensions to virtually all the life-support systems on which humanity depends.

All human activities affect the earth's physical condition, but two are disproportionately important: energy use and population growth. Heavy dependence on fossil fuels has caused a buildup of carbon dioxide in the atmosphere that threatens to warm the earth. Pollutants from fossil-fuel burning have also led to acidification and the death of lakes and forests. Advances in human health have led to unprecedented reproductive success and a growth of population that in many countries is overwhelming local life-support systems.

Many of the world's problems, including ozone depletion and climate protection, cannot be solved without international action. In these areas, any one country's efforts to change would be overwhelmed without global cooperation. This sense of international responsibility marked the September 1987 signing in Montreal of international accords to limit the production of chlorofluorocarbons to protect the earth's ozone layer. These accords, although modest in scope, were a signal achievement and could become a model for future agreements.

The world has come a long way from the mid-1970s, when environmental concerns were considered something that only the rich could afford to worry about. Today, they are concerns no one can afford to ignore.

From Lester R. Brown, Christopher Flavin, and Edward C. Wolf, "Earth's Vital Signs," *The Futurist* (July/August 1988). Adapted from Lester R. Brown et al., *State of the World 1988* (Norton, 1988). Copyright © 1988 by the Worldwatch Institute. Reprinted by permission.

THE EARTH'S ANNUAL PHYSICAL

Table 1 depicts the earth's vital signs—the current state of the world's physical health.

Tree cover is one of the most visible indicators of the earth's health and, because trees are an integral part of basic life-support systems, one of the most vital. The loss of trees on sloping land can accelerate rainfall runoff and increase soil erosion, diminishing land productivity and aggravating local flooding. Where tree cutting exceeds regrowth, deforestation releases carbon that contributes to the buildup of atmospheric CO_2 and a warming of the earth.

One consequence of declining tree cover and expanding agriculture is accelerated soil erosion. Despite topsoil's essential economic role, only a few countries regularly monitor these losses. As erosion continues, land gradually loses its inherent productivity, threatening the livelihood of those who depend on it.

The health of the earth's inhabitants cannot be separated from that of the planet itself. Contaminations by industrial chemicals in communities such as Love Canal in the United States and Seveso in Italy have led to permanent evacuations. In Brazil, where concentrations of industrial wastes along the

Table 1

Vital Signs

Forest Cover	Tropical forests shrinking by 11 million hectares per year; 31 million hectares in industrial countries damaged, apparently by air pollution or acid rain.
Topsoil on Cropland	An estimated 26 billion tons lost annually in excess of new soil formation.
Desert Area	Some 6 million hectares of new desert formed annually by land mismanagement.
Lakes	Thousands of lakes in the industrial north now biologically dead; thousands more dying.
Fresh Water	Underground water tables falling in parts of Africa, China, India, and North America as demand for water rises above aquifer recharge rates.
Species Diversity	Extinctions of plant and animal species together now estimated at several thousand per year; one-fifth of all species may disappear over next 20 years.
Ground-water Quality	Some 50 pesticides contaminate groundwater in 32 American states; some 2,500 U.S. toxic waste sites need cleanup; extent of toxic contamination unknown.
Climate	Mean temperature projected to rise between 1.5° and 4.5° C between now and 2050.
Sea Level	Projected to rise between 1.4 meters (4.7 feet) and 2.2 meters (7.1 feet) by 2100.
Ozone Layer in Upper Atmosphere	Growing "hole" in the earth's ozone layer over Antarctica each spring suggests gradual global depletion could be starting.

Source: Compiled by Worldwatch Institute from various sources.

southern coast have reached life-threatening levels, the industrial city of Cubatão is locally referred to as the "Valley of Death."

Another of the earth's vital indicators, the amount of carbon dioxide and other greenhouse gases in the atmosphere, can be measured rather precisely. Since 1958, careful recordings have shown that the atmospheric CO_2 concentration is rising each year. This increase, combined with that of trace gases, may be warming the earth more rapidly than had been anticipated.

As forests disappear, as soils erode, and as lakes and soil acidify and become polluted, the number of plant and animal species diminishes. This reduction in the diversity of life on earth may well have unforeseen long-term consequences.

POPULATION GROWTH AND LAND DEGRADATION

The annual increment of births over deaths has climbed from 74 million in 1970 to 83 million in 1987. During the 1990s, it is projected to surpass 90 million before moderating as the next century begins. Most of the annual increment has been concentrated in the Third World, where human demands often overtax local life-support systems already.

When annual population additions are coupled with heightened stress on local life-support systems, shortages of food, fodder, and fuel can emerge almost overnight. Development economists typically focus on changes in the rate of population growth, but a more vital sign is the relationship between population size and the sustainable yield of local forests, grasslands, and croplands. If the demands of a local population surpass these sustainable yields, the systems will continue to deteriorate even if population growth stops.

In the Third World, continuous population growth and skewed land distribution drive land-hungry farmers onto marginal land that is highly erodible and incapable of sustaining cultivation over the long term.

A DESTRUCTIVE ENERGY PATH

Energy trends are an important indicator of the world's economic and ecological health. The trends since early 1986 point to a partial resurgence of growth in world oil consumption and continued growth in coal use. Although oil ministers and coal operators are undoubtedly cheered by this turn of events, it is in fact an ominous one. Any additional energy growth will add to the dangerous chemistry experiment we are conducting on the earth's atmosphere. Lakes, estuaries, forests, human health, and the climate itself are now at risk.

By the early 1980s, activities such as generating electricity, driving automobiles, and producing steel were releasing into the atmosphere over 5 billion tons of carbon, close to 10 million tons of sulfur, and lesser quantities of nitrogen oxides each year. Carbon emissions closely track world energy trends, but because coal releases more carbon than does either oil or natural gas, the shift to coal accelerates the rise in carbon emissions. At a time when climatological evidence points to a need to reduce carbon emissions, they are actually rising.

Developing countries are also among the victims of environmental damage from the use of fossil fuels. China, for instance, is suffering from its massive use of coal. Since China generally lacks both tall smokestacks and pollution-control equipment, cities and surrounding farmland will likely suffer severe damage from coal-fired air pollution. The Third World as a whole will have to exert enormous effort in order to avoid the apparent environmental fate of Eastern Europe.

In developing energy strategies, policy makers should consider the benefits of reducing acidification and CO_2 emission together. The combined societal cost of acidification and climate warming of the sort projected may justify a more fundamental redirection of the world's energy systems than any seriously considered to date.

THE CLIMATIC CONSEQUENCES

As indicated in Table 1, the earth's mean temperature will rise over the next decades. Two of the most serious effects of the projected warming would be the impact on agriculture and sea level. Meteorological models, though they remain sketchy, suggest that two of the world's major food-producing regions—the North American heartland and the grain-growing regions of the Soviet Union—are likely to experience a decline in soil moisture during the summer growing season as a result of increased evaporation.

A somewhat more predictable result of a hotter earth is a rise in sea level. This would hurt most in Asia, where rice is produced on low-lying river deltas and floodplains. Without heavy investments in dikes and seawalls to protect the rice fields from saltwater intrusion, even a relatively modest one-meter rise would markedly reduce harvests.

The detailed effects of climate change cannot be predicted with great accuracy. We do know, however, that human civilization has evolved within a narrow range of climate conditions. Any major departure from those conditions will cause enormous hardship and require incalculable investments during the adjustment. Because some of the most important changes could occur abruptly, with little warning, most of the costs would simply have to be borne by an unwitting society. Ways to avoid massive climate change now deserve serious consideration.

RECLAIMING THE FUTURE

Assessing the threats to the future of the planet's life-support systems can easily lead to apathy or despair, particularly in view of policy makers' preoccupation with the East-West political conflict and global economic issues. Yet, we can do something about the planet's deteriorating physical condition. Some of the steps needed to restore its health, including investment in energy efficiency, reforestation, and population stabilization, can be sketched out.

A sustainable future requires that a series of interlocking issues be dealt with simultaneously. For instance, it may be impossible to avoid a mass extinction of species as long as the Third World is burdened with debt. And the resources needed to arrest the physical deterioration of the planet may not be available unless the international arms race can be reversed.

The immediate effects of population growth and land degradation are largely local, but the climate alteration linked to fossil-fuel combustion is incontestably global. Just as land degradation can threaten local efforts to raise living standards, so, too, climate alteration can overwhelm progress at the global level. Efforts to adjust the global economy to a much warmer earth—with the accompanying changes in rainfall patterns, evaporation rates, and sea level—eventually could absorb all available investment capital.

CONSERVING SOIL

Restoring two of the earth's life-support systems—its soil and trees—will require heavy capital investments and strong commitments by political leaders. The expenditures sketched here are rough estimates at best intended only to convey the magnitude of the effort needed.

As of the early 1980s, American farmers and the U.S. Department of Agriculture together were spending just over $1 billion per year to control erosion on cropland. Despite this effort, a detailed soil survey conducted in 1982 showed farmers were losing 3.1 billion tons of topsoil annually from water and wind erosion, some 2 billion tons in excess of tolerable levels of soil loss. For every ton of grain they produced, American farmers were losing six tons of their topsoil.

Congress responded to this clearly documented threat and the runaway costs of farm price-support programs with the landmark Conservation Reserve program. For the first time, policy was designed to control excessive production *and* to cut soil losses by idling land. The USDA agreed to pay farmers an average of $48 per acre each year for land enrolled in the reserve to compensate them for net income from the crops the land would otherwise have produced.

Reaching a goal of converting 40 million acres of highly erodible cropland to grassland or woodland by 1990 will cost the U.S. Treasury $2 billion per year once the full area is retired.

Erosion on the land planted to grass or trees during the first year of the cropland conversion program was estimated to decline from an average of 29 tons per acre to two tons. If this rate prevailed on all the land to be enrolled in the reserve, excessive erosion would be reduced by over 1 billion tons. This would leave just under 1 billion tons to be eliminated on the remaining 30% of the cropland still eroding excessively.

In summary, annual expenditures of roughly $3 billion would be required for the United States to stabilize the soils on its cropland once the program is fully in place by 1990.

Extrapolating these data, we estimate that global expenditures to protect the cropland base would total some $24 billion per year. Although this is obviously a large sum, it is less than the U.S. government paid farmers to support crop prices in 1986. As an investment in future food supplies for a world expecting 3–5 billion more people, $24 billion is one that humanity can ill afford not to make.

PLANTING TREES

Adding trees to the global forest stock is a valuable investment in our economic future, whether to satisfy growing firewood needs in the Third World or to stabilize soil and water regimes in watersheds where land degradation and disruptions of the hydrological cycle are undermining local economies.

Considering that some trees would serve both ecological and fuelwood objectives, a total of 120 million hectares might need to be planted. An additional 30 million hectares will be needed to satisfy demand for lumber, paper, and other forest products. If this tree-planting goal is to be achieved by the end of the century, the effort would need to reach total plantings of 17 million hectares, at a cost of $6.8 billion, per year.

It should be noted that tree planting which restores watersheds, thereby conserving soil and water, complements the expenditures on soil erosion by farmers on their cropland.

SLOWING POPULATION GROWTH

The success of efforts to save top-soil and restore tree cover both depend heavily on slowing population growth. Indeed, countries with populations expanding at 2%–4% per year may find it almost impossible to restore tree cover, protect their soils, and take other steps toward a sustainable development path.

Providing family-planning services in response to unsatisfied demand is often the quickest and most cost-effective step countries can take to secure life-support systems. World Bank surveys show that 50%–90% of the Third World women interviewed want either to stop childbearing altogether or to delay the birth of another child. This suggests an enormous unsatisfied demand for contraceptive services. The Bank estimates that providing family-planning services to all those in need would entail expenditures of roughly $8 billion per year by the end of the century.

Fertility declines most rapidly when family-planning services are introduced into a society already enjoying broad-based economic and social gains. The social indicator that correlates most closely with fertility decline is the education of women. Providing elementary education for the estimated 120 million school-age children not now in school would cost roughly $50 each or $6 billion per year. Providing literacy training for those women who are illiterate and be-

yond school age would require an additional estimated $2 billion per year.

A second social indicator that closely correlates with declines in birth rates is infant mortality. It is rare for birth rates to drop sharply if infant survival remains low. Substantial gains in reducing infant mortality can be achieved with relatively modest investments. Immunizing the 55% of the world's children not now protected from diphtheria, measles, polio, and tuberculosis would cost roughly $2 billion per year. Training mothers in oral rehydration therapy (used to treat infants with diarrhea), in basic hygiene, and in the health advantages of breastfeeding would cost another $1 billion per year. These efforts wold markedly lower infant death and in the process stimulate interest in reducing family size.

STABILIZING THE EARTH'S CLIMATE

The central issue for policy makers is whether to follow a business-as-usual energy policy and risk having to adapt the global economy to the changed climate, or to take steps to slow the warming. Unfortunately, the costs of adapting to the global warming could one day siphon off so much investment capital that economic progress would come to a halt and living standards would begin to decline.

The most costly adjustments now anticipated would be those needed to protect coastal areas from the rising sea. Some sense of the magnitude of these expenses is offered by Bangladesh.

Unlike the Netherlands, which spends 6% of its gross national product to maintain a complex set of dikes, seawalls, and other structures to protect the nation from the sea, Bangladesh cannot afford

Table 2

Investments Needed for Sustainability (Figures in billions of dollars)

Year	Protecting Topsoil on Cropland	Reforest-ing the Earth	Slowing Population Growth	Raising Energy Efficiency	Develop-ing Re-newable Energy	Retiring Third World Debt	Total
1990	4	2	13	5	2	20	46
1991	9	3	18	10	5	30	75
1992	14	4	22	15	8	40	103
1993	18	5	26	20	10	50	129
1994	24	6	28	25	12	50	145
1995	24	6	30	30	15	40	145
1996	24	6	31	35	18	30	144
1997	24	6	32	40	21	20	143
1998	24	7	32	45	24	10	142
1999	24	7	32	50	27	10	150
2000	24	7	33	55	30	0	149

Source: Worldwatch Institute.

this approach. Consequently, it has paid a heavy toll in human lives. In 1970, some 300,000 people were killed in a single cyclone; 10,000 people were killed and 1.3 million affected by a storm surge in 1985. The willingness of Bangladeshis to reset-tle in such high-risk areas reflects a keen land hunger—one that will intensify if the population increases, as projected, from 106 million in 1988 to 305 million late in the next century.

One thing is clear: If the projected warming is to be minimized, the buildup of CO_2 and the trace gases that contrib-ute to the greenhouse effect must be slowed, and quickly, by raising the effi-ciency of energy use, shifting from fossil fuels to renewable energy sources and reversing deforestation.

The United States uses twice as much energy to produce a dollar's worth of goods and services as Japan does. If the United States were to double fuel-effi-ciency standards for vehicles to over 50 miles per gallon by the end of the cen-tury—a level that can be achieved with cars now on the market—global carbon emissions would drop measurably.

Replacing existing technologies with more efficient ones is merely the first step. Beyond this, economic systems can be redesigned so that some sectors can be sustained with relatively little energy. For example, although fuel-inefficient cars can be replaced with more-efficient ones, the large gains in transport effi-ciency will come from designing commu-

Table 3

Alternative Global-Security Budgets (Figures in billions of dollars)

| Year | Global Security Defined in Military Terms | Global Security Defined in Sustainable Development Terms | | |
	Current Military Expenditures Continued	Military Expenditures	Expenditures to Achieve Sustainable Development	Total Security Expenditures
1990	900	854	46	900
1991	900	825	75	900
1992	900	797	103	900
1993	900	771	129	900
1994	900	755	145	900
1995	900	755	145	900
1996	900	756	144	900
1997	900	757	143	900
1998	900	758	142	900
1999	900	750	150	900
2000	900	751	149	900

Source: Worldwatch Institute.

nities where residents do not depend on automobiles.

Countries that rely heavily on renewable energy typically use several different sources. Among the largest is Brazil, a country that relies heavily on hydropower for electricity, alcohol fuels for transport, and charcoal for steel smelting. Altogether renewable energy sources account for some 60% of Brazil's total energy use, making it the first large industrializing economy to rely primarily on renewables.

But Brazil ranks fourth in CO_2 emissions. The reason is not because it is a heavy user of fossil fuels, but because it is burning its rain forest to make way for cattle ranching and crop production. The vast Amazon rain forest helps shape continental climate patterns; unrestrained forest clearing would therefore adversely affect rainfall and temperatures in the important agricultural regions to the south.

Expenditures in energy efficiency and renewable energy sufficient to head off the global warming cannot easily be estimated, in contrast to those on soil conservation and population stabilization. Having only a sense that the costs of climate change are enormous, we recommend a tripling in the annual investment in energy efficiency during the 1990s and a doubling in investment in developing renewable energy resources.

These investment levels, which offer immediate environmental and economic gains, should be viewed as minimal. If the economic disruption associated with the global warming passes the threshold of political acceptability, then investments far greater than those outlined here will be made to reduce fossil-fuel use.

INVESTING IN ENVIRONMENTAL SECURITY

To continue with a more or less business-as-usual attitude—to accept the loss of tree cover, the erosion of soil, the expansion of deserts, the loss of plant and animal species, the depletion of the ozone layer, and the buildup of greenhouse gases—implies acceptance of economic decline and social disintegration. In a world where progress depends on a complex set of national and international economic ties, such disintegration would bring human suffering on a scale that has no precedent. The threat posed by continuing environmental deterioration is no longer a hypothetical one. Dozens of countries will have lower living standards at the end of the 1980s than at the beginning.

The momentum inherent in population growth, the forces of land degradation, and the changing chemistry of the atmosphere make it difficult to get the world on a sustainable development path. The scale of these challenges and the urgency with which they must be addressed require that they be moved to the center of governmental agendas.

Through decisions about existing and prospective technologies, humanity has far more control over the rate of global warming than is commonly recognized. In addition to direct influence over the activities that produce CO_2 and the land uses that sequester carbon from the atmosphere, accelerating progress toward population stabilization can reduce the numbers dependent on activities that put climate stability at risk. The many factors that will shape future energy demand and the pattern of human activities in generations to come cannot be forecast with any certainty, but investing some $150 billion per year in areas that broaden human options in the face of enormous uncertainty would be a reasonable down payment on environmentally sustainable global economy. (See Table 2.)

Two barriers now stand in the way of ensuring that capital and political will are available on the scale needed. One is the profound misallocation of capital implicit in global military expenditures of $900 billion each year. (See Table 3.) The other is the unmanageable Third World debt that burdens the world economy. Unless these obstacles are overcome, funds on the scale needed to ensure sustainable development will not be available.

ENTERING A NEW ERA

In some important respects, the world situation today resembles that during the mid-1940s. The scale of human suffering as a result of the Great Depression and World War II gave the international community the resolve to address the weaknesses inherent in the global system.

This period of crisis produced some visionaries—leaders who were able to engineer an effective response to the new threats to progress. One was General George Marshall, U.S. Secretary of State from 1947 to 1949. When he proposed in 1947 that the United States launch a massive international assistance plan to rebuild Europe, including Germany, the conventional image of postwar relationships was turned upside down. Instead of plundering the defeated enemy, the United States held out a helping hand, launching a massive reconstruction of victors and vanquished alike, an effort that led to a generation of European prosperity.

Initiatives of comparable boldness are needed in the late 1980s. The world may not have the financial resources both to sustain the arms race and to make the investments needed to return the world to a sustainable development path. The deterioration of the earth's life-support systems is threatening, but the psychological toll of failing to reverse it could also be high. Such a failure would lead to a loss of confidence in political institutions and would risk widespread demoralization—a sense that our ability to control our destiny is slipping away.

If, on the other hand, the world can mobilize along the lines discussed here, the trends that threaten to undermine the human future can be reversed. If widespread concern motivates political action, and if the needed changes in national priorities, national policies, and individual lifestyles take root, then—and only then—can we expect sustained improvements in the human condition.

POSTSCRIPT

Is the Environment Improving?

Simon argues that the media misleads the public with frightening headlines of environmental problems and famines. In contrast to the media, he looks at scientific data that prove that the environment is improving and resources are becoming more available. He agrees that mankind has environmental and resource problems to work on, but he is confident that they will be taken care of by human effort and inventiveness. He expects necessity to give birth to inventions, because technological developments will reap substantial economic rewards as resources become scarce. Simon's problem-solving thesis is supported by Charles Maurice and Charles W. Smith with ten major historical examples in *The Doomsday Myth: Ten Thousand Years of Economic Crisis* (Hoover Institution Press, 1985).

Lester Brown, Christopher Flavin, and Edward C. Wolf would see Simon as a mythmaker whose optimism requires selective scanning of data on the environment. Furthermore, environmentalists such as Brown, Flavin, and Wolf think economists such as Simon fail to understand environmental principles, one of which is that the environment gives off few signals of population overshoot and other environmental dangers until it is too late for species to moderate their growth and come into balance with the environment. The environmentalists argue that many regional and local ecosystems throughout the world are decreasing their natural productivity and major ecocatastrophes loom on the horizon.

Some of the prominent optimists on the issues of the availability of resources and health of the environment include Herman Kahn, *World Economic Development 1979 and Beyond* (Westville Press, 1979); Christopher

Freeman and Marie Jahoda, eds., *World Futures: The Great Debate* (Universe Books, 1978); Julian L. Simon, *The Ultimate Resource* (Princeton University, 1981); and Julian L. Simon and Herman Kahn, eds., *The Resourceful Earth: A Response to Global 2000* (Basil Blackwell, 1984). Some of the prominent pessimists include Ferdinand E. Banks, *Scarcity, Energy, and Economic Progress* (Lexington Books, 1977); W. Jackson Davis, *The Seventh Year: Industrial Civilization in Transition* (Norton, 1979); S. R. Eye, *The Real Wealth of Nations* (St. Martin's Press, 1978); *The Global 2000 Report to the President* (Government Printing Office, 1980); William Catton, *Overshoot* (University of Illinois Press, 1980); and Lester R. Brown et al., *State of the World, 1989* (W. W. Norton, 1989). For a balanced review of both sides of the debate see Barry B. Hughes, *World Futures: A Critical Analysis of Alternatives* (Johns Hopkins University Press, 1985). For the volume with the greatest policy impact throughout the world see *Our Common Future*, produced by The World Commission on the Environment and Development (Oxford University Press, 1987).

ISSUE 19

Is America Declining?

YES: Paul Kennedy, from *The Rise and Fall of the Great Powers: Economic Change and Military Conflict from 1500 to 2000* (Random House, 1987)

NO: Samuel P. Huntington, from "The U.S.—Decline or Renewal?" *Foreign Affairs* (Winter 1988/89)

ISSUE SUMMARY

YES: Historian Paul Kennedy believes that the United States, like other great powers before it, has developed an imbalance between international military commitments and domestic economic development, which will inevitably result in America's decline in power.

NO: Samuel P. Huntington, a political scientist, maintains that the so-called U.S. decline is temporary and reversible and that a renewal is on the way.

The United States emerged after World War II as the most powerful nation in the world. In part this was the result of the cumulative economic costs of World Wars I and II for England, Germany, the Soviet Union, and Japan. America escaped the physical devastation of the wars that these nations suffered, and America's economy boomed during the war years and continued to grow in the post-war periods. Having become the most prosperous and powerful of nations, the United States assumed international leadership in armaments, investments, and aid.

Critics now argue that the costs of maintaining this leadership role have surpassed the nation's willingness to pay. In the last decade, the national debt has tripled. A nation that was long the world's greatest creditor is now the largest debtor nation in history.

It is difficult for Americans living today to accept the view that this nation's power and influence will not endure. Yet historians have always noted the "rise and fall of great powers," as does Paul Kennedy in his book. Kennedy's book has attracted great interest because it is an impressive survey of the past that also ventures to peer ahead to the near future, with direct relevance to the United States.

Kennedy summarized his thesis: "The historical record suggests that there is a very clear connection *in the long run* between an individual Great Power's economic rise and fall and its growth and decline as an important military power (or world empire)." Nations must spend to create the armies

342

and navies that protect their wealth and security; but if they spend too much, they weaken their economic competitiveness. "Imperial overstretch" is Kennedy's term for the tendency of great powers to commit too much wealth to overseas commitments and too little to domestic economic growth. This is the sociological law (probabilistic) that is at the heart of Kennedy's analysis.

Kennedy identifies the loss of power with the decline of economic competitiveness. In his account, the most powerful nations in the last five centuries—successively, Spain, the Netherlands, France, and England—were unable or unwilling to tax themselves sufficiently to pay for their armed forces and empires, and the United States now finds itself in a comparable position. The greater the power of a state, the greater the expenditure that must be made to support it.

There is an almost instinctive American rejection of any theory that even suggests that historical forces determine our fates independent of our wills. Public rhetoric expresses a conviction that there is little that Americans cannot achieve, if they will it and work to achieve it. The qualities that made it possible for earlier American generations to settle a subcontinent and make it prosper—idealism, dedication to a common purpose, a willingness to sacrifice for significant long-range goals—can enable this generation to keep America prosperous and powerful into the future.

A further objection is that Kennedy's generalizations confuse different cases. After all, the United States has not created an international empire similar to those established by Spain, France, or England. Far from trying to become the dominant nation in the world, the United States since World War I has sought to strengthen its allies to create an effective balance of power vis-à-vis the Soviet Union and its allies. To be sure, the United States, by virtue of its military and economic power, has exercised leadership; but that is very different from domination. American support for the United Nations, economic aid to rebuild war-torn Europe, and mutual security acts with the non-communist nations of Europe and Asia are the acts of an ally, not a conqueror.

In the following selections, Paul Kennedy applies his theory to the United States, while Samuel P. Huntington argues that the decline will soon turn into renewal and that the nation can continue to be both powerful and influential.

YES

Paul Kennedy

THE UNITED STATES: THE PROBLEM OF NUMBER ONE IN RELATIVE DECLINE

Although the United States is at present still in a class of its own economically and perhaps even militarily, it cannot avoid confronting the two great tests which challenge the *longevity* of every major power that occupies the "number one" position in world affairs: whether, in the military/strategic realm, it can preserve a reasonable balance between the nation's perceived defense requirements and the means it possesses to maintain those commitments; and whether, as an intimately related point, it can preserve the technological and economic bases of its power from relative erosion in the face of the ever-shifting patterns of global production. This test of American abilities will be the greater because it, like Imperial Spain around 1600 or the British Empire around 1900, is the inheritor of a vast array of strategical commitments which had been made decades earlier, when the nation's political, economic, and military capacity to influence world affairs seemed so much more assured. In consequence, the United States now runs the risk, so familiar to historians of the rise and fall of previous Great Powers, of what might roughly be called "imperial overstretch": that is to say, decision-makers in Washington must face the awkward and enduring fact that the sum total of the United States' global interests and obligations is nowadays far larger than the country's power to defend them all simultaneously. . . .

[T]he United States today has roughly the same massive array of military obligations across the globe as it had a quarter-century ago, when its shares of world GNP, manufacturing production, military spending, and armed forces personnel were so much larger than they are now. Even in 1985, forty years after its triumphs of the Second World War and over a decade after its pull-out from Vietnam, the United States had 520,000 members of its armed forces abroad (including 65,000 afloat). That total is, incidentally, substantially more than the overseas deployments in peacetime of the military and naval forces of the British Empire at the height of its power. Nevertheless, in the strongly expressed opinion of the Joint Chiefs of Staff, and of many civilian experts, it is simply not enough. Despite a near-trebling of the American defense budget since the late 1970s, there has occurred a "mere 5 percent increase in the numerical size of the armed forces on active duty." As the British and French military found in their time, a nation with extensive overseas obligations will always have a more difficult "manpower problem" than a state which keeps its armed forces solely for home defense; and a politically liberal and economically laissez-faire society—aware of the unpopularity of conscription—will have a greater problem than most.

Possibly this concern about the gap between American interests and capabilities in the world would be less acute had there not been so much doubt expressed—since at least the time of the Vietnam War—about the *efficiency* of the system itself. Since those doubts have been repeatedly aired in other studies, they will only be summarized here; this is not a further essay on the hot topic of "defense reform." One major area of contention, for example, has been the degree of interservice rivalry, which is of course common to most armed forces but seems more deeply entrenched in the American system—possibly because of the relatively modest powers of the chairman of the Joint Chiefs of Staff, possibly because so much more energy appears to be devoted to procurement as opposed to strategical and operational issues. In peacetime, this might merely be dismissed as an extreme example of "bureaucratic politics"; but in actual wartime operations—say in the emergency dispatch of the Rapid Deployment Joint Task Force, which contains elements from all four services—a lack of proper coordination could be fatal.

In the area of military procurement itself, allegations of "waste, fraud and abuse" have been commonplace. The various scandals over horrendously expensive, *under*performing weapons which have caught the public's attention in recent years have plausible explanations: the lack of proper competitive bidding and of market forces in the "military-industrial complex," and the tendency toward "gold-plated" weapon systems, not to mention the striving for large profits. It is difficult, however, to separate those deficiencies in the procurement process from what is clearly a more fundamental happening: the intensification of the impacts which new technological advances make upon the art of war. Given that it is in the high-technology field that the USSR usually appears most vulnerable—which suggests that American *quality* in weaponry can be employed to counter the superior Russian *quantity* of, say, tanks and aircraft—there is an obvious attraction in what Caspar Weinberger termed "competitive strategies" when ordering new armaments. Nevertheless, the fact that the Reagan administration in its first term spent over 75 percent more on new aircraft than the Carter regime but acquired only 9 percent more planes points to *the* appalling military-procurement problem of the late twentieth century: given the technologically driven tendency toward spending more and more money upon fewer and fewer weapon systems, would the United States and its allies really have enough sophisticated and highly expensive aircraft and tanks in reserve after the early stages of a ferociously fought conventional war? Does the U.S. Navy possess enough attack submarines, or frigates, if heavy losses were incurred in the early stages of a *third* Battle of the Atlantic? If not, the results would be grim; for it is clear that today's complex weaponry simply cannot be replaced in the short times which were achieved during the Second World War.

This dilemma is accentuated by two other elements in the complicated calculus of evolving an effective American defense policy. The first is the issue of budgetary constraints. Unless external circumstances became much more threatening, it would be a remarkable act of political persuasion to get national defense expenditures raised much above, say, 7.5 percent of GNP—the more especially since the size of the federal deficit . . . points to the need to balance governmental spending as the first priority of state. But if there is a slowing-down or even a halt in the increase in defense spending, coinciding with the continuous upward spiral in weapons costs, then the problem facing the Pentagon will become much more acute.

The second factor is the sheer variety of military contingencies that a global superpower like the United States has to plan for—all of which, in their way place differing demands upon the armed forces and the weaponry they are likely to employ. This again is not without precedent in the history of the Great Powers; the British army was frequently placed under strain by having to plan to fight on the Northwest Frontier of India *or* in Belgium. But even that challenge pales beside the task facing today's "number one." If the critical issue for the United States is preserving a nuclear deterrent against the Soviet Union at *all*

levels of escalation, then money will inevitably be poured into such weapons as the MX missile, the B-1 and "Stealth" bombers, Pershing IIs, cruise missiles, and Trident-bearing submarines. If a large-scale conventional war against the Warsaw Pact is the most probable scenario, then the funds presumably need to go in quite different directions: tactical aircraft, main battle tanks, large carriers, frigates, attack submarines and logistical services. If it is likely that the United States and the USSR will avoid a direct clash, but that both will become more active in the Third World, then the weapons mix changes again: small arms, helicopters, light carriers, an enhanced role for the U.S. Marine Corps become the chief items on the list. Already it is clear that a large part of the controversy over "defense reform" stems from differing assumptions about the *type* of war the United States might be called upon to fight. But what if those in authority make the wrong assumption? . . .

The final question about the proper relationship of "means and ends" in the defense of American global interests relates to the economic challenges bearing down upon the country, which, because they are so various, threaten to place immense strains upon decision-making in national policy. The extraordinary breadth and complexity of the American economy makes it difficult to summarize what is happening to all parts of it—especially in a period when it is sending out such contradictory signals. . . .

The first of these is the country's relative industrial decline, as measured against world production, not only in older manufactures such as textiles, iron and steel, shipbuilding, and basic chemicals, but also—although it is far less easy to judge the final outcome of this level of industrial-technological combat—in global shares of robotics, aerospace, automobiles, machine tools, and computers. Both of these pose immense problems: in traditional and basic manufacturing, the gap in wage scales between the United States and newly industrializing countries is probably such that no "efficiency measures" will close it; but to lose out in the competition in future technologies, if that indeed should occur, would be even more disastrous. In late, 1986, for example, a congressional study reported that the U.S. trade surplus in high-technology goods had plunged from $27 billion in 1980 to a mere $4 billion in 1985, and was swiftly heading into a deficit.

The second, and in many ways less expected, sector of decline is agriculture. Only a decade ago, experts in that subject were predicting a frightening global imbalance between feeding requirements and farming output. But such a scenario of famine and disaster stimulated two powerful responses. The first was a massive investment into American farming from the 1970's onward, fueled by the prospect of ever-larger overseas food sales; the second was the enormous (western-world-funded) investigation into scientific means of increasing Third World crop outputs, which has been so successful as to turn growing numbers of such countries into food *exporters*, and thus competitors of the United States. These two trends are separate from, but have coincided with, the transformation of the EEC into a major producer of agricultural surpluses, because of its price-support system. In consequence, experts now refer to a "world awash in food," which in turn leads to sharp declines in agricultural prices and in American food exports—and drives many farmers out of business.

It is not surprising, therefore, that these economic problems have led to a surge in protectionist sentiment throughout many sectors of the American economy, and among businessmen, unions, farmers, and their congressmen. As with the "tariff reform" agitation in Edwardian Britain, the advocates of increased protection complain of unfair foreign practices, of "dumping" below-cost manufactures on the American market, and of enormous subsidies to foreign farmers—which, they maintain, can only be answered by U.S. administrations abandoning their laissez-faire policy on trade and instituting tough countermeasures. Many of those individual complaints (e.g., of Japan shipping below-cost silicon chips to the American market) have been valid. More broadly, however, the surge in protectionist sentiment is also a reflection of the erosion of the previously unchallenged U.S. manufacturing supremacy. Like mid-Victorian Britons, Americans after 1945 favored free trade and open competition, not just because they held that global commerce and prosperity would be boosted in the process, but also because they knew that they were most likely to benefit from the abandonment of protectionism. Forty years later, with that confidence ebbing, there is a predictable shift of opinion in favor of protecting the domestic market and the domestic producer. And, just as in that earlier British case, defenders of the existing system point out that enhanced tariffs might not only make domestic products *less* competitive internationally, but that there also could be various external repercussions—a global tariff war, blows against American exports, the undermining of the currencies of certain newly industrializing countries, and a return to the economic crisis of the 1930s.

Along with these difficulties affecting American manufacturing and agriculture there are unprecedented turbulences in the nation's finances. The uncompetitiveness of U.S. industrial products abroad and the declining sales of agricultural exports have together produced staggering deficits in visible trade—$160 billion in the twelve months to May 1986—but what is more alarming is that such a gap can no longer be covered by American earnings on "invisibles," which is the traditional recourse of a mature economy (e.g. Great Britain before 1914). On the contrary, the only way the United States can pay its way in the world is by importing ever-larger sums of capital, which has transformed it from being the world's largest creditor to the world's largest debtor nation *in the space of a few years.*

Compounding this problem—in the view of many critics, *causing* this problem—have been the budgetary policies of the U.S. government itself. Even in the 1960s, there was a tendency for Washington to rely upon deficit finance, rather than additional taxes, to pay for the increasing cost of defense and social programs. But the decisions taken by the Reagan administration in the early 1980s —i.e., large-scale increases in defense expenditures, plus considerable decreases in taxation, but *without* significant reductions in federal spending elsewhere— have produced extraordinary rises in the deficit, and consequently in the national debt, as shown in Table 1.

The continuation of such trends, alarmed voices have pointed out, would push the U.S. national debt to around $13 *trillion* by the year 2000 (fourteen times that of 1980), and the interest payments

Table 1

U.S. Federal Deficit, Debt, and Interest, 1980–1985
(billions of dollars)

	Deficit	Debt	Interest on Debt
1980	59.6	914.3	52.5
1983	195.4	1,381.9	87.8
1985	202.8	1,823.1	129.0

on such debt to $1.5 *trillion* (twenty-nine times that of 1980). In fact, a lowering of interest rates could bring down those estimates, but the overall trend is still very unhealthy. Even if federal deficits could be reduced to a "mere" $100 billion annually, the compounding of national debt and interest payments by the early twenty-first century will still cause quite unprecedented totals of money to be diverted in that direction. Historically, the only other example which comes to mind of a Great Power so increasing its indebtedness in *peacetime* is France in the 1780s, where the fiscal crisis contributed to the domestic political crisis. . . .

[G]iven the worldwide array of military liabilities which the United States has assumed since 1945, its capacity to carry those burdens is obviously less than it was several decades ago, when its share of global manufacturing and GNP was much larger, its agriculture was not in crisis, its balance of payments was far healthier, the government budget was also in balance, and it was not so heavily in debt to the rest of the world. In that larger sense, there is something in the analogy which is made by certain political scientists between the United States' position today and that of previous "declining hegemons."

Here again, it is instructive to note the uncanny similarities between the growing mood of anxiety among thoughtful circles in the United States today and that which pervaded all political parties in Edwardian Britain and led to what has been termed the "national efficiency" movement: that is, a broad-based debate within the nation's decision-making, business, and educational elites over the various measures which could reverse what was seen to be a growing uncompetitiveness as compared with other advanced societies. In terms of commercial expertise, levels of training and education, efficiency of production, standards of income and (among the less well-off) of living, health, and housing, the "number one" power of 1900 seemed to be losing its position, with dire implications for the country's long-term *strategic* position; hence the fact that the calls for "renewal" and "reorganization" came at least as much from the Right as from the Left. Such campaigns usually do lead to reforms, here and there; but their very existence is, ironically, a confirmation of decline, in that such an agitation simply would not have been necessary a few decades earlier, when the nation's lead was unquestioned. A strong man, the writer G. K. Chesterton sardonically observed, does not worry about his bodily efficiency; only when he weakens does he begin to talk about health. In the same way, when a Great Power is strong and unchallenged, it will be much less likely to debate its capacity to meet its obligations than when it is relatively weaker. . . .

A quite different problem, but one equally important for the sustaining of a proper grand strategy, concerns the impact of slow economic growth upon the American social/political consensus. To a degree which amazes most Europeans, the United States in the twentieth century has managed to avoid ostensible "class" politics. This is due, one imagines, to the facts that so many of its immigrants were fleeing from socially rigid circumstances elsewhere; that the sheer size of the country allowed those who were disillusioned with their economic position to "escape" to the West, and simultaneously made the organization of labor much more difficult than in, say, France or Britain; and that those same geographical dimensions, and the entrepreneurial opportunities within them, encouraged the development of a largely unreconstructed form of laissez-faire capitalism which has dominated the political culture of the nation (despite occasional counterattacks from the left). In consequence, the "earnings gap" between rich and poor in the United States is significantly larger than in any other advanced industrial society; and, by the same token, state expenditures upon social services form a lower share of GNP than in comparable countries (except Japan, which appears to have a much stronger family-based form of support for the poor and the aged).

This lack of "class" politics despite the obvious socioeconomic disparities has obviously been helped by the fact that the United States' overall growth since the 1930s offered the prospect of individual betterment to a majority of the population; and by the more disturbing fact that the poorest *one-third* of American society has not been "mobilized" to become regular voters. But given the differentiated birthrate between the white ethnic groups on the one hand and the black and Hispanic groups on the other—not to mention the changing flow of immigrants into the United States, and given also the economic metamorphosis which is leading to the loss of millions of relatively high-earning jobs in manufacturing, and the creation of millions of poorly paid jobs in services, it may be unwise to assume that the prevailing norms of the American political economy (low governmental expenditures, low taxes on the rich) would be maintained if the nation entered a period of sustained economic difficulty caused by a plunging dollar and slow growth. What this also suggests is that an American polity which responds to external challenges by increasing defense expenditures, and reacts to the budgetary crisis by slashing the existing social expenditures, may run the risk of provoking an eventual political backlash. . . .

This brings us, inevitably, to the delicate relationship between slow economic growth and high defense spending. The debate upon "the economics of defense spending" is a highly controversial one, and—bearing in mind the size and variety of the American economy, the stimulus which can come from large government contracts, and the technical spin-offs from weapons research—the evidence does not point simply in one direction. But what is significant for our purposes is the comparative dimension. Even if (as is often pointed out) defense expenditures formed 10 percent of GNP under Eisenhower and 9 percent under Kennedy, the United States' relative share of global production and wealth was at that time around *twice* what it is today; and, more particularly, the American economy was not then facing the challenges to either its traditional or its high-technology manufactures. Moreover, if the United States at present continues to devote 7 percent or more of its GNP to defense spending while its major eco-

nomic rivals, especially Japan, allocate a far smaller proportion, then *ipso facto* the latter have potentially more funds "free" for civilian investment; if the United States continues to invest a massive amount of its R&D activities into military-related production while the Japanese and West Germans concentrate upon commerical R&D; and if the Pentagon's spending drains off the majority of the country's scientists and engineers from the design and production of goods for the world market while similar personnel in other countries are primarily engaged in bringing out better products for the civilian consumer, then it seems inevitable that the American share of world manufacturing will steadily decline, and also likely that its economic growth rates will be slower than in those countries dedicated to the marketplace and less eager to channel resources into defense.

It is almost superfluous to say that these tendencies place the United States on the horns of a most acute dilemma over the longer term. Simply because it is *the* global superpower, with far more extensive military commitments than a regional Power like Japan or West Germany, it requires much larger defense forces—in just the same way as imperial Spain felt it needed a far larger army than its contemporaries and Victorian Britain insisted upon a much bigger navy than any other country. Furthermore, since the USSR is seen to be the major military threat to American interests across the globe and is clearly devoting a far greater proportion of *its* GNP to defense, American decision-makers are inevitably worried about "losing" the arms race with Russia. Yet the more sensible among these decision-makers can also perceive that the burden of armaments is debilitating the Soviet economy; and that if the two superpowers continue to allocate ever-larger shares of their national wealth into the unproductive field of armaments, the critical question might soon be: "Whose economy will decline *fastest*, relative to such expanding states as Japan, China, etc.?" A low investment in armaments may, for a globally overstretched Power like the United States, leave it feeling vulnerable everywhere; but a very heavy investment in armaments, while bringing greater security in the short term, may so erode the commercial competitiveness of the American economy that the nation will be *less* secure in the long term.

Here, too, the historical precedents are not encouraging. For it has been a common dilemma facing previous "number-one" countries that even as their relative economic strength is ebbing, the growing foreign challenges to their position have compelled them to allocate more and more of their resources into the military sector, which in turn squeezes out productive investment and, over time, leads to the downward spiral of slower growth, heavier taxes, deepening domestic splits over spending priorities, and a weakening capacity to bear the burdens of defense. If this, indeed, is the pattern of history, one is tempted to paraphrase Shaw's deadly serious quip and say: "Rome fell; Babylon fell; Scarsdale's turn will come."

In the largest sense of all, therefore, the only answer to the question increasingly debated by the public of whether the United States can preserve its existing position is "no"—for it simply has not been given to any one society to remain *permanently* ahead of all the others, because that would imply a freezing of the differentiated pattern of growth rates, technological advance, and military developments which has existed since time immemorial. On the other hand, this reference to historical precedents does *not* imply that the United States is destined to shrink to the relative obscurity of former leading Powers such as Spain or the Netherlands, or to disintegrate like the Roman and Austro-Hungarian empires; it is simply too large to do the former, and presumably too homogeneous to do the latter. Even the British analogy, much favored in the current political-science literature, is not a good one if it ignores the differences in *scale*. This can be put another way: the geographical size, population, and natural resources of the British Isles would suggest that it ought to possess roughly 3 or 4 percent of the world's wealth and power, *all other things being equal;* but it is precisely because all other things are *never* equal that a peculiar set of historical and technological circumstances permitted the British Isles to expand to possess, say, 25 percent of the world's wealth and power in its prime; and since those favorable circumstances have disappeared, all that it has been doing is returning down to its more "natural" size. In the same way, it may be argued that the geographical extent, population, and natural resources of the United States suggest that it ought to possess perhaps 16 or 18 percent of the world's wealth and power, but because of historical and technical circumstances favorable to it, that share rose to 40 percent or more by 1945; and what we are witnessing at the moment is the early decades of the ebbing away from that extraordinarily high figure to a more "natural" share. That decline is being masked by the country's enormous military capabilities at present, and also by its success in "internationalizing" American capitalism and culture. Yet even when it declines to occupy its "natural" share of the world's wealth and power, a long time into the future, the United States will still be a very significant Power in a multipolar world, simply because of its size.

The task facing American statesmen over the next decades, therefore, is to recognize that broad trends are under way, and that there is a need to "manage" affairs so that the *relative* erosion of the United States' position takes place slowly and smoothly, and is not accelerated by policies which bring merely short-term advantage but longer-term disadvantage. This involves, from the president's office downward, an appreciation that technological and therefore socioeconomic change is occurring in the world faster than ever before; that the international community is much more politically and culturally diverse than has been assumed, and is defiant of simplistic remedies offered either by Washington or Moscow to its problems; that the economic and productive power balances are no longer as favorably tilted in the United States' direction as in 1945; and that, even in the military realm, there are signs of a certain redistribution of the balances, away from a bipolar to more of a multipolar system, in which the conglomeration of American economic-cum-military strength is likely to remain larger than that possessed by any one of the others individually, but will not be as disproportionate as in the decades which immediately followed the Second World War. This, in itself, is not a bad thing if one recalls Kissinger's observations about the disadvantages of carrying out policies in what is always seen to be a bipolar world . . . ; and it may seem still less of a bad thing when it is recognized how much more Russia may be affected by the changing dynamics of world power. In all of the discussions about the erosion of American leadership, it needs to be repeated again and again that the decline referred to is relative not absolute, and is therefore perfectly natural; and that the only serious threat to the real interests of the United States can come from a failure to adjust sensibly to the newer world order.

NO

Samuel P. Huntington

THE U.S.—DECLINE OR RENEWAL?

In 1988 the United States reached the zenith of its fifth wave of declinism since the 1950s. The roots of this phenomenon lie in the political economy literature of the early 1980s that analyzed the fading American economic hegemony and attempted to identify the consequences of its disappearance. These themes were picked up in more popular and policy-oriented writings, and the combination of the budget and trade deficits plus the October 1987 stock market crash produced the environment for the spectacular success of Paul Kennedy's scholarly historical analysis in early 1988. Decline has been on everyone's mind, and the arguments of the declinists have stimulated lively public debate.[1]

Although predominantly of a liberal-leftist hue, declinist writings reflect varying political philosophies and make many different claims. In general, however, they offer three core propositions.

First, the United States is declining economically compared to other market economy countries, most notably Japan but also Europe and the newly industrializing countries. The declinists focus on economic performance and on scientific, technological and educational factors presumably related to economic performance.

Second, economic power is the central element of a nation's strength, and hence a decline in economic power eventually affects the other dimensions of national power.

Third, the relative economic decline of the United States is caused primarily by its spending too much for military purposes, which in turn is the result, in Kennedy's phrase, of "imperial overstretch," of attempting to maintain commitments abroad that the country can no longer afford. In this respect, the problems the United States confronts are similar to those of previous imperial or hegemonic powers such as Britain, France and Spain.

Declinist literature sets forth images of a nation winding down economically, living beyond its means, losing its competitive edge to more dynamic peoples, sagging under the burdens of empire, and suffering from a variety of intensifying social, economic and political ills. It follows that American

From Samuel P. Huntington, "The U.S.—Decline or Renewal?" *Foreign Affairs*, vol. 67, no. 2 (Winter 1988/89). Copyright © 1988 by the Council on Foreign Relations, Inc. Reprinted by permission of *Foreign Affairs*.

leadership must recognize and acquiesce in these conditions and accept the "need to 'manage' affairs so that the *relative* erosion of the United States' position takes place slowly and smoothly, and is not accelerated by policies which bring merely short-term advantage but longer-term disadvantage."

Before one accepts the policy conclusions of the declinists, however, their basic propositions should be critically examined. Does their argument hold water? Is the United States fundamentally a nation in decline? Or is it a nation in the midst of renewal?

The declinists point to many urgent if transitory American problems and other serious if long-standing American weakness. Overall, however, their argument fails; it is seriously weak on both the extent and causes of decline. The image of renewal is far closer to the American truth than the image of decadence purveyed by the declinists.

II

With some exceptions, declinist writings do not elaborate testable propositions involving independent and dependent variables. With a rather broad brush, they tend to paint an impressionistic picture of economic decline, mixing references to economic trends and performance (economic growth, productivity), educational data (test scores, length of school year), fiscal matters (deficits), science and technology (R&D expenditures, output of engineers), international trade and capital flows, savings and investment, and other matters. In general, however, they point to three bodies of evidence to support their argument for decline:

• first, mounting U.S. trade and fiscal deficits which, to date, the U.S. political system has shown no signs of being able to correct;

• second, continuing and even accelerating declines in U.S. shares of global economic power and in U.S. rates of growth in key areas of economic performance;

• third, sustained systemic weaknesses, including research and development practices, primary and secondary education, production of scientists and engineers, and most seriously, savings and investment patterns.

Each body of evidence requires separate examination.

Deficits. Escalating current account and budgetary deficits have been the most important changes affecting the U.S. position in the world in the 1980s. They furnish dramatic immediacy to the declinist argument. In a few short years the United States was transformed from the principal creditor nation in the world to its largest debtor. The current account balance, which had a surplus of $6.9 billion in 1981 and a small deficit of $8.7 billion in 1982, plunged to deficits of almost $140 billion in 1986 and about $160 billion in 1987. In 1981 the United States had a net credit in its international investment position of $141 billion; by 1987 it was a net debtor to the tune of $400 billion. Assets in the United States owned by foreigners roughly doubled between 1982 and 1986 to $1.3 trillion.

Coincidental with this growth of U.S. international deficits and a major cause of them was the burgeoning of the U.S. budget deficit. The annual deficit had fluctuated in the vicinity of $50 billion to $75 billion in the Ford and Carter Administrations. In 1982 it began to increase rapidly, reaching a peak of $221 billion in

FY 1986. It dropped back to $150 billion in FY 1987 and was modestly higher at about $155 billion in FY 1988.

Declinists see these deficits as evidence of fundamental weaknesses in the American economic position. They correctly point out that the massive influx of foreign funds has largely gone not for investment but for private consumption and governmental spending for defense. Such borrowing will not generate revenues with which it can be liquidated. The United States is living in a style it cannot afford and is imbued with an "eat, drink and be merry" psychology. . . .

Several points must be made to disentangle the valid from the invalid elements of these declinist arguments.

First, trade and budget deficits were not a major problem before 1982. They then mushroomed. This development may in some small measure flow from underlying weaknesses in productivity, savings and investment, but it cannot primarily result from such causes. If the deficits did come from these causes, they would have developed slowly rather than rapidly and very probably would have manifested themselves before the advent of the Reagan Administration. Instead, the deficits are overwhelmingly the result of the economic policies of the Reagan Administration: reduction in tax rates, expansion of defense spending, a strong dollar. These policies were premised on the assumption that domestic governmental spending could be curtailed and that lower tax rates would stimulate investment, growth and revenues. These assumptions did not prove to be valid, and the policies that were based on them produced the surging deficits. A different Administration with different fiscal and economic policies would have produced different results.

The deficits stem from the weaknesses, not of the American economy, but of Reagan economics. Produced quickly by one set of policies, they can be reversed almost as quickly by another set of policies.

Second, that reversal has begun and is likely to intensify. The reversal results partly from changes in policy by the Reagan Administration, partly from policies adopted by other governments and partly from the workings of the international economy, which naturally generates equilibrating tendencies. President Bush will probably move to reinforce U.S. policies designed to reduce the deficits. Through tight controls on spending, promotion of economic growth, "revenue enhancements" and, at some point, new taxes (luxury taxes, gasoline taxes and a general value-added tax are most frequently mentioned), the budget deficit is likely to be brought down to a sustainable level at which it does not pose a threat to long-term economic growth. As it is, the deficit in 1988 is only about half of what it was in 1983 as a percent of gross national product (3.1 percent versus 6.3 percent).

The trade deficit began to decrease with the rapid expansion of American exports in 1988. Its further reduction will be facilitated by budget deficit reduction, increases in manufacturing productivity (which rose significantly in the 1980s), ceilings on the exchange rate of the dollar and pressure which the U.S. government will—and must—apply under the new trade law to open up foreign markets. Cutting the trade deficit will be further enhanced, of course, to the extent that oil prices do not increase, American wage levels remain below those of the principal U.S. competitors, the developing countries' debt problem is contained and foreign economies grow at healthy rates. The trade deficit, some analysts predict, will become a trade surplus in the coming decade.

Third, both the deficits and the processes of curing them impose significant costs on the American economy. The substantial increase—absolute and net— in American foreign indebtedness means that a larger portion of U.S. GNP will be paid to foreigners in debt service. These funds will not be available for either personal consumption or savings and domestic investment. The future American standard of living will be less than it would have been otherwise. . . .

In the coming years both deficits will probably be reduced to sustainable and nonmalign proportions. Their effects, however, will be around for some while to come. But it is a mistake to view them as open sores that will continue to bleed away American strength. They are wounds that will heal, although their scars will remain.

Declining Shares. This argument has been put most explicitly by Paul Kennedy. "The U.S.A.'s share of total GNP," he says, "of world manufacturing output, and of many other indices of national efficiency has steadily declined." The United States has suffered "relative industrial decline, as measured against world production, not only in older manufactures such as textiles, iron and steel, shipbuilding, and basic chemicals, but also—although it is far less easy to judge the final outcome of this level of industrial-technological combat—in global shares of robotics, aerospace, automobiles, machine tools, and computers." American agriculture has also declined. The decline in the U.S. share of world GNP was "natural" after 1945, but it "has declined much more quickly than it should have

over the last few years" and the decline has become "precipitous."

These propositions need serious qualification. Various estimates exist of global and national gross products for various times. All have to be used with caution. Virtually all, however, show a common pattern.

The United States produced 40 to 45 percent of the gross world product in the late 1940s and early 1950s. That share declined rapidly, reaching the vicinity of 20 to 25 percent of gross world product by the late 1960s. That is roughly where it has remained.

It certainly has not declined more rapidly in the past two decades than it did during the previous two decades. Figures of the U.S. Council on Competitiveness (whose mission is to voice alarm about declining U.S. competitiveness) and from other sources show, for instance, that:

• between 1970 and 1987 the U.S. share of the gross world product varied between 22 and 25 percent and most recently was 23 percent;

• the U.S. share of world exports was 12 percent in 1970 and ten percent in 1987, and varied between nine and 14 percent in the years between;

• the U.S. share of the exports of the seven economic summit countries was 24 percent in 1970 and 23 percent in 1987, varying between 20 and 25 percent in the intervening years;

• in 1965 the United States accounted for 27.5 percent of world exports of technology-intensive products; this dropped to a low of 22.9 percent in 1980 and was back at 25.2 percent in 1984.

Overall, the United States accounts for 22 to 25 percent of the major forms of global economic activity and has done so fairly consistently for twenty years or more. The declinists are clearly right in saying that this is much less than the U.S. shares according to the same indices during the decade after World War II. A situation in which one country accounted for up to 50 percent of the global economic action was clearly a temporary product of the war. The ending of that imbalance was a major and successful goal of U.S. policy. The shift from 40–45 percent of global economic activity to 20–25 percent had generally occurred by the late 1960s. It is an increasingly remote historical event. For about a quarter-century U.S. shares in global economic activity have fluctuated within a relatively narrow range. . . .

In short, if "hegemony" means having 40 percent or more of world economic activity (a percentage Britain never remotely approximated during its hegemonic years), American hegemony disappeared long ago. If hegemony means producing 20 to 25 percent of the world product and twice as much as any other individual country, American hegemony looks quite secure.

Systemic Failures. A third set of phenomena cited by declinists consists of what might be termed systemic failures. These involved the sustained inability of America's society and its economy to function either at the levels of comparable societies or at levels presumed necessary to sustain the American role in the world. Since systemic characteristics have, by definition, been present for a long period of time, their contributions to American decline presumably stem from their cumulative impact. Among other deficiencies, declinists point to the poor quality of American primary and secondary education (manifested, for instance in the low scores of American students in comparative tests of mathe-

matics and reading skills), the small numbers of scientists and engineers produced in the United States (particularly compared to the high production of lawyers), and the complexity and inefficiency of American governmental policymaking processes. The most heavily emphasized systemic weakness, however, concerns low savings and investment rates.

Americans clearly save less than most other people. During the 1970s and 1980s U.S. gross savings as a proportion of GDP varied between 14.8 and 19.1 percent. During this period Japanese savings varied between 27.1 percent and 32.9 percent of GDP. In 1970 the Japanese savings rate was more than twice that of the United States (32.9 versus 16.1 percent); in 1987 it was almost twice the U.S. rate (28.2 versus 14.8 percent). Throughout these years U.S. savings lagged behind those of the other major industrialized democracies. . . .

As one might expect, similar patterns across countries exist with respect to investment. Between 1965 and 1984 U.S. gross fixed capital formation varied between 17 percent and 19.8 percent of GNP. That for Japan varied between 27.8 percent and 35.5 percent of GNP. The OECD average, less the United States, varied between 21.6 and 26 percent. Other measures of investment yield comparable results: the U.S. rates tend to be slightly more than half those of Japan and perhaps 75 percent of those of the other major industrialized democracies.

The significance of these differences in savings and investment can be debated, and mitigating factors may explain and compensate for some low U.S. rates. In addition, the poor U.S. performance seems not to have noticeably affected U.S. economic growth as yet. Nonetheless, clearly the declinists are right in highlighting savings and investment as long-term systemic weaknesses that require correction if economic growth is to be maintained.

Many, although not all, declinists go wrong, however, when they identify the reasons for poor U.S. performance. They argue that overexpenditure for military purposes crowds out investment for economic growth and hence leads to economic decline. Decline flows from imperialism and militarism.

This argument has little to support it, especially as applied to the United States. Kennedy's historical examples themselves suggest that the burden of empire usually becomes onerous when it amounts to ten percent or more of the society's product. Defense, however, takes only six to seven percent of American GNP. The declinists' thesis is clearly more relevant to the Soviet Union, which apparently (Soviet officials themselves claim they do not know for sure) spends 17 to 18 percent or more of its GNP for military purposes. Is this, however, a cause of Soviet decline? Its military sector is widely held to be the most technically efficient sector of the Soviet economy, and it is the only sector that is able to compete internationally. More generally, there is little comparative evidence to suggest that military expenditures are necessarily a drag on economic development. Some analysts, indeed, have argued that defense spending stimulates economic growth. One does not necessarily have to buy that argument in order to reject its opposite.

In fact, of course, how much a country invests is influenced by, but not determined by, how much it spends on defense. The Soviet Union spends close to three times as much of its GNP on defense as does the United States. It also invests more of its GNP than does the United States. This occurs at the expense of Soviet consumption. In theory, a country can allocate its resources as it wishes among consumption, defense and investment. In fact, countries make different choices, and the countries with the three largest economies in the world do exactly that. It is difficult to get comparable figures for the Soviet Union and market economy countries, and the portions of government spending which are in fact investment do not always show up in national accounts. Nonetheless, a rough prototypical allocation of GNP for the three largest economies might be as follows:

• U.S. consumption (private and public) at about 78 percent of its GNP, Japan's at 67 percent, and the Soviet Union's 56 percent;

• U.S. defense spending at about seven percent of its GNP, Japan's about one percent, and the Soviet Union's 18 percent;

• U.S. investment at roughly 17 percent of GNP, Japan's at about 30 percent of its GNP, and the Soviets' about 26 percent.

In short, the Soviets arm, the United States consumes, Japan invests. . . .

In any event, even if half the resources the United States uses for defense were shifted to investment, the American investment ratio would still lag behind the ratios of Japan and the Soviet Union. If the United States is to increase its investment ratio significantly, that increase will have to come primarily from the 75 percent or more of the GNP devoted to consumption, not from the less than seven percent committed to defense. If the United States falters economically, it will not be because U.S. soldiers, sailors and airmen stand guard on the Elbe, the Strait of Hormuz and the 38th parallel; it will be because U.S. men, women and children overindulge themselves in the comforts of the good life. Consumerism, not militarism, is the threat to American strength. The declinists have it wrong; Montesquieu got it right: "Republics end with luxury; monarchies with poverty."

III

The predominant view among declinists points to external expansion rather than internal stagnation as the principal cause of the decline of nations. This argument runs counter to a tradition of political thought going back to Plato and Aristotle which focuses on the internal ability of a society to renew itself. According to modern formulations of this view, a society declines when bureaucratic stagnation, monopoly, caste, hierarchy, social rigidity, organizational obesity and arteriosclerosis make innovation and adaptation difficult or impossible. As societies age, these characteristics tend to become more predominant.

In his sophisticated theoretical analysis which departs from the declinist mainstream, Mancur Olson argues this point persuasively, explaining the decline of nations by the development of vested interests or "distributional coalitions" that reduce economic efficiency and constrain economic growth. Societies whose social, economic and political structures are substantially destroyed through war, revolution or other upheaval grow rapidly. Over time, however, distributional coalitions develop and economic dynamism wanes. Although Olson does not discuss it in his book, the prototypical contemporary case of an economy grinding to a halt because of the constrictions imposed by distributional coalitions is, of course, the Soviet Union under Brezhnev.

Successful societies, in contrast, are those that find ways short of their own destruction to sustain the dynamism of their youth. The structure of such societies will presumably encourage competition, mobility, fluidity, pluralism and openness—all qualities that prevent a society from becoming mired in a network of collusive deals in which everyone benefits to everyone's disadvantage.

Viewed from this perspective, the United States is less likely to decline than any other major country. It is distinguished by the openness of its economy, society and politics. Its engines of renewal are competition, mobility and immigration.

Competition and opposition to monopoly, both public and private, are hallmarks of American society. The United States led the way in the modern world in attempting to institutionalize antitrust and antimonopoly practices in business. Government bureaucracy in the United States is weaker and more divided against itself than bureaucracies in most other countries. State-owned enterprises are rare. New companies are created— and go bankrupt—on a scale unknown in European societies. Small, new companies have been responsible for the bulk of the twenty million new jobs created in the past decade.

Labor unions have never been strong and are declining. American universities, it has been argued, are the best in the world because of the intense competition among them for faculty, students and money. Secondary education, it might be noted, is, in contrast, overwhelmingly a public monopoly and is inferior as a result; widely considered proposals for improving it are to introduce competition among schools for students and state support.

In comparison to other societies, individual mobility, both horizontal and vertical, is extremely high. Far more rapidly than elsewhere, American workers shift from job to job, up and down the income scale, in and out of the poverty brackets. People move from region to region at about three times the rate they do in European countries. With the notable exception of race, ascriptive obstacles to upward mobility have been relatively minimal compared to other societies.

The continuing flow of immigrants into American society reflects the opportunities it offers and contributes to its renewal. Historically, first- and second-generation immigrants have been a dynamic force in American society. Under the Immigration Act of 1965, about 600,000 legal immigrants enter the United States each year. Thousands more enter illegally. These newcomers renew the pools of cheap labor, entrepreneurial skill, intellectual talent and driving ambition to succeed. Thirty-six of the 114 American citizens who won Nobel prizes in science and medicine between 1945 and 1984 were born elsewhere. In the 1940s and 1950s American scientific and intellectual life was tremendously enriched by Jewish refugees from Hitler and the children of East European Jewish immigrants before World War II. Today Asian-Americans sweep the intellectual honors. (About two percent of the total population, they make up 14 percent of the 1988 freshman class at Harvard.) In the coming decades, immigration also means that the American population will continue to grow, unlike those of many European countries and will remain relatively young, unlike that of Japan.

IV

The ultimate test of a great power is its ability to renew its power. The competition, mobility and immigration characteristic of American society enable the United States to meet this test to a far greater extent than any other great power, past or present. They are the central sources of American strength. They are supplemented by three aspects of the American position in international affairs.

First, in comparison to other major countries, American strength is peculiarly multidimensional. Mao Zedong reportedly said that power grows out of the barrel of a gun; the declinists see power coming out of a belching smokestack. In fact, power comes in various forms and international influence can stem from very different sources. The Soviet Union, it has often been said, is a one-dimensional superpower, its international position resting almost exclusively on its military might. Whatever influence Saudi Arabia has in international affairs flows from its oil reserves. Japan's influence has come first from its manufacturing performance and then from its control of financial resources. . . .

In contrast to other countries, the United States ranks extraordinarily high in almost all the major sources of national power: population size and education, natural resources, economic development, social cohesion, political stability, military strength, ideological appeal, diplomatic alliances, technological achievement. It is, consequently, able to sustain reverses in any one arena while maintaining its overall influence stemming from other sources. At present, no country can mount a multidimensional challenge to the United

States, and with one conceivable exception no country seems likely to be able to do so in the relevant future.

Second, U.S. influence also flows from its structural position in world politics. The United States benefits from being geographically distant from most major areas of world conflict, from having a past relatively free of overseas imperialism, from espousing an economic and political philosophy that is antistatist and, hence, less likely to be threatening to other peoples, from being involved in a historically uniquely diversified network of alliances and from having a sense, stronger in the past than more recently, of identification with universal international institutions.

These factors pull the United States into a leadership role in dealing with international problems and disputes. They help create a demand for the American presence overseas. Slogans of "U.S. go home!" may command headlines, but in many regions the underlying fear is that the United States might just do that. Neither Germans, French, Dutch nor (some say) the Soviets are eager for the United States to pull out of Europe. Many Filipinos act as if they wished the bases removed from their country, and some may actually want that to happen, but many others worry deeply that an American withdrawal from Southeast Asia would leave them to the tender mercies of the Soviets and the Japanese. Long before diplomatic relations existed between Washington and Beijing, China supported the American presence in Japan and Korea. . . .

Finally, no alternative to hegemonic power, with one possible exception, seems likely to emerge in the coming century. A short while ago, of course, it was widely thought that the Soviet Union would perform that role. Mr. Khrushchev talked confidently about the U.S.S.R. overtaking the United States economically and the grandchildren of Western capitalists playing under red flags.

These seem not just forlorn but bizarre hopes. The Soviet Union still has the resources, size and military strength of a superpower, but it has lost economically, ideologically and diplomatically. Conceivably, the Gorbachev reforms could start a process that would put the Soviet Union back into competition to become the number-one actor on the world stage, but at the moment the success of his efforts is in doubt and the impact of the reforms, if they are successful, will not necessarily enhance Soviet power.

Currently, the popular choice—and the choice of the declinists—for the country that will supersede the United States is, of course, Japan. "The American Century is over," a former U.S. official has said. "The big development in the latter part of the century is the emergence of Japan as a major superpower." With all due respect to Clyde Prestowitz, this proposition will not hold up. Japan has neither the size, natural resources, military strength, diplomatic affiliates nor, most important, the ideological appeal to be a twentieth-century superpower.

In a world of instant communication, widespread literacy and social mobilization, a superpower has to stand for an idea with appeal beyond its borders. In recent history the United States and the Soviet Union have done this. Today the message of the Soviet Union is tattered and apparently rejected, in part by its own leadership. The appeal of the American message of political democracy and economic liberalism has never been stronger Conceivably, Japan could also develop a message to the world, but that would require fundamental changes in Japanese culture and society. . . .

The declinists play an indispensable role in preventing what they are predicting. Contrary to Professor Kennedy, the more Americans worry about the health of their society, the healthier they are. The current wave will serve a useful historical function if it encourages the new president and Congress to take prompt and effective actions on the deficits and to inaugurate longer-term policies designed to promote saving and investment.

"If Sparta and Rome perished," asked Rousseau, "what State can hope to endure forever?" The obvious answer is "no state" and that may be the right answer. The United States is not immortal and American preeminence is not inevitable. Yet, some states endure for extraordinary lengths of time, and little reason exists to assume that recent prophecies of American decline are more accurate than earlier ones. Every reason exists, however, to encourage belief in such prophecies in order to disprove them. Happily, the self-renewing genius of American politics does exactly that

NOTES

1. Apart from the more academic international political economy literature, declinist works that have been widely discussed in policy debates and the general media include: Walter Russell Mead, *Mortal Splendor*, Boston: Houghton Mifflin, 1987; David P. Calleo, *Beyond American Hegemony*, New York: Basic Books, 1987; and, of course, Paul Kennedy, *The Rise and Fall of the Great Powers: Economic Change and Military Conflict from 1500 to 2000*, New York: Random House, 1987. In discussing declinist ideas, I will rely primarily on Kennedy's writings and statements, since they have had the greatest impact on public debate in the United States.

POSTSCRIPT

Is America Declining?

Despite disagreement over whether or not the United States is declining, it is inescapable that other nations are growing and are likely to continue to grow in productivity, military power, and international influence. These nations include those of the European Economic Community and, most impressively, those of Asia. It is also possible that the Soviet Union, Eastern Europe, and Latin America will revive and produce a larger share of the world output. Therefore, even if America continues to prosper, it is likely to represent a decreasing share of world productivity.

Does the United States strive to be *the* dominant power in the world? Or is the United States a powerful leader in an alliance of nations arrayed against another bloc in arrangements akin to traditional balance-of-power politics? Those who see an America in decline believe that U.S. policymakers hold the former view. Walter Russell Mead urges cutback in American commitments in *Mortal Splendor: The American Empire in Transition* (Houghton Mifflin, 1987). Like Kennedy, Mead traces parallels with past empires and concludes that decline is inevitable, but he maintains that America can shape its post-imperial future. David P. Calleo, in *Beyond American Hegemony: The Future of the Western Alliance* (Basic Books, 1987), argues that Europe must bear a greater share of military costs.

Decline theory is rejected by critics who conclude that America has been strengthened by its commitments abroad and economic policies at home. For Norman Podhoretz, the issue is not overstretching or overspending but national will. In *The Present Danger* (Simon & Schuster, 1980) he posed the question: "Do we have the will to reverse the decline of American power?" Owen Harries rejects Kennedy's arguments in "The Rise of American Decline," *Commentary* (May 1988). Barbara W. Tuchman, in "A Nation in Decline?" *The New York Times Magazine* (September 20, 1987), blames decline on the incompetence and inefficiency that have resulted from "a deteriorating ethic." Now that the Soviet bloc is being completely transformed, the American empire will be redefined as well. A volume that looks at American decline in terms of world system theory is Terry Boswell and Albert Bergesen, *America's Changing Role in the World System* (Praeger, 1987).

Whatever our conclusions, the debate prompted by the theory of decline compels us to examine the nature and consequences of American values and goals in relation to the rest of the world. As the rest of the world changes so dramatically, America has to redefine its values and mission in the world.

CONTRIBUTORS
TO THIS VOLUME

EDITORS

KURT FINSTERBUSCH received his bachelor's degree in history from Princeton University in 1957, and a bachelor of Divinity degree from Grace Theological Seminary in 1960. His Ph.D. in Sociology, from Columbia University, was conferred in 1969. He is the author of several books, including *Understanding Social Impacts* (Sage Publications, 1980), and *Social Research for Policy Decisions* (Wadsworth Publishing, 1980), with Annabelle Bender Motz. He is currently teaching at the University of Maryland, College Park, and is the academic editor for the Dushkin Publishing Group's *Annual Editions: Sociology.*

GEORGE McKENNA received his bachelor's degree from the University of Chicago in 1959, his M.A. from the University of Massachusetts in 1962, and his Ph.D. from Fordham University in 1967. He has been teaching political science at City College of New York since 1963. Among his publications are *American Populism* (Putnam, 1974) and *American Politics: Ideals and Realities* (McGraw-Hill, 1976). He has written articles in the fields of American government and political theory, and he is coeditor of *Taking Sides: Clashing Views on Controversial Political Issues.* He is the author of the textbook *The Drama of Democracy: American Government and Politics* (DPG, 1990).

STAFF

Marguerite L. Egan   Program Manager
Brenda S. Filley   Production Manager
Whit Vye   Designer
Libra Ann Cusack   Typesetting Supervisor
Juliana Arbo   Typesetter
Jean Bailey   Graphics Coordinator
Diane Barker   Editorial Assistant

AUTHORS

EDWARD BANFIELD is professor emeritus of urban studies at Harvard University and author of a number of articles and books on urban problems, including *The Unheavenly City* (Little, Brown, 1970).

DAVID L. BAZELON is a senior judge of the United States Court of Appeals for the District of Columbia circuit.

PETER L. BERGER is professor of sociology and religion and director of the Institute for the Study of Economic Culture at Boston University.

LESTER R. BROWN is president of the Worldwatch Institute, a research organization with an interdisciplinary approach to global environmental problem-solving.

HAL BURDETT is director of information at the Population Institute in Washington, D.C.

NOAM CHOMSKY is the Institute Professor in the Department of Linguistics and Philosophy at the Massachusetts Institute of Technology.

NICHOLAS DAVIDSON is a writer. He is author of *The Failure of Feminism* (Prometheus, 1988) and *Gender Sanity* (University Press of America, 1989).

JOHN J. DiIULIO, JR., is associate professor of politics and public affairs at Princeton University and was recently a guest scholar at The Brookings Institution.

CYNTHIA FUCHS EPSTEIN is professor of sociology at the Graduate Center of the City University of New York and resident scholar at the Russell Sage Foundation. She is the author of *Women in Law* (Basic Books, 1981).

CHRISTOPHER FLAVIN is vice president of research at the Worldwatch Institute.

WERNER FORNOS is president of the Population Institute, based in Washington, D.C.

MARILYN FRENCH is a novelist and literary critic. She is author of *The Women's Room* (Summit Books, 1977) and *James Joyce's Ulysses* (Harvard University Press, 1976). She received a Ph.D. from Harvard University and has taught at Harvard University, Hofstra University, and College of the Holy Cross.

JOHN KENNETH GALBRAITH is an internationally renowned economist who, before his retirement in 1975, was Paul M. Warburg Professor of Economics at Harvard University.

GEORGE GILDER is program director of the International Center for Economic Policy Studies. He was a fellow at the John F. Kennedy School of Government at Harvard University and a speechwriter for Nelson Rockefeller and Ronald Reagan. He is a widely published social commentator.

STEVEN GOLDBERG is associate professor and acting chair of the Department of Sociology at City College, City University of New York.

EDWARD S. HERMAN is professor emeritus of finance at the Wharton School of Business, University of Pennsylvania.

SAMUEL P. HUNTINGTON is professor of government and director of the John·M. Olin Institute for Strategic Studies at Harvard University.

CHRISTOPHER JENCKS is professor of sociology and urban affairs at Northwestern University. His books include *Who Gets Ahead?* and *Inequality*.

PAUL KENNEDY is the J. Richardson Dilworth Professor of History at Yale University and the author of several books on contemporary international relations.

SHEILA KINKADE is a free-lance writer for the *Washington Post* and the *Washington Times*. She is a former researcher for the Population Institute.

The late LAWRENCE KOHLBERG was professor of education and director of the Center for Moral Education at Harvard University. He wrote many articles based on his research into the relationship of cognitive growth and ethicality, and he compiled a volume entitled *Essays on the Philosophy of Moral Development*—which has become a classic.

The late GERALD J. KRUIJER was professor emeritus of applied sociology at the University of Amsterdam. He wrote about the problems of poverty and development, particularly in the Caribbean and Latin American countries.

CHARLES E. LINDBLOM is professor emeritus of political science at Yale University. He is currently writing a book about "how society fails to use knowledge and misuses knowledge, both lay and scientific."

GLENN C. LOURY is professor of political economy at Harvard University's John F. Kennedy School of Government.

DAVID MEYER is a former researcher for the Population Institute. He is currently studying law at the University of Michigan.

THOMAS A. W. MILLER is a senior vice president and the publication director at Roper, the polling organization, in New York City. He is also the editor of *The Public Pulse*,

Roper's newsletter on American attitudes, lifestyles, and behavior.

CLAUDIA MILLS is a graduate of Wellesley College and Princeton University, and she is currently engaged in doctoral studies in philosophy at the University of Maryland.

CHARLES MURRAY is a senior fellow at the Manhattan Institute for Policy Research.

RAY PERCIVAL is a Ph.D. student in philosophy at the London School of Economics.

JEFFREY H. REIMAN is professor of criminal justice at American University. He is a member of the American Society of Criminology and the American Philosophical Association. His writings include *In Defense of Political Philosophy* (Harper, 1972) and *The Police in Society* (Lexington, 1974).

WILLIAM RUSHER is a senior fellow at the Claremont Institute. He is a former publisher of the *National Review.*

WILLIAM RYAN is professor of psychology at Boston College and a consultant in the fields of mental health, community planning, and social problems. Besides *Blaming the Victim*, his publications include *Distress in the City* (UPB, 1969).

HERMAN SCHWARTZ teaches law at American University and is

the director of the Wm. O. Douglas Inquiry into the State of Individual Freedom.

JULIAN L. SIMON is a fellow at the Heritage Foundation and teaches economics at the University of Maryland.

WILLIAM SIMON is a former U.S. Treasury Department secretary who writes on topics of current social and economic interest.

DAVID VOGEL is a professor in the School of Business Administration at the University of California, Berkeley. He is author of *Fluxuating Fortunes: The Political Power of Business in America* (Basic Books, 1989).

SHIRLEY WILKINS is former president of Roper, the polling organization, and currently performs consulting work for the Virginia Slims American Women Opinion Poll, a series conducted annually by Roper since 1970.

CHARLES V. WILLIE, professor of education and urban studies at Harvard Graduate School of Education, is a former president of the Eastern Sociological Society. He has authored several books on minority relations, including *Black/Brown/White Relations* (Transaction Books, 1977).

JAMES Q. WILSON is the Collins Professor of Management at UCLA. Previously he was the Henry Lee

Shattuck Professor of Government at Harvard University for many years. He has published several successful books on crime and American government.

WILLIAM JULIUS WILSON is the Lucy Flower Distinguished Service Professor of Sociology and Public Policy at the University of Chicago.

EDWARD C. WOLF is an environmental consultant and a former researcher for the Worldwatch Institute.

EDWARD A. WYNNE is a professor in the College of Education at the University of Illinois, Chicago Circle.

INDEX

T'MOAN:
GUARDIANS
OF THE
SECRET TEMPLE OF GOD

AN AMAZING JUNGLE ADVENTURE TAKING THE
GOSPEL TO UNDISCOVERED TRIBES
IN THE 21ˢᵀ CENTURY

BY STEVE HYDE

Second Printing

Published by:
   Words of Life Ministries
   P.O. Box 2581
   Phnom Penh, 3
   Kingdom of Cambodia

Sketches by Phal Putti from photographs taken by Steven Hyde.

Cover Concept by Steve Miller.

Printed in the Kingdom of Cambodia

ISBN: 978-9-9963-4009-3
ISBN number issued by the National Library of Cambodia

TABLE OF CONTENTS

DEDICATION

I dedicate this work to the memory of two men who greatly influenced my life, giving me the godly motivation to take the gospel to the remotest parts of the earth. Both died serving God: one as a martyr and one passed away while serving the people he loved. First is my father, and the second is Pin Long, who was instrumental in leading the T'moan people to Christ.

William "Bill" Hyde, my father, was a great inspiration and model for my life as a teacher and effective trainer of church leaders. He lived and worked among those who desired to kill him and showed no fear. Without fear of man, he served in dangerous places. With the fear of God, he lived his life seeking always to be in the will of God to accomplish his divine purposes. His life demonstrated a willingness to remain in the perfect will of God no matter what sacrifices or burdens he would have to bear. His death as a martyr demonstrated the way he lived his life and gave witness to the Lord Jesus Christ. He is survived by his wife, who remained a missionary in the Philippines, two adult sons, their wives, and three grandchildren. He never had a chance to hold or play with his grandchildren.

WILLIAM PAUL HYDE

FEBRUARY 2, 1944 — MARCH 4, 2003

MARTYRED IN DAVAO CITY, PHILIPPINES

AFTER 25 YEARS OF SERVICE.

The second influential person is Pin Long, a great companion and fellow minister to the people of Kracheh province in Cambodia. His life was full of hardships after being given to the Khmer Rouge to become a child soldier at the age of nine and was wounded many times in battle. He achieved the rank of commander of a unit of about three-hundred men in the Khmer Rouge forces in Kracheh province. As a believer who heard the gospel late in his life, his passion for life and for people opened many doors for the gospel in the last few years of his life. Whole villages were opened to the gospel because of his fearless travels to remote villages and his compassion for people. Pin died in his sleep, lying in a hammock, at the young age of forty-five while caring for impoverished tribal children. He leaves behind a wife, eight children, and hundreds of believers, to carry on the passion of their father (spiritual or biological).

PIN LONG

1961 — OCTOBER 18, 2006

PIN DIED IN KRACHEH PROVINCE SERVING CHRIST.

ACKNOWLEDGEMENTS

May all glory and honor be for the Lord Jesus Christ. We are simply his servants and humble tools in His hands.

I would first like to acknowledge the willingness of the T'moan people to receive us as friends. Though they are ostracized and oppressed, they never cease to befriend anyone who comes to them. It is our prayer that more people would return their kindness with gratitude, rather than seeing an opportunity to exploit innocent people for the natural resources where they live.

To Pin, Ang and Poline, my colleagues and partners in seeking the T'moan—thank you for your hard work, passion and concern for the people who have not heard. Thank you to all our wives for enduring, supporting and encouraging us in God's work: Noit (Steve's wife), Khon Nic (Pin's wife), Chmran Milia (Ang's wife), and Raksmie (Poline's wife).

A special appreciation goes to my wife, Noit, who has always been a solid helper in the ministry whether it be taking care of the kids at home, overseeing the children's centers or teaching a discipleship class whenever it is needed. I could never have imagined a more wonderful life partner in all the world. And to my children, Paul, Anna, and Odom who missed their daddy and prayed for me when I was gone. I hope that when you are older you will have an even greater passion for the people who have not heard of Jesus. I love you all so much.

I would like to thank my Mom, Lyn Hyde, Shirley Seale, Mary Tice and Elisabeth Brooks for their hard work editing this manuscript as well as others who wish to remain anonymous.

Also a special thanks to Pastor Dave Bryan and the Church of Glad Tidings in Yuba City, California who have been such a wonderful blessing and encouragement. They even provided my family and me with time to rest and write so that others can hear about the mighty things God has done among the T'moan people. Thank you, GT, for being such supportive church family.

INTRODUCTION

What you are about to read is the true story of four men who had a passion to tell people about Jesus in one of the most remote places on this earth. They desired this, not in an effort for political gain or self-benefit, but in obedience to the final command of the Lord Jesus Christ before he ascended into heaven. Jesus commanded, *"Therefore go and make disciples of all nations, baptizing them in the name of the Father and of the Son and of the Holy Spirit, and teaching them to obey everything I have commanded you. And surely I am with you always, to the very end of the age"* (Matthew 28:19-20).

All of these men personally know the power of God to transform a person's life for the better. It is their desire that all who read this story may not exalt the instruments of God's hand, mere people, but be encouraged in their own lives to share Christ with others in obedience to the command of Christ . . . especially to those who have never heard. All glory belongs to the Lord Jesus Christ.

This is the story of how four persistent men, in obedience to Christ, were instrumental in leading nearly an entire nomadic people group to accept Christ at one time. This people group lives in the jungles of northeastern Cambodia. This is not a missionary tale of long ago; rather, it is a recent testimony of the acts of the Holy Spirit in the 21st century.

Cambodia has long been a country notorious for civil war, grotesque violence, and seemingly constant social and political upheaval. Since Cambodia became independent from the French colonialists in 1954, it has faced constant social transition, degradation, and often traumatic political maneuvering as elite families vie for power and money.

Cambodia has been in a period of relative peace and freedom since 1993, and currently has earned a reputation for being one the most corrupt countries in the world—a place where justice, personal security, and hope are rare commodities.

Yet, in spite of this, there has come a semblance of religious freedom, which in 1,200 years of recorded Cambodian history has never been known. In this brief era of freedom there has been an incredible hunger, openness, and desire for personal life change. This can only be explained as a powerful outpouring of the Holy Spirit.

This outpouring has not developed as Western culture would expect. Past Western revivals are often characterized by dramatic personal experiences of emotional and moving moments of repentance and seeking of holiness. In many well known Western revivals, such as the Welsh revival, Haystack revival, the Great Awakenings in America and Azusa Street revival, there was not only religious revival but also social transformation.

The Cambodian revival rarely exhibits emotional outbursts, but is characterized by people coming to the conclusion that Jesus is truly the only hope for their own sinful character and for their nation. In 1993, scarcely anyone in Cambodia had heard of Jesus, much less heard the message of the gospel of salvation. Freedom of religion had always been suppressed, so the name of Jesus had never been heard by the majority of the eleven million Cambodians.

Today when people hear about Jesus, their response usually falls into one of two categories, with little variation. One choice is to blindly follow old traditions and what they understand to be the religious culture of Cambodia (usually without having any real understanding of what that means). The other response is that Cambodians come to the realization that Jesus truly is the only hope for their lives and accept him whole-heartedly.

These responses today are representative of what we find in Scripture as well. During the passion of Christ, people were polarized in their understanding of him. At our Lord's crucifixion, two thieves were crucified along side Christ, and each chose a different path. One considered his own benefit, his wretched life, and passed on into eternal hell. The other saw his own helplessness and need for a savior. In his last moments of life, he accepted Jesus as his Savior and went on to eternity with the Messiah.

These two responses are the same basic responses seen today in Cambodia. It is either complete acceptance or complete rejection, but seldom apathy.

What this story will reveal, through the lives of the T'moan people, is that salvation truly is a process and a path toward righteousness. While the acceptance of the Lordship of Christ is instantaneous and the eternal balance is shifted, a holy life and maturity in Christ are not immediate. This is just as true in the heartland of America as it is in the jungles of Cambodia. Salvation for an entire people group is not a final spiritual victory, but is a milestone on a path following the perfect will of God to its divine conclusion. The Kingdom of God in its fullness is truly closer than ever before. This story is a jungle adventure, a struggle for survival, a story of stubborn persistence, and the courage of four men who had a vision to find and bring an encounter with Jesus to a remote tribe of people called 'T'moan'.

1

THE PHANTOM TRIBE

My face is pressed against the airplane window. I have a crick in my neck and I am straining to look into the jungle canopy below. I am looking for trails, houses, or for cultivated land. . . any signs of life. My hands are busily writing notes about the features of the land and any jungle paths I see while I dare not look away from the window. From twenty-seven thousand feet it is really hard to make out life below. When I fly over Cambodia I am always desperately looking for people who live beneath the vast jungle canopy. Many times I have gone back to the areas that the commercial flights have gone over and tried to find the trails to the villages.

THE JUNGLE SMASHER TRUCK!

In Cambodia, I have two modes of transport. First, I have an old, beat up Toyota four-wheel drive with a powerful winch on the front. That is my jungle smasher truck! I have driven through countless rivers, up mountain trails, around or through massive bomb craters and one time I even drove up a waterfall! Once I heard from a villager there was a seven-tiered waterfall in Northwest Cambodia that very few people had ever seen. I was shown the trail, and they said the falls were some three miles back into the mountains. I decided that I would rather smash through the jungle than walk three miles, so with our picnic gear and a load of friends we headed straight into the jungle brush. Small trees are easy to push over. Twice we came across illegal loggers who abandoned their chainsaws in the middle of the path as they heard our truck coming through the jungle. They probably thought forest rangers in a tank were bearing down on them. We called out to them not to fear and to come back and get their chainsaws. After crisscrossing back and forth across a shallow flowing creek for about an hour, we finally broke through to a beautiful, cascading waterfall. It was worth the drive!

The winch was my best investment ever for the pickup! There was a movie a few years back which showed a jeep getting winched up a tree. . . I want to assure you it was not a photographic trick, it is not only possible. . . I have done it! When we first traveled by road to Kracheh province back in the early nineties, we had to cross sixty-four make shift bridges. My wife was my guide the whole way. The "bridge" was only two trees cut down placed parallel across the ravines. My wife would help me to line the tires up to the tree trunks and drive across. My wife would never ride with me crossing those bridges, but would instead stand on the other side guiding me and watching the wheels closely. Only once did we slip off a bridge, but the vehicle did not fall completely down, it got hung up on the axle. After many hours, we were eventually able to jack the wheel back onto the bridge and make our way across the steep ravine.

STEVE'S MOTORCYCLE

My other mode of transport, and my favorite, is my motorcycle. It is a small dirt bike—a 250cc Honda. If the motorcycle was too big, it would be too heavy to pick up when I fall down, but if it is too small it does not have the power I need to drive through sandy jungle trails, cross through swollen rivers, or jump out of a ravine. Many times we have to walk or push our motorcycles, which is a miserable job, but when the motorcycles are going . . . it is a much faster way to travel.

Motorcycles in Cambodia are family vehicles. Like nearly every other Cambodian family, my wife Noit, and I have both driven motorcycles for all of our married life. The truck we keep for long distance travel and for when we take lots of people into a remote area. When we attend wedding parties, go to church, visit families, or just drive to work, we usually do so on our family motorcycle. Noit sits on the very back with Anna wedged between me and her, and our son Paul sits in front of me on the gas tank. The addition of our third child Odom makes motorcycle excursions more difficult. However, now that he is getting older, he is getting too tall to sit on the gas tank because then I cannot see.

Cambodians often joke that they are much smarter than the Japanese because the Japanese build their Honda motor- cycles for seating two people, but we can ride up to nine. For public

CAMBODIAN " Bus" (MOTORCYCLE CART)

transport, Cambodians will attach a small 150cc motorcycle to a cart with which they can pull up to forty people (as much as a school bus in America).

Working in rural Cambodia, if you want to go somewhere, it usually requires a significant effort. Often telephone service is not available, and since there is no postal system, even the simplest messages require a significant amount of travel. One night, Noit and I had our six month old baby Anna with us, but we needed to visit a Stieng family in a remote village near the Vietnamese border. We were rushed for time, so we decided we would head out before it was dark to stay in the village that night. We took our truck and on the way, our baby got a fever that rapidly got worse. Anna was in great pain and screaming constantly. We were six to eight hours from any hospital, but I recommended that we go ahead and press on to the village for the night and early the next morning we would head for the hospital in Phnom Penh. It is very dangerous to drive at night in Cambodia, not just because of the lack of electric lighting, but because of the prevalence of thieves and drunks.

As we headed off the main road down a slippery muddy trail, I knew we were going to be in trouble. I put on the brakes but we continued to slide down the slick muddy slope, finally resting in a muddy ditch halfway down the mountain. Noit just gave me one of those looks! After thirty minutes or so, we were free from the mud and I assured her that we were doing the right thing as we headed deeper into the jungle. Toward the bottom of the hill, the slippery mud again took over and we were stuck fast. We met one of the people from the village and I asked them if they could take my wife and baby into the village and let me worry about the truck. Walking on the slick mud was not easy either, and required bare feet, but it would be better to get Noit and Anna into a dry home in the village and let us men worry about getting the truck out of the mud. After what seemed like hours, we finally made it into the village. Anna was still screaming and in obvious pain, but all we could do was to pray for her. Noit looked at me and commented, "I think we are the only people in the world who, when their daughter is sick, go deeper into the jungle, rather than away from the jungle and toward a hospital."

"Well, wherever we go, we really only have Jesus, but I promise before dawn tomorrow I will get us out of the jungle," I said. It was not until the next day that Anna's fever finally broke. After another day's worth of driving we were able to get Anna to a hospital in Phnom Penh and soon she was fine.

Life in Cambodia is hard and the difficulties in travel just make it harder. There are few roads and plenty of villages. The population is scattered sparsely throughout the country.

Unofficially there are three classes of people in Cambodia: city people, rice farming people, and the jungle people. The city people are those who are often the most educated and wealthy and are those involved in business and politics. The rice farming people are the vast majority of the population, probably seventy percent, and they make their living in small villages scattered around flat areas good for planting rice. City people often look down on the rice farming people. The third class are the "untouchables" of Cambodia. They are called jungle people. Jungle people are mostly minorities. Cambodia has at least thirty-one small minority tribes who all have their own language and are the most uneducated and deprived of them all. They are looked down upon by everyone in Cambodia. To insult someone people will often call others "jungle people" to belittle them.

Jesus had a clear mission. "*The Spirit of the Lord is on me, because he has anointed me to preach good news to the poor. He has sent me to proclaim freedom for the prisoners and recovery of sight for the blind, to release the oppressed, to proclaim the year of the Lord's favor.*" (Luke 4:18-19). The minorities of Cambodia are the poorest, blinded in their ignorance, and the most oppressed of all Cambodians. Certainly Jesus has a special place in his heart for these.

Among the ethnic minorities in Cambodia there is a legend that tribes have passed from generation to generation. This is the legend of a jungle tribe called "*Pnong pahoung trung*" or literally in the Khmer language, "a minority group with a hole in their chest." Every tribe in Cambodia, especially in Northeastern Cambodia, speaks of this legendary people group convinced they exist.

For years, while visiting and working among many ethnic minorities in Cambodia, I have listened to people talk about the tribe with a hole in their chest. At those times it was quite hard for me to imagine an entire tribe with a literal hole in their chest. I suspected a child might have been born at one time with a defect, such as a 'pigeon chest' or other abnormality. Perhaps when seen by others, I speculated, the legend of "the people with a hole in their chest" was born. For whatever reason, this legend has passed through the generations among the tribal people.

When meeting new people, I have asked about the legend of this people group. When they confirmed they knew the legend, my follow-up question was, "Do you know where they are?" The answer was usually, "They are very far;" or "They live in the deep jungle." But no one knew the tribe's true location.

During my years in Cambodia, I have always desired to search for the next town, the next village, the next tribe, beyond where I had previously been. My life verse has come from the passion of the Apostle Paul in Romans 15:20. "*It has always been my ambition to preach the gospel where Christ was not known, so that I would not be building on someone else's foundation.*"

I can remember vividly one day, traveling through the jungle looking for unreached peoples, being stirred by a compelling fire burning within me. On that day, as I was navigating a rugged jungle path on my motorcycle, the gravity of what my companions and I were doing in the spiritual realm overcame me. Trudging through the jungle, sweating profusely in the stagnant hot air with wounds hurting from minor falls and side-swiping branches, suddenly it was as if all discomfort left and the presence of God came over me. I could view with my spiritual eyes the second return of Christ.

Jesus promised that when all the nations (ethnic groups) hear the gospel of the Kingdom, he will then return. I began to weep. Suddenly I thought, "What if the last people group to hear the gospel on the earth is around the next corner or across the next river? What if, after I share the gospel with the next person out here in the jungle, the heavens open up and Jesus comes riding on a white stallion through the sky with millions of angels following him in a vast, celestial army?" What a glorious day that would be! Jesus would return to fulfill the Kingdom of God on Earth!

Passion for the people who have never heard the gospel of Jesus Christ stirred me that day, no matter what pain, discomfort, and challenges we faced. That same passion continues to burn within me. It keeps me searching and going forward, regardless of the difficulties, until every person has heard the gospel.

2

EXPEDITION ONE:

NEEDLE IN A HAY STACK

At night back in my house in Phnom Penh, I would spend hours looking over terrain maps of Cambodia. I knew that people could live anywhere there was water, so I would look for possible streams or jungle depressions that could hold water and support a community. One place that always fascinated me was an area of Northeastern Cambodia. It was inaccessible due to lack of roads, but what captured my imagination was the presence of two fairly sizable rivers and the lack of villages (on the official maps). This area was in the heart of the Northeast, which is a region of many small ethnic minority groups. These minority groups are famous for being able to survive off of the land for generations without ever setting foot into a developed town. Electricity, paved roads, and motorcycles were all foreign to these people who relied on elephants for their heavy work and transportation.

ELEPHANT AT WORK

The land in this area was not flat. It was hilly, but with no large mountains. Khmer people are generally centered around the production of rice and as such require flat ground, not hills. However, ethnic minorities often have small farms, like plantations, in the jungle where they practice slash and burn agriculture and also harvest naturally growing jungle plants for food. I knew there would be people there. It was inconceivable that in a country where the population is extremely spread out, there could be such a large area completely devoid of any population centers, even though they may be very small villages.

The journey to find this isolated people group would not be easy. The search area alone was some fifty kilometers east to west and eighty kilometers north to south (4,000 square kilometers or approximately 1,500 square miles). Such an area is five times the size of the entire nation of Singapore or approximately half the size of Yellowstone National Park. The search area was almost the same size as Rhode Island, the smallest state in the United States. That is a big area to try and find a small village—an area defined by a massive jungle canopy, no roads, no landmarks and a gaping blank spot on the national map of Cambodia. . . a needle in a hay stack.

We had the heart for a jungle expedition, but we did not have the needed equipment. To walk would have taken weeks. I had a dirt bike, but my companions did not. The only motorcycles they had were made for use on Korean city streets. A 100cc Daelim motorcycle, with only a six-inch clearance, does not do very well in a jungle environment where the path is a treacherous combination of rotten tree stumps, rocks, and thorny vines crisscrossing animal paths. In spite of this, we decided to make plans to start off on our adventure.

In areas where people had made trails, the path was usually made for walking. So stumps were ignored. A little stump however, has a devastating shock on a small motor scooter, as we soon found out. Travel required constant zigzagging back and forth trying to avoid the stumps and other obstacles along the way. There is no such thing as a straight path in the jungle--not even for ten feet.

One of my companions, riding one of the small city scooters, hit the engine block so hard on a stump that it tore out the engine bolts that held it to the frame. The small tires caused other problems with the scooters. They often bogged down in sand or slipped on slick mud, depending on the season. After only a day of driving the small motorcycles, we had cramps in our arms from the constant maneuvering to avoid hitting damaging obstacles.

UNKNOWN TRAILS

The desire to find the people with holes in their chests was set in our heart. Were they legend or reality? The year was 2004. The jungle was dry and haze from jungle fires filled the sky. Those were both good signs. The haze of jungle fires told us the paths would be very dry, and the intentionally lit fires would burn the underbrush that grows so rapidly in a wet, tropical environment like Cambodia. Because the fires are lit every year, most of the jungle gets a good burn. These regular forest fires rarely kill the large trees and do not burn hot enough to destroy the younger trees, palms, and ferns. The fires simply clear away dead leaves, dead branches, clusters of bamboo, and open the paths for easier traveling. The time was right to begin our search.

We wanted to travel while it was still cool. "Cool" in Cambodia means temperatures in the 70's and 80's, rather than the usual 90's and 100's. Cool season is usually December and January, while the hot season reaches its maximum temperature during March and April. By the end of April and the beginning of May, the monsoon rains begin to start their regular cycle. So February, being a good transition month, was selected as the date to go.

Only two companions and myself made the first trip into the jungle. We decided to take only two motorcycles, both little 100cc scooters. The two smaller Cambodian men used one motorcycle, and I used one motorcycle by myself, carrying most of our equipment and food.

We knew the way to a river called "O Krieng," but from there on we would be in unexplored territory. The road to O Krieng is part of a famous old highway: the Ho Chi Minh trail. The Ho Chi Minh trail was a well known supply line used by the North Vietnamese to supply Viet Cong soldiers who were fighting the Americans in southern Vietnam during the Vietnam War. South Vietnam and Cambodia share a long common border. Kracheh province, where we were searching, sits on that border.

We soon discovered that the only thing remaining from this historic trail was a devastated path that had gone unused for more than thirty years. Its bridges had long been destroyed or collapsed. Even the old pavement was unrecognizable, except for a few patches not more than ten feet in length every few miles. It was difficult to imagine that this rocky path used to be "National Highway Number Seven." The weather had also greatly eroded what was left. Pot holes were larger than vehicles.

Littered along the sides of the road were sleeping warriors. These sleeping warriors didn't care who they killed or even that the war had ended decades earlier. The sleeping warriors came in the form of landmines and unexploded bombs dropped from American B-52's while carpet-bombing the area

B-52 Carpet Bombing

during the war. The worst sleeping warriors were unexploded bomblets from cluster bombs. Cluster bombs were used for wiping out infantry and convoys. Typically one single bomb dropped from an aircraft would deliver hundreds of smaller baseball-sized bomblets, each with an explosive power similar to that of a grenade. They were dispersed in the air above a target and would blanket a large area. Out of hundreds of bomblets dropped from each single cluster bomb, many did not explode and still remain active today. In Cambodia, hundreds of people have been killed decades after these bombs were dropped. Most casualties are children because the bomblets are round in shape and are sometimes painted bright colors, looking like a harmless toy.

Cluster Bomb

Disabled Victim

For the journey, Ang and Pin, my two best church planters, met me in Kracheh province where they lived. I traveled from Phnom Penh by pickup truck to join them. The ten to twelve hour journey was a difficult beginning to an even harder and longer trip to come. However, the road was familiar to me and the road conditions, though difficult in places, were no match for my 4x4 with its heavy-duty winch. I had previously made the journey hundreds of times since beginning ministry in Kracheh province. The last leg of the trip went from the Vietnam border town of Snoul, eighty-three kilometers away, inland to the provincial capital of Kracheh province (a town with the same name).

When I first made the trip (in reverse) during 1996, the area was under the control of the Khmer Rouge. The entire province, except for the provincial capital and a small area to the south of it, was dominated by Khmer Rouge soldiers and their families. By 1996 the Khmer Rouge were a spent force, but the Cambodian government military was also weak. Neither had the weapons, manpower, nor the willpower to overthrow the other. The Khmer Rouge, once die-hard communists, no longer cared or could remember their ideology. They simply robbed, looted, and ambushed people for profit.

In 1996, I was being led to another tribe, the Stieng people, who had been partially evangelized through Vietnamese Montengards, not through people in Cambodia. Years earlier, the Stieng homeland had been divided along the Cambodian-Vietnamese border by the French. Therefore, my companion and I had to gain permission from the Khmer Rouge soldiers controlling the jungle in between the two areas. This journey also consisted of crossing sixty-four creeks or rivers, only one of which had a bridge which had, remarkably, had been missed by American bombers. Interestingly, that bridge, only twenty kilometers from the Vietnamese border, was the only crossing point of a major river called *Chlong*. Had the Americans taken out that bridge, the flow of weapons down the Ho Chi Minh trail would have been severely restricted, though certainly not stopped.

A taxi driver with good relations among the Khmer Rouge (he knew how to "grease" the right people's palms) agreed to take us down the dilapidated road and through the area to reach the Stieng people. The taxi, an old beat up Nissan pickup truck, bounced and weaved down the jungle path. At each bend in the road, a Khmer Rouge soldier holding an AK-47 greeted the taxi by holding out his hand for money. With each progressive turn, more money was given. At one particular bend in the road, an irate Khmer Rouge soldier far away began yelling at us as we were approaching. He was clearly very angry. He pointed at our taxi, screaming many curse words. However, our taxi driver kept coming closer, unable to drive more than ten miles per hour because of the condition of the road. Suddenly the soldier stepped up to a tree where a B-40 rocket was propped. He raised the unmistakable mushroom cone rocket to his shoulder and pointed it directly at us.

Total fear and panic hit me. I immediately ducked down in the bed of the pickup. I knew that a direct hit on the pickup would kill every one of us, and it would reduce the pickup to a mangled burning wreck. I held

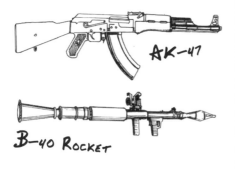

AK-47

B-40 ROCKET

my breath and gripped the truck as hard as I could (as if that would protect me). After the next second, that seemed to last an eternity, I saw the soldier struggling to fire the rocket trigger. The taxi driver floored the accelerator and headed straight toward the fighter, who was standing slightly off the side of the road. The old Nissan pickup was our only weapon.

The Khmer Rouge soldier cursed the rocket as we neared. Dropping it to the ground, he took off running to his house where he had an AK-47 hanging in the doorway. The taxi didn't slow down. Our driver continued as fast as possible. From my position in the rear bed of the pickup, I saw the soldier grab his AK-47 and run toward the road. The taxi continued to move further away and out of range from the gun's bullets. The soldier raised the weapon to his shoulder, but by that time we were several hundred yards away and continued to move rapidly. Due to the noise of the rattling old truck and the roar of its diesel engine, I didn't hear the weapon fire. I suspect his gun jammed as well.

The people living in that area, including the Khmer Rouge soldiers, rarely had transportation other than a broken down bicycle. So we knew we only had to get out of the gun's firing range. In 1996, the Khmer Rouge in the area did not have radios to communicate with each other since there was no electricity to charge batteries. Even today, only commanders carry radios in the Cambodian military.

I immediately began thanking Jesus for his protection. Jesus, my Jehovah Sabaoth, my protector, the Lord of Hosts! My brief missionary career of about three years could have instantly come to an end on that lonely, deserted road in northeastern Cambodia. That would not have been my idea of a good ending! Clearly the Lord had jammed the rocket and prevented it from firing, and possibly the AK-47 as well. I never knew why the soldier was so angry. I speculated that perhaps the taxi driver, on a previous trip, had not given money to the soldier.

Just as my heart rate began returning to normal, a few hours later down the narrow, rough road, our vehicle was stopped by two more Khmer Rouge soldiers. Each of them carried a gun that was nearly as big as they were. One had an AK-47 and the other had an American made M-16. The taxi stopped and the two armed Khmer Rouge soldiers climbed into the back of the pickup with me. I politely greeted them, but quickly began to develop escape plans in my mind if they tried to kidnap me.

As I watched the soldiers, I realized the guns they carried were not actually all that big. The soldiers were just very young boys. Their small stature made the automatic weapons look much larger than they were. Their behavior was far from pleasant. They were rude to the other people in the truck, and their words very vulgar.

Young Khmer Rouge Soldiers

Trying to ease the tension, I began making "small talk" with the soldiers. I asked them which gun they liked more, the Soviet AK-47 or the American M-16. I thought later that such a provocative question was probably not a good beginning to our conversation. One of them snapped back that the M-16 is lighter and easier to carry, but in combat the AK-47 is much better. Just the powerful sound of the AK alone can cause an enemy to lose his bowels, he informed me. The M-16, he continued, sounds like a pea-shooter comparatively, though actually the calibers of the bullets are similar.

Eventually I asked the soldiers their age. One boy was fifteen years old, and the other fourteen. I asked them how long they had been soldiers. Both responded that they had been fighting since they were nine years of age. One added that the first time he fired an AK-47, it knocked him down. The older soldiers mocked him. However, after a few months of carrying the older men's weapons for them, he became accustomed to firing the guns as well.

As we drove toward a village, the two soldiers saw some old people standing along the road in front of a recently cleared field. In the middle of the field was a small wood building with a pointed roof. I instantly recognized the structure as the beginnings of a Buddhist temple.

As we approached the elderly people standing near the road, the two boy-soldiers stood up in the truck and began screaming curse words at them. It was shocking to witness this behavior in Cambodia. It is forbidden in Khmer culture to say anything bad to any elder, or even disagree with them, much less curse them. Yet they continued to curse them. In the midst of the shouted vulgarities, I realized they were mocking the old people because they were building a temple. The boy-soldiers still clung to some communist ideology. Lenin had considered religions "the opiate of the people." In later years, I would meet the ideological head of the Khmer Rouge named *Khieu Samphan*, who told me that he considered all religion to be a tool used by the ruling classes for their own corruption and oppression of the people. Clearly, this teaching was deeply entrenched in the minds of these two young boy-soldiers.

As we neared our destination, the boys called for the taxi to stop. They both jumped off the back and slipped off the side of the road and disappeared into the trees. The taxi continued on down the road. As we headed on our way, the driver called back to me and asked, "Were you scared?" I replied that I wasn't. He said, "You should have been. Those two Khmer Rouge soldiers are the two most notorious killers in the area. They often ambush civilians traveling along the road, burning their vehicles, stealing all their possessions, and then killing everyone." Again Jesus was my Jehovah Sabaoth, my protection.

We finally arrived in Snoul, one of the main towns of the Stieng people, where we would begin a long and close relationship with the tribe. That journey through the Khmer Rouge-controlled area would be a journey I would never forget. The dangers, the fears, as well as the confidence that Jesus would also be there to protect me would give me strength to go into the jungles in search of lost tribes for many years to come.

BACK ON THE JOURNEY TO THE PHANTOM TRIBE

As I joined the rest of the team in Kracheh province, we made our travel plans and purchased last minute supplies, such as Ramen noodles and bottled water. At five o'clock the following morning, we gathered below the Kracheh training center, which was set on stilts, to pray before setting out. It was still dark out and very quiet. The prayer was quite simple, "Lord, guide our paths to people who have never heard of you, so we can bring them the gospel of the Kingdom, that they may know you and receive your salvation. Lord, protect us and keep us from harm along the path. Guide us to the people you would have us to meet. Amen!" Off we went, kicking up a cloud of dust behind our two scooters on the dirt road.

The first couple of hours were the easy part. We drove along the Mekong River on a pre-existing road that was in pretty good condition for a jungle road. After a couple of hours, the road turned away from the Mekong River and headed northeast toward the Lao border (the communist country known in French as Laos).

When the road turned into the jungle, the condition of the road deteriorated quickly. At the last fuel point, we filled our motor scooters to the brim and also carried an extra two and a half gallons of gas with us. Since the scooters only had 100cc engines, they didn't use much fuel. They also didn't have much power!

A CAMBODIAN GAS STATION

Once we turned away from the Mekong River, only Pin had previously traveled into this area as a former Khmer Rouge commander many years earlier. The road was rocky and driving was difficult. Most of the bridges were gone, so we had to cross through creeks which still had some water in them. Our small motor scooters only had a six inch clearance. If water went up the tailpipe into the engine and the pistons the scooters would die and refuse to start. If that happened in the jungle, it would be a trip-ending breakdown. The only thing we would be able to do would be to take the entire engine apart and re-lubricate it. That would take hours and require more specialized tools than we carried with us.

After several hours, we arrived at a crossroad. There were a few houses at the junction. A sandy trail shot off to the east and the main road continued north.

We stopped to ask the people for some water. They gladly gave us some tea. We were grateful for the tea, because we knew the water had been boiled and the tea flavor masked the bad taste of the pond water they used. We asked the people where the sandy trail led. "To *Ra-lu-ah* village" they responded. "Where the *Mel* people live."

That was just what we wanted to hear! I had read a government report mentioning the *Mel* people, but the language and the number of people in the tribe were unknown. As we were preparing to leave the junction in the road, an old woman rushed up to me concealing something in her skirt. She told me she had something to show me. I told her to go ahead and reveal what she was hiding. She grabbed my arm and asked me to come behind the house. I was curious. What could be so secretive to the old lady? Looking around to see that no one was watching, she cautiously pulled out an object. I started to laugh. It was a funny looking brass statue of Jesus. I asked, "Do you know what this is?" She quietly answered, "It is a valuable idol with magic power."

I laughed again. "No", I explained, "It is not valuable. It is an idol of Jesus on the cross, but it has no power." I asked the old woman if she knew who Jesus was. She did not. Buddhists believe all images have magic power, so she assumed this idol had magic power as well.

Since the image was brass I considered buying it, as she was requesting. Her selling price was 2,000 Riel   (the Cambodian currency) which was about $0.50. I decided to purchase it, to give the old woman a little money, and also to get it out of her hands. However, when I pulled out the 2000 Riel she cried, "No! No! $2,000 dollars! It is magic!" I couldn't restrain my laughter.

After finally gaining some composure, I was determined to make this a teachable moment for the old woman. Looking more carefully at the idol, I realized why it looked funny to me. Jesus' arms were supposed to be outstretched on the cross. It was an old catholic crucifix. However, the arms had broken off and had been re-melted. They were attached on the opposite side so that the arms were bent up toward the sky rather than in an outstretched position.   In re-attaching the arms they had gotten mixed up. The thumbs were facing outward and down, yet the palms facing forward. I explained the error, and asked her to examine the thumbs on the image, then look at her own hands. I told her that the real Jesus is alive. I told her Jesus doesn't allow people to worship idols. I also explained that no idol of Jesus could have any power, especially one that was handicapped!

The old woman had never heard the name of Jesus. Her only belief was that power could come from an inanimate object. How blind the evil one has made people. We gave the woman a booklet about Jesus, asked her to read it, and told her we would be back along that road and we would tell her more about the real Jesus.

If we were going to make it to a village by nightfall, we had to keep moving. So we set off down the sandy path. We were already being affected by the heat of the afternoon. We had only gone about fifty feet when we became completely bogged down in sand. This sand seemed to be unending and no way to get around it. The worst possible surface for motorcycles is soft sand. The wheels sink and cannot get traction. Worse yet, it is very difficult to steer or keep the motorcycle upright. The engines were heating up quickly with the high revs, and one-by-one we fell in the sand. We would get up and fall again, repeatedly trying to get through the soft merciless sand. It seemed to go on without end.

The sandy stretch turned out to be about three miles of backbreaking work, slugging through incredibly soft sand. Once we reached harder ground, we collapsed to rest. The motorcycles needed a rest too, to cool down or the pistons would be in danger of seizing up. Nearly all our water had been used because of our exhaustion and the incredible heat we had been through. We had not expected such grueling work to travel only three miles and didn't know what would be ahead.

Following a brief rest, we continued traveling. The next few miles were a mixture of sand and loose rocks, both very difficult to ride on. By this time we had all become accustomed to falling down. At our slow speed, we were not normally hurt and suffered only from scratches and bruises. We even teased each other from time to time about who had the best fall.

However, the absolute worst falls, were yet to come when we mistakenly hit exposed tree stumps. When that occurred, without warning the motorcycles instantly stopped. Then the built up momentum slammed the driver into the handlebars. If the cycle had been moving fast enough, the driver flew over the handlebars and made a face plant in the weeds and ground. Each time one of us performed this undesirable acrobatic maneuver, the others stopped to check for injuries, and then burst into laughter as they graded the fall.

As we continued the trip, more and more pieces of the motorcycles were sacrificed along the way. The turn signals were the first to go, along with the front hand brake, fairings, rear lights and headlight. Sometimes the clutch pedal and brake pedal would get bent backward. We had to carefully force them back into a position where we could use them without completely breaking them off. One trip into the jungle like this took years off the life of our scooters.

We traveled like this hour after hour. We had not seen a single person since entering the trail at the junction earlier in the day. We began to wonder if we would have to spend the night in the open jungle. Our water was almost gone. We had only about one liter (approximately one quart) between the three of us. One more rest stop and the water would be finished.

Suddenly, up ahead we saw thick smoke and heard the roar of a forest fire. As we pressed closer we realized we had a problem! The fire was directly in front of us and burning very strong. We waited and watched for awhile, but the fire began to shift toward us, burning in our direction. We could see that the fire had burned out behind the blazing flames coming toward us. We discussed our options: drive through the fire, or head back where we had come from. We determined that driving through the fire would be easier than trying to go backward. Since our water was nearly gone, we knew it was unlikely we could make it back to the cross-road without water and rest.

We discussed our plan and lined up on the path, waiting for the best moment to ride through the flames. One, two, three and we were off. We held our breath while speeding through the flames. The heat seared our bodies. As we popped out the other side, we were still engulfed in smoke. The thick smoke made breathing difficult. Quickly we checked to see that we were not on fire and continued to ride hard to get away from the smoke. We had to keep moving. Finally we reached a clearing and stopped to suck up our last bit of water.

After a brief rest and an attempt to clear our lungs from the smoke, we continued down the trail and came to a flowing river. Fortunately, it was only about two to three feet deep. We carried our motorcycles across one by one, keeping the exhaust pipes out of the water. We stopped to rest in the middle of the stream by placing the wheels of the motorcycle on some stones, continuing to keep the exhaust and spark plug above the water level. The rocks, covered with yellow and green slime, were very slippery. It was no easy task to keep our balance.

Once across the river, we headed up the bank on the other side and continued moving. We were thirsty, but the water was a brown tea color. We also saw thousands of frog tadpoles moving about in the basins that didn't have flowing water. So, we didn't want to drink the water. The color was caused by millions of leaves that had fallen into the water. Not only did the leaves discolor the water, but later we discovered the leaves also gave the water a bitter taste.

Evening was approaching and the sun was nearly gone, then suddenly we heard music! It was Khmer music, not tribal music. Somewhere ahead of us had to be a village. As the music became louder, we grew more excited. The sound of music ignited a new burst of energy in us. We had been traveling on our motorcycles, with only a few short breaks, for more than twelve hours. We were pumped, knowing we would soon find people in the jungle.

Our excitement, however, was short lived. While the music grew louder, we came to a river, larger than the one we had previously crossed. This time however, the river was much further across and also much deeper. This meant we could not stop in the middle of the river to set the heavy motorcycles down to rest our muscles. We would have to carry the motorcycles the entire width of the river without resting; a distance of more than one hundred yards. It takes all of us to move one motorcycle across the river, so we have to make a trip back and forth across the river for each motorcycle. After so many hours of rugged travel we were already exhausted.

This time there was no other option for getting beyond another obstacle. We began carrying the first motorcycle through the water, but soon realized we were in trouble. We were all much too tired to keep the motorcycle up out of the water. We scrambled, slipped and slid, continually losing our footing on the rocks beneath the water.

We noticed a herd of twenty cows heading down the river bank toward us. Some of the cows started to become spooked when they saw us.   We worried what the animals might do, never having seen three men carrying a motorcycle across the river in the place that they normally drink in peace. As we quickly considered what to do, we saw a young shepherd boy following the herd, skipping down the river bank. The moment he saw us, he froze in his tracks. We greeted him, but he didn't respond. We wondered if he couldn't understand,   or maybe he was just too afraid to speak to us. He didn't run from us but stayed at a distance just staring at us.

After great effort, we finally got the first motorcycle across the river and headed back to get the second one. By this time, more and more children were beginning to appear. They began chattering and stirring up a commotion.   We were excited, because we could understand them!   They were speaking Khmer, not the Mel language.

We asked the children if someone had drinking water. They pointed up the hill. As we reached the top of the bank, we

CURIOUS VILLAGERS

saw the first house only fifty feet from the river bank, then another and another. We kept inquiring where the village chief lived. As we passed house after house, we were all in shock. This was no small village. It had to have a few thousand people, with hundreds of houses stretching along a sandy road for a couple of miles. We wondered how thousands of people and a village this size could sustain itself in such a remote and isolated location.

As we slowly moved through the village followed by an ever-growing crowd of people, we finally saw a make-shift store with little bags of hanging candy out in front of a small hut. We greeted the people and asked if they had drinking water and food we could buy. Fortunately, they did. The girls selling the goods began to make us some noodles while we rested on a wood bench. We were exhausted and the sky was now almost black. Night had come.

The father of the house asked us where we were going to stay. We politely said that we did not know, but asked if we could sleep under his house. We knew that this was very humbling. The bottom of a stilted house is open, and reserved for animals and people who are not trusted. We didn't want to ask to sleep inside a person's home unless they first invited us. A neighbor heard we did not have a place to sleep, so he approached us. He told us we could sleep at his house, since his wife was gone to a relative's house.

Climbing up the stairs, we entered the house. The house had walls, but no windows. It had an open section for a doorway, but no door. It was so hot, so we all hoped to sleep in the doorway. That would be the only possible way to get some airflow from outside. We put our things in the house and decided to clean up before going to bed.

A community water well was located a few hundred yards from where we were staying, so we walked over to it to take a bath. It was an open well in full public view. There were no buildings, only a flat open space so the villagers had easy access to the well water. Even though it was dark with the night sky, many villagers came out of their houses, watching at a distance to see the big foreign guy take a bath. To the dark-skinned onlookers, I appeared so white that I almost glowed. None of the village homes have electricity, so even my white skin in the moonlight seemed very bright to them. For the entire length of my bath, the crowd continued to swell to nearly one hundred people. Everyone watched intently as I soaped up, rinsed off and nervously strained to keep a small loin cloth in place, not wanting to reveal all to the ever growing crowd.

After finishing our bath, we headed back to the house and prepared to sleep. I hung my hammock, as did Ang. Pin, however, preferred to sleep on the bamboo slat floor. As soon as my head was resting in the

STEVE IN THE HAMMOCK

hammock I fell asleep. I was so tired, I didn't wake up until the sun came up at 5:30 the next morning.

The next morning, we went back to the house that sold us drinking water and noodles the night before. By now the entire village knew a foreigner was present. As we ate our breakfast, a few hundred people gradually gathered around. The people were curious why a foreigner had come to their village. They were also curious about the two Khmer men who had brought the foreigner there.

With such a large gathering, I seized the moment to ask about the ethnic groups in the area. They explained that there were two different ethnic groups, Mel people and Kroawl people. Among them were also a few Khmers.

I asked if they had ever heard of Jesus (*Preah Yesu* in Khmer). "Yes," they all responded. But then they tried to explain to me that their sandy soil was not good. I chuckled inside. My pronunciation was absolutely correct, but they had never heard of Jesus. They thought I was trying to say, "*Prey Kowsu.*" "Prey Kowsu" means "rubber plantation." Rubber trees are very common in eastern Cambodia and grow very well in red clay but not in sandy soil. We then spent the morning telling the people about Jesus. They were curious, and politely listened to us. However, we didn't sense an open door.

After talking all morning, we asked if there were any tribes still farther away. They responded immediately informing us that there was another tribe down the river a bit further. The people living further down the river toward the east they said, they were called the *Kraowl* people.

We decided to leave our newly-made friends and begin looking for the next village. After driving two hours on sandy paths again, we arrived at a second village. We were impressed with the huge, beautiful mango trees. These trees were so big it seemed that it would require four or five guys holding hands simply to encircle them. I had never seen mango trees so big. Mango trees are not indigenous to the area, they are planted. The massive mango trees gave evidence that the isolated tribal village is a very old settlement.

We continued driving through the village, noticing that this also was a large village of a few thousand people. Then the path headed toward another river bank. A crowd gathered at the end of the village, so we began to speak to them. Some could speak the Khmer language, but others could not. They spoke to each other in their own language, unlike the Mel in the previous village who could speak the national language of Khmer quite easily.

This village was called *Srie Chi* (meaning fertile rice field). In the middle of the village stood a dilapidated Buddhist temple. It didn't look like anyone lived there. The absence of monks meant that the people were not really Buddhist. They only gave the appearance of being Buddhist for the sake of the majority Khmer people. All ethnic minorities are under the political authority of the Khmers who have made Buddhism the national religion; therefore minority villages which "adopt" Buddhism can gain humanitarian assistance, schools, and medical care but continued traditional animistic practices will lead to continued isolation within the nation.

After developing some trust, we asked the people around us if they knew about the man named Jesus. Like the previous village, they also did not know who or what we were taking about. We felt warmly received by the people in this village. We asked to meet the village chief but were told he was gone. This meant we would need to return to the village of *Ro-lou-uh* to spend the night once again.

If the village chief does not give an outsider permission to stay, that person cannot remain in the village. Since the village chief was away, we were unable to get the needed permission. One of the ways that communist countries control their populations is by limiting travel. Upon arrival in any village in Cambodia, a visitor, whether Cambodian or foreigner, must present his passport or national ID card at the local police station or village chief's house and state his purpose for being in the village. Only after the chief or police department grants permission can the visitor proceed to a villager's home. Suspicious people, political activists, or simply undesirables are simply refused permission and sent away. After further discussion, we decided to stay back in the ·other village where we had stayed the previous night. Before leaving we asked if there were any other people living beyond their village. "Oh yes," they replied, "the *Bu-nong* people are a few more hours ahead."

We also asked if they had heard about the people with a hole in their chest. They replied that of course they had heard of them, but had no idea where they lived. At that, we headed back to the main village of *Ra-lou-uh* where we had stayed the previous night.

Once back in the village, we returned to the same house that had welcomed us the night before. Again the villagers gathered and we continued talking about Jesus where we had left off earlier. However, they didn't seem to want to hear about Jesus anymore.

After spending the second night in *Ro-lou-uh,* we met a young man who had just returned from another village. "Where did you come from?" I asked.

"From far away," he replied.

I asked him the name of the tribe and village where he had been. I had not heard of them but marked it down on paper so I could check maps later. I then asked, "Have you ever heard of the people with a hole in their chest?"

"Oh yes, they are very far. About a day's journey from here," he said.

"Really!" I said, surprised. "Can you take us there?" I asked.

"Sure, but I will only go there in a week or so," he replied.

After begging him to take us now, he stubbornly refused. So we backed down and asked if he could take us another time. He agreed. He said he would take us when we returned. Pin, Ang, and I discussed the information we had received and decided to return to Kracheh for now. However, we would soon return to meet "the people with a hole in their chest."

As we were getting on our motorcycles, I asked the young man, "Do the people with a hole in their chest have a name?"

"T'moan," he answered.

I have never forgotten the moment I first heard the name of this legendary people group. I had never heard the name of this tribe, nor had my friends or even most villagers.

We left the village thrilled that we had found information as to the location of the T'moan. In the process, we had also found two new tribes that had never heard the gospel. We had discovered two very large villages in the jungle, completely cut off and isolated from the rest of Cambodia. Neither had a road in or out of their village and neither had communication. We speculated that there could be ten thousand people in that area, and none of them had ever heard of Jesus until we shared him with them. Though we tried to share briefly about Jesus, they still didn't understand the gospel of the Kingdom. There was much work ahead to be done.

We still did not know exactly where the legendary tribe was located. However, for the first time we had found someone who knew where they were and was willing to take us to them. We were all excited as we headed back toward Kracheh town again.

We crossed back through the countless rivers, creeks, and gullies. After some time, we stopped to take a break. Since there was also a small hill, I recommended we climb to the top of the hill so we could look over the jungle. Traveling in the jungle, we rarely knew where we were, which direction we were facing, much less what could be ahead. Even though the area was quite hilly, we were never high enough to see above the trees. This tall hill, I thought, might give us a vantage point above the trees. Everyone agreed, so we hiked up the hill, leaving our motorcycles at the bottom. The hilltop was also tree covered, but there were some rock formations that we could climb up on. From that vantage point, we were finally above most of the trees. As we looked across the land all we could see was a vast jungle canopy, with no signs of life anywhere. As far as we could see, it was just the tops of trees.

I recommended to Pin and Ang that we not waste the view. I suggested we worship the Lord and pray loudly claiming this jungle for our Lord Jesus Christ. After singing to the Lord at the tops of our voices, we prayed a simple prayer:

"Lord, we claim this jungle for you. Please help us find all the people that live in this jungle so they can believe in you. And Lord, next time . . . help us find the T'moan people! Amen."

3

EXPEDITION TWO:

SATANIC ATTACK

Returning back to our home base in Phnom Penh we began to make plans for our second expedition to find the T'moan people. Poline, my assistant in Words of Life Ministries, would join us this time in the adventurous search. Nearly every waking moment I thought of the people we had found. The Mel and the Kraowl, with villages numbering in the thousands, were quite accessible to us, but completely isolated in the jungle. The thought of an even further tribe, the legendary "tribe with the hole in their chest" burned in my heart. It was as if the name of the tribe echoed in my ears. . . T'moan, T'moan, T'moan. I was anxious to return to find the tribe.

The first priority for the trip was to prepare the motorcycles. From our first trip, we had learned that the 100cc motor scooters were slow and ineffective in the jungle. We prayed, asking God whether we should invest in some larger dirt bikes that are made for rough terrain. Sensing His confirmation, we purchased two used dirt bikes and made plans to head back into the jungle. We made sure the bikes were tuned properly and that we had the necessary tools to fix any repairs that might be needed in the jungle.

Since there are no repair shops deep in the jungle, we knew we had to carry with us everything we might need. We packed spare inner-tubes, patch kits, air pumps, and every tool we thought would be helpful.

JUNGLE THORNS CAN BE AS LONG AS A FINGER. OUCH!

In jungle travel, flat tires are very common. Most jungle plants have their natural built-in protection: long and very sharp thorns. Some tree branches and bushes have thorns up to two inches long. When a thorny branch falls across a path or gets buried in the sand, a motorcycle tire becomes its instant victim when it crosses the hidden barbs. Some simple journeys that should take only four or five hours have been stretched to as long as eight hours due to the sheer number of flat tires.

I was a Boy Scout when I was young, achieving the rank of Eagle Scout with several additional palms (levels) beyond that. The main motto of the Boy Scouts is "be prepared." We were taught to prepare everything from snake-bite kits, food, utensils, bedding, first-aid kits, tools . . . and even pictures of Mom and Dad at home!

While loading up everything I thought was necessary for our second jungle expedition, my wife just shook her head. "You would think you are going to the moon," she said. We both laughed.

My Cambodian colleagues had a different idea of what to bring. Everything they needed was packed into a small bag. They each had one change of clothes, a hammock, a few tools and a single water bottle.

On the other hand, this Eagle Scout had a buck knife, machete, Leatherman, matches, lighters and topographical maps of the area that were US combat maps used during the Vietnam War. I had five changes of clothes plus a pile of extra socks and underwear. I had even purchased an entire tool-kit of more than one-hundred different tools that needed to be carried, just in case we had to overhaul an engine in the jungle. Several inner tubes, patch kits, and an air pump for tire punctures were included as well. I also had a case of noodles (forty packets), instant coffee, jolly rancher candies, and even a can of Pringles. Tied to the motorcycle I had two canteens filled with water and twelve additional bottles of water in my luggage to be used and discarded along the way. For sleeping gear I had my hammock, a blanket, an extra sleeping bag just in case it became cold at night and a small pillow. Obviously, all of my things wouldn't fit on my motorcycle, so I tied the excess on Poline's motorcycle. I would have made the Boy Scouts of America proud. I was prepared--prepared for everything except nuclear war!

Since we had two big motorcycles this time, we decided not to drive the pickup as we had done before from Phnom Penh to Kracheh where we would meet Pin and Ang once again. Instead, we would drive our heavy duty dirt-bikes. By using motorcycles, we could avoid the national road that went to the Vietnam border before turning north toward where we needed to go. On our dirt-bikes, we could take a village trail that followed the Mekong River, making the trip shorter in distance. We knew it was only a dirt road that had some bad places along the way. The trip from Phnom Penh to the base in Kracheh was about 220 miles, mostly on unpaved village trails. So we had a long way to travel, and it would not be easy driving. However, if everything went well, we should reach Pin and Ang in about eight hours.

Cambodia has two very distinct seasons: wet season and dry season. As expected, in the wet season it rains every day, almost without fail. The flat areas of Cambodia receive about sixty inches per year, while the mountainous areas can receive two hundred inches. The total rainfall comes only between the months of May until early November. From late November to April there is no rain whatsoever. It was still dry season as we departed, once again, in search of the T'moan. Normally, when going to Kracheh, we start the drive quite early in the morning. This time we decided to leave at about eight o'clock, so we wouldn't begin our travel already tired.

As we headed out, it seemed that the most dangerous part of the trip would be negotiating the traffic in Phnom Penh, the capital city, at that time of the day. Finally, after an hour or more, we broke free of the traffic. Our 250cc dirt-bikes could really go fast. However, the tread on our tires was not designed for paved roads. They were designed for dirt and muddy roads, which we wouldn't reach for awhile. On the pavement we couldn't get good traction. Even the painted lines on the road caused our tires to slip a little, making us feel unstable.

Everything, however, was going well. At high speeds, the sustained roar of the engine with higher revs made for good singing along the way. I sang in harmony with the motorcycle's pitch, enjoying every minute of the trip. The only really negative part about the trip was the heat. It was made worse by the extra clothes we had to wear for protection. I wore a jacket and long pants. Unfortunately they were both made for the cool weather in the United States, not the hot weather in Cambodia. The lining of the jacket and pants caused me to sweat profusely, but it was better than having exposed flesh to become severely sunburned. It was a regular hot day in the blazing tropical sun, around ninety-five degrees. If it was not for the wind generated by riding the motorcycle fast, the heat would have been unbearable.

Hour upon hour we drove, rarely stopping except to fill up the gas tanks. Finally, we came to the shortcut along the Mekong River. I knew the road and villages well, since we had planted several churches along the river. The road was very dusty, so Poline and I allowed some space between us so that we could see the road though the thick dust. There was also some traffic on the road. Since the road was only about ten feet wide, the traffic proved to be a challenge. When a vehicle came in the opposite direction, they forced us off the narrow road. The dust cloud that ensued caused a "white out" that lasted for nearly a minute until the dust settled. Each time this occurred, we knocked the dust off of our clothes and continued our journey until the next vehicle, usually a public taxi, ran us off the road. Poline struggled with his motorcycle on the rocky dirt road. He often began to fishtail but was able to recover and continue down the road. I chose to stay behind him, because I was worried about him falling down.

We were excited about the trip and anxious to get to Kracheh to join the others. We could hardly wait to get into the jungle. All along the way, I was constantly singing and praying as we drove. I knew that this was going to be a great trip. I was praying that we could find the T'moan people and tell them the gospel message. Emotionally I was on top of the world, yet I knew that Satan would surely be working overtime against us. For thousands of years he had been able to keep the T'moan people in the darkness, blinded to God and the message of true salvation. As I drove, I prayed more intensely and worshiped our Lord, more focused than I had done in the past. I knew Satan had many different tricks he could use against us.

Our journey was pretty uneventful as we traveled hour after hour. Now and again, both Poline and I felt the motorcycle tires lose their grip on the rocky road beneath us and begin to fishtail. Because of this, we reduced our speed, staying between thirty and forty miles per hour. We were not going too fast but also not too slow, as we had a long way to go. Eventually I felt a sense of relief, knowing we only had about ten miles remaining until we reached the Words of Life Training Center in Kracheh where we would meet Pin and Ang. Poline was in the lead.

The road ran very close to the Mekong River. I especially enjoyed looking at the beauty down the bank of the river, and across the massive Mekong. Much of the Mekong River is three to four miles wide. The river bank was about thirty to forty feet high above the river below us. The road had been built up another ten to fifteen feet higher than the plain around us because of the flooding of the Mekong in the rainy season. It was quite a massive drop down to the river; it was nearly straight down.

Ahead of us was a small bridge stretched across a dry creek bed that drained water into the Mekong during rainy season. Still following behind, I watched Poline cross the bridge and suddenly fishtail, a cloud of dust rising from his path. The out-of-control motorcycle was heading straight for the drop-off. Fortunately, he quickly regained control of the motorcycle and turned into the bend of the road and out of my sight.

I had no idea what Poline had just hit to cause the mishap, perhaps some sand or something else. I decided I would not take his same path to avoid whatever was hidden from my view. To me the smooth dirt road looked fine. But something in the road had nearly caused Poline to have a terrible accident. I saw the sharp bend in the road after the bridge, but nothing that a slight shifting of my weight into the corner couldn't fix. So I crossed the bridge on a different track line than Poline had just driven.

As I crossed the bridge suddenly the beautiful scenery changed. I was no longer sitting high in my motorcycle saddle. I was sliding head first on the ground. What happened! My hands, legs, stomach were all sliding on the ground and little rocks were bouncing off my helmet visor. I realized quickly that I should roll rather than slide because I was sliding on the palms of my hands. A couple of rolls later I stopped moving, with half my body in the bushes and the other half lying in the road, right at the road's bend. I tried to look for Poline, but could not see through the dust kicked up by my motorcycle. The engine on my motorcycle had died and was completely silent.

Looking up at the sky through my dirt-covered helmet, I thought to myself, "in the next second this is going to really hurt." Sure enough, at that moment my entire body burned like fire. My right leg and arm hurt the worst. I had never felt such pain as I was feeling in my leg. I reached down to feel my bone to see if it was broken. I tried to move my leg but couldn't.

I held my hands up to the facemask on my helmet that was still covered with dirt. Through the dust I could see a dark red color on the palms of my hands. The skin was gone. The gravel had ripped the skin from my palms like sandpaper. I knew that was going to hurt as well, and it did. I tried to pry open my facemask so I could breathe. Just as I got it open I saw a terrifying sight. Out of the corner of my eye I saw another provincial taxi

PROVINCIAL TAXI VAN (OFTEN HOLD UP TO 30 PEOPLE!)

barreling down on my position and he wasn't stopping. I realized that he could not see me because only my head was visible around the bend. The road was not big enough for him to miss me. I could not move to get out of the way because of the shock of the fall. "Oh perfect," my thoughts mocked, "I survived the fall only to be hit by a taxi!"

I tried to raise my hand to signal the car to stop. At that moment I saw a passenger grab the driver's hand while pointing at me. The taxi came to a stop only a few feet from my head. The doors quickly opened and the people jumped out, including two Buddhist monks. I asked the people to help me to my feet. Three or four men began to tug on my injured arms pulling me up. I asked another to help get my helmet off so I could breathe better. My hands were hurting so badly that I could not release the clip. They all worked to help. Some of the passengers walked over to my motorcycle that was still lying in the middle of the road about twenty feet away. Poline was still nowhere in sight.

The passengers asked if I had anyone traveling with me. I informed them that they had probably passed my friend on another motorcycle just ahead of me. Surely Poline would be back soon, I thought.

The people were very surprised that this bloody and filthy dirty American could speak fluent Cambodian. The monks looked at my injuries. I was most concerned about my leg that I still couldn't move. However, the monks were all looking at my arm. They were making terrible facial expressions and commenting to each other about the piece of my arm that was missing. "That is a big chunk which is gone," one said.

Another said, "You can see right into the bone. That must hurt!"

When I was in Boy Scouts, I was taught never to tell the real condition of injuries to the person lying in pain. Instead, we were instructed to say encouraging things like "Oh it's not bad," or "It's only a little flesh wound." Certainly we were not to give a detailed description of blood, tissue, and bone damage in the presence of the victim. It just makes them hurt worse and lose hope.

Finally, Poline had realized I was not trailing him and had turned back. As he arrived, the crowd of passengers was still gathered around me. When Poline pulled up and looked at my arm, he told me he thought it was broken. My arm was receiving everyone's attention. I really couldn't tell the extent of the injury because of its location at the back of my elbow and arm. However, I was able to move my arm

The taxi driver came to me and said, "You're in luck. Today I have some medicine with me to stop the bleeding and clean out your wound."

"Great!" I said. Then I saw him open a bottle of brake fluid. "What are you doing?" I quickly said.

He went on to explain that pouring brake fluid on open wounds worked really well to stop bleeding and assured me that my arm was in need of his quick medical attention.

I remembered a missionary friend of mine in the Philippines I call "Uncle Darrel." One time, when Uncle Darrel and I were doing something together, he accidentally cut his hand very deeply with a knife. He asked me drive him quickly to a gas station. I questioned him if he hadn't misspoken and meant the emergency room. He assured me that the gas station would be fine. At the station, while still bleeding profusely, Uncle Darrel asked the attendant to fill a container with a gallon of kerosene fuel. He then plunged his hand into the fuel. It turned red with his blood but soon began to clear. Sure enough, the bleeding stopped.

My missionary uncle was from Houston, Texas. He didn't seem to be too much of a red neck, but that sure seemed to me to be a very red-neck medical treatment! It worked though. Now, needing treatment for injuries in the middle of Cambodia where there are few medical facilities, I remembered that kerosene had helped my Uncle Darrel. So, perhaps another petroleum product would work equally well.

The village medic/ taxi driver smothered a cloth with brake fluid and swabbed my wound. Then he poured it right into the wound and tied the cloth to my arm. It burned for just a second, then a warm sensation took over and it actually felt quite good. They assured me I would be alright. Several men moved my motorcycle off the road. Everyone boarded the taxi again and continue on their way. I imagine those people are still talking about the day they saved the life of a big Cambodian- speaking American who had been lying in the road from a motorcycle accident. I can just hear the magnified description of my injuries.

Dust filled the air as the taxi pulled away. Poline and I were now left standing in the road by ourselves, with no way to call someone for help. But I was alive. I looked over to my motorcycle. The front lights were bent ninety degrees and wedged into the front tire. The turn signals were shattered. There were scratches down one side of the bike but amazingly all my luggage had prevented the motorcycle from being severely damaged. One sleeping bag was shredded and all my water bottles had burst open, but I considered that pretty minor.

With the headlight pinned against the front wheel I couldn't drive. We were still ten miles from where we needed to be. We would have to fix the bike. I knew that we needed to do it as quickly as possible before additional intense pain from my injuries set in. Blood was dripping from both knees and from my toes. One whole shoe had been ripped off as I slid on the ground. Both my stomach and back were in a lot of pain and bleeding, as was much of my body. Since the palms of my hands were bloody, I could only hold the handle bars by my fingertips.   I was a mess, and probably looked even worse to other people.

We needed to get the bike running so I could get to the hospital in the town up ahead.   Together, we tried to twist and pull the headlight into position and get it off of the front wheel.   Finally, we were able to partially bend the steel frame off the wheel. With this, I could turn the wheel to the left but not to the right.   We could do no more with our tools and limited time. I had to drive the motorcycle as it was into town.

The next job was to get the engine started.   Gas had leaked out of the engine and tank all over the motorcycle. We worked on the carburetor to clean it out.   After a minute or so, the engine kicked back to life. I climbed on and headed down the road, much slower than before. Since I could only steer to the left, any needed movement to the right required me to lean into the turn to try and get the motorcycle to go in that direction.   Slowly we made our way.   The handle bars were soon covered with sticky blood that ran down my arms.   It was very painful to turn the throttle, but I knew I had to keep moving.

Upon entering the town, I remembered I had burned my hand a couple years earlier. I had gone to a private medical clinic for treatment. The doctor was nice and if I went there, I thought he would perhaps treat me quickly. I would certainly have to wait for hours in the government hospital. So I signaled Poline to follow me as we passed the hospital and went toward the clinic.

I could see that the medical clinic was full of people.   A crowd quickly gathered upon seeing a bleeding foreigner, covered in dirt, straggle into their clinic. The people inside cleared a bed and I sat down. The wife of the doctor quickly came to me and called for her husband, while helping me out of my jacket. I could hear the swelling crowd talk about how terrible my arm looked, which I still could not see.

People helped peel the layers of clothes off that I was wearing, so all my wounds could be cleaned and treated.   It was a relief to have cooler air blowing on my sweaty body once the outer clothes were off. As I looked over my wounds, I was thankful for my choice of thick winter clothes. They had helped protect my body from much more damage.

As I examined my wounds, I became discouraged.   I could see that each wound was embedded with little pebbles and large amounts of dirt and sand. I knew that each wound would have to be completely cleaned out, and that would be much more painful than the initial accident.

I asked Poline to help me call my wife. As the doctor was cleaning the first wound I called Noit to let her know that I was hurt.   I tried to minimize the injuries as we talked. She asked if we would continue into the jungle the next day. I told her I would see how the night went. My plan was to continue, because I didn't want Satan to win. Poline then called our teammates and within minutes they were at my side. Over the next hour the doctor worked to clean out each wound. Every moment was extremely painful.

After I had been cleaned up, I drove the motorcycle to our training center where my teammates and I would spend the night. Pin, who was trained to be a medic in the Khmer Rouge, stayed by my side to help me recover. I asked what he thought about going to the jungle the next day. He said, "Look at yourself, tonight you will break out in a fever and your whole body will be in great pain so that you will not even be able to walk tomorrow."

I didn't think that sounded very encouraging. But he was right. In only a few minutes after his medical prophecy, the fever hit and excruciating pain set in. The men tied up my hammock so I could lie down.

As I lay there, I prayed that the Lord would bring healing to me quickly. I was especially angry that Satan was trying to stop us. We talked about the accident and Poline explained to everyone that there was absolutely nothing in the road that could have caused us to crash. Yet, moments before my accident, Poline had nearly plummeted down the steep roadside leading to the river bank. As we described the location of the accident, the others remembered that a week earlier a taxi had driven off the road and down into the Mekong River in exactly the same place. Two people had been killed. A week after my accident, we later learned that a husband and wife going home from the market had wiped out in the same place, killing both of them as well.

After years of ministry in Cambodia, I have learned that it seems there are some demons that control certain territories. In another part of Cambodia, over a period of four years every time I approached a certain bridge, my car, truck or motorcycle would stall. It would take thirty minutes to an hour to restart the engine and continue. This happened no matter what month or year I was passing by. After a few years, I just came to expect it, and whoever was onboard with me would begin praying. When the engine died, we would gather around the engine and pray and demand the demon that was affecting our travel leave, and within minutes it would start up again. This happened nearly ten times over many years, at the exact same location in Western Cambodia. I believe that this fall which stopped our journey to the T'moan people was a similar kind of territorial spirit, especially since others had died in the same location for suspicious reasons.

That night as my pain and fever continued to increase, we decided to postpone our trip into the jungle to find the T'moan people. There was no way I would be able ride a motorcycle. Poline made arrangements for a taxi to drive us back to Phnom Penh.   We intentionally left our motorcycles at the Kracheh training center so we would be motivated to come back quickly.

Very early the next morning we headed back to Phnom Penh. The taxi took the same road we had ridden the day before. We asked him to stop at the place where I had wrecked so I could look at the road for some explanation for the cause. Upon examining the road, we could find nothing that could have caused a wreck. The bridge was concrete and flat and the exit onto the gravel road was fine as well. There was no sand, just gravel and dirt that covered the whole rest of the road. Compared to the rest of the road that we had traveled on, it was actually a very good section.

Satan had won a round, but we were not going to be stopped. We were determined to continue our search for the T'moan at another time.

When we reached Phnom Penh, I went to a hospital to have my arm x-rayed. There are no x-ray machines in the entire Northeastern Cambodia. After the x-ray was taken, the doctor said there was no break. I asked him what the dozen or so white pieces on the x-ray were, as well as the dark line that looked like a crack on my bone. The x-ray technician spoke up and said that it was probably just a problem in the developing.

My arm was too sore to touch, causing me a lot of pain. Over a long period of time it finally healed. Sometime later we learned that the x-ray technician had probably just been a janitor. My arm had definitely been broken. In fact there was a hole in the bone about an inch wide. The white pieces were bone chips that later re-attached in many different places along the bone, giving my arm a textured feel!

I was determined that my injuries would only be a temporary setback in our search for the T'moan to tell them about Jesus Christ. My colleagues and I made plans to return to the jungle as quickly as possible.

4

EXPEDITION THREE:

TRAVERSING THE RIVER OF GOD

After a week of recovery following my motorcycle accident, I was emotionally ready to return to the jungle. By this time my wounds were scabbed over, except for my arm. My entire right arm was still extremely painful and swollen. I was still taking several Tylenol a day, trying to reduce the pain and swelling. Even the slightest touch to my arm sent a sharp pain, like a knife cutting through my body. Physically, because of my arm, I knew I could not go back into the jungle yet. Each day, however, I became more and more anxious to go. On the tenth day toward recovery, I called Pin and Ang in Kracheh. I asked them if they were ready to try again to find the T'moan. They were quick to respond, "Yes."

Though it was much hotter in only two weeks time, the rains had not yet come. The absence of rain would make our travel easier, since we had many rivers and creeks to cross. I made a bandage for my arm using a volleyball kneepad. However, the elastic strap cut off the circulation in my arm, so the kneepad soon had to be discarded.

Since Poline and I had left our motorcycles in Kracheh, we needed to return to our "base" at the training center, riding in one of the infamous Cambodian taxis. We had planned an extra day at the center to work on our motorcycles, to get them repaired and ready for the jungle trails. We knew my bike would require a lot of work before it would be usable in the jungle terrain. After a day of working on the motorcycle, we were ready to head into the jungle.

We were all excited the morning of our departure. We pulled away from the training center fully determined to find the T'moan no matter what it took. We left early because we knew it was almost a day's journey to the Mel tribe, where we had met the man willing to lead us to the T'moan.

ME AND MY MOTORCYCLE

The journey was much the same as our first trip into the jungle, although the path was more familiar to us. The creek crossings became easier because this time we knew which parts were rocky, which were sandy, and which were muddy. As before, navigating the sandy sections remained exhausting. We were thankful that this time there were no major motorcycle spills. After successfully making it across all the rivers and creeks, we finally arrived in the Mel village once again.

When we arrived in the Mel village, we inquired about the man who had told us he would show us the way to the T'moan village. We soon found him and asked if he would now guide us to the village. His story suddenly changed. He confessed that he knew the T'moan people lived somewhere around the *River of God*, but he had not actually been to their village. A few years earlier he had come across some of the T'moan people by chance in the jungle. We were greatly disappointed.

After a quick huddle, we realized we were not going to get much help from the man we had expected to guide us. So we decided to go on to the Kraowl village to see if we could find someone there who could help us. We traveled through more sand and crossed a few more creeks and finally arrived in *Srie Chi*.

I suggested we find the village chief before going anywhere else, since the people did not know us in the village. We went house by house, asking for the location of their chief. Each time the people pointed further and further away. Eventually, it seemed to us that we had left the village. However, after crossing another deep creek, we came upon another section of houses. We continued to inquire about the location of their chief and eventually we found his house. The chief was not home, but an old women welcomed us into the house and sent a boy running to find the chief.

Within a short time a friendly old man arrived. We greeted each other politely. I made a point to shake the man's hand, and he responded with a big smile. There are two different styles of greeting in Cambodia. Khmer people do not traditionally shake hands. They greet each other by putting their hands together, as if to pray, and then bow slightly. Tribal people, however, greet each other by shaking each other's hand with both hands, not unlike a typical friendly American handshake. This simple gesture, knowing the culturally appropriate way to shake the chief's hand, got us miles into a good relationship.

We sat drinking tea and talking for a few hours. We explained why we were there. We told the chief we were Christians, and we were very interested in finding ways to help the ethnic minorities. We were especially interested in the T'moan people, as we heard they lived far away and were very isolated.

The chief told us that he knew the T'moan. During the oppressive years of the Khmer Rouge, the T'moan people had been gathered up and forced to live in a new village called *Koun Va*. That village was only a few kilometers from where we were sitting. However, the chief went on, once the Khmer Rouge military rule ended, the T'moan moved back into the jungle. The chief did not know where they were located, but he knew the chief's name was *Vi*, if he was still living.

Technically, *Koun Va* village was under the jurisdiction of the district chief we were talking to, so, wherever the T'moan now lived, they would still be under his jurisdiction, he reasoned. The Kraowl chief in *Srie Chi* went on to tell us that there was only one T'moan family remaining in *Koun Va*, where the Khmer Rouge had once forced them to live. A T'moan man had inter-married with a Kroawl wife and chose to remain in and live his life as a Kroawl, rather than to go farther back into the jungle with the T'moan people.

The Kraowl chief told us that no one in his village knew the way to the T'moan village. However, he would give us a letter, as well as one guide to help us reach the next village. In his letter, the chief would instruct the villagers to find a guide who could take us on to the next village. From that village a new guide would be secured to take us on to the next, and so on. At each new village we were to be given a new guide until we found someone who could lead us to the T'moan. Each guide would travel with us on one of our motorcycles. Then the guide would have to walk back to his own village. I thought that it was terrible to make the guides walk back after riding with us on the motorcycle, but the chief figured they would love the chance to ride on a motorcycle, and they could always gather some extra food from the leaves on the trees on their walk back to their village.

The Kraowl chief invited us to spend the evening and sleep at his house that night before leaving the next morning with the guide. The chief's house was still being built, so it did not have walls. However, we were happy to have the invitation and a place to stay for the night.

The chief informed us they would be having a celebration in the village. The Khmers wanted the tribal villagers to become Buddhist. So the Khmers gave the people of *Srie Chi* money once a year to conduct a ceremony. I asked the chief what kind of ceremony it was, but he wasn't sure. He explained that there was an old statute with a lion on it in the village, built fifty years earlier around the time of the country's independence from France. When the Khmer provincial leaders gave money for a celebration, they bought alcohol and rented a generator and sound system. Then they played music at its highest volume all night, drinking as they danced around the statue. By doing this, the chief assumed they were being good Buddhists, just like the Khmer wanted.

The chief went on to explain that if they did not become Buddhist, they would not receive help from the government. There would be no schools, no roads, and no income. Even he as the district chief, which is a fairly prestigious title in Cambodia, received no salary from the government.

The chief was a farmer and raised cows just like all the other people in his village. When he complained to the government that he was not receiving a salary for the work he was doing as district chief, he was told to use his position to create money. He was told to get money from the village people every time he signed his name on a document, on land titles, on sales, and so on. In that way, he was told he could support himself.

The chief was angry about the instructions that had been given to him. As a tribal person he could not do that to his people. They were his family and he loved them. "How could I possibly extort money from them?" he said to us.

The four of us from outside the jungle, knowing common practices in government, did not share our thoughts with the chief. There was nothing we could do about his situation. However, we were all confident that the Khmer provincial leaders were likely stealing his salary and probably any development money for the region as well.

After we had finished talking and made our travel plans for the next day, the chief invited the four of us to join him at the village well to take a bath. Much like foot washing in the Bible, people who have been on a journey are often invited to take a bath. It's a sign of hospitality in most village homes. While this used to be extremely uncomfortable for me, as I would much prefer to bathe privately and on my own terms, now it is a welcome event to cool off and clean up after a long hot day. Getting practically naked in front of the entire village does wonders for "breaking the ice" and building close relationships in the village. (It also gives an isolated village some entertainment in the absence of any other form of entertainment, such as TV, radio or other entertainment activities.) We gathered our clothes, soap, and towels and headed toward the village well. As we walked with the chief, a line of people filed in behind us. Of course, they were all curious to see what a foreigner looked like taking a bath! Anyone else taking a public bath wouldn't have been noticed at all, since a giant foreigner was invading their communal bathing site.

As we approached the well, the chief called out to the people who were pumping water. He commanded them to move away and make room for his special visitors to take a bath. Before we could even fill one pail of water, a crowd of nearly one hundred people had gathered to watch my every move. I wrapped the traditional red and white-checkered loin-cloth around my waist and carefully removed my shirt and pants. As I lifted my shirt the crowd shrieked with laughter and sounded like a swarm of bees as they talked among themselves. My companions were used to the attention I drew when people saw so much white skin for the first time, so they tried their best to act as if nothing unusual was taking place. Down the road the ceremonial dance had already begun. However, my bath was a much bigger attraction than their party. Eventually I finished my bath and the people moved on to their celebration.

As night came, the music geared up more and more. The loud speakers were more than one kilometer away, but the music was so loud it seemed like it was in the house next door to us. The Kraowl chief wrote us a letter of introduction to be given to all the villages under his jurisdiction. He instructed them to receive us and help us find the T'moan.

The chief apologized that he must leave us to attend the party, since he was the chief. He also asked us to please forgive him because he would have to get drunk with all the village people that night. He knew we would leave the next morning before he awakened. We thanked the chief and said our good-byes so he could attend the ceremony that had no meaning. We needed to try to sleep, even though the distant music was blasting in our ears.

Early the next morning we set off with our prearranged guide. After a couple of hours of driving though the jungle we entered a small village of about thirty houses. These people were also from the Kroawl tribe, but very few spoke Khmer, the national language. We presented our letter from the Kroawl chief to the village leader.

We rested for an hour while the villagers tried to decide who would guide us to the next village. We continued with a new guide and within a few hours, we arrived in the next village called *Phnom Pi* or "Two Mountains Village." This was a *Bunong* village, not Kroawl. Outside the town, as the name indicated, there were two small mountains.

We had underestimated the amount of fuel we needed, so we asked if anyone in the village had gas. One man replied that he had some, so we asked to buy it from him. We filled up two motorcycles and began the next leg of our journey with our new guide. Before reaching the end of the village boundary, Poline's motorcycle died. Up ahead, Pin's motorcycle also died at about the same time. We were not even outside the village.

Both motorcycles were the two we had just filled with village gas. We proceeded to drain out all the fuel which was previously no good. It was obvious we could not continue until we worked on the engines. I was glad I was prepared! I had all the tools I needed! It required a couple of hours of our labor to get the engines running again. We determined that the gas we had just purchased may have been for chainsaws, so it was mixed with oil--although the man who had sold us the gas swore he had not mixed oil into it. However, after draining the fuel out and replenishing the tanks with our own reserve fuel, the motorcycles started right up.

Our guide in this village had his own motorcycle, a small 100cc motorcycle similar to what we had used the first time we drove into the jungle. We observed that most of the parts of his motorcycle appeared to be tied together with bailing wire and string. It was a mix and match of many colors. I was worried that our guide may not be able to make it to where we needed to go with his motorcycle in that condition. He told us we were going to the River of God. He assured us that along the river, there was a village. He assumed it was the T'moan people. He had seen the village one time while hunting, so he knew where the village sat.

The remaining distance we had to travel was only about thirty miles, but the trail became harder and harder to follow. There were numerous small trails that crisscrossed in the jungle. Some were animal trails; some were trails to other villages; some were trails that went to remote rice fields or jungle ponds; some were trails that were just shortcuts to other trails. With so many trails here and there, it was easy to become confused. However, our guide seemed to know the way, so we followed.

After about twenty minutes on these difficult trails, the guide got a flat tire. We all stopped, spending thirty minutes patching the tire. After proceeding for another thirty minutes, the guide had another flat tire.

One of his tires was so thin and bald that every little sharp stone and twig caused it to go flat. We were becoming frustrated, but we had no choice but to work together to get to the village. The four of us had no idea where we were.

It was nearly dark and we had seen no sign of people. Then we came to a clearing. In the clearing lay hundreds of felled trees. This was an illegal logging camp that had been abandoned. Trees were lying everywhere. They were all hardwood trees, like Mahogany and Resin trees. Because the illegal loggers had been discovered, all the trees had been abandoned. Each felled tree was thirty to forty feet long and up to five and six feet thick. They were huge.

Over the next few years we would pass through the abandoned camp regularly. Each year the jungle fires would burn into the logs. Some of the logs were so big they would burn for months on end. We observed that even after two years of annual burning, the logs remain only partially burned. It may take ten years before they are completely burned up.

It was sad to see the ruin of valuable hardwood by illegal loggers. However, even sadder was and is the fact that this destruction of trees lies only two miles from a T'moan village.

The T'moan people have nothing for cutting timber. Their houses are made of bamboo, and therefore need regular repairs and have to be rebuilt every few years. If the people had been given a saw, they could have cut the illegally felled trees into lumber for building each family a beautiful house with the wood. Instead the wood is left to rot and burn over the span of a decade.

Minorities are often blamed for deforestation because of their use of the "slash and burn" agricultural method. From my experience, the minorities living in grass and bamboo huts are almost never to blame for most deforestation. It is the chainsaws, bulldozers and excavators of the majority people group seeking financial gain who wipe out hundreds and thousands of acres of forest in short order.

Directly after passing the logging camp, we came upon the River of God. The water was flowing but only about knee high. Since the water was not any higher than that, we would be able to cross with our larger motorcycles, even though the uneasy rock bottom of the river would be a challenge. The smaller motorcycles, however, would have to be carried above the water.

We had a different and more improved strategy for carrying motorcycles across rivers than we had during our first expedition. We cut down branches to use as poles. One pole went through the front tire frame and one pole tied onto the motorcycle frame. Four guys could

MOTORCYCLE RIVER CROSSING

then pick the motorcycle up and walk across the river. Since the water was only knee deep, we did not have to get the motorcycle very high. We could actually rest the poles on our shoulders.

Occasionally one person would slip on the uneven rocks in the river bed. When that happened the other three struggled to keep the motorcycle out of the water. The person who had fallen would have to fight to keep his portion of the cycle up out of the water as well as regain his footing at the same time. It was a very physically demanding task, but we were thankful we did not have to carry the larger motorcycles. We drove those through the river.

It was significant to me that the river was called the River of God. It was a long river, but on the map there were no villages listed or marked along its path. The entire river had bedrock as its base. Although it was uneven, it was solid. We learned that when the river stops flowing in the height of dry season, the water does not completely drain from the river bed because of the bedrock. The banks of the river were about twenty to twenty-five feet high. During flash floods, the river could quickly rise to the top of the banks.

Going down to the river bed was usually quite easy. Even if we didn't begin our descent correctly, the momentum and the steep grade brought us to the bottom – sometimes head first! Getting up the other side of the bank was the tricky part.

After a lot of hard work, we made it up over the other side of the bank. The trail was even more narrow here than before, and the trees had grown thicker and closer together, making it difficult to ride our motorcycles. Our guide assured us we were very close to the village. We began to see some isolated rice fields. Surely we were now close!

It was hard to drive, since our concentration was drawn away from the road. We were looking through the trees ahead to see if we could see houses or people. As a result, we had several mishaps, smashing into tree stumps the last two miles. Our attention was drawn to looking for signs of human life, not on the trail.

We were like little children waiting to open Christmas presents. We had waited and worked so hard to find these people and were now apparently only minutes away. Suddenly, we broke through the trees and drove out into a grassy meadow. We were in awe. There it was — a village!

We headed into the village and stopped in front of one of the houses. At first no one came out to look at the noisy motorcycle intruders. Cautiously a few men emerged from other houses, followed by some children. Eventually the older women appeared as well. The people began to gather looking curiously at their unexpected visitors. It was obvious that the men were drunk. They were talking very loud but didn't realize it. They had conducted a sacrifice to the spirits the night before. As in all tribal villages, drinking and dancing are part of making a sacrifice to the spirits. They told us the name of the village was *Srie Hiew*.

We noticed that everyone was smoking, even some of the children. The cigarettes were their own homegrown leaves wrapped on the outside with a green leaf. As I watched the people, I couldn't help but laugh as I observed one particular old woman. The older village people had large holes in their ear lobes. We were told that during ceremonies the people put large ivory earrings into their lobes. But the old woman who had caught my attention had another use for the hole in her ear lobe. She smoked a little bit and then put the cigarette butt into her ear lobe. When she felt like smoking again, she pulled the cigarette out of her ear lobe to take a few more drags on the cigarette before putting it back into her ear lobe. It was hilarious to watch her with her very unique cigarette holder!

As we talked with the people we learned that this was not the main village. The main village was still ahead a few more miles. The village we had entered was just a gathering of a few families who had moved out of the main village. Even though it was getting dark, we decided to press on to the main village. We wanted to avoid a possible problem, since the men in the village were drunk. We did not know them, and they did not know us.

In some local tribal groups, especially further north, the people take pride in their ability to be very friendly-- enabling them to woo people into their village. These tribal groups have earned a frightening reputation--whether true or

An EARLOBE CIGARETTE
HOLDER! (CREATIVE)

not, I do not know. In these villages it is said that the men play an evil game. During the night the men try to tie a string on the toe of a visitor while he is sleeping without awakening him. At day-break, if a visitor has a string tied on his toe, he will be killed by the villagers. It is a type of hunting game. The people we had just located were probably the most remote tribe in all of Cambodia. We knew nothing about them and prayed they didn't have a hunting game that they wanted to play!

It also would be proper for us to meet the chief of the tribe first, so we apologized to the people for leaving suddenly. We promised we would return (after their homebrew moonshine had worn off).

Later we discovered that it was because of the alcohol that we were actually able to talk to the people. It made them braver. The standard practice, we would soon discover, was to run into the jungle and hide if a stranger came into the village.

The path between the two villages became my favorite section of the entire trail. This stretch had six river crossings, as well as one small waterfall during rainy season. Each crossing was a steep, narrow gorge.

These crossings provided the thrill every motorcyclist enjoys. The only way to get from one side to the other was to dive into the gorge, and rapidly accelerate out of it, with a final launch up and over the lip. It was more fun than an amusement park! This was the real thing, in the middle of a jungle.

We had been told that the main village was only two miles ahead. However, it turned out to be about an additional five miles that would take us about forty-five minutes to an hour in jungle travel.

As we pulled into the next village, we could immediately tell that it was much larger than the first. We later learned that it had over three hundred people living there. The village was in a row, with a clump of houses at one end. As soon as we drove into the village, the people scattered. Some hid in their houses, but most of them ran into the jungle when they heard the sound of our motorcycles coming.

When we saw what was happening, we stopped our motorcycles and quickly dismounted. We could tell that our presence was perceived as a threat to them. By getting off of our motorcycles, we hoped to minimize their concern that we might bring them harm.

We moved away from our motorcycles and squatted down. After a short while, an elderly man moved toward us and squatted down as well. We told him that we had a note from the district chief. We read the note that instructed the villages to welcome us and concluded by reading the name of the district chief. When the elderly man heard the name of the district chief, he knew we were all right. He then stood up to greet us. Darkness was coming very quickly now.

Our greeter was the village chief of the T'moan people. He led us to the middle of the village and pointed to a house that had no walls and huge holes in the roof. It looked like it was about to fall down. "You can sleep there," he told us. We were not sure if it was an honor or an insult, but since it was the building in the center of the village we suspected it was an honor.

We asked the chief if someone could boil water for us. We had not eaten all day, but we had carried dry instant noodles with us to eat. The chief sent his wife to boil some water. People stood around our sleeping quarters as darkness fell, staring into the house to see what we were like. Some of the men were squatting next to our motorcycles, just looking at them. Some of them sat staring at the motorcycles for hours, even late into the night. I would have given a hundred dollars to know what they were thinking as they stared at the motorcycles! We didn't even take the keys out of the ignition, because we knew they would be completely safe. Since the house we were sleeping in had no walls, we knew it must be a very safe village.

As the chief's wife came back with boiled water, we invited the chief to eat noodles with us. He invited some of the other elders and asked his wife to boil more water. Once again it paid off to "be prepared," packing a large quantity of dried noodles.

The chief spoke good Khmer. We had to be careful not to use complex words, but we did not have difficulty communicating with him. We talked until it was pitch dark. The village chief told us to get some sleep and he would see us in the morning.

We strung up our hammocks, careful not to hang them all together. We were certain that the house we were staying in could not support the weight of all our hammocks tied to its main beams. The main beams were filled with termite holes and looked like they provided housing for a whole community of termites. The termite-eaten beams were less than four inches across.

After we each had our hammocks securely tied, we climbed in, ready for a quiet night of sleep in the jungle, (unlike the previous night with the blaring sound of ceremonial music). As we put our weight into the hammocks, the whole building moved! We laughed in relief that the building stayed standing.

Soon we were all looking up through the rotten roof at millions of stars in the sky. The village roofs were made of grass. After a year or two, bugs and termites eat the grass away, making it necessary for them to be replaced. This roof had been almost completely eaten away but never replaced.

The night sky was beautiful. I thought about Abraham when God told him that he would make Abraham's descendants more numerous than the stars in the sky. I couldn't believe how many stars there were-- millions upon millions. The awesome beauty of the stars was mesmerizing. In the city of Phnom Penh, it is difficult to see stars. That night as I lay in my hammock looking at God's incredible creation, I was sure I had never seen so many stars in my lifetime.

We were about thirty miles from the closest light source, so nothing was blocking the radiance of the stars. As I contemplated that the stars were probably the same ones that Abraham looked up at, I recalled the promise that God gave to Abraham. *"I will make you into a great nation and I will bless you; I will make your name great, and you will be a blessing. I will bless those who bless you, and whoever curses you I will curse; and all peoples on earth will be blessed through you"* (Genesis 12:2-3). We were here, in the T'moan village in response to that covenant God had made with Abraham. Hopefully, the T'moan would be added to the descendants of Abraham as a result of our trip. Though it was a stifling hot night with no breeze, I thanked God for helping us to persevere in finding the T'moan people. Quickly we all drifted off into a deep sleep. We were all exhausted.

The next morning we were up bright and early. By 5:00 in the morning the whole village was also awake and back in front of our rickety house. We spent time talking to the people while we ate our noodles for breakfast. Culturally it was important for us to share our food with everyone. So by the end of breakfast our forty packets of noodles were gone. We didn't mind. It gave us a lot of time to fellowship with the people and ask questions.

We asked about their contact with the outside world. They told us that we were the first outsiders who had come to visit them. We asked how some of them had learned Khmer. They told us that under Sihanouk's regime (in the 1950's and 1960's) they were forced to live like Khmer people and were sent for education in the Khmer language.

The village chief was only a boy during that time, but he learned Khmer and could actually read a little as well. They spoke of the Khmer people, using a term usually reserved for Europeans (*bori-teh*) that means foreigners.

They told us of one Khmer by the name of "Thai Boon Roong." It is a funny sounding Khmer name, more like a name one would hear in Thailand. However, we all recognized the name of the person. He was the owner of the Inter-Continental Hotel in Phnom Penh and an influential businessman in Cambodia. The villager revealed to us that Thai Bong Roong was the owner of the logging camp that we had come through that had devastated the forest.

We asked if the people knew the name of the Prime Minister of Cambodia. They did not. They were really isolated! Only a few of them had been to the closest village and none of them had ever been to the provincial capitol of Kracheh, much less the capitol of Cambodia, Phnom Penh.

By ten o'clock we were getting hungry, as we had already been up for five hours. A small package of noodles the night before, after a hard day of travel, and a small packet of noodles for breakfast wasn't enough to satisfy our hunger. So we asked the chief if they had food we could buy. They didn't.

The entire village was out of food. They were only gathering leaves in the jungle to eat. We saw lots of chickens and pigs in the village, but they were reserved for sacrifices, not for human consumption.

We spent the day just talking and fellowshipping with the people. It was another extremely hot day. We walked around the village to see how they lived and met people who had been too shy to come to the center house where we stayed.

We knew we had a problem. It was three o'clock in the afternoon, we had only one bottle of water left between us, and we still did not have food. Since it was the middle of dry season, it was burning hot. The heat, and lack of food and water made us feel exhausted. We prayed and asked God to help us. We needed water, food, and strength. God answered our prayer but not in the way we expected it.

At five o'clock toward evening, dark clouds starting rolling in above the trees and a strong cold wind began to blow. That was a sure sign that we were about to get rain! We looked up at our decrepit roof and thought . . . "What on earth do we do now?"

We climbed into our hammocks and covered ourselves with blankets as the first sprinkles began to fall. We put all of our important belongings below our hanging bodies trying to protect them from the rain. We were using our own bodies as a raincoat. Then the water came, a massive monsoon downpour. As it forced its way through our nearly non-existent roof we became soaked within seconds. But that wasn't all. With the strong blowing cold wind, the rain didn't need to come through the roof. It was coming into the house horizontally. Our house didn't have any walls either!

We didn't say much to each other, we just tried to stay warm hugging our soaking wet blankets. The rain did not let up. It rained all night long (which was the longest night any of us had ever gone through). Only out of sheer exhaustion did anyone sleep, and then it was for only a few minutes at a time.

By day-break the rain had still not stopped, though the wind had died down considerably. We were starving! Our spirits were lifted with the new sound in the air. Frogs! We could also hear the belching critters, everywhere.

The rainstorm had come two months earlier than normal. The hard rain had also triggered the frogs to come out of their dry season hibernation. When it is extremely hot the frogs dig into the moist river banks and wait for months for water to come. However, at the first rain, frogs come out to mate and that was exactly what was happening. Pin, our jungle expert, smiled real big and said "FOOD! Let's go, everyone," he called. God had done a miracle for us and the villagers who were without food.

Boiled Frogs. . . Yum!

Off we went down to the river bank. Sure enough, frogs were everywhere in the water, piggybacked in pairs. The water was higher and flowing stronger than when we had crossed the day we entered the village. We began gathering frogs, stuffing them into bags. Within an hour, we had gathered a hundred pounds of frogs. Ang was our cook and eagerly went to work preparing the food God had provided for us. Ang boiled water, chopped all the frogs into pieces and dropped them in to the water to cook. Since we had not eaten for nearly twenty-four hours, anything tasted good. All day long we ate frogs!

That night we talked long into the night with the village people. We told them we would have to leave the next day, but we would come back again. We told them we were their friends. The next time they saw us or heard our motorcycles coming, they didn't need to be afraid. They agreed with us and asked us to come back to their village anytime. I specifically told my team not to share with them a typical "four spiritual laws" plan of salvation, and not to even talk about Jesus. Before we came on the trip, I was praying and the Lord spoke to me and told me not to seek people coming to Him one by one. He had impressed on me that if we were patient, the whole tribe could come to Christ at once. Building a relationship with these people and trying to understand their culture, way of thinking, and belief system would be crucial to knowing how to approach them with the gospel. Simply talking about a "Jesus" would be just the same as talking about the logger "Thai Boon Roong." They could not comprehend either.

When I was a young minister and recent seminary graduate, my understanding of "preaching the gospel" was more like a helicopter flying over an "unreached" village dumping tracts out on the "lost" people below. As I grew in the Lord, I came to the realization that the gospel is not about some magic words, formulas, or a simple historical acceptance that Jesus was indeed born in Israel, but it must be a message of repentance from sin and a message of complete life transformation. If the message we brought to them did not change their lives, then we brought the wrong message. I strongly believe that just introducing someone to the name of Jesus and his historical attributes is not nearly enough to bring about true salvation. Salvation comes when they take the gospel of the Kingdom and that gospel replaces their own self-destructive belief system, bringing transformation. Across the world, in tribes and larger people groups who have "converted to Christ," there are significant problems with mixing multiple religious practices (technically called syncretism). This might involve tribal people dressing up in suits and ties on Sunday to worship Jesus, yet on the other days of the week continuing their veneration of ancient spirits, demons, and witchcraft. Though they accepted the historical Jesus, there was never a transformation of the heart, a righteous character, or repentance from sin and ungodly practices. This is what I desperately wanted to avoid with the T'moan. Revealing to them the true Jesus, his message, and their need for him could not be done in a few hours or days, but would require an ongoing relationship and openness with the village.

Although it was a very wet day, the villagers wanted to show us their tribal dances. One man went to get a set of gongs, while the women dressed in their brightest and most colorful clothing--whatever it might be. Their dance was very unique. It reminded me of a Texas line dance, but this was performed in a circle. The female dancers held hands behind their backs and slowly moved in unison. The elders played the gongs, moving in a counter-clockwise circle outside the circle of girls. We were told that the female dancers were the single girls in the village. This was a way for them to show themselves off to the guys. It was very unique in comparison to tribal dances I have

T'MOAN WOMEN "LINE DANCING"

Men Playing Gongs

seen in other places. We appreciated their kindness to us through this presentation.

The next morning we got up early and said our goodbyes. We promised to return to their village as soon as possible. We put our remaining fuel in the motorcycles and started down the path. We had gone only a few hundred yards outside the village when suddenly Poline's motorcycle died. It would not respond at all and simply would not start. All of the electrical connections were dead. Poline's motorcycle was new. We had failed to get tools that might be needed to work on his bike. We needed to get to the battery, but it was under the seat. The bolts holding it all together required specialized "hex" keys, which we did not have.

We tried pushing the motorcycle to start it, but due to the rain the jungle was now a slick mud hole. No matter what we did, we could not get traction for the tire to spin that would hopefully start the engine. After almost an hour of work, we decided to go on to the river. I pulled Poline's motorcycle by linking our motorcycles together with hammock cords. It was very difficult to pull the bike, because the path was not level or straight. The dry creek beds we had crossed going into the village were now three to four feet deep with water because of the heavy monsoon rain. When we reached the River of God, our jaws dropped in disbelief. What was once a knee-deep gently flowing river was now incredibly deep, with fast rushing rapids!

We looked in amazement at the river, contemplating what we needed to do. We reviewed the fact that we did not have drinking water or food, so we needed to get to a place with supplies. We had no choice but to carry the motorcycles again, all four of them this time, one by one across the river. This was going to be difficult.

We found a rock path across the river that was only about waist deep. We knew it was going to be very hard to keep the motorcycles above the water for one-hundred yards. We began cutting poles to put through the tire frames as we had done before, so we could lift the motorcycles. The two new 250cc motorcycles were twice the weight of the two smaller motorcycles as well as the guide's. We struggled to keep all of them out of the raging river. It was excruciatingly painful and took nearly every ounce of our strength.

Poline's motorcycle was still not working by the time we reached the river. When one of the men slipped on the river rocks causing the motorcycle to plunge into the water, we had even less hope that we would get it started. We worked for two hours lifting the heavy motorcycles, cautiously making our way back and forth across the River of God.

We had said our goodbyes to the T'moan people early that morning. We had thought we would have little difficulty getting back to the last village. We were even thinking that if everything went well, we might be able to reach the Kracheh training center where our families were waiting for us by that night. That was wishful thinking!

Once we had carried all the motorcycles across the river, we began working on Poline's bike again. After two more fruitless hours of labor, we decided I would continue to pull Poline's motorcycle out of the jungle. Since Poline's motorcycle was new (to us that is) we were not about to abandon it in the jungle. So we reconnected our bikes with the hammock cords and proceeded along the path.

It was not long before the difficulty of the travel back to the training center set in our minds. We realized we still had to cross about fifty creeks. Although many had been dry on our trip into the jungle, it was likely they would now be full of water. Driving across a creek bed was difficult enough without pulling a motorcycle. It would be much more difficult with the creek full of water, with muddy banks, and with myself trying to pull another motorcycle at the same time.

Poline was often sideswiped by trees and branches, since he was being pulled down the winding path. When he fell, it forced my motorcycle to the ground as well. Time and time again, when one of us fell the other fell. So we tried to keep our speed low while riding on the muddy trail to prevent personal injury. If I was the one to fall first, the results were generally worse. Before Poline could stop, he would run over me or fall on me. Other than the damage the sheer weight of the motorcycle can cause, the bigger dangers are the extremely hot engine and muffler that can instantly burn skin.

The rain finally stopped. However, we were soaking wet and the whole jungle was wet as well. As we suspected, all the creeks were full of water. That meant that we had to carry all the motorcycles in more places than we normally would have needed to. It was very slow going.

After many hours in the jungle, our guide told us he was going to leave us and take a different trail to his village. As he pointed down a path, he said that if we kept going straight, we would get back to the main Mel village in no time. I was very uneasy with his announcement, but we had no other choice than to proceed according to his instructions.

As we kept moving forward, the trail became much more tricky. It seemed that Poline and I were falling every few hundred yards. We always tried to make light of the falls. I have always said, "It is better to laugh than to cry!" To mask the pain of the falls, we often graded the falls based on impact and form. We didn't really have a system; we just did it for fun. The best acrobatic fall award went to Poline. As darkness was coming on us, we came to a sharp turn in the path. I slowed down and looked backward to make sure I was giving him room to clear the trees on the corner. He was doing fine until he slipped in the mud. His motorcycle went down. I immediately braced myself so I would not fall as well. Poline went right over the handlebars and made a high arch in the air as he headed back down to the muddy path. When he hit the ground headfirst, he rolled, did three summersaults and rolled up to his feet. He was so tired that he never said one word. He didn't grunt, moan, or make any sounds. He just walked back to his motorcycle, picked it up and signaled for me to keep going. I chuckled at the time, but we all laughed and laughed repeatedly about Poline's fall later. It had been the best-looking fall we had seen. However, the funniest part about the whole scene was the fact that we were all so exhausted that not a sound was made from any one of us. It was by far the most graceful fall we saw. Most falls were not that easy.

Though my polite companions would never admit it, the award for the best jungle-temper-tantrum-after-a-fall goes to me. My fall was *not my fault* (point of contention). I was hit from behind by Poline! When he hit me, my motorcycle seized up and I was launched over the handle bars. Now Poline, a whopping 115 pounds, flying over the handlebars is not that big of a deal. The Cambodian "Big Show" going airborne, however, is another story. Let's just say that three hundred and fifty pounds of sheer body mass does not fly well! Somehow in the fall, I also rolled around in the dirt but ended up back on my feet sucking some wind! My helmet was constraining my airflow, so I (in a moment of frustration) ripped it off my head and started to throw it down into a small ravine. . . instantly registering in my mind what a bad idea that was. . . as it launched away from my grip. As it hit the bottom of the ravine, it multiplied by dividing! Pieces of the face mask, inner cushions and other parts littered the bottom of the ravine. What I had realized was that I actually needed that helmet! What followed are what are known as "consequences," which brought me great remorse. I had to walk down that ravine and try to put my helmet back together. My team members were absolutely silent as I walked down and tried to piece my helmet together. The face mask was shattered, so all I got back was the hard shell. I walked back up the ravine, sitting and resting at the top. Poline came up to me with a very apologetic "sorry." This was a difficult day that seemed to have no end.

I responded with, "I was pretty stupid." With that, we headed out again. (To this day, when we pass one of our memorable sites, we laugh and reminisce about the falls that took place. No one will forget what is now known as the "helmet graveyard.") Of course we all realize that it is better that there is a helmet graveyard there rather than a real graveyard!

After my big fall, I was really tired. I was just too tired to go on, but I knew we had to keep going. Night was approaching as we continued down the unfamiliar trail. At each trail crossing we huddled to discuss which way we needed to go. The entire journey to the next village should only have taken about six hours, but we had been traveling for more than ten hours. We had not seen a single person or any sign of life. We feared we were lost in the vast northern Cambodian jungle, and our guide had left us hours earlier. The sky was cloudy, so we could not even discern by the setting sun the direction we were traveling.

We had no choice but to continue on, stumbling and falling as we went. We continued down the path, into the darkness. We felt miserable. We had no idea where we were. The lack of water was painful. It was the worst feeling I have ever had, going without water for an entire day. The reality was that we had no idea when we would be able to get drinking water. We were lost.

After driving a couple more hours in darkness, we saw a small light through the trees ahead. What a moment! Finally, we had found a village. As we drove into the dark village, we recognized that it was the Mel village. The guide had been right; we did make it there.

We immediately went to a house where we knew we could get water. As we drove through the sleeping village, the sound of our motorcycles woke the people. They began to peer out of their houses to see what was happening. To have motorcycles come through any village was rare. Coming during the night was even more rare and caused quit a stir. Before we did anything, we all sat down to drink water. I drank a full gallon of water in less than five minutes. The thirst was unbearable.

The same family that had invited us to sleep in their house previously invited us back to spend the night. We were covered with mud and dirt from head to toe. We went to the open public well to wash our bodies and clothes quickly, then climbed into our hammocks to sleep. During the night, my legs cramped from the days rigorous travel and dehydration, causing great pain. Although exhausted, I had to get out of my hammock to stretch out my legs.

By morning we had regained some energy. We bought some noodles from the villagers to eat. We recounted to the villagers what we had learned about the T'moan. They listened with great interest as we shared story after story.

As we discussed our need to return to the training center in Kracheh, the Mel people told us that the water level in the *O Krieng* River had risen in the storm. The only possible way across the river now was by boat. They offered to help us get across so we could go home. We were very grateful. The boat was one big log that had been dug out like a canoe. Many people cannot imagine how it is possible to put a motorcycle in such an unstable boat and not tip over. I had made river crossings in dug-out canoes before, so I told my team not to worry, it was easier than it looked.

MOTORCYCLE FERRY IN A CANOE.
(BALANCE IS CRUCIAL!)

The only way to take a motorcycle in a dug out canoe is to sit on the motorcycle. A person's equilibrium works like a series of gyros. The motorcycle is in the center of the boat, with the rider's feet on the sides of the boat. As the weight of the motorcycle shifts, a person's mental equilibrium takes effect and the feet automatically adjust the canoe so that the motorcycle stays upright. It is really amazing to do, and it is not difficult at all. The only difficult part is driving the motorcycle out of the canoe when getting to the other side. I have heard of some foolish "know it all types" (i.e. Westerner tourists) who tried to tie a motorcycle upright in a canoe rather than sit on it. Everyone of those "smart guys" with their motorcycles ended up at the bottom of the river! The center of gravity is so high that the boat immediately capsizes. The jungle people know how to do it.

After an exciting and successful canoe crossing, we continued on our way, knowing that we were still far from getting out of the jungle. It had rained again during the night. We still had many creeks to cross, and with more rain we knew the creeks would be getting deeper and more treacherous to cross.

This was March, two months before the normal rainy season begins in Cambodia. We knew Satan was working overtime to prevent us from ever wanting to take the gospel of Jesus Christ back to the people living in the jungle. We did not know that the worst was yet to come.

I was still pulling Poline, so he was trailing me as we approached another creek bed. It had a steep, muddy slope down to the creek. It was straight so we wouldn't have to make any turns. However, Poline fell as I headed down the incline. As always, his fall caused me to fall.

Because we were headed down a slope, I had shifted my weight backward, so I wouldn't go over the handlebars. As the motorcycle went down, my leg was caught under the engine and the exhaust pipe. My leg instantly began to burn. The burn sent incredible searing pain through my leg. It burned through my nylon pants. I tried to pull my leg out but it was trapped. The pain was so great that I was frantic for the guys to help me.

I screamed for the guys to help me. They didn't realize that my leg was being burned on the exhaust pipe, and I was trapped underneath the motorcycle. I tried to get the motorcycle up, but I had no leverage to be able to get the several-hundred-pound motorcycle off of my leg. The muffler and engine continued to burn into my leg with the smell of burning flesh permeating the air.

Poline ran to me and tried to pick up my motorcycle. There was instant relief as he separated my skin from the exhaust pipe. His motorcycle, however, was still trapping my motorcycle, keeping it down because they were tied together. So he had to drop my motorcycle on my leg again as he worked to get his motorcycle off of mine.

When Poline dropped the motorcycle back down, the terrible burning pain shot through my body. Once again my leg was being burned. I screamed with pain. Finally Pin and Ang also came to help. The three of them were able to pull the motorcycles off of my leg and get my leg untangled. As I lay in the mud, I grabbed my leg in pain. The nylon pants were burned completely through and I could see my pink, burned skin below. The pain was extremely intense. I pulled my nylon pants off and slid down the mud into the creek below. I hoped the water would ease the pain. My whole body throbbed with pain as I lay in the creek water.

A tribal hunter soon appeared out of the woods. He had heard my screams and thought a tiger or bear had attacked someone and was being eaten. He was surprised to see a big foreigner, not a bear, sitting in the creek below. The burns were severe. The flowing water of the creek was soothing, but I also knew that I was infecting my wounds with the muddy water.

I asked the guys if they could get the motorcycles across the creek while I continued to soak in the water as it reduced the intensity of the pain. Once they were across, I would get out of the creek and begin the drive, pulling Poline again.

I knew that sitting in the creek was only a temporary solution for the pain. We needed to examine the wounds more closely before trying to get back on the motorcycle. Three oval shaped burns were quite severe. The outer skin was burned completely away with only pieces of dead skin still attached. A fourth burn was blistered but had not broken. Each burn was about four to five inches long on my left calf. I am thankful to have strong legs. Once the initial intense pain of the burns began to subside, I was able to get back on the motorcycle and keep going. While riding, the heat from the engine continued to cause discomfort, but we had to keep moving. There was no one who could help us, we had to do it alone, regardless of pain.

After a few more hours and a few more creek crossings, we emerged out of the jungle. We were a ragged mess! But we had accomplished what we had set out to do. We found the T'moan people! The mystery of the legendary "people with a whole in their chest" had been solved. The people were not jungle ghosts but a real people called "T'moan". In our search for this legendary people everything that could possibly go wrong did, but we never quit; we just kept pressing forward. We had found the T'moan people and made it back to our home base.

Before the trip, the Lord had spoken to me about the T'moan people. He told me that if we were patient and waited for the Holy Spirit to work in the hearts of the T'moan, the entire tribe could come into the Kingdom of God all at one time. In the meantime, the Lord instructed me that we were to pray for them, and learn as much as we could about their customs, traditions, and beliefs. We were to become their friends. Then we would find a way to present the gospel to them in a way that they could understand.

Because I had been given this word from the Lord, we restrained ourselves from presenting the gospel during our first encounter with the T'moan. Our goal was to find them, begin to build friendship with them, and develop their trust. We were determined and committed to return to the T'moan people, no matter what obstacles Satan put in our path.

During our third expedition, the spiritual attacks against us were constant, just as they had been on previous expeditions, but more intense. We knew Satan was not going to give up the T'moan easily. We also knew that we were going to make sure they heard about salvation through Jesus Christ that would transform their lives completely!

5

EXPEDITION FOUR:

JUNGLE FRIENDS

I am certain that the isolated T'moan people were shocked the day four men and their guide riding motorcycles suddenly drove into their village. We knew it would take time for the tribal people to get to know us and trust us. So we scheduled several more trips to their village to establish a bond with them and to learn their culture, customs, and traditions.

If we had immediately shared Jesus, they would possibly not have understood the gospel or accepted it from us. We knew we had to build much closer relationships with the people before sharing this life changing message of eternal salvation through Jesus Christ. During future visits, we began learning some of their tribal language as well. It was actually quite simple to learn, because it has a fairly small vocabulary.

On the next trip, Pin and Ang went into the village alone. They prepared to stay with the people for two weeks. Poline and I ran our ministry's Bible school, among other projects, in Phnom Penh, so we had to plan our schedule carefully to make time for going to the T'moan village.

The Words of Life Ministries actually has a diverse role throughout Cambodia that includes church planting, Bible translation, producing

Christian literature and training materials, producing radio and video Bible teaching programs, as well as regional teaching and ministry. Directing the large staff working in all these roles and building better capacity in them as well, Poline and I are often pressed for time. Although we could not join Pin and Ang on this trip, we prayed continually for them during those two weeks.

The day Pin and Ang headed into the jungle I received an email from a church in the States that was new to us. The message stated that they were interested in supporting ministries to unreached people groups. I immediately replied with a simple message. "Pray for the T'moan people. We just sent a team in today who will be with them for two weeks."

The church responded by asking what the needs were for reaching this unreached people group. My answer was again simple: we needed equipment.

We now knew where the people were located; we had the passion, but we needed better equipment for going in and out of the jungle. We needed well-functioning motorcycles and medicine for the people. Since Pin had been trained as a Khmer Rouge medic and was familiar with jungle living, he knew exactly what medicines these isolated people needed. However, the greatest need that outsiders could help us with was faithful and persistent prayer.

Going into areas of unreached people for the purpose of sharing the gospel of Jesus Christ brings on intense spiritual attack from the Evil One. He had successfully kept these people in darkness for thousands of years. We knew that the demonic forces would fight to the end trying to maintain their territory.

It has always been my experience in serving the Lord that when we are faithful to do what God has called us to do, without fundraising or relying on advertising, the Lord faithfully supplies our needs. He truly is our Jehovah Jireh; Jesus always provides for what he commissions. He is our provider. To go in and out of the jungle on a regular basis requires good equipment, funds for ministry, and practical assistance in meeting the needs that we observed during our ministry in the village.

Pin and Ang went all over the jungle with the tribal chief and his family during their stay. The T'moan village chief showed them their fields, their graveyard, and talked about their contact with other tribes. They used to have contact with the *Jarai* tribe, but only every few years. The *Jarai* people used to sell them things, such as gongs and even elephants. A few months before our first visit into the tribe, their last elephant had died. They said the elephant died of old age. They were certain of the cause of death, because the elephant had outlived three generations of T'moan people. It was likely more than one hundred years old when it died. The stories that elephant could have told!

After nearly two weeks of friendly dialogue with the tribal people, they began to share more personal things about their contact with other tribes. The Mel tribe, in the past two years since our first trip into the tribe, had begun to have more contact with the T'moan for the purpose of trading goods.

The Mel people bought wild animals, horns, antlers, wild boar tusks, and such from the T'moan in exchange for things that the T'moan desired. One of the foods the T'moan people really liked was mangoes. They were sweet and delicious. Every mango season the *Mel* people carried in bushels of mangoes in exchange for whatever they valued. As outsiders we knew that the trades were never fair and the other tribes were taking advantage of the T'moan people's ignorance.

For example, they convinced the T'moan that a plow with a diesel engine (what the Khmer's call a "mechanical cow") would be better than plowing the ground with water buffaloes. A water buffalo is worth $400-500. A brand new mechanical cow costs $900. The Mel people convinced the T'moan that trading five to six buffaloes was a good trade in exchange for their old, rusty and  beat up plow. Some of the plows that were traded did not even work when they were delivered. The T'moan had basically paid $2,000 for a rusted piece of junk that they could have purchased in the next village with the trade of one water buffalo.

The T'moan knew absolutely nothing about engines. They did not have diesel fuel and didn't know anything about engine maintenance, such as changing oil and water. Within a short time, the mechanical plows became useless. The T'moan didn't even have a way to fix a flat tire or weld a broken piece of metal. There are now a couple of rusted "mechanical cows" that are only used as a perch for roosting chickens, because they don't work and they don't have the fuel to run them.

Another jungle commodity is natural resin. It is very valuable in Cambodia and around the world, because it is a natural sealer used for sealing boats to make them water-tight. Resin is found in the jungles and, in Kracheh province, it can be sold for about 40,000 Riel per kilo (which is about $5.00 per pound).

The Mel people were giving the T'moan a "great deal" paying 500 Riel per kilo ($0.07 per pound). Every "deal" the Mel made ensured that the T'moan worked hard and were given little or no profit. The T'moan didn't know any better and really had no choice but to take what was offered.

In cases of "businesses" that were downright illegal, such as illegal logging or trading in wildlife, those dressed as soldiers and police officers from the Mel and Kraowl tribes made the T'moan village their jungle base. The uninvited "business men" demanded food and supplies from the T'moan people for their hunting teams. All the men carried weapons and because of their apparent official authority they intimidated the local villagers. The T'moan people were helpless to do anything other than obey the commands.

The T'moan didn't have weapons, so they could not protect themselves from such invasions. These "fake officials" would go into the jungle and onto the T'moan farmland. They cut down their trees and captured wildlife such as monkeys, bears, tigers, wild buffalo, wild cows, porcupines, otters, snakes, and deer. In return, the men gave the T'moan nothing--not even money for the T'moan food they had eaten when staying uninvited in their village.

A monkey, for example, could be sold for $50-$300 depending on the species. The hunting teams captured fifty to one hundred monkeys during each hunt. Live tigers and bears were worth hundreds if not thousands of dollars. Those that had been killed were sold for their meat and bones to be used in Chinese medicines.

WOMAN GATHERING
FIREWOOD

The T'moan poured out their aching hearts as they told the stories of being abused. We were angered by their reports. The military and government authorities are supposed to be the protectors of the people, but those involved in schemes of illegal financial gain were further oppressing the T'moan.

The T'moan were once a nomadic tribe. They moved freely throughout the jungle, not maintaining a fixed location. Because of this movement, they rarely came into contact with others. In previous generations they were called "hunter-gathers"--just living off the land. However, they were unable to maintain the nomadic lifestyle as outsiders destroyed their natural resources. In the last five years, the T'moan stopped roaming, trying instead to establish a village and cultivate land.

The nation of Cambodia has had a turbulent history. Since the 1950s, they have been in almost constant civil war. During the 1950s, as in other time periods, the minority groups were the biggest losers in the battle for control in the country.

Before independence in 1954 (independence from the colonial power France), there were few Khmer people living in Northeast Cambodia. The area was part of a hill-tribe minority region that included the central highlands of Vietnam. The Stieng people, living in that region still had their own independent nation until not so long ago.

At the time of the nation's independence from France, the French had ruled all of Laos, Vietnam, and Cambodia, which were collectively called "Indochina." In 1953 the French were forced out of Indochina by the Vietnamese. They were finally forced out in the epic battle of Dien Bien Phu in which the villager army of Vietnam decimated the French forces. The region was then divided, giving half of the territory to Vietnam and the other half to the Khmers and Laotians. The French and later the governments of Vietnam, Laos, and Cambodia ignored the ancestral lands and territory of the other hundreds of minority groups and began a process of occupying minority lands. This practice of assimilating the tribes and occupying their lands is still continuing.

Previous to 1954 the Khmer had little influence in Northeast Cambodia. However, from that time on, the Khmer have been moving more and more people into the area, taking over the land and natural resources. Under the Khmer Rouge, the minority groups suffered greatly. They were forced to be soldiers or be killed. Their villages were burned, and the people were relocated to centralized areas to grow rice. Minority groups had never been rice growers before the Khmer influence. The minorities lived primarily in hilly and remote mountainous sections of the country, while the Khmers, who centuries ago were jungle-based, have usually lived in flatlands which is ideal for growing rice.

During the Khmer Rouge regime, the minority region was devastated. Northeastern Cambodia was a battle ground for the communist Khmer Rouge from the 1960s until 1998 when Pol Pot died. While *Analong Veng* was the last stronghold of the Khmer Rouge leadership and the last battleground, the "105" Khmer Rouge detachment remained active for several years after that as thugs and bandits. During this time, there was no order.

Any living animal was shot for food. Most of the animals were nocturnal animals so they were quite easy to hunt at night. Even now those with weapons go out at night, hunting with an AK-47 and a flashlight. Nocturnal animals' eyes glow at night because they are able to see in the dark. The eyes of animals light up like reflectors when the hunters use flashlights. All a hunter has to do is shoot toward the eyes and he kills whatever is behind the eyes. It is indiscriminate killing of all animals--male, female, or babies. This manner of hunting has left very few wild animals in Cambodia.

The tribal leaders told us that when they were young, they remember herds of wild elephants, wild buffalo, and wild oxen. They saw more deer than they could count. Today even a small squirrel or rabbit is a rare sight.

The tribal leaders can no longer depend on being able to provide for their people by living off of the land, even though they are the only village in a 2,500 square- kilometer area (1,000 square miles). The large number of hunters coming into their area has made life quite difficult.

The T'moan people have continued to plant rice, since they were forced to learn how to do it under the brutal Khmer Rouge government. However, they have never been taught how to grow other foods. Therefore, they do not grow vegetables or other edible plants.

The T'moan people have also never been taught agricultural principles for proper cultivation of the land and methods to keep the land healthy. That is why the T'moan people practice "slash and burn" agriculture. All they know to do is burn sections of the forest so they can plant rice. They get a pretty good harvest for a couple of years following a fresh burn because of the ashes which provide nutrients to the soil. However, once the nutrients have been depleted from the soil, the ground becomes useless. Because they do not know how to add nutrients back into the soil, they simply burn another area for planting their rice.

There is plenty of jungle remaining in this part of Cambodia. However, the T'moan don't need to continue their "slash and burn" farming practice. If the people were taught good agricultural principles and techniques, they could use the land they have already cultivated to its best potential.

Often the jungle trees that are burned down are worth thousands of dollars. Mahogany, Teak, and other hardwood trees needed for building homes and beautiful furniture grow in abundance in their area. The T'moan don't have saws for cutting trees; but even if they did, the people would be arrested by the military for trying to harvest the lumber themselves. The military, on the other hand, boldly come in and cut all the trees they want. They have even cut the trees shading the people's homes. The men then cart off the logs to sell through their military contacts.

I sat listening to the injustices, one after another, as the tribal chief talked to me one day about his people. With a downcast face he said to me, "We are the minority of the minorities. I am so ashamed when I meet a person of another tribe. I look like a tribal person, so they call me an ignorant person. I can read and write the national language, but because I have big earlobes, and I am missing most of my front teeth, they know I am tribal and they persecute me."

My heart sank as I listened to the chief share his heart. Since finding the T'moan people and hearing how they have been terribly abused and mistreated, I have kept their location a secret in Cambodia. Many people have wanted to visit the T'moan, but I do not take people other than my team to their location. I want to protect them,

THE T'MOAN CHIEF

because I fear they will be further exploited. I want these people to be respected and lifted up. They are human beings, created by God and just as valuable as any other human being on this earth. I do not want them to become showcased like museum pieces or zoo animals. Even worse, I do not want more people to take advantage of them because they are poor and ignorant. Too much has already been done against this innocent people group by those who know where they live.

The purpose in writing this book, from its conception, is two-fold: First, I want the story of the T'moan people to encourage and motivate others to go to the places where people still have not heard about Jesus and make Him known. Along that same line, I want the story of the T'moan to ignite the hearts of people to do more to reach their own communities with the gospel of the Kingdom. The second purpose I have in writing this book is so that the hearts of people will be stirred by the miracle read in the coming pages, the miracle of an entire unreached people group coming to Christ at one time. It is my desire that considerable resources can be procured for the purpose of developing the T'moan village and providing education for its people. It is my desire that the Bible also be translated into the T'moan language, enabling them to gain strength for daily life.

Jesus Christ will bring them salvation by giving them forgiveness of their sins and changing them from their destructive habits. Education will lift them out of ignorance, so they will not be so easily exploited.

Ever since we first went into the T'moan tribe, we have sought only to bless the people rather than to take advantage of them. I believe they see that we are very different from others who have come to their village to take from them and use them. We want to learn from them and help them to have a better life. That better life begins with a transformation in their lives that can only come from God, beginning with his salvation. We have been patient, waiting for the Lord's timing as we have continually prayed for the salvation and transformation of the T'moan people.

After nearly two weeks in the village, Pin and Ang said their goodbyes and promised to return soon. On their way back, they had some difficulties; but as time passed, they began to learn the trail well. On this expedition, Pin and Ang both rode on one small 100cc motorcycle. Since there was no rain, they made better time than our third expedition. The motorcycle, however, was very old and unreliable. About half way to the training center, the pistons seized up. The pistons were damaged, so they knew that they had to walk out.

Walking in the jungle is quite difficult because of the uneven ground. Walking in the jungle and pushing a motorcycle is even more difficult and definitely not fun! Pin and Ang ended up walking and pushing the motorcycle nearly twenty miles.

As tired as they were, once Pin and Ang reached the Kracheh training center they immediately called me. "Steve," they said, "We believe the time is right for us to share the gospel with them. They accept us like brothers."

"Ok", I said, I sensed the time was right as well. "Let's go in two weeks. This time we will share the gospel to the people."

T'MOAN CHILDREN

From that moment, we began making our plans--a plan to share the gospel to the whole village. We prepared the stories from the Bible so that the T'moan would be able to accept the gospel as something intended specifically for their people. I believed that if we prepared everything right and if the Holy Spirit was working in the lives of the villagers, they could all accept Christ at the same time. That had been the word God had given me many months earlier.

It was obvious to us that the T'moan were a very close-knit people. I sensed that looking for an opportunity for the whole village to accept Christ would be better in the long run than seeking individual decisions, as that might bring extensive and long-lasting division to the village rather than unity.

We all prepared our hearts, minds, bodies, and physical gear for the next trip into the village. We were excited about the opportunity that lay ahead. We prayed that the hearts of the T'moan would be ready to receive the gospel message.

6

EXPEDITION FIVE:

THE GOSPEL

March of 2006 was a memorable month. It had taken a couple of years to build relationships with the T'moan people and learn about their culture, traditions, and folklore. We believed the time was now right for us to present the gospel to these people.

The greatest challenge was to present the truth of the Bible and Jesus as God, however, they had previously not heard any of it before. They did not know what the Bible was, much less any book, so we could not simply present the Bible as truth and expect them to believe us.

In their folklore, they have two key stories which support the truth in God's Word. These two stories provide a common point of understanding in how we view the world. The first is a flood story. The second is a story about the end of the world coming because of a great fire. Our presentation to them would hinge on these two key stories, but it was supported by our two years of building a close friendship with the people.

The apostle Paul said, "*Though I am free and belong to no man, I make myself a slave to everyone, to win as many as possible. To the Jews I became like a Jew, to win the Jews. To those under the law I became like one under the law (though I myself am not under the law), so as to win those under the law. To those not having the law I became like one not having the law (though I am not free from God's law but am under Christ's law), so as to win those not having the law. To the weak I became weak, to win the weak. I have become all things to all men so that by all possible means I might save some. I do all this for the sake of the gospel, that I may share in its blessings"* (1 Corinthians 9:22-23). Paul would do whatever it took to share the gospel, and we would do our best to eliminate any personal cultural elements that might be a barrier to their receiving the gospel. It was our desire to become like a T'moan tribal person to be able to save the T'moan. If we would come to them as outsiders bringing our own dominant culture, we feared alienating the people and causing them to reject our culture--preventing them from hearing the gospel message.

There was much we had to do before leaving for the T'moan village again. The spiritual warfare before departure was intense. I had a massive headache for two weeks. It was so painful that I could not sleep at night. I would pace the house praying that the pain would leave. No medication helped to relieve the pain. Tylenol, aspirin, migraine medicine, codeine, and even de-worming medicine had no effect at all.

All of us believed that the time was right to return to the village. We also believed that the Holy Spirit had prepared our every step to this point. I knew that my headache was a demonic attack. I also knew that I could not allow anything to deter the plan God had put in our hearts. The fate of an entire people group rested on what we would do or not do. How could I allow people to die and spend eternity in hell just because I had a lingering headache?

A few months earlier, a mission team from Texas had given me a GPS (Global Positioning System) that is used by the military, campers, and fishermen to find an exact position on the earth. It is the modern replacement of a compass. With a GPS we would never have to wander aimlessly in the jungle as we had done during our early expeditions. Once we marked the course, we could re-trace our steps precisely. We wanted to determine where the village was actually located. The topographical terrain map with hundreds of little hills and dozens of creeks all looked the same, so it was not very helpful.

Most importantly, I contacted close friends of our ministry in California. I told them we needed prayer and how we were going into the jungle to share Jesus to a whole tribe. We believed that the Holy Spirit was preparing the entire tribe to come to Christ at the same time. The pastor told me that the whole church would be in a three-day prayer and fasting time at the exact time of our expedition into the jungle. The pastor committed the church to pray for us during that time.

We prepared the motorcycles once again. We bought two bigger motorcycles (250cc) for the two church planters, even though we did not really have the finances to do so. I knew the owner of the motorcycle shop, so I asked him permission to take the motorcycles on a "test drive." In the end I only paid for one and took two! (I just conveniently left out the details of our "test drive," saying I was going to try out the motorcycles "up north!" My word was good enough for him. This time we would have four dirt bikes, one for each person on the team. This would help to speed up our progress and comfort on the trail. The dirt bikes are built with a suspension to handle bumps and jumps, tires designed to dig into mud and sand and keep their grip, and enough power to force ourselves through any mud hole. The only draw backs are weight and fuel consumption, and with more power comes more acrobatic falls!

We prepared a gospel film and the story of Noah that paralleled Noah to Jesus. The gospel film climaxed with the judgment of God and the destruction of the world by fire, being the judgment of God. The T'moan people, who had never seen a TV much less a movie, were going to see a big screen presentation of the gospel using their own stories as a storyline. We took a screen, amplifier, DVD player, LCD projector and a generator. We were weighed down with equipment, but we knew we would only get one shot to do it right--presenting the gospel to the entire village during this one trip.

READY TO GO!

We had all the motorcycles checked out and repaired. Chains were tightened and greased, oil changed, and tires and inner tubes checked and replaced if needed. Weak batteries were replaced with new ones. Nothing was left to chance. We knew that many people's spiritual lives depended on what we would do, and that thought consumed us. Some of us on the team fasted. We all spent many hours in prayer as part of our preparation. We were totally dependant on the Holy Spirit to convict the people of their own sin and their need for Jesus. However, we wanted to make sure that we covered any elements that we could.

The morning of our departure came. My ever-present headache was extremely painful. I did not sleep much the night before, partially because of the anticipation of the next day's events, but also because of the extreme pain. I have had bad headaches before, but never for days on end like this. They usually last just a few hours.

We packed all of the motorcycles and began to start our engines. Mine didn't start! I laughed. "Nice trick, Satan!" I said. I asked the guys to push me and follow me to the mechanic. "I know exactly what this is," I thought to myself. The Holy Spirit had prompted me that morning that something would happen to my battery. I didn't need to waste any time trying to figure anything out. I drove straight to the mechanic, took out the battery, replaced it, and in less than five minutes we were underway. I spent the entire time worshipping the Lord and praying as we drove down the highway out of Phnom Penh and toward Kracheh. As we came to the border of the next province, my headache instantly disappeared. I believe that the number of people praying for us was making a great difference. Yet as the road would get much worse ahead, we would find out the extent of the difference when we got to the jungle and had to go off of the road.

The first leg of the trip was two hundred twenty miles long. Though it was a long day, we had no problems. As we approached the spot where I had broken my arm, I prayed the Lord would protect us all. As we passed the spot, I continued worshipping the Lord at the top of my lungs. We arrived in Kracheh and with the other team members, we stocked up on food and other things we would need before going into the jungle.

I had decided this time that I would give much of my "equipment" away to the village people when we departed, like my buck knives, backpacks, and such. My wife usually laughed at my Boy Scout preparedness when I went anywhere. The Cambodian mindset is that you solve a problem when it arises. Why bother yourself before there is a problem, they reason. I am beginning to see a lot of wisdom in that thinking. Previously I took a lot of extra clothes for the "just in case" moments. This time I took only a couple changes of clothes and washed some each day.

One great addition on this trip was a backpacker's water filter. It was designed for clear mountain streams in America. I was not sure if it would work on stagnant ponds that were black with the pollution that three hundred people and dozens of cattle cause.

One important addition on this trip was a video camera. I wanted to record the conditions of the village, the travel, and anything exciting that might happen. I was secretly thinking that perhaps some supernatural event would take place, and I wanted to be able to capture it on tape. Surely if an entire people group would come to Jesus at one time, it would be deserving of an angelic choir descending from heaven to serenade us!

After a day of travel to the Kracheh training center, we headed into the jungle the next morning. What used to be a full day trip was now made easier by the construction of a new highway to China that was nearly completed. That gave us a two lane paved highway where there once was a broken gravel track.

Over the last ten years of working to start churches in Northeastern Cambodia, we have noticed a special divine blessing--roads. Time and time again, where we started churches, the government would come in and build roads, without knowing that they were building them so we could more easily reach our congregations. Sometimes the road went right up to the church property and stopped. Even this new road to China was built through the jungle many kilometers away from the old road. We had worked for many years planting churches in the jungle, and when they put the new road in, it crossed many of the villages in which we had previously started churches, making them more accessible. I believe that the roads were a divine blessing from God to help transform the lives of the people who believe in Jesus. I have no doubt that within a few years there will even be a road to the T'moan village.

Once we exited from the new road, the path to the village was just the same as it had always been. The sand was especially deep and difficult to maneuver in. The creeks were dry, the ravines were as steep as before, but it was as if we were flying through in record time. In fact, it usually took us a day to reach the Mel village, but this time we were there by ten o'clock in the morning. It seemed as if we would have no problem making the trip in one day!

So we continued on our way to the T'moan village. We kept traveling in single file, one after another, on the narrow path. Then all of a sudden we realized that Poline was missing. He had been bringing up the rear. We waited a few minutes, wondering what had happened to him. When he eventually rejoined us, he told us his motorcycle had simply died. He could see fuel dripping out of the carburetor. He didn't know what to do, but then suddenly the dripping stopped. The engine restarted with ease, so he continued in the direction the rest of us had gone. Poline's motorcycle didn't have any other problems during the entire trip.

Halfway into this leg of our trip, we came across a group of three hunters. They had bags filled with turtles. They were burning the grass around dried creek beds. As the fires burned, the holes where the turtles were nesting were revealed. That was one way the men could collect a lot of turtles at one time.

Pin noticed another bag under everything else they had. It was a monitor lizard. Our jungle expert, Pin said, "Those are delicious!" He continued, asking the hunters, "How much do you want for it?" They said $5.00 but Pin said he would give them $2.00. The hunters agreed on the lesser price.

A monitor lizard looks like a normal small lizard found anywhere, but monitor lizards are at least three feet long. Since it was still alive, Pin gave it a whack on the head to kill it. He then tied it to his motorcycle right behind where he sat. Pin told us we needed to cook it within a few hours from the time he had killed it or it would stink. Eyeing our "delicious meal" I had doubts about the quality of our food, but I was sure it would be better than frogs!

We continued on our way until we came to the River of God. At the river, the water level was low so we knew we would be able to easily drive our motorcycles across. We stopped to rest in the shade, knowing that we were just minutes away from the first T'moan village. Once we arrived there, we would have to devote our full attention to the people. So we drove down into the river bed to sit on some dead logs. Pin went over to the water and washed off his face while we sat in the shade. Suddenly the monitor lizard squirmed on the back of his motorcycle. "Pin!" I said, "It's not dead."

"Sure it is. You saw me smash him in the head." he replied. The lizard lay still again as Pin looked at it from a distance. "See," he joked, "he was just rolling over in his grave. He's dead."

However, I noticed that it moved again, and again. I called out to Pin, "Do you think he is having nightmares in the grave? He is moving a lot!"

Pin rushed over; thoroughly convinced that it was just a dead lizard twitch. The head was tied into a black plastic bag. Pin loosened the ropes that had the lizard tied to the motorcycle. With the release of the pressure the lizard stopped moving. Then Pin slipped the bag from the lizard's head while holding the tail. When the bag came off the head, the monitor lizard lunged at Pin with its mouth wide open. It was mad! Pin jumped away, still holding the tail. Its legs, with one-inch claws started trying to rip into Pin's arm. Pin threw the fighting creature into the water, instantly realizing that had been a bad idea. Monitor lizards can swim very well. As the monitor lizard hit the water Pin jumped into the water after it. The lizard had started swimming immediately. Pin grabbed it again by the tail and swung it forcefully like a wet towel into the water again. He kept swinging it harder and harder, hoping to knock the lizard unconscious. Pin eventually made his way to the rocky shoreline with his angry purchase and gave it another big swing. It was still not dead, but not as aggressive by this time. Pin quickly picked up a large rock and smashed its head. The rest of us were laughing as we watched Pin's battle with the monitor lizard. Pin gave a sigh of relief that the lizard was finally dead, looked up at his laughing audience and said, "Now it will really be fresh. They are much more delicious fresh!"

We all laughed some more. I commented how funny it would have been if the lizard had bit Pin in the backside while he was driving, since Pin had tied it to the back of his motorcycle seat! It was a good day!

Within minutes we were in the village. Along the whole way, not one person's motorcycle had slipped or fallen. Not one person had engine trouble. Not one person felt tired. Here it was 3:00 pm on what was previously a two to three-day journey. We had made it in one day and felt very refreshed. There was even a wonderful, cool breeze blowing in the jungle where usually there was hot, stagnant air. The prayers of believers were making a significant and tangible difference on this expedition.

The villagers came out to greet us as soon as we entered the village. They were looking forward to our coming. They were also happy to see the monitor lizard, as they knew that meant they would have some good food too. The chief gestured for us to look under his house. He wanted to show us what he had caught. We had been pleased with our three-foot monitor lizard. However, there under the house, tied by

its neck and in a mesh bag was a six-foot monitor lizard that probably weighed between seventy and one-hundred pounds. The chief told us they were going to sell it to the military the next time they came through their village.

That night as darkness came, our lizard was ready to eat. I cautiously took my first bite while every one else dug right into their meal for the day. I was surprised that it actually tasted good. It tasted like a very delicious chicken! I have eaten many odd things during my many years in Cambodia, all of which I was told were supposed to taste like chicken...but they didn't. However, this monitor lizard tasted exactly like chicken, although it was very boney.

FRESH MEAT: LIZARD!

Our monitor lizard meat lasted until the last day when we then had our traditional rooster meal. In the T'moan village, hundreds of chickens ran around; but they were not for food--they were for sacrifice. Occasionally the T'moan would kill a rooster for us to eat, usually a very old rooster. I have yet to be able to chew old rooster meat. It is quite literally like trying to bite through a car tire.

We used a machete to cut the uncooked meat so it would not be so tough. We hacked the rooster into small pieces, bones and all, so that we could swallow the meat. By the end of our rooster meal, our jaws were sore from being overworked.

POT-BELLIED PIGS

The T'moan also have a lot of native pigs (pot-bellied pigs). The bellies on some of the pigs literally drag on the ground. They are very funny to look at. Some of them even have piglets, but the nipples are nearly dragging on the ground, so I am not sure how the piglets nurse.

That night we made preparations to show the T'moan their first movie. They were not sure what to expect as we put the screen up on the side of one of the houses. It filled the entire wall of the house. As we set up all of the equipment, we realized we had forgotten an extension cord that would enable us to place the small portable generator away from the other equipment. This would lower the noise level by the speakers. We knew that the sound was slightly muffled on the DVD. Since it was in Khmer, only about half of the village would understand the words that were being said.

As darkness came, the people wanted no delay. They all ate their evening meal quickly then came out and sat on the ground in front of the screen. Before long the entire village of three hundred people was sitting on the ground waiting in anticipation of what was to come. Sitting in the middle of the village in total darkness, unable to see the faces of the people, we started the generator and turned on our LCD projector. The whole village lit up. The screen (ok, it was a bed sheet) covered the entire side of one house.

The movie began with creation, showing a little boy looking into the sky. "Have you ever wondered who made the stars in the sky?" the narrator said. Looking up at the stars in the sky that night, I realized once again that there were so many. How could anyone not just naturally

PREMIER NIGHT... FIRST MOVIE EVER!

assume that there was a God who created everything their eyes could see? The story continued with a summary of how the world was created and the creation of Adam and Eve. Then it explained that people became wicked and became enemies of God. God then destroyed the world with a flood, but some people who were in a boat were saved--just like the T'moan story had said.

The middle section of the movie was a summary of the life of Christ and explained why Jesus is God and why we need him to forgive us of our sins. The end of the movie culminated with a parallel between what will happen to those who do not receive Jesus' salvation and those who do. Since the T'moan had a story about the end of the world coming with a great fire, we showed that in the movie. The closing of the movie ended with the promise of eternal life and avoiding the fire for all of those who receive Jesus Christ.

When the hour-long movie finished the people called out . . . "Can we please watch it again?" Why not? So we played it one more time.

We had a second movie made specifically for dealing with the life of Noah and the great flood. After the gospel movie finished a second time, we began the life of Noah. The story went into detail about the condition of the people and how they had become very wicked and rejected God, who had created them. The movie explained the faithfulness and obedience of Noah to God's instructions to make the boat, and as a result how he was saved when the flood came.

The T'moan folklore flood story stated that the boat had been tied by a rope to the earth where the T'moan people lived. Some of the T'moan people got into the boat. Then the flood waters rose and the rope broke. The story goes on to say that the T'moan people in the boat sailed away and never came back.

Using their flood story as a connection to understand God's Word, we introduced ourselves to the T'moan as the long-lost relatives of the T'moan who were saved by the boat and have now returned to share with them about Jesus who saved them. All the villagers were very happy to hear the great news.

It was late in the evening when we finished answering the questions of the people about the gospel message they had just seen. For a people who get up with the sun and go down with the sun every day, they were getting sleepy. We were all tired by now as well. The nice, cool weather was a great blessing. I knew we would sleep very well that night in the little house with no walls or roof.

As we tied up our hammock, we talked about our agenda for the next day. We planned to gather the elders and the rest of the people to share more about Jesus. Pin and I would spend our time with the elders answering every question they had about Jesus Christ and what they had seen in the movies the night before. Poline said he wanted to talk with the young people, especially the young men who have a unique position in their society. Ang said he wanted to spend time with the families, the children and women to share Christ with them.

The plan was set and we quickly drifted off into a nice rest as the cool breeze continued to blow on us all night. Just before dawn, it became quite cold for us. The temperature was probably only about seventy degrees, but we only had shorts and t-shirts and we were sleeping in nylon hammocks, which become quite cold as well.

In the morning we had some more monitor lizard for breakfast and asked the chief if he wanted to invite the people to ask questions about what they had heard the night before. He said, "Oh yes, they have many questions they want to ask."

Soon all the elders came to the chief's house. Ang went to another house where the children and women often gathered to watch what we were doing in the center house. Poline called all the young people to another house on another side of the village. We were all set to present the gospel to the people in whatever way we could so that each group of villagers could easily understand. We could hear Poline teaching the young people some Christian songs and explaining the meanings. Ang was using a tract with beautiful pictures to share the gospel to the children and women.

Before Pin and I could start, the chief told us that a lady had become very sick in a house across the river. The chief said, "I think she will die soon." The spirits were upset with this family, he told us. Two weeks previously, a little boy in the family died. One week earlier, the grandfather died. Now the grandmother had become sick that morning. The symptoms were the same each time. They each developed a high fever and their neck began to swell until their windpipe was choked off and they died. It had not taken long for them to die. Silently I prayed that God would protect the lady so that she could hear the gospel. Pin and I felt this was clearly a case of evil spirits attacking the family.

With all the elders together, Pin and I told them we were going to review what they had seen the night before in the movie. Then we told them they could ask us any questions they had about the things we were saying. Using a picture book we had helped make a few years earlier, we went through the creation, flood, life of Jesus, and the eternal judgments all people will face. When we finished, we asked if they had any questions. The chief asked, "So, if we believe in Jesus, He will forgive our sins?"

"Yes, that is right," we replied and continued by saying, "And He will also protect you from the spirits that want to keep you poor and make you have a difficult life." Pin explained to them that they actually had lots of food to eat. There were hundreds of chickens and pigs running around the village. We knew they were reserved for sacrifice and were not being eaten by the people. The chief spoke up and said, "Last year we sacrificed nearly forty cows and water buffaloes also. Now we have very few left."

After a few hours of talking and fellowship I could hear Poline ask the youth in another house, "Do you want to believe in Jesus?" I could here them responded, "yes". At almost the same moment I saw Ang bowing his head to pray with the women and children. They were accepting Christ. I motioned to Pin that now seemed to be a good time. Pin said, "Now that you have heard the truth about Jesus, do you want to believe in him?"

Everyone looked to the chief to speak and he said to Pin, "We have seen everything with our own eyes. We know that Jesus is the true God. Of course I will believe in him." I wanted to jump with excitement.

"What about the others?" Pin asked.

The chief said, "They can decide for themselves. You ask them."

One by one all the elders said they would like to believe in Jesus as well. Pin then led them in a prayer to commit their lives to Christ and to ask divine protection over the village. We were all so thrilled.

Pin Explaining About Jesus

I thought to myself. . . that was sure easy. Though it took a couple of years to get to this point, when it was the Lord's timing, the Holy Spirit just took over. Everyone in the village, nearly an entire people group had accepted Jesus into their lives at one moment. There had been zero percent Christians among the T'moan one day, and the next day the entire village had became followers of Jesus Christ! At that moment I also began to ponder, what if we missed something? What if they were confused by all we had taught?

While thinking about the possibility, a young man came up to the chief and reported that the sick lady in the house across the river had just died. They talked among themselves for a moment, and then I asked the chief, "What will you do now?"

He answered quickly, "Before we would always offer a sacrifice to appease the spirits, but we will never do that again. We will do a funeral, but we will not do a sacrifice to the spirits."

With those statements I knew their acceptance of Jesus was genuine. Only minutes after they had accepted Christ, their first test had come. Now we would see whether they would truly believe in Christ or simply syncretize Christ into their animistic spirit veneration. We spent the rest of the day with the village people teaching them the very basics of the Christian life.

There was one more T'moan village that had not yet heard the Good News of Jesus Christ. Previously, we had spent little time there because the men drank heavily. However, this time we wanted to spend a couple days with them before leaving the jungle. We told the people in the first village that we would return soon. We invited the village people to go with us to the second village if they wanted to join us to show the movie. The second village was only about forty-five minutes away. A few of the young people headed off to the village, and we followed by motorcycle once we got all our equipment packed up.

It was almost nightfall when we arrived in the second village, so we quickly set up our equipment to show the movie. The village leader was not there, but the people wanted to see the movie. The young people from the first village told them how wonderful it was to see the movie about Jesus. Everyone quickly ate, as did we, having plain leftover rice and nothing more. The village was much smaller than the first, with only a dozen houses, but we still managed to have close to a hundred people sitting on the ground watching the gospel movie.

The next morning, Pin recommended leaving because we did not have a close relationship with the people and the village chief was not there. I insisted that since we had come so far, we needed to spend some time with them to explain what they had seen the night before in the movie. This time Pin sat down and called the people to him. He opened up a tract that had a similar story line and began to explain the gospel, answering their questions as they were raised. Once Pin finished explaining the gospel story he asked them, "Do you want to become followers of Jesus?"

One by one, they all said they did. Every last one of them, from the eldest to the children wanted to become followers of Jesus. It was quite evident that this village had been under the bondage of spirits for generations. It was evident by the strings that were tied around the children's necks and the strings tied around the waists of most of the adults. Attached to the strings were small metal strips made from lead that had magic words or signs written on them to invoke the powers of certain spirits.

In Christian terminology and understanding, these strings are fetishes, for the purpose of inviting demons to possess the individual. The strings are a sign of the covenant between that person and the demons. Ang told them that those who now believed in Jesus had the Holy Spirit, who is all-powerful, to protect them. He told them they should cut their strings off. One by one the mothers cut the strings off their children, and from around their own waists and then the men did the same. When the cutting was finished, there was a huge pile of strings. By that one act of faith in the power of the one true God, many demonic strongholds in their lives had been broken.

It was amazing! Over a period of a couple of days, two whole villages and nearly every T'moan person in the whole world had accepted Jesus Christ into their lives.

Later we learned that two more small villages exist in different parts of the jungle. These other villages are not pure T'moan and are comprised mainly of those who have left the T'moan villages over the years and inter-married with other tribes. However, there has been little or no contact between the two groups. As I thought about this new information, it occurred to me that it was perhaps good that some T'moan had still not heard the Good News. It is God's intention for all people, even the T'moan, to be missionaries--sharing the gospel with those who do not know Him. If all T'moan had accepted Christ within those two days, they may have become stagnant in their faith and not become evangelistic, as Jesus commands them to be.

With great joy and excitement about the future, the following day we headed out of the jungle. We made good time weaving our way through the jungle paths arriving back at our Kracheh training center. I couldn't wait to call my wife and let her know what wonderful events had occurred. My son answered the phone and the first thing he said was, "Daddy, how may people did you tell about Jesus?"

With a lump in my throat, I said, "So many in fact, that two whole villages believed in Jesus!"

"Wow!" he said, "Next time can I go with you to help you?"

"Sure, when you are a little older." I said to my six year old son, named Paul. I had named him Paul for a reason, after Paul the missionary of the Bible!

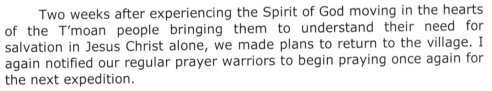

7

EXPEDITION SIX:

IMMERSED

Two weeks after experiencing the Spirit of God moving in the hearts of the T'moan people bringing them to understand their need for salvation in Jesus Christ alone, we made plans to return to the village. I again notified our regular prayer warriors to begin praying once again for the next expedition.

There would be only three of us making the journey this time. Poline had decided not to join us. Since His marriage five months earlier, he had spent only one weekend at home. His involvement with all of the T'moan ministry and our Bible school had consumed much of his life. Understandably, as a newlywed, Poline was missing his wife.

My wife Noit planned to join this expedition. However, as the time neared, our young daughter developed a fever. We felt it best that Noit postpone going into the jungle with me this time, so she could care for our children.

Once again we got the motorcycles tuned up and ready to go. This time, since I would be going alone from Phnom Penh to Kracheh, I loaded my motorcycle onto the pickup for the first 220 miles. Noit and my daughter went with me as far as the training center in Kracheh. My son remained in Phnom Penh so he would not miss school. While I was in the jungle, my wife would do some teaching and discipleship among the local churches. We reached the training center without difficulty.

THE RIVER OF GOD

The following morning after praying together with the staff, Pin, Ang and I headed for the jungle, fully expecting this to be a marvelous trip. When I first came to Cambodia in 1994, I discovered something I had not previously seen in the States. In Cambodia when a person is baptized, a great spiritual change takes place. From my observation, until people had been baptized, they tended to be nice people but were not really committed to Christ in every aspect of their lives. Also, I noticed that before a Cambodian was baptized, there were few overt spiritual attacks taking place. Since baptism is commanded by the Lord, and in the New Testament church believers were baptized immediately after they were saved, I figured two weeks was long enough to wait before baptizing the T'moan. We did not intend to force the T'moan people who had prayed to receive Christ in their lives to be baptized. However, we planned to teach what God's Word says about baptism and see what their response would be. We would allow the Holy Spirit to once again work in their hearts and give them understanding.

Ang had previously always used a little 100cc motorcycle or ridden with someone else on a big motorcycle, but this time he was getting up his nerve to drive one of the big motorcycles. We joked with him that this would be a good time to learn, because we would be driving off-road through the jungle for more than one hundred twenty miles each way. We teased him every time he crashed, as long as we saw it was not a serious fall. We figured by the time he had flown over the handlebars ten times or had done a face-plant into a river bed, he would figure out how to drive the bigger motorcycle. He had no idea what he was in for. The main difference between a 100cc scooter and 250cc dirt bike is the addition of a lot more power and a clutch. The balance between changing the gears, operating the clutch, and how much power to give the engine is crucial to driving smoothly. Not enough power will kill the engine and too much power will leave you hanging on for dear life as the motorcycle launches out from under you. He got to experience both!

Shortly after we entered the jungle, the excitement began. We put him on point so we would not drive off and leave him. All of a sudden, he slipped in some sand and the motorcycle launched to the left and then up in the air as it hit a giant termite mound. Ang was helpless as the motorcycle jumped into the air. He bailed off one side and the motorcycle came crashing down. We just laughed and laughed. When he slipped in the sand, he jerked the throttle, which on a 100cc bike would do almost nothing. However, on a 250cc bike, the tires got traction and launched him into the air. It was a cool wipeout! We told him that a few more times like that and he would definitely be an expert.

He often forgot to change gears. The little scooters have a rotary clutch with no hand clutch—just an automatic one. The big dirt bikes, however, have a hand clutch which must be used carefully so that the engine does not stall. A few times when crossing the creek, he would come down the creek in 3rd or 4th gear and forget to put it into 1st gear to get up the other side. The result was a brief climb and the engine dying. Watching him try and stay upright while he backed down an incline was always a funny sight. Ang really broke up the travel time for us with some humorous wipeouts. Fortunately, he was not hurt, or we wouldn't have thought it was so funny. We had all done the same thing many years ago when we were first learning. Other than Ang's beginner mistakes, we didn't have any troubles on the trip going there and again made record time getting to the village.

As we got to the village, Pin snuck off with one of the young T'moan guys. I was suspicious because I knew he had something up his sleeve. When he came back, I asked what was going on. Then he opened up a small bag that was in his pocket. It had ten AK-47 bullets, which were illegal to carry.

"What are you doing?" I asked.

"Somebody is going to shoot all the deer out here, so it might as well be us," Pin answered.

I thought about it a minute, but I felt uneasy about it. It is true that the military always comes and shoots what they want, but should we do the same? I inquired as to whether he had a gun or not, and he

said he didn't, but one of the villagers had told him he had a gun left over from the war but had no bullets. Every time we came, there was a lack of food when we went into the village, so he was just trying to help.

That night we ate our noodles and fellowshipped with the elders. Everything was going well. As we were lying down to sleep, we heard a sharp sound, "BAMM!" An AK is extremely loud but only the villagers would hear the shot. Pin looked over at me and said, "We are going to eat good tomorrow!" He smiled big and lay back down. A few seconds later there was another shot. Pin looked over at me again and said, "We are going to have a feast!"

Unlike the previous time we were in the village, this time it was typical jungle weather. Jungle weather is usually hot, sticky, and without a breeze. Sleeping was going to be very uncomfortable. After a long day, we were ready to sleep, and we

FRESH DEER MEAT crawled into our hammocks thinking about the great food we were going to eat the next day.

In the morning we had some good news and some bad news. The good news was the hunters had shot two deer and two otters. They only shot five of the bullets. That was good shooting with only a flashlight for light. Pin took one deer and gave them the rest. All the men in the village came around as Pin skinned the deer and cut the meat off. They were all excited about having meat to eat. The deer is a special kind of deer called a barking deer because of the sound it makes. It is very delicious to eat. There is little fat on this kind of deer and the meat is very tender. I have had it many times before, and it is my personal favorite as far as meat. The otter however, was also very delicious. It was my first time to have it. The meat had a good taste, but it also had a thin layer of fat which added to the taste.

Later I thought about bringing the bullets into the village. The American in me knew it was a bad idea. Especially since both the barking deer and otter were endangered animals. The Cambodian in me knew that the military would not quit killing them and selling the meat to restaurants until there were none left, so if someone was going to get to eat them, we might as well as enjoy the delicacy with the villagers. As I thought later, it was a good idea to have meat to eat, but it was a bad idea because it put us on the same moral ground as the military and police who were killing off the animals. We wanted to demonstrate that we had a different purpose for being there, and it was not to use the T'moan for our own benefit as everyone else did, but to bring them the blessing of eternal life and salvation that only comes from Jesus Christ. I decided we wouldn't bring bullets anymore to the village.

The next day we got some bad news. The last family member of the family across the river had fallen sick. We had already taught the villagers that morning about baptism and they decided they wanted to be baptized, but when it was cooler in the day, around three o'clock in the afternoon. The bad news came just before noon that the last family member had gotten a fever and his throat was beginning to swell. A fear came over many of the younger people. We had all seen the power of the evil one wipe out an entire family. We prayed for the young man, only twenty-four years old, and the village chief tried to get an antibiotic (ciprofloxin) that I had with me down him, but his throat was already too tight to swallow. At one o'clock in the afternoon, we got word he died. I was shocked. What made the villagers especially sad was that this was the last family member who had died. The entire family was now gone.

Immediately upon a death, the whole village goes into funeral preparations. They immediately cover the body so that no one looks at the face of a dead person. The relatives and other villagers gather around the body and wail. That was actually very unique to us because they were not just crying spontaneously but they were almost chanting phrases. Later we found out that the words were saying how sad they were and what a pity it was that such a young boy died. They just repeated the phrase over and over while holding their head and crying loudly. That evening the entire village would be expected to stay with the body until daylight, when they would bury the body. They would spend the night dancing and before they accepted Jesus, they would also give sacrifices.

I knew better than to question the Lord as to why a death happened, but I was certain it was a last-ditch effort of the evil one to put fear into the people so that they would recant their faith.

When it got to be about three o'clock, the village chief came over to the center house and said that most of the people needed to go make funeral arrangements. We understood and said we would like to help in the funeral as well. After a brief huddle, we were convinced that we needed to push through with the baptism with as many people as possible without affecting the funeral arrangements going on. The village chief thought it was a good idea, and he called around to different families in the village to send those who were free for baptism.

We all headed down to the River of God. What is normally a daily exercise to haul water, bathe, wash clothes, or water the livestock turned into a special meeting to demonstrate their commitment to Jesus. We had learned over the years in Cambodia to avoid certain things which cause problems later. First of all, we always had men baptizing men and women baptizing women. We didn't have any baptized women since my wife didn't come. In Cambodia, non-believers often spread rumors that men baptizing women were actually improperly touching the women

AN ELDER BEING BAPTIZED
IN THE RIVER OF GOD

under the water. It wasn't true, of course, but just to avoid any rumors, we never do it. Also, we found having at least two people doing the baptism was best because later some people thought the baptism was more or less effective based on the person who was the "baptizer." As the Bible never says who can or cannot baptize, we have always used multiple people to baptize so that there is not one personality which people focus on. The most important individual is the person being baptized, not the person who is conducting the baptism.

For the T'moan, we had a special case. The entire village, two villages in fact, had accepted Christ at the same time. It was a community decision to follow Christ. We felt that the entire community should have the opportunity to be baptized at the same time, even whole families at a time. So that is what happened. The tribal chief went first, followed by his family and other families. Sometimes they were baptized in pairs, sometimes whole families at a time including mother, father, and children.

Another thing that I discovered was that Cambodians felt like being baptized by a foreigner was more special than being baptized by a Cambodian leader. I know some churches who baptize the entire church every time another group of Americans come on a mission trip to their area. It makes for a great fund-raising video to show baptisms after only a weekend's worth of work! Pretty much in those churches, baptism has no meaning at all. Because of this trend, I have chosen not to baptize any people in Cambodia, but instead leave it to my local leaders. The only person I have baptized was Pin, and that was because as we were going to baptize his church members that he had led to Christ he leaned over and whispered to me. . . "I have not been baptized yet!"

"No problem," I told him, "I will baptize you first and then you can baptize the others." I have personally seen this same scenario more than twenty times where the person who is the "pastor" led his village to Christ so very quickly after he was saved that when it was time to baptize the new

AN ENTIRE FAMILY BAPTIZED AT ONCE!

congregation, the leader had to be baptized first. While he was still wet from his own baptism, he would baptize his congregation. This is a testimony to how fast the church is growing in Cambodia.

As Pin and Ang were baptizing, I was taking pictures of those who were baptized and also recording the moment on a video camera. At such a historic moment, I wondered if we were deserving of an angelic visitation. After all, the place was called the River of God and the entire tribe had accepted Christ at one time. Surely that would bring about a visit from Gabriel, I thought! After a time of praying and anxiously waiting for that angelic visitation I decided it would probably not happen. We would just have to be content with the hot, sticky jungle air.

Immediately after the baptism was completed, we could hear thunder and flashes of lightning in the sky. It was the sign of a storm-- right in the middle of the dry season again. Fortunately, in the couple of weeks that we were gone, they had put a roof on half of the building we were staying in, but there were still no walls. We prayed passionately that it would not rain hard, just enough to wet down the dust would be fine with us. With heavy rains, the rivers and creeks rise, and travel becomes very difficult.

For hours on end, the lightning flashed and thunder roared. The whole sky was black with rain clouds. At one point the wind picked up, a sure sign that the rain would soon fall. We all prayed very loudly together, "Lord, please. . . just a little, not too much! Have mercy on us!" The wind got stronger and stronger. The villagers started running for cover, knowing that a huge rain storm was coming. We covered our belongings and got into our hammocks, hoping the nylon would repel some of the water. We continued to pray. All of a sudden, it started to sprinkle and after a few minutes, the rain was gone--followed by a cool breeze. It was not even a significant amount of rain.

Not only was the light rain very cooling but I believed it had a spiritual significance. Later, as we left the jungle, we found out that the villages belonging to the Mel and Kroawl tribes had been pummeled with a huge downpour that flooded the main dirt path in the village. Some houses had their roofs blown off, it was so bad. Satan wanted to keep the whole jungle region in darkness and under his oppression, but God was going to bless the T'moan people. God was indeed moving through the jungle.

Late that night one of the young people came and told us to come to his house quickly. They caught a wild cow (gaur). When we arrived, we were told the story. One of the villagers saw a wild cow and its calf. The mother gaur burst into the jungle cover, but the baby could not get away, since it was a newborn. The baby was bigger than the barking deer, or about the size of a large German Shepherd dog. It looked exactly like a domesticated baby calf, except that it had no bone on its neck so it could not be yoked. Being separated from its mother, it could not survive. I asked if they had any cows which recently had babies that we could try and put the wild calf on the domesticated cow's utter. They didn't. The next morning, they cut its throat and divided up the meat among the villagers. The poverty was so apparent. They were so hungry that they would even kill and eat a newborn baby calf.

As we drove back, our emotions were mixed. We had no trouble driving until we got to the Mel village where Ang got more practice in crashing into mud puddles! We continued to have a good time with him and his driving experience. I couldn't help but think of the loss of an entire family due to a demonic attack. I think any doctor would admit that a disease which kills very quickly by choking the windpipe and striking and killing an entire family over a period of a month is quite strange. As I was feeling pretty bad about the situation, the Holy Spirit comforted me and said, "You are only seeing the death of the young man as a terrible loss, but today the first T'moan believer has entered heaven. He was one of those who two weeks ago had committed his life to be a follower of Jesus and received the gift of salvation."

That's right! He is the first T'moan to enter heaven. I could just visualize that T'moan believer coming into the presence of Jesus the King and worshipping around the throne in his own T'moan way.

As we arrived at the Kracheh training center and recounted Ang's falls, we proudly proclaimed him an expert after traversing more than three hundred miles of jungle with only minor falls. He had a good laugh with all of us.

As we reminisced about all that had happened with the T'moan people, we reaffirmed the commitment that we made in the beginning. We had made a promise that if the T'moan were to accept Christ, then we would commit ourselves to them to ensure that they are discipled into mature Christians who will reach out to other tribal people. Our commitment was deep, realizing that no matter how difficult it might be, and no matter what we might have to give up to ensure their discipleship, we were willing. We all knew the rains would be coming soon. We could not abandon these new Christians for six months until the next dry season came. One by one we affirmed our commitment to the T'moan, no matter what it took, even if we had to swim to get there or walk the entire distance. We committed to regularly go back to disciple the T'moan so that they could grow strong in their newfound faith in Jesus Christ. Ultimately we knew that we were just tools of the Holy Spirit to do the work of the Lord and that the Holy Spirit would continue to teach and convict the people in our absence.

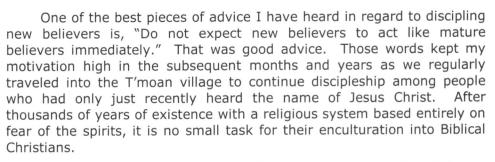

8

SUBSEQUENT JOURNEYS

One of the best pieces of advice I have heard in regard to discipling new believers is, "Do not expect new believers to act like mature believers immediately." That was good advice. Those words kept my motivation high in the subsequent months and years as we regularly traveled into the T'moan village to continue discipleship among people who had only just recently heard the name of Jesus Christ. After thousands of years of existence with a religious system based entirely on fear of the spirits, it is no small task for their enculturation into Biblical Christians.

The entire T'moan existence is based on survival. Everything is against them. The weather brings flash floods and periods of drought. Food comes and goes during the seasons at the whim of the natural elements. Sickness, even simple colds, can bring death easily and infect the entire village due to the lack of medicine and hygienic understanding.

Sadly, outsiders come and cheat the T'moan people out of everything they possibly can. They steal their few possessions, their natural resources, and ancestral lands. In the T'moan worldview (their understanding of the world), everything happens because of spiritual forces. Every sickness, every rainstorm, and even "bad hair days" are because of spiritual forces. Likewise, everything good that happens is because of devotion and respect to jungle spirits. Spirits are found in

DEATH WRAP OF A
STRANGLER FIG

trees, rocks, and even animals that wander in the deep jungle.

They believe certain trees possess more spirits than other trees. These trees, like the *Strangler Fig,* are well known throughout Asia to be the homes of spirits. It is also called a *Banyan Tree* regionally. This tree lives by killing a host tree. Its seeds are blown by the wind or transported by birds. The seed germinates high in the branches of a host tree and begins by dropping roots down from the high branches into the ground for nourishment. As soon as the initial roots are imbedded into the ground, the tree rapidly grows by surrounding the host tree until the host tree is only barely visible in the middle of the *Strangler Fig*. Eventually the host tree will die as all visible light, water, and nourishment are choked off. After many years, the dead tree will rot and be eaten by termites while the strangler fig becomes an impressive giant tree, living hundreds of years.

This fully mature tree, however, usually remains hollow in the center where the only reminder of the host is just an empty void straight up through the center. What happens in the physical development of the strangler fig is a perfect illustration of how the demonic forces operate. Initially, the presence is barely noticeable as a small seed, but eventually it germinates and begins to grow roots that suck the life out of the host. Over time, the host is completely covered by the presence of this demonic force until eventually nothing is left of the host.

Paul explained that in the beginning, all people knew God. . . the true God. *"For since the creation of the world God's invisible qualities—his eternal power and divine nature—have been clearly seen, being understood from what has been made, so that men are without excuse. For*

OVER TIME HOLLOW
CENTER: HOST DEAD

although they knew God, they neither glorified him as God nor gave thanks to him, but their thinking became futile and their foolish hearts were darkened" (Romans 1:20-21).

People did not always worship spirits and demons. This happened as a result of sin in people's lives. God has never forced people to follow him and, it is completely voluntary. After generations of people forgetting about God, demonic forces have been able to grow in strength and power until the entire knowledge of God is all but lost to people. From that time, the people have then lived in constant fear and under the control of evil spirits. Just as the *Strangler Fig* tree is hollow at the center, after generations of ignorance and being in bondage to demons, people have lost their connection to God.

In societies which are majority Christian, there seems to be a common moral background. We believe minors should not smoke or drink; drunkenness is socially unacceptable; deceiving others for personal gain is wrong; sex before marriage is wrong; etc. Even the idea that Jesus loves the world has been taught in our society for generations. We know these things instinctively because of our cultural background. Even many non-believers in societies which have many Christians often agree with these things as well.

The T'moan, who have been isolated in the jungle for centuries, do not share the same cultural heritage as Christian peoples. In taking Christ to the T'moan people group, it was very important that we learned about their cultural background in order to approach them in ways that would be culturally acceptable. It was important to speak to the negative influences of their culture, while on the other hand, bring out the positive elements within their culture. Our task is not to eliminate their culture. That would be morally wrong. However, it is important that we help eliminate negative and destructive elements of their culture, while enhancing and promoting positive elements.

The T'moan culture is very different from my own and other cultures. No matter how hard I try to learn about another people group's culture, unfortunately it seems that I often learn by making mistakes. For example: T'moan houses are made entirely of bamboo and have no furniture. The people sit on the floor, eat on the floor, and sleep on the floor. I am a very large-framed American with

A T'MOAN HOUSE

limited flexibility in my joints. It is a struggle for me to sit on an uneven bamboo floor for hours and hours with nothing to lean against. It is actually quite painful. When possible, I like to talk with people outside their simple house, sitting on a fallen log or on a tree stump.

While visiting in a T'moan house one day, I noticed a big rice sack on the floor. A Cambodian pastor, knowing my discomfort when I sit for a long time on the floor, motioned that I should go and sit on the rice sack. So I did.

At the time, only one T'moan grandmother was in the house, busy boiling water in a corner. After a few minutes, she turned around and saw me sitting on the rice sack. She immediately changed from a quiet, gentle grandmother into an aggressive and angry woman, screaming at me in T'moan to get off the rice sack. Immediately and with great embarrassment, I removed myself and apologized. Later we re-grouped to try and figure out what went wrong and politely asked a village elder about the situation. He explained that the rice is offered to the spirits, and my sitting on the rice was a great offense to the spirits. The spirits might take revenge on the people of that household and cause sickness to overcome them.

Our response was not to go against their belief but to pray, asking God to protect the people from the spirits. Demonic forces are very aggressive in areas they have claimed as their territory. We apologized to the family for our misunderstanding so that we would have further opportunities to disciple them in the truth. If we remained culturally offensive to them, it could cause a break in our relationship.

When I go into a T'moan house I now know that the best cultural response for me is to simply not sit on rice sacks. Does that mean I am respecting evil spirits? No, not at all. I despise the evil spirits, but I love the people who come from that cultural understanding. Hygienically, it is not ideal to sit on a rice sack. However, the rice will later be cooked which will purify it from any germ contamination. In the culture I grew up in, it is common to see men sleeping on bags of rice or a cat finding a cozy place to rest during the heat of the day on top of a bag of rice that is propped in the shade. However, among the T'moan people I simply want to avoid cultural offenses so I can have the best possible relationship with them.

If I insist on interpreting everything I experience from my personal cultural worldview, I would close the door to ever being able to share the gospel to people of another culture. Had I not humbled myself to their cultural worldview, I might have told them that sitting on a rice sack is beneficial for me so I would no longer have pain sitting on the floor. I might also have informed them that germ contamination would be negligible, and I (as a Christian) would not respect nor yield to any evil spirits.

Had I said those things, the response of the T'moan family to my cultural understanding would be very predictable and very negative! If anyone would get sick in that house in the days following my misguided actions, the illness would be blamed on me and the door of opportunity for discipling people into the Christian life would have been slammed shut--all because of a cultural misunderstanding about sitting on a rice sack. The T'moan would not reject me (and reject following Jesus) because of a theological reason, nor a rationalistic reason, but simply because I showed disdain and insensitivity to what they believe.

Discipling the T'moan people to become mature children of God will be a slow and difficult task. We have to slowly introduce them into an entirely new Christian understanding of life, while at the same time eliminating Cambodian and American culture, so they can freely respond to the leading of the Holy Spirit in their own culture.

My American culture determines what is proper in a Christian environment in America; however, my challenge with the T'moan is to share the gospel and teach Biblical truth in a completely different context. God has not called me to model American Christian culture to the T'moan, but rather to teach them Biblical truths and allow them to express themselves in a Christian way inside their culture.

In many churches in America, it is improper to wear a hat inside the church. It is also improper to ask questions directly to the pastor while he is preaching. Some church cultures even dictate what a person should wear to a church service. Culturally, it is expected in some places that a person have a new outfit to wear on Easter Sunday!

Churches in America generally design their buildings for the proclamation of a message and therefore have pews or chairs facing a front platform, much like a theater. If I would simply replicate what is done traditionally in America, I would rob the T'moan of their own cultural expressions.

We know that none of the above mentioned illustrations are Biblical teachings. They are simply cultural expressions. Unlike average American culture, tribal people usually sit in a circle around their leaders. If I requested the T'moan to sit in rows it would be a disservice to the value of their culture. Another area of difference is that whole families worship together in Cambodia, allowing children to be children. Where as, in the States, children are often ushered out to attend a culturally relevant "children's church" so they will not disturb the adults. People in Cambodia often speak up in services and ask the preacher questions about what he has said. The service resembles more of an interactive discussion than a lecture or speech-type presentation that is generally seen in America.

The process of discipleship in Cambodia is also much more than simply teaching through an American systematic theology book. It is more than details about the historical content of the Bible. It involves teaching the truths of the Bible in a way that brings change to the lives and culture of the people for the better. The best way to teach the Bible may not be in a systematic way, but by using stories, multi-media, drama, memorization or even chanting. It is not important "how" they learn, but it is far more important that they apply the Bible in their lives in a meaningful and relevant way to their culture.

In my travels to more than fifty countries through the years, I have tried to learn as much as I can about minority groups and their churches. What I have found is that in most cases, when culture is not extensively considered, what develops is a double culture (or a culture within a culture). The animistic fear of spirits remains, but on Sundays the people give the impression of a "good" Christian life.

In a far away mountain village, a pastor wearing a suit coat and tie leads a service mimicking a 1950s rural American worship service, complete with the old hymns, identical order of worship and rituals just as the church in America did fifty years ago. When a "Christian" gets sick, however, they immediately sacrifice a chicken or pig to the spirits. Why? I have discovered that in the 1950s, not much emphasis was given to spiritual gifts and the power of Christ to heal and deliver; therefore, when the believers have a physical need, they continue in their old demonic practices because they were never given an alternative. What has developed is technically called "syncretism," which means the blending of two different cultures and religions. Pure animists will accuse them of not being faithful to the spirits. True Christians will criticize them for not being fully committed to Christ. Both statements are true. This is why culture is so important in discipleship.

EMPTY RICE WINE POTS

On one of our trips to the T'moan people, this very issue was brought up. We arrived at the village late in the day completely exhausted from our travel. The people immediately wanted us to teach them. So while some went to the central water supply to clean up and then rest, a couple of us started teaching the people. As we looked around we saw evidence in the village of heavy drinking, suggesting that some of the people had engaged in more sacrifices.

When sacrifices are made to the spirits, there is always heavy drinking of a communal rice wine concoction. Their "moonshine" is made from rice and bark taken from a particular tree, then left to ferment. On days of ceremonies, the people communally drink the wine using a long reed straw. Everyone uses the same straw and they do not stop drinking until everyone is drunk. This behavior, they believe, makes them more sensitive to the spirits. It also temporarily releases them from the harsh lives they live.

Immediately upon seeing that some people in the village were continuing their sacrifices to the spirits, we began to teach them about the fact that God is a jealous God and will not be shared with others. Conviction came upon some of the people. They understood the teaching from God's Word and began crying out to God for forgiveness for their participation in the sacrifices.

We finished teaching as darkness surrounded us. We had seen God work in the lives of some of the people and we promised we would continue to teach them the next morning. Night had fallen and we were exhausted. We prayed before we climbed into our hammocks that the people would continue to grow in their understanding. That night we all slept well.

As teachers, we often get discouraged when the people we are discipling do not readily apply what they are being taught. When my mind begins to think in this negative manner, I remind myself that new believers cannot be expected to act as mature Christians immediately. It takes time for them to change the old practices of many generations. I know the enemy wants to discourage me in the hopes that I will give up.

The next morning we continued our teaching. We taught them in detail about people in the Bible who were not faithful to God. They were people who had worshiped both God and other spirits. We told them the story of the people of Israel who came out of Egypt and were completely dedicated to God until they thought Moses had gotten lost in the mountains of Sinai. While Moses was gone to the mountaintop to receive the Ten Commandments, the people built a statue to God. The Israelites then began to worship the idol in very evil ways, just like they had observed and experienced for more than four hundred years while living in Egypt. The people of Israel had quickly reverted to their old practices when there was a forty day break in Moses' presence with the people. God was not impressed with the people of Israel when they reverted back to Egyptian practices. In fact, the leaders and those involved were killed because of it.

The T'moan people understood very clearly what God thought of their sacrifices, as they listened to the teaching of the Word of God. One of the elders spoke up and said to us, "We are very sorry. We know that our sacrifices to spirits are not good and are also worthless. But we have been doing them for generations, and it is very hard to stop all these things immediately. We will stop all sacrifices in time, but I know that there are some who will take more time to stop the sacrifices. Please be patient with us."

A T'MOAN ELDER

I was happy to hear those sincere words of the elder. I knew that they saw the error of their ways and that they were convicted by the power of God. I also knew that we would need to be persistent in our discipleship with them in this area of sin as in other new teachings for them.

About noon we began to prepare our lunch (i.e. a can of sardines we had brought), and were looking forward to resting during the heat of the day. While we were preparing our things, one of the older elders came to us. He asked the young men to go with him to offer a sacrifice. His granddaughter, he said, had come down with a fever and he was going to offer a sacrifice to the spirits so she would be well.

The village witchdoctor, who always stayed away from us, had told the family that the spirit affecting the girl had come from the deep jungle. Therefore, the witchdoctor told them that they needed to go to the trail that went into the deep jungle to offer a sacrifice to the spirit there. The girl would get better if the spirit was pleased with the sacrifice, they were told. However, if the girl continued to be sick with fever, that meant they had offended another spirit and they would have to inquire of the spirits (i.e. witchdoctor) to discover what sacrifice they would have to make. Either way, the spirits win! Hearing all of this, many of the young men refused to go to offer sacrifices. We pleaded with the elder not to do a sacrifice and told him we would ask Jesus to heal the girl.

The elder told us we could pray for the girl, but he was still going to offer a sacrifice. In his mind, two were better than one. We tried to explain that Jesus would not help them if they gave sacrifices, because he would not be honored in that. The old man was determined to stick with his old ways, so off he went to the jungle trail.

We went to the home of the sick girl to pray for her, but they were not interested in praying for the girl. Because of their disbelief, we did not expect a miraculous recovery of the child and there was none.

Such events are discouraging to us. On the other hand, we were encouraged that some of the young men were steadfast in what they had just learned about God, and the sin of making sacrifices. These young men had stood up to the elder and refused to be a part of making sacrifices.

Another time when we arrived in the village, we were told the village chief was sick. We were so busy with our teaching that we were not able to spend time with the chief for two days. The third day we went to visit him in his house. The tribal chief had been the first one to accept Jesus among the T'moan. We were shocked to see that he appeared near death. His wife helped him to sit up, and he explained that he had been having very high fever for two days and had not been able to eat because he was so sick. His body was in much pain.

We were sad to see that on his wrists the chief had tied strings we knew to be charms which are tied in respect of a vow made to spirits. We asked him about the strings. He looked down and said sadly, "I know they are worthless; it is just tradition." Upon saying that, the chief ripped the strings off of his wrists and neck and threw them into the pig's wallow below his house. We prayed for the chief's healing and gave him a couple of tablets of Tylenol that we had with us. We said our goodbyes and immediately went back to our house to continue teaching. Fifteen minutes later, the chief walked over to where we were teaching. He looked like a refreshed man. Jesus had healed him!

We travel to the T'moan village as often as possible to teach and disciple. We are praying that one of our Cambodian teachers will be willing to live among the T'moan to disciple them daily. This would enable the people to grow in the Lord more steadily. This would also help them resist the temptation to fall back into traditional practices that prevent them from having true freedom in Christ.

Such a position, however, requires a clear call of God. With such isolation in the jungle, along with disease, danger, and lack of food, an outsider could easily die before word got out to us that there was a problem. Only the strongest of character and faith dare try to attempt such a mission.

We will not abandon the T'moan people. We will continue to disciple them. We want them to grow closer to Christ, and to be a tool in the hand of Almighty God to reach other remote tribes.

The T'moan...

The Oldest T'moan:
The stories this man could tell!

GUARDIANS OF THE SECRET TEMPLE OF GOD

LIFE IN COMMUNITY: MUCH OF T'MOAN LIFE IS EXPERIENCED AROUND A FIRE

THOUGH T'MOAN LIFE IS VERY HARD
THEY ARE VERY PLEASANT PEOPLE

The ox cart, important transportation for the T'moan.

My T'moan Guesthouse!

Grass for Roof,
Jars for Moonshine

A Lesson on Re-building an Axle
in the Middle of the Jungle

Getting the rice ready...

PLANT, GROW, HARVEST, DRY, BEAT, SIFT, CLEAN, COOK, EAT. . . SIX MONTHS TO EAT A MEAL!

THE STAPLE OF THE T'MOAN DIET is the RICE they spend their LIVES GROWING, SUPPLIMENTED BY OTHER FOOD THEY GATHER IN THE JUNGLE.

THE T'MOAN CHILDREN...

Jesus Christ Provides a Brighter Future for these Beautiful Children

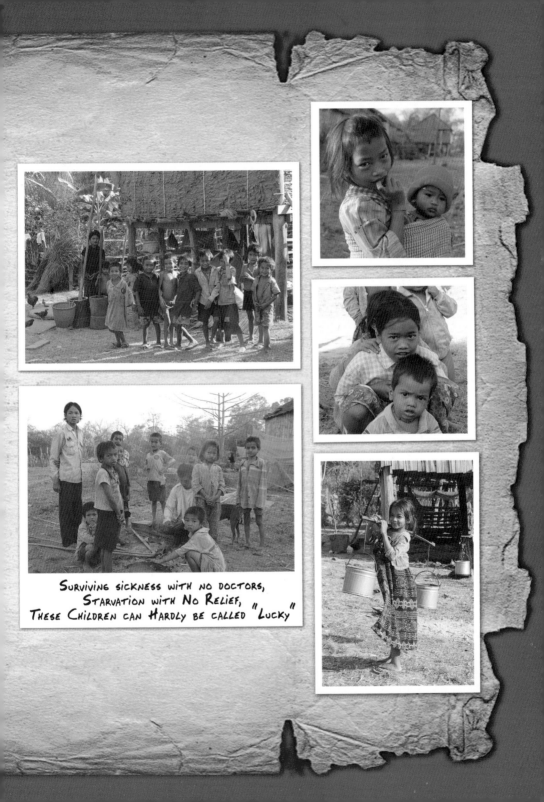

SURVIVING SICKNESS WITH NO DOCTORS,
STARVATION WITH NO RELIEF,
THESE CHILDREN CAN HARDLY BE CALLED "LUCKY"

THE T'MOAN DANCING INTO HEAVEN!

9

FOUR PERSISTENT MEN

During these jungle expeditions there have been four men who have been committed to finding and reaching the T'moan for Jesus Christ. All four men are very different but work extremely well together as a team. Each of their gifts complement one another, forming a solid ministry team. The following is a brief snapshot of each of the four men.

POLINE

Poline is a "city boy" of Chinese descent. Poline's grandfather moved to Cambodia from China. He is the third generation in his family to live in Cambodia. Poline is not a pure Cambodian, but he speaks only Khmer and English. He does not speak Chinese. Most Chinese are considered to be Cambodian because they assimilate well into the culture.

Poline is from a wealthy family. However, he lost everything when he became a Christian. His family practices Chinese traditional religion combined with Buddhism. This combination of religious practices mixed with veneration of spirits has many superstitions. Buddhism is basically veneration of spirits with the addition of idols of Buddha and other mythical beings. Most of their festivals and ceremonies are for appeasing spirits, just like pure animists.

Poline became a Christian through sports. I first came to Cambodia as the Cambodian National Basketball Coach. The title sounded impressive; however, the government gave me twelve military guys who knew nothing about sports. My job was to form them into a national basketball team. Because we had no one to play against, I began teaching in churches as well. One pastor, named Thavy, loved sports and was anxious for me to help his church, which I willingly did. Poline became a Christian through the sports ministry of Thavy's church. I have known Poline for many years. Later, Poline came to work for me in Words of Life Ministries and was my very first staff member.

Poline is very intelligent and also very good with the English language. He finished a bachelor's degree in Business Administration in Phnom Penh. I was later able to arrange for him to complete a Master's degree in Singapore. Eventually we both received Master's degrees from Bethany International University located in Singapore. Poline was only the second local Cambodian church leader to ever earn a Master's degree in theology.

When Poline became a Christian, he met a girl name Raksmie, who was the leader of the youth group at church. They fell in love with one another and never loved anyone else. Although the church youth knew about their love for one another for several years, Poline's parents did not know about his commitment to Raksmie.

As is typical in Chinese families, Poline's parents had big plans for him. Since Poline is the eldest son of a wealthy Chinese family, he is considered the most important child. Poline's position also means that he is expected to carry on the inheritance and family businesses.

After Poline became a Christian, his parents didn't mind so much, just as long as he always did what they wanted. Poline's mother was not a typical mother. She was deep into a combination of the black magic aspects of Buddhism and animism. They wanted Poline to marry someone of the same or higher class, as do most people. For some reason they did not think Raksmie was good enough for Poline, even though her father was an Army General.

Poline's parents insisted that he break the relationship with Raksmie and marry someone of their choice. Poline refused because he knew that Raksmie was the one God had prepared for him. When Poline refused to obey his parents, they banished him from the family. Poline's parents also forbade all their relatives to have any contact with him. The parents tried to create additional persecution by going to a church Christmas party where Poline and his friends were present and causing a painful scene. At one point, they hired a witchdoctor to kill Raksmie. She was deathly ill for nearly a month and doctors could find no cause for her sickness. After continual prayer, one night the demons left and she was free of the sickness and immediately returned to health.

Poline was determined, however, to marry the young woman God had placed in his life. Therefore, Poline was completely cut off from his family. He has never given up trying to bring reconciliation with his family, but they have refused any relationship with him and Raksmie.

Poline's mother had previously given him large tracts of land, gold jewelry, diamonds and other heirlooms since he was the oldest son. She demanded everything back, which he obliged.

In December of 2005, Poline was married in a beautiful Christian ceremony with many friends attending. However, no one from Poline's family was present. In March of 2007, Poline and Raksmie had their first child, a boy, named Immanuel, "God is with us". In January of 2009 he had a daughter and named her "Jubilee" meaning freedom and restoration. On August of 2010 they were blessed with a third child they named "Rene" which is a Greek word which means "Peace".

Poline has been a faithful servant of the Lord, no matter what the situation or difficulty confronting him.

ANG

Ang lives in a remote village in Kracheh province, though he is not originally from Kracheh province. He is from the rice-growing region of Cambodia in the south. He went to Kracheh during the Khmer Rouge reign as a worker, not a soldier. After the Khmer Rouge era ended, he stayed. He was assigned in a tribal village called *Beung Reun*, a very isolated village with no road. In the rainy season the village is only accessible by the flooded Kapi river. In the dry season, when the river runs dry, villagers make temporary jungle paths and cross rice fields to get to the village. The village is about half Khmer and half tribal people. There are some Stieng people, but the majority of the people in the village are Bunong people. Ang married a Bunong woman and they now have two sons, Chiva and Tola.

Ang was led to Christ by Pin. The very first day I met Ang, I knew he would be a leader. He is talented, has charisma, and is a dedicated follower of Christ. Through much hardship and persecution, he strives to be the shining light of Jesus Christ because of his love for the people. After being a Christian and receiving training for one year, he was commissioned to be an evangelist and start new churches. Ang has created many opportunities in villages for starting new churches. Since Pin passed away in late 2006, Ang (his disciple) has taken over responsibility for all the churches of Kracheh province.

PIN

Pin was the most colorful member of the team. He was the oldest one on the team and the father of eight children. A constant jokester, he masked his background for those that didn't know him. Up until 1998 he was a commander in the Khmer Rouge! We always joked with him that he was such a good evangelist because the villagers recognize him! He did not want to be in the Khmer Rouge, but the curse of poverty determined his fate. The Khmer Rouge took over Kracheh province, where Pin was born, long before Phnom Penh was conquered in 1975. Back in the 1960s, Kracheh province was already controlled by the Khmer Rouge forces. Pin was one son of a large family.

One day Pin's mother did something which offended the Khmer Rouge leaders and they said she must be punished. Punishment (which they called "*kaw-sang*" or literally "building up" really meant execution) was severe under the Khmer Rouge. Pin's mother was probably guilty of doing something like stealing some rice to feed her family. Under the Khmer Rouge, they didn't care if people starved and died as a result. All the Khmer Rouge rice was shipped off to China in exchange for weapons from Mao Tse Tong.   Private property and personal interests were eliminated by the Khmer Rouge, which was called *Ongka*. *Ongka* owned everything.   To take rice, even if it was from your own field, was considered stealing from *Ongka*.

As Pin's mother stood before the Khmer Rouge commander, she begged for her life and eventually offered her son to the Khmer Rouge as a retribution for her crime. They agreed to her offer, so Pin was taken to become a child soldier.   At nine years of age, Pin was removed from his family and trained to be a killer. Pin later commented to me that his mother's crime cost him thirty years under the Khmer Rouge. It was a living hell. Pin never saw his family again until after the Khmer Rouge reign was over. It was not until 1998 after the cease-fire agreement that he was finally able to reunite with his mother. When he returned home, no one recognized him. Pin cared for his mother until the day she died in 2005 and never once talked to his mother about what her decision had cost him.

Under the Khmer Rouge, Pin eventually was known for being fearless and an excellent fighter. He was an expert in ambush. He never talked about how many people he killed or any missions. However, one day he was reading in the newspaper that the Vietnamese were offering $300 per body for their missing-in-action soldiers. Pin commented that he would be a millionaire if he could remember where he dumped all the Vietnamese bodies he killed. More than 60,000 Vietnamese soldiers were killed in the liberation of Cambodia by the Khmer Rouge.

While serving with the Khmer Rouge, Pin learned how to be a medic. In one conversation about his 'doctoring' he said, "Medical care is easy. When I got shot in the leg, I dug the bullet out. Soon others wanted me to dig bullets out of them." Pin went on to tell about getting shot right through the neck. He was happy to show people his scars. He also tells a story about the time some Vietnamese soldiers shot a B-40 rocket that exploded at his feet. That blast left him with a bunch of holes, but he patched himself up. Living in the jungle for so many years, Pin learned how to treat malaria and other sicknesses. He also learned how to live off of the land and survive on almost nothing.

Until Pin's death, he was constantly sought after for his medical skills. He had no formal education, but most people went to him when they were sick. The sick always said that if they went to the government doctors, all their money would be taken and they would still die. However, Pin made sure the sick person was getting well before he asked for money. Even then he usually only charged for the price of the medicine. Sometimes the people didn't have money to pay for the medicine, so Pin paid for it himself. Pin was a good-hearted guy who was willing to help anyone.

When going into the jungle, there was no better person to have by your side than Pin. He could find food when there appeared to be none. He could heal any sickness or injury, and people just loved him because of his pleasant personality. Pin had never been to school one day in his life, but no one would notice when just meeting him.

On October 18, 2006, we received a telephone call at five o'clock in the morning from the Kracheh Children's Center. On the phone, Saret (our staff member responsible for the training center) told us that Pin was dead. He had been watching a few sick children during the night and was sleeping in his hammock near the youngsters. The staff tried to wake Pin, but he didn't wake up. He had died in his sleep. It was a shock that none of us could believe at Words of Life. Pin was only forty-five years old, with a wife and eight children.

Noit and I had just spent the previous two days with Pin and his health was fine. The night before Pin died, he was playing volleyball (he won!) and later went out with the other church planters for a fruit shake before bed. Pin stayed up caring for three very sick kids until about two o'clock in the morning. That was the last time he spoke to the other leaders. After checking the medical condition of the children, he went back to sleep and did not wake up. Not a sound had been heard from him. The following day we buried Pin at the Kracheh Center.

Pin was greatly respected as a Christian leader. Nearly every Christian from every denomination in the province attended his funeral. There were just as many Buddhists as Christians who attended. Along the three mile journey from his home to the training center to be buried, people came out of their homes to join in the funeral procession. The school dismissed early so the kids could line the street in respect as Pin's casket came by. Christ was truly honored in and through Pin, both during his life and at his death.

PIN'S SIX YEARS FOLLOWING CHRIST

In Cambodia, at the death of a person, we read out loud a short family history of the deceased. The story usually details the basic events of his life and the achievements of him and his children. Pin became a Christian in the year 2000 at 39 years of age. He only lived as a Christian for six years but had a greater impact bringing people to Jesus Christ than many Christians do in a 30 to 50 year lifespan as a believer.

After becoming a Christian, Pin led his mother to Christ and most of his family. Immediately after becoming a Christian, Pin asked to study the Bible with me. He completed the basic eight course Bible training we conduct at Words of Life in his first year as a Christian. By the time we got to level six which deals with how to start a new church, he had already started one.

After Pin's graduation, we went to Kracheh to help him baptize the people in his new church. As everyone lined up to go in the water, Pin leaned over to me and said. . . "I haven't been baptized yet!"

"Oh", I said, "Then I better baptize you first." So off the two of us went into the water. I baptized him while his congregation looked on.

After coming up out of the water he shouted, "Hallelujah!" and then immediately baptized his own congregation.

In his six years as a Christian, Pin had a direct hand in starting more than ten new churches from among people who were formerly Buddhist! He had a direct role in leading the entire tribe of the T'moan to Christ, as well as another whole Khmer village of *Chu-turn*. In all, I would estimate that Pin led close to one thousand people to Christ.

Perhaps one of the most remarkable individuals Pin led to Christ was the village chief of *Srie Chi*. Pin had personally burned the village down in 1995 (as a Khmer Rouge soldier) starting with the chief's house. Almost a decade later, Pin sat in the village chief's new house and shared with him about Jesus.

Pin also refused to let family members accept Christ without them first talking to their own family about the decision. They then made a family decision together. Without exception, when an individual was first turned down by Pin to accept Christ, the entire family came to receive the Lord within a few short days. If you think about it, in just six short years Pin literally led a person to Christ every other day!

Pin's life is a model of what a life completely sold out to Christ can look like. Pin always carried a Bible, hammock, and an extra shirt with him so that he could travel to where he needed to go at a moment's notice. He feared no one, except the Lord Jesus Christ, and it showed by how he lived his life. He was humble, kind, and always had a funny joke or story to tell. Many nights Pin and I would lie in our hammocks looking up at the stars in the sky and share our experiences and plan trips to places that still had never heard about Jesus. He was constantly thinking about finding more people who had never heard about Jesus, as well as thinking how to keep the ones who had already believed living a righteous life. Paul said, *"Follow me as I follow Christ."* (I Corinthians 11:1). I could honestly tell people in Kracheh to "follow Pin as he follows Christ." In only six years as a Christian, he shamed almost all of us. I think the only difference between Pin's life and anyone else's is that Pin was completely dedicated to being a follower of Christ, every single day he lived. What a challenge his life is to us all.

STEVE

Steve Hyde was born in the state of Iowa in the United States in 1971. His parents were living in the town of Barnum, Iowa (population 94) when Steve was born. When he was six years old, Steve moved with his family to the Philippines where his parents began their missionary career. Steve lived in the Philippines until he went to college in the United States.

In 1994 at Hardin-Simmons University, in Abilene, Texas, he earned a Bachelor of Business Administration degree and upon completion of his university education he moved to Cambodia.   Initially Steve went to Cambodia to work as a missionary for two years with the Southern Baptists.   However, he has remained in Cambodia since that time, starting his own ministry there.

Steve married Noit in 1999. Noit was the Cambodian director of World Relief's children's ministry for several years before they married. Steve and Noit have three children, Paul, born in December of 1999 and Anna born in June of 2005 and Odom born in June of 2007.

Words of Life Ministries was started in 1997 in order to develop training materials for church leaders in Cambodia.   Over the years, not only has Words of Life become the largest publisher of Christian literature in Cambodia, but also operates a nation-wide training program which currently has around four thousand church leaders being trained. The focus of the training is to give pastors and church leaders foundational training which will strengthen them in their personal lives, ministry, and in church planting.   Hundreds of churches have been started in Cambodia as a result of their training. Words of Life Ministries has trained leaders from nineteen different denominations. As well as training leaders, Words of Life Ministries also works actively in church planting and providing resources for local evangelists to reach the lost for Jesus Christ.

On March 4, 2003, Muslim terrorists killed Steve's father in a bomb attack at the Davao International Airport in Davao City, Philippines after twenty-five years of service as a missionary. Steve's mother continued her missionary work in the Philippines as a widow.

Although Steve was previously committed to missions, the death of his father had a significant impact on his understanding of his purpose in life. Steve has dedicated his entire life to see that those who have been blinded by the evil one can be shown the light of the gospel of the Kingdom.

Steve has completed additional educational milestones. At the end of 2003, Steve received a Master of Arts in Inter-Cultural Education from Bethany International University in Singapore.   In 2005, Steve received a Master of Arts in Missiology from Southwestern Baptist Theological Seminary in Ft. Worth, Texas, USA.   Steve's father had received his Master of Divinity degree from Southwestern many years prior. Steve is currently a Ph.D. Candidate at Bethany International University, where he also regularly lectures. His Ph.D. thesis is researching the correlation between culture and church growth, using Cambodia's rapid church growth as the primary country of study.

POWER OF THE HOLY SPIRIT

Some people may try to read this book to uncover some hidden secret formula about how to target a remote tribe and bring them to Christ. I want to assure you there is no formula, and I would be highly surprised if anything we did with the T'moan people would work anywhere else. The reason that it won't work is that the key element is the creative power of the Holy Spirit and our submission to him. There is no procedure to follow. The only formula that will work to lead others to Christ in mass is complete surrender of a person's will, ambitions, methodologies, and desires to the complete direction of God's Holy Spirit.

Along with submission to the Holy Spirit is stubborn persistence to fulfill all that God has called us to, no matter what the costs or sacrifices involved. I have never been in favor of "global" strategies or a "perfect program" to follow. Everything we do needs to be adapted and submitted to the full guidance of the Holy Spirit. What may produce fruit in one location will not necessarily produce fruit in another.

A perfect illustration of this can be explained by the packets of seeds that can be bought in many stores in America. If you plant flowers or vegetables at the right season (as the packet instructions read), you are most likely going to get the flowers or vegetables you expect. The seed company guarantees the results. If you buy a packet of snow peas, you will get snow peas. As they grow, they will look very similar to the picture of snow peas on the packet. If you buy a sunflower seed packet and plant them in the United States, you are going to get sunflowers. Take those same seeds, which have been processed and treated to work in most home gardens in the United States and try to plant them in Cambodia, and the seed will not even germinate. Sometimes, if something does come up, there will be no flower or no fruit, just a small leaf. That is because even a seed knows the difference between soil, weather, and climate in the United States and the hot tropical climate of Cambodia. To get seeds that grow in Cambodia requires seeds that have been prepared in Cambodia--especially for Cambodian soil, weather, and climate. In technical terms, we say that it has to be "contextualized" or adapted to the culture of Cambodia.

The same is true of methodology, training, theology, and evangelism. It all must be contextualized, or adapted, to produce good results in Cambodia. The gardener does not pride himself in how well he can plant a seed; that is easy. He prides himself in the fruit that grows. The same is true of the ministries of the Church. It is easy to launch a program based on methodology that worked somewhere else, but it will usually yield little fruit in a completely different location. The goal needs to be the fruit, not the planting itself.

Also, no fruit grows instantly. It takes time to germinate. It requires watering and care to nurture the plant into maturity so that it can produce fruit. The same is true of evangelism and sharing the gospel. While we are always glad to share the gospel (sowing seed), we are committed to the long term goal of discipling believers to maturity in Christ (producing fruit) who will be equipped and trained for ministry (making more seeds). This all takes time. It cannot be done on a weekend trip or even with a year-long commitment. It requires God's perfect timing and our persistence and faithfulness.

We spent nearly two years with the T'moan before we shared the gospel with them because we were looking for lasting fruit. In fact, it is Jesus who has called us to produce lasting fruit. He says so Himself in John 15:16 by saying, "*You did not choose me, but I chose you and appointed you to go and bear fruit—fruit that will last.*" Now that the T'moan have accepted and heard the gospel, it will take more time to nurture, guide, and lead them in becoming mature believers. We are committed to this call, no matter how long it takes. In order to be successful in the mission God has given us, it requires us to be completely dependent on the Holy Spirit every step of the way.

STRATEGY FOR REACHING THE T'MOAN

When we considered working with the T'moan people, we did not make a general strategy to cover the entire people group. We were looking for multiple ways to approach the T'moan according to various distinctives which we would observe in them. Knowing that the T'moan were a very isolated group, we knew that we would have to use a different methodology to share the gospel with them than we would normally use in other areas of Cambodia.

It cannot be said enough that it is the Holy Spirit who convicts of sin and brings a person to salvation. Our team was only the instrument used in the hands of a powerful and merciful God to be given the opportunity to lead the T'moan people to Christ.

Four of us worked for over two years to get to a point of being able to share Jesus with

SHOWING THE LOVE OF GOD By CUTTING HAIR

this tribe who had never even heard of Jesus before we introduced Him to them. Their religious practices are organized but are based on fear and appeasement of spirits who live in the jungles of Cambodia and involve sacrifices to these spirits to appease them.

Of the four people in our team, two had no formal education at all. One lives in a different tribal village, the other was a former Khmer Rouge commander. The third is a Chinese Cambodian with a higher educational level and the fourth is myself. Each brought his own value and gifts to the endeavor. My gifts were primarily strategy and finances because of my experience in working with a variety of ethnic minorities. I found out, however, that those who had a lower formal educational level were much more effective evangelists. There have been thousands of books written about how to share the gospel effectively with others. Some people swear by mass evangelism as the best method, but to others it's all about personal relationships and spending time with people. Others are passionate about literature, such as tracts, pamphlets, and the written Word of God. The current trend is oral learning where story telling and oral presentation are promoted as the ultimate method to win people to Christ. There are as many methods as people promoting them and all of them sound like "the" perfect solution.

What was our methodology to lead an entire tribe to Christ? Apart from the inexplicable power and working of the Holy Spirit, we used personal relationships developed over two years, we also used written tracts, media in the form of a gospel film, mass evangelism, small groups for discussions, and we even used pictures. It was the most diversified presentation focused on one people that I have personally ever been a part of or even heard of. Most of all, we were open to the working of the Holy Spirit and flexible as we were led by Him, not depending on one specific methodology. Instead, we used every possible way to reach the people. In the end, I would say the Holy Spirit did it, not us!

GOING BEYOND THE "WARM FUZZIES"

On many occasions during our time of reaching the T'moan for Christ, I had what could be called *warm fuzzy* moments. *Warm fuzzy* moments are awesome! Many times praying and singing to the Lord, I would be overcome by emotion as I thought of reaching the T'moan. Climbing on top of the small hill looking over the jungle canopy and claiming the jungle for Jesus was a significant *warm fuzzy* moment.

Another powerful *warm fuzzy* moment was the looking up at the millions of stars in the sky and feeling knowing I was an integral part of God's eternal plan since the time of Abraham. The point when the whole T'moan village accepted Christ was a powerful *warm fuzzy* moment which I will never forget. Then, only a few months later, baptizing some of the key leaders in the River of God continued to conjure up powerful *warm fuzzy* feelings in me. It is easy to be a Christian at those times. It is easy to volunteer to lay down my life during a *warm fuzzy* moment.

Conversely, falling into a ravine, breaking my arm, being trapped under a burning-hot motorcycle, sweating profusely at every moment, or trying to sleep through a torrential rain storm are examples of events which I would much rather forget. Like most people, I would much prefer to live in the *warm fuzzy* moments.

I love going to American churches, because they are built to ooze *warm fuzziness*. The sermons are beautiful, eloquent, multi-media enhanced presentations of the highest caliber. The worship times are models of perfection. The latest sound equipment, musical instruments, and other digital enhancements are top quality. Buildings are acoustically designed for the optimal experience. Musicians are professional and technical experts in their artistry. The worship teams quite easily usher people into an awe-inspiring *warm fuzzy* experience. I could stay in a service for hours on end without leaving such an environment.

As someone on the front lines of building the Kingdom of God, these *warm fuzzy* moments are few and far between. Most days it is just patient persistence adhering to the plan of God which keeps me going. During services, there is rarely anyone in a village church who even knows how to play a musical instrument or sing any song. We sit on uneven bamboo floors. After only a few minutes, my legs and backside are numb with pain. There is no electricity, so we sit, soaking in sweltering heat. I have become accustomed to being wet with sweat most of the time. Day in and day out, this is the challenge on the front lines.

FAITH AND PERSISTENCE

With the ease of global travel now-a-days, some people recklessly consider eliminating funding to long-term ministers, or incarnational missionaries who live among the people. It seems they have so few results. The families sacrifice the comforts of American living; the children sacrifice by missing their relatives, and they seem to have so many struggles and problems. Learning the languages is hard work and humiliating. On top of that, "hit-and-run mission trips" (the weekend warriors of missions) fly into a country for a weekend. None of them speak the language, and few are actually involved in their local churches but they have vacation time and would like to give of their time for a worthy cause. You can only go to the mall so many times, but mission trips are cool! It is an adventure every time! A brief mission trip is full of *warm fuzzy* moments, but leaves little lasting fruit. After just a week in the country, a typical mission trip will report several hundred "conversions" to Christ (i.e. they prayed the prayer or raised their hand at a public invitation). No one was discipled. It took the incarnational missionary twenty years to be able to give a similar report. Back on the home front and after the powerful three-minute DVD presentation, no one wants to support the long-term incarnational missionary. Then half the church signs up to go on the next *warm fuzzy* packed week long mission trip.

In reality, the impact for the Kingdom of God was negligible. There was not a hundred-fold jump in attendance; instead there is usually a decrease right after a team leaves due to the lack of fresh foreign faces. The tendency is to try and continually experience *warm fuzzy* moments. Short-term mission teams are needed, and are a great opportunity to expose people to the needs of the world at large, but these short term teams will never replace incarnational missionaries which continue to be severely lacking in numbers and under-funded.

The danger of trying to live in continual *warm fuzzy* moments is that eventually, what previously excited you no longer does; it becomes routine. Then considerable effort has to be made to "one-up" the last one to make the experience more enjoyable and satisfying. Jesus specifically said in John 15:16 that He has called us to produce lasting fruit. The focus needs to shift from a powerful experience, to lasting fruit --real and tangible fruit. To get this kind of fruit requires patience, hard work, self-sacrifice, and a willingness to deal intimately with the lives of people. That is so much more than a *warm fuzzy* moment can bring. Thank God for the *warm fuzzy* moments we have, but let us not focus on them.

YOU DON'T HAVE TO BE A JUNGLE EXPLORER; GOD CALLS YOU WHERE YOU ARE.

After reading a book like this one, people are excited and want to do something for God. They want to discover the adventure of being a jungle explorer. It seems the grass is always greener on the other side! In most cases, God has called people to the place they are living. I am not against short-term mission's trips, but I am against diverting the efforts of the church from long-term, lasting benefits for the Kingdom of God, to a short-term *warm fuzzy* moment! I know from experience that most people who come on a mission trip are ill-equipped to be there. Most have never led a children's Bible study in the church, but when they come to Cambodia they want to teach pastors how to plant churches.

God has called you to be a blessing where he has planted you!

Take an active role in your local church (your Jerusalem). Share the gospel through showing love to your neighbors, those at Wal-mart, and at your place of work. Be concerned for unreached communities, or segments of your community (your Judea and Samaria). Be involved in reaching the world for him. Intercede on behalf of the servants of God around the world who sacrifice for the gospel and have few *warm fuzzy* moments. Give to help meet their needs. If you can help in a specific area by going to a country, do so; but know your limitations and seek to build up the body of Christ wherever you are.

THE LAW OF THE HARVEST

The Apostle Paul speaks of the Law of the Harvest. "*⁷ Do not be deceived: God cannot be mocked. A man reaps what he sows. ⁸ The one who sows to please his sinful nature, from that nature will reap destruction; the one who sows to please the Spirit, from the Spirit will reap eternal life. ⁹ Let us not become weary in doing good, for at the proper time we will reap a harvest if we do not give up. ¹⁰ Therefore, as we have opportunity, let us do good to all people, especially to those who belong to the family of believers.*" (Galatians 6:7-10) It is true for agriculture, and it is true for the work of the Kingdom of God as well. It is for missions just as it is for locally-based ministries.

1. If you do not sow, you cannot reap a harvest.

2. You reap what you sow. (Like you cannot harvest beans from corn seed, you cannot get good fruit from bad seed.)

3. You reap after you sow. (There is always a period of germination and growth that must take place before the harvest; it is not instant.)

4. You reap more than you sow. (While you may only sow one seed, the fruit of that one seed can produce many more seeds.) Matthew 13:8 says that seed planted in good soil can produce 30, 60, and 100 times as much as was planted.

SEPARATING THE
CHAFF FROM
THE GRAINS

Consider the law of the harvest in your kingdom ventures! It is not so much a matter of the amount that people give, but the heart which is giving and receiving.

FACING THE ULTIMATE LOSS IN THE MIDST OF THE WILL OF GOD.

Some people say that the safest place you can be is in the will of God. Yet, somehow our *warm fuzzy* theology has shunned the idea that a bad thing, much less a tragic death, could be a part of the will of God. Psalms says, *"Those who sow in tears will reap with songs of joy. He who goes out weeping, carrying seed to sow, will return with songs of joy, carrying sheaves with him."* (Psalms 126:5,6) To assume that serving God should be full of *warm fuzzy* moments is simply not realistic.

This book is dedicated to two people who lived their lives completely surrendered to the work of God. They lived in the center of His will. They were both a significant threat to the work of the kingdom of evil. My own father was blown up by Muslim terrorists in the Philippines while faithfully serving God. He will never accomplish the American dream. He will never be able to sit back in a rocking chair in a mountain cabin; he will never be able to play golf with his sons; he will never be able to enjoy his grandchildren. He spent a lifetime separated from his parents and siblings and never got to enjoy holidays with his whole family. Yet, far more than most, he was in the center of God's will. Thousands of people came to Christ because of his efforts. Hundreds of churches were started which will continue to reach out to others long after his death.

Pin lived only six years of his life as a Christian. The transformation of his life is one which is a testimony to the restoration power of the gospel of Jesus. In only six years as a Christian, he personally led more than one thousand people to Christ. Right before he died, there was an intense spiritual attack. A festival was held at a nearby abandoned Buddhist temple where some people rallied together to counteract the Christian influence in the area. At the festival, they concluded by releasing their offerings to the spirits in the sky by way of homemade hot air balloons. Usually when these balloons are launched, they go so high into the sky that they cannot be seen, and will travel for miles before they come down. In October, the winds are coming out of the northeast and the Buddhist temple is to the southwest of our center. When they released the two balloons with their blessings (i.e. demonic curses) the balloons traveled against the wind directly toward our center, one landing on the roof of the main building and another landing on a secondary building on the back of the property. From that moment there was a massive spiritual attack on our center with Pin at the heart of it. All of our forty-seven children got high fevers and their blood work showed three horrible diseases: malaria, dengue fever (i.e. a type of Hemorrhagic Fever), and typhoid. It is nearly impossible to get all three of these at the same time. All of the children were near death. Pin did not have any of the fever or symptoms, but was treating the children until he died. To this day I believe he was killed by demons. There were no physical signs or evidence to the contrary. Pin was a warrior for God, living each day at the very center of God's will and purpose for Cambodia. Pin left behind eight young children, a wife, and only two worldly possessions: an old cell phone and a motorcycle.

Both men died tragically, yet were humble servants of God. In the world's eyes, they were misfits. Neither one accomplished the American dream. Neither one was honored by men for their service on earth. While both had *warm fuzzy* moments in their lives, their ministry ensured that they faced many trials, headaches, physical pains, poverty, and anonymity. However, what they accomplished for the Kingdom of God will be spoken about for generations to come and rewarded abundantly in heaven!

10

REDEMPTIVE ANALOGIES

Don Richardson, who wrote the famous missionary and anthropological books titled *"Peace Child"* and *"Eternity in their Hearts,"* coined the term "redemptive analogies." In the last fifty years, the progression of missionary study has brought scholars and practitioners to a point of seeing the importance of culture and tradition in the presentation of the gospel. Every person understands the gospel according to their own culture. When Americans think about the church, they have in their minds a beautiful building with a steeple on the top. Even American non-believers think of the church in this way. When we talk of the gospel, many people think of the intellectual arguments which they heard, allowing them to reason that Jesus is God. Based on those logical arguments, they ascertain that they and any other "reasonable person" should accept Jesus and become a Christian, too. Becoming a Christian is considered a very private and individual decision in American culture, which places much emphasis on the individual's rights and independence from others.

When a missionary leaves American culture or whatever their home culture might be, they enter a world which does not think or reason in the same way. It is not wrong or uncivilized; it is simply a different way. Because of this, the gospel message would not be clearly understood in a foreign setting if it were presented in an American way. A missionary needs to study the culture, traditions, and even folklore to find any common ground or ways to present the message of the gospel in a way that the receptor culture (in our case the T'moan people) can understand the true message of Jesus and respond to that accordingly.

In order to aid in bringing the gospel, the message of salvation, to other cultures it is essential to find ways to be able to compare the Biblical teachings with that culture. For the T'moan, a very isolated people group, we needed to find points of common interest, events, behaviors, or folklore which helped support the authenticity of the Biblical message we were bringing to them. We found many points which were relevant to the gospel message.

THE GREAT FLOOD

There were several redemptive analogies that we were able to use to complement and substantiate the gospel message. It is said that in every culture of the world there are stories of a great flood. The T'moan, we quickly discovered, were no exception. The T'moan have always lived in a hilly area of Northeastern Cambodia and the only floods they know about are the annual rainy-season flash floods that come down the River of God, and other small creeks which are dry for much of the year. None of these flash floods could possibly flood a significant area of the jungle because of the hilly nature of the region. The "original" T'moan people, the village elders explained, were separated during a great flood.

The tribal chief explained that many years ago there were many more ancestors who lived in the jungle, but one day a great flood came. The T'moan do not have boats, nor do they know how to build them. So, they are not sure where their ancestors got a boat. Some of the ancestors, they say, got into a big boat because they were afraid the flood waters would rise. Others, however, stayed on the ground, assuming the water would be only a brief flash-flood and would soon go down. The large boat was anchored by a strong vine to the T'moan village. The water continued to rise. As the water rose higher and higher, the boat rose above the village, leaving the other villagers climbing trees to try to get out of the water. The water did not go down and continued to rise higher and higher. The vine was stretched to the maximum until the force of the water became too great and the boat broke away. The people on the boat and those left in the trees cried out to each other, but it was no use. The boat sailed far away. Many people who were left on the land died, but some survived. "We are the ancestors of those who survived the flood and remained in the trees," the tribal chief explained. He then paused thoughtfully and added, "We have never seen our other ancestors again, but we know that somewhere in this world there are other T'moan people."

A door was open. I explained that we have a similar story. Although they do not know what happened to their ancestors who sailed off in the boat, we have a story about our ancestors who sailed off in a boat, and we do know what happened. Then I explained to them the story of our Biblical ancestors. . .

Many years ago, one of the elders in the village named Noah saw that the people were sinning very much and did not care about God. God told Noah to build a big boat. God told Noah exactly how to build the boat, because Noah had never seen a boat. He didn't know how to make it. God told Noah to tell the people to stop sinning, or he was going to destroy them with a flood. Noah continued to build the boat, but the other people were always making fun of him. He told them that God wanted them to repent of their sins and to live a good live, but they didn't listen. They just laughed at Noah and his family. Finally, after many years of preparing a boat the floods did indeed come. Noah and his family got in the boat.

As the flood waters rose, the people on the land called out to Noah and his family in the boat, but there was no way they could help them. Noah never saw his neighbors again. When the flood waters came down Noah ended up on a mountain far away from his homeland. There he settled and started a new family.

"And do you know what?", I asked the chief and quickly responded to my own question, "We are the descendants of Noah, the family in the boat." With a big smile I continued, "That means we are relatives."

A big smile came across the chief's face and the other villagers too.

LIFE FROM A TREE

One area that could have created a problem if we had been unaware of it was from the origin of life. We have the story of Adam and Eve, but they have a story about life coming out of a tree. The specific tree is a *salaw* tree, which is a very tall and beautiful white trunked tree. By simply debating with them over whether Adam and Eve were the first humans compared to their understanding of life coming from a tree, we would only have lost ground. So we agreed with them. Life came from a tree. In America we call it "The Old Rugged Cross." On that rugged cross, Jesus died and paid for our sins so that we could all live.

What could have been a negative belief was turned into a positive one. There is not much use in debating someone's firm beliefs that can neither be proven nor disproven. It just takes careful thinking and guidance from the Holy Spirit.

END OF THE WORLD BY FIRE

In the jungle, fires are very common. Actually, those who travel in the jungle are the ones who start the fires. In the tropics, we get hundreds of inches of rain a year. We get all that rain during one of our three seasons, aptly called the rainy season. We have a winter (or cool season) which lasts about two months with little or no rain. The hot season lasts three to four months and there is also no rain. The rainy season lasts the longest and is about six months long in a normal year cycle. Sometimes the rainy season is called a monsoon, as the rains are very predictable. When we get so much rain in a few months, the jungle grows very quickly. Normally it is the underbrush, bamboo, ferns, and thorn bushes which grow the fastest. When the cool season hits, the lush green underbrush turns a dead brown very quickly in the absence of water. This dry underbrush is often very thorny and dense, making travel in the jungle very difficult. As the entire jungle is covered with the underbrush, the easiest thing to do to get rid of it is just light some fires. Across Cambodia during dry season, the sky appears foggy. It is not fog, however, it is smoke from all the jungles burning.

Unlike forest fires in the United States which are mainly pine trees burning, in Cambodia the jungles are burned off each year, so the fire never gets hot enough to kill the larger trees. It is said that a hundred years ago in the United States they used to burn the forests in the same way, annually, but over the last few decades as people are more concerned with pollution, they use fire-suppression techniques. Now when there is a forest fire in the States, with a massive accumulation of underbrush and dead trees, it is devastating. Everything is destroyed. Remember the forest fires that burned Yellowstone National Park in 1988? They burned off almost everything, both the young trees and the dead ones. In my generation, and probably my son's as well, they will never know the former beauty of Yellowstone previous to the fires that engulfed the park. Because the fires burn annually in Cambodia, we don't get massive forest fires at all. The jungle replenishes itself every year very quickly.

For life in the jungle in Cambodia, though, one of the worst fears is that an uncontrolled forest fire might accidentally burn down a person's home or village, it happens often. When a fire reaches an area with houses, it will often burn quickly. When it reaches the grass and bamboo -made houses, it takes only a few minutes to destroy the entire house. This is a great fear that people live with in the jungle.

When the T'moan told us they had a story about the end of the world and its destruction by fire, I could imagine what they faced. Many times we had to cross fires or flee from oncoming forest fires in the jungle. We had even been guilty of starting a few where the bamboo and grasses were especially thick. When a fire comes, everything in its path is at the mercy of the flames.

Of course, our Bible speaks clearly about a coming day of judgment in which everyone will be judged for their sins. Those who have rejected Christ and those who followed Satan will be cast into the lake of fire where there will be constant burning and no relief. The T'moan could relate to that also, as they knew there would be a day of judgment. It was not a point we dwelt on, but we simply compared the two stories to demonstrate the truth of what we were saying.

THE RIVER OF GOD

The river that all T'moan people live on is called *O Preah,* which literally means The River of God. This is actually quite an odd occurrence to have a river named after God in general. Historically, Cambodia has always been polytheistic (meaning they worship many gods). They are culturally Buddhist, yet most of their temples and statues are built to honor Hindu gods, as well as Buddha. They also worship many spirits which often are given divine names. The Mekong River, for example, is a Cambodian word which means Mother of Waters, referring to a water deity. *"Me"* means mother and *"kong"* means water. There are many places along the Mekong River where they offer sacrifices and prayer to this water deity. The River of God, however, is a general term for God and not specific like the Mekong river is.

In the jungle, water is life. Without the River of God, the T'moan people could not possibly live where they do. Even when Cambodia is at the height of the hot season when there is no rain, the bed of the River of God never runs completely dry. The entire bed of the river, as far as I have explored it, is all bedrock. There is little dirt or sand; it is just solid rock. Because of the rock, little water can soak into the soil, but once it gets to the River of God, it stays there. There are numerous pools of water, some quite deep, along the river which never run dry. This is where they build their villages and spend most of their days.

Just the fact that their river was named the River of God was a point of contact for us. Somehow they knew about a single God who was greater than any other god. On the surface, the T'moan would be tempted to say they don't believe in any one God, per se. The T'moan do not worship Hindu and Buddhist gods like other Khmers, but they were living right along a river which they called the River of God.

The Apostle Paul spoke of what he had observed and learned as it pertained to the ethnic groups that he worked among when he was living out the New Testament. In Romans he says:

"*For since the creation of the world God's invisible qualities—his eternal power and divine nature—have been clearly seen, being understood from what has been made, so that men are without excuse. For although they knew God, they neither glorified him as God nor gave thanks to him, but their thinking became futile and their foolish hearts were darkened. Although they claimed to be wise, they became fools and exchanged the glory of the immortal God for images made to look like mortal man and birds and animals and reptiles. Therefore God gave them over to the sinful desires of their hearts, to sexual impurity for the degrading of their bodies with one another. They exchanged the truth of God for a lie, and worshiped and served created things rather than the Creator—who is forever praised. Amen*" (Romans 1:20-25).

Paul said, "*they knew God.*" At one time they had a witness in the natural elements as to the creator God and their need to worship him, but they followed other ways. Why would the T'moan, who did not know of a supreme God, live along a river they called the "River of God"? Because at one time, they did know God. . . we were simply leading them back to the God they had forgotten.

OTHER HELPFUL CULTURAL ELEMENTS

There are numerous points of comparison that can be made to the truths of the Bible and positive T'moan cultural elements as well. Some of these may seem like minor things, like the fact that T'moan people are monogamous and marry only one wife for life. That is actually highly unusual among tribal groups in the region, where often they will have more wives based on their position in the society. Often chiefs can easily have a dozen wives, while poor people will have one or two and can exchange them for others at times. The T'moan, however, once married, were committed to one wife for their whole life. There are other elements as well such as:

No IDOLS BUT FEAR SPIRITS. . .

NO IDOLATRY

Buddhism is all about ritual idol worship and the worship of religious relics. The Buddha is worshipped in his idol form. They have big ones, small ones, fat ones, skinny ones, twenty

-cent ones made from plastic, and others worth millions of dollars made from sapphires, emeralds or other precious stones. The Khmers have idols everywhere, which is what has been passed down through their religion and culture. The T'moan people, however, have no idols of any god. The second commandment that God gave to Moses for the people of Israel was to not ever worship idols. Idol worship is a great bondage, and it is difficult to break the ritualistic habits and even spiritual powers associated with those idols. As the T'moan did not have idols, this was one less problem we had to deal with and would go a long way toward discipling them into mature believers.

BURIAL OF THE DEAD

You might not think that burial rights would be that significant of an issue. In Asia, nearly everyone cremates bodies. There are certain Buddhist and Hindu sects that do bury, but it is usually an exception rather than a rule. Almost everyone cremates dead bodies. In Cambodia, though we have been through the genocide which wiped out more than two million people, there are very few cemeteries around the country. Usually cemeteries are those belonging to Chinese or Vietnamese people, not Khmers.

A T'MOAN GRAVE

I remember one day going to a photocopy shop near the center of Phnom Penh. On that day, there was a strong breeze. When I got near the photocopy shop, there was a lot of smoke that filled the air. I thought there must be a house fire or something. As I got into the smoke, it really smelled awful. With very few regulations on chemicals and such, I assumed that there was a chemical fire or something because of the odd, pungent smell. People were all holding their noses and covering their mouths along the road, so I did the same, trying to drive my motorcycle at the same time. When I got to the photocopy shop around lunch time, I joked with the staff that they were burning their *prahok* (a pungent fish paste that the Khmers love which is made from rotten fish that are left to decompose in the sun for three days). They assured me that it was not their *prahok*, but it was a dead body that they were burning at the temple across the street. Because of the winds, the smoke, ashes, and smell of the dead body were being forced down the street. I almost vomited when they told me that.

One day I happened to mention to the T'moan that in my country, America, most people do not cremate, but they bury their dead and make beautiful cemeteries and plots to honor their lives. Their faces lit up! They told me how wonderful that was, and they explained their perspective on cremation. They said that life is very difficult and hard, and when a person dies, it is never pleasant. . . they often go through great suffering. How awful, they figured, to then take the body of a friend or relative that has been going through so much suffering before their death and then set them on fire and burn them up. It was disgraceful for them to even consider that. To burn a body, they reasoned, showed they had no love for them.

When I shared with them about Jesus, I stressed the fact that he was placed in a brand new tomb by his friends and that there was even a guard at the tomb. They thought that was a great honor and proper way to bury the dead. To them, the fact that Jesus was buried showed that he was loved, appreciated, and confirmed to them that the Bible was a true and holy book.

SACRIFICES

Explaining sacrifices to a culture that does not make sacrifices, like the United States, is only understood as an imagined metaphorical concept. When the early church struggled with the issue of whether or not it was permissible to eat food which was sacrificed to idols, to the American church, this has little meaning. When the concept of believers being a "living sacrifice" is discussed, they imagine images of going without McDonalds for a week for the purpose of sacrificing the saved money for missions. While that may be a sacrifice, it is the not a sacrifice in terms of what it is really talking about. Sacrifice was the ritual killing of an animal to offer to God, a pagan god, or spirit, for some religious purpose. We have one whole book of the Bible, Leviticus, nearly completely dedicated to what types of sacrifices are required for which trespasses and situations. In a culture which does not have sacrifices, this is often overlooked.

A Sacrifice to the Spirits

How many American Christians could discuss off-hand the various sacrifices, their purposes, and their meaning given in the book of Leviticus? Probably one in a million. As it is not part of American culture, it has little meaning.

For the T'moan, they have a very well-established ritual sacrificial system. They understand the meanings and purposes of sacrifices. While they don't know what a lamb is, they do understand that sacrifices of large animals are more important than those of small ones. For a simple fever or disagreement in the village, they may sacrifice a chicken to the spirits. For a death, they may sacrifice a pig. For the annual sacrifice to the dead ancestors, they will never sacrifice anything less than a water buffalo.

When John the Baptist saw Jesus, he shouted, "*Look, the Lamb of God, who takes away the sin of the world!*" (John 1:29) Why did John refer to Jesus as the "Lamb of God?" Was it because Jesus was a warm and fuzzy friend, as many Americans might be tempted to understand? No, it was because lambs were used for sacrifices, and Jesus would be sacrificed and His blood spilled for the sins of the whole world. This verse has great meaning for the T'moan, as they could easily comprehend the death of Jesus as a sacrifice--a very important sacrifice--for their sins. Because the T'moan had a culture which already had a sacrificial system, they could easily comprehend and relate to the Biblical teachings about sacrifice.

UNDERSTANDING THE SPIRIT REALM

In my reporting on the ministry in Cambodia, sharing prayer requests and preaching in the United States, I often omit sharing about demonic encounters we face in the ministry. I am afraid many people would freak out, or think I had gone mad.

The Bible clearly teaches that we are in a spiritual battle. The Apostle Paul taught, "*For our struggle is not against flesh and blood, but against the rulers, against the authorities, against the powers of this dark world and against the spiritual forces of evil in the heavenly realms.*" (Ephesians 6:12). Throughout the Bible there were strange, supernatural events which occurred. Most cannot be explained other than to assume that there were supernatural forces involved. Have you seen a sea parted recently? Have you seen anyone walk on water? Can you even imagine what Jesus "transfigured" looked like? The Greek word used is so odd in the original text that it is just rendered "transfigured" in English, because they had no idea how to translate it! The Bible is full of incredible and amazing supernatural events, because people are part of a supernatural battle going on between Satan and God over establishing the Kingdom of God universally. One of the key purposes of the Holy Spirit is to provide believers with supernatural guidance, protection, and power!

Modern stories of demons speaking through a person spooks people out. Supernatural healings are usually questioned and blamed on medical mistakes. Demons affecting equipment or holding territories captive sounds very odd indeed. When demons are visible, living in tree tops, and having conversations with people, this sounds more like a Hollywood horror film than real life.

The spiritual realm was very real to the people of the Old and New Testaments. They understood the physical world they were in was also affected by the spiritual realm. Even when the church was birthed, Jesus told the Apostle Peter, "And I tell you that you are Peter, and on this rock I will build my church, and the gates of Hades will not overcome it. I will give you the keys of the kingdom of heaven; whatever you bind on earth will be bound in heaven, and whatever you loose on earth will be loosed in heaven" (Matthew 16:18-19). Jesus was not speaking figuratively; he was speaking literally. Hades, the realm of death (i.e. hell), would not overcome the church, the bride of Christ. What Peter bound or loosed on earth (in the physical), would be bound or loosed in heaven (in the spiritual realm). For many Americans who have been bombarded with an anti-religious message for generations in their educational systems, political systems, and business systems. . . to even consider a real spiritual realm is absurd. The sanity of those who claim to see spiritual beings, much less converse with them, would be instantly questioned. Americans have a very hard time because of their cultural background in understanding the spiritual realm. Because of this, much of the Bible is understood to be simple folklore, myths, and superstition--not truth. The Bible, however, is true and everything in the Bible is true. The T'moan can understand the spiritual aspects of the Bible much easier than most educated Americans, and therefore it is much easier for them to comprehend and believe all the teachings of the Bible. Their understanding of the spiritual realm was very positive in teaching them spiritual things from the Bible.

All of these elements were helpful redemptive analogies which allowed the T'moan people to be able to understand the life transforming message of the gospel of Jesus in their culture.

11

THE SECRET TEMPLE
OF GOD

After working among ethnic minority hill tribes in Cambodia for more than ten years, I have often heard about a secret temple which the tribal consider to be a most sacred place. Along with the legend of the *Pnong pahoung trung* (the tribal people with a hole in their chest) I figured it to have some truth but not much. Cambodia, as the world has recently discovered, has thousands of ancient temples. Scattered across

ANGKOR WAT

Cambodia are more than one hundred massive stone temples, with literally tens of thousands of other smaller shrines and monuments. All these temples were built between the years AD 802 and AD 1220. The famous *Angkor Wat* temple is the largest religious temple in the world. This single temple stands as tall as the cathedrals of Europe, but stretches for miles and is surrounded by a massive man-made mote. It was built to be a model of heaven, albeit a Hindu concept of heaven.

Most of these temples are in northern Cambodia, though nearly all are on the western side of the Mekong River, while the T'moan lands are located deep in the jungles on the eastern side. Periodically, they find more temples and sites buried in the jungles. In fact, the main complex, a massive city, was lost to the jungles from the 1400's until 1860 when a French explorer, Henri Mouhot, revealed it to the West. The temples of Cambodia are not inferior in any way to the ancient Egyptian pyramids and temples. Most of the history of *Angkor Wat* and the ancient temples of Cambodia were lost during the Thai invasions in the 1400's, and very little of note has survived regarding the locations, names, or meanings of the temples. With so many ancient worship sites that are still being found, it would not be surprising that there would be more.

All the ethnic minorities talk about a secret temple complex, and this has remained a heavily-guarded secret. I have personally heard about the temples from four different tribes in different provinces in northeastern Cambodia. Friends that work with other tribes have also confirmed to me the stories about the existence of such a temple complex. However, no one has ever revealed the location or any details about this temple.

Kracheh province was a major part of the old Ho Chi Minh Trail and therefore, was heavily bombed by B-52 carpet bombing. It is also where the United States Army invaded Cambodia in May of 1970. In addition, numerous smaller missions by helicopters, fighter aircraft, and reconnaissance aircraft were flown over Kracheh. There are still numerous soldiers, mostly pilots, who are considered as missing-in-action in Kracheh province. Over the years of traveling for hours upon hours through the jungle in Kracheh, I have often wondered if one day I would come across a crash-site or evidence that could help return a serviceman's body to America. I know that many who lived through the Vietnam era in the 1960s and 1970s still think that there are servicemen who are still being held. I would highly doubt it. Most certainly they would not be in Kracheh province, as they could easily walk out (in any direction) to a friendly village. I think it is highly probable that there are remains of serviceman who went down with their aircraft deep in the jungle. Near the T'moan village is a thick jungle area where the T'moan have told me there are 2,000 pound bombs which were dropped by B-52's that did not explode and remain, half-buried in the ground and still active, nearly forty years later. The T'moan talk of the whole jungle shaking when the Americans carpet-bombed the area. Even if the bombing was several miles away, the whole earth would shake when the bombs exploded. They were devastating explosives. My curious mind thinks about how they could be safely detonated, not just for the need of disposing of unexploded ordinance, but to find out personally how big an explosion a 2,000 pound bomb makes! These bombs, though they were dropped nearly forty years ago, remain as active and deadly as the day they were dropped. It would be fun (ha ha ha. . . *sinister laughing*) to explode one. I think that a very hot bonfire under the explosive should do the trick, as the detonator is most likely so rusted that it is of no use. I am quite certain my mother would be totally against that plan! Come to think of it, my wife wouldn't think that was a good idea either. Wouldn't it be cool though. . . as long as no one got hurt? Hmm. . .

After the T'moan leaders had gotten to know us and receive us well, the chief mentioned that they know of an ancient temple, the location of which, they keep secret. I was instantly intrigued. I asked them to describe the temple, if they would. They were a little reluctant, but they are the ones who started sharing with us. In great detail, the chief talked about the main sanctuary being a massive tower greater than anything the Khmer had ever dreamed of. There were beautifully-carved elephants which were as big as the authentic likenesses that they represent. The temple complex was huge and would require many days to explore completely. In the main sanctuary, he recalled, there was an inner chamber. A few people he knew had tried to venture into the inner chamber, but no one ever returned.

He explained that this was the greatest temple of all and was without equal. We were fascinated, and so I asked him, "Could you take us there?"

He said, "Oh no, I am much too old for the journey." He explained that they don't take outsiders to this temple, and they keep its location secret.

The chief, knowing we were very curious about this temple, told us that there is even an inscription with a date. There is a number which is inscribed on one of the doors which says "1322." That is old! Then he told us what our ears were dying to hear. . . "I will have my son take you; he knows the way. It is one day away and a very difficult journey."

"No problem," I said. "It was not easy getting here, so I am sure we can go further as well." We decided to make preparations in the village that day and leave the next day for the temple.

"I want to warn you though," the chief warned, "the temples have been taken over by snakes. There are cobras and pythons everywhere. This is their home. You have to be very careful. I suspect that those who went into the inner chamber were killed by snakes or lost their way in the complete darkness."

We sent one motorcycle back to *Ralough* village to buy as much gas as they had so we could keep our motorcycles going as we drove through the jungle. That night I could hardly sleep. What if we become famous explorers. . .? How can I contact National Geographic. . .? Would Discovery Channel be better. . .? My mind was racing all night. I knew from the Bible that the python snake was a demonic symbol and even in

Cambodia, it is worshipped. I tried to imagine what the temple would be like. Would it be a temple dedicated to a Hindu god, or would it be the "Unknown God" that the people had previously worshipped? Could this temple be the key to bringing the tribes of Cambodia to Christ? Somewhere in my thinking and pondering, I fell asleep.

I woke up ready to go, probably about six in the morning. In the jungle we rarely even look at a watch and I usually take mine off. I remember the first time I met the Chief, he was wearing a watch. I was quite impressed. At the end of our trip he asked me if I could help him with the watch. It had quit working. I asked when it stopped and he told me it had quit five years previously. So I asked him if he wore it all that time. He assured me he did because he was the chief, and it made him look very important to have a watch. I chuckled inside. When we took the watch to a repair shop in Phnom Penh, we discovered the whole inside of the watch had been sprayed with super glue to hold it together. It was beyond hope. On our next trip, we brought him a new watch. He was ecstatic to have such a nice watch, one that actually worked.

We got up early and cooked some noodles for our breakfast. As we headed off that morning, we found out quickly that it was going to be a long day. We traveled for a few hours on a small path, but clearly no vehicles ever used this path, not even an ox cart. It was small and the brush had not been burned off. Much of the underbrush is bamboo which, when we brush against it with the motorcycle, it snaps back and whips our body. It was like being stuck in an eternal spanking machine. My legs and forearms, which took the brunt of the whipping, were numb with pain. The path was very rocky with sections of sand and the elevation continued to climb. Though we were traveling up and down hills, overall I could tell we were climbing from the readings on the GPS. The T'moan village was at about two hundred and fifty feet above sea level, but now we had climbed to five and six hundred feet above sea level. It does not sound like much, but for a country which is nearly completely flat, this is considered mountainous. After a few hours, we broke into a clearing with a pond of water right in the middle of it. The clearing was surrounded by grasses and jungle trees. It looked like an ideal spot for wildlife. I decided to stop and explore. Sure enough, there were tracks everywhere. I was looking for tiger tracks. I found wild gaur, deer, wild bore, and bird tracks but no tiger tracks. Then I noticed a small campsite. I motioned to my friends. . . that it seemed we were not

COOKING BREAKFAST

alone. Everyone stopped talking and looked to the jungle around us, wondering if someone was watching us.

Pin called out into the jungle. "It is ok, we are not going to hurt anyone. We are just resting. . . please come out." Slowly, out of the jungle emerged a whole family, a few at a time. There were a few men, their wives, and even small children. When they heard motorcycles, they were scared so they ran away into the jungle for safety. They had in their hands two large animals, which I easily recognized, but had never seen in the wild--porcupines. They were quite big, as big as dogs; but were both dead. They were just about to eat them. Pin assured me that porcupine was not a very good meal and we would be better to stick to our noodles and not try to swap our food for theirs. I was curious but deferred to his judgment.

As most of the animals in the jungle are nocturnal, I imagine it would be a great place to set up some night vision equipment to see what straggled in overnight to the waterhole. There was obviously still some wildlife. After a brief rest, we continued on our way. . . I am sure the hunting family was glad to see us leave. Jungle encounters are usually very tense because you never know who you will meet.

We continued on our way with much of the same--painful snaps from bamboo branches, bogging down in sand, and a few hill crossings which were quite challenging. In one of them, we came up a hill into a very dense forest. There must have been a water source high on the hill, because the massive trees were growing well on the top of the hill but were only sparse below the hill. Coming down the hill was a great challenge to dirt-bike riding. The whole hillside was loose rocks, causing the motorcycles to continually want to slide out of control. It was not a huge hill though and soon we were down at its base. Our guides told us at that point we were close. The scenery began to change slightly. We were clearly on the edge of a small plateau. It was not incredibly high, but we could see over the jungle, so we were probably fifty to one hundred feet higher than the rest of the jungle. There were large rock formations every fifty to one hundred feet that were very interesting. Huge rock formations, mostly granite, just jutted out of the ground. The whole area was sparsely covered in trees, so we could see up to half a mile through the trees (which is unusual as normally we can only see a dozen yards or so between the trees). I could imagine that it would be easy for the builders to get rock, as this area was very rocky. Also, most of the rock was granite, as opposed to the limestone and sandstone which covers most of Kracheh.

As we looked around we couldn't help but notice the beauty of the area. High in the trees there were gorgeous, wild orchids. The jungle orchids usually bloom in the hot season, and we were in the peak of it.

As my wife and I had collected orchids for many years, I was keen to get a wild orchid (or a few) from this area of the jungle. I spotted a beautiful red one which was not so high in the tree branches that I hoped I could get it down by using a stick or bamboo pole to knock it out of the tree. We decided to stop and rest for a few minutes. It had been a long day, but our guides assured us the sacred temple was not far away. We stopped at one of the rock formations which was about forty feet high. It looked like a spire shooting up out of the ground. I joked with our team that there is evidence that there was never any Khmer people here. They asked, "What was the evidence?" It was a lack of incense. Anything this beautiful and unique would certainly be worshipped by the Khmer. By not seeing any evidence of worship, it was clear that no Khmers had ever been here.

I decided that before I was going to lay down on the rock and rest I had better make sure there were no cobras or other snakes hiding near me since the chief had told us about so many snakes in the temple area. It looked to me like an ideal location for snakes. After satisfactorily looking around and taking a few pictures of the rocks, I laid down on one of the huge slabs of granite and looked up at the sky. It was a hot day and sitting on the rocks was refreshing, though it was still hot. Pin continued to look around the rocks, but I didn't care because I was tired.

Eventually he gave up his hunt and lay down by the rest of us. Lying down, he looked under one of the rocks that was near his head. It was very dark under the rock, but there was a space under the rock about six inches high. He looked and looked, determined to find a snake. I hoped he would not succeed. After a couple of minutes he said, "I need to get a stick. There is a small hole at the very back. I think it is a snake hole." After he got a long stick, he began poking into the hole and with great joy he shouted, "There is a snake in there!"

My rest was over. I immediately jumped up and moved away from his work area! I wasn't going to be on the receiving end of a mad cobra or another snake coming out of the small hole. Eventually Pin saw the head. It was about five feet under the rock and so it was very hard to see. Only the head was visible through the small hole. Pin took off his shoelaces. He had bought a new pair of shoes for this trip, which was a luxury item for him. He said he had bought them so he would have nice shoes to wear to a wedding which was coming in the next week. Time and again he kept telling us he was worried that his shoes might get dirty. . . and we would laugh at him. What did he expect, wearing them into the jungle? He smiled big and proclaimed, "See, my wedding shoes are coming in useful." He made a small lasso with his shoe laces and fastened it firmly to the stick. We all teased him. How did he think he was going to lasso a snake?

He worked by himself while we mocked his efforts. After only a few moments he proclaimed, "I got him!" We all rushed to his side as he pulled with all his might on the stick. The snake wasn't budging and Pin was a strong guy. It seems either the snake is stuck, or he was bigger than we thought. Pin assured us that he would not get free.

"Either he will let go and come out of the hole or his head is going to pop off," he explained.

Pretty good shoelaces, I figured. Pin's pull on the snake's head was relentless. As it came out, he was more and more excited. He called for all of us to help him. Being a brave man, I said he could count me out! I wasn't going to travel days in the jungle to be bitten by a snake.

Pin assured me, "Don't worry. It is not a cobra; it is a python. It's not poisonous."

It was huge. As he pulled, eventually the head came out from under the rock. . . and it was still not out. That meant that the snake was longer than five or six feet. He kept pulling and the other tribal guys excitedly helped him hold onto the snake as it came out. Finally, he got the whole snake out. Now I was

10 FOOT PYTHON CAUGHT WITH A SHOESTRING

really backing away. I was relieved it was not a cobra, but it was a huge python. I had never seen such a huge snake, not even in a zoo. I had seen a dead one when I was a kid that was much bigger, but not a living one. Wow!

They stretched it out and posed for pictures. It took four of the men to hold onto the snake. It was more than ten feet long! They decided that they were going to take it back to the village alive, so they tied it up into a rice sack. I knew I was not going to put it on my motorcycle. Pin assured me that by tying it tightly into a rice sack it could not get out, because it could not stretch out its body. I was glad for the information, but I still was not going to take it on my motorcycle!

After collecting a few orchids, which I had no trouble tying to my motorcycle, we headed on toward the secret temple. I continued to be amazed at the rock structures as we traveled. I thought to myself, "How would the tribal chief know what the number '1322' was? As the modern calendar would not have been known in Cambodia at that time, how would they know they were living in the year '1322'?" I pondered, "These tribal people have no knowledge of the Khmer temples, like *Angkor Wat*, because they have never been out of the jungle. Having never seen the Khmer temples, how could they possibly compare them? I tried to lower my expectations of what I was expecting to see. Maybe it is only a small shrine next to a big rock? Maybe it is only a cave? My mind was working overtime thinking of the possibilities of what was coming.

I was bringing up the rear. I usually volunteered to go last, because the last person got to eat everyone else's dust, literally. I seemed to be the least susceptible to breathing problems and colds which come from long exposures to dust, so it seemed best if I take the tail of the group. Up ahead the guides were motioning everyone to stop as we came to a small hill, surrounded by large rock features. They were pointing ahead. I pulled up with the other motorcycles and asked if we were there. The guides pointed to a large rock structure ahead.

Pin, Ang, and Poline dropped their heads. "It is a rock!" they exclaimed, "Not a temple." I stared, somewhat in disbelief, but also aware that every word we were saying was most likely offending our guides, who had been careful to keep the temple a secret for generations. I asked them, "What about the carved elephants and tall buildings?" The guides motioned that everything was up ahead in the "temple".

I proceeded ahead alone and shouted to the others as I pulled out, "Let's explore!" The ground was very rocky and difficult to drive on. We crossed a small dry creek bed which clearly dropped off into a waterfall when there was water. I could imagine the creeks rocky outcrops, when flowing, would have had very beautiful rapids and waterfalls. I continued ahead and the stones seemed to be growing out of the earth as I approached the largest of them. I continued driving toward it, with some anticipation, wondering what would be behind the rock structure. The main rock appeared to be one piece of granite, which soared to fifty or sixty feet in the air. It was massive.

As I rounded the base of the rock I could imagine what these simple people were imagining in their minds. It truly was incredible: one massive granite rock soaring high into the air. What a magnificent temple. Surrounding it were minor temples in odd clusters

STONE ELEPHANT GRAZING

of rock. I parked my motorcycle and looked around the complex, completely alone. Then I saw the elephant. It was a massive granite rock the size of a full grown elephant. It has a crevice in the rock which looked like a large ear and trunk coming down to the ground. Yes, this was the elephant they mentioned for sure!

ROCK FACE

My companions were less enthusiastic than I was and were more concerned that their precious snake might die before they could go back. I was astounded with the beauty of the temple and didn't want to leave before exploring more. They agreed to let me wander for a few minutes. Pin found a group of fragrant orchids and called out asking if I wanted to take them back with me. "Of course," I said. He spent his time collecting orchids while I looked for a cave entrance or space between the rocks. I asked our guides if they knew where the hole was. They did not. Only the elders knew were the entrance to the cavern was. My companions did not want to stay long, so I made a quick look around the rocks and headed down to the dry river bed to meet my friends.

At the river I talked with them. "I am glad it was a natural rock," I said. Can you imagine what would happen if there was a man-made temple complex back here. Scholars would come to study them, to find out who the great "makers" were and everything would lead them farther and farther away from the true God. *Angkor Wat*, just one temple, took four hundred years to build. It is the greatest temple in the world (I was appealing to their nationalism!) and an honor to the builders. Look at this place. Clearly it was built by God. It is amazing! No human hand could fashion such a temple complex. There is not a crane strong enough to move the massive central tower out of place! I told them about a similar place that God had made in the United States. We called it the "Garden of the Gods" in America. They are massive stone structures in the state of Colorado which are completely natural and point to a creative God, hence the name: "Garden of the Gods." Fortunately the Khmer language does not have singular and plural, so it can only be translated as the "Garden of God." It shows me that the tribal people are indeed searching for God. For them to keep this secret temple hidden for generations spoke of its importance to all the peoples of the region.

Some scholars point out that it is quite likely that the Khmer came originally from the east side of the Mekong River, but traveled west to get out of the mountains for better agricultural lands. It is likely that the original Khmer people even knew of this site and tried to build greater and greater temples by their own hands which would bring glory to themselves, not to the Creator God. The T'moan have guarded the secret of the location for generations so that it would not be destroyed or defiled.

We ate lunch using giant leaves from trees as our plates and our hands as utensils and drank stagnant water from the river bed.   I continued to be amazed as I looked around. God is truly faithful to His word. He left people plenty of evidence of Himself so that they would seek Him. I have seen many beautiful places around the world, but the secret temple of the T'moan would be one that would count among the most beautiful because of its natural beauty. I could have spent several days there looking among the stones.

We spent a time of prayer and worshipped the Lord there, thanking him for His glory and creative power to build such a place, unmatched by human hands. We also thanked him for allowing us to capture the python. Because the python is a symbol of demonic power, we prayed that the demonic forces which have bound the T'moan people for generations would be forever bound and cast out of the T'moan jungle.

We traveled back through the same rocky and treacherous path to the T'moan village. Late at night we arrived. The people all came out to greet us and to get our impression of their secret temple. I knew it was a great honor they had given to us to show us their temple. Immediately the chief came to me and said, "Did you see the temple?"

I said, "Oh yes, it was just as you said. It was big and beautiful. I saw the stone elephants and the massive spires going high into the sky. It was so beautiful. Thank you for allowing us to see it." He then asked me if I went inside the temple and saw the inscriptions. "No, I am sorry, I didn't see it. We looked for an entrance but we didn't find one. Maybe next time you can show us," I said.

"They captured a snake also--a very big one!" I shared. All of the people gathered around to look at the snake. It was one of the biggest they had ever captured live. They asked us if we were going to take it, but we assured him that we wanted them to have the snake and do with it what they wanted, either to eat it or sell it. We knew such a snake was valuable. They were very thankful, and as they share everything, there would be plenty to go around. Everyone in the village was glad that we had a wonderful trip to their sacred place.

God certainly made a beautiful temple for the T'moan people to point them to himself. We decided then that we would keep the location of the temple a secret. It is an important place to many tribes, the T'moan being the closest to it, and we wanted to respect their secret that they had entrusted to us. I am sure it will be found eventually, but I do not want to be the person to reveal it. As I had a GPS with me, I know exactly where the temple is and could find it again quite easily.

12

THE FUTURE

I would like to say that the future looks very bright for the T'moan people, but it does not. As I write this book, Chinese and Vietnamese bulldozers are demolishing the jungle and getting ever closer to the unsuspecting T'moan people. Recently, they have been contacted by a group of soldiers, telling them that their village will have to move, as the area has been given over to loggers. So they are trespassing on state land. The T'moan have lived in the jungle and in that small area for thousands of years. Their ancestors are buried across the jungle, and they will not disrespect their ancestors by leaving the jungle. The Khmer Rouge had forced them into villages thirty years ago, and it devastated the people. As soon as the Khmer Rouge were defeated, they immediately escaped back into their ancestral lands deep into the jungle.

ILLEGALLY CUT WOOD

I have personally seen loggers come into the village, protected by high-powered weapons, and cut down the hardwood trees directly in front of the T'moan people's homes. Their shade trees were mutilated by the high-pitched screams of chainsaw blades ripping through their trunks. As the wood was loaded onto oxcarts for the journey to overseas homes of the wealthy, elite, or powerful leaders in the city, the T'moan were never compensated for their trees. All that remains is the outer bark of centuries-old trees. I have seen other groups of soldiers enter the village and demand the location of monkey families from the T'moan people. Within a few short hours, the soldiers would return through the jungle with bags of monkeys, young and old, male and female alike. Some bags were full of terrified infant baby monkeys still clutching their mother's breasts. These monkeys are sold at the Vietnamese border for between $50 and $80 each. A typical catch will be fifty to one hundred monkeys which are caught using large fishnets. Again the T'moan received nothing in return.

The secret temple of God will eventually be discovered, and as it is not in a protected area, it will most likely draw the attention of rock cutters from China and Vietnam. There is a new road underway into the capital area of Ratanakiri province which passes quite close to the temple complex area. The Chinese are building the road, which will connect directly to Vietnam. I have no doubt that the granite of which the temple complex is formed will be soon sold around the world to cover table tops and cover floors of the rich and powerful. What God made and has remained hidden for generations will no doubt be cut into millions of pieces and spread out all over the world bringing praise, not to God, but to architects and designers to integrate the granite into their creative architectural themes.

Soon the jungle resources will be gone. When the resources are gone, the T'moan will still live an impoverished life deep in a devastated jungle. They will still live in grass houses with no roads, no electricity, no clean water, no access to proper medical care, and no education for their children. Eventually their language, or the people themselves, will die out and the T'moan will be swallowed up either into the majority race or back into the earth. It is doubtful that the T'moan, as a unique people, will survive much longer.

I consider one of God's divine callings on my life to help the T'moan people. God would not lead me far into

Impoverished Villager

the jungles of Cambodia just to reveal the location of their secret temple. God would not call me to seek to benefit off of the backs of the innocent T'moan people like nearly everyone else has done who has encountered them. God's Holy Spirit would not open the hearts of a whole people to receive his salvation for the purpose of simply being abandoned once again to the distant jungles. I have no desire to meddle in the politics of the land, and it is not my right as a visitor in their land. I see my role to help the T'moan as one who can bring education to the next generation of T'moan. God can use me to provide developmental resources to the people for improving their lives. With education they can preserve their culture, their language, and their ancient history. They could even promote their culture to others.

Most importantly, God has called me, and the ones who traveled with me, to find the T'moan, to disciple them into mature believers in Jesus. Jesus was always interested in individual's lives, not building a religious system. Christ has called us to assist the T'moan to become believers who once again seek the one true God and worship Him-- believers who are transformed by the love of Christ and demonstrate that love among themselves and to other tribes with whom they come in contact.

WOMAN MAKING A ROOF OUT OF GRASS (THATCH)

I have no doubt that the journey to disciple and help the T'moan people will be much like the path that we traveled to find the T'moan. At times it will be smooth going, but most likely it will be difficult, challenging, and full of obstacles. The journey will be full of dangerous crossings, snares which entangle us, and painful moments. With divine stubbornness we will not back down. *We will not quit* and we will help transform this remote jungle people for the glory of God.

13

FINAL CHALLENGE:

PASSION

It is easy to have passion for the lost when you see a missionary video showing the poverty and despair of people outside of America and other developed countries. One look at the tiny, emaciated body of a little dirty baby with flies hovering around his glistening eyes triggers a deep emotional response in any society. The shocking pictures, plus a message of the need for evangelism, makes people subconsciously see poverty and spiritual lost-ness as invariably linked. At such a time of deep emotional appeal, it is easy to have a temporary passion for the cause of Christ. After a hefty lunch and watching a ball game from the comfort of the couch, the passion seems to have dwindled away just as quickly as it came.

Having a genuine and deep passion for the lost can only come from understanding the plan of God and having a personal commitment to God's eternal plan for the earth. This chapter will show the ideological or theological reason that led four men into the jungles of Cambodia looking for isolated tribes. While this chapter is not action-packed, it is compelling to unravel the reason people should search for remote tribes and share Jesus with them.

The acceptance and complete belief that the Bible is wholly inspired by God is necessary before the study and acceptance of the mission of God for any individual. The Bible is completely authoritative and is essential in understanding the will of God. Without the Bible, as God's revelation to people, there would be no standard by which to live and to develop an understanding of the plan of God for all peoples everywhere.

The central focus of God can be described in terms of a compass. Like a compass which points to the magnetic north, no matter where you are on the earth, the needle always points true. While a compass is designed to give direction in relation to an unchanging point, the magnetic attraction and pull determines that the magnetic center will always stay true. Jesus Christ, the unchanging God, is the magnetic center. The mission of God can clearly be seen at all times in the limited history of the peoples of the earth.

No person was ever intended to be a spectator in the plan of God. People are the very ones whom God has appointed to complete the task of restoring the presence of God in the hearts of all other peoples of this world. While God raised up an entire nation to follow after him, it was only a remnant, a small few, who lived their lives with absolute purpose and determination to lead others and to pursue the mission of God on this earth.

The central focus of the lives of Abraham, Isaac, Jacob and subsequently to every following generation throughout the Old Testament was inhabiting the land of Israel--the Promised Land. Jesus was born in the small village of Bethlehem, only a few kilometers from the Temple Mount in Jerusalem. Jesus lived most of his life, and ministered completely in the land of Israel. It was only by the command of Christ that Jesus' disciples continued the mission of God by taking the Good News to all peoples. The focus became the "ends of the earth," rather than being centralized in Jerusalem.

In the New Testament, the message of the Kingdom of God was the same for both the Jews and Gentiles (non-Jews). Paul preached the same message to both; however, other nationalities received it more readily than the Jews. Paul was not only theologically committed to taking the gospel to non-Jewish people, but he was committed personally to seeing people of every nationality come to Christ. His efforts earned him the title "Apostle to the Gentiles."

Jesus, in a parable describing the Kingdom of God said, "*People will come from east and west and north and south, and will take their places at the feast in the kingdom of God.*" (Luke 13:29). The book of Revelation describes what the Apostle John saw in the future at the culmination of time (as we humanly understand 'time'). The completion of the mission task was realized with the kingdom of God being established in full, and the peoples of the earth encircling the throne of God. John described what he saw by saying, "*After this I looked and there before me was a great multitude that no one could count, from every nation, tribe, people, and language, standing before the throne* and in front of the Lamb. They were wearing white robes and were holding palm branches in their hands." (Revelation 7:9)

Throughout the entire Bible and the history of the earth, there has been a war between two opposing powers: God and Satan. One is completely good and holy--the other completely evil and rebellious.

In the book of Revelation, the power of Satan is referred to as "Babylon." During the actual reign of the Kingdom of Babylon, people of every language and tribe bowed down to Nebuchadnezzar. Daniel and his three friends remained faithful to God, and Daniel saw a reversal of the situation in the future. Daniel said, "In my vision at night I looked, and there before me was one like a son of man, coming with the clouds of heaven. He approached the Ancient of Days and was led into his presence. He was given authority, glory and sovereign power; all peoples, nations and men of every language worshiped him. His dominion is an everlasting dominion that will not pass away, and his kingdom is one that will never be destroyed." (Daniel 7:13-14). The Kingdom of God will be unified as one Body of Christ, where God will forever reign on the throne and all the peoples of the earth will freely worship the Lord forever.

As the world approached the third millennium a few years back, many people questioned, "When will Jesus return?"

"Why didn't Jesus return after the first millennium, a full one thousand years after he departed following his resurrection?" Others pondered, "Why didn't the Lord return in the year 2000?"

The answer is very clear. People have not finished the job! Jesus also will not return before the year 3000 if the job has not been finished! Jesus' return is promised, but it is a promise with a condition. When we have done our part (preaching the gospel to all the peoples of the world and to all creation) then Jesus will do as he promised (return and bind all the powers of evil and complete the Kingdom of God for all eternity to come).

There are many topics that are not clear in the Bible like the unclear reference to 'baptism of the dead' in I Corinthians 15:29. Yet, there are other things that are perfectly clear: from the beginning of time, God has been shaping and guiding the path of the nations to complete the Kingdom of God. The historical significance of the creation and the origins of all peoples of the earth are known through the records of the Bible, a most ancient of books inspired directly from God. The story of Jesus, the Son of God, coming to redeem all the peoples of the world is known and its meaning is clearly understood. The end of the world and the culmination of all history are also known. In the end, Jesus will win over the enemies of God and the Kingdom of God will be established in full. The reign of God will stretch from Jerusalem to every corner of the earth, to every lost tribe, and to people living along every jungle path. The reign of God will encompass every place on this earth and in the heavens above.

What is not clearly known is the space of time between the ascension of Jesus into heaven, after issuing his final commands and the point of Jesus' return to earth in the future. The Apostle Paul said that the task of spreading the Good News of Jesus must continue until "*at the name of Jesus every knee should bow, in heaven and on earth and under the earth, and every tongue confess that Jesus Christ is Lord, to the glory of God the Father*" (Philippians 2:10-11). In fact, Paul was quoting the same message which had been spoken since the Prophet Isaiah in Isaiah 45:23.

The message goes as far back as the struggle between God and Satan, before the beginning of time. Satan challenged God that people would not choose to worship Him (submitting to his Lordship) if God did not bless them (the book of Job). As Job remained faithful to God, unknowingly undergoing a test of his submission to the Kingdom of God, also in the future all people everywhere will willingly bow the knee and submit to the Lordship of Jesus Christ. Then Satan's power will be gone forever and the absolute fullness of the Kingdom will have come. Until that day, believers everywhere must continue to be obedient to the plan of God for establishing His Kingdom among all the nations and peoples of the earth.

God has entrusted believers with the most important task of all time. If people do not do it, it will not get done and the ending will be delayed. His return will continue to be delayed until a generation of people seeking the heart of God are able to convince believers of their responsibility. Jesus said, "*Go into all the world,*" (whether by physically going, praying, sending others, supporting. . . however God leads) and "*preach the good news to all creation.*" (Mark 16). There are still four billion people who have not heard the Good News and that number is growing by 208,218 people every day.[2]

In today's world, as "the ends of the earth" are being reached, the focus has shifted once again toward Jerusalem, to complete the mission mandate of God for all the peoples of the earth. While many areas of the world are reached, a saturation of the Good News is far from complete. The history of all peoples will culminate with the completion of the mission mandate of God. Then the second triumphal entry into Jerusalem will mark its conclusion.

It is out of the Biblical understanding of the mission heart of God and a personal calling to make Jesus Christ known to the people of Cambodia, that predicated the strategy and deliberate action to search for the T'moan. The mission heart of God yearns for and calls every believer to action in the pursuit of fulfilling the mission mandate. This mandate is for all believers around the world.

God's mandate is that every tribe, every tongue, and every nation have a chance to hear and respond to the Good News of Jesus Christ. That is why four men ventured into a dangerous region in the jungles of Cambodia.

My father was drafted into the Army during the Vietnam War before I was born. As a young man, my curious mind wanted to know the details of that war. All that my Dad told me about the war was that it was extremely boring. He explained that there were hours, and even days, of nothing but sitting around. These long periods of pure boredom were then followed by seconds of sheer terror, as a mortar round whistled through the air. Then boredom would return again.

Searching for a lost tribe is much the same as war. There are moments of great joy and exhilaration. However, it is primarily long hours of boring preparation, followed by hard work and difficult travel.

The only possible motorized travel into Cambodian jungles is by motorcycle. As a team of

FOUR MEN WITH A "WORLD" PERSPECTIVE

four maneuvering through rough terrain, we rarely talked to one another. Because of the need for safety we wore helmets which limited our communication. The easiest way to occupy one's mind while traveling is to pray and worship the Lord. Singing while wearing a motorcycle helmet is much like singing in the shower--just a little more muffled than echoed. My personal favorite time to worship the Lord is spontaneously singing to the Lord, accompanied by the revving sound of my motorcycle engine. Hour upon hour of travel provides plenty of time to think upon and worship the Lord. To share the gospel meaningfully to a person can take months, or years of preparation. An effective presentation of the gospel requires us to first build relationships with the people, while finding the best means for presenting the gospel in a way that is clear and understandable to the people.

Acts 1:8 gives Christians a geographical goal for the presentation of the gospel. It says, *"But you will receive power when the Holy Spirit* comes on you; and you will be my witnesses in Jerusalem, and in all Judea and Samaria, and to the ends of the earth." As Jesus was talking to his own disciples on the outskirts of Jerusalem, they were probably not intimidated by going to Jerusalem or Judea. Samaria, would be a little more challenging, but the ends of the earth was definitely far and would be a nearly unimaginable challenge.

All of the apostles, and the believers after them, have continued to go farther and farther to the ends of the earth. Yet, after more than two thousand years and with more than two billion people professing to be Christians, there are still many tribes in Cambodia and other countries who have never seen an outsider, much less heard the gospel message.

T' MOAN WOMEN IN TRADITIONAL DRESS

There has always been a grave misinterpretation of Acts 1:8, which has stagnated the expansion of the gospel. I have heard preachers say the plan of God is for Christians to reach Jerusalem (one's hometown) first. Then when that has been accomplished, they instruct their congregations to expand to Judea and Samaria (identified as the surrounding towns and counties). Once those places have been saturated with the gospel and the church is strong and financially secure, then they can pursue going to the ends of the earth. A quick look back at Acts 1:8 will reveal the flaw. This verse is not talking about a progressive path to preaching the gospel, but it is talking about the command of Christ for believers to reach the whole world. Notice, it is Jerusalem AND Judea AND Samaria AND to the ends of the earth. This is not a progression but a responsibility for believers and churches everywhere to not only reach their own communities and the neighboring towns, but at the same time to be engaged in reaching every person, all the way to the ends of the earth. If everyone waited for their entire hometown to be reached before they began their focus on others, this world would never get reached.

Because the global mandate of Christ has been largely ignored (being implemented by only a few), there are still thousands and even millions of people who after two thousand years have not heard about Jesus. Churches have been so negligent in obedience to the mission mandate of God that they have often relegated missions to external church entities.

Consider a good example of a rural church from the Northern California hills. Back in the 70's when everyone was growing their hair down to their waists, a group of dope-smoking, tree-huggers got touched by the Holy Spirit. They began a Christian community reaching out to other dope smokers, hitch-hikers, and hillbillies out in the Sierra Nevada Mountains in a small town called Smartville (population about 1000 souls). Fortunately, they did not have a "Jerusalem only" vision. They didn't want to change only Smartville, but they wanted to change the whole of Yuba county, the State of California, and while they were at it... the whole world. That is how big and important Jesus was to them. Now, some forty years later, their local church--the Church of Glad Tidings--sits out among walnut and pomegranate orchards, about three miles from the nearest town. Yet, nearly every day people in the area flood to the church for prayer, counseling, deliverance, and ministry at the church--which has become a launching pad for ministries and missionaries around the world. They have more than forty specific ministries for impacting and helping the community in which they live. They are involved with a deliverance ministry and anti-abortion causes across the nation. Globally, they have had tremendous impact in places like Cambodia, where they help to feed thousands of orphans, finance pastoral training, church planting, and support local missionaries. In other places like Uganda, Romania, Bangladesh, the Philippines, China, and Vietnam, they also have done significant things. Their efforts have directly brought thousands of people to Christ. Because they refused to be limited to their "Jerusalem," they have impacted populations and nations far beyond what the average citizen of Smartville could have comprehend forty years ago. Praise God they were never confused that they had to reach their "Jerusalem" first, before they engaged the "Judea and Samaria" and the "ends of the earth."

You see, Jesus repeatedly told believers to be involved in taking the gospel to the whole world. The church was His created body to accomplish this task. Yet the church has often relegated their call to para-church organizations. Unfortunately, many have diluted the gospel message and turned missions into a kind of social ministry for Christian 'tourists' to become involved. Local churches stress the importance of their own local "needs" and ignore the call to go outside their own communities. No wonder the world is not being saved! No wonder there are still entire tribes who have never heard of Jesus!

In Cambodia, there are at least thirty-one different linguistic ethnic tribes. Tribes are not always determined by language. They are also determined by clans or geographical location. None-the-less, categorizing tribes by languages alone creates a list of nearly 7,000 tribes in the world. In Southeast Asia alone there are roughly 1,500 different tribes among only eleven small countries.[1] Southeast Asia is an extremely diverse area of the world, and also highly volatile; therefore there is still so much to be done, even in the twenty-first century.

The task before us is immense and the size of the task is growing rapidly everyday. This divine calling to spread the Good News of Jesus will not be changed, it will not be altered or re-defined, and it will not be cancelled nor postponed for a more convenient time. The return of Christ is entirely hinged on our faithfulness in accomplishing Christ's global mandate.

The only way for it to be accomplished in our lifetime is that believers make the mission of Christ their personal passion and life goal.

14

JOURNEY IN THE PRESENCE OF GOD

Though I have been a Christian since I was about thirteen years old, it was in 1997 that I had the most significant spiritual turning point in my life. It culminated from a year of civil war in Cambodia, in which the entire foreign population was evacuated, a traumatic plane crash near my home, ministry difficulties and strained relationships. It was a tough year. Then God showed up! I will never forget it.

Truly God opened the doors to heaven and came down on me and my staff in a way that brought us to our knees. Over two months God did a thorough cleaning of all our lives and we have completely turned directions in our life and ministry. I had hesitated in the past to try and explain this dramatic shift because it was very difficult to put into words and so personal. Each day God continues to pour out his Spirit on our lives in new ways. From that point in 1997 there was more fruit coming out of that outpouring in one month than in all previous fourteen years that I had been a Christian. In the following pages I will attempt, by the Spirit's guidance, not to explain but to show some of the fruit that has come from this mighty outpouring of God into our lives.

If you have ever worked a potter's wheel you know that if you were the clay it would not always be enjoyable. Forming the clay is not always being spun around in joyful bliss. It involves numerous deformities which must be broken down; there are lop-sided bases which have to be re-spun. When the molding is all finished. . . it gets cooked! Ouch. Then it is what the potter has intended it to be.

Consider a life. God is our potter, we are the clay. The problem is that we like to wiggle around a lot and get off center. When that happens, the whole process must begin again. Other times a beautiful life begins to form, but then we get too thin (busy), or our foundation is faulty (based on emotions rather than solid truth), or we want the potter to stop working (our pride repels the Spirit of God). Getting spun is never fun, especially when it doesn't work out the way we like it. *It is much easier to trust the potter!*

One thing we can definitely glean from the scriptures is that God blesses obedience. As the clay we must simply respond to the potter. Questioning his work in another life would be utterly disastrous, so we do not look for outward signs, emotions or manifestations but at the heart. Since 1997 my staff and I have looked to see how God has changed our lives and what fruit has been born out of it. We have seen God working in a moment to change our whole worldview; not God working in a moment to make us bubble with emotion. It is here where I feel many may misunderstand the working of the Spirit. The fullness of the Spirit is not only about an attitude change, it is not a rediscovered biblical truth. It is not necessarily an emotional outburst. The fullness of the Spirit, when truly orchestrated by the Spirit, is a complete life change, regardless of external manifestations. It is a hunger and thirst for Jesus everyday. It is a shift away from human effort to divine power; from self-knowledge to Spiritually revealed truth; from arrogance and pride to humbleness; from pious holiness to absolute reverence and awe of God; from self-glorification to being crucified with Christ; from a prayer list of wants and desires to seeking only the will of God. The list of life changing and transforming values could go on and on.

Back in 1997 between October and December, the struggles and pain of the previous four months all hit a tremendous climax as my staff and I sought spiritual guidance and instruction from gifted Cambodian pastors. I, personally, came to a crisis of belief. Either church planting really is about God building his church (Matthew 16:18) and God alone or it is about tremendous human effort. I put my vote with God. But as I examined my life I discovered the hidden corrupted character I had. Did I really believe that "*He who is in me is greater than he who is in the world*" (I John 4:4)?

If this was true then why was I continually under demonic pressure? I had been told numerous times in Sunday School that Satan can not touch believers. Was my faith merely a list of Sunday School phrases and cute little songs? Did I really believe Jesus was really alive and working today? Does he have the same power to heal the sick, cast out demons and destroy the curses of this world today as he did two thousand years ago? In Cambodia I deal with the sick and dying every day. Demon possession is as common as the flu in America. Did I really believe that poverty could be alleviated by education, technology, health care and small business loans? Was God irrelevant? Can I give people the abundant life that was promised *by Jesus* (John 10:10)? Everything I could remember about my faith was now under my own internal investigation.

When I came to this crisis in my belief system, I asked one last difficult question. If I can alleviate poverty, if God does not manifest his power like he did two thousand years ago, if the sick simply lack proper health care and I can, with my own knowledge and motivation, start a church anywhere I want; and if I can lead church planters with my own ability; *do I really need God?*

Please, do not fear. I know the question is difficult to swallow, but this truly was a crisis. I had prepared for years to be a church planter. I had studied under the best scholars and church planters, walked in the footsteps of the most capable and studied the Bible looking for the most intricate details that might reveal more insight. None of this was wrong in itself, but collectively it was lacking the only essential ingredient. . . divine power! I had studied at the largest theological institution in the world, I had read the best books, I had the best opportunities but all this had done was to develop a deep-seated human pride. Invisible by human eyes, but grossly ugly when cast into the crucible of fire by the Spirit. I think I read somewhere once that pride was sin!

I always had good intentions and tried to do the right things, but clearly it wasn't the best thing. I lived a life as pure as humanly possible (though I have since learned that absolute purity is only found in the grace and cleansing power of God). God even had a hand in many things I had done. Sometimes he would even bless me or my work. But I could no longer, in good conscience, continue a life and ministry of human effort and ask God to sanctify it when I was finished. If anything, this was a time of repentance. My sin was not against myself, it was against all. I, the servant, was trying to be the master while still calling myself the 'humble servant.' I had to first ask God to forgive me, then my staff, then the children's ministry I was attached with, then my boss, then my church, and my friends and supporters.

I was on my own road before. I was still going to heaven, but not to the throne room of God. I might have made it to the outer courts. Then God showed me his road. This is an incredible story because it actually involves a literal journey, led completely by the Spirit. Humanly speaking, you will laugh or wonder at the stupidity of it, but please remember what I tried to explain earlier: If your focus is on the outside appearance when God is working in a life you will only see a silly story about a man who took a jog, got completely lost and misplaced his shirt in a passionate desire to go swimming at the beach. In the true reality I was being led by the very word of the Holy Spirit as he showed me the life I was now to live. This life was the exact opposite of the life I had been living. Looking only at the outside you would probably surmise that I have lost my mind. Trust me, I have not. I am fully in control of my senses and full of joy and the Spirit. My life has been changed and there is a lot of fruit! So sit back, relax and join me on my spiritual journey. Maybe God will have a word for you too.

GOD'S ROAD, NOT MINE

We had just finished a three day intensive workshop on the Holy Spirit and God was moving in mighty ways in all of our lives. I had repented publicly of my pride and how I had lived my own life by my own power. During that time God told me that I was no longer to depend on my own knowledge, ideas, insights or even money. During that time God had me give all my money for the trip away, so I had nothing. I had no choice but to depend on him.

The final meeting concluded and all of us were going to meet at the beach for about an hour before we left to go back to Phnom Penh. Then God told me, "Steve, in your human wisdom you would ride a motorcycle or catch a ride to go to the beach... but today you will depend on my strength. You must run to the beach!" While as a youngster I loved to run, I still am a big guy and running is not my forte. Especially when the beach was about five miles away. In fact, I don't think I had run that far since I was playing soccer in college. I did not question God though, I simply ran. But a puzzling thing happened. . .

I have been to this beach several times and I knew there was only one road in and out. From our meeting place I should take a left and simply follow the road. But the Spirit told me that my ways were not his, so go *right*. I had learned the importance of obedience now, so I simply ran right. I did not even question where I was going. This was no ordinary run. This run represented the life that God intends me to live. So I ran.

It was easy at first. Downhill. After the initial few hundred meters my energy began to wear off. It was very hot. It was now nearly noon and the blaring tropical sun was cooking me. Within two minutes all of my clothes were soaked with sweat. I was still clipping along when I came to the uphill part. Very few people in Cambodia publicly exercise, so they are not accustomed to seeing people running. Many people were laughing and curiously wondering what the crazy foreigner was doing. I plodded along, hardly running, but not wanting to stop. Uphill was hard!

I came to a school. The biggest school in town. The students were coming out and walking home. Here there was a split in the road and they were walking every which way, but not the way to the ocean. Then God had another message for me. "You went to a big seminary, the biggest. Many times people pause along their spiritual journeys and go into a school. They learn a lot of stuff, fill their heads and get officially ordained. Then when they leave the seminary, they quit following the road that God intended and start following other paths. Paths of self-understanding, theological debate, criticizing other Christians who are different, arrogance. . . or some never even come out. They stay in the school forever!" God showed me my arrogance. Was I willing to give up a seminary degree forever to follow God, even though I am only one semester from finishing? The answer is YES!

A KHMER TEMPLE

I continued on the path toward the ocean, but the wrong beach. The road was quiet now. There were not many people here. A few people were walking or riding motorcycles back from the ocean, but none going my way. Then I saw huge temple on a hill. (The word in Khmer for temple, pagoda, church and mosque is identical—"*Preah Vihear.*" I usually think in the Khmer language now.) It reminded me of American churches. It was a beautiful church, with a tall steeple, and a beautiful garden surrounding it. As I looked I could see there were people going in, but no one coming out. Then God spoke again. "At one time the people believed and were following the true way, then they started following the big church. They followed programs and eloquent pastors. Church became a social activity and it was fun. They quit following Me and now followed their own interests. They would never reach the ocean." Then a shocking thing hit me. In that "church" the people were singing songs to God, but their hearts were not worshipping. They were reading the Bible, but not finding truth. They were praying, but only talking to themselves.

I continued on. It was hard now. I was breathing heavy. My legs were like anchors trying to hold me back. My body was trying to pull me into mediocrity. I pressed on looking down the long, quiet and hilly road. Finally I saw the ocean. It looked wonderful. The trees, water, sand. . . it could have been a post card. But. . . it was the wrong beach! I knew

THE BEAUTIFUL CAMBODIAN BEACH

this beach, I had swam here by mistake once before. While it looked beautiful on the surface, under the water was jagged coral and sea urchins waiting for the unsuspecting foot. Jelly fish often swarmed here. It also had strong currents that would suck a weak person out into the vast ocean. In short. . . it looked like heaven, but it was far from it.

Then God said, "go left." I knew the beach I needed to go to was toward the left, but there was no road, only a narrow animal path. The path went through the grass and up a big hill in front of me. I obeyed and went. I chugged up the hill, slipping and sliding on loose gravel and sharp weeds slashing away at my legs. The road to heaven surely was narrow and few found it.

Finally I reached the top of the hill. Looking down was a wonderful sight. *The right beach*! As I stood at the top of the hill, I pondered the journey that God had brought me on. I was almost there. Almost to the Promised Land! Then another message came: "Moses could not enter the Promised Land because he liked to do things his way. He tried to be a warrior and free his people. Then he did not glorify me by assuming I had forgotten my people and asked for water. Moses did things his way and he wandered in the wilderness. Joshua was obedient and he went in. Are you going to be a Moses or a Joshua." *"Joshua,"* I called out. I started down the hill, but there was only one problem. The small path that I was on ended. There was no more road, no path to follow, only a grassy slope and a river between the Promised Beach and me. There was a small boy near me so I asked him, "which is the easiest way to the beach?"

The little boy told me to follow him. So I walked behind the small little boy. He was too poor to own a shirt or shoes; there was a stark contrast between him and me. Though my clothing would not be nice compared to American standards, they were luxurious compared to his. I actually had a pair of socks and shoes other than flip flops. This little boy had no false motives, he had no corrupted character, he was so innocent. This was the life that God has called me to. True purity, not a façade put up on Sunday mornings, or a fake smile always protruding from my face. True purity must ooze from within to be real.

Then the most interesting thing happened. The Spirit told me to give up my shirt. Immediately I obeyed. When I handed over my shirt I was completely free! Naked we come into the world, and naked we leave it (I Timothy 6:7)! I ran down the grassy hill, plunged into the river and forged my way across. Now totally soaked I ran, bursting with joy, excitement and happiness. *I was truly free!*

My friends saw me coming, running out of the forest half naked and glowing with excitement. I was so happy I had forgotten about being tired. God had showed me the life I was now to live. I may have to be penniless and shirtless. . . but I would be full of joy when I was obedient to the Spirit's direction. What a release.

The law, human effort, and church tradition were all broken away revealing the precious truth about God. Now I knew what hunger and thirsting after righteousness was about. It has nothing to do with forcing yourself to study, nothing to do with your position in the church, and nothing to do with your past life. It has everything to do with being obedient to every word of God (written and living). My whole life has changed! *Praise the Lord!*

WHERE FROM HERE?

Though I have the title of "Director" I submit myself to the Holy Spirit's leadership. **The Holy Spirit is in charge of the ministry.** When he says "go", we go; when he says "stay", we stay. We pray and pray and pray. Not just talking, but listening. Not asking, but seeking. We worship together sometimes two and three times a day and then privately at night. We continually call out to God to build *His Church*, to prepare the way and to show us what to say and where to go. We rely on inspiration from on high rather than our own understanding. We truly believe Isaiah 55:8,9 when it says that our ways are not God's ways, and our thought are not His thoughts. His ways are so much higher than ours! We cannot even understand them.

When obediently presenting the truth that God gives us, we see lives changed. Pastors publicly confessing sins, and youth leaders asking forgiveness for their wrongs. People are accepting Christ. In one church eight out of ten leaders publicly repented of their sin. All the way from the pastor, elders, deacons, and youth and children's leaders. One had done so the night before and the other was just in awe. In the churches I grew up in I have never seen ten people repent at a time, much less the leaders! *This is the fruit that the Spirit brings.*

Where previously we worked so hard by teaching, persuading, pleading, and enticing just to see one person come to Christ, now we were seeing dozens come to Christ without any effort. I have never seen that before in my life. So I say, it may look silly on the outside, but on the inside the Holy Spirit did a thorough cleaning. There is plenty of real spiritual fruit to prove it!

I have always been very honest in how God is working in my life and ministry. I would have it no other way. I could simply hide my new life and stay away from any kind of controversy and no one would ever know. If I did that, no one would know how to pray for me, nor how to help me. My life would become a new façade. I have trouble believing God blesses secret Christians. God can't bless this ministry if I am ashamed of it, and God cannot bless my life if I hide it.

Since 1997, I have approached life, ministry and every decision by seeking after God's heart. I desire to be his servant, not just someone who wants God to bless his own ideas and efforts. I think that is why God took me, along with my three friends, deep into the Cambodian jungle, just to show us it can still be done. Tribes can still be reached, in their entirety, in the 21st century because Jesus is the one who does it. We are just his servants.

We didn't initially set out to try and reach an entire tribe for Christ. It just happened, not by accident, but by the daily submission of our will to Christ's. The fruit, a whole tribe coming to Christ, is just a by-product of lives completely surrendered. It is the fruit of faith in Jesus and his power!

HOW CAN YOU ACCOMPLISH GREAT THINGS FOR GOD?

GET ON GOD'S ROAD!

I PROMISE THE JOURNEY HE WILL TAKE YOU ON,

IF YOU REMAIN FAITHFUL,

WILL BE THE GREATEST JOURNEY OF YOUR LIFE.

ENDNOTES

[1] According to Wycliffe Bible Translators Ethnologue. 2008
   http://www.ethnologue.com/ (SIL International: Dallas, Texas)
[2] United Nations Population Fund, Electronic document